PHOTO **1** KATIE STERN

PHOTO 1 KATIE STERN

DELMAR
CENGAGE Learning™

Australia • Brazil • Japan • Korea • Mexico • Singapore • Spain • United Kingdom • United States

Photo 1: An Introduction to the Art of Photography

Katie Stern

Vice President, Editorial: Dave Garza

Director of Learning Solutions: Sandy Clark

Senior Acquisitions Editor: Jim Gish

Managing Editor: Larry Main

Associate Product Manager: Meaghan Tomaso

Editorial Assistant: Sarah Timm

Vice President, Marketing: Jennifer Baker

Marketing Director: Deborah S. Yarnell

Marketing Manager: Erin Brennan

Marketing Coordinator: Erin DeAngelo

Production Director: Wendy Troeger

Senior Content Product Manager:
    Kathryn B. Kucharek

Senior Art Director: Joy Kocsis

Technology Project Manager:
    Christopher Catalina

> For product information and technology assistance, contact us at
> **Cengage Learning Customer & Sales Support, 1-800-354-9706**
> For permission to use material from this text or product,
> submit all requests online at **www.cengage.com/permissions.**
> Further permissions questions can be e-mailed to
> **permissionrequest@cengage.com**

Library of Congress Control Number: 2010937204

ISBN-13: 978-1-111-03641-6
ISBN-10: 1-111-03641-1

Delmar
5 Maxwell Drive
Clifton Park, NY 12065-2919
USA

Cengage Learning is a leading provider of customized learning solutions with office locations around the globe, including Singapore, the United Kingdom, Australia, Mexico, Brazil, and Japan. Locate your local office at: **international.cengage.com/region**

Cengage Learning products are represented in Canada by Nelson Education, Ltd.

To learn more about Delmar, visit **www.cengage.com/delmar**

Purchase any of our products at your local college store or at our preferred online store **www.cengagebrain.com**

Notice to the Reader

Publisher does not warrant or guarantee any of the products described herein or perform any independent analysis in connection with any of the product information contained herein. Publisher does not assume, and expressly disclaims, any obligation to obtain and include information other than that provided to it by the manufacturer. The reader is expressly warned to consider and adopt all safety precautions that might be indicated by the activities described herein and to avoid all potential hazards. By following the instructions contained herein, the reader willingly assumes all risks in connection with such instructions. The publisher makes no representations or warranties of any kind, including but not limited to, the warranties of fitness for particular purpose or merchantability, nor are any such representations implied with respect to the material set forth herein, and the publisher takes no responsibility with respect to such material. The publisher shall not be liable for any special, consequential, or exemplary damages resulting, in whole or part, from the readers' use of, or reliance upon, this material.

Printed in the United States of America
1 2 3 4 5 6 7 15 14 13 12 11

Contents

Preface   xi

1 What Is a Photograph?   2

Photography in Your Life
Purposes of Photography
Photography in Our Society
Why Study Photography?
Finding Photographic Opportunities
About the Textbook
How to Learn Photography
Summary

2 Getting to Know Cameras   20

Early Cameras
Viewfinder Cameras
SLR Cameras
Camera Body
Shutters and Shutter Speed
Specifics of Digital Cameras
Medium-Format Cameras
Plastic Cameras
Pinhole Cameras
Large-Format Cameras
Cell Phone Cameras
Caring for Your Camera
Summary

3 **What Is a Good Photographic Exposure?** 56

The Three Elements of Exposure
Exposure Equivalents
Your Camera's Definition of a Good Exposure
Camera Metering Modes
The Zone System
Handheld Light Meters
The Sunny f/16 Rule
Dynamic Range
Camera Mode Settings
Over- and Underexposure
Aesthetic Considerations
The Histogram in Photoshop
Bit Depth
The Aesthetic Aspects of Making Good Exposures
Film Speed (ISO or ASA)
So What Is a Good Exposure?
Summary

 4 **Film and Film Processing** 96

Why Use Black-and-White Film?
Varieties of Black-and-White Print Film
Characteristic Curves of Film
Black-and-White Film Processing
How Black-and-White Film Developing Chemicals Work
The Steps of Black-and-White Film Processing
Loading and Developing 4 × 5 Sheet Film
Identifying Underexposed and Overexposed Negatives
Beyond Basic Film Development
Color Film and Film Processing
Color Perception
How Color Is Created in Film and Print
C-41 Processing for Color Print Films
E-6 Processing
Infrared Film
Summary

5 Traditional Darkroom Printing   128

The Artistry of Darkroom Printing
Black-and-White Darkroom Requirements
Photographic Papers and Filters
Preparation for Print Processing
The Contact Print
The Test Print
The Straight Print
Archival Processing
Retouching the Print
Traditional Darkroom Color Printing
Summary

6 Finishing, Mounting, and Storing of Prints   160

Print Mounting Considerations
Techniques for Print Mounting and Matting
Cold Mount Technique
An Alternative Mounting Method
Presentation Portfolios
Summary

7 The Digital Darkroom   176

History of the Digital Photographer's Workflow
Image Quality
Digital Displays
Resolution
Opening the Digital File
File Organization in Bridge
Opening a File in Adobe Camera Raw
Color Quality Adjustments
Setting the Color Space, Resolution, and Bit Depth
Straightening and Cropping in Adobe Camera Raw
Saving and Opening Options
Working in Adobe Photoshop
Saving Files
Summary

8 Image Development in Photoshop   206

Evaluating a Scene
Aesthetic and Compositional Assessment of Your Photograph
Selections and Adjustment Layers
Alpha Channels
Fine-Tuning Edges
Adjustment Layers
Tonal Value Adjustments
Levels and Curves Adjustments
Quick Mask Mode
Pixel-Based Layers
Continuing the Artistic Process
Summary

9 Final Touches and Creative Options   238

Cleaning and Fine-Tuning Tools
The History Panel
Handling Dust and Noise
Sharpening Images
Photoshop Sharpening Tools
Straightening Images in Photoshop
Combining Photographs
Transforming Pixels
Layer Blending Modes
Learning More While Being Careful
Summary

10 Digital Color Management and Printing   270

History of Digital Color Management
The Role of Digital Color Management
Mechanical Means of Measuring Color
Color Spaces, Gamuts, and Profiling Devices
Photoshop's Color Modes
The Human Factor in Digital Color Management
Steps in Digital Color Management
Making Digital Color Prints
Preparing Your Printer
Digital Print Permanence
Summary

11 **Working with Light** 290

Human Vision
Human Vision and the Camera
Light and Electromagnetic Radiation
Pay Attention to Light
Fast and Slow Falloff
Contrast of Tonal Values
Color Temperature
Directional Light
Surface Quality
Polarizing Filter
Ultraviolet (UV) Filter
A Sense of Play
Portrait and Commercial Photography
The Classic Portrait
Basic Classic Lighting
Lighting Ratios
Summary

 12 **Composition** 332

Composition and Visual Communication
Gestalt and Image Composition
Additional Issues of Perception
Composing a Photograph
Remove Clutter
Experiment with Your Compositions
Summary

 13 **Critiquing Photographs** 366

Reasons for Making Photographs
Steps in Critiquing Individual Photographs
Critiquing a Collection of Photographs
Thoughts on Being Critiqued or Judged
Summary

14 Copyright Law   384

What Works Can Be Copyrighted?

Registering Your Photographs

Fair Use Doctrine

Use of Copyrighted Photographs for Collage Work

Royalty-Free Photographs

Derivatives

The Best Copyright Solution

Copyright License Conditions

Wikimedia Commons

Protecting Your Copyrighted Images

Summary

 15 Best Practices   400

Orphan Works Act: Protecting Your Copyrighted Images

Photographer Registry

Electronic Identification of Photographs

Keywords

Creating Metadata Templates

Business-Related Forms

Summary

Appendix A: By the Decade   419

Appendix B: List of Photographers   457

Glossary   459

Index   471

Preface

Introduction

Photo 1: An Introduction to the Artistry of Photography is written for anyone who wants to learn about photography. It is written especially for film-based photographers entering digital photography and for student photographers who dream of one day seeing their photographs in publications or art galleries. Camera and film/digital darkroom chapters are accompanied by chapters on matting and framing, color management, best business practices, and copyright law to expand readers' knowledge of the field and to help them become safe and secure businesspeople early in their careers.

This text fully discusses photography from the standpoint of the visual communicator and examines photography from technical, artistic, and cultural viewpoints. My goal is to help photographers find new avenues for visual self-expression while they also learn best practices in photography.

Emerging Trends

Few artistic fields have changed as rapidly as photography has over the past five years. The digital industry has developed well-documented industry standards that dissolve lingering doubts on how to work with digital photographs. This timely textbook clearly introduces you to these new standards and fully explains how to apply them.

Many software-based photography textbooks don't explain *why* you use specific software functions. It's hard to know when to use a software tool if you aren't sure of its purpose or ramifications, much less its dangers. This text explains *why* you would do something in Photoshop or Adobe Camera Raw, resulting in an increased understanding of how the software "thinks." The more you understand how a software function works, the better practitioner you will become. This information can be applied regardless of the version of Photoshop available to you.

Background of This Text

I wrote this text out of a sincere passion for photography and a strong belief in its potential for self-expression. It is difficult to define a photographic "beginner" in today's society; yet despite its ubiquity, photography as a storytelling medium offers much more than the general public is aware.

Research for the text encompassed many modes. I thank my photography educators, including Dr. Roger Grant, John Sexton, Eddie Tapp, Jane Connor-Ziser, John Paul Caponigro, Christopher James, David Arnold, Greg Stangl, and Huth & Booth Photography for their courses and/or workshops I have attended. These people are my mentors, and I am deeply grateful to them.

Online resources have burgeoned over the past few years. Lynda.com (www.lynda.com) provides online tutorials covering Photoshop, Bridge, and digital photography. Tutorials by Chris Orwig, Jan Kabili, and Deke McClelland have been particularly valuable to me. The people at X-Rite (www.xrite.com) have developed many hour-long free online seminars on digital color management and best practices in digital asset management. Norman Koren (www.imatest.com), the Image Permanence Institute (www.imagepermanenceinstitute.org), and Digital Photography Review (www.dpreview.com) were invaluable in providing up-to-date information. Websites like www.photo.net and www.behance.net provided a world view of photographers and their portfolios. Online photographic competitions like the Black and White Spider Awards (www.thespiderawards.com) and the Photography Masters Cup (www.thecolorawards.com) provided me with more photographers and portfolios to explore. Websites of the Photographers Association of America (www.ppa.com), the U. S. Copyright Office (www.copyright.gov), and the American Society of Media Photographers (www.asmp.org) proved to be excellent resources for copyright law and business practices. In addition, I directly consulted professional photographers and photographic manufacturers and read art history and general photography books.

Recent texts have come forward as excellent resources for authors, professionals, and students alike. I am indebted to Martin Evening, author of *Adobe Photoshop CS5 for Photographers*; David Nightingale, author of *Practical HDR*; Fil Hunter, Steven Biver, and Paul Fuqua for their book, *Light: Science & Magic, Third Edition*; Peter Krogh for his book, *The DAM Book: Digital Asset Management for Photographers*; the authors at the American Society of Media Photographers for *Professional Business Practices in Photography, Seventh Edition*; and Patricia Russotti and Richard Anderson, authors of *Digital Photography Best Practices and Workflow Handbook*. In addition, the Adobe Photoshop task force has developed an excellent online Photoshop Help resource that I consulted many times.

No doubt, countless other educators have trained my mentors and the authors of the aforementioned books. One in particular deserves mention. Although I never had the pleasure of meeting or studying directly under Bruce Fraser, I have long benefitted from his devotion to educating people about Photoshop and digital photography. He was a world leader in helping all of us understand the digital darkroom.

On a final note, I wrote this text because I wanted to update my knowledge of photography. I have met and had conversations with photographers from around the world, with industry leaders, and with true experts in film-based and digital photography. It has been a phenomenal journey.

Organization of the Text

The text is organized into information that readers might need when they first start learning and practicing photography. The camera and exposure are discussed first, followed by traditional darkroom work and print finishing. Traditional darkroom instructions precede digital darkroom instruction so that the student studying both can see the parallels between the two. The remaining chapters help students improve their photography and become good practitioners and businesspeople, regardless of whether they use film-based or digital cameras.

Chapter 1: What Is a Photograph?
As an introduction to the role photography plays in our life, culture, and society, Chapter 1 gives suggestions on how best to learn photography.

Chapter 2: Getting to Know Cameras
Chapter 2 describes the parts of cameras and lenses, as well as the parts of SLR cameras and their functions, and addresses how to care for photographic equipment.

Chapter 3: What Is a Good Photographic Exposure

Explaining the three major components of exposure, Chapter 3 also covers how a camera's light meter works and how/when a light meter can be overridden to obtain proper exposures. The concept of "proper exposure" is defined in terms of the photographer's intentions for the photograph and whether highlight/shadow information is needed.

Chapter 4: Film and Film Processing

Covering the components of black-and-white and chromogenic films, characteristic curves, and exposure latitude, Chapter 4 includes information about the requirements for a traditional black-and-white darkroom, darkroom safety, and mixing and storing of chemistry. Students progress through a step-by-step film development process for 35 mm and 4 × 5 sheet film. Chapter 4 also describes color film and film processing, C-41 print processing, E-6 processing, and information on working with and developing infrared film.

Chapter 5: Traditional Darkroom Printing

Chapter 5 presents further information on darkroom requirements for black-and-white printing, as well as descriptions of various aspects of black-and-white printing papers and chemistry. This chapter takes students through the steps of printing, including burning, dodging, washing, and retouching, and introduces the Zone System of printing and archival processing.

Chapter 6: Finishing, Mounting, and Storing Prints

In Chapter 6, students learn about different types of mount boards, overmats, glazing, and frames for print matting and framing, and describes the archival characteristics of common matting materials, Chapter 6 also gives step-by-step instructions for mounting and matting prints using a variety of methods.

Chapter 7: The Digital Darkroom

Chapter 7 covers image quality, digital displays and resolution, file organization in Adobe Bridge, as well as opening and working with photographs in Adobe Camera Raw. The chapter also describes resolution in Photoshop and how to save files in various formats.

Chapter 8: Image Development in Photoshop

In Chapter 8, students look at photographs from an aesthetic standpoint. Chapter 8 describes the Merge to HDR functions in Photoshop. It also discusses selection tools, alpha channels, and working with adjustment layers.

Chapter 9: Final Touches and Creative Options

In addition to describing the use of retouching tools in Adobe Camera Raw and Photoshop, Chapter 9 also covers the use of the History Panel and dust and noise filters. This chapter gives a thorough description of various sharpening tools in Photoshop and also introduces concepts of pixel layers, transforming pixels, and layer blending modes.

Chapter 10: Digital Color Management and Printing

In Chapter 10, students are presented a brief history of digital color management and its role within the digital workflow. Color models and color modes are described, and the human factor in digital color management is also discussed. The steps in digital color management are clearly spelled out, including monitor calibration and selection of industry-standard Photoshop settings. Chapter 10 familiarizes readers with printer profiles and color printing methods, and also summarizes how prints should be cared for and stored.

Chapter 11: Working with Light

Chapter 11 begins with a primer on human vision and visual perception and then describes light in terms of physics and visual characteristics, including falloff, color temperature, direction, and surface quality. The benefits and use of polarizing and UV filters are explained. Basic portraiture lighting is thoroughly covered, including examples of correct and incorrect light applications.

Chapter 12: Composition

Chapter 12 introduces readers to gestalt and image composition and other issues of perception. Factors include value, shapes, texture, perspective, mergers, rule of thirds, and movement. The author has provided photographic examples of each concept.

Chapter 13: Critiquing Photographs

As an introduction to how photographs are critiqued, Chapter 13 includes reasons for making photographs and steps in critiquing photographs. This chapter encourages discussion, rather than statements about likes and dislikes.

Chapter 14: Copyright Law

Chapter 14 gives readers the fundamentals of copyright law, including infractions, derivatives, fair use, and Creative Commons. Further resources are made available to readers.

Chapter 15: Best Practices

So that readers have the tools to be safe business practitioners, Chapter 15 discusses business practices and business forms pertaining to the photographic profession. File naming policies, metadata information, keywords, and model and property releases are also covered.

Features of the Text

The following provides some of the salient features of the text:

■ Objectives clearly state the learning goals of each chapter. For those using WIDS (the Wisconsin Instructional Design System), these objectives are written specifically at the appropriate learning levels for educational activities.

■ Uses of Adobe Photoshop, Adobe Bridge, and Adobe Camera Raw present the most recent advances in digital workflow, aligning student activities with industry best practices, while also maintaining a concentration toward meeting the photographer's visual intentions.

■ Artist Statements accompany many photographs so readers can better understand the intentions of the artists. Exposure information accompanies some photographs so students can assess the effects of aperture and shutter speed.

■ Profiles feature insights and thoughtful advice from various specialty photographers.

■ Exercises at the end of chapters give ideas on how to practice photographic/darkroom skills and also investigate photography as a medium of visual communication.

- Additional reading assignments broaden the learning experience and encourage students to continue lifelong learning of photography.

- The By the Decade section of this text (Appendix A) helps students comprehend the sociopolitical and cultural times in which photography was maturing, hence encouraging a greater understanding of the impact of the medium.

- The List of Photographers (Appendix B) is a launching point for further investigation into all eras and styles of photography.

- Chapters on copyright law and photography business practices add to the student experience and answer questions that many students, especially those who are novices to photography, may have.

Photography CourseMate

Photo 1 includes a Photography CourseMate, which helps you make the grade.

This CourseMate includes:

- an interactive eBook, with highlighting, note taking and search capabilities

- interactive learning tools including:
  - Quizzes
  - Flashcards
  - Videos
  - and more!

To access additional course materials including CourseMate, please visit www.cengagebrain.com. At the CengageBrain.com home page, search for the ISBN of your title (from the back cover of your book) using the search box at the top of the page. This will take you to the product page where these resources can be found.

Instructor Resources

To assist instructors with planning and implementing their instructional programs, several instructor resources are available. The CD offers many helpful features to compliment the text, including:

- PowerPoint lecture slides highlighting the main topics of each chapter;

- Sample syllabi for both 11- and 15-week semesters; and

- Teaching and grading philosophy resources.

Photo copyright © Huth & Booth Photography

About the Author

Katie Stern is an Associate Professor of Web and Digital Media Development at the University of Wisconsin-Stevens Point. The owner of a successful photography business, Katie has taught university-level classes in traditional darkroom and digital photography, graphic design, and art appreciation for more than a decade. Her photographs have been published nationwide in magazines, calendars, brochures, posters, and postcards. Her fine art photographs have won awards in national competitions. Katie holds an Individual Master of Arts Degree (I.M.A.) from Antioch University McGregor and a Masters of Fine Arts Degree from the University of Wisconsin-Madison. She is active in the Society for Photographic Education and the Professional Photographers of America. She is an Adobe Certified Expert for Photoshop CS5.

Acknowledgments

This text could not have been written without the incredible assistance of the professional team at Delmar, Cengage Learning. Jim Gish's confidence and energy were contagious and very much appreciated. The constant, near-daily support of Meaghan Tomaso over the period of a year and more was indispensable and deeply appreciated. Terri Wright procured images from around the world when I couldn't find the proper sources. Joy Kocsis provided much needed technical guidance at critical moments, and Sarah Timm assisted me with the required paperwork. Kathryn Kucharek in production was instrumental in producing a well-designed, highly readable text, other active Cengage team members included Joe Pliss in technology and Erin Brennan in marketing. Please accept my sincere thanks for your help and support.

Working with photographers around the world occasionally presented language barriers. I sincerely thank Belkis Kalayoglu for assistance with translations and Elyane Steeves for recommending Belkis to me.

Thanks also to Justyna Badach at the University of Wisconsin—La Crosse for her support, Daniel Goscha at Nicolet College for his feedback and valuable input, and Barbara Buckle at Nicolet College for helping to organize photo sessions. Thanks also go to Katie, Nikki, Ally, Kevin, Jessica, and Blane for modeling in several photographs, and to David and Lauren Stern for allowing me to use photos of their daughter, Evie.

Thanks to Jay Arend and Dale Reichert of Intevation Food Group, LLC, for their willingness to let me photograph within their manufacturing plant in Plover, Wisconsin.

Professional photographers are incredibly busy people. I sincerely thank Jeff Richter, Dick and Barbara Waltenberry, Betty Huth and Ed Booth, Felice Frankel, W. Morgan Rockhill, Chuck Pefley, R. J. Hinkle, and Michael Kamber, for contributing their time and expertise in the Professional Profiles. Special thanks go to Phil Ziesemer who made many of the photographs for the chapter on light.

I am grateful for the support of my colleagues in the Department of Computing and New Media Technologies at the University of Wisconsin-Stevens Point. Along with my current colleagues, other educators have given their support during the writing of this text. Thanks go to Roger Grant, Professor Emeritus of the University of Wisconsin—La Crosse, for his support of my photographic endeavors over the years and with this text in particular. Bob Kanyusik has been a colleague, supporter, and mentor of the highest level during my years at Nicolet College and beyond. These two people have instilled me with a passion for photography and teaching, and I am forever grateful.

To my father, John Bockoven, my sister, Beverly Doyle, Phyllis, Paul, and Pam Stern and Laura Smith, thank you for your moral support. And to my husband, Ed, I have deeply appreciated your unwavering support of my work on this project. I am so glad all of you are in my life.

Delmar, Cengage Learning and the author would like to thank the following reviewers for their valuable suggestions and expertise:

Elizabeth Amidon
Santa Barbara City College
Santa Barbara, California

Jeff Curto
College of DuPage
Glen Ellyn, Illinois

Daniel Goscha
Nicolet Area Technical College
Rhinelander, Wisconsin

Craig McMonigal
Parkland College
Champaign, Illinois

Paul Pelak
International Academy of Design & Technology
Tampa, Florida

Seantel Saunders
Santa Barbara City College
Santa Barbara, California

Peggy Shaw
Parkland College
Champaign, Illinois

Lynn Wright
Savannah College of Art and Design
Savannah, Georgia

Phil Ziesemer
Freelance Photographer
Merrill, Wisconsin

About the Cover Photo

To select a front cover photograph for this book, the author and the Cengage team searched for a visual story depicting photography's capacity to change the way people think about their lives and the lives of those around them. When Art Director Joy Kocsis discovered this image among the photographs created by JR, an undercover French photographer who won the 2011 TED Prize (www.tedprize.org), we knew we had found our cover photo.

From Parisian slums to the walls of the Middle East to the favelas of Brazil, JR works in areas typically not touched by art, with the goal of provoking change by fostering a sense of community. He asks community members to model for him, and then he mounts massive prints of the people he photographs onto walls, bridges, and buildings. His installations invite a visual dialogue between passers-by and their families, their neighbors, and themselves. As he notes on his website, "JR owns the biggest gallery in the world. He exhibits freely in the streets of the world." Read more about JR and his work at http://jr-art.net.

Questions and Feedback

Delmar, Cengage Learning and the author welcome your questions and feedback. If you have suggestions that you think you and others would benefit from, please let us know and we will try to include them in the next edition.

To send us your questions and/or feedback, you can contact the publisher at:

Delmar, Cengage Learning
Executive Woods
5 Maxwell Drive
Clifton Park, NY 12065
Attn: Media Arts & Design Team
800-998-7498

Cedar River at Night, 2009.

CHAPTER

What Is a Photograph?

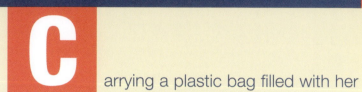arrying a plastic bag filled with her family's severely damaged photo album, a woman entered the volunteers' room at the African American Museum in Cedar Rapids, Iowa. The odor of "flood" emanated from the bag. As the woman approached the volunteers' table, she began, "I have some pictures…" Her voice faltered. Tears welled in the woman's eyes and in the eyes of the volunteers.

June 2008 in Cedar Rapids, Iowa, spelled disaster for thousands of residents, businesses, religious centers, museums, libraries, bridges, and roads. Unusually heavy rains caused heavy flooding of the river running directly through the city.

Figure 1-1

Cedar Rapids, Iowa, June 13, 2008.
© David K. Purdy/epa/Corbis.

More than 1,200 blocks of the city were flooded, forcing 30,000 residents to evacuate their homes. The floods continued for a span of three weeks. More than 4,000 homes were underwater. Of the 90 counties in Iowa, 83 were declared disaster areas. The cost of the damage was more than $6 billion.

Upon their return after the waters receded, residents and businesspeople had to clean up the devastation left behind by the floods. One victim identified the unforgettable smell of "flood" as the combined odors of water, mud, and mold. The ingredients had intermingled and coated everything in the flood's path, including family albums and photographs that their owners had treasured for decades.

About 15 months after the flood waters receded, a nonprofit grassroots organization called Operation Photo Rescue came to Cedar Rapids. The organization's mission was to photograph, digitally retouch, and reprint damaged photos not covered by insurance free of charge to the flood victims.

After the long and painful pause, the tearful woman at the African American Museum in Cedar Rapids, Iowa, continued her story. She described her family's sense of loss over the damaged photo album. Operation Photo Rescue volunteers paged through the album and found some prints that could be saved.

More flood victims came with equally moving stories. Volunteers carefully photographed dozens of damaged prints and immediately returned the prints to their owners. The images were later uploaded to an online catalog where approximately 2,000 volunteers from around the world viewed the images.

The volunteers compared the damage on each photograph to their own level of retouching skills, downloaded the images they could repair, and painstakingly retouched the damaged areas. After the repaired images were uploaded to Operation Photo Rescue, they were printed and returned to the owners at absolutely no cost to the families.

Photography in Your Life

We see them everywhere. Photographs are printed on magazines, newspapers, billboards, brochures, packages, bags, and toys. The World Wide Web is filled with photographs. The wildly popular Flickr website holds more than four billion photographs. Snapfish.com and Picasa.com help people share their photos with friends and families around the world. Facebook members upload more than two billion photographs per month.

There are literally hundreds of digital camera models available for purchase at any given time. You can take photographs with your digital camera or cell phone and immediately share them with friends or send them out for printing. Photos are attached to e-mails and sent to all corners of the earth. People's daily lives in most of the world are inundated with photographs (Figure 1-2).

From a technical standpoint, a photograph on the wall or in an album is simply a piece of paper with a gelatinous surface containing silver or colored dyes. A photograph on the World Wide Web is simply a series of digits, either 0 or 1, organized in a specific way to create a visual image on a computer or handheld device. These dry, unemotional descriptions do nothing to endear us to our personal collection of photographs. Nor do they entice us to pick up a camera and create more images!

Purposes of Photography

There are four general purposes for photography. First, decade after decade, people have turned to photography for its decorative function (Figure 1-3). Satisfying their own creative urges, photographers capture the beauty of their surroundings and share with viewers what they find as beautiful or visually interesting. Helping others see what might otherwise go completely unnoticed, photographers select

Figure 1-2

Magazine stand, Rome, Italy.
© Richard T. Nowrtz/Corbis.

Figure 1-3

Magnolia Blossom, 1925.

Image Courtesy of the Imogen
Cunningham Trust © 1925, 2010
Imogen Cunningham Trust/www.
ImogenCunningham.com.

subject matter existing in their everyday world or find beautiful scenes available only in exotic locations.

Second, other people like to create images that include very personal symbolism, something deeply personal. If the image was created with the intention of reflecting inner thoughts, we call it **expressive photography** (Figure 1-4).

A third purpose for photography is persuasion or propaganda. Thousands of advertising and political photographs seek

Figure 1-4

Familia. Abades,
Segovia, 2009.

Courtesy of Dánae Cuesta
(www.danaecuesta.com),
Barcelona, Spain.

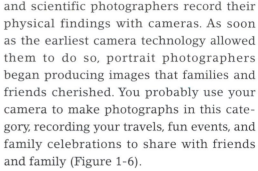

and scientific photographers record their physical findings with cameras. As soon as the earliest camera technology allowed them to do so, portrait photographers began producing images that families and friends cherished. You probably use your camera to make photographs in this category, recording your travels, fun events, and family celebrations to share with friends and family (Figure 1-6).

The society of the twenty-first century is a multimedia society. Photographs are combined with sound, motion, text, and video. Technologists and engineers are constantly coming up with new inventions to create more diverse photographs. As such, photography is an ever-changing art form.

Photography in Our Society

Throughout history, art has helped us understand the social and political aspects of past and current cultures. Art inevitably mirrors the culture that created it. As far back as when humans dwelled in caves, we learned about society through the art made by that more primitive society.

The painting by Jan van Eyck in 1434, as shown in Figure 1-7, is one example

Figure 1-5

Nawaz Sharif's Election Campaign—Meeting of Nawaz Sharif during his campaign for the general election in Pakistan. Leader of the Islamic Democratic Alliance (IJI), he won the election and became Prime Minister on November 1, 1990. Supporters hold up photographs of Pakistan's Former President Muhammad Zia-ul-Haq® and Nawaz Sharif.

Photograph © Derek Hudson/ Sygma/Corbis.

to persuade you to believe their message. This is particularly true during election years when political candidates flood the print media with photos and posters (Figure 1-5). Well aware of the persuasive aspect of photographs, marketing professionals use the medium to sell their products.

A fourth purpose of photography is to record an event, scene, or object. This includes by far the majority of photographs today. Photojournalists record events as they're happening, helping us better understand the world and current events. Medical

Figure 1-6 (left)

Visitors to San Francisco, 2009.

Photo © KS.

Figure 1-7 (right)

Portrait of Giovanni Arnolfini and his wife Giovanna Cenami (*The Arnolfini Marriage*) 1434 (oil on panel), Eyck, Jan van (c.1390–1441).

© National Gallery, London, UK/ The Bridgeman Art Library.

of how art mirrors culture. Filled with symbolism, this painting tells us about the culture and beliefs of the couple depicted and the society in which they lived. We learn about their clothing, what their homes looked like, their beliefs surrounding the wedding ceremony, and their place in society. The bride appears to be pregnant, but research suggests that the portrayal of the woman in this manner reveals the fashionable look for women's dresses at that time. There are several symbols of wealth in the painting, including the room's chandelier, the oranges on the table behind the man, and the fur on the couple's clothing.

Culturally revealing drawings, paintings, and sculptures have survived throughout modern history. The study of these art pieces enrich our understanding of how people thought and lived during those times. Photography takes a similar role in our society, dramatically increasing the number of images and art pieces that show us what our society was like a few decades ago and who we have become. But instead of being available only to fine artists, photography is available to millions of people. As a result, we have an unprecedented record of who we are today.

Because of the ubiquitous and instantaneous nature of digital photography, cultures are being documented at a pace unapproachable by other art forms. *National Geographic* magazine sends photographers around the world to visually document cultures we could otherwise only read about (Figure 1-8).

Photography plays a reflective role that shows others who we are, what we think is important, or who we want to be. It can decorate a wall; it can educate. It can persuade; it can intimidate. Photography can also encourage or discourage behaviors in others. Advertisers, newspaper editors, package

Figure 1-8

Women use their bare feet to thresh rice on mats spread on grass.

© J. BAYLOR ROBERTS/National Geographic Stock.

designers, graphic designers, marketing experts, individual artists, special interest groups, families, friends, politicians, sports enthusiasts, greeting card companies—all these people use photography to promote a cause or to celebrate an event.

By creating brochures, posters, and advertisements containing photography, medical organizations encourage people to take care of their health. Thousands of not-for-profit organizations use photographic advertising to encourage the public to give to worthy causes. Entertainment and fine art organizations use photography to showcase cultural events (Figure 1-9).

Why Study Photography?

It is incredibly easy to take a picture. Pick up a digital camera, turn it on, and push a button. If photography is so easy to do, why study the subject at all? What is there to learn? Will your spontaneity be hampered by all of the steps you study in this text? Will it take forever to set up a photo, forcing you to miss that magic moment? Surely, if you take enough pictures, some of them will be spectacular, right?

The process of learning about photography forces you to slow down and use your brain more than your camera's internal computer chip. You will need to become much more methodical and thoughtful when using your camera for a while. It's like learning how to ride a bicycle. At first riding a bike was really challenging and you made lots of mistakes, fell off, and perhaps got a little scratched up. But as you improved, your skills became second nature. You no longer thought about the process. The same thing will happen with photography. Concentrate on studying the basic skills for a long time, and then add new skills as you improve. Challenge yourself to gain more control over your camera's functions. Take long hours to learn how to see as photographers see.

Eventually, you will be able to return to a spontaneous method of working with your camera. You will still go through all of the thought processes you've learned, but you'll go through them very quickly. Instead of thinking for ten minutes, for example, you'll think for a tenth of a second. You will be far more prepared for that spontaneous moment, and your photographs will no longer look like everyday snapshots. Instead, you will create images that capture a visual story worthy of being appreciated and remembered.

The goal of this text is to help you visually communicate your thoughts and ideas to viewers, a skill that improves with training and practice. It takes time and effort to learn the skills, but it will be worthwhile when you see your pho-tographs improve. Throughout this textbook, you will learn the language of photography. You will see elements of photographs you had not noticed before. By studying design elements like line, texture, form, highlights, and shadows, you will create photographs that meet your own personal goals—be they to decorate, to record events, to persuade, or to create strong personal visual messages.

Finding Photographic Opportunities

The exercises at the end of each chapter will introduce you to techniques and thought processes that will make you a better photographer. You may wonder at times *what* to photograph, and that is a valid question. It's most helpful to begin with something that particularly interests you, say, a hobby, a profession, or a true passion. For example, see Figure 1-10 through Figure 1-14.

Being a photography student opens doors. People tend to give student photographers permission to photograph subjects for a class assignment. Find the courage to ask permission to photograph in situations that you might otherwise feel uneasy about. Many people are willing to help photographers, and especially student photographers, achieve their goals.

NOTE

Photography Opens Doors

Remember this: Photography opens doors. Ask permission to photograph in places you might not otherwise go. You might be turned down, in which case be gracious and move on. But if you are given permission, go and make the best photographs you can. When you are granted special photographic opportunities, always remain considerate of other people's property and possessions. Thank the people who helped you.

Andrew Moore

Detroit Disassembled

No longer the Motor City of boom-time industry, the city of Detroit has fallen into an incredible state of dilapidation since the decline of the American auto industry after the World War II. Today, whole sections of the city resemble a war zone, its once-spectacular architectural grandeur reduced to vacant ruins. Moore's photographs record a territory in which the ordinary flow of time—or the forward march of the assembly line—appears to have been thrown spectacularly into reverse. For Moore, who throughout his career has been drawn to all that contradicts or seems to threaten America's postwar self-image (his previous projects include portraits of Cuba and Soviet Russia), Detroit's decline affirms the carnivorousness of our earth, as it seeps into and overruns the buildings of a city that once epitomized humankind's supposed supremacy. Beyond their jaw-dropping content, Moore's photographs raise the uneasy question of the long-term future of a country in which such extreme degradation can exist unchecked.

Figure 1-10

The Rouge, Dearborn, 2008.

Photo © Andrew Moore.

Figure 1-11

Detroit Dry Dock, Rivertown, 2009.

Photo © Andrew Moore.

Figure 1-12

Kinga, Eastside, 2009.

Photo © Andrew Moore.

Figure 1-13

Model T Headquarters,
Highland Park, 2009.

Photo © Andrew Moore.

Figure 1-14

Roofparty, Broderick
Tower, 2009.

Photo © Andrew Moore.

Learn everything you can about the subject you are photographing. If you get an opportunity to photograph farm machinery, study everything you can about that subject before making your photographs. Not only will you add to your own general knowledge, but you will also make better photographs because you understand the subject.

Photographing People

Rather than "taking" photographs, which implies a taking of something from someone, "make" photographs with the consent of those you photograph. If you're photographing in a foreign country, smile and use hand gestures, pointing to your camera and then to the person to request permission to photograph. Not only does this help your reputation, but it will also gain the cooperation of people you're photographing. The end results will be better photographs and a more positive experience for everyone.

There is one particular issue you need to especially consider: You must ask permission before photographing children. Ask the parent's or guardian's permission and explain the purpose of your photography. If you carry a business card, give your card to the parent or guardian.

Creating Goodwill

If it is feasible, offer to send the person who gave you the photographic opportunity a free print of one of your photographs as thanks for allowing you to make the photographs. *Follow through with that offer*. Don't forget about it or set it aside for a later date. This practice will increase your credibility as a photographer and may open a similar door for another photographer in the future.

About the Textbook

This text will ask you to think about how a photograph affects you and how a photograph you make can affect others. In our media-rich culture, it's important to realize that people *are* affected by the photographs they see. The techniques you decide to use when making images will have an impact on the message your viewers receive from your photographs.

You will ask questions like: What do you want to photograph? Why do you want to photograph it? What message are you trying to send to your viewers? What action or reaction do you want from your viewers? Such thought processes are called **intentions**.

If you can ask yourself these questions and translate the answers into the visual photograph, your images will be stronger and more dynamic. Your camera and computer will be tools at your command, rather than machines working independently of your thoughts and ideas.

You will also be introduced to the history of photography. Because photographic history is best understood within the context of when it took place, the By the Decade section of this text (Appendix A) lists important dates and information from the fields of photography, world and U.S. history, and art history. Use this information as a springboard for your study of the history of photography.

You will learn about copyright law and best business practices for photographers. This knowledge will help protect you as a photographer and consumer of visual media.

Along this learning road, you will meet some professional photographers working in a variety of photographic specialties. They will give you a little background about themselves and will also give some advice targeted at budding professional photographers. You'll also see photographs by professionals and amateurs, who have taken the time to master their craft, and you'll read their own thoughts about how or why they made their photographs.

Finally, you will find references in this text at the end of chapters giving direction on where to find more information. No introductory textbook can cover all the information available on any subject.

Susan Lirakis

Although all photographic work, at some level, is a mirror for who we are, I work additionally and more directly with myself through an exploration of my personal mythology. I make self-portraits using long exposures and little available light. With the advent of digital processes, I have delighted in making combined imagery and new stories.

In my effort to find sanctuary, I meditate in and photograph the landscape, both in a traditional manner and with plastic cameras—which help in the interpretation of the places photographed. The blurred quality of these cameras helps create images filled with spirit, feeling, mystery, and the language of dreaming.

Figure 1-15

Tempest by Susan Lirakis.

Photo courtesy of Susan Lirakis.

However, if you pursue the references listed at the end of each chapter, you will quickly gain more valuable information.

How to Learn Photography

- Make photographs. Make hundreds of thousands of photographs. There is no substitute for experience when learning photography.
- Select a theme and follow it, taking as many photos on that theme as you can. Later, refine your selection of photos and explore new avenues to visually express your thoughts about that theme.
- Keep track of what you do. Record the lighting conditions, your camera settings, the way you set up a still life. Then evaluate the resulting photograph. You'll quickly learn what works and what doesn't work.
- Read and reread your camera manual. Keep it with you when you go out to photograph. Keep it handy when you read this text so you can apply your new knowledge to your own camera.
- Seek examples of professional photography on the Internet. Compare the images of professionals to the images you make. How are they similar? How are they different? Be inspired by the images you find.
- Read about other photographers and why they make the images they do. Good photography tells stories. It brings to light the ideas, thoughts, and concerns of others. Taking the time to read information about the photographers themselves will help you understand their images. It will also give you ideas for photographic series of your own.

Summary

People have been in love with photography for more than 170 years. Photographs have gone from highly rare and delicate prints to constant bombardments of our visual everyday lives. They are used for decoration, persuasion, personal symbolism, and a means to save memories.

Being a photography student opens doors to new opportunities. Photograph what you care about. Those images will likely be stronger because of your own emotional investment in the subject.

Viewers better remember photographs that tell a story. This textbook will teach you techniques that help your photographs tell the visual story you want to portray. There's a lot to learn. Let's get started!

EXERCISES

1. Write a single-page paper on what you think about photography. What is the role of photography in your life right now? Why have you chosen to study photography?

2. Do one of the following:

   a. Use one roll of print film and make a series of photographs on a theme of your choosing. Select a theme that you care about. Have the film processed and printed.

   b. Take 30 digital photographs of your choosing. Create a PowerPoint slide show of your images to share with others.

3. Go onto the Internet and look at as many photos as you can find on the same subject that you photographed for Exercise 2. How do those photographs differ from the photographs you made? How are they similar?

4. Think about the media and how images you see on television and in magazines influence your life. Which images stand out to you? Why do you think they remain in your memory?

5. Take this opportunity to talk with your family members about what your family album means to them. From an emotional standpoint, what is the value of your family's photo collection?

6. Carefully read the Artists' Statements written by Andrew Moore and Susan Lirakis in this chapter. Then look again at their photographs. What connections can you draw between the photographs and the Artists' Statements? Evaluate how the photographs relate to the corresponding Artist's Statement.

FURTHER READING

■ RESEARCH art forms from the impressionism, romanticism, and neoclassical art movements. They were prevalent in the 1800s, around the time photography was invented. Use the following keywords: "impressionistic art," "impressionism art history," "Romantic art," "neoclassical art," and "photography history."

■ LOOK AT ARTWORK by Claude Monet, Paul Cézanne, Georges Seurat, Vincent van Gogh, and Jacques-Louis David.

■ DO RESEARCH ON Louis Daguerre and William Henry Fox Talbot. Learn about the beginnings of photography.

■ IN THE BY THE DECADE SECTION, refer to the 1850–1860 and 1860–1870 eras to relate your research to what was happening in the world when photography was invented.

Positioning a Camera for Mars Reconnaissance Orbiter January 7, 2005. Workers at Lockheed Martin Space Systems, Denver, position a telescopic camera for installation onto NASA's Mars Reconnaissance Orbiter spacecraft on Dec. 11, 2004. Ball Aerospace and Technology Corp., Boulder, Colo., built this camera, called the High Resolution Imaging Science Experiment, or HiRISE, for the University of Arizona, Tucson, to supply for the mission.

Photo courtesy of NASA Jet Propulsion Laboratory (NASA-JPL).

2

Getting to Know Cameras

Chapter Learning Objectives

■ Observe the difference between 35 mm viewfinder cameras and SLR cameras.

■ List the components of a camera body.

■ Identify the important parts of lenses and learn how they work.

■ Describe how the camera's built-in light meter obtains proper exposure.

■ Explain how CMOS sensors work within digital cameras.

■ Identify medium-format, plastic, pinhole, large-format (4 × 5-inch), and cell phone cameras, and describe different scenarios in which each might be used.

■ Prevent problems with your camera by taking good care of it.

The role of any camera is simple: Capture a scene in front of the camera and record it onto film or a digital storage device. It is the tool you will use to create images of interest to you. Your challenge as a student of photography isn't simply to capture an image. The challenge is to use the camera in ways that enhance your subject matter and help you convey meaning in your photographs. In this chapter, you will learn how your camera can help you meet these challenges and how you can gain the photographic control you need to achieve your goals.

Many photographers begin with a thought process of deciding what to photograph and how to photograph it. Their intentions for the photographic work will dictate their selection of equipment and camera settings. They will consider what kind of camera to use, what settings would work best for their purposes, what conditions they will encounter, and what obstacles might arise. All of these factors impact the photographer's choice of equipment and camera settings.

The more you can learn about how your camera works, the better decisions you will be able to make when creating your own images. Camera technology goes hand in hand with the photographer's thought process. One inherently influences the other. The impact of using a camera in ways that meet and enhance the photographer's intention can't be overstated. Learning about the technical aspects of your camera is the first step in becoming a better photographer.

Many elements of traditional film-based and digital cameras are very similar, if not identical. You will first learn about the elements that are similar between the two styles of cameras. Later you will learn about elements that pertain only to digital cameras.

Early Cameras

All cameras have one thing in common: they record light. In fact, "photography" is derived from Greek root words meaning "recording of light."

Most people think that all cameras have a lens. However, the earliest cameras weren't even that sophisticated. The simplest of all cameras is a **pinhole camera** (Figure 2-1), a light-tight box with a tiny hole on one side. On the other side of the box is a flat plane where film or light-sensitive paper can be held in position. During an exposure, light is allowed in through the hole and hits the film or paper. When the exposure is complete, the photographer closes the hole to block out any more light.

The photographer takes the film or paper out of the camera and develops it in chemistry. This produces a **negative**. On a negative, all objects that reflected a lot of light (which bright or lightly-colored objects in a scene do) appear as dark areas. Objects that reflect very little light (which dark or dark-colored objects do) appear very light on the negative (Figure 2-2).

To create a positive photographic print from a traditional photographic negative, a light is projected through the negative and lands on a piece of light-sensitive paper. After the proper exposure time, the paper is placed in a liquid developing solution producing the **positive**, or the print (Figure 2-3). Areas that were dark in the scene appear dark on the print, and

Figure 2-1

A manufactured pinhole camera.

Photo © KS.

Figure 2-2 (left)

This negative measures 4 × 5 inches, considerably larger than film used by 35 mm cameras. The negative was exposed using a pinhole camera in a garden shop. The exposure was approximately 2½ minutes.

Figure 2-3 (right)

This is the positive image of the negative shown in Figure 2-2.

Photos 2-2 and 2-3 © KS.

A viewfinder-style camera.

Photo © Justin Maresch/
iStockphoto.

they are either viewfinder (Figure 2-4) or SLR (single-lens reflex) cameras.

Viewfinder Cameras

All cameras have a **viewfinder**, a small window through which you look to compose and focus the scene you are photographing. Where that viewfinder is located and how it functions within the camera differentiates viewfinder cameras from SLR cameras.

Viewfinder cameras use a **rangefinder optical system** that separates the viewfinder from the lens. In viewfinder cameras, the viewfinder itself is placed above and often to the side of the lens. Because the window goes completely through the camera, it allows you to see directly to the scene in front of you. You look through the viewfinder to compose your image, but the viewfinder doesn't show you the same scene as the lens captures.

If your subject is close to you, a phenomenon called **parallax** causes a visual miscalculation between what you see through the viewfinder and what your camera ultimately records. You run the risk of taking pictures slightly low and off center, even though you thought your scene was perfectly composed when you looked through the viewfinder (Figure 2-5).

Parallax can be problematic unless you're aware of the situation. By moving your camera so the lens is positioned where your viewfinder was when you composed the scene, you can quickly overcome this problem. Typically this requires only an inch or so of repositioning.

Unlike SLR cameras (which are discussed in the next section), the lenses on many viewfinder cameras can't be removed.

areas that were light in the scene appear light in the print.

The pinhole camera is one of the simplest and earliest forms of photography. Although it can create beautiful images, it gives the photographer very little control. Modern cameras have lenses, light meters, apertures, and other controls to give you many ways in which to create images.

It's very important to realize that all camera brands differ slightly in design. We'll be discussing elements that are common to (almost) all cameras, but your camera manual will tell you how this information relates to your camera. Refer often to your manual as you read this chapter.

There is one distinguishing feature between all 35 mm cameras, both film and digital:

Figure 2-5

Viewfinder cameras cause a misalignment of what you see through the viewfinder and what the camera lens captures. By moving the camera slightly, you can compensate for the misalignment.

© Cengage Learning 2012.

What the viewfinder shows.

What the camera captures.

NOTE

The issue of parallax has been minimized with the live view capabilities available on some digital cameras. The image you see in the live view is the same scene your camera will record.

A viewfinder camera's lens may be a **fixed focal length** (or **prime**) **lens**, such as 50 mm, or it may have a **zoom lens** that can cover a variety of focal lengths, such as 35 mm to 70 mm or from 28 mm to 105 mm. Fixed focal length lenses can only give you a single view of your scene. A zoom lens can give you a **wide-angle view**, showing more of the scene in your photo, or it can give a **telephoto view**, showing less of the scene in your photo. A telephoto view makes it seem like you are closer to your subject than you really are.

Viewfinder cameras can be either film-based or digital, and there are dozens of brands and styles available. The most basic viewfinder cameras offer very few controls for you to use. They make most of the decisions for you, therefore falling into the **point-and-shoot** classification of cameras. Although this is fine for some situations, it doesn't give you the control needed to make deliberate decisions about how your photographs will look.

SLR Cameras

SLR ("single-lens reflex") **cameras** are constructed quite differently from viewfinder cameras and can be film-based or digital (Figure 2-6). An image coming through an SLR camera lens is reflected off a mirror, goes through a prism of glass, and then appears through the viewfinder on the back of your camera. The image you see in your viewfinder is very close to being the exact image your lens is taking in. This allows you to make much more accurate decisions on what parts of the scene will end up in your photograph. Parallax is not an issue with SLR cameras.

When the scene first hits the internal mirror, it is upside down from the original scene. This is a result of the bending, or refraction, of the light as it travels through the lens. A **pentaprism** (a piece of glass with five sides) located above the mirror reverts the image to right-side up so you can see the image as it is in real life (Figure 2-7).

The film-based SLR camera's mirror blocks the light coming through the lens from reaching the **shutter** (a series of

metal strips that open and close to allow light to expose the film) and film in the back of the camera. As a result, the mirror must be moved out of the way so the light can reach the shutter and ultimately the film. When you push the shutter button, the mirror flips up and the shutter opens, moving out of the light's path. When the exposure is complete, the shutter closes and the mirror falls back into its original position. This movement of the mirror causes you to temporarily lose sight of your scene during the exposure. It also causes, in part, the clicking sound you hear when you push the shutter button.

The mirror of an SLR camera is very delicate and should not be touched. If the mirror becomes dirty, a professional camera repair shop should repair it. Dirt on the mirror or the pentaprism will not show up in your photographs.

Figure 2-6

A digital SLR camera.

Photo © Nicolas Hansen/ iStockphoto.

Figure 2-7

Path and orientation of an image traveling through an SLR camera.

© Cengage Learning 2012.

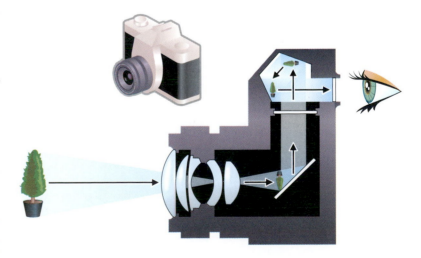

Camera Body

The body of the camera is essentially a light-tight box. **Light-tight** means that light coming through the lens during an exposure is the only light that can reach the camera's internal parts.

SLR camera bodies have a hole to which the lens is attached via a mounting style specific to that brand of camera. Modern film-based camera bodies also have a battery, an on-off switch, a viewfinder, and a shutter. The dials and screens on the camera's exterior give you information about the settings within the camera. Each brand and model of camera differs in what settings are available. It is important to frequently refer to your camera's manual as you learn about those settings in this chapter.

The Light Meter

Every modern, battery-run camera has a built-in light meter that registers the amount of light coming through the lens. Its purpose is to help you make correctly exposed photographs. A **correct exposure** means that the film negative (or digital information) produces a print in which the light areas and light-colored objects are as light as you would expect, and the shadows and dark objects are as dark as you would expect from the scene you photographed.

Most in-camera light meters automatically take a reading when you push the shutter button halfway down. Different brands of cameras have different styles of light meters; so, consult your owner's manual to learn how your camera's light meter works.

Camera Lenses

All cameras other than pinhole cameras use a lens to focus the image. Although lenses appear to be a single piece of glass, they are actually made of several pieces of convex or concave glass within a cylinder. Studies of physics have shown that light passing through just one lens may not focus properly, rendering a slightly blurry image. By using multiple pieces of glass, lenses can render a very clear, sharp picture onto the film or digital sensor.

All lenses have **focal lengths**. The focal length of a lens is a measurement of the distance from the **principal plane** (outer edge) of the lens to where the light rays converge. Just as with the human eye, light rays coming through a lens (either human or camera) bend as they travel toward the back of the eye, or toward the back of the camera lens. The point at which the image converges to a single point is called the **rear nodal point**. The distance (usually measured in millimeters) from the principal plane of the lens to the rear nodal point is called the *focal length of the lens* (Figure 2-8).

Types of Camera Lenses

On 35 mm cameras, a 50 mm lens is considered to be **normal**. That means the angle of view from left to right within the photographed scene approximates your visual field of view with only one eye open. The normal focal length of a lens can also be thought of as the approximate distance of the diagonal of the camera's format. The diagonal length of a single frame of 35 mm film (a single negative on a roll of 35 mm film) is approximately 50 mm.

Telephoto lenses are longer than 50 mm in the 35 mm-format cameras and range from 70 mm to 800 mm or longer. Telephoto lenses act like binoculars in that they narrow your field of view and also magnify

Figure 2-8

The focal length of a lens is the distance from the front (principal plane) of the lens to the point where the image converges to a single point (rear nodal point).

© Cengage Learning 2012.

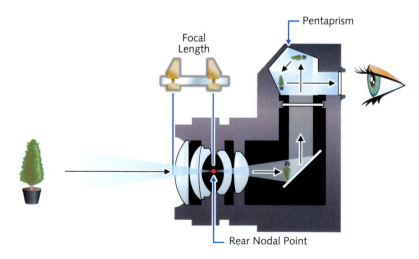

Focal Length

Pentaprism

Rear Nodal Point

Figure 2-9

Diagram of fields of view for various 35 mm lenses.

© Cengage Learning 2012.

23°

105mm

47°

50mm

75°

28mm

the scene (Figure 2-9). A 100 mm lens will make a scene appear twice as close as does a 50 mm lens. One side effect of telephoto lenses is that they tend to make objects behind other objects look somewhat stacked together without an appropriate amount of distance between them. This optical illusion causes differences in the apparent (not real) depth of field of an image. You'll learn more about depth of field later.

Wide-angle lenses have focal lengths shorter than 50mm in the 35 mm-format cameras and range from 35 mm down to 4.5 mm (also called *fisheye lenses*). Wide-angle lenses allow you to photograph large areas, such as mountains or football stadiums, from shorter distances. Your photographs will show a much wider scene than you can see with one eye open. Wide-angle lenses can distort images. Photographing a person close to the camera with a wide-angle lens will cause facial distortions. Any lines within your scene can also be distorted—straight lines can appear curved at the edges of the photograph.

Zoom lenses are relatively complex lenses that allow you to alter the focal length of a lens according to your needs. There are several zoom lenses available, including 28–80 mm or 24–105 mm, 100–300 mm, or 70–210 mm.

If you're using a 35 mm camera and the first number is less than 50, and the second number is greater than 50, the lens has a range from wide-angle to telephoto. It's a wide-angle zoom lens if both numbers are less than 50 on a 35 mm camera. It's a telephoto zoom lens if both numbers are greater than 50 on a 35 mm camera. Zoom lenses have the tremendous advantage of giving you more opportunities to choose what portion of a scene to photograph. By staying in one place and zooming in or out, you can decide how much of your scene to photograph without needing to move.

Prime lenses, the opposite of a zoom lens, are fixed focal length lenses. These lenses are listed as having only one focal length. If you are using a fixed focal length lens and want to change how much to photograph within your scene, you need to move toward or away from that scene to make the change—your lens can't do the leg work for you. However, fixed focal length lenses may render sharper photographs than some less-expensive zoom lenses.

Focusing Distances of Lenses

All lenses have a **minimum focusing distance**. If your subject is closer than this distance to your lens, you can't focus on it. If you are interested in doing close-up photography, it's worth asking about

the minimum focusing distance for a lens before you purchase it. Fixed focal length lenses frequently have a shorter minimum focusing distance than do zoom lenses set at the same focal length. In other words, you might be able to focus closer to an object using a 100 mm fixed focal length lens than with a 28–105 zoom lens set at 100 mm.

Some lenses, including zoom lenses, come with a **macro setting**. This feature allows an even shorter minimum focusing distance than the same lens without a macro setting. It's still worth your while to research the actual minimum focusing distance for any lens before you purchase it, as a macro feature on a zoom lens may not match the minimum focusing distance of fixed focal length lenses, whether they have macro settings or not.

Optional Lens Functions and Accessories

Some lenses are fitted with special **image stabilization (IS)** functions. If your lens has IS, it will steady itself enough to compensate for natural *camera shake,* or movement from handholding your camera. However, you can't trust the IS function to remove all risk of camera shake—far from it! Experiment with IS before trusting it to help you in your standard photographic situations.

Many camera manufacturers also make lenses for their cameras. Each company has a style of mount that connects the lens onto that company's cameras. If you purchase a lens from a company that didn't make your camera, you may not be able to connect that lens to your camera. If you make such a purchase, be sure to order the lens with a lens mount made specifically for your brand of camera. Some companies only make lenses, not cameras. These companies have a variety of lens mounts available for customers. Be sure to tell the seller what kind of camera you will be using. The seller will make sure you get the proper type of lens mount on your new lens.

Lenses are sold with lens covers to protect the expensive glass of the lens (Figure 2-10). Although many people lose

Figure 2-10

Lens covers protect lenses from dirt and damage.

Photo © KS.

and never replace their lens covers, such practices aren't recommended. Lenses are expensive. Protect your lenses by keeping their lens covers on whenever you are not making photographs. If you lose a lens cover, replace it.

Some lenses are sold with lens shades. These plastic tubes are attached to the front of the lens whenever you are using the camera (Figure 2-11). Their purpose is to prevent rays from a light source from hitting the lens at an obtuse angle, scattering the light and causing **lens flare** (Figure 2-12). Lens flare can wash out your image, leaving it lighter than you intended. It can also create unexpected polygonal bright spots within your image that are created by the diaphragm reflecting through the lens elements.

Lens shades have the added value of protecting the glass of a lens that might accidentally be dropped. They can be uniformly shaped for longer focal length lenses, or they can be tulip-shaped for shorter focal length and/or zoom lenses. The tulip-shaped shades prevent **vignetting**, or cutting off a portion of the scene.

If you use a tulip-shaped lens shade, be sure that the shorter portions of the shade are placed parallel with the widest format of the film plane. In other words, when you're holding the camera horizontally, the shorter portions of the shade are to the left and right of the lens. If your camera is being held in the vertical position, the shorter portions of the shade should be above and below the lens. This will automatically take place when you turn the camera to the vertical position (Figure 2-13).

Figure 2-11

A lens shade placed on the front of the lens helps prevent lens flare and also protects the lens if it's dropped.

Photo © EML/Shutterstock.

Figure 2-12

Lens flare is caused by a light source hitting the lens at an angle. Some photographers like the effect; others do not. Lens flare is more likely to occur with inexpensive glass or plastic lenses.

Photo by Janaka Dharmasena/ Shutterstock.

A third way to protect your lens is to purchase a relatively inexpensive filter, such as an ultraviolet (UV) filter, and keep it on your lens. The UV filter helps to filter out some of the ultraviolet light entering your lens, but it has no effect on exposure and rarely has any effect on the color balance of your images. If something spills onto your lens or if the lens is accidentally

Figure 2-13a (left)

Incorrect application of a tulip-shaped lens shade. The short sides are perpendicular to the horizontally positioned camera.

Figure 2-13b (right)

Correct application of a tulip-shaped lens shade. The short sides are parallel to the horizontally positioned camera.

Photos 2-13a and 2-13b © KS.

bumped or dropped, the UV filter will protect the much more expensive lens. Check the size you need before you purchase a filter for a lens. It's the number in millimeters printed on the inside rim of the front of your lens (Figure 2-14).

Good lenses have **optical coatings** that increase the actual transmission of light so the lens is more efficient. Optical coatings also reduce the amount of scattered light within the lens itself, therefore reducing the chance of lens flare.

An optical coating is a thin layer of material placed on a lens. The most common type is an antireflection coating that reduces unwanted reflections from surfaces. When light goes from one medium (such as air) to another (such as the glass lens), some percentage of the light is

reflected from the surface between the two media. The amount of light reflected back from the lens is known as the **reflection loss**. The percentage of reflection loss when light goes from air to glass is typically about 7.7%. Modern antireflection optical coatings are capable of reducing the reflection loss to less than 0.5%.

Aperture

Modern camera lenses are made of a series of pieces of glass stacked together in a light-tight cylinder. There is also an arrangement of flat, thin pieces of metal that overlap and work together inside the lens to create an opening for the light to pass through the lens. This is the **diaphragm** of the lens, and the size of its opening can change in similar fashion to the iris of your eye (Figures 2-15 and 2-16). If it's a very bright day, the diaphragm opening can become smaller to keep too much light from entering the camera. If it's dark, the diaphragm opening can become larger to allow more light to enter the camera. Note that even though the shape of the diaphragm is similar to that of a leaf shutter, these two parts of a camera and lens are completely separate and different from each other in position and function.

The **aperture** is the actual opening created by the diaphragm. Its size dictates the amount of light allowed through the lens as you make a photograph. An **f-stop** (also called the **relative aperture**) is a

Figure 2-14

A relatively inexpensive UV filter protects your lens from scratches, dirt, or actual breakage if you drop it.

Photo 11-21-09 © CANER ÖDEN/istockphoto.

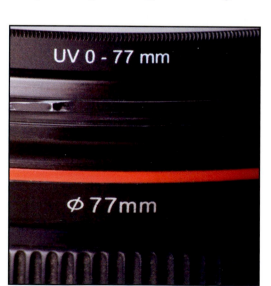

measurement of the aperture expressed as a fraction of the focal length of the lens. The f-stop is found by dividing the focal length of a lens by the effective diameter of its aperture. F-stops are, therefore, fractions of the lens diameter.

For example, a lens with a focal length of 100 mm and an aperture diameter set at 25 mm has an f-stop of 4. The same 100 mm lens with an aperture diameter set at 12.5 mm has an f-stop of 8. Notice that the smaller the aperture for a given lens, the higher the f-stop number associated with it.

The *amount* of light entering the lens is actually measured as the area of the aperture, which equals the square of the aperture's diameter. As an example, the f/4 aperture is twice the diameter of an f/8 aperture, but the f/4 transmits *four times as much light* as the f/8 aperture. Therefore, it is wrong to think that going from f/8 to f/4 would double the amount of light passing through the lens. Going from f/8 to f/4 quadruples the amount of light passing through the lens.

Typical f-stops are f/2.8, f/4.0, f/5.6, f/8, f/11, f/16, and f/22 (Figure 2-17). There is a mathematical relationship between these numbers. Each jump from one aperture number to the next either doubles or cuts in half the amount of light passing through the lens. Each time the aperture is changed by one jump, it is considered a change of 1

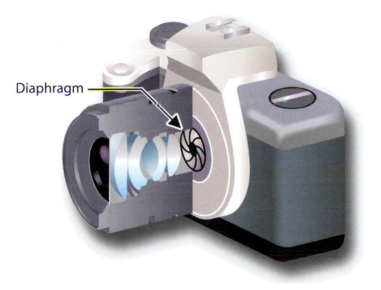

Diaphragm

NOTE

Memorizing the Different Values of Apertures

To help you memorize the different values of apertures, note that a change from f/4 to f/8 (a change of 2 full stops) doubles the number (4 × 2 = 8). A change from f/11 to f/22 (a change of 2 full stops) doubles the number (11 × 2 = 22) and quadruples the amount of light. A change from f/5.6 to f/11 (a change of 2 full stops) isn't exactly doubling the number, but it's very close. Again, this change quadruples the amount of light.

NOTE

Calculating f-Stops

A 100 mm lens with an aperture of 25 mm has an f-stop of 4 (100/25 = 4). A 100 mm lens with an aperture of 12.5 mm has an f-stop of 8 (100/12.5 = 8).

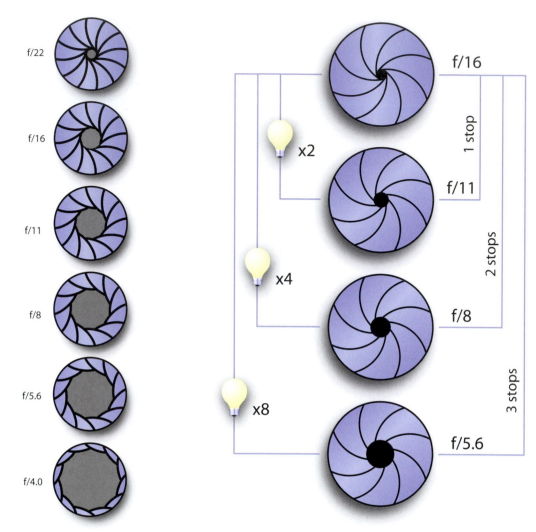

full stop. An aperture of f/5.6 allows twice as much light to pass through the lens as does an aperture of f/8; so, there is a 1-stop difference between f/5.6 and f/8. An aperture of f/22 allows half as much light to pass through the lens as does an aperture of f/16. There is a 1-stop difference between f/16 and f/22 (Figure 2-18).

Most cameras are capable of f-stops that fall between these basic full-stop values. Numbers such as f/3.5 and f/9.6 are considered half-stops. To find half-stops, multiply the f-number by 1.2, or simply add the previous two f-numbers together. As an example, f/4 + f/5.6 = f/9.6. A change from f/8 to f/9.6 is a change of ½-stop. Other cameras are capable of ⅓-stop values. Check your camera's manual to see what fractions of f-stops your camera will be using.

Camera lenses are identified in part by their maximum aperture opening size. A **fast lens** is capable of a very large opening, such as f/2.8, and can use faster shutter speeds to stop action. Sports and wildlife photographers tend to purchase fast lenses because they have a greater chance of stopping the action in their photographs. A **slow lens** is a lens with a maximum aperture of f/5.6 or f/8.0. A slow lens requires longer shutter speeds to compensate for its smaller maximum apertures. Slower lenses tend to be lighter in weight and less expensive than fast lenses.

Shutters and Shutter Speed

All modern cameras have a mechanism that either reveals and then covers the film during exposure or activates and deactivates the digital light sensor.

Film-based SLR and viewfinder cameras use **focal-plane shutters**, which are mounted toward the back of the camera body, just in front of the **film plane**, the plane where the film rests. Older cameras may have a two-curtain system. Each curtain has adjustable spring tensions that alter the speed at which the curtain moves across the film plane.

During a short exposure time, a slit is created between the two curtains, allowing for an exposure of varying speeds, depending on how fast the curtains move across the film plane. During longer exposure times, the first curtain travels across, allowing the entire scene to be captured on film, before the second curtain comes across.

Focal-plane shutters were installed in the earliest cameras. In the early designs, two cloth curtains were moved immediately in front of the image plane. A thin slot separated the two curtains. As the slot moved across the focal plane, light entered the camera and fell on the photographic film. The exposure time, or shutter speed, was equal to the time it took for the cloth curtains to cover the width of the slot (Figure 2-19).

Modern focal-plane shutters are completely suitable for fast-action photography and are installed in many 35 mm, medium-format, and instant cameras. They are typically made of metal or

Figure 2-19

Movement of a two-curtain shutter system.

Photo © KS.

plastic composite blades overlapping Venetian-like blinds instead of a curtain (Figure 2-20). These blades can move much faster and form a very narrow slit. **Shutter speeds** (the length of time the shutter remains open during an exposure) up to 1/8000 second or faster are possible with this technology.

Leaf Shutter

Leaf shutters are built into some lenses. A series of individual metal leaves move in a synchronous pattern to allow light into the camera. The leaves are spring-mounted and move extremely fast, allowing almost all of the light from the scene to enter the camera at the same time (Figure 2-21). Large-format cameras frequently use lenses with leaf shutters (Figure 2-22).

NOTE

A leaf shutter is not the same as the similar-appearing leaf-shaped diaphragm visible in your 35 mm lenses. The diaphragm sets the aperture for the lens, not the shutter speed.

Digital "Shutter"

Digital cameras don't actually have shutters. Instead, your digital camera's sensor allows for an on/off function called **gating**. During the gating time, the sensor is collecting light information coming through the lens. At the end of the gating period, the sensor no longer collects that information. Your camera's circuitry adjusts the exact period of time. Even so,

the term "shutter speed" is still used on digital cameras.

In film-based SLR cameras, the shutter is located inside the camera body (the box part of the camera) and is activated by pushing the shutter button all the way down. The "click" you hear when you've pushed the shutter button down is a combination of the sound of the mirror going up and down and a sound created by the shutter opening and closing.

Shutter Speeds

Shutter speeds are measured in fractions of time. Each doubling or cutting in half of the shutter speed either doubles or cuts in half the amount of light hitting the film or light sensor. A change from ½- to ¼-second is a change of 1 full stop. A change from 1/60- to 1/30-second is a change of 1 full stop. The directional change doesn't matter, as a full stop can designate either a longer or a shorter amount of time. It's the *amount of change* that matters (Figure 2-23).

When reading the shutter speed in your camera, note that a quote mark (") is used to designate a second. If you do not see a quote mark, then the reading is a fraction of a second. For example, 4 is actually ¼ second, but 4" designates 4 seconds.

Specifics of Digital Cameras

Digital and traditional cameras have a lot in common. The information discussed thus far in this chapter applies to both digital and film-based cameras. Digital cameras have some components not found in traditional film-based cameras. We'll go through these components one by one.

Digital Camera Sensors

Digital camera sensors are the "film" of digital cameras. Sensors are responsible for gathering two kinds of information: values (brightness) and colors. With a few exceptions, most modern cameras use CCD or CMOS sensors. At least one manufacturer uses a hybrid sensor, called NMOS (n-channel metal oxide semiconductor).

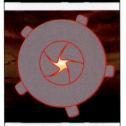

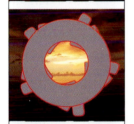

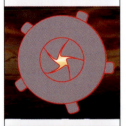

Figure 2-21

Movement of a leaf shutter.

Photo © KS.

Figure 2-22

A large-format lens' leaf shutter is built into the lens and is manually controlled by the silver knob (circled).

Photo © KS.

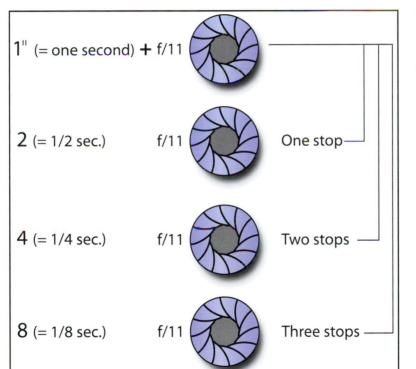

1" (= one second) **+** f/11

2 (= 1/2 sec.)   f/11   One stop

4 (= 1/4 sec.)   f/11   Two stops

8 (= 1/8 sec.)   f/11   Three stops

Figure 2-23

Each doubling or cutting in half of the shutter speed gives a change of 1 full stop, doubling or cutting in half the amount of captured light. Note that the aperture in this illustration remains unchanged.

© Cengage Learning 2012.

CCD

A **charge-coupled device (CCD)** is a solid-state imager (sensor) that converts light coming through the lens into electronic signals. CCDs were the earliest light-converting devices in digital cameras. Although they cost less now, CCDs had a high price tag, which became a big limiting factor for their use,. They are still frequently used in applications demanding high quality, such as scientific and medical applications and high-end consumer cameras. Many digital camera manufacturers have switched to a different solid-state sensor called CMOS for consumer-level cameras.

CMOS

Like a CCD, a **CMOS (complementary metal-oxide semiconductor)** is a sensor that collects light coming through the lens and converts it to electronic signals. In a CMOS sensor, each tiny portion of light coming through a lens has its own charge-to-voltage conversion node. In addition, many CMOS sensors include special circuitry allowing them to create digital bits of information readable by digital cameras (Figure 2-24).

CMOS sensors are dramatically improving in performance as research continues in the industry. Newer sensors boast greater clarity as a result of increased numbers of conversion nodes and other factors that affect quality. As companies continue to improve CMOS technology, digital photography will continue to improve in quality.

Sensor Sizes

Sensor sizes differ dramatically, depending on their ultimate use, their price, and their portability. The smallest digital cameras require small sensors, sometimes one-quarter or less the size of a full-frame sensor. A full-frame sensor in a digital SLR camera is 36 mm × 24 mm. The full-frame sensors in digital medium-format cameras are significantly larger.

The ability of a sensor to capture an entire scene is based in part on its size, but it is also based on the size of the lens being used. Some lens/camera combinations result in a portion of a scene falling beyond the physical position of the sensor. As a result, smaller sensors may capture only the portion of the scene that

---

Shutter Speed Decisions

- **I want to stop the action of my 2-year old child.** FAST shutter speed, faster than 1/250 second if possible.

- **I want to photograph an adult standing still.** RELATIVELY FAST shutter speed, anywhere from 1/30 second or faster.

- **I want to photograph a flower in my garden.** RELATIVELY FAST shutter speed, but use 1/30 second or faster to help stop any motion from breeze.

- **I want to photograph a waterfall and make the water look flowing and milky.** SLOW shutter speed, anywhere from 2–8 seconds. Use a tripod!

- **I want to photograph fireworks.** VERY SLOW shutter speed such as 15–30 seconds. Use a tripod!

- **Is there a rule of thumb for preventing camera shake with lenses of different focal lengths?** YES. Make a fraction out of the lens focal length. If your focal length is 100 mm, your fraction becomes 1/100. That is the slowest shutter speed you should use to prevent camera shake if you are handholding your camera. If you need a slower shutter speed than this rule of thumb suggests, use a tripod.

Figure 2-24

Left: KODAK KAF-10500 Image Sensor, an APS-sized sensor used in the Leica M8 camera. Center: KODAK KAF-18500 Image Sensor, a 35 mm-format sensor used in the Leica M9 camera. Right: KODAK KAF-37500 Image Sensor, which is larger than 35 mm and used in the Leica S2 camera.

Image courtesy of Eastman Kodak Company.

falls on them. The remainder of the scene is not recorded (Figure 2-25).

Sensors, along with any necessary converters, translate visual information into digital strings of 1s and 0s, or digital **bits** of information in binary code. These bits of information, arranged on a computer screen, form the photographic image.

How Does a CMOS Sensor Work?

The light coming through the lens is made up of tiny particles of light called **photons**. As these photons come through the lens, they fall on the CMOS sensor. Each sensor is made up of a grid of light-sensitive sections called **photosites**, sometimes loosely called **pixels**, an acronym for picture elements or tiny parts of a picture. Each individual photosite creates 1 pixel of information in the final image (Figure 2-26).

During an exposure, the camera uncovers or activates the photosites so they can react to the light particles (photons). Once the exposure is over, the camera covers or deactivates the photosites so that no more light can strike them. The brighter the light hitting any one photosite, the greater the electrical charge that is collected at that site.

Each individual photosite does two things. First, it measures the strength or intensity of the light hitting it. Second, it captures the red, green, or blue components of the scene via a single red, green,

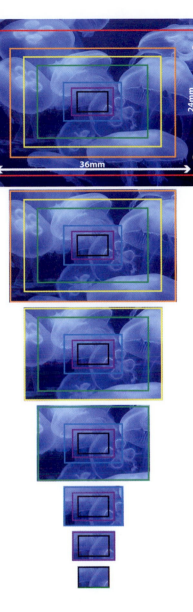

Figure 2-25

Full-frame sensor capture (top) and the capture of smaller sensors below.

Photo © KS.

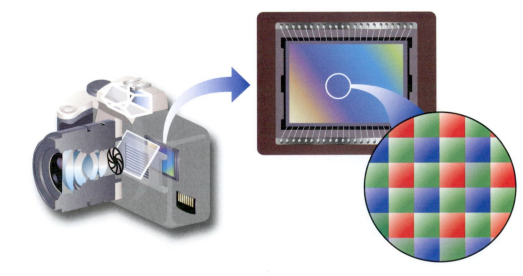

Figure 2-26

Photosites react to the light coming through the lens. Each photosite generates roughly 1 pixel of information in your digital file.

© Cengage Learning 2012.

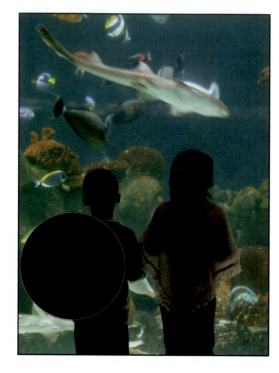

or blue filter covering its surface. Most sensors have more green photosites than they do red or blue, as the human eye is more sensitive to green than it is to the other colors. Having more green-filtered photosites allows digital cameras to more accurately read the green in your scenes.

During the exposure, transistors at each photosite amplify and, by using small wires, transport the electronic signal to the converter where it is converted to digital information. Each photosite is individually read, but these readings aren't perfect. CMOS chips are susceptible to misreadings of the electronic information creating a phenomenon called **noise**, or visual flecks that don't match the rest of your image (Figures 2-27 and 2-28).

Saving the Image

Digital information is stored on a removable memory card (Figure 2-29) that digital cameras require to save your images. Not having a memory card in your digital camera is the equivalent of not putting film into a film-based camera.

There are several styles of memory cards available. Check your camera's manual to learn what your camera's manufacturer recommends. Some printers will accept memory cards so you can immediately print your images directly from the memory card. At some stage, though, you'll want to save those files for printing or viewing in the future.

There are two common methods to transfer your images to your computer. The first method is by connecting a wire between your camera and your computer. Consult your owner's manual and follow the directions to transfer your files. A second method is to use a memory card reader that attaches to your computer via USB port. Memory card readers can be purchased from office supply and computer stores. Take the memory card from your camera and insert it into the reader. Insert the reader into your computer's USB port. Then transfer the images as you would transfer any other file (Figure 2-30).

Medium-Format Cameras

Several varieties of medium-format film-based cameras are available. Many work basically the same as 35 mm cameras, except that they use the medium-format film. Mamiya and Hasselblad (Figure 2-31) are manufacturers of excellent medium-format film-based cameras.

All film-based medium-format cameras use larger film sizes than do 35 mm cameras. The result is improved sharpness and less film grain visible in enlarged prints. Beautiful prints can be made from this larger film.

The manufacturer and style of a medium-format camera determine the actual film size it will use. The most common medium-format film sizes are 2¼ × 2¼-inch square (6 × 6 cm) to 15/8 × 2¼ inches (4.5 × 6 cm), and 2¼ × 2¾ inches (6 × 7 cm). The rectangular-proportioned films lend themselves better to the customary rectangular 8 × 10-inch or 11 × 14-inch prints.

Medium-format film comes in rolls of 120 size, capable of taking 5–15 **frames** (separate images recorded on the film) per roll, depending on the image size for the camera being used. Many medium-format cameras can use 220 size film, which can up to double the number of frames per roll.

Digital Medium-Format Cameras

Some companies have developed digital medium-format cameras as well. Because the sensors are so large on these cameras, the image quality typically exceeds that of a professional level 35 mm digital camera. Digital camera backs are an alternative for owners of film-based medium-format cameras. The camera back is attached to the camera in a way that allows digital capture, instead of film capture.

Manufacturers are also now building fully digital medium format cameras. Hasselblad and Mamiya are two manufacturers offering digital medium-format cameras (Figure 2-32). Sensor sizes go up to 40 megapixels, so each photograph can be close to 120 MB in size.

Figure 2-29

Memory cards come in a variety of sizes and memory capacity. Check your owner's manual to learn what size card your camera requires.

Photo © KS.

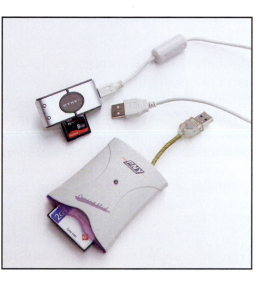

Figure 2-30

Memory card readers like these plug into your computer's USB port. Make sure you purchase the size that reads the memory cards your camera uses.

Photo © KS.

Figure 2-31

The Hasselblad 503CW film-based medium-format camera.

Courtesy of Hasselblad PR.

Figure 2-32

The Hasselblad H4D-40 digital medium-format camera.

Courtesy of Hasselblad PR.

Figure 2-33

A plastic camera.

Photo © KS.

Plastic Cameras

Some people consider plastic cameras to be toys. They're very inexpensive, usually costing between $30 and $75. Plastic cameras can be purchased through camera supply companies (Figure 2-33).

Plastic cameras use 120 or 220 size (medium-format) film. Incredibly simple, nonelectronic cameras, they have a lens made of plastic and have minimal mechanical parts. Each camera has a unique (but rarely perfect) focusing capability—they sometimes show light leaks and frequently have flaws that give a strong sense of mood and personality to the images (Figure 2-34).

Medium-Format Cameras and Focal Length

Remember that the normal focal length lens for a 35 mm camera is 50 mm. Because of the larger film/sensor size for medium-format cameras, a normal focal length lens for medium-format cameras is 80–90 mm, depending on the actual film format. The approximate distance of the diagonal of a single frame of the camera's square format is 80 mm. Medium-format cameras using rectangular film formats may have frames measuring up to 90 mm. For these cameras, a lens shorter than 90 mm lens is considered wide-angle; a lens longer than 90 mm, telephoto.

Pinhole Cameras

Among the first cameras built, pinhole cameras can be made in a variety of sizes. Many are made from common household items, such as oatmeal boxes. Others are manufactured and can use sheet film in 4 × 5-inch, 8 × 10-inch, or 11 × 14-inch sizes. These cameras use sheets of film (or photographic paper) that must be individually inserted, exposed, and then removed from the camera.

Pinhole cameras are comprised of a single tiny hole on the front of a light-tight box.

Figure 2-34

Fine art photographers sometimes use plastic cameras because of their unique characteristics. Jami Tucker uses her plastic camera for multiple images, because her camera allows her to manually *advance* her film.

Photo © Jamie Tucker

The film or paper is placed in the back of the box, and the box is placed in position for making a photograph. There is no focusing or previewing of the image. Because the size of the hole is so small, pinhole cameras tend to put everything in as much focus as is possible without a lens. Everything directly in front of the camera all the way to the background is in relatively good focus. Because there is no lens, the photographs tend to remain a little soft, giving them a surrealistic, gentle feel (Figure 2-35). Pinhole cameras have been enjoying a revival in recent years as their soft focus capabilities give photographers a distinctive tool for self-expression.

Large-Format Cameras

Large-format cameras come in a variety of sizes and two different styles. The sizes refer to the size of sheet film used in each camera. Cameras that measure 4 × 5 inches use individual sheets of 4 × 5-inch film. Cameras that measure 8 × 10 inches use individual sheets of 8 × 10-inch film. Less common large format cameras come in 11 × 14-inch and 16 × 20-inch sizes.

Field cameras, one style of large-format cameras, consist of the camera front onto which a lens is attached, a bellows that allows extension and contraction of the camera, and the camera back that holds the film and the focusing glass. The front and back parts of the camera are attached to a flat camera base. These cameras can be partially folded up for easy storage (Figure 2-36a).

Monorail cameras, the second style of large-format cameras, are mounted onto a straight horizontal rail (Figure 2-36b). These cameras are typically found in commercial studios. Having the same camera parts as the field cameras, with the addition of the monorail, monorail cameras are capable of more camera movements than are field cameras.

What Makes Large-Format Cameras Different?

The front (lens plane) and back (image plane or film plane) of all large-format cameras move independently of each other

Figure 2-35 (top)

Image made with a pinhole camera. The exposure time was about 2 minutes. The long exposure gave a milky texture to the water.

Photo © KS.

Figure 2-36a (bottom)

A 4 × 5 field camera.

Photo © KS.

and independently of the camera body. The front lens can be raised, lowered, tilted, or swung on its bracket without needing to tip the entire camera forward or backward or left to right. There are distinct advantages to having these capabilities.

Figure 2-36b

Large-format monorail cameras are most frequently found in commercial photography studios and are highly acclaimed for architectural photography.

Photo © Roger Grant.

Figure 2-37a

Demonstration of Scheimpflug principle. Both of these photos were made at an aperture of f/5.6 on a large-format camera. For the left ruler, the lens was on the same plane as the back of the camera, just as if the image had been made with a 35 mm camera. For the right ruler, the lens was tilted forward so it was no longer on the same plane as the back of the camera. This allows for greater depth of field at the same aperture.

Photo © KS.

Figure 2-37b

Illustration of the Scheimpflug principle. The lens plane is no longer parallel with the film plane.

The Scheimpflug Principle

Large-format cameras take advantage of the **Scheimpflug principle**, a law of physics that describes the increased depth of field you get by tilting the lens forward (Figures 2-37a and 2-37b). Depth of field increases if the lens plane (the front of the camera) is tilted forward in relation to the film plane (in the back of the camera). Photographers are able to use a wider aperture and still get the depth of field they need.

Perspective Control

When you tilt a 35 mm camera upward to photograph a tall building, the top of the building appears narrower than the bottom of the building. This is a phenomenon called **keystoning** (Figure 2-38a). It occurs because the film plane is at a different angle than the perpendicular building.

If a large-format camera body is tilted back to look up toward a tall building, the camera back can remain parallel to the building to prevent keystoning. The back of the camera can be tilted independently of the camera's base (Figure 2-38b). The camera positions for Figures 2-38a and 2-38b are shown in Figure 2-39.

Because the independent camera movements are crucial in architectural and commercial photography, large-format cameras are very popular with this group of photographers.

Figure 2-38a (left)

An example of keystoning. The camera's film plane was not parallel with the building.

Photo © sal - Fotolia.com.

Figure 2-38b (right)

This similar image shows *correct perspective without keystoning.* The film/sensor plane was parallel with the building.

Photo © anweber - Fotolia.com.

Figure 2-39

Camera position for Figure 2-38a (left) and Figure 2-38b (right).

Earlier you learned that a normal lens for a 35 mm camera is 50 mm, and a normal lens for a medium-format camera is approximately 80–90 mm. A normal lens for a large format camera is 150 mm. Any large-format lens less than a focal length of 150 mm is considered wide-angle; any greater than a focal length of 150 mm, telephoto.

Angle of View and Angle of Coverage

The **angle of view** is the portion of the scene that the lens sees. Measured in degrees, the angle of view is sometimes called the **image circle**. A wide-angle lens sees a greater degree of the scene than does a telephoto lens.

The **angle of coverage** or **covering power** of a lens is a measurement of what the film or sensor sees. Because lenses are round and film/sensors are rectangular or square, lenses must be manufactured to cover a greater area than the film or sensor size alone. Otherwise, you could get black areas in the corners of your film/sensor on every photograph. Different lenses of the same focal length are manufactured to produce a variety of angles of coverage.

In large-format cameras, a greater area of the image needs to be available to the photographer than it is for a 35 mm camera. As the photographer raises or lowers the front of the camera, a different portion of the scene falls on the film. If the lens coverage doesn't include that area, that portion of the final photograph will be black.

Photographers purchasing lenses for large-format cameras research both the angle of view and the diameter of the image circle in the technical data for each lens.

Figure 2-40

The image circle (the yellow circle in each of these images) changes, depending on the height setting of the lens on the camera. The image on the left shows an image circle that completely covers the film or sensor. If the image circle is small and the photographer raises or lowers the front lens without moving the back of the camera, the image circle may not cover the film or sensor (center and right images). The portion of the film/sensor that doesn't fit within the image circle will be black on the resulting photograph.

Photo © KS.

Prospective buyers can use the image circle measurement to gauge how much of the image will fall on the film or sensor. Lenses with larger image circles in relation to the angle of view will offer photographers greater flexibility in using camera movements such as rise, tilt, and shift (Figure 2-40).

Cell Phone Cameras

Many cell phones now contain digital cameras. Sony/Ericsson, Motorola, Sanyo, HP, Palm, and Nokia, among other companies, are making cell phones with integrated cameras. Several of the more than 25 available models also have a video camera and an audio player. Cell phone cameras currently use fixed-focus lenses and contain smaller sensors than do other digital cameras.

You will be learning about resolution in another chapter. For those of you who already understand resolution, the following information will help you understand the quality of cell phone images. The resolution for cell phone cameras is quite small. They are suitable only for printing at small print sizes because they don't contain enough digital information to create a good print. Nevertheless, they are sufficient size and quality to be sent over the Internet to friends and family.

Because of the advances in online sharing of photographs, cell phone cameras are dramatically adding to the ubiquity of digital photography. A young couple can photograph their newborn baby minutes after birth and, within a few minutes, have the image available to family and friends around the world. People witnessing important events capture fleeting moments for themselves, their friends and families, and even for law enforcement agencies. Medical personnel can use cell phone cameras for the greater good (Figure 2-41).

Caring for Your Camera

You've purchased a camera and all of the accessories you need to make photographs. Now it's time to learn how to protect your investment. Modern cameras are sturdy, but there are a lot of physical conditions that can damage your camera (Figures 2-42 and 2-43). The following is a synopsis of some of the worst offenders.

Figure 2-41

A Palestinian nurse in Amman, Jordan, uses a cell phone to send pictures of a patient to a doctor for an additional opinion.

Photo © Karen Kasmauski/Corbis.

Figure 2-42

Clark Little uses a specialized underwater housing to protect his camera from the Hawaiian surf. See his collection of photos at www.clarklittle.com.

Photo © Clark Little.

Weather-Related Issues

Since the technical quality of photography depends to a certain extent on the quality of your camera, it's important to know how to deal with weather-related issues. This information will be helpful in preventing camera malfunctions.

Heat

Heat causes problems for cameras, sensors, and film. The following is a list of possible issues with heat:

- Cameras and batteries can be damaged if left in an enclosed car during a hot summer day. Don't allow your photographic equipment to overheat.

- Use of hot film can cause color shifts in the film's emulsion and softening of the film itself. Refrigerate film if you're traveling through hot areas or storing film in a car.

- Hot sensors in digital cameras produce linear aberrations called *heat noise* in your photographs.

- Digital sensors heat up during each exposure, so a series of exposures taken in quick succession can increase the digital noise in the image. Some high-end cameras have a noise reduction function for long exposures.

- Aside from long exposures, digital noise also increases with higher temperatures. Keep your camera as cool as possible. If it's sitting in the hot sun for long periods, cover it with a light-colored hat or cloth.

Cold Conditions

- Cameras and lenses fog up, just like your eyeglasses, when you bring cold equipment into a warmer room.

- Solution: Put your camera into a camera bag and close the bag while you're still in the cold environment. Then bring the camera bag into the warmer environment and let it sit for an hour or two. After the camera has had a chance to warm up, you can take it out of the bag and have no problems with fogging.

- Camera batteries don't last as long if they're cold. Always carry extra batteries with you. Store extra batteries in a pocket close to your body.

- Cold film is prone to breakage. Auto-wind cameras, in particular, may wind film so fast that it breaks. Keep your camera and film as warm as possible when working in cold conditions.

- Static electricity can be an issue in very cold conditions. A shock of static electricity can create a streak across your film's emulsion. Keeping your camera as warm as possible will reduce this risk.

Humidity

High humidity leads to a variety of problems for lenses and film. It is best to keep your cameras, lenses, and processed film away from high humidity during long-term storage.

- Mold can cause damage to camera lenses and film, either processed or unprocessed. Lenses can grow mold between the glass pieces in places that are difficult or impossible to clean.

- High humidity can accelerate the fading of color dyes in film, damage the gelatin in film, and promote the growth of mold. It also speeds shrinkage, doubling the permanent shrinkage in some films when the humidity goes from 60–90% for extended periods.

Hints to Protect Your Film

Follow these procedures to protect your film:

- Unused film should be kept in its foil or plastic wrapping until you're ready to use it.
- Use your film before the expiration date. If that isn't possible, refrigerate or freeze the film until a couple of days before you plan to use it. Keep the film in its wrapper and slowly bring it up to room temperature over a period of a few days before planning to use it. Don't open the wrapper until it has remained at room temperature for at least 2 hours. Otherwise, your film could have streaks or spots on it from moisture condensation.
- Processed film should be cut into strips, stored in archival-quality plastic sleeves, and kept in a cool, dry storage container in total darkness away from all light.
- All film, unprocessed or processed, should be stored away from typical household solvents and cleaners. Vapors from these products can damage film.
- Always use your film as soon as you
- can after purchasing it and process it as soon as possible thereafter. The normal amounts of radiation in our environment can fog the film over long periods of time, decreasing the contrast of your images. It can also make your film less sensitive to light (requiring more light to make proper exposures) and can increase the appearance of film grain.

Travel Concerns with Film

- For travelers in the United States: High- and medium-ISO film should be han-dinspected at airports to prevent radia-tion damage to the film. It's helpful to put the film into plastic bags to decrease inspection time. Many photog-raphers have all of their film handin-spected regardless of ISO, as the effects of radiation are cumulative.
- Travelers outside the United States may face the additional risk of having airport personnel open actual film con-tainers, hence ruining their exposed film. If possible, have your film pro-cessed before taking another flight.
- If you can't get the film processed before taking another flight, write or speak to the airport manager well in advance of your arrival and give your arrival time, flight number, and departure time. List the equipment and film you're bringing with you. Ask if there are any steps you can take to expedite matters and ensure the safety of the film.

Fresh Water

- If you drop your camera into fresh water or if your camera is exposed to rain, immediately remove the camera's battery and memory card.
- Allow the camera to dry for several days. It's imperative that your camera is completely dry before trying to use it again, as electricity conducted via the water inside the camera can destroy it.
- Call your camera's manufacturer for more advice.

Salt Conditions and Problems

- Using your camera around saltwater or other high salt conditions can cause cor-rosion on the metal parts of your camera.
- Keep your camera in its bag unless you're actively making photographs.
- Keep the neck strap around your neck to prevent dropping the camera into water.
- If possible, cover the camera and lens (other than the lens front) with plastic to avoid contact with saltwater.
- Wipe down your camera with a clean cloth dampened with fresh water after photographing in salty conditions.
- If your camera falls into salt water, your camera may short circuit because salt conducts electricity. Quickly remove the battery and memory card and immediately immerse the camera in fresh, clean water. Keep the camera immersed and get it to a professional repair shop.

Figure 2-43

Dusty Curtain, on the road to
Old Bagan, Mayanmar.

Photo © Andreas Urban.

Protecting Your Camera from Dirt and Dust

- Always carry your camera and lenses in enclosed bags. Keep the bags closed until you need equipment inside them.
- Be aware of your surroundings when inserting batteries or inserting/removing your memory card. These are times when dust and sand can easily enter your camera and cause damage.
- If there are small particles of dust on the exterior of your lens or camera, use a soft brush or air blower specifically made for cameras to remove them. Do this before using cleaning cloths or cleaning paper on the lens to prevent scratching.
- Clean the glass on your lenses. Use an optical cleaning cloth, or use paper and cleaning fluid made specifically for glasses or photo lenses. Do not use tissue, clothing fabric, or kitchen/household cleaners.

- Place a few drops of lens cleaning fluid on a piece of optical cleaning paper, and then use that paper to gently clean the lens surface. Never put drops directly on the lens, as the fluid could leak behind the first lens element and allow mold to grow between the elements.
- Consider purchasing UV or Haze filters for your lenses. If a filter gets scratched or damaged, it can be replaced far less expensively than purchasing a new lens.
- In film-based cameras, hold the camera upside down and brush out the film compartments every time you load new film. Never touch the shutter curtain, as you could easily damage it.
- When changing lenses on an SLR camera, point the camera toward the floor to prevent dust from entering the camera and landing on the mirror and/or sensor.

Figure 2-44

If you have dust on your sensor, you will see tiny dots like these magnified here.

Photo © KS.

Dust on Your Internal Mirror

If you see a speck of dust while looking through the viewfinder of an SLR camera, the dust is on the internal mirror that inverts the image, not on your sensor. Do not blow on the mirror. The air pressure could damage the mirror's surface and/or displace the mirror, destroying any chance to focus the lens. Take your camera to a professional to have the mirror cleaned.

Dust on Your Digital Sensor

If you get dust on your sensor, you will see small dark spots in your photos (Figure 2-44). To test your sensor for dust:

- Set your camera at the smallest aperture for your camera and lens.
- Switch your lens to manual focus and set it so the image is completely out of focus.
- Clean your computer monitor's glass so there is no dust or dirt on it.
- Open Photoshop and start a new document with a white background. Zoom in on the background until white fills the computer screen.

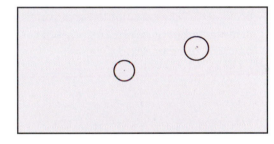

Figure 2-45

Examine the resulting photograph. If you see tiny black dots anywhere in the image (as those circled here), your sensor needs to be cleaned.

Photo © KS.

- You are going to photograph the white screen. You may need to change your autofocus lens to manual focus. There is no need to focus on the screen. Photograph the white screen, making sure the white area fills your camera's field of view.
- Download and look carefully at the photograph of the white screen. If you see dark spots, you know your sensor needs cleaning (Figure 2-45).
- If your sensor needs cleaning, send your camera to a professional. Although there are products on the market for cleaning sensors, they are not recommended and may violate your camera's warranty.

Sunscreen and Insect Repellent

- Keep sunscreen and insect repellent off of your camera body and lenses. These products can cause damage to your camera.
- Do not store sunscreen or insect repellent containers in your camera bag.
- Wash your hands after applying sunscreen or insect repellent before you touch your camera.

Battery Care

- Take batteries out of your camera before storing it for long periods of time. Otherwise your camera can be damaged by corrosion.
- Batteries tend to lose strength more quickly in lower temperatures. Keep a battery close to your body while doing outdoor winter photography. Be sure to bring along spare batteries in case you need them.
- Overheated batteries can be damaged or ruined. Take care not to leave your camera and batteries in an enclosed car on a hot summer day.

Summary

It's amazing to think that the first successful photographs were taken less than 200 years ago. The growth in technology has been very fast-paced. Although the explanations of camera functions can be long and involved, it's important to remember that the camera is a tool for your own artistic vision. Think about how you want your images to look, and then learn what you need to know to make those images. Little by little, the process of using your camera as a tool will become second nature.

This chapter has been an introduction to the many varieties of cameras. Each type of camera has its own function in the photographic world. Whether the cameras are simple or complex, they are of secondary importance to the eye and thought processes of the photographer making the photographs. The photographer's sense of vision and decision to make a specific style of photograph are the most important tools of all.

EXERCISES

1. Identify the following components on your camera. Use your manual to learn how these functions work.

   - ON/OFF button

   - Viewfinder

   - Lens

   - Focus

   - Aperture setting, and how to change it

   - Shutter speed, and how to change it

   - Lens cap

   - Shutter button

   - Place for film (or a memory card for digital cameras)

2. Compile a list of the aperture settings your camera is capable of using.

3. Compile a list of the shutter speeds your camera is capable of using.

4. Compare the images you found after doing the Internet searches listed under the Further Reading section to most photographs you have seen or made yourself. How are they similar to typical photos? How are they different?

FURTHER READING

- ADAMS, Ansel. *The Camera*. Boston: Little, Brown, and Co., 1995.

- LONG, Ben. *Complete Digital Photography*. 3rd ed. Hingham, MA: Charles River Media, Inc., 2004.

- WARREN, Bruce. *Photography*. 2nd ed. Clifton Park, NY: Thomson Delmar Learning, 2001.

- PERFORM INTERNET SEARCHES FOR IMAGES made with pinhole, Holga, and Diana cameras. Use the following search engine keywords: "pinhole photographs," "Holga photographs," and "Diana camera photographs."

NOTES

Dick and Barbara Waltenberry
Event Photographers

Dick and Barbara Waltenberry specialize in photographing horse competitions around the United States. Their photographs routinely appear in international trade magazines, and they are in high demand for national and regional championship shows. Although this Professional Profile showcases photographers of horse shows, the couple's wisdom and advice pertain to any aspiring event photographer.

Dick, how did you get started in photography?

I learned photography while in high school. I had a horse and joined a local riding club. After I put on slide shows for the club, people started asking for photos. Then I started watching how professional photographers worked at big shows. I started a part-time photography business while maintaining a full-time job as a mechanical draftsman, and then quit the day job when the photography business took off. I started with transparency (slide) film, then print film (negatives), added video in the 1980s and then went entirely to digital photography in 2002.

How did you build customer trust?

Well, we didn't take the money and run as some other photographers had done. We had to deal with other people's bad reputations. Integrity is imperative in our business! When we first started, we actually made prints overnight at the shows. We had a portable darkroom with two to three enlargers, and we printed during the night so we could deliver the prints the next day. Eventually, people started to trust that we would deliver. Now we use a professional lab for everything other than canvas prints.

Tell me about your thought process as you're photographing horses.

I'm constantly changing camera and strobe settings throughout the event. I turn strobes on and off to get the best lighting effects. I adjust my exposure for white or black horses because I can't afford blasted out highlights or black shadows. I have to use a fast enough shutter speed to prevent ambient light coming in, or I'll have problems with color balance and motion blur.

I also keep written records while I'm photographing. I jot down a short description of the horse and rider and the corresponding camera frames. Later, my notes help Barbara identify the horse and rider.

Barbara adds:

We're taking pictures of the *person* and the horse. You need to know the sport well enough to know the critical moments for that event. People won't buy a photo if the angle or timing of photo makes a horse look faulty, even if the lighting and composition are beautiful. Neither will customers buy a picture if their clothes or facial expressions don't look good. We pay attention to *all* the details, including the person's clothing. We'll tell a person to tuck in a shirt, stand straight, etc.

Your photos show an expertise in strobe lighting. How did you develop your lighting techniques?

At first, I watched what my competitors were doing. All horse show photographers light an arena differently. Then we were inspired by some photos we had taken at one show. The serendipitous late afternoon sunlight created strong front light, a little rim lighting, and a warm color tone. We decided to develop strobe lighting to create that effect.

Mandy McCutcheon winning the NonPro National Reining Breeder's Classic in 2007 on a horse called I Spin for Chics.

Photo © Waltenberry Photography, Ripon, WI.

Sometimes we need more lights in different places. We use several strobes on high stands around the arena. With the transmitter on the camera, I regulate individual strobes regardless of how far away they are. I can power up or power down strobes as needed during the event.

You're dealing with horses, which are easily startled. How does that safety issue factor into your photography?

I first take a photo when the horse is farther away. Horses don't know where a flash came from unless they hear the click of the camera. I watch for any nervous signs before trying anything close up. Sometimes I'm asked not to photograph a

particular horse, and I honor that request. I also have to watch for kids along the rail of the arena, as they can spook the horses, too.

Barb, you do the file management, photo retouching, and sales. Tell us about your work.

I keep things organized so we can find them again. We have 350,000 negatives filed in envelopes with file information on the front. Now that we're totally digital, our website has over 500,000 images available to horse owners. Everything is carefully named and organized so that owners can quickly find the images of their horses. The file management alone is a highly specialized process.

Dick's lighting techniques are geared toward minimizing the amount of retouching I need to do. Even so, every photograph gets retouched. The horses' eyes often need retouching when flash is used. I also do burning and dodging in every photo, and I clean up or minimize any issues with the arena itself, such as ventilation grates or garbage on the ground. Every photo also needs to be sharpened. I also do additional retouching if a customer requests it. Most requested? "Can you make me look thinner?"

What advice do you have for aspiring event photographers?

Learn the photography business, not just how to take pictures. You need to understand file management, payroll, insurance, marketing and accounting, even if you hire office help and an accountant.

Communication with the customers is critical. As you get started, listen to them to find out what they want. Your customers will tell you what they like and don't like if you ask them.

Putting something away for retirement is critically important. Plan ahead, even though it's hard. We haven't made a lot of money, and we've had to spend a lot. This business isn't likely to leave you very wealthy, but is satisfying and rewarding in many ways, including the many personal friendships gained along the way.

"I like to take a section of the lives of my models and emerge this into my own imagination. I feel this gives them an extra power and they are no longer mere photos. This is what I do most of the time. . . . I need to get to know my models a little before I photograph them. . . . I have to know their strengths and their weaknesses and what impresses them the most. . . . I say "I have to" because the photos are their photos; they cannot just be in the picture as images. . . . They should also have a meaning. . . . The "meaning" is hidden in their expression, the way they look at things, and the way they carry themselves. This photo's title is *Victory*. . . . She should have confronted herself, now she has a new gained respect of herself and can look up . . . she is victorious . . . she can sing at the moonlight . . . or, she can transform the moon itself into a song."

Photo © Kemal Kamil, Istanbul, Turkey.

CHAPTER

What Is a Good Photographic Exposure?

Chapter Learning Objectives

- Recognize the difference between your camera's definition of and your aesthetic definition of a *good exposure*.

- Identify scenes that reflect an 18% gray value of light.

- Understand when to use a variety of different in-camera light metering modes.

- Identify your camera's exposure lock metering capabilities.

- Summarize how to work with your camera's exposure compensation feature.

- Describe the Sunny f/16 Rule.

- Define *dynamic range* and discuss its implications for exposures with film and digital cameras.

- List what questions you should ask when evaluating a photographic exposure.

- Define *aperture* and *film speed* and their relationships to photographic aesthetics.

A creative photograph tells a story. It gives viewers a sense of time, place, action, mood, characters, and even plot. It gives them something to think about, perhaps something they can relate to in their own lives. A photograph may startle viewers, elicit their memories, or allow them to share a special moment with others. It may answer a question, or it may give only enough information to evoke a question without revealing an answer.

The photographer who makes memorable images creates stories on a two-dimensional plane. Every square inch is like a canvas, awaiting the photographer's decision on what portion of a scene to reveal there and what intensity of light will reveal it.

The amount of illumination in the scene directly influences the mood a photograph elicits. If the photographer intends the mood to be serious, sad, or frightening, a relatively dark image can support that intention. Photographs meant to be happy or exciting benefit from brighter illumination. An image portraying happy people in a dark environment (or sad people in a bright environment) can create an emotional contrast within that photograph. The contrast between the subject and its environment will, in itself, tell a story.

Most people point their cameras toward a subject and make a photograph. They don't take control over their environment or consider changes in lighting or exposure. Their environment and their cameras control the quality of images they make.

To be a creative photographer, you must become aware of your photographic environment and how your camera works within that environment. Your camera's exposure level needs to support your intentions for your photographs. Knowing how to control the quality and quantity of light used to create an exposure is a vital step, and this control requires both a technical and an aesthetic study of light.

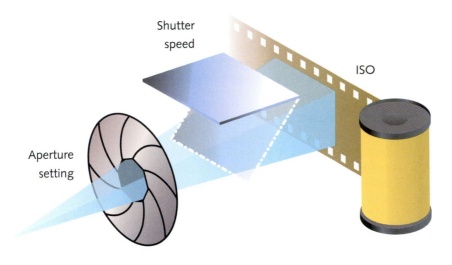

Shutter
speed

Aperture
setting

ISO

Figure 3-1

The three elements
of an exposure.

© Cengage Learning 2012.

The Three Elements of Exposure

Exposure is the result of three critical elements:

1. A specified sensitivity of the film or sensor to light (ISO),
2. A specific amount of light through a camera's lens (aperture), and
3. A specified period of time (shutter speed).

The **ISO** (International Standards Organization) is a numerical description of the sensitivity of film or a digital sensor to light. Film is manufactured at different ISO values. Digital sensors are manually set to different ISO values. You will learn more about ISO later in the chapter.

Aperture is the scalable hole, formed by the diaphragm in the lens, which allows light to enter the camera through the lens. The aperture size controls the amount of light traveling through the lens and also affects the depth of field in your image.

Shutter speed is the speed at which the shutter opens and closes in a film-based camera or the amount of time that a digital sensor is activated and able to record light.

When you set your camera to Program (Automatic) mode, your camera's light meter selects settings for ISO, aperture, and shutter speed that will often give you a good exposure, depending on what you're photographing.

Exposure Equivalents

If you change any one of the elements of exposure, your camera will adjust the other two elements accordingly to yield the same exposure. This allows you to make creative decisions such as how fast to set your shutter speed or how wide to set your aperture. With digital cameras, you can change your ISO in low-light conditions, thereby allowing for faster shutter speeds (Figure 3-2). Photographers using film-based cameras select a film with an ISO suitable for the conditions under which they will be photographing. If those conditions change, they must use a different roll of film with a different ISO.

Your Camera's Definition of a Good Exposure

Your camera is a great tool, but it's only a machine and can't help you make aesthetic decisions. You need to understand

Figure 3-2

Your digital camera has a variety of ISO settings. Consult your camera's manual to learn how to set the ISO on your camera.

Photo © KS.

Quality	
Red-eye on/off	
AEB	▶100
ISO speed	200
LCD illumi.	400
Beep	800
Custom WB	1000

how your camera makes what it considers "good" exposures and how you can use your camera's functions to your aesthetic advantage. You and your camera will often disagree on the concept of what constitutes a "good exposure."

Reflected Light

When you take a photograph, you aren't recording an object, person, or scene. Rather, you are recording the *light reflecting off* that object, person, or scene. Your camera's meter measures the light *reflecting off* that subject. How that meter renders exposure information—and what you do with that information—is an important aspect of learning creative photography.

Photographers observe light. They look at light reflecting off of objects, paying attention to the direction, intensity, and color of the light falling on their subjects. They watch how the time of day changes the color of sunlight falling on an object; the shape, intensity, and direction of shadows cast by the object; and the influence of other surrounding objects that bounce additional reflected light onto the object.

Good photography requires exceptional light. It is the most basic component of a photograph, but light's influence goes well beyond the basics. Light can create a mood, a sense of joy or sorrow, or a sense of urgency or calm. Many of the photographs selected for this textbook were chosen because of the exceptional light in them. Uninspiring light makes for an uninspiring photograph. Beautiful light is a helpful component of a memorable photograph.

The process of seeing light does not require a camera. It requires only your eyes and your mind. It is a matter of paying attention to how the light in your surroundings is being reflected by the objects in your surroundings. It is a skill you can practice any time of day or night. Everyone who can see, *sees* reflected light. Photographers and artists learn to pay close attention to reflected light.

Examining Reflected Light

It's easy to imagine what things should look like. When you think of trains, you might think of dark or black engines. When you think of clouds, you might think of light or white clouds.

Reality, on the other hand, might differ greatly from our imagination. It's quite possible that train tracks reflect so much light that the resulting image actually renders the tracks in a midtone or highlight range (Figure 3-3). A cloud may be so dark that it is rendered as middle gray (or even darker) within an image. A **midtone** is a reflected light value that falls between the highlights and the shadows, whereas **middle gray** is the halfway point between the brightest possible value (white) and the darkest possible value (black). **Value** is the range of black through progressively lighter grays to white within an image.

Values are described as *light, medium,* or *dark*. Values are always discussed independent of hue (color) in this textbook. A dark

Figure 3-3

Train tracks reflecting light at night. Chicago, 1961.

Photo © Kenneth Josephson/ Higher Pictures

red flower can have the same value as a dark green leaf or a purple flower. A light green leaf can have the same value as a dark pink or orange flower.

Taking Special Note of Reflected Light

It's important to look carefully at the objects you're photographing and to take special note of the light reflecting off of those objects. The amount, direction, and quality of reflected light are all important.

The Light Meter

Every modern 35 mm camera has a light meter. Its task is to choose an aperture and shutter speed that will give you a "correct" exposure for a scene. In-camera light meters are considered **reflective meters** because they measure the light reflecting off the objects being photographed.

Your camera's light meter plays a critical role in selecting a good exposure, but it's important to understand the limitations of that role. A camera's light meter does one thing, and one thing only. It gives you a combination of ISO, aperture, and shutter speed that renders your scene as if it were a middle gray or 18% gray reflectance value. The term **18% gray** is a synonym for middle gray, even though you would expect middle gray to be called 50% gray. An object that produces a middle gray rendering within a photograph actually reflects 18% of the light falling on it. Therefore, *middle gray* is a term referring to how your eye reads the brightness of a portion of the photograph, not the more technical percentage of light bouncing off of the object in the photograph.

After assessing the ISO of your film or the digital ISO setting, the light meter chooses an aperture and shutter speed that, in tandem, allows a specific amount of light into the camera. It quantifies the amount of light required to yield an "average" scene for exposure purposes.

Most scenes have some highlights, some shadows, and some midtones. **Highlights** are bright areas in a scene or photograph.

Most highlights contain details that add to your understanding of the image. For instance, a bride's white dress, when properly photographed, will still hold enough detail for you to see the texture of its fabric or lace.

Specular highlights are a subset of highlights produced by light sources, such as street lights or car headlights, or very bright reflections of sunlight from windows or mirrors. Specular highlights are so bright that they don't contain detail and aren't considered highlights. They typically print as pure white within a photograph.

Shadows are dark areas in a scene, slide (transparency), or print. Shadows may contain detail, or they may be too dark to hold any detail. It doesn't make any difference if the dark areas are created by a man's black tuxedo or the dark shadow of someone standing under a streetlight. "Shadow" means dark, regardless of the photograph's subject. Midtones are areas of medium brightness in a scene or photograph. The majority of visual information within most photographs falls in the midtone range.

The role of the light meter is to read the scene you want to photograph and to take an average all of those values. It then gives you its best guess on what combination of ISO, aperture, and shutter speed will render a correct exposure for the scene.

Camera Metering Modes

Modern 35 mm cameras have two common types of metering systems: spot meters and matrix meters. Depending on its manufacturer, your camera could be using either one or both of these systems.

Spot Meters

Spot metering systems are reflected light metering systems that measure varying amounts (or angles) of your scene. A typical spot metering system has two different settings: center-weighted averaging and some smaller percentage of spot metering.

Center-Weighted Averaging

The oldest and most common type of in-camera light metering system, **center-weighted averaging** assumes that your subject of greatest interest is in the middle of your photograph. It meters the amount of light bouncing off the subject (the reflected light) and chooses an aperture and shutter speed to render that scene as a well-exposed photograph. Center-weighted averaging assumes that the periphery of your scene is less important and considers the light readings in that area as less important (Figure 3-4).

Center-weighted averaging is good for many photographic conditions. It works well if you are photographing friends in daylight or cloudy days when the sun is overhead. It doesn't work as well if your light source (the sun or an artificial light source) is behind the person or object you are photographing. In that situation, a spot metering system may work better.

20% or 10% Spot Metering

Another setting within the spot metering system takes into consideration a smaller circle within the middle of the scene. The amount of space is often stated in terms of percentages of the scene. A 20% or 10% area will give a different, often more accurate, reading of the light bouncing off the subject in the middle of the scene. This helps you ensure that your subject will be properly exposed.

Imagine that you are photographing a person at sunset, you are facing the sun, and the person is standing directly between you and the sun. If your camera is set to center-weighted averaging, the bright sunlight will tell your camera to select an aperture and shutter speed to make that bright light middle gray. In the meantime, your subject is not being illuminated by the sunlight and could be rendered as very dark within the photograph.

Figure 3-4

This illustrates the amount of a scene the light meter reads for center-weighted averaging (outer circle) versus spot metering (inner circle).

Photo © KS.

🟩 Center-weighted averaging

🟦 Spot metering

A spot metering system will read only the centermost portion of the **frame**, the area visible within your viewfinder. You can point your camera directly toward the person and take a spot meter reading, not allowing the camera's meter to take into account the bright sunlight in the background. Your camera's meter will select settings that will record the person with a proper exposure but will wash out and make the sunset very light. That's the trade-off in this situation.

Matrix Meters

Many camera manufacturers have gone to complex matrix meters for 35 mm cameras. These meters divide the scene into segments and use formulas to derive a proper exposure level for the entire scene (Figure 3-5). Many photographers find matrix meters useful for point-and-shoot photography or for making photographs in complex lighting conditions. Read your camera's manual to see what kind of metering system(s) your camera has and how to select the system you want to use.

Exposure Lock Metering

Unfortunately, not all the scenes you photograph are going to be "average" scenes. Most photographs made in broad daylight will be properly rendered using the in-camera light metering system. But what about night photographs? What about photographs that you take on bright snowy days? Your camera's light meter will read these scenes as if they were 18% gray, severely misjudging what a "good" exposure might be. Dark scenes taken at night will be rendered as if they were made in daylight. Bright snowy scenes will be rendered as middle gray.

These are aesthetic issues. Your camera is doing what it was designed to do, but you need something different. You know what the photo should look like, but your camera can't take this information into consideration.

If you photograph a black car, that car will be rendered middle gray, not black. The camera assumes the dark image needs to be photographed as middle gray and will choose an aperture and shutter speed to

Figure 3-5

Matrix metering involves dividing the scene into a series of sections. Readings are taken from each section to derive a proper exposure.

Photo © KS.

render the car as gray in the photograph. The entire photograph will be too light, or **overexposed**. Overexposed is a term that takes into consideration your intentions for the photograph. It means that the film or sensor has recorded the scene at a brighter level than what is appropriate for the subject matter or for your intentions.

If you photograph a field of bright white snow, the camera's meter will try to render the snow as if it were middle gray. It will choose an aperture and shutter speed that will only allow enough light into the camera to create a gray scene. The resulting photograph will appear too dark, or **underexposed**. Underexposure means that the film or sensor recorded a scene that is darker than what is appropriate for the subject matter or for your intentions.

You can trick your camera's light meter into giving you an appropriate meter reading even though the scene you are trying to record isn't of middle gray value. This procedure makes use of the exposure lock button on your camera (Figure 3-6). Look at your owner's manual to find and read about this feature. The exposure lock button allows you to lock in the exposure for a middle gray object and then turn the camera to photograph a different scene.

To use the exposure lock feature, first point the camera toward something that has

a middle gray reflectance value *and* is illuminated by the same light source as your subject. Then lock in the meter reading. A **gray card**, manufactured to give 18% gray reflectance, is frequently used and is available at camera stores (Figure 3-7). Meter the light reflecting off of the gray card only, allowing it to fill your screen. Once you have metered the gray card, remove it from the scene and move the camera to the proper position to photograph your desired scene. Even if your new scene is brighter or darker than middle gray, the aperture and shutter speed won't change as you change the position of your camera.

The object you meter and your photographed subject *must* have very similar lighting conditions! It does you absolutely no good to meter an 18% gray object in the

NOTE

Changing the Focal Length Can Alter the Meter Reading

If you are using a zoom lens, do not change the focal length of the lens to take the meter reading off the gray card. Instead, walk up to the gray card to take the meter reading. A change in the focal length of your lens can alter the meter reading.

Figure 3-8

Either of these scenes— blue sky or green grass— could be used to get an 18% gray meter reading.

Photo © KS.

shade and then photograph a sunlit scene. The correct exposure for those two scenes will be very different, and this metering method will not work.

You may not always have a gray card; therefore it's worth your time to memorize some common objects that usually reflect a middle gray amount of light. These objects include slightly faded blue jeans, green grass, wet cement, dry tree bark of a maple or oak tree, and a midday blue sky (Figure 3-8). You can meter on these items, lock in your exposure, and then move your camera to photograph your scene.

Whichever object you choose for metering, the concept is the same. Check your owner's manual for specific instructions on how to take a meter reading. Many cameras use the following technique:

- Look through your viewfinder and come close enough to the middle gray object so the object completely fills the visual field. Be careful not to cast a shadow onto the scene!
- Push the shutter button halfway down and keep it pressed at that level.
- Now turn your camera until the scene you want to photograph is in your viewfinder and push the shutter button all the way down.

When following this procedure, make sure that the object you're metering (such as blue jeans or green grass) is in the same lighting condition as your ultimate subject matter for the photograph. This is critical. It's not going to help you to meter green grass in bright sunlight and then photograph a person standing in the shadow of a building. Those are two different lighting conditions, and your camera's exposure setting would be wrong. Be sure to match the lighting conditions between the object you're metering and your final scene.

It's also important that you do not change the focal length on your lens by zooming in or out as you make the middle gray exposure. As your focal length changes, the physical length of your lens changes as well. Because light falls off as it travels through a lens, your exposure could change slightly as you change the focal length. Use the same focal length for your exposure lock metering as you will use for the actual photograph.

Overriding the Light Meter (Exposure Compensation)

There will be times when you want to photograph a scene, but you can't find anything

Figure 3-9

Exposure compensation is used when you have nothing on which to meter a middle gray value.

Photo © KS.

Another example is if you're taking a photograph of a black car. There is nothing of middle gray value in the area, and you know your camera's meter will render the black car as middle gray in the photograph. Here are the steps to correct these problems:

1. Learn which buttons to push on your camera to override your light meter. You might find a chapter called "Exposure Compensation" in your camera's manual. Read that chapter and become comfortable with changing the light meter readings.

2. Get a feel for how many stops of light brighter or darker than middle gray your scene is. In this example, the snow scene may be 2½ to 3 stops brighter than middle gray. The black car may be 2 stops darker than middle gray.

3. Take a meter reading of the snow in your snow scene and give 2 additional stops of light to your camera. You can either open the aperture by 3 stops or lengthen the shutter speed by 3 stops. If the black car fills your viewing screen when you're taking a meter reading, give 3 fewer stops of light to your camera. You can stop down the aperture by 3 stops, or shorten the shutter speed by 3 stops, or do a combination of changing the aperture and shutter speed to equal a change of 3 stops. Then make the exposure.

of middle gray value to help you get a good meter reading. In that case, you'll need to use another method to obtain a good aperture and shutter speed combination.

Many modern cameras have the capacity of allowing the photographer to override the light meter. You will want to do this if, for example, you want to photograph a field of snow (Figure 3-9). There is nothing of middle gray value in the area, and you know your camera's meter is going to give you an aperture and shutter speed combination that will render your white field middle gray in the photograph.

4. Here's the most important rule to remember: If you are using a reflective light meter and your subject matter is lighter than middle gray, you must add light. If your subject matter is darker than middle gray, you must subtract light (Figure 3-10). Note that this rule works only for a reflected light meter. It does not work with a handheld incident light meter (discussed later in this chapter).

Figure 3-10

If you are using a reflective light meter and your subject is lighter than middle gray, *add light* to your exposure. If you are using a reflective light meter and your subject is darker than middle gray, *subtract light* from your exposure. If you remember this rule, you'll always know what to do if you can't meter off of an object with middle gray value.

Photo © KS.

Exposure

Exposure

If this rule doesn't make sense, remember that the only thing your camera's meter can do is render all of your subjects middle gray in value. A black car or a white wedding gown becomes middle gray in value. By subtracting light from the photo with the dark car, the image becomes purposely "underexposed," as far as the light meter is concerned.

But you know that the car will look properly dark in the resulting photograph.

A wedding gown, brought down to middle gray by the light meter, needs more light to make it white. Adding light to the camera meter's suggested exposure will brighten the white gown. The camera will indicate that you're overexposing the photograph, but you will know that you're making the gown white (actually very light gray with detail) instead of middle gray.

The Zone System

It will be helpful for you to think of different values using the **Zone System**, a system of evaluating reflected light and exposure values that Ansel Adams introduced to the photographic world in his book, *The Negative*, in 1981. The Zone System breaks all of the possible values into discrete zones. Each change from one zone to another zone represents a 1-stop change in exposure. The Zone System applies to exposure of both film-based and digital photography. We will begin by introducing the different zones and thinking about how to identify each zone in a scene you are photographing. The examples listed here are generalities meant to get you started working with the Zone System. You will without doubt find exceptions to these examples.

- **Zone 0:** This portion of the image is totally black. There is no detail at all, and no object can be discerned.
- **Zone I:** This zone is the first change away from pure black. A Zone I object is very dark gray, and any texture within the object is still invisible.
- **Zone II:** A very dark object can be discerned, but the texture of the object is barely visible.
- **Zone III:** A typically dark object and its texture are easily discerned. Zone III objects include black electrical cord or black clothing in shade (not direct sunlight).
- **Zone IV:** Dark foliage such as grass in shade, wet pavement, dark blue jeans, or a dark gray camera bag in bright sunlight—these objects fall into Zone IV.
- **Zone V:** This is middle gray (18% gray) reflectance and includes objects such as dry and worn black pavement, the dry bark of a maple or oak tree, wet concrete, blue sky overhead (not directly into the sun), bright red flowers, green grass in sunlight, medium (not faded or dark blue) blue jeans, or a gray card manufactured specifically for photographers.
- **Zone VI:** Caucasian skin in overcast conditions, dry concrete, orange flowers, and slightly faded blue jeans—these objects fall into Zone VI.
- **Zone VII:** This zone includes objects such as Caucasian skin in sunlight conditions, light gray rocks, a snow field in shadow, pink flowers, light gray gravel, or a white car in shadow.
- **Zone VIII:** White objects with texture and detail—white clothing, white flowers, or a white car in sunlight—are Zone VIII objects.
- **Zone IX:** Objects in this zone are white with no texture. Zone IX is still not pure white, but an object rendered at Zone IX can't be easily identified.
- **Zone X:** Pure white objects fall into Zone X, as do specular highlights that print as pure white. There is no detail or texture.

If you are photographing an object that is anything other than Zone V, you need to override the camera's light meter by the number of stops that your object varies from Zone V. If you are photographing dark red flowers, subtract 1 stop of light. If you are photographing a wedding gown, add 3 stops of light.

Use One Method or the Other

So far we have discussed two separate methods to meter reflected light. The first is to meter off of something that reflects middle gray and to lock in your exposure. Once your exposure is locked in, move your camera so it is pointing to the subject you want to photograph and push the shutter button.

Figure 3-11

Bracketing exposures using print film. (left) − 1 stop; (center) as metered; (right) + 1 stop.
Photo © KS.

The second method is to meter directly off of the object you want to photograph, regardless of its reflectance value. Lock in that exposure, and then make alterations in your aperture and/or shutter speed to add to or subtract light from your exposure. Then push the shutter button. This is the exposure compensation method.

It's important to use one method or the other to get a good exposure. Don't try to mix the two methods, or you can easily get confused.

Bracketing Exposures

You must experiment to learn how your camera's film or sensor responds to different lighting conditions. It makes sense to bracket your exposures whenever possible, in case your exposures are not quite on target.

To compensate for the inevitable variations from this list of examples, take more than one exposure for each scene. Start with your best guess for aperture and shutter speed for your scene and make a photograph. Then, if you're using a film-based camera and print film, add 1 stop's worth of exposure. Make another photograph. Now go back to the origi-nal aperture and shutter speed. Before making a third picture, subtract 1 stop's worth of exposure. Then make the third picture (Figure 3-11).

Some cameras have an autobracketing feature that will automatically make three consecutive images with different exposures, bracketing the second and third exposures. Check your camera's manual to see if your camera has this capability.

If you're using a digital camera or if you're using slide (transparency) film in a film-based camera, add or subtract a ½-stop's worth of exposure instead of a full stop (Figure 3-12). Digital cameras and transparency film are far more sensitive to changes in exposure than is print film. A ½-stop change in exposure will give you a far better chance to achieve a correct exposure.

When making these various "bracketed" exposures, remember that you can change either the aperture or shutter speed to create the 1 stop's difference in exposure. If you choose to change the aperture, though, you're also going to get the side effect of changing the depth of field within your scene. Changing the aperture value always changes the depth of field.

Handheld Light Meters

Not all light meters on the market are attached to a camera. Although most often used in photographic studios, handheld light meters can also be used out in the field.

Some photographers purchase handheld light meters that allow spot readings of only 1% of a scene. Photographers point to a portion of the scene that they want to render as middle gray in their photographs. The light meter gives suggested readings for the aperture and shutter speed settings. Then photographers manually set the camera's aperture and shutter speed to match those settings and make the photograph. In this manner, the handheld light meter is being used as a reflected light meter.

Incident Lighting

Most handheld light meters can read either reflective light or incident light (Figure 3-13). **Incident light** is the available light that happens to be falling onto your object, regardless of what the light source is. It could be the sun, fluorescent lights, or headlights of a car.

If you are working with a handheld meter that has an attachment to read the incident light of your scene, first dial in the current ISO setting of your film or digital camera. Then dial in an aperture or shutter

speed that you will set in your camera. If you dial in an aperture value, the shutter speed becomes the variable for your exposure. If you dial in a shutter speed value, the aperture becomes the variable. The handheld light meter reads the light falling on it and suggests an aperture or shutter speed (whichever is the variable) that will render your photograph middle gray.

When you make incident readings, it doesn't matter if your subject's tonal values are light, dark, or middle gray. The light meter is simply reading the amount

Figure 3-14

The Sunny f/16 Rule.

© Cengage Learning 2012.

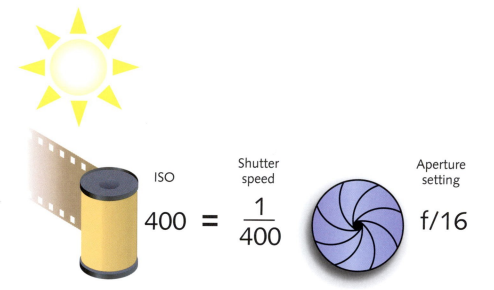

ISO   Shutter speed   Aperture setting

$$400 = \frac{1}{400} \qquad f/16$$

of light in that geographical region and is ignoring the fact that objects reflect different amounts of light. Incident light meters have no regard for the light reflecting off of objects in your scene.

Which Kind of Meter Should You Use?

The reflected light meter in your camera is the meter of choice under most circumstances. It can read differences in reflectance values of different objects, allowing you to make adjustments to your overall exposure.

Handheld incident light meters are particularly useful in studio lighting situations. Photographers can set the duration of different flash strobes, giving them a tremendous amount of control over the contrast of light hitting the subject from multiple light sources. The photographer measures the output of each flash strobe independently of any other light falling on the subject. Provided the photographer uses a fast shutter speed that doesn't allow ambient light to affect the exposure, the strobes will create all of the light captured by the camera.

The Sunny f/16 Rule

If all else fails, there is one final method to select an aperture and shutter speed. It is called the **Sunny f/16 Rule**. This rule

states that when photographing outdoors on a sunny day, you can use the following formula: 1/ISO is your shutter speed at an aperture of f/16 (Figure 3-14).

If your film's ISO (or the ISO setting on your digital camera) is 400, you can assume that your correct exposure for a sunny outdoor photo will be 1/400 second at f/16. If you're using film with an ISO of 100, you can assume that a shutter speed of 1/100 second and an aperture of f/16 will work.

Because these exact shutter speeds aren't usually available on cameras, you will need to make some compromise. The 1/400 second might change to 1/500 second, and the 1/100 second may change to 1/125 second. Bracketing these exposures is good insurance that you will obtain a good exposure.

The Sunny f/16 Rule works best during the day ranging from an hour after sunrise until an hour before sunset.

Dynamic Range

Dynamic range is a measurement of the range from darkness to brightness that a sensor or film can record. Many scenes in nature contain a far greater range from pure darkness (black) to pure brightness (white) than either film or digital sensors can capture. If you measure the number of stops between the brightest highlights

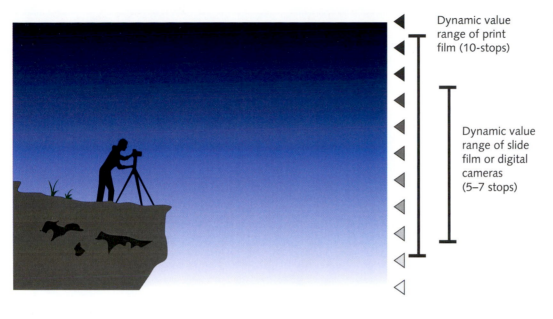

Figure 3-15

Illustration of the differences
in dynamic range between
print film and slide film or
the digital camera capture.

© Cengage Learning 2012.

Dynamic value
range of print
film (10-stops)

Dynamic value
range of slide
film or digital
cameras
(5–7 stops)

and the deepest shadows, a bright summer scene might measure 15 or more stops of light. Whereas high-end digital cameras might be able to capture a 10–12 stop range of light, compact digital cameras have sensors that may only be able to capture a 4–6 stop range. If a scene has more dynamic range than your film or sensor, something has to give. Your photographs will have areas that go pure white and/or pure black despite the fact that your eyes can see highlight and shadow details in the actual scene (Figure 3-15).

Until recently, film-based photography has led digital photography in its ability to capture a wider range of contrast than digital cameras can handle. Traditional photographic color print film can record up to 10 f-stops of light, depending on the type and brand of film. Now the more expensive digital cameras can approach this level of dynamic range.

Dynamic range is one aspect of digital cameras that differentiates the best cameras from lesser-quality cameras. The higher the dynamic range that a camera can record, the greater the range of values you will have between pure white and pure black in your image.

The high limit of a digital sensor's dynamic range is set at the point where light information hitting photosites starts to spill over to other photosites, producing a featureless white spot with purple fringing around the edge; this is called **blooming** (Figure 3-16). The low point of the dynamic range is set at the point where digital noise (visual speckles) overtakes the very weak signal that the small number of photons hitting the sensor generates, causing noise to become evident within the shadows.

The dynamic range of film varies, depending on the type and brand of film. Black-and-white film can have up to 12 or more f-stops of light. Color film's dynamic range is slightly less but still in that ballpark. However, color slide (transparency) film's dynamic range is only approximately

Figure 3-16

Example of blooming. The
specular highlight caused
by the sun hitting the wire
created a high contrast area.
Blooming discolored the
surrounding pixels.

Photo © KS.

Figure 3-17

The fence posts in this image have plenty of detail, but the overexposure made most of the sand void of detail.

Photo © KS.

5–6 f-stops of light, similar to that of inexpensive to moderately expensive digital cameras.

Film-based photography has an additional handicap. Even though film can handle a wide range of values, the photographic paper used for printing can only handle about 5 or 6 stops of contrast. Despite the fact that print film can capture a significant range of values, we don't currently have the technology to render all of those values onto the printed page.

You can ensure detail in your shadows by slightly overexposing an image. Again, that amount of overexposure will affect the entire image, including the highlights. Your highlights may be recorded as pure white, void of detail (Figure 3-17).

On the other hand, you might want to create a **silhouette**. In a silhouette, the subject is so dark as to be totally void of detail. The surrounding scene is lighter and almost always contains much more visual information (Figure 3-18). In this case, your goal is to purposely make the

photograph underexposed. It all depends on your intention. How do you intend your photograph to look?

Camera Mode Settings

Specific mode settings on your camera give you control over the artistic aspects of photography. Let's look at these settings one by one.

Program Mode

If you're new to photography and want to get started quickly, set your camera to Automatic or **Program (P) mode** (Figures 3-19a and 3-19b). This mode typically reads the film's or camera's ISO setting and then invokes your camera's light meter to select the proper aperture and shutter speed for the exposure. Your camera's light meter reads the amount of light coming through the lens and sets a combination of shutter speed and aperture to render the scene a middle gray value. All you need to do is push the shutter button.

Figure 3-18

A swimmer stands at the lip of a hidden pool at Victoria Falls in Zambia. A silhouette is made by having the light source behind the subject and metering toward the light source instead of toward the subject.

Photo © Annie Griffiths/National Geographic Stock.

Aperture Priority Mode

Aperture Priority (Av) mode setting allows you to select an aperture setting according to the depth of field you want for your photo (Figures 3-20a and 3-20b). Once you've set the aperture, your camera's light meter reads the ISO and selects the proper shutter speed to render the scene a middle gray value.

Changing the f-stop from a smaller opening (such as f/16 or f/22) to a larger opening (such as f/4 or f/2.8) is called **opening up the aperture**. Changing the f-stop from a larger opening (such as f/4.0 or f/5.6) to a smaller opening (such as f/16 or f/22) is

called **closing down**, or **stopping down, the aperture**.

Every lens has a maximum aperture opening. Many lenses are only capable of an opening of f/5.6 or f/4.0; other lenses can achieve larger aperture openings, such as f/2.8 or f/1.4. These are known as *fast lenses* because photographers can use faster shutter speeds with the larger apertures. Lenses with a maximum aperture of f/5.6 or smaller are considered slower lenses.

Aperture is a major component in controlling depth of field, which will be discussed in greater detail later in this chapter.

Figure 3-19

The Program mode is often represented by a "P" on cameras. (left) Film-based camera; (right) Digital camera.

Photo © KS.

Figure 3-20

The Aperture Priority (Av) mode setting on a camera. (left) Film-based camera; (right) Digital camera.

Photo © KS.

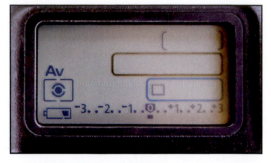

Figure 3-21

Shutter Priority (Tv) mode setting on a camera. (left) Film-based camera; (right) Digital camera.

Photo © KS.

Shutter Priority Mode

Shutter Priority (Tv) mode setting allows you to select a shutter speed setting according to your need to stop action in your scene. Once you've set the shutter speed, your camera's light meter reads the ISO and selects the proper aperture to render the scene a middle gray value (Figures 3-21a and 3-21b). The shutter speed remains the same until you change it.

Sports photographers frequently use Shutter Priority mode. They select a shutter speed capable of stopping the action of the sport participants. In so doing, they sacrifice their control over the aperture the camera's light meter sets for them.

Manual Mode

You are responsible for setting both the aperture and shutter speed when you use **Manual (M) mode**. You may choose to invoke the camera's light meter at some stage to see what it recommends for the aperture and shutter speed, but then you must set those values manually (Figures 3-22a and 3-22b).

Manual mode is the mode of choice under many circumstances. Nearly all studio photography is done in Manual mode because you have total control over the lights. If the lighting doesn't change, there is no need to recalculate exposure settings every time you take another photo. If you are working indoors or outdoors in conditions where the lighting doesn't change, Manual mode helps ensure that all of your images will be properly exposed.

Manual mode is also very useful if you're making panorama photographs. You don't want the aperture or shutter speed to change while making a series of photos you intend to stitch together. If either the aperture or the shutter speed was to change, your resulting panorama wouldn't be realistically exposed.

Bulb Mode

In **Bulb mode**, your camera's shutter will remain open as long as you're pushing the shutter button (Figure 3-23). Hold the shutter button down for 2 seconds and you have a 2-second exposure. Hold the shutter

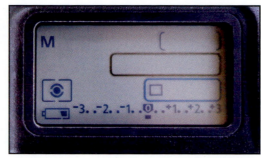

button down for 30 minutes, and you have a 30-minute exposure.

Bulb mode is helpful for low light situations. Use Bulb mode when photographing fireworks or star trails or when trying to capture lightning during a storm. Use a tripod to keep the camera steady during a long exposure.

Figure 3-24 is an example of how photographers write with light using the Bulb mode. If you wear dark clothes and photograph in a location with little or no ambient light, your camera will record whatever type of light you can use. Try penlights, flashlights, black lights, or any other light source you can safely use in that environment.

Over- and Underexposure

An overexposure means that the film or sensor recorded more light than appropriate. It happens when any one (or more) of the three elements of exposure allows more than the optimal amount of light to be recorded the camera. Overexposure can cause a loss of detail in the lightest portion of your photograph, also known as **blown-out highlights**. Overexposure also causes the shadows and middle values in your scene to be too light as seen earlier in Figure 3-17.

An underexposure means that the film or sensor recorded less light than appropriate. It happens when any one (or more) of the three elements of exposure allows less than the optimal amount of light to be recorded the camera. Underexposure can cause a

loss of detail in the darkest portion of your photograph, also known as **blocked-up shadows**. Underexposure also causes the middle values and the highlights to be too dark (Figure 3-25).

The importance of a correct exposure can't be overstated. Although minor tweaking of an exposure is possible in either the traditional or digital darkroom, your best image will present itself when the highlights and shadows are properly exposed at the time of image capture.

Light Writing

"This piece of light writing (or "Light Graffiti" as it is more commonly known) was created using a selection of torches to paint "light effects" into a real environment and captured using a digital SLR (Canon 5D mark 2, Lens Canon EF 16-35 mm L mark 2) set to Bulb mode. The abandoned rail tunnel is ideal for light graffiti as it is near complete darkness, free from obstacles and interruption, and allows exposures to run for over an hour, if needed." —Michael Bosanko.

Figure 3-24

Fire in Tunnel. Bulb mode is the mode of choice of you are photographing light in dark ambient conditions. This photographer uses small light sources to paint with light, creating what he calls "light graffiti."

Photo © Michael Bosanko. See more of his creative work at www.michaelbosanko.com.

Figure 3-25

An underexposed photograph of the Hoh National Rainforest in Washington. Note the lack of detail in the shadows.

Photo © KS.

Aesthetic Considerations

One aesthetic definition of a good exposure might be: "The exposure is good when the photograph looks realistic." However, unless you were at the scene when the photograph was made, how do you know what the "reality" of the moment was? And even if the print looks very realistic and "perfect" to some people, how do we know that's what the photographer intended?

Perhaps the photographer hoped to make a dark and moody scene out of a daylight photograph—such prints could easily come out of both traditional and digital environments. Just because the resulting photograph is darker than some people would expect does not make the photographer wrong; nor does it show poor craft (Figure 3-26). It means the photographer is using the camera to make images that match the intentions. That is an admirable goal!

Evaluating Your Photographic Exposures

It is up to you to decide if a photograph is correctly exposed. Here are some questions you might ask as you view your images:

Figure 3-26

This photographer took special care to make sure the exposure allowed the light inside the box to illuminate its sides. The background was purposely exposed at darker values to prevent the illuminated box from being overpowered.

Photo by Kemal Kamil, Istanbul, Turkey.

- Are the highlights as light as you want them to be?
- Are the shadows as dark as you want them to be?
- Are the areas that you wanted to be midtones at what you consider to be the proper tonal values?
- How wide is the range of values between the lightest highlight and the darkest shadow? Are you pleased with that range of values, or would you prefer something different?
- Where is the area of greatest contrast within the scene? Do you want your readers' eyes drawn to that area?
- How do the highlights and shadows help direct the viewer's eyes through the photograph? Do those highlights and shadows help or hurt your intentions of leading the viewer through the photograph?
- Do the values within the photograph help to express the mood you're trying to convey?

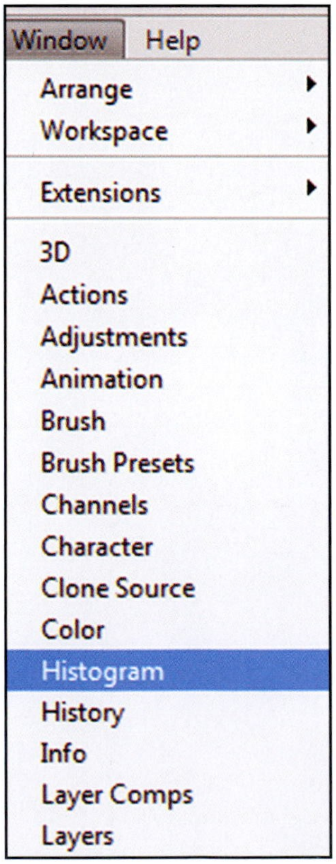

- When you look into the shadow areas, do you see detail or solid black? If all you see is solid black, is that what you intended to see, or would you prefer to see more detail?
- When you look into the highlight areas, do you see detail or is it solid white? If all you can see is solid white, does that fit with your intention, or would you prefer to see more detail?

Evaluating Exposures on the Computer

Photoshop is an excellent tool to evaluate photographic exposures. Photoshop's histogram is a graphical representation of the values of the various pixels within an image. It is used to determine whether your photographic exposure was successful. To understand a histogram, you need to understand how Photoshop thinks about exposures.

The Histogram in Photoshop

This section is designed to introduce you to the digital darkroom's method of evaluating values and exposures using Adobe Photoshop. You will get more detailed instruction on how to work with these Photoshop features in a later chapter. For now, try to understand the concepts being presented, as they are of paramount importance in evaluating the exposures of your digital photographs.

Levels of Brightness

The histogram (Figure 3-27) is a method of quantifying the contents of an image as those contents relate to values. Each color channel (Red, Green, and Blue) is capable of 256 levels of value, or **brightness**. The darkest value is pure darkness, or what we consider black. The brightest value is pure brightness, or what we consider white. A Photoshop function called Levels is an excellent tool for both evaluating and tweaking your digital exposures.

Let's examine a photograph and its corresponding histogram. Figure 3-28 is an image of rooftops during a rain/sun-mixed sky.

Figure 3-27

Window > Histogram.

Photo © KS.

This histogram shows pixels falling across the entire graph. The different peaks show the volume (not physical location) of pixels that fall on that particular level of brightness. The left side of the graph represents black-to-dark pixels (shadows). The center region represents middle value pixels (midtones). The right side of the graph represents light-to-white pixels (highlights).

By examining this histogram, you can see that there are no pure black areas within this photograph. We know that because there is no sharp peak of pixels climbing up the left side of the histogram. There are no pure white areas in the photograph, either. If there were, you would see a vertical line going up the right side of the histogram box.

All of the pixels in Figure 3-28 fall between pure darkness (black) and pure brightness (white). Because there are pixels representing nearly all of the possible levels of brightness between the black point and white point on the histogram, this photograph has what is called a *full range of tonal values*.

The photograph in Figure 3-29 was made shortly after the previous image. The rain-soaked shingles had dried; but the sun was shrouded by heavy clouds, which created low-contrast lighting. The histogram shows the number of pixels that fall on each value. Because there are more low- to midtone-value pixels in this image than there are shadows or highlights, the histogram shows a higher volume of pixels in the low- to midtone area of the graph.

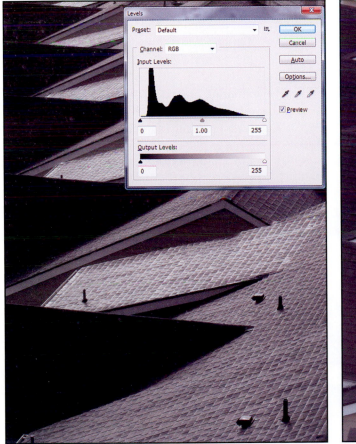

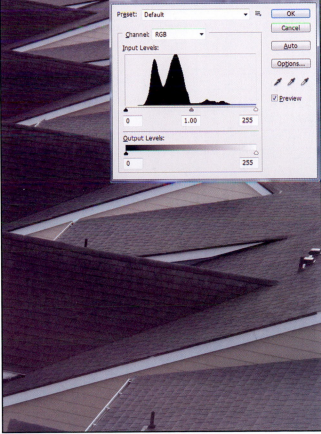

Figure 3-28

This histogram shows the distribution of pixels along each level of brightness values.

Photo © KS.

Figure 3-29

The histogram of this image shows that more pixels fall in the low- to midtone range. There are no pure black pixels in this photograph.

Photo © KS.

Interpreting the Histogram

"How do I know when the histogram is right?" is a common question, but it actually looks at the issue from the wrong direction. A better question would be: "What is this histogram telling me about my exposure?" Your goal as a photographer is to make an exposure that places the pixel values where you want them to be on the histogram.

If you want your image to be mostly light in value, you'll know you have the correct exposure when the histogram shows that most of the pixels fall on the right side of the graph. If the histogram of that same image shows that your pixels are falling across the middle of the histogram, your photograph is underexposed, or too dark in value, for your own intentions.

If you want your image to be mostly dark in value, most of your pixels should fall on the left side of the histogram. If they fall in the midtone range (in the middle of the histogram) instead, you know your photograph is overexposed, or too bright in value, for your own intentions.

Some digital cameras have histogram functions that allow you to view a histogram immediately after making a photograph. If your camera has this capability, use it. Evaluate each exposure you make. Then make adjustments to your camera's aperture and/or shutter speed settings, if the histogram doesn't match your intentions, and make another photograph.

Bit Depth

Most cameras collect 8 bits of information per color channel (Red, Green, and Blue) in a JPEG capture. That results in the 256 values available within each color channel of the histogram and allows approximately 16.7 million possible colors within a photograph.

Photoshop breaks 8-bit images into levels ranging from 0 to 255, making a total of 256 levels of brightness available for any image. The value of 0 is considered the **black point** or pure darkness. The value of 255 is considered the **white point** or pure brightness.

In reality, it's the **bit depth** of your image that determines the number of tonal values that are available within that range of 0 to 255. Some cameras and film scanners can collect 12 or 16 bits of information per color channel, creating considerably more tonal information for each image (Figure 3-30). A 12-bit pixel can portray any one of 4,096 tonal values. A 16-bit pixel can portray any one of 65,536 tonal values! Although a 12- or 16-bit photograph has the potential of having thousands more tonal values,

Figure 3-30

This illustrates a magnification of a histogram of an 8-bit image (top) and a 16-bit image (bottom).

© Cengage Learning 2012.

8-bit (256 individual levels)

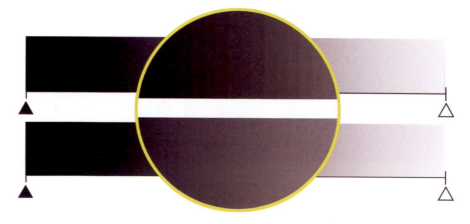

16-bit (32,769 levels)

the dynamic range of the photograph doesn't change between the 8-bit per pixel setting and the 12- or 16-bit per pixel setting. The 12- or 16-bit per pixel setting just offers far more separate tonal values within that camera's dynamic range.

To illustrate this point, think about the keys on a piano. Imagine the highest-sounding key is the white point, and the lowest-sounding key is the black point. If we can imagine an "8-bit piano," there would be 256 keys set at predetermined audible tones. Now, imagine a "16-bit piano"—there would be 65,536 potential keys/audible tones and therefore much smaller jumps in tone from one key to its adjacent neighbor. The top and bottom keys, though, would retain their original tonal values.

All of the pixels within a digital photograph fall within the range of values between 0 and 255, regardless of bit depth. Darker areas of an image have pixels that fall on the left side of the histogram and are considered shadows. Lighter areas of an image have pixels that fall on the right side of the histogram and are considered highlights. The middle-range values are considered midtones.

The importance of using 16-bit images, instead of 8-bit images, is revealed when you alter the values within a digital image. In the Levels dialog box of Photoshop, you can change the values of the pixels to lighten or darken the image (Figures 3-31 and 3-32). An 8-bit image lightened or darkened in Levels will leave gaps in the histogram that denote a shift in values. The gaps show the fact that no pixels have those particular values of brightness, a phenomenon called *posterization*.

Although this isn't a bad thing, it's better to use a 16-bit image when you can. Changes made to a 16-bit file will show no gaps in values because the image started off with so many more available values (Figures 3-33 and 3-34). However, it is possible to alter a 16-bit image so much that posterization will still occur. That's why it is far better to get a correct exposure when you capture the scene with your camera than it is to ask Photoshop to alter the exposure for you.

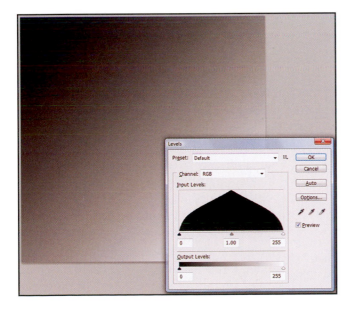

Figure 3-31

This is the original histogram for an 8-bit image. By changing the position of the center gray triangle (middle input slider moved toward the left), you're lightening the midtones of the image.

Photo © KS.

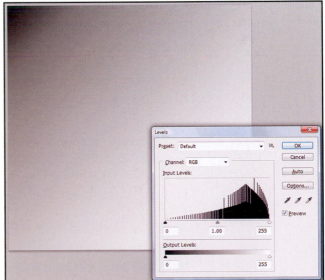

Figure 3-32

After the change is made and the Levels dialog box is reopened, you can see a shift in the values of the pixels. The blank spaces show values that contain no pixels.

Photo © KS.

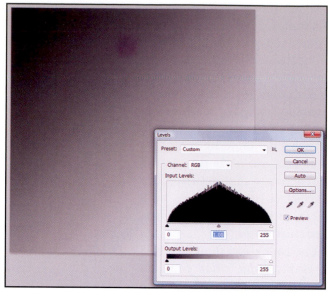

Figure 3-33

This is a 16-bit image. The histogram looks the same as for the 8-bit image, but there is actually far more information available for making smoother changes.

Photo © KS.

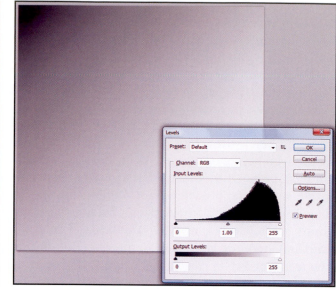

Figure 3-34

Note how much smoother the histogram looks after the change. The greater bit depth prevents the empty levels that were seen in Figure 3-32. You can see very little difference in the actual images of Figures 3-32 and 3-34. Your histogram is always your best diagnostic tool for posterization, as your monitor's resolution can mask banding that would typically show up in a final print.

Photo © KS.

Most consumer-level digital cameras don't make 16-bit images. However, any digital camera capable of making raw exposures can make 16-bit images. You will learn more about raw image captures in a later chapter.

The Aesthetic Aspects of Making Good Exposures

Now that you understand the complexities of exposure, it's time to examine the aesthetic ramifications of your choice of aperture and ISO. Both aperture and ISO have considerations beyond exposure alone.

Aperture and Depth of Field

Your aperture controls the amount of light through your camera's lens. The smaller the aperture, the less light that comes through the lens. A side effect of an aperture setting is **depth of field**. A small aperture hole yields a great depth of field. A large aperture hole yields a shallow depth of field (Figure 3-35).

When discussing depth of field, you're evaluating areas close to the camera (closest foreground) all the way back to the areas farthest from the camera. As the aperture is closed down, more of the scene becomes in focus.

The wider the opening in the lens, the less depth of field there is in the scene. Using an aperture of f/4.0 will result in a shallow depth of field. When you use a wide aperture and focus on a single object, the area directly between the camera and that object—and the area beyond that object—will be out of focus.

Depth of field issues become much more noticeable when you are photographing a subject within a few feet of the camera *and* have a long distance, such as a field or long road, in back of the subject. You won't see much difference in depth of field if you're photographing a person leaning against a tree 75 feet away from you. Depth of field increases as the camera-to-subject distance increases, even for wider open aperture settings (Figures 3-36 and 3-37).

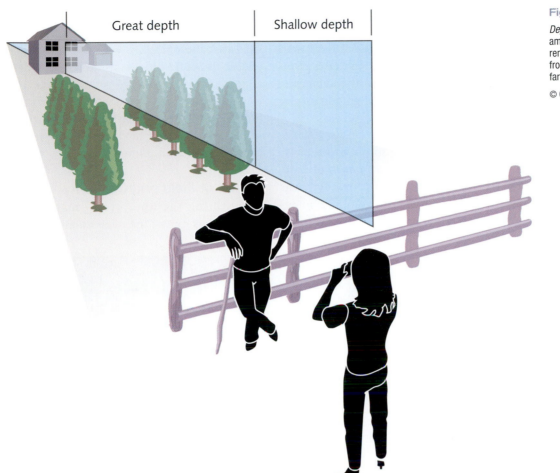

Great depth | Shallow depth

Figure 3-35

Depth of field refers to the amount of your scene that's rendered in sharp focus from close to your camera to far away from it.

© Cengage Learning 2012.

Figure 3-36 (left)

This photograph was made with a small aperture opening (f/22), resulting in a great depth of field.

Photo © KS.

Figure 3-37 (right)

A photograph of the same image as Figure 3-36, but made with a wide-open aperture (f/3.5) resulting in a more shallow depth of field.

Photo © KS.

Another variable in depth of field is your choice of lens. A telephoto lens has much more visible effect on depth of field than does a wide-angle lens. Although the physics of depth of field remain the same, the visible results do change when going from one lens to the other.

Telephoto lenses tend to create a stacking effect of elements within a scene, altering the *perceived* (not real) depth of field. The first photograph (Figure 3-38) was made with a 200 mm lens, and the photographer was standing several feet away from the closest model. The second photograph (Figure 3-39) was made with a 28 mm lens, and the photographer was standing much closer to the first model to keep the models' sizes similar in the two photographs. The models didn't move from their original positions. The photographer moved her position to keep the closest model the approximate same size in both photographs.

Depth of Field and Creativity

Controlling the aperture to match your intention is one of the most creative things

Figure 3-38

A photograph made with a 200 mm lens. Notice the stacking effect in comparison to Figure 3-39.

Photo © KS.

Figure 3-39

A photograph made with a 28 mm lens and the same aperture setting as Figure 3-38. Notice the greater depth of field. The models didn't move from their original positions.

Photo © KS.

you can do with your camera. By selecting specific areas to be in or out of focus, you create a visual hierarchy within your scene. Viewers first notice areas of sharp focus within an image. You can help guide your viewers to specific areas within your scene by using depth of field to your advantage.

If you are trying to separate a person or object from the surrounding environment, a shallow depth of field can help make that happen. Viewers see well-focused objects as physically (and perhaps emotionally) separate from out-of-focus objects. If everything within the scene is in equal focus, the various elements within the scene seem to have a more connected relationship.

If you want to creatively work with depth of field, you will find the Aperture Priority (Av) mode of your camera very helpful. Think about how you want the various elements within your photograph to connect on an emotional level and select your aperture/depth of field accordingly. As you focus your lens, focus directly on the most important element of your photograph. That element will be in focus. Other elements will be in less focus, depending on their proximity to the focused element.

Portrait photographers use apertures in the range of f/5.6 to f/16, depending on the size of the group being photographed. A single person might benefit from a relatively shallow depth of field. A group of people four rows deep will probably need the greater depth of field given by f/16 to make sure everyone will be in focus.

Sports and wildlife photographers frequently use the widest possible apertures on their lenses (f/2.8 or f/4), because those settings allow the fastest shutter speeds to stop action. Depth of field is sacrificed in hopes of stopping the action. Shallow depth of field also blurs foregrounds and backgrounds that might detract from the wildlife within the image.

Landscape photographers may use a much smaller aperture opening (f/16 or f/22) to get the greatest possible depth of field. Many of the landscape photographs

published in calendars are taken with very great depths of field.

Fine art and commercial photographers use varying depths of field, depending on their intention for each photograph. By having some parts of an image in focus and other parts out of focus, they can lead a viewer's eye through the photograph.

Preview Depth of Field

The depth of field you see while looking through your camera's viewfinder isn't necessarily what you will get when you make a photograph. All 35 mm cameras set the aperture wide open for focusing and compositional purposes. The aperture doesn't move to your selected setting until you press the shutter button all the way down. If this weren't the case and you selected f/22, the scene would be so dark in the viewfinder that you would have trouble seeing it.

Preview Depth of Field Button

Some cameras have a preview depth of field button (Figure 3-40). Pushing this button will close down the aperture before you push the shutter button. This allows a better preview of how much of your scene will be in focus. Be prepared to watch your scene go very dark if you are using an aperture like f/16 or f/22. These smaller apertures don't allow enough light

Figure 3-40

A preview depth of field button.

Photo © KS.

Figure 3-41

A photographic negative.

Photo © KS.

negative, and areas that received progressively less light during the exposure will be progressively lighter on the negative. The relative darkness of the different areas in the negative is called **density** (Figure 3-41). The darker areas within the negative are considered denser (e.g., contain more silver) than the lighter areas.

ISO is a numeric representation of a film's sensitivity to light and also is the acronym of the International Standards Organization, the current film speed rating system. ISO is related to the size of the silver halide particles within the film. Very small silver halide particles produce very clean, nongrainy prints. The finer the particles, the more light needed to transform the silver halide particles into the latent image state. Progressively larger silver particles within film require progressively less light to create the latent image. Faster exposures are possible, which helps photographers to stop action within their scenes.

Every box of film has the ISO clearly marked on its label. Older systems used a rating system called ASA (American Standards Association). Both of these systems use the same numerical progression—as the film sensitivity doubles, the ISO rating number also doubles. Higher numbers always denote faster film.

The trade-off for film speed is **film grain**. Film grain is negligible on prints from slow film. However, when negatives from faster film are enlarged to prints, the empty space between the particles of silver on the film can make the prints appear gritty, or grainy. Although some photographers are comfortable with this trade-off, other photographers avoid this situation by using only slow speed (very fine-grained) film.

Color film has all the silver removed from it during the film development process. Colored dyes replace the silver used to make the exposures. However, clouds of dye in the color film appear to separate slightly in space on large prints, giving

in to easily view the scene. It might be helpful to shield sunlight from your viewfinder to help you see your scene while using the preview depth of field button. Release the preview depth of field button before pushing your shutter button to make the actual photograph.

Film Speed (ISO or ASA)

We have discussed at length how aperture and shutter speed affect your photographic exposures. Now it's time to learn more about ISO, the third element of any photographic exposure.

Traditional black-and-white film, such as that manufactured by Kodak or Ilford, is made up of an acetate or polyester base and a gelatin-type substance that holds tiny particles of light-sensitive silver halide crystals. Photons of light from your scene enter the lens and hit the film inside your camera, converting the silver halide particles into a latent (potential) image that will eventually become the black or gray portion of the negative.

After photographic negative film is developed in a darkroom, the silver particles become metallic silver within the negative. Areas that received a lot of light during the exposure will be dark on the

the same effect as film grain in traditional black-and-white film (Figure 3-42).

Film grain often shows up on large-sized prints. A 5 × 7-inch print made from a 35 mm negative may show no grain. But if that same negative is printed at 20 × 24 inches, the degree of enlargement of such a small piece of film results in the film grain becoming much more visible.

If you plan to make big prints, you will be better off using the slowest film possible and also the largest film format possible. You might use a medium-format camera or, under more stringent circumstances, a 4 × 5 camera to take advantage of the larger film sizes.

Traditional ISO rating numbers include the following:

- Slow speed films: 50, 100
- Moderate speed films: 200, 400
- Fast speed films: 800, 1600, 3200

For each doubling of the ISO number, the required amount of light to create a good exposure is reduced by half. In other words, a scene requiring an exposure of f/8 at 1/60 second with ISO 200 film would only require f/8 at 1/125 second when using ISO 400 speed film. As another example in the opposite direction: An exposure of f/16 at 1/30 second with ISO 200 speed film would require f/16 at 1/15 second with ISO 100 speed film.

Modern 35 mm film cameras have the capability of reading the **DX code** on the canister of your film (Figure 3-43). This code tells the camera the film's speed. If your camera doesn't have the capacity to read the DX code, you must use a dial on your camera to select the proper film speed. Consult your camera's manual to see what you need to do.

If your camera doesn't automatically read the DX code and you forget to use the dial to tell your camera the speed of your film, you could grossly over- or underexpose all of the images you make with that roll of film. It's very important to keep track of the film speed you are using!

Figure 3-43

DX code on a canister of film.

Photo © KS.

Figure 3-42

(top) Photo made with 100 ISO film. Note the fine grain, but the swimmer's hands are blurred. (center) Photo made with 800 ISO film, 3 stops faster than the 100 ISO film. Now the swimmer's action is almost stopped, but there is increased film grain. (bottom) Photo made with 1600 ISO film, 1 stop faster than the 800 ISO film. The swimmer's action is stopped, but the film grain is increased and the colors have lost saturation.

Photo © KS.

Digital ISO

Digital cameras also have ISO settings similar to those of film. Increasing the ISO setting increases the sensitivity of the sensor to light. The values work the same as for film: Each increase (e.g., from 100 to 200 ISO) doubles the sensitivity to light and is considered a change of 1 full stop.

Although digital cameras don't need to deal with film grain, they do have digital noise. As the ISO setting increases, the amount of digital noise in your photograph also increases.

Types of Digital Noise

Noise is a visual flaw similar to film grain that appears in digitally produced photographs. Higher ISO speed levels will lead to an increased amount of noise in your prints.

Random Noise

Remember that CCDs or CMOS sensors have photosites that collect light photons. Random noise occurs when the photosites are relatively close together or small, as they are in the older or less expensive cameras. Light information overflows to other photosites, resulting in specks of light in images that weren't in the original scene. The larger the individual photosites on your CCD or CMOS, the less problem you'll have with noise.

Random noise (Figure 3-44) increases with progressively higher ISO settings of any digital camera. Changing the ISO increases the sensitivity of the entire semiconductor to light. As the sensitivity to light increases, so does the sensitivity to random noise. The result is increased visual random noise in photographs that are made with higher ISO settings.

Random noise tends to be visible first in the darker-value areas of your photograph. This is because of the way sensors are set to capture light. If your CMOS sensor is capable of capturing 6 stops (its dynamic range), it can capture 4,096 levels of brightness between pure white and pure black. Half of those 4,096 levels are devoted to capturing information in the brightest stop, half of the remaining 2,048 levels (which is 1,024 levels) are devoted to the next darker stop, half of the remaining 1,024 levels (which is 512 levels) are devoted to the next darker stop, and so on. The final darkest stop, the capture of extreme shadows, is devoted to only 64 levels of brightness.

Because of this linear method of capture, obtaining the highest quality, least noisy exposure means keeping the highlights as light as possible without allowing them to overexpose to pure white. This is called "Expose to the Right" because you want your highlights to fall toward the right side of the histogram where there are more available levels on the sensor to capture the information.

However, if you expose your highlights so far to the right that the histogram shows a peak climbing the right side, you have clipped the highlights; and that visual information will display as pure white in the photograph. Under these circumstances, you cannot retrieve your highlight details.

Because you may slightly overexpose your shadow areas in the process of capturing your highlights where you want them in the histogram, you may be frustrated by the brightness of your shadows' values. In later chapters, you will learn how to work within Photoshop to bring the shadows of

Figure 3-44

Example of random noise. This photograph was made at an ISO of 1250 on a digital camera.

Photo © KS.

your photographs back down to their correct level of brightness while maintaining the highlights where you want them.

Leakage (or Dark) Current

Leakage current is the result of heat generated in the CCD or CMOS sensor. The heat creates an electrical signal indistinguishable from the signal originating from light coming through the lens. It is sometimes called *dark current* because it isn't related to light originating from the scene being photographed (Figure 3-45).

Leakage current is increased under hot conditions (temperatures greater than 90° Fahrenheit), such as photographing on a very hot day or after leaving your camera in a hot car. It becomes most visible with long exposures (greater than 1 second) because the light signals from your scene are very small, and the leakage current becomes a greater percentage of the information gathered by the CCD or CMOS chip.

Luckily, leakage current is relatively repeatable from one photographic frame to another, so it is more easily repaired. Digital camera manufactures have created ways to deal with leakage current by installing photosites that are intentionally never exposed to light. The camera compares the values it sees from these photosites with the values it sees from photosites that are exposed to light. By subtracting the values of the nonexposed photosites from the values of the exposed photosites, the camera itself can remove much of the potential damage from leakage current.

These extra, nonexposed photosites take up space on the CMOS chip. This is the reason why chips that are supposed to create a specific sized megapixel file (such as 6 megapixel) don't actually quite reach 18 MB (6 × 3 channels [Red, Green, Blue] = 18 MB) in file size.

Some higher-end digital cameras actually take two photographs for each long-exposure photograph taken. They take one photograph that is **not** exposed to light and one photograph that *is* exposed to light. By subtracting the values of one image from

Figure 3-45

An example of leakage current. The camera had been purposely kept in a hot car for an hour before the photograph was made.

the other, the camera can dramatically reduce leakage current.

Row and Column Noise

CCD or CMOS sensors are created in a pattern of rows and columns. Random sensor defects can alter the quality of a final image. The technique of how the semiconductor reads the circuits can also cause problems. Row and column noise creates a noticeable pattern (horizontal, vertical, or both) in the final image. Because this kind of noise isn't at all like film grain, people can quickly differentiate this noise as being digitally produced.

Row and column noise was more prevalent in the earliest digital cameras. Manufacturers now produce much better camera components, so severe row and column noise is now uncommon.

So What Is a Good Exposure?

A "good" exposure is clearly more complex than you might think. Don't automatically assume that your camera will give you a good exposure. A good exposure takes both technique and aesthetics into consideration. It might be best described as camera settings that give you the exact visual information you need within your negative or digital file to create the photograph you see in your mind. It is the exposure that gives you the best raw materials for your final print.

Learning How to Make Good Exposures

It should be clear by now that the definition of a good exposure depends on the photographer's intention. You need to gain the knowledge and skills to use the camera in ways that will capture the image you want at the exposure you desire. Anything short of that puts the camera in control over you!

Writing down your aperture setting and shutter speed for every photograph you make is the best way of learning how to create the exposures you want. Consider purchasing a small notebook that fits inside your camera bag, and keep a pen with it. Then discipline yourself to write down the exposure information every time you make photographs.

If you are using a film-based camera, use slide (transparency) film instead of print film. Slide film is much less forgiving than print film, and it also has the advantage of showing you the direct results of your exposure without the intervention of a printer. A professional printer might tweak the exposures to compensate for a slightly over- or underexposed negative. When you're studying photography, sometimes it's better not to have that "help."

Summary

Photographic exposures have three components; ISO, shutter speed, and aperture. The aperture has a side effect of depth of field, one of the most creative aspects of photography.

The photographer, according to the intention for the photograph, determines a good exposure. The image may be overall dark or overall light, fall only in the midtone range, or it can contain a full range of values, depending on the photographer's intentions.

There is no substitute for practice to learn how to make proper exposures. Consider each over- or underexposure a success if it taught you something about how to make better exposures. Before long, this information will become second nature, and you won't have to think so long and hard about it.

1. In your camera's manual, read about its metering system. Experiment with Aperture Priority (Av), Shutter Priority (Tv), Manual, and Bulb modes, if your camera has them.

2. In your camera's manual, read how to set an exposure lock. Practice locking in middle gray exposures and then moving your camera to photograph your subjects.

3. Make a series of photographs by doing the following:

   a. Make a photograph of a light subject that totally or nearly fills your viewing screen. Let the camera's meter determine the exposure.

   b. Use the exposure lock metering function and meter on an object reflecting an 18% gray reflectance. Lock in that exposure. Then repeat the photograph you made of the light subject.

   c. Make a photograph of a dark subject that totally or nearly fills your viewing screen. Let the camera's meter determine the exposure.

   d. Use the exposure lock metering function and meter on an object reflecting an 18% gray reflectance. Lock in that exposure. Then repeat the photograph you made of the dark subject.

   e. Compare the various photographs you made. In particular, look at the negatives (if using film) or histograms (if using a digital camera) of those images. Look for differences in values within the images.

4. Examine photographs you have made and determine whether the exposure rendered the images you wanted. What would you change? Why?

5. Look through the other chapters in this textbook and examine the photographs for depth of field and the lighting conditions within the images. Select one or more images and write about what makes them powerful. If the photographer had chosen a different aperture setting for a different depth of field, or if the lighting conditions had been vastly different, how would those changes have altered the mood or impact of the resulting photograph?

6. Collect belongings that are meaningful to you and create still life scenes with them. Select lighting that both illuminates the belongings and helps to create a sense of mood for the photograph. In essence, use lighting that will help you tell your story of those belongings.

7. Create an informal portrait of a friend or relative who is willing to act as a model for you. Select lighting that matches your model's personality. Ask your model to wear clothing that will match your intentions. After making the photographs, study the resulting images and look for detail in highlights and shadows. Look at the midtones and decide if they are as light or as dark as you intended them to be. Does your exposure match your intentions for the photographs? If not, try adding or subtracting light from your camera's exposure (whichever is needed) and make more images.

8. Research paintings by Rembrandt van Rijn, Michelangelo Caravaggio, and Joseph Mallord William Turner. Look at how each of these painting masters used light to create a mood within their images. Look for contrasts between the highlights and shadows. Take note of when Turner was practicing his craft, and then look in the By the Decade section (Appendix A) in this textbook to learn more about the times in which he lived.

9. Look at images by the photographers listed below. Observe how these photographers used exposure to create a mood for their photographs.

   a. Ansel Adams

   b. John Paul Caponigro

   c. Yousuf Karsch

   d. Sally Mann

   e. Arnold Newman

   f. John Sexton

   g. Alfred Stieglitz

   h. Paul Strand

FURTHER READING

- ADAMS, Ansel. *The Camera.* Boston: Little, Brown, and Co., 1995.

- ADAMS, Ansel. *The Negative.* Boston: Little, Brown, and Co., 1981.

- YOUR CAMERA'S MANUAL will be an important resource as you learn about metering. Be sure to read about metering, exposure lock metering, and overriding the light meter.

- FRASER, Bruce. *Raw Capture, Linear Gamma, and Exposure.* San Jose, CA: Adobe Press, 2004. Adapted from his book, *Real World Camera Raw.* Peachpit Press, 2004.

R. J. Hinkle

Manager and photographer for QuadPhoto – Dallas

Photo by R.J. Hinkle ©2010.

Please describe your photographic background and how you prepared yourself for your current position.

I started by working on my high school's yearbook. During college I took a job as a photojournalist for the *University Daily*, Texas Tech's student-run daily newspaper. I also worked in the University News and Publications office at Texas Tech. Later I worked for various newspapers and became a stringer (a frequent freelancer) for AP (The Associated Press) and UPI (United Press International). After 13 years as a photojournalist, I started working for Quad Graphics, a large print production corporation. I was hired to photograph people and be the official corporate photographer. It didn't keep me as busy as I wanted to be, but I was lucky enough to have an office in the photographic studio. I started helping the other photographers and learned the studio part of the business.

That was essentially my "assistant" time. I learned about large-format and medium-format photography and became proficient in the more formal lighting techniques. I worked into a leadership role. In 2000, Quad Graphics opened four new studios across the country. The last one was in Dallas, and I moved down to work in that studio.

When you need photographic assistants, what kind of knowledge and training do you expect them to have, both photographically and computer-related (file management, Photoshop, etc.)?

The first and most critical thing I look for is a strong work ethic. It's extremely unfair, but your photo skills don't matter as much as your willingness to work. As an assistant photographer, you will fetch coffee, get lunch, carry heavy things, and do whatever is needed.

Here's a success story: A student from Texas Tech contacted me. She arrived for an interview dressed nicely. She brought her photo books and asked for work. We had a project coming up, so I let her come and observe the photo shoot. She jumped at the chance and did everything we asked her to do. She was even sweeping the floor, organizing things, and putting things away without being asked. She found things to do that helped the team. We were very impressed; so, we hired her again for subsequent jobs.

Macintosh skills are very important, and I trust only a few assistants to deal with the files. A photographic assistant needs to know the software being used on a particular project. Other software skills depend on your market and the job as to what workflow is used. Phase One camera backs and Capture One software are common, as are Lightroom and Bridge. An assistant must be familiar with downloading, adding metadata, and backing up files, all of which happen during the photo shoot.

In a lot of big markets, many of the camera stores and production rental houses will have either online resources or classes on Capture

One software (www.phaseone.com). Some manufacturers have tutorials online for people to learn the software or lighting equipment. Ask studio photographers what equipment they use, and take the initiative to go out and learn about that equipment before asking to be an assistant.

Overall, though, a good work ethic is most important. I can't say that enough.

We also look for students to be the experts in newer technologies. Universities often have the latest new equipment for students to learn on. Perhaps a student has used CS5 and a studio is still on CS4. By virtue of their age, students just coming out of school need to be computer experts. Some studios actually hire assistants they call Digital Techs and put them in charge of all file management.

Do any photographic assistants actually work with photo equipment during the actual photo shoot?

Yes. More advanced and experienced assistants do work with the lighting and product. One photo assistant I work with on a regular basis has years of experience and can do it all. On a large production with several assistants, he may be considered the first assistant and other assistants are under him. I really need the top assistant to be someone who knows lighting techniques very well. I need to be able to explain a concept and the assistant can nail it without further input from me. This is something photographic assistants can aspire to, but it doesn't happen in the beginning. You can't expect to come on board as a new assistant at that level.

How do you find good assistant photographers? Do they knock on your door with portfolios? What do you expect to see within their portfolios?

I don't have any preconceived ideas. I just enjoy looking at their work. Are they serious about photography? Do they have photo skills? A person's portfolio may not be the major criterion to be an assistant, although sometimes

an assistant can act as a second shooter. It depends on the studio.

Many students don't realize that professional photographers talk with each other. If I'm in a bind, I may call another studio and ask for the name of a good assistant. Assistants that act professional and have good reputations are well known, as are those who don't.

Can you give a description of what "acting professional" means?

Say appropriate things, don't say inappropriate things, fit in, follow all rules that exist. Even if you come to a more relaxed studio, you still need to be professional. Clients can influence the firing of assistants during a photo shoot. I can't argue with the client.

Know your place, and that can be very ambiguous. Don't try to join in on informal conversations between client and the photographer. Don't take on a familiarity with a client or photographer that isn't appropriate. Be respectful and don't assume anything. I was raised in Texas, so I say "sir" and "ma'am." Acting professional goes hand in hand with that work ethic. Don't walk into a studio with a sense of entitlement, thinking you deserve to be treated in a certain way. Everyone works hard.

Do you have any other words of wisdom for aspiring photographic assistants?

This is a business, it's tough to learn, and there is no silver bullet. It isn't glamorous work.

A photographer and a photographer's assistant have to do a lot of hard work. If you aren't shooting, you're selling. Be up on the new technology. Further your career by photographing during nights and weekends. Push your own envelope. Shoot every day. You need to be passionate about it, although vacations are allowed. It's all about improvement, changes, new technologies, new trends, and new looks (some of which might be old coming around again). You always need to be learning and experimenting. Today's experiments may be tomorrow's drudgery. Luckily, I really enjoy it.

Garden Archway is a photo made with infrared film.

Photo © Bob St. Cyr, Alberta, Canada.

CHAPTER

4

Film and Film Processing

Chapter Learning Objectives

- Differentiate between black-and-white, color print and slide, and chromogenic films.

- Explain the significance of a film's characteristic curve.

- Compare exposure latitudes of print film, slide film, and digital photographs.

- Study the steps of black-and-white film processing.

- Become acquainted with infrared film and its capabilities.

Film has been the raw material for making photographs ever since Kodak introduced the first plastic-based film to the public. Learning the basics about film and film processing will help you make informed decisions about which film to purchase. In this chapter, you will learn about different kinds of film, their different characteristics, and how they are processed.

Figure 4-1
Breakfast.
Photo © Anna Danilochkina.

Why Use Black-and-White Film?

When working with black-and-white photography, you will learn to change your visual perception of a scene. Black-and-white photography deals with tonal values and tonal contrast only. There is no color to separate objects within a photograph. There is also no color to distract viewers from the essence of the captured image. Black-and-white photography simplifies a scene and brings out the form and dimensions within that scene.

Black-and-white films have evolved over time. Improvements in dynamic range, sharpness, and the ability to capture detail in highlights and shadows have shaped the photographic community's passion for black-and-white films. Photographers select films according to their ability to create the final image desired.

Varieties of Black-and-White Print Film

There are two popular categories of black-and-white print film. To understand the process of developing the film, you need to be aware of the basic components and characteristics of each category.

Black-and-White Negative Film

Many manufacturers make black-and-white negative film. Ilford, Agfa, Kodak, and others have been making many popular brands of black-and-white film for decades.

Black-and-white negative film consists of six different layers (Figure 4-2). They are:

- A scratch resistant coating to prevent the emulsion from being damaged;
- An emulsion consisting of about 60% gelatin and 40% light-sensitive silver halide crystals; it is within the emulsion that the negative transforms after light falls onto it;
- An adhesive layer attaching the base coat to the emulsion;
- A base coat, which is a firm but flexible plastic, that provides the necessary support to the film;
- Another adhesive layer; and
- An **antihalation coating** that prevents light from reflecting back through the emulsion and further exposing the silver halide crystals.

Chromogenic Film

Chromogenic film is black-and-white film containing dye couplers along with silver halide. The dye couplers in chromogenic film produce black dye during the development process. Again, the silver is removed during the film development process, leaving only black dyes in the emulsion.

Chromogenic black-and-white film is processed in the same manner as color print film, making it a very popular choice for black-and-white photographers. It can be processed and printed at any one-hour photo facility capable of processing color print film.

Chromogenic films may not be as archival (last as long without damage) as traditional black-and-white films. If you make an image you want to last forever, scan the film using a good film scanner soon after the negative has been processed. Otherwise, your negative may experience fading.

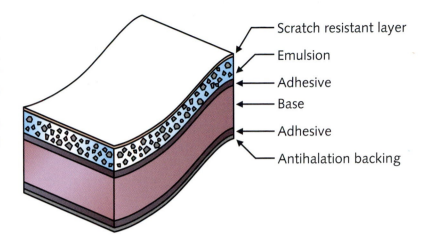

Scratch resistant layer
Emulsion
Adhesive
Base
Adhesive
Antihalation backing

Do not process chromogenic film with the traditional black-and-white film processing method described later in this chapter. The film is not manufactured to be processed in this manner.

Figure 4-2

Black-and-white print film.

© Cengage Learning 2012.

Characteristic Curves of Film

Different kinds of film have different reactions to light, beyond the discussion of a film's ISO. Some films are high-contrast; some are lower in contrast. High-contrast films have a very short tonal range between black and white. Lower-contrast films have a longer tonal range between black and white.

These tonal ranges can be graphed out to form a film's **characteristic curve**. A **densitometer**, a device used to measure the density of a substance, is used to discover the shape of a film's characteristic curve. The more light that makes contact with the film, the denser the silver (or dyes in chromogenic or color film) will be on the developed negative.

Characteristic curves of film include a toe, a slope, and a shoulder (Figure 4-3). Shadows are recorded in the toe, midtones on the slope, and highlights in the shoulder of the curve. As films become lower in contrast, the slopes of their characteristic curves become longer and shallower. Higher-contrast films may completely lose a toe and/or shoulder (Figure 4-4).

The toe of the curve represents the first response of film to the light falling on it. Films require at least a small amount of

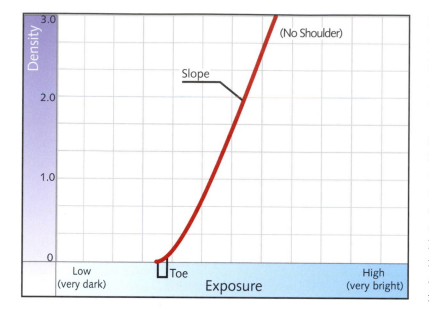

Figure 4-3

Characteristic curve of a film that records a significant amount of detail in highlights and shadows. Because of the sharp slope, this film would be considered a high contrast film.

© Cengage Learning 2012.

exposure before the silver halide crystals are activated to form a latent image. The toe of the film's characteristic curve represents the amount of exposure required before the film begins to form the latent image. An underexposed photograph may fall onto the toe of the characteristic curve, therefore losing detail in shadow areas of the photograph.

The slope of the curve represents the reaction of the film to the light that later represents the midtones of the image. Once

you have enough light to get past the toe of the curve, additional light causes a proportional increase in density on the film. There is no additional waiting for the film to become activated to light as there was in the toe portion.

The shoulder of the curve has a slower reaction to light, just as the toe did. An increase in light hitting the shoulder causes a much smaller increase in density. Areas of a photograph that are overexposed (have received too much light) are recorded in the shoulder of the curve. Eventually, additional light makes no difference in the density of the negative, as all of the available silver halide has been fully exposed.

An exposure that falls on the slope of a characteristic curve will have good separation between tonal values, allowing a considerable amount of detail to be rendered in the photograph. A part of the exposure that falls on the toe or shoulder of the curve will not be able to render clear separation between the tones—this phenomenon is called *blocking up* if it takes place in shadow areas. Blocked-up shadows in a resulting print are near-black or black with little or no detail. If it takes place in highlight areas, the phenomenon is called *blown-out*.

Figure 4-4

Characteristic curve of a normal-contrast film.

Photo © KS.

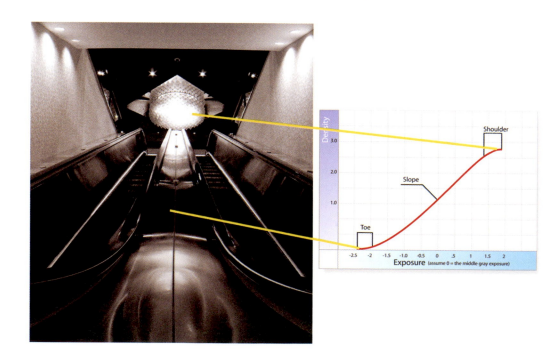

NOTE

Expose for the Shadows in Print Film

A good rule of thumb is to expose for the shadows and make sure the shadow information is well represented on your print film. You may have to sacrifice the highlights, but print film may have enough exposure latitude to hold detail in those highlights.

Blown-out highlights in a resulting print are white with little or no detail.

If your scene is mainly comprised of midtones, it might help you to use a film with a steeper slope to help separate those midtones when you print the negative. If your scene has a lot of detail in the shadows and highlights, it may not be necessary to use a film with a steeper slope. Instead, select a film with a long toe and shoulder to help maintain shadow and highlight detail within your print.

Most film manufacturers have films' characteristic curve information printed in their technical data documents or on their websites. You can look at these documents to select film that will best record the scene you want to photograph.

NOTE

Expose for the Highlights in Transparency Film

The rule of thumb for transparency film is to expose for the highlights and make sure the highlight information is well represented on your film. Visual information in the shadows may need to be sacrificed to maintain detail in the highlights.

Exposure Latitude

Exposure latitude is a measure of the forgiveness of a film subjected to overexposure or underexposure and its ability to still produce a relatively good print. Print film often has enough exposure latitude that if you overexpose or underexpose your film by a full stop, you will still be able to make a print. It won't be the same quality as a properly exposed print, but you'll be able to get at least some image from the negative. It is generally safer to slightly overexpose print film than it is to underexpose the film.

Slide or transparency film has less exposure latitude than does print film. If your exposure is off as little as a ½-stop with these films, you may lose detail in bright highlights or dark shadows. These films require much more care when choosing your aperture and shutter speed. You must be right on target to create a good exposure. If a compromise must be made, it's better to slightly underexpose transparency film by a $1/3$-stop or ½-stop to make sure you aren't overexposing your highlights.

Black-and-White Film Processing

To process black-and-white film, you need a darkroom. There are many darkroom plans available on the Internet. Darkrooms needn't be terribly expensive, and they can actually be built in a modified area of a basement or a laundry room.

Film development can be performed without a complete darkroom, but it's probably easier if both film development and print processing are done in one room. The information provided in this chapter will apply to both film and print processing. First, you'll learn about what a well-equipped darkroom includes. Then you'll learn about safety issues that apply to any darkroom. Finally, you'll learn how to develop black-and-white film. In Chapter 5, you'll learn about enlargers and the black-and-white printing process.

What's In a Darkroom?

Darkrooms are commonly built with a dry side and a wet side (Figure 4-5). The dry side includes a counter and drawers for holding materials. You would typically have your enlarger and easel, print paper, film development tools, and notebook/writing materials on the dry side of the darkroom.

The wet side of the darkroom includes a sink large enough for at least three large developing trays, a tray for washing prints, a source of fresh water, and a well-functioning drain. The wet side of the darkroom must also have enough space to mix and store chemicals.

Darkroom Safety

Even amateur photographers will find the physical requirements for developing black-and-white film to be relatively simple and attainable. However, you need to adhere to specific physical and safety requirements. Black-and-white darkroom chemistry includes strong acids, basic solutions, heavy metals, and sulfur chemicals. Safety must be a primary issue if you want to process and print black-and-white film.

Some chemicals used in film and print processing are common chemicals used in a variety of products. The differences are in the quantity and in the forms of chemicals used. Some chemicals that might be dangerous when used as a powder are much safer when used in a solution. The major issues are possible ingestion, penetration through broken skin, absorption through the skin, and inhalation of vapors from the chemistry.

Penetration and Absorption

As you mix them, chemicals could **penetrate** broken skin or be **absorbed** through your skin. Such hazards can be minimized by wearing rubber gloves and eye protection. Although the chemistry used in black-and-white darkrooms is not as hazardous as that used for color film and print processing, you still may experience some skin or eye irritation. Take steps to prevent splashing of chemicals into your face or eyes. Rubber gloves and protective eye wear are strongly recommended when you are working with darkroom chemistry.

Some photographers use tongs for lifting prints out of processing trays. Many photographers use their bare hands for processing black-and-white prints through the various chemical trays, but there is a risk of developing an allergy to metol, the active ingredient in many developers.

Figure 4-5

Diagram of a typical black-and-white darkroom.

© Cengage Learning 2012.

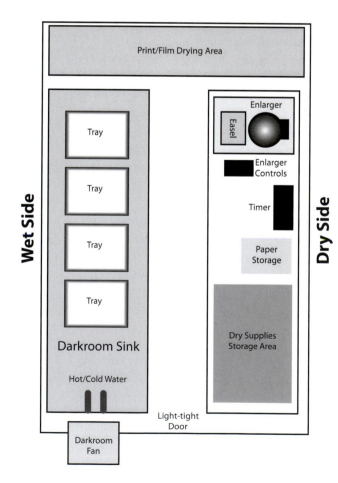

> ### NOTE
>
> **Ingestion**
>
> **Ingestion** takes place if you mix food or beverages with darkroom chemistry. It is always dangerous to have food or beverages in your darkroom. Likewise, it is always dangerous to use your kitchen as a darkroom. Do not use labeled food containers as darkroom chemical storage containers.

Inhalation

Inhalation of chemical vapors is a common hazard in darkrooms. Install a fan manufactured specifically for photographic darkrooms, and route the ventilated air through ductwork that directly exits your residence. You will also need an air intake that allows fresh air to enter your darkroom without allowing light to come in.

An exhaust fan is most effectively installed just above the level of the chemical trays in the darkroom. Because the trays are typically used in a darkroom sink, a fan placed close to the height of the darkroom sink will pull the vapors away from you. A fan installed close to the ceiling will draw the vapors directly past your face, increasing your exposure to the vapors.

Exhaust fans are sold according to the number of cubic feet of air exchanged per minute. Manufacturers of darkroom exhaust fans also specify the maximum size a darkroom can be for efficient operation of each fan. Select a fan manufactured for the size of your darkroom.

Materials Safety Data Sheets (MSDS)

Manufacturers of chemicals are required to have Materials Safety Data Sheets available to users. You can find MSDS for your chemistry online, or you can request written MSDS information from the manufacturer. These informational sheets tell you what chemistry is included in the formula, the proper working conditions for mixing and using the chemistry, and what to do in case of spills, contamination, or ingestion of the chemistry. You are strongly encouraged to have MSDS information on hand for every darkroom chemical you purchase.

Pregnancy, Children, and Pets

Pregnant women should consult with their physicians before working in any darkroom environment. Because some chemicals may be harmful or toxic to the fetus, pregnant women need to be especially mindful of this possibility. As with any other chemicals, keep all darkroom chemicals out of reach of children and pets. Ingestion of these chemicals can be very dangerous.

Getting Started with Black-and-White Film Development

Having read all of this, you may be frightened of working in a darkroom. Basic black-and-white film and print processing is really quite safe and simple, provided you take the precautions described above. It is incredibly fun to develop your own film and see the results when you pull the film from the developing reel. And there is nothing, *absolutely nothing*, like watching an image appear on a plain white sheet of paper as you develop your own black-and-white print. It's like magic; and for those who love black-and-white darkroom photography, it never grows old. Add to that the fact that you can gain considerable control over the final prints you make, and you may find black-and-white film developing and print processing enormously gratifying.

Here is what you'll need to get started with black-and-white film development:

- A room without a window. You must be able to achieve total darkness in this room. Even the slightest light leak can ruin an unprocessed roll of film.
- A place where you can hang your film to dry. This should be as dust-free an environment as possible.
- A clean, dry counter on which you can place your tools and materials.
- Access to a sink and source of fresh water. This *cannot* be your kitchen!
- A storage area for equipment and chemistry.
- Chemistry, including:
  - Developer, either purchased as a powder or liquid and mixed with water according to the manufacturer's instructions.
  - Stop bath is optional, but many photographers use it between the developer and fixer stages.
  - Fixer, either purchased as a powder or liquid and mixed with water according to the manufacturer's instructions.
  - Hypo clearing agent.
  - Wetting agent.

- At least two plastic measuring cylinders (1000 ml).
- Plastic funnel.
- A thermometer that can measure at least a range from 60–80 degrees Fahrenheit. You need to be able to easily read the individual degrees. Film processes faster in warmer water, so it's critical that you can monitor the temperature of your chemistry.
- Gallon-sized dark plastic containers manufactured for storing chemistry and a permanent writing marker for labeling the containers.
- Scissors.
- Bottle cap opener (not the same one you use in your kitchen) for removing the flat side of the film canister.
- Film reel and developing container manufactured for your film size (35 mm or medium format film). Processing of sheet film requires a different style of film holder than the film holders used for 35 mm or medium-format film rolls.
- A watch or timer with a second hand.
- A line or hanger from which to hang your processed film.
- A film clip (offered commercially) or clothespin to help your processed film hang straight.
- Negative storage bags.

Mixing and Storing Chemicals

You can purchase black-and-white chemicals from several manufacturers, including Kodak and Ilford. There are many popular film developers, and each has advantages and disadvantages, depending on your needs and interests. Different film developers will frequently alter the characteristic curve of your film. Go online to search for conversations about the pros and cons of different film developers. Be sure to read the manufacturer's technical data sheet for your film for information on which film developer to use and how to mix the solutions.

Stock and Working Solutions

You will purchase either a package of powder (such as Kodak D-76) or a bottle of developer concentrate (such as Ilford Ilfotec DD-X) to develop your film. There are a variety of fixers on the market, both in powder and liquid concentrate form. They all need to be mixed with water and stored as **stock solutions** in dark (brown or black) plastic containers. The stock solution is considerably stronger than the solution you will actually use to develop your film.

Working solutions are stock solutions further diluted with water. Mix only as much working solution as you need to completely fill your film developer container. Film developer working solution should only be used once. Fixer working solution can be reused. Follow the manufacturer's instructions for mixing your stock and working solutions.

Labeling Containers

Proper labeling of containers is important from both a production and a safety standpoint. You need to identify the chemical and mixing date on each chemical storage container. Because developer reacts with air over time, you need to keep track of how old your stock solution is before developing film with it.

Be sure your various containers are clearly labeled. If you happen to pour in fixer before you use developer on your film, your film will be irretrievably ruined. The fixer removes all of the unprocessed silver from the film and puts it into solution. When you pour out your fixer, you pour out all of your silver. There's nothing left to make an image on your negative.

How Black-and-White Film Developing Chemicals Work

Black-and-white film processing requires four steps: development, stop, fix, and wash.

Developer

When light strikes the film inside your camera, it produces an electrochemical effect on the tiny silver halide crystals within the emulsion. The light basically changes the electrical charge of the crystals so they will be responsive to the action of the chemical **developer**. This change results in a latent image—an invisible image on the film that is prepared to undergo film processing.

Crystals that have been struck by a lot of light will be more responsive to the developers than crystals that have been struck by less light. Crystals that have not been struck by any light will not be responsive to the chemical developer.

Chemical developers are made by companies such as Kodak and Ilford. Each developer reacts a little differently with the film. Most film manufacturers recommend that you use their own developer product with their brand of film in an effort to balance various factors; including emulsion characteristics, efficient processing times, and factors involving film grain. The following information applies to any brand of developer. The term "developer" in this context is generic to any brand of developing chemistry.

Developer contains a **developing agent**, an organic compound that reduces the exposed silver halide crystals to metallic silver. The most common developing agents in developer are metol, phenidone-hydroquinone, amidol, or glycin. Sometimes a specific developer will have a blend of these agents.

Developer also contains a **preservative** to maintain freshness over time. Developer tends to oxidize rapidly in water, rendering it useless for film processing. The preservative helps to slow this oxidation process. Developer includes an **accelerator** to provide the alkaline environment required by the developing agent. The accelerator has an effect on the contrast of the resulting negative. The **restrainer** included in developer prevents the developing agents from affecting any silver halide crystals that have not been exposed to very much light. Without the restrainer, some of this slightly exposed silver halide would change to metallic silver.

Developers may be sold in liquid or powder form. If you purchase the powder form, you need to mix the powder with water

according to the manufacturer's instructions. Liquid developer is sold as a concentrate that must be diluted with water, according to manufacturer's instructions, before use.

Replenisher

Film can be processed in two general ways: using developer as a one-time shot or dipping film into a tank of developer that is reused later. If the developer will be reused, a **replenisher** is added to the tank to help restore the developer to full activity.

Replenisher is most frequently used in large production labs that process several rolls of film per day. It is added according to a schedule based on the number of square inches of film that have gone through the developer. Therefore, the production lab must keep careful records regarding the amount of film that it has developed in each tank of developer.

Stop Bath

The stop bath serves three important functions:

1. Because it is acidic, the stop bath neutralizes the alkaline developer still in the emulsion.
2. Because the next step (fixing) is an acidic process, the stop bath helps create a more acidic environment for the film, rather than going straight from the developer (alkaline) to the fixer (acidic).
3. The stop bath helps to prevent staining and scum formation on the negative.

Many people simply use water as the stop bath when developing film. Water serves the same function as a commercially available stop bath, but it does so with much less strength because water's pH is not as acidic as the commercially available stop bath.

Fixer

Fixer removes the unreduced silver halide that remains in the film emulsion after development. Without the fixer to remove this silver halide, the entire roll of film would still be sensitive to light after the film had been processed. Fixing film, then, is a crucial step in film processing.

Some fixers include a substance called a **hardening agent** that hardens the emulsion of the film to help protect it from scratching. Although there may be some extenuating circumstances for not using fixer with a hardening agent, most student photographers take advantage of the benefits that a hardening agent can offer. It's important to fix, but not excessively fix, your negatives. Keeping film in a fixer too long can lead to bleaching of the image by removing unreduced silver *and* some of the metallic silver that forms your image.

After the film is fixed according to the manufacturer's recommendations, it is safe to bring it into light. At this point, you can see the images on the film for the first time. This is not, however, the end of the processing procedures.

Wash

After fixing, film needs to be washed with clean water. This can be accomplished in many ways, including running water through a **film washer**, a specialized film reel holder with a connecting tube hooked up to a water faucet. If a film washer isn't available, you can run water directly from a faucet to the film development canister. Longer wash times are likely necessary, though, to make sure the film is thoroughly rinsed.

Hypo Clearing Agents

Hypo clearing agents contain inorganic salts that remove fixer more quickly than washing in plain water alone. Use of a hypo clearing agent ensures that all of the fixer has been removed from the negatives. Instructions for these agents usually include a wash time for completion of the film development.

The Steps of Black-and-White Film Processing

Follow the steps in this section to process your black-and-white film. Because of the importance of keeping your film safe during processing, you will start with practice sessions.

Practice Before Working with Exposed Film

Film processing begins by removing the exposed film from its canister and placing it on a metal or plastic reel, which is spiral and prevents the film from touching any other portion of film during the development process. If different areas of film touch each other during development, that portion of the film will be ruined.

Threading your film onto a film reel takes practice. Before trying to develop exposed film, sacrifice a roll of new film or use processed film to practice threading the film onto your film reel. Once you're comfortable doing this with the lights on, turn out the lights and practice threading the film onto the film reel. Only when you're proficient with this procedure should you proceed to developing exposed film.

Measure the Volume of Your Film Development Canister

During the film development process, you will be frequently adding and pouring out a variety of fluids. It's most economical to know beforehand how much fluid your canister holds before mixing your chemistry.

Test this by adding a film reel to your film developing canister and filling it with tap water. Then empty the canister into a measuring beaker and read the amount of fluid your canister holds. Write this number down so you can mix just enough of your chemistry to match this amount. Be sure to thoroughly dry your film reel before proceeding.

Prepare Your Chemistry

Before you prepare your film for processing, mix the required amount of developer and fixer you will need to process your film. Make sure the chemistry is fresh and at the required temperature recommended by the film manufacturer. The temperature of the solutions and water used in the development process is very important and must be judiciously maintained.

Most black-and-white print films can be processed at a variety of temperatures, but the processing times will vary, depending on the chemistry's temperature. Consult the literature that accompanies the film to select the proper development time for the chemistry's temperature.

Select a Location

Traditional black-and-white film starts its development process in a totally dark room. It can be a closet or bathroom without windows, a basement room with a door that doesn't allow light leaks, or a small room adjacent to a traditional darkroom. The requirements of the room are simple in that you need space to stand, a table or counter on which to place your supplies, and a light switch for an overhead light or lamp.

Before actually processing film, test the room to make sure it is dark. Go into the room, close the door, turn the light off, and stand there for several minutes until your eyes adjust to the dark. Look for cracks around the door or along the walls that allow light into the room. Any light coming into the room could damage or ruin your film. Once you are sure the room is light-tight, you can proceed.

Prepare Your Film for Processing

Begin by gathering all the equipment you'll need: scissors, bottle opener, a film developing canister and lid made for your size film (either 35 mm or medium-format), a film reel, and, of course, your film (Figure 4-6).

Once you assemble your equipment, close the door, turn off the light, and use the bottle opener to remove the flat end of your film canister (Figure 4-7). Trim off the tab of film with the scissors (Figures 4-8). It is most helpful to cut between the sprocket holes in the film so the film's edge is perfectly smooth. This will make it easier to load onto the film reel.

Thread the film onto the film reel (Figure 4-9). Some film reels have a

> ### NOTE
>
> ### Turn Off Lights!
>
> Don't forget to turn off the light! Any light in the room will destroy the images on your film. Do not use a safelight, as safelights can only be used during print processing (described in Chapter 5).

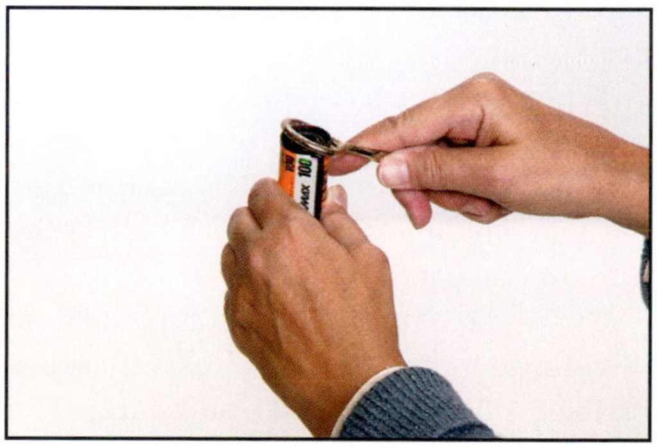

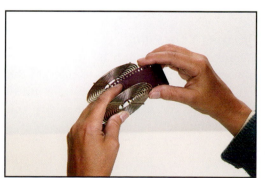

**Figure 4-6
(top left)**

Assemble your supplies in a light-tight room. Turn out the lights and make sure there are no light leaks coming into the room from windows or cracks around the door. Use towels to block out any light leaks.

**Figure 4-7
(top right)**

Using the bottle opener, remove the flat end of the film canister.

**Figure 4-8
(bottom left)**

Use the scissors to cut off the film leader.

**Figure 4-9
(bottom right)**

Wind the film onto the film reel.

Photos 4-6 through 4-9 © Kitty Sookochoff.

> ## NOTE
>
> ### Keep the Lid Closed!
>
> From this point forward, keep the developing canister lid tightly on the canister. The only portion of the lid you will remove is the small removable cap in the lid's center. If you remove the entire canister lid and expose the film to light, you will destroy your images on the film.

threading system that starts on the perimeter of the reel; others require you to start at the center of the reel. Some center-loading reels have clips under which you slide the film to hold the film in position. Whatever style you use, take extreme care to avoid letting the film layers touch each other.

When you reach the end of the film, trim away the film spool (Figure 4-10). A small amount of paper may be left on the film, but that isn't a problem. It won't affect the film processing.

Then place the film reel into your film developing canister and close the specialized lid (Figures 4-11 and 4-12). The lid allows fluid to flow into and out of the canister while blocking light from the film.

Process Your Film

When the canister top is firmly on the film canister, you are free to turn on the lights and, if you need to, go into a utility room where you have your chemistry and water source.

Measure the temperature of your chemistry (Figure 4-13). Your goal should be to have all chemistry, including your wash water, the same temperature.

Remove the topmost center lid, *not the entire lid*, of the film development canister and fill it with 68° F. water (Figure 4-14). Replace the lid and shake the canister (Figures 4-15 and 4-16). Tap the canister on the counter a few times to remove any air bubbles from the film surface (Figure 4-17).

Continue this process for 2 minutes. After 2 minutes, pour out the water and pour the developing solution into the canister (Figures 4-18 and 4-19).

Repeat the combination of shaking (also called *agitating*) and tapping against a hard surface for the first 30 seconds to ensure that air bubbles (also called *air bells*) don't remain on the film surface. If the air bubbles prevent a chemical solution from reaching the film surface, that area of the

film will not be properly developed, and that negative will have small circular spots on it. Those spots show up as flaws when the negative is printed.

After the initial 30 seconds, place the canister on the counter and let it rest (Figure 4-20). After another 25 seconds, lift and agitate the canister for 5 seconds,

Figure 4-21 (left)

When the development time is up, pour the developer out of the canister.

Figure 4-22 (right)

Fill the canister with water. Agitate the canister for 30 seconds. As you did before, periodically tap the canister against the counter to remove air bubbles from the surface of the film.

Photos 4-21 and 4-22
© Kitty Sookochoff.

then let it rest again. Continue this process of agitation 5 out of every 30 seconds of the remaining developing time. The reason for this pattern is to make sure the developer that's touching the film is frequently replenished during the processing time.

When the developing time is over, remove the topmost lid (*not the entire lid)* and pour the developer out of the canister (Figure 4-21). The negatives contain the images in their final form, but it is still not safe to take the film out of the light-tight canister. All of the silver originally contained in the film's emulsion is still present, and it will still react to light and ruin the images.

Fill the canister with 68° F water, and agitate the water for about 1 minute to stop the action of the film developer. Tap the canister on the counter occasionally during this period to remove any air bubbles on the film (Figure 4-22).

After a minute, empty the water and pour enough fixer into the canister to completely fill it to the top. After you have

poured the fixer into the canister, shake the canister and tap it against a hard surface to remove air bubbles as you did before. Using the same agitate/rest procedure that you did for the developer, process the film in the fixer for 5–7 minutes, or according to the film manufacturer's instructions. The first 30 seconds involves agitating and tapping the canister. Beyond that time, agitate and tap the canister against a counter for 5 out of every 30 seconds. Rest the canister on the counter for the next 25 seconds, then repeat the 5 second/25 second cycle for the recommended time period.

Fixer contains silver after it has processed film. Silver is an environmental hazard and *must* be disposed of in a responsible fashion, according to EPA standards. Film processing laboratories have filtration systems that filter the silver out of the fixer. Recycling companies recycle the silver. Be especially careful not

NOTE

Stop Bath—Stops the Developing Process

Although water is most commonly used as a stop bath, some photographers use a mild acidic stop bath to more quickly and effectively stop the developing process.

NOTE

Silver Filtration Systems for Home Darkrooms

Some photographic suppliers sell smaller, easily used silver filtration systems for home darkroom use. These relatively inexpensive units help to keep the environment safe from the hazards of silver. *Under no circumstances should silver-laden fixer be drained into a septic tank!*

to allow silver-laden fixer to drain into a septic tank because silver kills the beneficial bacteria there.

When the fixing is complete, pour the fixer out of the canister. Now you can remove the entire canister lid, as it is safe to let light hit the film. But don't make the mistake of removing the film from the film reel yet!

Some photographers use a hypo clearing agent at this stage. This agent, used as a final wash, helps to clear the fixer from the film. After you have completed the hypo wash, you need to wash the film with clean running water for at least 5 minutes (Figure 4-23).

One last step remains. If the film were removed from the reel and hung to dry at this stage, water droplets remaining on the film can leave tiny mineral deposits on the film as it dries. These deposits cause white marks on your prints where the enlarger's light couldn't reach the printing paper.

Fill your film developing canister with clean water, add a few drops of a wetting agent to the rinse water, and very gently stir it (Figure 4-24). You don't want bubbles

to form in the solution. Drop the film reel back into the canister and let it rest without any agitation.

After a 30-second soak in the wetting agent, remove the film reel from the developing canister and unroll the film from the processing reel (Figure 4-25). Photographers use a sponge, squeegee, or even their fingers to rid the film of excessive moisture. The film is then hung vertically in a dust-free cabinet to dry (Figure 4-26). A weight, such as a wooden clothespin clipped to the bottom of the film roll, can be used to prevent the film from curling. Avoid letting the clothespin come anywhere near the image portion of your film.

Storage of Processed Film

Film is best stored in negative sleeves available through photographic supply stores or photographic archival supply stores. Negative sleeves are available for 35 mm, medium-format, or 4 × 5 film. Be sure to purchase archival quality sleeves to prevent damage to the negatives.

Once your 35 mm or medium-format film is dry, use scissors to cut it into strips, round off the sharp corners of the film to make it easy to slip into the negative sleeve used for long-term storage (Figure 4-27). Large-format film does not need to be trimmed before placing it in a negative sleeve.

Moisture, dust, and light are your film's worst enemies. Moisture leads to mold growth on the film's surface. Dust is challenging to deal with when printing, because dust on the negative will leave tiny white spots where light was blocked from reaching the printing paper. Light will eventually fade your negatives and, in the case of color film, can cause color shifts that lead to prints that can't easily be color balanced. Store your film in a dry, dark storage area to protect it from these hazards.

Film sleeves typically have a place to write identifying information. Develop a system of identification so you can quickly find a negative you need. Be judicious in your practice of this identification system, as it can save you hours when you are looking for a specific image.

Loading and Developing 4 × 5 Sheet Film

If you use sheet film for either 4 × 5 pinhole or large-format camera photography, you will need to use a slightly different approach to film development. The chemistry and process are the same. The only major difference is the container in which you load and process your film.

Sheet Film Holders

Large format cameras use two-sided sheet film holders. Each side holds one sheet of 4" × 5" film (Figure 4-28).

Loading sheet film holders requires careful cleaning and preparation, as any dust on the film will prevent light from your scene from exposing that portion of the film. The result is a white dot on your film that creates a black dot on your prints.

Start by carefully cleaning all dust and debris from the film holder and the two film covers (Figure 4-29). Insert the two film covers into their respective slots at the top of the film holder (Figure 4-30). By convention, photographers insert the cover so the side with the white bar across the top (the left film cover in Figure 4-28) faces outward. After the film has been exposed, the film cover is inserted so the white bar faces inward toward the film holder (the right film cover in Figure 4-28). That way you will reduce the chance for double exposures.

So far, there is no film in the film holders. Store the film holders in a vertical position, if possible, to prevent dust from getting inside when the film covers are removed.

Sheet film is packaged in a light-tight box. Every type of sheet film has its own coding of notches cut into the bottom edge of the film. You can identify each type of film by reading the manufacturer's instructions included in the film package. The notches also help you identify the emulsion side of the sheet film. When you are loading the film, you should be able to feel

the notches along the left lower corner of the sheet. This tells you that the emulsion is facing toward you. The emulsion must be facing the film cover, *not* the film holder, when it is loaded.

To load film into your sheet film holders, take your clean film holders and box of film into a light-tight room. Turn off the lights and check for light leaks. Remove the lid of the film box. You will find another lid immediately inside. Remove that lid as well, and you will find a package of film. Tear off the top of the package and remove one sheet of film. Do not take all of the film out of the box, as you increase your risk of getting dust on the film. Feel the edge of the film to find the notches, and rotate or flip the film so the notches are along the bottom left side of the sheet. Now the film is in the proper position to be placed in the film holder (Figure 4-31).

Slide the film cover up enough to be able to flip the bottom lip of the film holder downward. It is hinged to the film holder and won't fall off. Slide the film into the film holder, being careful to push the top of the film underneath both of the grooves on

either side of the film holder (Figure 4-32). Those grooves hold the film covers in place. If your film is placed within those grooves, you won't be able to easily slide the film cover down over the film. Use clean hands, but not gloves, for this procedure. Lint from gloves will cause the same problems as dust on your film.

When you have pushed the film high enough, lift the bottom lip of the film holder back into its original upright position (Figure 4-33). Then push the film cover down into its closed position. Turn the film holder over and repeat the film loading process for the other side. Each film holder holds two sheets of film.

Figure 4-34 (left)

This sheet film development tank system will develop six, 4 × 5 sheets at a time.

Figure 4-35 (right)

Place the sheet film guide on top of the grooves on one side of the film holder.

Figure 4-36 (left)

Insert one sheet into each groove.

Figure 4-37 (right)

Place the plastic stop piece on top of the holder to hold the sheets of film in position.

Photos 4-34 through 4-37 © KS.

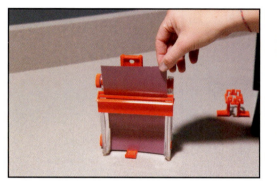

Manufacturers make a variety of sheet film developing tanks (Figure 4-34). These are relatively small containers that come with a sheet film holder and specialized lid, similar to that of a 35 mm developing container. The major difference is that the film is loaded one sheet at a time onto an immersible sheet film holder.

A developing tank will come with instructions on how much fluid to add during the film development process. Be sure to adhere to these recommendations, as proper agitation may require a small amount of empty space within the tank.

To begin, bring your sheet film holders and film developing tank and lid into your light-tight room. Remove the sheet film holder from the developing tank and place it on the counter (Figure 4-35). Place the plastic guide on top of the grooves on one side of the sheet film holder. Make a note of where the tank's lid is for later use. Turn off the lights.

Carefully withdraw each sheet of film from its film holder and slide it into the slot on the developing tank's sheet film holder (Figure 4-36). When you have completed the first three sheets, remove the film guide and place it on the other side of the film holder and load the remaining three sheets. Then remove the film guide.

When all of the slots are filled, place the plastic stop piece on the top of the holder (Figure 4-37). Lift the entire holder and place it in the developer tank (Figure 4-38). Place the lid tightly onto the tank. Your film is ready to be processed (Figure 4-39).

The remainder of the process is very similar to processing 35 mm or medium-format film. Follow the same instructions as those for 35 mm film described earlier in this chapter.

> ### NOTE
>
> **Removing Lids in Light-Tight Rooms**
>
> If you need to pour out the chemistry faster than the small opening allows, *work in a completely dark room with no light leaks* and remove the entire lid to remove or add chemistry.

You can purchase 4 × 5 film storage sheets to protect your film. Store your 4 × 5 negatives the same way you would your 35 mm or medium-format negatives.

Identifying Underexposed and Overexposed Negatives

The following are examples of underexposed, overexposed, and properly exposed films. Learning to evaluate the exposure quality of your negatives will help you make better exposure decisions when photographing in the future.

When you examine your negatives, do so by looking through a magnifying loupe (Figure 4-40). It is difficult to see the detail within a negative without this device. Magnifying loupes are available through many camera supply stores.

Underexposed negatives look thin, and no area looks particularly dark. You can't see any detail in areas that you expected to show detail. Properly exposed negatives have the expected range from light areas to dark areas within the frame. There is detail where you want detail in both highlights and shadows. Overexposed negatives look thick and dark. There are very few, if any, transparent areas.

Figure 4-41 is a series of photographs of a white blouse on the left and a black blouse on the right. A grayscale chart and color chart are included for reference. Frame #11 was 2 stops overexposed. Frame #12 was 1 stop overexposed. Frame #13 was properly exposed. Frame #14 was 1 stop underexposed, and Frame #15 was 2 stops underexposed. The resulting prints are shown directly above the corresponding negatives.

Figure 4-40

A magnifying loupe for examining negatives.

Photo © Richard Mirro/iStockphoto.

Figure 4-41

Five different exposures of one scene, with 1 stop difference in each exposure. The center frame was correctly exposed. The resulting prints are directly above each corresponding photograph.

Photo © KS.

Beyond Basic Film Development

The information provided so far has been an introduction to film processing. There are several variables, including different developers, developing times and temperatures, and film types that can dramatically alter the resulting negatives. Serious black-and-white photographers will find a wealth of possibilities by going beyond the basics of film processing.

Contrast Control in Film Development

As you gain experience with black-and-white photography, you'll develop an ability to predict how much contrast within a scene will be recorded on your film. This skill is valuable for several reasons. First, you will learn to adjust the lighting conditions so your entire scene will fall within the dynamic range of your film. Your resulting exposure will contain the desired details within your highlight and shadow areas.

Predicting how your highlights and shadows will be recorded by film will also allow you to make adjustments when you process you film. If you increase the amount of time your film remains in the developer by 20%, you will increase the contrast of the resulting images. This is very helpful if you've made photographs in low-contrast conditions (Figure 4-42).

Conversely, if you decrease the amount of time your film remains in the developer by 20%, you will decrease the contrast in the resulting images. Again, this is very helpful if you have photographed scenes containing contrast beyond your film's dynamic range.

Push Processing

Push processing of black-and-white film involves manually setting your camera's ISO to a speed higher than your film's ISO. When you expose your film, your camera will be fooled into recommending a faster shutter speed than your film would typically need. Your result is an underexposed roll of film. You need to identify that film roll in some way so you know how many stops you underexposed the roll.

When you process the film, give the film extended time in the developer, about 20% extra time for each stop of exposure you underexposed your film. For example, if your film has a recommended ISO of 400 and you set your camera's ISO to 800, you have underexposed your film by 1 stop and should increase your development time by 20%. If your film's recommended ISO is 400 and you set your camera's ISO to 1600, you have underexposed your film by 2 stops and should increase your development time by 40%. There is no need to change the stop bath or fixer times during the development process.

Figure 4-42

A change in development time results in a contrast change in the negatives. "N" denotes the standard length of time for processing the film. "N + 1" denotes that length of time, plus an additional 20% of time, resulting in higher contrast. "N − 1" denotes the standard length of time, minus 20% of time, resulting in lower contrast.

Photo © KS.

N+20

N-20

Because films vary in their response to push processing, you should experiment with these procedures with all of the film brands and ISO speeds you use. Manufacturers may give recommendations for push processing times, as well. Consult the manufacturer's product data sheets, and keep a record of your experiences with push processing.

Push processing does have limits. The absolute limit for push processing is 3 stops, and the film you use may not have good results with such an extreme underexposure. Image quality decreases to the point that using a faster film in the first place would have yielded better results.

Traditional black-and white, chromogenic, color print, and transparency films can all be push processed to a lesser or greater extent. Some manufacturers recommend that you don't add development time to color print films, as their exposure latitude is already great enough to cover an underexposure of 1 stop.

If you don't process your own film, you will need to work directly with a photo lab willing to push process your film as a separate order. One-hour labs are set up to run several rolls of film through their processors for the same time period, so a roll that requires push processing becomes a special order. Ask the lab manager if push processing is available before dropping off your film. Be careful to clearly mark your film envelope for push processing, making a special note in the Special Instructions section, if possible.

If there is any question that your request won't be honored, find a professional lab that will push process your film instead of a one-hour lab. Otherwise, your film can be ruined by insufficient processing.

Exposing for Different Film Types

Your goal, under all circumstances, is to correctly expose your film so detail is

Old Axiom for Print Film

Expose for the shadows, develop for the highlights.

Old Axiom for Slide Film

Expose for the highlights, develop for the shadows.

preserved as you want it in both highlight and shadow areas. Following the manufacturer's instructions for ISO ratings and keeping in mind how your camera's meter reads middle gray will help you do this. Beyond that, there is an old photographic axiom that can be helpful to you: *Expose for the shadows, develop for the highlights* is a practice many film-based photographers use to make sure their print film captures enough detail in the shadows to print properly. Changing the development time of print film (as in push processing) has little effect on the shadow areas. If it's important that your shadows contain visual detail, you must expose your film long enough that those shadow details are recorded.

Changing the development time of print film has a much greater effect on highlight areas on a negative. The longer your film stays in the developer, the denser the highlight areas become. This causes a greater difference between the density of the highlight and shadow areas on the negative, which is equivalent to increasing the contrast of the negative.

The axiom is reversed if you are using slide film. It's vital that you maintain detail in the highlights of slide film, sacrificing shadow detail if necessary. For slide film, you should *expose for the highlights and develop for the shadows.*

Color Film and Film Processing

Color film comes in two versions: print and transparency. Processing of print film results in a negative image that is printed onto color print paper. Transparency film is also called *slide, positive,* or *reversal* film. The processing of transparency film results in a positive image, meaning that the film shows the original scene. Transparency film was the film of choice for publishing photographs in magazines, calendars, and other print media; however, when high-quality digital cameras became affordable for professional photographers, the use of transparency film dramatically decreased.

Both print and transparency films come in a variety of film sizes and speeds. Just as with black-and-white film, color film is available for 35 mm, medium-format, and large-format cameras. Transparency film comes in speeds as slow as ISO 50 and as fast as ISO 200. Color print film comes as slow as ISO 100 and as fast as ISO 3200.

Film grain is extremely fine and colors are very saturated in slow transparency film, making it the film of choice for color reproduction in the printing process before digital photography took over. As film speeds increase, film grain becomes more apparent in enlarged prints, just as it does for black-and-white film.

Color print film is composed of a base and silver particle emulsion layer very similar to black-and-white film. In addition to these components, color film emulsions contain dye couplers (Figure 4-43). Each layer contains silver halide plus one color, either red, green, or blue. During the development of color film, the silver halide crystals that were exposed to light cause a buildup of the color dyes. The silver itself is ultimately removed, leaving the dyes to create the image on the negative. During the processing phase, the red dye changes to cyan, green dye changes to magenta, and blue dye changes to yellow.

Figure 4-43

Diagram of color print film.
© Cengage Learning 2012.

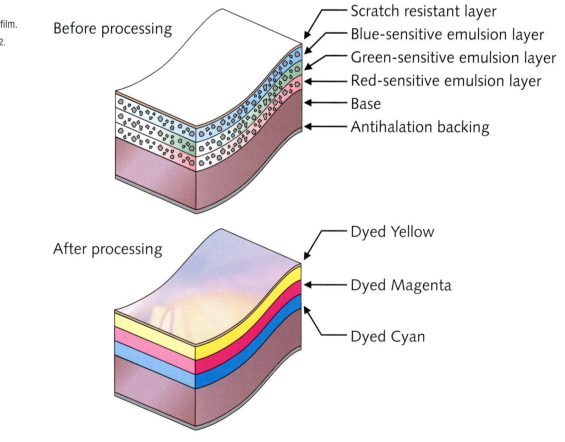

Before processing

- Scratch resistant layer
- Blue-sensitive emulsion layer
- Green-sensitive emulsion layer
- Red-sensitive emulsion layer
- Base
- Antihalation backing

After processing

- Dyed Yellow
- Dyed Magenta
- Dyed Cyan

Why Use Color Film?

Color isn't simply one additional dimension to photography—it can be carefully used to change a photograph's mood, aesthetics, symbolism, and overall impact to the viewer. It is a highly complex element that can both make your photographs more visually interesting *and* complicate your photographic endeavors in many ways. Although none of these issues is insurmountable, it does take time and effort to learn about and understand them.

Different cultures have different emotional responses to specific colors, creating a major potential gap between your intentions for your photograph and the viewer's understanding of that image. For example, Native Americans attach a great deal of symbolism to colors (Figure 4-44). This symbolism is often overlooked or misunderstood by European Americans.

Color can also evoke a subtle physical response. It can change the energy level of people. Think about the bright red color on the walls and carpets of casinos. That same color of red might not be the best color choice for a preschool room where teachers want children to be well-behaved and relatively quiet. The calming colors of light blue and green might be more welcomed there.

Psychologists and artists have performed multitudes of studies on the human response to color. See the books listed in the Further Reading section at the end of this chapter for a start on how to study color and its effects on viewers.

Color Perception

Working with color is even more difficult when you realize that our perception of a single color changes depending on its surrounding colors. Dull, relatively low-saturated colors appear more saturated when surrounded by even duller colors. Colors, including gray, appear darker when surrounded by lighter colors, and vice versa (Figures 4-45 and 4-46). Colors also appear warmer when surrounded by cooler colors and vice versa (Figures 4-47 and 4-48).

This has significant impact when you are compositing images that have different overall color palettes. Although a person's red shirt might appear orange-red in a predominately blue photograph, that same shirt may appear blue-red when it is brought into a predominately yellow or orange photograph. The color of the shirt doesn't actually change—it's your *perception* of the color that shifts.

Ojibwe Ceremonial Colors Also known as the four directions or the four winds	
Blue	West
Red	North
Yellow	East
Green	South

Ojibwe Medicine Wheel Colors represent all people of the world	
White	White brothers
Yellow	Asian brothers
Black	Black brothers
Red	Native American, Latino, and Aboriginal brothers

Figure 4-44

Color chart and significance of color for Ojibwa Native Americans residing in northern Wisconsin.

© Cengage Learning 2012.

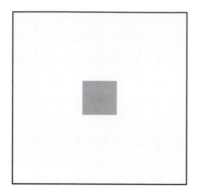

Figure 4-45

Compare the center gray square to the center gray square in Figure 4-46.

Photos 4-45 through 4-49 © Cengage Learning 2012.

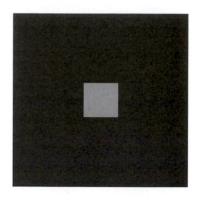

Figure 4-46

The two center squares in Figures 4-45 and 4-46 are exactly the same color. They appear different because of the difference in value of their surroundings.

Figure 4-47 (left)

Compare the color of the diagonal row of green squares to the green squares in Figure 4-48.

Figure 4-48 (right)

The two diagonal rows in Figures 4-47 and 4-48 are exactly the same color and value. They appear different because of the difference in color of their surroundings.

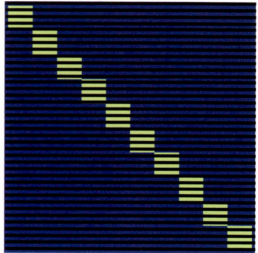

Figure 4-49

In a traditional color wheel used by artists, red, blue, and yellow are primary colors. On computer monitors, red, green, and blue are the primary colors.

Color wheel

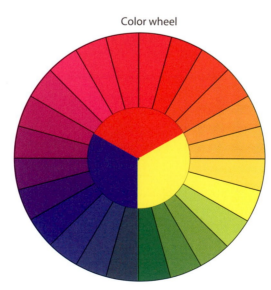

How Color Is Created in Film and Print

It is helpful to know a little about the color wheel when developing and printing color film. The **color wheel** is an artistic tool that painters use to choose and mix various colors. The wheel includes the same categories of color as a rainbow: red, orange, yellow, green, blue, and violet (or what some call magenta). Placed on a color wheel, the colors can be analyzed and compared by their respective positions on the wheel (Figure 4-49).

Three primary colors—red, green, and blue—constitute the *additive* color process. When you add red, green, and blue light together at full strength, you see white light (Figure 4-50). Other colors are mixed from these primary colors to produce the remainder of the visible color spectrum.

For every color of light in the color wheel, there is an opposite or "complementary" (not *complimentary*) color. When a color and its complement are mixed together, they cancel each other out, and you are left with gray (Figure 4-51). It is worth your while to memorize the color complements, as they have many applications in both film-based color printing and all of digital photography.

C-41 Processing for Color Print Films

Processing of color print film involves the C-41 process available at almost all photo labs. **C-41** is a rather general term given to the process for developing many kinds of color print film. It is known as CN-16 by Fuji and AP-70 by AGFA. Kodak manufactures Flexicolor chemicals for processing

Figure 4-50

The additive color system of light. A mix of red plus green light produces yellow light. A mix of green plus blue light produces cyan-colored light.

© Cengage Learning 2012.

Kodak color print film. Temperature control and consistent agitation of the film while it's in the developer are critical to the success of C-41 film development.

Figure 4-51

Color complements of light.

© Cengage Learning 2012.

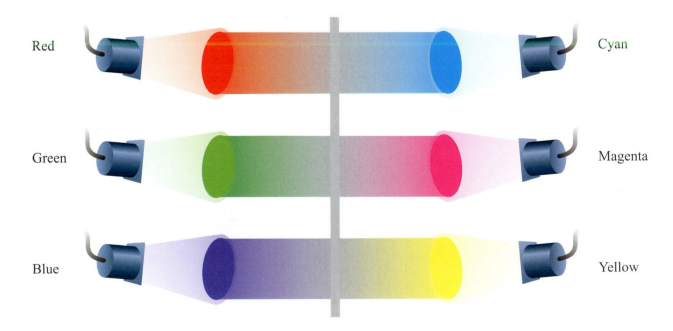

Red   Cyan

Green   Magenta

Blue   Yellow

Figure 4-52

The steps for C-41 rotary tube processing with Kodak Flexicolor chemicals.

© Cengage Learning 2012.

Solution/Step	Time* (min:sec)	Temperature °C (°F)	Comment
Flexicolor Developer	3:15	37.8 ± 0.15 (100.0 ± 0.25)†	Agitate with nitrogen and/or manual agitation
Flexicolor Bleach III‡ Bleach III‡	6:30	24 to 41 (75 to 105)	Agitate and aerate with oil-free air and/or manual agitation
Wash	3:15	24 to 41 (75 to 105)	Agitate with oil-free air or nitrogen or manual agitation
Flexicolor Fixer and Replenisher	6:30	24 to 41	Agitate with oil-free air or nitrogen or manual agitation
Wash	3:15	24 to 41 (75 to 105)	Agitate with oil-free air or nitrogen or manual agitation
Flexicolor Stabilizer III	1:30	24 to 41 (75 to 105)	Manual agitation only
Dry	As needed	24 to 43 (75 to 110)	Remove roll film from reel

* Times include a 10-second drain time at the end of each step.

† The developer temperature given is the recommended temperature during development; it is not the recommended starting temperature for the developer (see Developer Starting Temperature).

‡ You can turn on the lights after the bleach step.

C-41 processing can be accomplished in the home darkroom. The greatest issue facing the darkroom photographer is temperature control. A slight variation in temperature during processing will affect the color balance of the resulting negatives.

Water quality is also an issue in the home darkroom. The water should be free of color or suspended materials. It should not have any heavy metals and should not be very hard.

Check with your local authorities regarding disposal of the post-processing chemicals before doing C-41 processing in your home darkroom. Just as with black-and-white film processing, the fixer will be laden with silver. The silver should be removed from the fixer before disposing of it. Some communities may require a license before you dispose of C-41 chemicals into a wastewater treatment system.

The actual C-41 developing process is very similar to the processing of black-and-white film. C-41 developers work in similar fashion to black-and-white film developers, but they also contain additions to develop the dye-couplers nested in the film emulsion. When developed,

these dye-couplers change to visible cyan, magenta, and yellow dyes.

After development, film is immersed in a mildly acidic stop bath to stop the development process. Finally, a bleach-fix solution (or sometimes a bleach followed by a fixer) dissolves the silver generated by development and removes the undeveloped silver halide particles. The last bath includes chemicals that stabilize and wet the film so it will dry without streaks. A final wash completes the C-41 process (Figure 4-52).

Because different manufacturers produce C-41 chemicals, read the manufacturer's instructions for processing times, temperatures, and solution strengths.

E-6 Processing

E-6 processing is required for most slide (transparency) film. The major exception is Kodachrome film, which requires a much more involved development process. When you purchase slide film, read the required process on the film box. It should say "Process E-6" to be processed in the manner described in this chapter.

Many labs across the country can do E-6 processing. Local one-hour labs may not be able to process E-6 film and instead will send it to a larger regional lab for processing. Turnaround time is generally within 48 hours, depending on where you live.

Photographers with darkrooms can also do E-6 processing, although it can be tricky. Temperature control must be precise (within 0.2° Centigrade) to maintain proper color balance in the final film.

There are six steps to the E-6 film development process:

1. First Developer converts the exposed silver halide within the film's emulsion to metallic silver. This is similar to what happens in black-and-white film development. It is the most critical step in the E-6 process. After the prescribed amount of time has passed, the first developer is removed and a water wash stops the first developer action and removes the solution from the film.
2. Reversal Bath involves using a reversal agent to prepare the film for the color developer step.
3. Color Developer is a developing agent that reacts with the silver halide to form metallic silver.
4. Pre-Bleach prepares the film for the bleach step.
5. Bleach converts the metallic silver back to silver halide in preparation for the fixing step.
6. Fixer converts all of the silver bromide into soluble silver compounds so the unused silver compounds can be washed away. After the fixer time is up, it is removed and the film is thoroughly washed with water.

Infrared Film

You've learned how to process black-and-white, color negative, and color print film. Another popular type of film that invites experimentation and discovery is infrared (IR) film.

IR film captures a portion of the light spectrum just beyond the wavelengths visible to humans. Infrared film's extended red sensitivity captures wavelengths up to 740 nm in length, longer than wavelengths captured by conventional film.

Effects of Using Infrared Film

When black-and-white IR film is used with yellow, orange, or red color filters in front of the lens, blue sky will print very dark, and green foliage will print unusually light. The opening photograph at the beginning of this chapter was made with infrared film.

The reason IR film produces unexpected results is that IR light reflects from objects differently than does light with shorter wavelengths. Objects that are rendered a dark value by standard films may reflect much more IR wavelengths, rendering the dark object very light.

Living foliage such as green leaves and grass reflect infrared light very strongly, as does human skin. These appear very light when photographed with IR film. In addition, overexposure of IR film can cause an ethereal-looking glow around these objects. But blue sky reflects very little infrared wavelengths, so it appears unusually dark in IR photographs.

This effect is enhanced if you use colored filters in front of the lens to block out visible color wavelengths. Yellow filters, such as Kodak Wratten 3, 8, 12, or 15, yield succeedingly greater effects. Orange-to-red filters such as Kodak Wratten 21, 23a, and 25 increase the IR effects even more. Deep red filters such as Kodak Wratten 25, 29, and 89B yield the greatest results. Other deep red filters made by other manufacturers include B+W 091, Heliopan 29, and Rodenstock 29. These filters give an even more dramatic effect than red filters. Cokin, Hitech, and Hoya also make red filters suitable for infrared photography.

Purchasing, Storing, and Traveling with Infrared Film

Infrared film is highly sensitive to heat and radiation. If possible, have IR film shipped during cooler months instead of during the hot summer months. Store the film in a cool, dry place (no warmer than 68° F) in its original packaging. Always have IR film hand-checked at airports. Process the film as soon as it is practical for you to do so.

Film Speed of Infrared Film

Speed ratings for infrared film are typically ISO 200 or ISO 400. However, you should enter the world of infrared film with a great deal of patience and an experimental approach. Camera light meters don't accurately measure infrared light, so metering your scene is only partially helpful. You will need to experiment a lot when first using IR film. As a guide, begin by bracketing 1 stop, and then up to 2 stops, both overexposing and underexposing each scene with your filter in front of the lens.

Because the color gel filters increase in density as you go from filter 3 through filter 89B, exposure times must increase to factor in the loss of light. If your camera does through-the-lens metering (as all modern 35 mm cameras do), your camera's meter will give you the required exposure adjustment. If it doesn't, you will need to make manual adjustments to your exposures.

Focusing Your Camera While Using Infrared Film

Some lenses focus red light slightly differently than other visible light. As a result, you may experience a slight focusing problem when using IR film. In addition, it is very difficult to focus an autofocus lens with a dark red filter because it blocks so much light.

If you have problems with focusing of your images when using IR film, first focus as you usually would. Then set your lens to manual focus and rotate the lens barrel very slightly as if you want to focus on something slightly closer to you.

Another way to adjust for this focus issue is to use an aperture capable of giving you a greater depth of field than you would otherwise use.

Developing Infrared Film

The process for developing IR film is similar to that of standard black-and-white film. The film manufacturers make recommendations on the type of developer to use, temperature for the chemistry, and specific development times.

Printing Infrared Film

Infrared film can be printed in similar fashion to any other black-and-white films. Again, approach the printing of IR film with patience and a willingness to experiment. You may find yourself using an unexpected grade of paper or a different filter (for multigrade and variable contrast papers) than you would typically use. You can also expect more film grain in your prints than conventional film will give you.

Capturing Infrared with Digital Cameras

Even though this is a chapter on film development, you are probably wondering if digital cameras are capable of acting like infrared film. It is possible to capture infrared wavelengths with digital cameras. In fact, digital sensors can be as sensitive to IR light as they are to visible light. However, manufacturers cover the sensors with an infrared-removing filter to prevent the typical visual changes caused by infrared wavelength capture. Most people don't want the IR effect.

It is possible to replace the IR-removing filter with a filter that will enhance your camera's ability to capture IR wavelengths. This is a distinct advantage over the use of IR film, as you get immediate results you can see while still on the scene. If you need to alter your exposure, you can do so right away.

Some companies, such as LifePixel, offer services including the replacement of your camera sensor's IR filter.

The company's website lists which camera models have sensors that can be altered for use in IR photography. Not all cameras can be altered.

If you do an online search for digital infrared photography, you will find several resources that will guide you through the possibilities.

Summary

This chapter has introduced the basics of film and film processing. It's not at all unusual to find photographers who have home darkrooms. The major cautions need to be safety-related. Darkrooms need good ventilation to rid them of airborne chemicals. Chemicals must be properly disposed of to ensure the health of the environment. All darkroom activity must be in a place where food is not a factor; it is *never* safe to use a kitchen sink for film processing.

If these safety factors are taken into consideration, traditional black-and-white film processing can be easily done in a home darkroom. Photographers who can control the processing of their own film have the advantage of controlling the length of time the film remains in the developer, thus altering the amount of contrast within the resulting negatives.

Film manufacturers include a lot of information on the material inside the film boxes. This information should be read and applied to the film development process. Manufacturers' websites are excellent sources of additional and more detailed information.

1. This is an opportunity for you to make photographs of subjects that interest you. Make two or three dozen photographs using traditional (*not* chromogenic) black-and-white film, such as Tri-X or Tmax. Practice some of the exposure techniques discussed in earlier chapters. As you make your selection of subjects, approach them from a variety of vantage points and distances from the subject.

   ■ Try to find angles that produce unusual photographs of the subject.

   ■ Use different lighting to find what kind of lighting conditions best enhance the emotion you feel about the subject.

   ■ Look at the entire photograph to see if background and surrounding areas enhance or detract from the story you are trying to tell with the photographs.

2. Process the black-and-white film using this chapter's information as a reference.

3. Store the negatives in negative sleeves.

4. Read the manufacturer's technical data sheet for your film to learn more about different film developers available for that brand of film. Use at least two different developers to develop different rolls of film and compare the contrast, exposure, grain, and image quality of the developed film.

5. Research the work of infrared photographers. Discuss with your peers how infrared film might be used to strengthen the emotional connection between your images and their viewers.

6. Experiment with infrared film, making several bracketed exposures of scenes that include people and/or living flora.

7. Go online and research the available methods for changing a digital camera to an infrared digital camera.

8. Make a series of photographs about a person you know well. Talk with that person and select one aspect of his/her life that can be photographically portrayed. As you collaborate to make the photographs, consider how the person's story is best told by including or excluding his/her surroundings, the lighting used, where you position the camera, and your choice of close-up versus more wide-angle lens.

FURTHER READING

■ ADAMS, Ansel. *The Negative.* Boston: Little, Brown, and Co., 1995.

■ AIREY, Theresa. *Creative Photo Printmaking.* New York: Amphoto Books, 1996.

■ MCKENZIE, Joy. *Exploring Basic Black & White Photography.* Clifton Park, NY: Thomson Delmar Learning, 2003.

Soup Beggar.

Photograph by Elliot Ross.

CHAPTER

5

Traditional Darkroom Printing

Chapter Learning Objectives

- Use the information in this chapter to print your black-and-white and color negatives.

- Identify the different parts of an enlarger.

- Choose a proper exposure from a test print of your negative, and make a straight print of the negative.

- Select specific areas of the print for burning and dodging procedures.

- Print the negative using burning and dodging techniques.

- Make a contact print of your negatives.

- Use spotting techniques to retouch dust spots.

- Apply archival printing techniques to your final prints.

Your negative is the raw material from which your print will evolve. Darkroom printing isn't difficult, given proper equipment and practice, but the nuances available to darkroom photographers bring the printing process to a new level of intention. Your visual story will come alive within the luminosity of your midtones and highlights and in the depth of your shadows. Translating the highlight, midtone, and shadow information from your negative to your print is an art form that takes considerable thought and practice.

The Artistry of Darkroom Printing

Darkroom printing gives you the artistic opportunity to decide how various portions of your negative will appear on the printed page. The difference in dynamic range between negatives and prints leaves much more visual highlight and shadow information on the negative than can be directly printed onto paper. It is up to you to pick and choose which areas to keep at the same value that they initially print and which areas to manually lighten or darken so all of the desired visual information on your negative is represented on the print.

As you print your negatives, keep your intention in mind. Why did you make this photograph? What did you see within the scene that interested you? What story are you trying to share with viewers?

Then ask yourself what areas of your print should be highlights. How bright should each highlight area be to convey your message? Should they hold textural detail? Which areas of the print should be in shadow? How dark should each shadow area be? Should they hold textural detail? Thinking about your visual story in terms of highlights, midtones, and shadows will help you create a stronger print. Remember that the word *shadows* as used here is a general term for any dark area of your photograph. A black tuxedo, a black dog, or any dark object would be considered shadow areas within a print.

Black-and-White Darkroom Requirements

Many of the requirements for black-and-white film processing also apply to black-and-white printing. As you learned in Chapter 4, there is typically a dry side and a wet side to every darkroom. The dry side of a well-equipped darkroom includes a counter on which the enlarger, easel, focusing magnifier, and paper are kept (Figure 5-1); the wet side includes a sink in which trays for the developer, stop bath, fixer, and wash water reside (Figure 5-2).

Safelights

The only light source allowed in a black-and-white printing darkroom is an amber-colored (yellow) light called a **safelight**. The safelight very minimally exposes black-and-white photographic paper. All black-and-white photographic paper is more sensitive to the blue end of the light spectrum. Recalling the color theory you learned in Chapter 4, you know that blue and yellow are opposite colors when produced by light. The blue-sensitive paper's slow response time to the amber-colored light gives you enough time to process the paper. The safelight's purpose is to give you as much working light as possible without affecting your print.

A phenomenon called **safelight fog** occurs if your photographic paper is exposed to a safelight for a long period of time or if your darkroom safelight is too bright. The safelight gives a very small

Figure 5-1

The dry side of Dave Butcher's darkroom holds his Durst 138S enlarger with an Ilford MG500H Multigrade head on the right and a 3 Durst M670 enlargers further back.

Photo © Dave Butcher
www.davebutcher.co.uk.

overall exposure to the blue-sensitive paper. If the paper is exposed to the safe-light too long, or if the safelight is too bright, your resulting print's highlights will be darker than expected. The result is a decrease in the overall contrast of your print.

The Enlarger

The **enlarger** is the machine used to print negatives (Figure 5-3). It sits on a sturdy table or counter in the darkroom. Enlargers are manufactured to print 35 mm film (called a *35 mm enlarger*), either 35 mm or medium-format film (called a *medium-format enlarger*), or 35 mm, medium-format, and 4 × 5 film (called a *large-format enlarger*). Negative carriers created for the various sizes of film hold the film in place during printing.

Enlargers come in two basic types: condenser and diffusion. Both styles are basically projectors mounted on a strong vertical column. Light from the enlarger

Figure 5-2

Dave Butcher's black-and-white darkroom wet processing area, 2008.

Photo © Dave Butcher
www.davebutcher.co.uk.

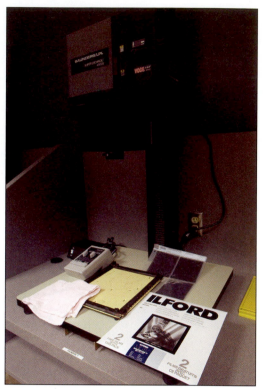

head (topmost portion) shines through your negative. The image from the negative is focused with a lens similar to your camera's lens. The resulting image falls on the photographic paper lying in an easel on the enlarger's base (Figure 5-4).

A timer is tethered to the enlarger, allowing you to control the length of time the enlarger light source is turned on. The longer the light source is on, the darker your resulting print will be. Enlarger timers have toggle switches that allow you to have the enlarger light on while you crop and focus the image before placing paper into the easel. When you're ready to place the light-sensitive photographic paper in the easel, turn off the enlarger light to prevent exposure to the paper until you're ready to start the printing process.

Condenser Enlargers

The major difference in the appearance of prints made with condenser and diffusion enlargers is the amount of contrast produced in the final black-and-white images. Condenser enlargers contain two convex lenses that spread the light evenly over the negative (Figure 5-5). This allows for shorter exposures and higher overall contrast than a black-and-white print made from diffusion enlargers.

Condenser enlargers can have color filters inserted in them, allowing for color printing. Because color negatives produce colored dyes, color prints don't have the same contrast issue that black-and-white prints have when printed with condenser enlargers.

The heat of some enlarger light sources can warm the negative enough to make it bend or buckle, which can occasionally cause a portion of your negative to appear

Photographic Printing—A Process

Photographic printing is a process, not something that begins and ends with the first print you produce. You will probably make several prints of varying exposures and alterations before you finalize the print. Take your time. Be prepared to go back into the darkroom over and over as the process evolves.

out of focus. It's a good practice to allow your negative to warm up in the enlarger for a few minutes and then refocus the image on the easel again before making your print.

Diffusion Enlargers

Diffusion enlargers (Figure 5-6a) contain a flat ground-glass diffuser (a translucent white plate of glass) that scatters the light over the negative, decreasing the contrast in the resulting print. One advantage of a diffusion enlarger is that dust spots on your prints are minimal in comparison to those on prints made with a condenser enlarger.

Some diffusion enlargers use incandescent bulbs as their light source. Others, called *cold-light systems* (Figure 5-6b), use a set of neon-like tubes instead of incandescent bulbs. Cold-light diffusion enlargers can only be used for black-and-white printing. Although the heat of some enlarger light sources can warm the negative enough to make it bend or buckle, a cold-light enlarger will remain cool, allowing the film to remain more flat.

Another advantage is the cold-light system's larger light source that more evenly illuminates your negative. Condenser enlargers are somewhat prone to increased illumination in the middle of your image and less illumination along its edges. Cold-light diffusion enlargers help resolve this issue.

A third variety of diffusion enlargers uses a high-intensity bulb in a chamber directly adjacent to the enlarger head. Colored filters (cyan, magenta, and yellow) placed in the light beam create the required filtration for a color print. This is the style of enlarger required for color printing.

Enlarger Lens and Aperture

The lens on the enlarger focuses the image onto the easel. The aperture of an enlarger lens works exactly the same as

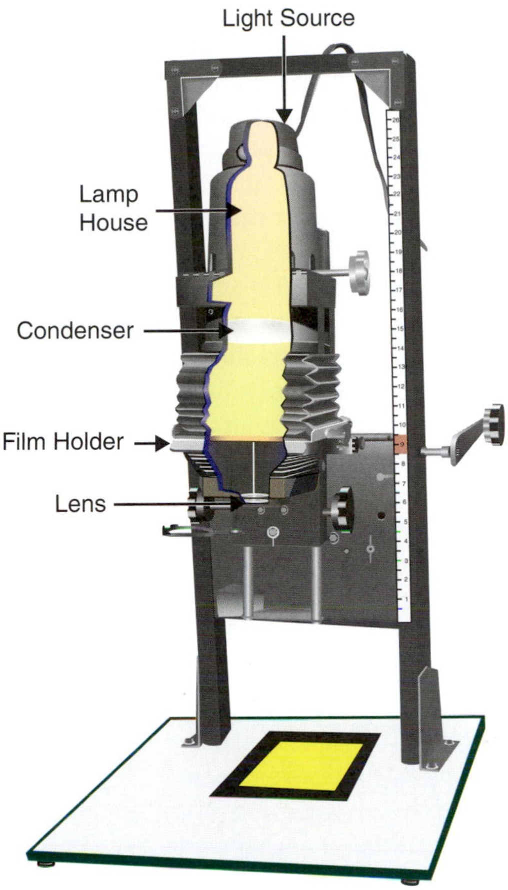

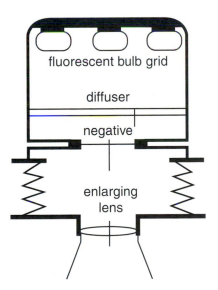

Figure 5-5

Illustration of a condenser enlarger head.

© Cengage Learning 2012.

Light Source

Lamp House

Condenser

Film Holder

Lens

Figure 5-6

Illustration of a cold-light diffusion enlarger head.

© Cengage Learning 2012.

fluorescent bulb grid

diffuser

negative

enlarging lens

the aperture in a camera lens (Figure 5-7). Higher f-stop values create a smaller hole through which the light will fall onto the paper; lower f-stop values create a larger hole. It takes less time to print a negative using a lower f-stop value than it takes to print the same negative using a higher f-stop value.

Lens aperture also affects depth of field in the darkroom, just as it does in camera lenses. In the darkroom, a moderate aperture setting will prevent any portion of a negative from going out of focus—a setting of f/8 to f/16 is generally sufficient.

The Easel

The easel holds your photographic paper flat and in position on the base of the enlarger. Adjustable easels, those with adjustable metal strips on each side, can accommodate various sizes of printing paper. Other easels are manufactured to accept only one size of paper. A good easel will have a frame or series of metal strips that hold the paper edges flat during the exposure period.

If the horizon line of your photograph is slightly tilted, you can rotate the easel underneath the enlarger head to straighten out the horizon line. You can also rotate the easel to introduce a creative new angle to your photograph.

Enlarger-Easel Alignment

It is imperative that the image being delivered by your enlarger head be exactly parallel with the plane of the easel. If your enlarger is out of alignment, or if your easel isn't perfectly flat, the two planes will not match and your print will be out of focus.

Using a higher aperture number (such as f/16 or f/22) can help alleviate this issue, but it also forces you to use longer exposure times. A better method is to read your enlarger's instruction manual on how to align your enlarger head. Also check the base of the enlarger to make sure it is not warped. Finally, be sure that your easel is not bent. Place small pieces of paper or cardboard under a corner, if necessary, to make sure the easel is flat. When you print a well-focused negative, your print should also be in good focus throughout.

Print Size and Cropping the Image

The distance from the enlarger head to the easel determines the size of your print. Enlargers have a vertical post to allow raising and lowering of the head. Higher elevations of the enlarger head create a larger image falling on the easel. If the size of the image is larger than your photographic paper and easel, only the portion of the image falling on the paper will be printed. You can purposely raise the enlarger head and reposition the easel to crop a portion of the negative (Figure 5-8).

Photographic Papers and Filters

Photographic papers come in two general categories: **graded** and **variable contrast** (sometimes called *multicontrast*). Graded papers have numbers associated with them.

Figure 5-7

The aperture on the enlarger works in similar fashion to the aperture in your camera's lens.

Photo © KS.

The numbers refer to the amount of contrast you can expect when printing a typical negative. A grade 1 paper translates the information in the negative into a very low-contrast image. Use grade 1 paper if you know you have a negative containing a lot of contrast.

Grade 2 papers are manufactured to create as much contrast as you would expect to see from a typical negative. You should be able to print a well-exposed negative with moderate contrast onto a grade 2 paper. Grade 3 papers produce more contrast than grade 2 papers. Use a grade 3 paper if your negative doesn't contain as much contrast as you would like. Grade 4 papers produce even more contrast than grade 3 papers and are used with negatives containing very little contrast. When graded papers are used, no filtration is required on black-and-white enlargers.

Many photographers prefer to use variable contrast papers. When these papers are used, a filter is inserted under the lens on the enlarger head. The choice of filter will dictate the resulting contrast of the negative. Kodak filter sets range from grade 1 (to dramatically lower contrast) by half-grades to grade 4 (to dramatically increase contrast).

Grades 1 and 1½ are yellow, with grade 1 being a more saturated yellow than grade 1½. Grade 2 is a very light magenta, which becomes progressively more saturated for grades 2½ through 4 (Figure 5-9). Because the higher numbered filters are somewhat dark, they lengthen the required printing exposure time.

Neither variable contrast nor graded papers are available for printing color negative or slide film. Contrast control of color images is more easily handled on the computer by scanning the film and working with the images in a software program like Adobe Photoshop.

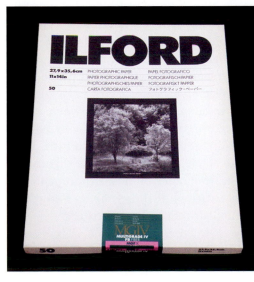

Figure 5-8 (top)

The photographer clearly selected a tight crop for this photograph. As you look at it, observe the contrast between the model's serene face and the tension created by the tight crop. Contrasts like this create visual interest.

Photo © Jeff Tse.

Figure 5-9 (bottom)

Variable contrast paper is used with a variety of filters to control contrast. This is one of many brands and styles of variable contrast papers on the market.

Photo © Roger Grant.

Differences Among Various Photographic Papers

There are several black-and-white printing papers on the market. Whether a photographic paper is variable contrast or graded is only one factor in selecting which paper to use. Other factors include paper weight, surface texture, fiber-based versus resin-coated (RC), and the color tone of the paper.

Paper is manufactured as either single-weight or double-weight. Single-weight paper is thinner and more likely to crease during print processing, whereas double-weight papers are much heavier and are typically used for fine art printing.

The surface texture of papers varies according to the manufacturer. A variety of names are given to paper textures (also called **finishes**), depending on the manufacturer, and the actual finish varies dramatically from one brand to another. There are some generalities, though. Glossy paper is always shiny, and surrounding light produces reflections on its surface. It holds a wide range of tones, contrast, and sharpness. The paper of choice for printing rich, dark blacks, glossy paper is more prone to showing fingerprints and scratches.

The least glossy and the most forgiving to fingerprints and scratches, matte paper typically prints with less contrast than glossy paper. It is difficult to print a pure black on matte paper. However, matte paper also produces less reflection, allowing for better visibility when framed and displayed on a wall.

Low-luster papers fall between glossy and matte and have a variety of names, including semimatte, pearl, and satin. Each brand of low-luster paper looks slightly different from other brands. Experimentation with a variety of these papers is the best way to learn their characteristics.

Fiber-Based and Resin-Coated Papers

Most photographers begin their darkroom careers using resin-coated, rather than fiber-based, papers. Resin-coated (RC) papers have a paper base, plus an emulsion layer containing light-sensitive silver halide crystals similar to black-and-white film. Both sides of the paper are sealed by two polyethylene layers, making it impermeable to liquids. Because the paper base cannot absorb the developing chemistry, RC papers only need a washing time of 10 minutes and a shorter drying time than do fiber-based papers. However, it is not advisable to send a final RC print through a heated print dryer, as excessive heat can damage the polyethylene layer.

Fiber-based papers also consist of a paper base coated with a light-sensitive emulsion. However, there is no protective gelatin layer over the top of the emulsion, so these papers must be carefully handled. They are preferred for high-quality fine art printing. They also require a much longer washing time of 1 hour after printing.

Because both RC and fiber-based papers have a gelatin coating that contains the silver particles, black-and-white prints are also frequently called **silver gelatin prints**. This differentiates a traditional darkroom black-and-white print from an inkjet print that might look similar to it.

Most black-and-white printing papers print color-neutral blacks and grays. However, cool tone and warm tone papers are also available. A cool tone paper prints grays with a hint of blue. A warm tone paper prints grays with a hint of brown.

Preparation for Print Processing

Before beginning to print, set up the darkroom so everything runs smoothly once you turn out the overhead lights. Begin by mixing the chemistry used for print processing. Your first step should always be to ensure your safety. Turn on the darkroom fan to ensure adequate air exchange in the darkroom. Make sure there is no food or drink in the darkroom.

Have tongs or rubber gloves available for handling your prints in the printing trays. Many people develop a sensitivity to metol (an ingredient in many print developers), resulting in an itchy, painful rash lasting days or weeks. Although some photographers prefer not to use tongs or rubber gloves, they are still recommended.

Darkroom printing uses chemistry similar to the chemistry used in negative processing. A developer changes the silver halide crystals exposed to light to metallic silver. The stop bath is an acidic solution that stops the developing process. The fixer removes the silver halide particles not converted to metallic silver.

Set up four trays in a large sink that has access to hot and cold running water and a properly functioning drain. Each tray should be used specifically for developer, stop bath, or fixer and should not be interchanged. Labeling each tray helps ensure that you don't get them mixed up.

Mix your chemicals according to the manufacturer's instructions for print processing. The ratio of chemistry to water will likely be different than that for negative processing, so read the instructions carefully.

The temperature of your developer will influence your print's exposure and should be kept at a constant level, usually 68° F. Many photographers set their trays in a water bath kept at a constant temperature. Others keep the room temperature at a constant level. In this case, the developer, stop bath, and fixer must all be allowed to reach room temperature before print processing begins.

A fourth tray should be set up as a fresh water bath. Both hot and cold water should be accessible to obtain a 68° F temperature for the running water. Excessively warm water can soften the emulsion of photographic paper, making scratches more likely.

The size of each tray should be larger than the size of paper you will print. Add enough chemistry to each tray to easily cover the paper, but not so much as to cause splashing during print processing. It is helpful to have a large tray for the water bath, regardless of the size of paper you are using.

Some photographers use a specialized timer created for darkroom use (Figure 5-10).

Figure 5-10

A darkroom timer.

© Cengage Learning 2012.

If you have access to a freestanding timer, have the timer accessible but not in a place where it will get wet.

The Contact Print

A **contact print** is a single print made of a series of negatives. The photographs are printed at the exact same size as the negatives. A contact print allows you to see all of your images without going to the effort of printing each individual negative at a time. A contact print is most easily made if you have stored your negative in a negative sleeve. It requires a **contact print frame**, a combination of glass plus a sturdy backing between which you can place your negatives and photographic paper. There must be immediate contact between negative sleeve and printing paper (hence the phrase "contact print").

Contact Print Exposure

To create a contact print, turn off the overhead light in the darkroom so that only the safelight is on. Place an empty negative carrier in its holder within the enlarger head. Take a sheet of photographic paper out of its box and place it behind your negative sleeve. The side of the paper containing the light-sensitive emulsion should face the negative sleeve.

Make sure your negatives are faced emulsion side down toward the paper (also known as *printing emulsion to emulsion*). You'll know the emulsion side is down if

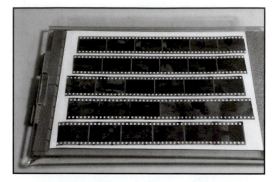

you can properly read the writing on the film edge when you look down onto the film. Be sure to close the paper box to prevent exposure of the remaining paper to light.

Place the negative sheet and paper into the contact print frame so that the negative sheet is pressing against the glass in the frame (Figure 5-11). Attach the backing of the frame, if your style of contact frame requires it.

Place the contact print frame on the base of the enlarger, glass side up. With the enlarger light turned off, remove the negative carrier from the enlarger head to increase the diameter of the coverage of light when the enlarger is turned on. Close the bracket that holds the negative carrier in place. Set the aperture between f/8 and f/16, depending on the density of your negatives. Denser negatives will require a lower aperture number.

Set the enlarger's timer for 5 seconds. Give the first exposure by pushing the timer button. When the 5-second exposure is over, the enlarger light will go out and the timer will reset itself.

Cover about one-eighth of your negatives with an opaque board to hide that portion from further exposure. Then give a second exposure. When that exposure is up, cover up another inch or so of your negatives with the opaque board and give a third exposure. Continue this process until you have created a series of 8–10 exposure times across the negatives (Figures 5-12 and 5-13).

Print Processing

After you have made 8–10 exposures across the negatives, remove the photographic paper from the contact print frame and move to the wet side of the darkroom.

Quickly immerse the paper in the paper developer (Figure 5-14) and turn on your timer (or look at your watch) for 1 minute. Try to immerse the paper as quickly as possible in the developer to ensure even development. If necessary, push all four corners down to immerse the paper in the developer solution. During this time, gently lift a corner of the tray up and down repeatedly to create a rocking motion in the liquid (Figure 5-15). This replenishes the developer that is falling on the paper and prevents exhaustion of the developer in any area of the image. There is no need to rock the tray so hard as to spill the chemistry.

It will be to your benefit to standardize your tray rocking speed. Faster rocking can increase the contrast in your print. If you get accustomed to rocking the tray at one speed, your printing will be more consistent.

Figure 5-14
(top left)

Try to immerse the paper as quickly as possible in the developer to ensure even development. If necessary, push all four corners of the paper down into the solution.

Figure 5-15
(top right)

Gently rock the tray to continually replenish the developer solution on the print.

Figure 5-16
(middle left)

Lift the print out and allow it to drip for 10 seconds.

Figure 5-17
(middle right)

Immerse the print into the stop bath and gently rock the tray for 30 seconds. During the last ten seconds, lift the paper and allow it to drip. Then immerse it in the Fixer tray for one minute.

Figure 5-18
(bottom left)

After fixing the print for at least one minute, rinse it in clean running water for at least one minute. This is enough time for a basic wash, but a permanent wash requires ten minutes for resin coated paper and one hour for fiber based paper.

Photos 5-14 through 5-18 © KS.

Ten seconds before the minute is up, curl a corner of the paper toward its center, then lift the paper. Allow the paper to drip into the developer tray for the remainder of the 10 seconds (Figure 5-16).

When the full minute is up, immerse the paper into the stop bath (Figure 5-17). Set the timer for 30 seconds and again rock the tray back and forth to prevent exhaustion of the developer. Ten seconds before the time is up, remove the paper from the tray and allow it to drip into the stop bath tray for the remainder of the 30 seconds.

Next, immerse the paper into the fixer and set the timer for 1 minute. Again, gently rock the tray during that minute. Ten seconds before the time is up, lift the paper out of the fixer and allow it to drip into the tray for those final 10 seconds.

Place the paper into a tray of clean water (Figure 5-18) and run 68° F water over it for a full minute. It is now safe for you to turn on the overhead light in the room to evaluate the test print. This period of washing time does not sufficiently wash your print, but it is enough to take a look at it and move on to more prints.

It will be important for you to return the contact print to the fixer for an additional 3 minutes to fully fix the image. After fixing the image, a print made on RC paper requires a 10-minute wash under clean running water. A print made on double-weight fiber paper requires an hour-long wash under clean running water. Any remaining fixer will yellow that portion of the print over time. This is permanent damage that can't be repaired.

Contact Print Evaluation

Remove the paper from the water and place it on a smooth surface; wipe the excess water from it. Then look at the print and determine which exposure time was best for your negatives. You will use this information as a starting point for your test print.

The Test Print

The test print is your first print of a single negative. The process will determine the best exposure for your negative and will also give you an opportunity to determine how to handle the amount of contrast within that negative.

Start by selecting one negative to print. Remove that negative strip from the negative sleeve. It is easier to handle the entire strip, rather than an individual negative, so photographers generally don't trim a negative strip into individual negatives. Instead, they cut strips of 4–6 negatives per strip.

Remove the negative carrier from the enlarger. Use the same size negative carrier as the size of your film (35 mm, medium-format, or 4 × 5). Place your negative in the negative carrier, emulsion side down. You'll know the emulsion side is down if you can properly read the writing along the film edge when you look down onto the film. Make sure the negative is properly positioned so that the edges of the frame match the edges of the opening in the negative carrier. You shouldn't be able to see any light along the edges of the frame. Then place the negative carrier back into its position in the enlarger (Figure 5-19) and turn off all room lights except the safelight.

Set your easel under the lens on the table. If your easel doesn't have a single set size, move the blades until the proper paper size is achieved. Then move the blades $1/8$–$1/4$-inch closer to each other to cover the edges of the paper. This will help to hold the paper flat and in position when you load paper into the easel. It will also give you a white border on the edges of your print.

Start by placing an old photograph, print side down, in the easel. The purpose of this is to make sure the image will focus correctly when you put new photographic paper into the easel. If you don't do this step, your focus could be slightly off.

Turn on the light source in the enlarger head by setting the enlarger's timer to the preview setting. Use the enlarger's focusing adjustment to focus the image falling onto the paper (Figure 5-20). It's sometimes easier to use a wide-open aperture when focusing your image, as the details

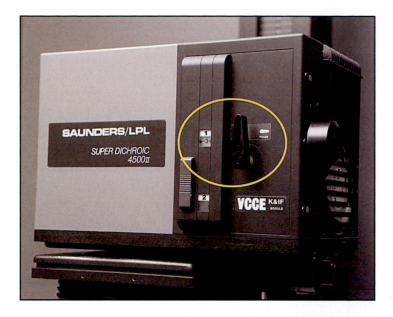

Figure 5-21

This enlarger's filters are dialed in (left side of circled area). The built-in timer's toggle switch is on the right. Other standalone timers plug into the enlarger via a wire.

Photo © Roger Grant.

of the image are easier to see. Move the enlarger up and down until the photograph is cropped the way you want it. This is also a good time to rotate the easel, if necessary, to straighten the horizon line in the image.

Step-by-Step Printing

Once the image is in focus and your enlarger head is set to the desired height, turn the lens aperture to the same setting you used for the contact print.

Place a contrast filter into position directly under the enlarger lens, or dial the desired contrast filter into the enlarger head (Figure 5-21). A grade 2 filter (if you're using Kodak contrast filters) will render good contrast for a negative with normal contrast. Filter numbers less than 2 will progressively decrease the amount of contrast in your print, and filter numbers greater than 2 will progressively increase the amount of contrast.

When you have finished focusing the image, remove the old print from the easel. Move the toggle switch on the enlarger timer until the enlarger's preview light goes off and the timer is activated.

Now, you are ready to open the box of printing paper and its inner plastic bag and remove one sheet of paper. Close the plastic bag and return it to the box. Then close the box. Developing this habit will prevent

Figure 5-22

Set the enlarger timer to five seconds.

Photo © KS.

you from accidentally turning on a light and ruining a box of paper.

Place the paper in the easel, shiny (emulsion) side up, being careful not to move the easel from its position. If you do move the easel by accident, return the paper to the box and turn on the enlarger's preview light again. Readjust the easel's positioning and then reset the enlarger light. Then you can take the paper from the box and position it within the easel.

Set the enlarger timer to 5 seconds (Figure 5-22) or for the same duration you used for the contact print. Maintain this time on the enlarger and continue pushing the timer button to make additional exposures, just as you did for the contact print.

The rest of the process is very similar to that of the contact printing process. The only difference is that you will take into consideration the exposure level of your contact print. Start by pushing the timer button the number of times *minus 3* of your contact

Figure 5-23

Test print showing exposure steps.

Photo © KS.

Figure 5-24

These filters can be used in enlarger heads that don't have built-in filters. Kodak filters are on the left and bottom, and a package containing an Ilford filter on the upper right.

Photo © KS.

Each time you move the dark paper, make another exposure. Your goal is to have 6–8 consecutive exposures of your image on that single sheet of paper (Figure 5-23).

Process the exposed paper in the same manner as for the contact print. When the print has been briefly washed and the excess water removed, determine the best exposure for the print. Look for an area that properly exposed your highlights. They should be the exact value you want them to be. Make note of how many times the enlarger timer was pushed to obtain that exposure.

At this time, you can also determine if the contrast of the image was correct. Your exposure time is determined by the appearance of your highlights. Selection of a contrast filter is determined by the shadow values you see in that same exposure strip on the test print. Do not look at different areas of exposure when evaluating the shadow values.

If the shadows in that exposure strip are too light in value, the contrast is too low—this is called a *flat image*—and you will benefit from using a higher-contrast filter (Figure 5-24). If the shadows in that exposure strip are too dark in value, the

print's best exposure time. If your contact print's best exposure time was 5 pushes of the timer button, begin your test print with 2 pushes of the timer button before covering any portion of the print. Then cover a small portion (perhaps an inch or so) of the image with an opaque board to shield the enlarger light from falling on that portion of the image. Push the timer button again for an additional 5-second exposure.

When that exposure is over, move the opaque board to cover up more of the image.

142 CHAPTER 5

contrast is too high and you need a lower-contrast filter. Note that the filter you use affects the exposure time for your print. If you make a filter adjustment at this stage, it is best to go back and create another test print with the new filter.

If you are satisfied with the contrast in your image, make note of the exposure time that works best for the highlights in your image. It's important to know that prints tend to darken slightly as they dry. Different brands of paper darken to varying degrees. This phenomenon is called **dry down**, and it needs to be taken into consideration when you evaluate your print. Once you have chosen an exposure time, return your test print to the fixer to become fully fixed (this generally takes 4 minutes). Do not discard the test print, as you will find it useful again when it comes time to work on your final print.

The Straight Print

The **straight print** is a print made of an entire negative at a single exposure. All of the printing you have done thus far is in preparation for your straight print.

Rinse any fixer from your hands and thoroughly dry them. Then turn off the overhead light and place a new sheet of paper in the easel. This time, push the enlarger timer button for the number of times that produced a good highlight exposure on your test print. Although you can change the enlarger timer to the full number of seconds needed for an exposure, it's more accurate to push the timer button for the same number of times you did during the test print, allowing the timer to reset between each exposure.

When you have completed the exposures, take the paper out of the tray and develop it as before. This is your straight print. Your next step will be to decide which areas of your image are too light and which are too dark for your intentions.

Printing and the Zone System

It is helpful to return to your contact print and the Zone System when evaluating your straight print. When looking at prints, Zone X is an area that has absolutely no density. It is as white as the paper's border that was covered by the easel's frame or blades. Zone 0 is pure black, or as dark as the paper can be physically printed (RC papers can generally produce a deeper black than matte papers). All of the other zones still match the descriptions given in Chapter 3.

As you look at your straight print, evaluate the image according to the zones of different areas within it. Look at Figure 5-25 as an example. This image of Lake Superior's rocky, ice- and snow-covered shoreline was made with a 4 × 5 field camera on a very cloudy, foggy day in mid-April. The photographer was concerned that the white snow and ice might be too bright when printing the light snow, so she erred on the side of caution and selected an exposure that would render the snow at Zone VII. This is how the negative would have looked when straight printed onto variable contrast paper with a grade 2 filter.

The tops of the snow/ice caps are at Zone VII, and the icicles are at approximately Zone VI. The snow and ice have the expected amount of detail and value, so the print's exposure is adequate. However, the image now looks flat. The darkest shadow areas between and underneath the rocks are no darker than Zone IV, which is too light a value for the photographer's intention. The next step would be to print the image with a different filter, still maintaining the highlight value where it is. Another test print is required because the change to a denser filter results in a change of the exposure time.

A straight print made with a grade 3 filter and revised exposure time would look much better (Figure 5-26). The highlights are still at approximately Zone VII, but the shadows have darkened to Zone II or III. Now there is considerably more contrast within the print.

The photographer still isn't satisfied with the print. She would like some areas to be darker and some areas to be lighter than those in the straight print. The next step will be to selectively darken (burn) or lighten (dodge) specific areas within the print.

Figure 5-25 (left)

A straight print made of a 4 × 5 black-and-white negative made with a grade 2 filter.

Figure 5-26 (right)

Note the deeper shadows on this image when printed with a grade 3 filter.

Photos 5-25 and 5-26 © KS.

Artist Statement

Emphasizing the Elements

The weather along the shores of Lake Superior is relentless and harsh much of the year. With this photograph, I wanted to emphasize the destructive nature of the ice, snow, and water as these elements eternally erode the ancient faces of rock (Figures 5-25 through 5-28).

Burning and Dodging

This is where your artistic vision is of foremost importance. What mood are you trying to convey? What do you want the viewers to pay attention to within the photograph? How do you want the viewers' eyes to travel through the photograph? Which elements of the photograph are most important and which are less important for conveying the intended message? The answers to these questions will help you make burning and dodging decisions.

It is ultimately your task to decide how you want your photograph to look, regardless of how the photo first looked without burning or dodging. The systematic, artistic processes of burning and dodging will turn the final print into a visual testament to your artistic intention for the photograph.

The photographer wanted more contrast between the rocks and the ice, without sacrificing a significant amount of detail within the shadow areas. The solution was to make a straight print with slightly less exposure given to the top surfaces of rocks and slightly more exposure given to the sides of rocks. Giving slightly less exposure than for a straight print is **dodging**, whereas giving slightly more exposure than for a straight print is **burning**.

How much more or less exposure? Go back to your test print and observe the exposure that gave you the amount of brightness you want in specific areas. Note the exposure time for those areas. This will be the exposure you will use as you dodge or burn specific areas.

Figure 5-27 is a simulated test strip of the image, simplified for illustration purposes. The center strip is the exposure chosen, as it holds a significant amount of detail in the highlights (Zone VII). The photographer can look at various areas in the separate exposure strips, deciding which exposure will be correct for the ice and rocks.

The photographer varied the different exposures by 5 seconds when making this test print. Making a personal artistic decision, the photographer chooses to subtract 1 exposure time (−5 seconds) from the straight print time for the rock tops (dodge) and add 1 straight print exposure time (+5 seconds) for the areas of rock, icicles, and water she wants to have darker (burn). Wherever necessary, she could do a little more or a little less dodging and burning according to her personal tastes. After making these decisions, the photographer went back into the darkroom for another printing session. The results of the burning and dodging are shown in Figure 5-28. You may or may not agree with her decisions.

Now, go back to your own print to learn how to burn and dodge (Figure 5-29). Look at your straight print and determine which areas need to be burned or dodged (Figure 5-30). Turn off the room light, dry your hands, place another piece of photographic paper under the enlarger, and focus it. Make sure the enlarger timer is still set for 5 seconds.

During some of that exposure time, create shadows with your fingers, hands, or other instruments (such as paper cut-outs) to block the light from hitting the paper (Figure 5-31). As a result, those areas become lighter than they were in the original print. This is the act of dodging. Dodging results in areas printing lighter because they have not received the full straight exposure.

For areas that need to be darkened more, complete the straight exposure.

Larger Negative—Better Crop

For these examples, the photographer used a 4 × 5 negative that he wanted to enlarge. The enlarger head was raised high enough to allow much of the image to be projected beyond the easel. In this way, the photographer was able to crop his image. His resulting photograph was still of good quality because of the large size of the original negative. A 35 mm negative would not have fared so well.

Figure 5-29

This is the straight print being used to demonstrate burning and dodging techniques.

Photo © KS.

Figure 5-30

The red areas shown here will be burned by the percentage of straight exposure time listed. The yellow areas will be dodged by the percentage of straight exposure time listed.

Photo © KS.

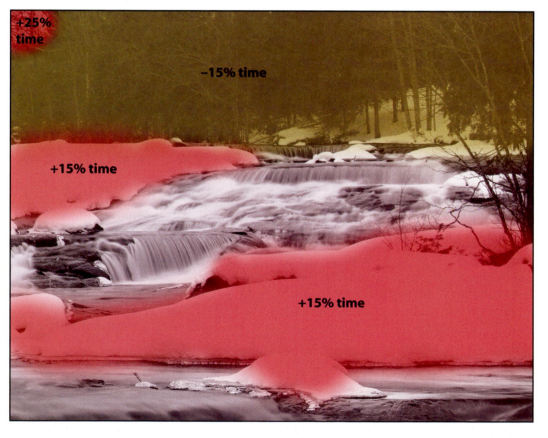

+25% time

−15% time

+15% time

+15% time

Figure 5-31 (left)

Dodging an area during the straight exposure time. You can select any five-second interval during which to dodge various areas.

Figure 5-32 (right)

Burning in an area after the straight exposure is complete.

Photos 5-31 and 5-32 © KS.

Then push the enlarger timer and give the print additional time. During this additional time, block the light from the majority of the print to prevent the properly exposed areas from going too dark. This additional exposure to chosen parts of the paper is the technique of burning (Figure 5-32).

After the straight exposures, burning, and dodging are completed, develop the paper as usual. Figure 5-33 shows the results of this demonstration's burning and dodging.

Although you might hope to perfectly burn and dodge all areas and end up with a great print the first time, it usually

Figure 5-33

The resulting print, burned and dodged.

Photo © KS.

Figure 5-34

There is a limit to how much change dodging or burning can make. In this example, dodging an area without any detail on the negative just gives a lighter shade of gray. It doesn't introduce any detail.

Photo © KS.

takes several attempts and much testing. Then, if more prints are desired, you must repeat all of the burning and dodging procedures on future prints. If you don't exactly repeat the position of the shadows created for burning and dodging, each print will look slightly different.

Documenting Your Burning and Dodging

The goal of burning and dodging is to make the photograph look the way you want it to without being obvious about your changes. It's important to carefully adhere to the shapes of areas of your photograph. In other words, be sure to dodge or burn exactly the areas you wish to change without allowing the extra light or shadow to fall onto surrounding areas. This is one of the most difficult aspects of burning and dodging.

As you become comfortable with printing, use a pencil on the back of your prints to write down information about the printing and development process before placing the paper in the easel. Document information such as the aperture and contrast filter to be used, the straight exposure time, and the amount and position of any burning or dodging you will do. That way it will be far easier to repeat the printing process in the future.

Note that burning and dodging can't fix all problems. If there was no visual detail in the light or dark areas of the negative, burning or dodging will not bring detail into the print. The initial negative must have some visual information in the highlights and shadows in order for burning and dodging to benefit your final print. Otherwise, you will be left with a light (if burning was attempted) or dark (if dodging was attempted) blob on your print (Figures 5-34 and 5-35).

The final steps are washing and drying your prints (Figure 5-36). It is critical that prints be thoroughly washed in clean water before being hung to dry—any fixer left on the prints can bleach them or cause them to discolor. RC papers must be thoroughly washed for 10 minutes; fiber-based paper must be thoroughly washed for a full hour.

It is not sufficient to set a group of prints in a tray and run water over them for the specified time. Prints must be rotated from the top to the bottom of the stack or placed in a specialized print washer that will ensure that every print will be cleaned.

After the prints have been washed for a specified period of time, squeegee off the prints and place them in a dust-free environment to dry. RC prints can be carefully hung from hangers to dry or placed face up on print drying screens such as those in Figure 5-37. Fiber-based prints should be laid face down and flat to dry on print drying screens. Place a second screen on top of the first one to prevent curling of the print.

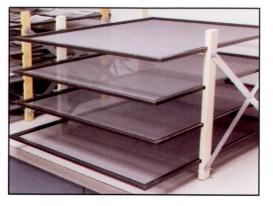

Figure 5-37

Print drying screens.

Photo © KS.

NOTE

Keep a List of Your Burn/Dodge Requirements

It's not unusual to compile a list of areas that need various amounts of burning and dodging. Keep a list of your burn/dodge requirements stored with each negative for future printing needs.

Archival Processing

It takes a little more time and effort to process a black-and-white print so it will truly last for decades. The silver in your prints can tarnish over time. Any residual fixer on the print can cause damage. The procedures described in this chapter will preserve your prints for several years, but fine artists need to go beyond these steps to ensure greater print life. The additional care taken by these photographers is called **archival processing.**

Archival processing applies only to fiber-based prints. RC prints have not historically been as long-lasting as fiber-based prints, even if photographers go through the added steps of archival print processing. Archival printing starts with the choice of paper and works its way throughout the printing process. In many ways, it is simply a stepped-up version of what you have already learned.

Steps to Archival Print Processing

Always use a fiber-based paper, preferably double-weight, for your fine art printing.

There are several brands on the market. You will print your negative as usual, but give your printing paper at least a 1-inch border around the entire print. The larger border will act as a shield from any contaminants penetrating the print over time.

Develop the print as has been described earlier, making sure that you keep the print in the developer for the full prescribed time. Give the print a full 30 seconds in the stop bath.

You will use two different fixer baths to fix the print. Always use fresh fixer, not fixer that has already processed many prints. Keep the print in the first fixer bath and constantly rock the tray for 3–5 minutes. Then place the print in the second bath and rock the tray for an additional 4 minutes.

Wash the print in fresh 75°–80° F water for a full 5 minutes. Allow the excess water to spill out of the tray. You can also use an archival print washer that exchanges the water at frequent intervals for you. Ideally, you should have a complete water exchange within the tray or print washer at least once every 5 minutes.

The next step is to tone your print to convert the silver in your print to a more stable compound. A common toning agent is selenium. Another is gold, but the cost of gold prevents many photographers from using it. Follow the toner manufacturer's instructions for diluting the toner.

Set up three trays. Fill the first with water and place the print in it. Fill the second tray with the properly diluted toner. Fill the third tray with clean, gently running water. Allow the water to continue running during the toning process.

Lift the print out of the first tray and allow it to drip for about 10 seconds. Place it in the tray containing the toner and immediately begin to rock the tray. Watch for a very slight shift in color balance. If you are using Kodak's Rapid Selenium Toner, you will see a shift toward brown if you're using a warm-tone paper, a shift toward purple if you're using neutral-tone papers, and little or no color shift if you are using cold-tone papers. It is helpful to keep a second print of the same negative in the first tray so your eyes will more quickly notice a shift in color balance.

Just before the print shifts to the color you want, remove it from the toning tray and place it in the third tray with its clean running water. Then give it an hour-long wash. You may notice a continuation of the color shift from the toner. Experience will teach you how early to remove a print before it achieves the color shift you desire.

Some photographers use a hypo test kit available through photographic supply stores to test for residual fixer. Any fixer remaining on your print can permanently stain it over time, so this is a worthwhile practice. It requires you to obtain Kodak's Black-and-White Darkroom Dataguide, Publication R-20. Trim a small amount of your print's margin and blot it dry. Place one drop of the test solution on the strip and allow it to sit for 2 minutes. Blot off any excess and compare the residual stain with the comparison chart in the R-20 publication. The stain on your test area should be no darker than that recommended in the Dataguide.

Archival print drying should be done on clean fiberglass drying screens. Always use acid-free, archival quality supplies to mount and mat your prints.

Retouching the Print

Once a print is dry, it may need some touch-up work. Despite your best efforts, dust or lint may have settled on your negative. The result will be a small white mark on your print. You may also see a fine white line somewhere in your print. This could be a result of a scratch on your negative. The cure for either situation is spotting (Figure 5-38).

Retouching involves using a permanent ink specifically made for retouching, and applying that ink to your print with a very fine brush. Marshall's and Peerless are two common brands of inks for photo retouching. You can purchase them in a variety of hues from cool black to warm black. You need to be careful to choose a hue that matches your print.

Figure 5-38

Spotting a print requires a fine haired brush and a lot of patience.

Photo © KS.

Apply the retouching ink very carefully, using a size 000 camel hair brush. Some photographers use magnifying glasses to better view the area needing spotting. Consider wearing white gloves to protect your print. Place a drop of ink on a nonporous surface such as Styrofoam or Plexiglas and mix in a few drops of water. Once your brush is filled with this mixture, wipe the brush on a clean, dry paper towel to absorb most of the mixture. When the brush is relatively dry, dab the tip of the brush onto the white spot of your print. It is far better to go slowly and build up the density of ink rather than try to apply a lot of ink at once.

Repair a scratch mark in the same manner. Slowly dab individual dots of ink along the white mark, never dragging a line of ink. Slowly connecting the dots and increasing the density by adding layers of ink will make a better repair.

Be very careful not to overpaint the boundary of a dust mark or scratch. It's very easy to overdo spotting on a print, and the result can be equally as destructive as the original mark.

This spotting process can also create a purposeful accent for very small areas that you wish to darken on your print. As always, this is a judgment call, depending on your intention for the photograph. If a small area was too tiny to burn during the printing process, consider using a little ink to darken that area of the print.

The goal when spotting a print is to have your work invisible to the viewer's eye. You will probably always notice where you retouched your prints, but other viewers won't be aware of your handiwork if you do a careful job.

Traditional Darkroom Color Printing

Color enlargers are very similar to black-and-white enlargers, with one important difference: The head of the color enlarger contains a filtration system that allows you to alter the color balance of the light projected onto the color photographic paper (Figure 5-39).

This color filtration system includes separate controls for the cyan, magenta, and yellow filters. Color control uses the same complementary color system used on computers. If the initial print appears too red, increase the cyan filter value. If it's too green, increase the magenta filter value. If it's too blue, increase the yellow filter value.

Paper used for color printing is sensitive to all light, regardless of color temperature. Loading the paper from its box into the easel must be done in total darkness. Only the enlarger light can be used during the exposure period.

Color print processing must also be completed in total darkness. There are several processors available for color printing. Most are covered containers that have separate internal trays for the different required chemicals, allowing you to keep a room light on after the print has completely entered the light-tight processor.

Another alternative is to use a tube processor such as the JOBO processor (Figure 5-40). After exposing the color print paper to light under the color enlarger, the print is loaded into a print drum and attached to a rotation mechanism on the processor. Chemistry can be poured in and out of the drum without casting light onto the paper.

The processing of both color film and color paper must be completed at specific temperatures for all of the involved chemicals. If the temperature is off by as little as 0.3° C, the color balance of the resulting film will be off. Color processors frequently employ a highly temperature-controlled water bath that circulates around the chemical trays (as with the JOBO processor).

Color chemicals, especially the fixer, are very caustic to the touch. They are also potentially harmful to the environment and must be discarded according to manufacturer's instructions. Just as with black-and-white fixer, the color fixer contains unused silver and should not be allowed to enter a septic tank.

Color Print Processing

Color printing almost always involves the RA-4 chemical process. Kodak Ektacolor RA processing has a total of six steps. All printing of color papers must be completed in total darkness. Safelights of any color or strength are strongly discouraged. Be cautious about any glow-in-the-dark materials present in the darkroom, as the glow can cause damage to unprocessed film and paper.

The processing of color prints requires information from two sources. Your processor's manufacturer will give instructions on the volume of liquid to use in your processor. When you purchase RA-4 chemicals,

Figure 5-39

Color enlargers have three sets of filters, each capable of being changed to achieve proper color balance for the print.

Photo © Roger Grant.

Figure 5-40

The JOBO CPP-2 processor rotates the film inside a drum. The drum rests in a warmed-water bath to carefully maintain the temperature of the chemistry.

Photo © Gregory W. Blank Photography.

the accompanying instructions will tell you how to mix the chemicals to obtain a working solution and for what time and at what temperature the chemicals should be used. The temperature of the developer is most critical.

After you have printed the paper under the enlarger, place the print into a light-tight processing drum. The steps to follow will depend on the type of processor you are using. The following instructions apply to processing color papers in small tube processors.

- Prewet the paper by adding water and manually rolling the tube on its side to coat the entire sheet(s) of paper for 30 seconds.
- Pour out the water and add the developer. Again, roll the tube on its side— this time for 55 seconds. Pour out the developer (the assumption is that this will take 5 seconds, giving the paper 1 full minute of development time).
- You have the option of using a stop bath for 30 seconds, followed by an optional wash for 30 seconds. Roll the tube as before during these times.

- Pour in the bleach-fix and roll the tube for 1 minute. During the final 5 seconds, drain the tube.
- Wash the paper for 1 minute and 30 seconds. When the wash time is over, you may remove the lid of the tube and remove the print. Dry the print by placing it on a print drying screen.
- Once the print is dry (and not before), evaluate it for density and color balance. If a color cast exists, adjust the color filtration on the enlarger head and print again.

Summary

It takes a relatively short amount of training to print your first black-and-white print; it can take years of experimentation and practice to perfect the process. We have barely scratched the surface of possibilities in this chapter. Different paper and chemical combinations will yield different results. Burning and dodging take practice. Be sure to read the books listed at the end of this chapter to continue your education in this field.

NOTES

1. Read the entire chapter before starting your first print. Then follow all of the steps to print a negative of your choice. Start with a test print, then create a straight print, using the best exposure.

2. Examine your straight print for areas you would like to lighten or darken. Then make another print using burning and dodging to produce a print that reflects your intentions.

3. Create a contact print of your negatives. Again, start with a test print, then make a straight print of the entire set of negatives.

FURTHER READING

- ADAMS, Ansel. *The Print.* Boston: Little, Brown, and Co., 1995. This is an extensive resource for the traditional black-and-white darkroom printer. Ansel Adams was a very important photographer in the early- to mid-1900s. His photographs were instrumental in defining the potential of black-and-white photography. His technical advisor, John Sexton, has continued practicing the techniques Adams used in his photography.

- MORA, Gilles. *Edward Weston: Forms of Passion.* New York: Harry N. Abrams, Inc., 1995. Weston was a pioneer of photography in the early 1900s. His darkroom control of contrast and exposure produced magnificent images.

- SEXTON, John. *Listen to the Trees.* Boston: Little, Brown & Co., 1994. This beautiful book showcases Sexton's insightful and sensitive use of darkroom skills to create black-and-white images.

- UELSMANN, Jerry N., and John Ames. *Uelsmann: Process and Perception.* Gainesville, FL: University of Florida Press, 1986. In this book, Uelsmann shares his thoughts on the photographic collages he creates in the traditional black-and-white darkroom.

FURTHER READING (CONTINUED)

- USING THE BY THE DECADE SECTION (Appendix A), research the 1920s, 1930s, and 1940s. Go on the Internet and learn about the Group F/64, of which Adams was a member. Look also at the photography of Alfred Stieglitz, Paul Strand, and Edward Weston. All three were active in photography during these times.

Michael Kamber
Photojournalist

ADVICE FOR YOUNG PHOTOGRAPHERS

by Michael Kamber

10 June, 07

I am writing this from the Baghdad bureau of the *New York Times* where I am on assignment.

I have received dozens of queries from photojournalists starting out in the business. I am writing this in response, partly so I can refer others to it in the future and not spend time on lengthy replies.

Some beginners ask for advice on gear; others, on how to get started finding assignments and selling their work. I will describe my own path into photojournalism here and give some general advice that may be useful.

This is not definitive in any way. It is simply my experience and opinion formulated from 20 years' experience as a photojournalist. No doubt others can weigh in and improve this with their comments and ideas.

I started as a photojournalist by going to art school. I thought I would be a fine art or landscape photographer, but I took a photojournalism course and was quickly hooked. When my money ran out after a year, I dropped out of school, but continued to work as a teaching assistant for photojournalism classes. I may have learned more in this way than I did as a student. I received no credit, but photography is a meritocracy. In over 20 years, I have never been asked for my degree; in the world of photojournalism, your portfolio is your degree.

I also learned a great deal from spending days in the library, reading about photojournalism and looking up, and discovering, each new name that I chanced upon. In this way, I found Robert Capa, Robert Frank, Larry Clark, Alex Webb and dozens of others.

If you are going to be a photojournalist, you should have a good working knowledge of the history of photojournalism, and of the medium's iconic images. You can show me nearly any often published photograph from the twentieth century, and I can tell you who took it and where. I've studied the pictures carefully and memorized details about them. This is extremely useful and will help you later as you shoot.

As you study images, you should think about where the photographer is in relation to the subjects, study how he or she has managed the light and the angle of the camera. Is the photo effective because it is compressed with a telephoto, or opened up with a wide-angle lens? And how did they get access? How will you gain access to a similar situation?

I believe that the written word, still photos, and film are connected. Artists in the above disciplines are telling stories, whatever the medium. It is important for those in one area to study the work of documentarians and artists in the others. At the bottom of this page is a list of recommended writers, photographers and filmmakers, all personal favorites.

To be a photojournalist, you should be informed. I'm was appalled at a group of photographers who showed up in Haiti a few years ago, but did not know who the Duvalier's were, or know even the most rudimentary history of the country. These countries are not there for you to practice photo-tourism and have an extended holiday. These are people's lives you are documenting. Be knowledgeable and show respect.

At the very least, you should read the front page or lead Web stories each day from either *The Washington Post*, *LA Times*, or *NY Times*. *The New Yorker* has the best long-form journalism in the English language. I read it every week.

A second language is probably the most important skill you can acquire, far more important than the latest camera gear or a diploma from a photo school. It takes time,

Iraq.
Photo © Michael Kamber/
New York Times.

but you should speak at least basic French or Spanish, in addition to English. Arabic, or a language spoken in China, would be an excellent choice also, especially as I write this in 2007.

I began my "career" by photographing street demonstrations in New York and taking the pictures around to newspapers and wire services. There was easy access to what was happening, which is important when you're starting out. And even the pictures I was not able to sell helped me to build a portfolio. I also began, almost immediately, to work on long-term projects.

I cannot overstate the importance of long-term projects. Rather than run around taking hundreds of pictures of dozens of subjects, it is much better to spend a few weeks or a month with a family, or a group of people, and get to know them. Your pictures will reveal your commitment as subjects become comfortable with you. Choose your projects carefully. There are hundreds of important projects out there waiting to be discovered and photographed. Photo editors know the commitment behind this kind of in-depth work, and they respect it. A good photo-essay on one project will be remembered and will help to get you assignments.

You are going to have to promote yourself and your work. If you're afraid of rejection, find another line of work. You have to take your work around, or send it out to editors constantly. Most will turn you away. That's the nature of the business. Get used to it and don't take it personally. I was crushed in 1985 when Fred McDarrah, an editor at *The Village Voice*, spent 30 seconds flipping through a portfolio I had spent months creating, then dismissed me with a flip of his hand. It took me a long time to get my courage up again, but I eventually did "break in" to *The Village Voice*, then a major photo publication.

So you must be persistent. And remember that editors are extremely busy. Expect them to take a few minutes to see your work, not more. They don't need to see hundreds of photos on many subjects. Show them 20 or 25 photos they will remember and you'll be much better off.

Notes on Technique

When I am photographing, I often approach my subjects and explain what I am doing, then ask permission to take their picture. In the ideal situation, I will spend hours or days with a subject; they become comfortable with my presence and I can capture what I want. Sometimes I will carry a small album with my pictures, which I will show to people. This helps them to understand who I am and what I'm working on—there is some give and take. People always want to feel that you are not there to exploit them. Be sensitive to this.

In a news situation, I never ask permission, nor do I do anything to alter the situation as it is happening. Likewise, if I am on the street and see a moment in time that would be destroyed by my asking permission, I shoot without asking. I feel that this is my art and I have the right to practice it. I do not pay my subjects—it is unethical and makes it impossible for those who come after you to work without paying also.

Notes on Equipment

There is no magic camera that will make you take great pictures. Use what works for you. Develop a system that is reliable and that you are comfortable with. Never, under any circumstances, go on a major assignment with brand new equipment that you have not used. I don't care if it is the latest and greatest. Often there will be glitches and growing pains; you don't want these when you're under the gun.

For two decades I used primarily Leica rangefinders. I'm now doing a lot of work with Canon digital EOS models, mostly a 5D and a 24-70 zoom lens. In Africa, where I'm based, I always have a Hasselblad for portraits and usually a Leica as well. I still believe in film but have to acknowledge that for a newspaper photographer, it is impractical at best.

I'm a bit of a "techie"; I carry a lot of gear when doing long assignments and am always experimenting with some new piece that will give me an edge. I know photographers far better than me that walk around with one battered body and a single lens and do great work. I hate flash and avoid it at all cost. Other photographers who I admire shoot with flash all the time. There is no right way to do it. I would say that a low light lens, preferably a wide-angle f/1.4, or at least an f/2, is a good investment.

I shoot at night frequently, and here in Baghdad I am out with soldiers on night raids inside homes; flash is out of the question.

There are exceptions to what I wrote above: in a combat situation, I do not carry a lot of gear. Usually one camera and one lens. Under fire is not a time to be fumbling with gear. Shoot what you can with what you have.

I will update this as I get new ideas and suggestions and post it on my website: Kamberphoto.com.

Some of My recommended Materials

Photo Books

- Eugene Richards, *Cocaine True*
- Luc Delahaye, *WinterRiesse*
- Robert Frank, *The Americans*
- Gilles Peress, *Telex Iran*
- Mary Ellen Mark—anything by her
- William Klein—anything you can find

Movies

- *Harlan County, USA*, a documentary movie by Barbara Koppel
- *My American Girls*, a documentary video about a Dominican family
- Anything by the Maysle brothers
- Anything by D.A. Pennebaker

Journalism

- Joseph Mitchell, *Up in the Old Hotel*
- Joan Didion—anything she's ever done
- Michael Herr, *Dispatches*
- Guy Trebay, *In The Place To Be*
- William Finnegan, *Cold New World*
- Anything by Charlie Leduff or Barry Bearak in the *New York Times*
- George Orwell—anything he's ever written; *Down and Out in Paris and London* and *Homage to Catalonia* are particularly good.

Muhammad Ali, boxing world heavy weight champion. Ali, suffering from Parkinson's disease, is being driven to his home in Berrien Springs, Mich. He holds photo by Thomas Hoepker, taken in 1966. Imagine the personal value to Ali of these photographs made earlier in his career.

Photo © Thomas Koepker/Magnum Photos.

CHAPTER

6

Finishing, Mounting, and Storing of Prints

Chapter Learning Objectives

- List both the physical and chemical needs for print protection.

- Describe the difference in processes for traditional darkroom print mounting versus digital print mounting.

- Define *pH* and describe how it relates to archival print mounting and matting materials.

- Describe the difference between various types of mount boards.

- Define *glazing* and describe the difference between common glazing materials.

- Mount a print using the dry mount technique.

- Mount a print using a cold mount technique.

- Mount a print using a spray mount technique.

The process of mounting and matting your prints is an extension of everything you have done so far. It should be approached from both the practical and the aesthetic viewpoints, with an added creative dimension to further your intention for your photograph.

In this chapter, you will learn how to mount and mat your prints. The aesthetic and practical decisions you make will enhance your images and protect them from environmental dangers. First, you will learn about why print mounting is important. Later, you will be introduced to step-by-step instructions for mounting and matting your photographs.

The techniques taught in this chapter are excellent for all photographers. However, they are only the beginning of what is actually possible. Frames are being made of all kinds of materials; including glass, plastic, fiberglass, polymer clay, wood, metal, stone, and porcelain.

Print Mounting Considerations

Prints need two types of stability: physical and chemical. Prints that are mounted, matted, and framed remain in better condition. They are protected from dust, fingerprints, and light; and they tend not to bend or crease from accidental bumps. They are also protected from chemical contaminants such as acid, air pollution, and humidity. You've worked hard for your images, so why not protect and display them?

Consider several factors before choosing the best mounting technique for your prints. Are they traditional darkroom prints, either black-and-white or color? If so, you can use either museum mounting or dry mount techniques. But if your prints come from an inkjet printer, they are more safely mounted with spray mount or cold mount techniques. Here are some terms to know.

pH

pH is a measurement of the acidity or alkalinity of a substance. A neutral pH has a value of 7.0.

A substance with a pH less than 7.0 is considered acidic; with a pH greater than 7.0, alkaline. pH is an important aspect of archival materials because photographic prints are subject to damage if mounted with acidic or alkaline materials. Look for materials listed as archival with neutral pH.

Archival Materials

Archival materials withstand the test of time without discoloring, turning brown, or damaging a print. They are used for limited-edition prints and prints that shouldn't be glued to a board or subjected to high heat. Use archival materials when matting and mounting your prints.

The concept of what defines archival changes as technology changes. Any products advertised as archival should follow the Photographic Activity Test (PAT). The PAT is a worldwide standard for archival quality of materials used in photographic printing, mounting, and matting. The test predicts possible interactions between photographic prints and their storage devices.

The Image Permanence Institute, or IPI, is a nonprofit, university-based laboratory devoted to preservation research. The Institute developed ISO 18916 and ISO 18902, two tests for enclosure (matting, mounting, and framing) materials. Industry manufacturers use these simple tests to determine if their products will cause yellowing or fading of photographs.

Although products that pass both tests are considered acceptable, those that pass ISO 18902 have been tested more stringently and are more archival than the others. ISO 18902 requires that all paper and paperboard materials have a pH between 7.0 and 9.5, be buffered with at least 2% calcium carbonate, and be lignin-free. **Lignin** is a naturally occurring substance in wood that can damage prints. The lignin is removed from wooden frames that pass the ISO 18902 standards.

In this chapter, you will learn some of the most common manufacturing terms used in matting products. It's important to note that although these terms imply archival quality, they are not standardized or legal terms. Check with the manufacturer to make sure you understand the terms used for its products. The ultimate test of any product is whether or not it passes the ISO tests listed above.

Conservation Mount Board

A **conservation mount board** is made of chemically treated wood pulp and comes in buffered and unbuffered versions. *Buffering* is the process of making the board alkaline. This is important to photographers because alkaline materials can affect some types of photographs. Do not use buffered conservation mount board with photographs. Unbuffered conservation mount board is fine.

Cotton Museum Mount Board

A **cotton museum mount board** is made of 100% cotton fiber, a material known to be stable over decades of use. If you want to use cotton museum mount board, make sure it is unbuffered (neutral pH). The product comes in both buffered (alkaline) and unbuffered varieties.

Standard mount board is made of unpurified wood pulp. This product slowly breaks down over time, subjecting a print to acidity and potential damage. Many standard mount boards are now treated with an alkaline substance to decrease the chance of acid damage and are marketed as acid-free. They are still not the first choice for a print you want to preserve for decades. Standard mount board comes in a wide variety of colors. Whatever mount board you select should pass either the ISO 18916 or the ISO 18902 test.

Mat Board

A **mat board** is a mount board with a colored and/or textured surface on one side. Mat boards are typically smooth, white, and acid-free on one side, with colored and/or textured paper on the other side. The colored/textured paper is not acid-free and should not be used for mounting prints. Mat board is best used for overmats.

Overmat

An **overmat** (Figure 6-1) covers the borders of the photograph and ensures that the print lies flat. The overmat can be made of any of the types of board listed above and is simply another mat with a window cut in it. One major benefit of using an overmat is that the added height protects the print from touching the glass or acrylic sheet. The overmat can also be easily replaced if it becomes soiled or damaged.

Figure 6-1

This overmat will protect the print from damage.

Photo © KS.

Glazing

Glazing is the covering of the mat board and typically consists of glass or acrylic sheets. Both glass and acrylic can be purchased with an added ultraviolet (UV) filtering component to protect your prints from ultraviolet light. This is a significant improvement, as UV radiation causes fading and discoloration in color prints. Glazing with the added UV filtering component is also considerably more expensive.

Glass

Glass comes in two forms: standard and nonglare etched glass. Although nonglare glass makes it easier to see a print without reflections, manufacturers typically use acid to etch the glass. There are no guarantees that the acid has been completely neutralized, so you risk print contamination if you use this form of glass.

Acrylic Glazing

Acrylic glazing is an excellent choice when shipping framed photographs. There is much less chance for breakage than if glass were used. Acrylic scratches very easily, so it is sold with a cellophane-like cover that you must remove before you frame your print. Be extremely cautious not to scratch the acrylic during the framing process.

Frames

Frames are typically made of wood or metal. Wood frames are acidic by nature, so you need to use a vapor barrier (either aluminum or plastic tape) between the mat boards and the wood to avoid damaging the mat boards.

Aluminum is the most common metal used for framing. Frames are usually sold in sections and packaged by length. One package typically contains two sides for a frame. You would purchase one package of 8-inch sections and one package of 10-inch sections to make a complete 8 × 10-inch frame.

The hardware required to put the frame sections together is usually included in the packages. If you purchase aluminum sections through a catalog or online, be sure to order the separate hardware required

to assemble the frame sections if it isn't included with the aluminum sections.

Filler Board

A **filler board** is a mat board placed behind the mounted print to take up any empty space between the mounted print and the back edge of the frame. The filler board should meet the same standards as all other materials, despite the fact that it doesn't come in contact with the print. An acidic board can still cause damage by giving off harmful gases that permeate the print.

Back Paper

Many framers attach an archival liner paper, or **back paper**, to the back of wooden frames to keep out dust and insects. The liner paper also decreases fluctuations in humidity and limits the intake of airborne pollutants.

Metal frames are not designed to accept liner paper. When you use a metal frame, apply polyester tape around the edge of the entire inner framing package, including the glazing, photograph, and mat board. Be careful not to apply the tape beyond the position of the frame's edge on the glazing, or the tape will show when you add the frame. Place the taped package into the frame and insert a filler board as needed. Be sure to use an acid-free, archival quality tape.

Hanging Accessories

Accessories for hanging your framed photograph range from simple brackets nailed to the top of a wood frame, to wire that stretches across the back of an aluminum frame. When you purchase your framing supplies, check to see if the packages include these accessories. You may need to purchase them separately.

Techniques for Print Mounting and Matting

There are several techniques for mounting your prints. Those discussed here are low cost and/or available as supplies in many art and photography programs. This is not meant to be a complete discussion of all possible print mounting techniques.

Dry Mount Technique

Although excellent for traditional dark-room prints, the dry mount technique is *not* for inkjet prints, as the heat of the press can damage those prints.

A clean environment is very important when dry mounting prints. Begin by wiping off any counters or tables you will be using. Make sure all surfaces are dry before you begin. Here is a list of the materials you will need:

- Clean, smooth surface such as a clean, dry counter on a utility table;
- Cutting board or smooth mat board that can be sacrificed as a cutting surface;
- Mount board, double weight (4-ply);
- Dry mount tissue, a thin sheet of paper coated on both sides with a heat-sensitive adhesive, slightly larger than the size of your print so you can trim any excess before mounting the print;
- Mounting press, a flat-surfaced heating plate with top and bottom heating surfaces;
- Tacking iron, a small iron used to bond the center and corners of the dry mount tissue to the mount board;
- Metal weights, 20" × 20" specially made for dry mounting, or a couple of very large, heavy books;
- Utility knife with a very sharp cutting blade (you can't cut a clean line with a dull blade);
- Straight metal cutting edge, but not a wooden or plastic ruler, as the utility knife can cut into it;
- Mat cutter, which can be as simple as a metal ruler and utility knife, a handheld mat cutter, or a professional mat cutter used in frame shops; and
- Clean cotton gloves.

Heat the mounting press to the temperature required for your dry mount tissue (Figure 6-2). This temperature varies by brand, so carefully read the instructions accompanying your dry mount tissue package.

Select two pieces of clean, smooth-surfaced mount board sized at least 2 inches larger than the finished width and height of your mounted print. These mount boards will protect your print from the surface of the mounting press and, later, from the weights

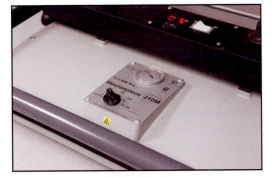

Figure 6-2

Heat the press to the temperature required for your dry mount tissue.

Photo © KS.

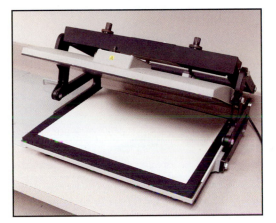

Figure 6-3

Heat two sheets of smooth-surfaced mount board in the mounting press and close the press to preheat them for 1–2 minutes.

Photo © KS.

or books used during the cooling process. Be absolutely certain that there is no dust, grit, or debris on the boards, as this could cause permanent dents in the emulsion of your print.

Place the two sheets of mount board in the mounting press, lower the press top, and preheat the boards to the required temperature for 1–2 minutes (Figure 6-3). Open the mounting press briefly two or three times during this period to allow steam to escape. Your goal is to extract all moisture from the two boards. If the boards still feel moist when you bring them out of the press, repeat the process until they feel dry.

Heat the tacking iron (Figure 6-4) to the temperature recommended by the dry mount tissue manufacturer. Check your print to make sure it is free of dust or dirt particles.

Figure 6-4

A tacking iron with adjustable heat settings. Consult your dry mount tissue manufacturer's instructions to learn what temperature to use.

Photo © KS.

Any particle on the print can cause a high point (not-so-affectionately known as a *mountain*) on the print surface.

Place the print between the two pieces of dried mount board, and close the mounting press for about 30 seconds (Figure 6-5). Then remove the print and close the mounting press. This both dries and flattens

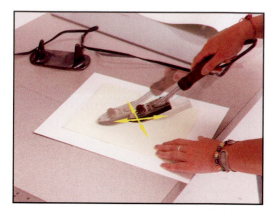

the print. Again, your goal is to remove all moisture from the print. Keep the two large mat boards in the press to keep them dry while you complete the next steps.

Remove the print from the mounting press and place it face down on a clean, smooth surface. Pick up the dry mount tissue and make sure there is no dirt or debris on it (Figure 6-6).

Center the dry mount tissue over the back of the print and gently drag an *X* beginning in the middle of the tissue and continuing about an inch toward a corner, bonding the tissue to the print. Use only the minimum required pressure to adhere the print and tissue together. Then return to the center and drag in the opposite direction for about an inch. Repeat until you have created an *X*-shaped bonded area. Always drag from the center outward toward a corner. Carefully and gently lift the tissue to make sure it is adhered to the print before going to the next step.

Trim the excess dry mount tissue and the white print borders (Figure 6-7). Use a utility knife and straight-edge metal ruler, or use a rotary cutter to evenly trim the borders. Do not use a plastic or wooden ruler as your knife can cut into this instrument,

making an irregular cut on your print border. A rotary cutter is excellent for this task.

Carefully position the print on the mount board, image side up (Figure 6-8). Measure the side margins to make sure they are even at both the top and bottom of the print. Some photographers prefer to leave a slightly greater space at the bottom of the mount board than at the top. If you need to lay the ruler on top of your print, protect the print first with a clean, white strip of paper placed loosely on the print surface.

Carefully lift each print corner individually, without moving the print position, and use the tacking iron to tack the dry mount tissue to the mount board (Figure 6-9). Start about an inch toward the print center and drag outward toward the corner. Do this on all four corners, using only enough pressure to adhere the tissue to the board. Do not allow the tissue to wrinkle under the print, and be especially careful not to let any of the glue from the dry mount tissue extend beyond the print's edge. Very carefully test the adhesion of the dry mount tissue to the board (Figure 6-10).

Place the print, tissue, and mount board between the two sheets of smooth-surfaced mount board you dried earlier (Figure 6-11).

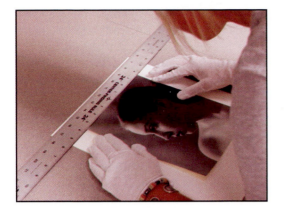

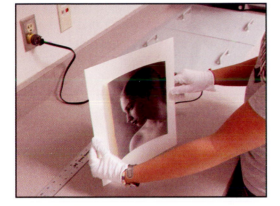

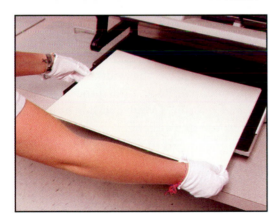

Close the mounting press. Keep the mounting press tightly closed for the recommended time period for your dry mount tissue.

Remove the two sheets of smooth-surfaced mount board (with the print and mount board still inside) from the mounting press (Figure 6-12). Place the sandwiched boards on the counter and gently place the mounting weights or heavy books close to each other on top of the boards (Figure 6-13). Allow the print to cool for a few minutes.

Figure 6-8 (top left)

Place the print on your mount board and carefully measure the margins.

Figure 6-9 (top right)

Tack down each corner of the dry mount tissue. Always gently drag the tacking iron from about an inch from the tissue border out toward the corner. The strip of paper you see over the center of the print was used to protect the print from the ruler placed over it. This paper strip can be removed at any time in the process.

Figure 6-10 (middle left)

Carefully test the adhesion of the dry mount tissue to make sure the print won't fall off. Be gentle in the process!

Figure 6-11 (middle right)

Place the print/mount board between the two large, smooth boards in your mounting press. Make sure the print is far from the borders of the large boards. Otherwise, you could end up with a dent across your print.

Figure 6-12 (bottom left)

When the time is up, open the mounting press and pull out all of the boards sandwiched together. Do not separate the boards at this time. Be rather quick as you do this, because the edges of your print will quickly start to curl away from the mounting board.

Figure 6-13 (bottom right)

Immediately place the sandwiched boards under a large, flat weight. You can use weights made specifically for this purpose, or you can use oversized, smooth-surfaced books. You must be certain that the weight is evenly distributed so no pressure points affect the print surface.

Figure 6-14

The final mounted print.

Photos 6-8 through 6-14 © KS.

Do not set the books directly on the print without the protective mount boards, as you could put a crease in the print. Be very careful to keep even pressure on the prints during the cool-down period.

Once the print has had time to completely cool (which will take several minutes), remove the weights and outer mount boards. Lift the mounted print and gently bend a corner of the mount board. The print should not dislodge from the board (Figure 6-14).

Cut an Overmat

A mat board with a window cut into it, an overmat creates a professional-appearing display and also separates your print from the glass in the frame. Using the technique described here, the overmat can be replaced if it gets dirty or damaged. The overmat can be measured and cut before or after mounting your print, depending on the mounting process you use.

Mat boards come in a large variety of colors and textures. Because of its archival quality, unbuffered museum mount board is commonly used for fine art prints, but you can decide if you would prefer a mat board with a colored and/or textured surface.

One consideration to think about is whether your print will be displayed in a collection with other photographs. If so, you may be expected to use a consistent color and texture of mat board across your entire collection. This will give your collection a cohesive look.

Begin by wiping off any counters or tables you will be using. Make sure all surfaces are dry before you begin. Here is a list of the materials you will need:

- Your mounted print;
- Straight-edge cutting tool such as a metal ruler;
- Utility knife, or specialized mat cutting knife, with a sharp blade (dull blades tend to tear mat boards);
- Safe, clean cutting surface;
- Pencil and soft eraser; and
- Mat cutter (professional or handheld).

Begin by cutting two boards to the width and height you want for your final mounted print (Figure 6-15). The first will be the mount board. The second will be the mat board you have selected for this project. The sizes of the two boards should match.

If your print has a white border, you can decide whether you want to show any of that border within the overmat window. If you don't want any border showing, you may trim it off before proceeding.

Take Measurements

Measure the width and height of your print, excluding any areas that you want covered by the mount board (Figure 6-16). Decide whether you want your top and bottom margins to be equal. Many photographers choose to have a larger margin on the bottom. If this is what you want, the top and two side margins can be equal. Allow for at least a $1/8$-inch covered area along each edge unless you want the print edges to show within the mat window.

Next, measure the width and height of your mount board, and write down those values (Figure 6-17). Subtract the width of the image area from the total width of the mount board. Divide this number by two. The result will be the width of each side of the overmat. Repeat this process for the top and bottom if your overmat's top and bottom margins are equal.

You may need to alter your measuring process to determine the height of the window top and bottom. If you left more space at the top than at the bottom when you mounted your print, you will need to directly measure the height of the top separately from the height of the bottom.

Place your overmat face down on a clean cutting surface. Use a ruler and pencil to transfer your measurements to the back of the overmat.

**Figure 6-15
(top left)**

Cut your mount board and mat board to the finished exterior width and height you want for your final mounted print.

**Figure 6-16
(top right)**

Measure the image area of your mounted print. If you want the border of your print to show through the mat window, include as much of the border as you want to have visible in your measurement.

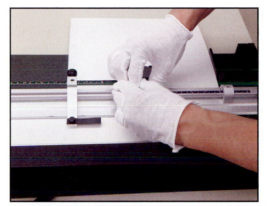

**Figure 6-17
(middle left)**

Measure all four sides of the window of your mat board.

**Figure 6-18
(middle right)**

Cut all four sides. If you are using a commercial mat cutter like this one, place the board face up in the cutter and set the measurements along the cutter's ruler.

Cut the Overmat

Keep your overmat face down. Using a straight-edged metal ruler and a sharp blade, make all four cuts, repositioning the board for each cut. Be careful to stop your blade at the proper point to avoid overcuts.

If you are using a commercial mat cutter such as that shown in Figure 6-18, you do not need to mark the board with your measurements. Instead, set the cutter's width to the measurements you took earlier, taking into consideration any changes required by your mat cutter's manufacturer. If you have different measurements for your window's top and bottom, make sure to make those changes on the mat cutter before making those cuts. Place the board face up in the commercial mat cutter to make the cuts.

**Figure 6-19
(bottom right)**

Carefully trim out any corners with a sharp knife as needed. Do not try to tear a corner loose.

Photos 6-15 through 6-19 © KS.

After the board has been cut, you may need to carefully come in with a sharp blade and gently cut the board's corners (Figure 6-19). DO NOT try to pop out the center piece, as you will tear the board and leave an uneven corner.

Figure 6-20
(top left)

Lay the two boards together along the top edge of the mounted print. The finished side of the overmat should be face down on the table.

Figure 6-21
(top right)

Use artist's tape to bind the two boards together. The yellow pattern shown as an overlay here is a suggested pattern to lay down the tape. Smaller pieces of tape reinforce the larger ones. The tape extending beyond the boards can be trimmed off.

Figure 6-22
(bottom left)

The finished mounted print can stand on its own, or you can place it in a frame.

Photos 6-20 through 6-22 © KS.

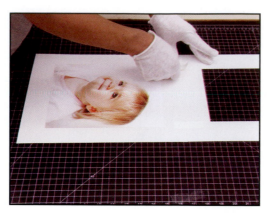

> **NOTE**
>
> ### Signing the Mount Board
>
> Some photographers sign the mount board just below the print. If you want your signature to show, add enough space for your signature in your measurement before cutting the overmat.

Hinge Mounting an Overmat to a Mat Board

Place your second mat board against the top of your finished print mat board (Figure 6-20). Make sure the edges touch tightly. Use a long piece of artist's tape across the juncture. If you like, you can bring your tape all the way past the edges of the mat board. Use a metal ruler and sharp knife to trim off the excess.

Reinforce the first piece by applying shorter pieces of tape at a perpendicular angle to the first tape. Be sure the two boards are tightly pressed together before applying these pieces of tape. Finally, reinforce each of those pieces with one small piece of tape as shown in Figure 6-21.

Now you're ready to fold the top mat over the print. You can either display the print in this manner, or you can place it in a frame (Figure 6-22).

Cold Mount Technique

The cold mount technique is best for inkjet prints or any print that can be damaged by the heat of the mounting press. There are several brands of cold mount materials, falling into three general categories: spray adhesives, transfer adhesives, and two-sided adhesive sheets. Spray adhesives are available at a relatively low cost and will be discussed here. Consult the manufacturers of transfer adhesives and two-sided adhesive sheets to learn more about them.

Spray adhesives must be carefully applied in well-ventilated conditions. A spray booth and respirator are strongly recommended. Spray adhesives include products like Scotch® Photo Mount or 3M™ Photo Mount Spray Adhesive. They are not considered to be quite as permanent as other transfer adhesive techniques, but you shouldn't plan on being able to remove your print after adhering the print to the mount board. Some spray adhesives allow more repositioning on the mount board than others. Be sure to read and follow the manufacturer's instructions on the container.

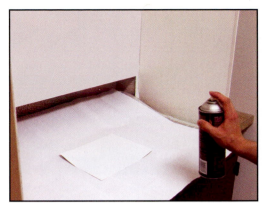

A clean environment is very important when using spray adhesive with prints. Begin by wiping off any counters or tables you will be using. Make sure all surfaces are dry before you begin. Here is a list of the materials you will need:

- Clean, smooth surface such as a clean, dry counter or utility table;
- Mount board, double weight (4-ply), cut to the finished size you want for your mounted print;
- Adhesive spray specially formulated for photographic use;
- Freezer paper to use as a protective base to catch the edge spray in the spray booth or outdoors;
- Ruler to measure your print and the margins of your mount board; and
- Small sticky notes to mark your corners for print placement.

The Technique

Begin by cutting your mount board and overmat to the width and height you want for your final mounted print as described earlier. If your print has a white border, you can decide whether or not you want to show any of that border within the overmat window. If you don't want any border showing, you may trim it off before proceeding.

Place your print loosely on your mount board, face up. Lay the overmat over the print and line up the print so it shows through the overmat window. Holding the print carefully in place, remove the mat board and set it aside.

Use sticky notes to mark the edges of each corner of your print (Figure 6-23). Start with eight sticky notes, one for each corner's side. As your confidence grows, you can mark as few or as many corners as you need.

Prepare your spray booth or well-ventilated area for the spraying process (Figure 6-24). Use pieces of newspaper on the booth counter to protect its surface from adhesive spray. Then use a large white sheet of paper over the newspaper to keep newspaper ink from damaging your print.

Place your print face down on the clean white paper and spray the adhesive onto the print's back. Hold the can vertically and allow the spray to come out parallel to the print surface. The spray will gently fall onto the print and cover it without creating puddles. Be sure to cover the entire surface without allowing the spray to seep onto the front of the print.

When the print surface is coated (the adhesive should not be pooling), carefully lift the print. You don't want to get adhesive stuck on your fingers and later transferred to

Remove Sticky Notes from Mount Board

CAUTION: DO NOT leave the sticky notes on your mount board for a long period of time (hours or days). Even though they are supposed to be easily removable, sticky notes can eventually become permanently adhered to the surface of the mount board.

the print. Carefully position the photograph on the mount board, using the sticky notes as a guide (Figure 6-25). Put clean gloves on and smooth the photograph down from the center to the edges. Finally, remove the sticky notes from the mount board.

An Alternative Mounting Method

If you do not have access to either a dry mount press or cold mount supplies, you can still mount your print using artist's tape. This method uses a new print mounting technique, in conjunction with mat cutting and hinge mounting techniques previously discussed.

Cut two boards to the width and height dimensions of your final mounted print. Measure and cut a window in your overmat as discussed earlier.

Place your print face up on the mount board, and lay the mat board over the print. Arrange the edges of the two boards so they are directly lined up with each other. Using clean gloves, adjust the position of the print until you get the exact composition you want to show through the mat window.

Carefully holding the print in place, remove the mat board. Take a measurement of the direction and distance you offset the print (if at all) from the center of the mount board. Using a pencil, make tiny marks on the outer edge of your print where the print will later line up with the window's edge.

Place your overmat face down on the table. Position your print face down on the overmat, lining up the pencil marks with the window edges. Place tape all the way around the print, using artist's tape or other archival tape (Figure 6-26).

Still keeping the print side down, place your mount board face up along the top edge of your overmat. Make sure the edges touch tightly. Use the hinge mount technique discussed earlier to attach the two boards together.

Presentation Portfolios

Another method for sharing your prints is to purchase a protective container suitable for long-term print storage. It's important to purchase a container made with archival materials to prevent damage to your photographs. Presentation containers can be soft-sided with three-ring or spiral notebook-style interiors, or they can be hard-shell boxes in which you can store mounted and matted prints.

Presentation portfolios are frequently used for showing photographs to current or prospective clients. They come in a variety of sizes, so be sure to purchase one that will carry the largest size print you plan to create.

You can also purchase padded, hard-shell mailing cases for mailing matted and framed prints to galleries or photographic competitions. If you need to ship prints in this manner, be sure to use protective cardboard corners and use Plexiglass instead of regular glass for the glazing.

Summary

Protecting your prints means more than keeping them free of dirt and moisture. Protecting your prints also requires you to think about pH and the archivability of the products you use for matting and mounting. Taking care of these issues will help ensure a long life for your prints.

EXERCISES

1. Take your finished print (either black-and-white or color) to a local framing shop and experiment with the overmat samples. Which overmat best enhances your print? What overmat colors detract from your print?

2. Search online for photography galleries and look at how the prints have been mounted and matted.

3. Experiment with unusual placement of your print on a mount board. Consider the content of your image. Is something falling? Is a person looking up or down? Prints don't necessarily have to be centered on a mount board. An unusual position might be a way to enhance the message of your image.

FURTHER READING

- VIEW http://www.larsonjuhl.com/; click on Ideas and Inspiration, and then select Interactive Frame Design to try a variety of frames for your photographs. Click also on For the Trade, and then select Design Students. The list on the left leads you to informative pages.

- VIEW http://www.lightimpressions-direct.com/; look through their catalog of archival supplies.

- VIEW http://www.printfile.com/PAT-information.aspx; read more about the Photographic Activity Test.

- VIEW http://www.printfile.com/archival-dictionary.aspx; use this dictionary to learn more about archival properties and supplies.

- VIEW http://www.imagepermanenceinstitute.org/; browse the navigation links on the left to learn more about projects, education, and ISO standards.

Betty Huth and Ed Booth

Huth & Booth Photographic Artists, LLC

How did you become involved with wedding and portrait photography?

Betty: I had been a registered nurse, but found I had a good eye for photography. I didn't enjoy nursing; so, I began to do photography. I worked out of my home at first, as I could do that while raising kids. Most of my education in photography was from the Professional Photographers of America (PPofA), a national organization that offers seminar-like classes through local or state chapters.

Ed: I was a surfer dude and photographed sports and sold them to the kids on the beach. I was hired by a studio and learned a lot there. Later I earned a degree in photography. There wasn't a lot of money in surfing photography, so I went into wedding photography. It's a good fit. I'm a people person. If your clients like you, they will like your work. If the experience was a good one for them, they'll be happy with your work. Happiness builds loyalty.

What advice do you have for prospective wedding photographers?

Get a good foundation. Study everything from lighting to posing, business, and camera work. You will need a lot of technical knowledge. You will also need a lot of business basics if you want to freelance. You might be good with a camera, but you won't make it if you don't have business knowledge and savvy. Either get marketing training or hire a marketer. That will teach you how to keep your name in front of people.

Don't plan on surviving on wedding photography alone. The market has changed, and it's very difficult to earn enough from wedding photography alone to survive. Think about the possibility of doing this work on the side, and have another job for additional salary and benefits.

How does a student know when he/she's good enough to photograph weddings?

Weddings are the most difficult of events to photograph. When you go out to do a wedding, you're taking a once in a lifetime experience and capturing it. Unless you know what you're doing and are confident you can handle anything that happens, you aren't being fair to your client. Don't tell them you can handle their memories without full knowledge of the craft. You would be doing the photography profession a disservice as well.

It's difficult to find photographers to take you on as an apprentice, but an apprenticeship is a great way to learn the craft. If you can, work for knowledge instead of pay. That means you would need to be able to support yourself during that period of time. It's important that you not start your own business in the same geographic region as the studio under which you apprenticed!

When you understand lighting, posing, what is needed when photographing a wedding, and can design an album, you're ready to take on wedding photography. You need to understand Photoshop or know someone who can do Photoshop procedures well. Weddings are the one field that you can't go back and re-create. If you blow a portrait session, you can go back and redo it. You can't do that at weddings. A wedding photographer has more responsibility on his shoulders than portrait photographers.

What professional organizations or magazines would be of benefit for prospective wedding and portrait photographers?

- *Rangefinder* Magazine, 1312 Lincoln Blvd., Santa Monica, CA 90406.
- Wedding and Portrait Photographers International (WPPI). This group holds a convention every March in Las Vegas. They hold classes beforehand, run extra classes, and have competitions during the convention.
- Professional Photographers of America (PPA) www.ppa.com.

Wedding photographers capture priceless moments.

Photograph © Huth & Booth Photography.

Concerned Photographers at an Official Inauguration Ball for President Barack Obama, Washington, DC, January 2009.

Photo © André S. Solidor (aka Elliott Erwitt)/Magnum Photos.

7

The Digital Darkroom

Chapter Learning Objectives

- Describe image quality and how it relates to digital camera settings.

- Describe the factors that determine the quality of a digital photograph.

- Use Adobe Camera Raw to adjust files before opening them in Photoshop.

- Organize your files, including using Ratings and Collections, in Adobe Bridge.

- Define resolution as it is applied to photographs in Adobe Camera Raw and Photoshop.

- Use the exposure adjustments within Adobe Camera Raw before opening your photograph in Photoshop.

- Change your file's resolution in Photoshop.

- Become familiar with different file formats and when to use them.

In this chapter, you'll learn about the methods used to download and edit a digital photograph. You'll be introduced to Adobe Bridge, Adobe Camera Raw, and Adobe Photoshop. Resolution, a very important aspect of digital photography, will be discussed at length.

It is challenging to use the digital darkroom without a large knowledge base, and this chapter will get you started. Chapters 8 and 9 will give you additional tools to fine-tune your image. As soon as you begin feeling comfortable with the information presented in these chapters, read Chapters 10 and 11. The information in these chapters will make a big difference in the artistic and technical quality of your photographs.

Although any discussion of a digital workflow seems completely technical in nature, never forget that your goal is to match the appearance of your photograph to your intentions for your image. This chapter teaches the controls available to you. How and when you apply those controls to your images is totally up to you.

History of the Digital Photographer's Workflow

When consumer-level digital cameras first came on the market, professional photographers rarely used them because of image-quality issues. Early digital sensors simply couldn't capture enough information to create a high-quality photograph. Image quality has been at the forefront of the digital revolution ever since, with photographers demanding and receiving more from camera engineers and software developers every year.

The digital darkroom revolution began with the development of Photoshop in the 1980s and the release of its first full version in 1990. The first version was relatively primitive and included only a small fraction of the capabilities it has today. All editing changes were completed by directly altering the existing pixels within a photograph.

Through research, photographers realized that multiple alterations of the pixels' colors and values could damage the image quality of the digital file. Photographers were encouraged to think in terms of **pixel preservation**, or working methods designed to maintain the integrity of the original pixels.

Newer generations of image-editing software have addressed the pixel preservation issue in several ways. Most recently, Adobe has developed software programs like Adobe Camera Raw (ACR) and Lightroom to give photographers powerful **nondestructive editing** capabilities. Nondestructive editing changes the *appearance* of the pixels without changing the actual color or values of the original pixels. Using nondestructive editing techniques, you can alter your photograph any number of times using the same tools over again until you have fine-tuned your image. Only after you have finalized everything will the original color and value of pixels be altered. This prevents the pixels from being changed many times over, hence degrading the image quality.

Although all image editing used to be completed in Photoshop, the new digital workflow places Adobe Camera Raw or Adobe Lightroom before Photoshop in the chronological sequence of image editing. Because Adobe Camera Raw ships with Adobe Photoshop, this chapter will address the Adobe Camera Raw digital darkroom.

You will also be introduced to Adobe Bridge, a program that installs with nearly all Adobe products. Bridge organizes your files and gives you the ability to open and work with files in Adobe Camera Raw while keeping Photoshop available for other tasks.

Because image quality is of paramount importance throughout the digital work-flow, you will begin by learning what factors play into the quality of your digital images.

Image Quality

Many factors affect the image quality of a digital photograph. The megapixel size of your camera's digital sensor is a major component. If you have a 6-megapixel camera, your largest potential file size is about 18 MB. An 8-megapixel camera will produce an approximate 24 MB file. The quality of your sensor is related to, but not totally dependent on, its size. Sensor manufacturers have developed proprietary features that also affect the image quality. Although articles and advertisements about digital cameras are valuable, the best way to judge the quality of an image is to see an enlarged print of a camera's digital file.

Other image-quality factors include the quality of your lens, whether you held the camera still while you were making the photograph, and the exposure of your image. Using a tripod is always a good idea if you are concerned about image quality. As you learned in Chapter 3, getting a good exposure without over- or underexposing your image is critically important.

Quality Control Variables

Many digital cameras offer a variety of quality settings. Small, medium, and large JPEG settings are common. Although the small setting is adequate for making images to be shared over the Internet, resulting photographs do not contain enough information to create good enlarged prints. Consult your camera manual to learn how to set file size and/or file quality, and always use the largest and best file setting available for your camera. You can throw away pixels to downsize your files later. Inventing pixels to compensate for a small original file size will never yield the same quality image.

Color balance is important in digital photography. Different light sources can affect the color balance of your photographs and make the colors look unnatural. If you are photographing under lighting conditions other than daylight, change your camera's color balance setting to match your light source. Even if you need to tweak your color balance later, your changes won't be as severe as they would have been with a daylight-balanced camera. Refer to your camera's manual to learn about the different color balance settings. An Automatic White Balance setting is frequently adequate for starters because the camera makes an effort to properly balance colors in your scene, but creating a custom white balance is better. Creating and using a custom white balance is discussed in Chapter 11.

To ensure a good digital capture, format your memory card on a regular basis. Consult your camera manual to learn about the format function on your camera. All existing images are erased when you format your card, so be sure you have them copied elsewhere before performing the format function. The author formats her card every time she inserts it into her camera during an important photo session.

Camera Raw Image Captures

Digital cameras collect light information to create the digital image. Your camera sends the exposure's light intensity (analog) information from the sensor to an analog-to-digital converter (ADC). The ADC is an in-camera microprocessor that converts the analog information to digital information, conducts a variety of image-altering procedures, and creates a JPEG image (called a **raw conversion**). JPEG (Joint Photographic Experts Group) is a very common standard for compression of digital images. The quality of the final JPEG image is highly dependent on the quality of that built-in microprocessor. A **camera raw file** has had its analog information digitized, but the image-altering procedures used to create a JPEG capture

were never applied. A camera raw file is, in essence, the digital equivalent to film that has been exposed but has not yet been processed.

As an analogy to film processing, JPEG images are "processed" by the settings you have chosen for your camera, including compression, file size, white balance, highlight and shadow values, and color mode. Digital information initially captured by your camera is compressed and/or discarded by the microprocessor during the JPEG image capture. This may include discarding a portion of the dynamic range of tonal values your camera's sensor is capable of capturing. Highlights and shadow information is initially recorded, but the lighter highlights and darker shadows may be compressed and/or discarded during the JPEG save, forcing those pixels to pure white or pure black. If you want to take advantage of the full dynamic range of your camera's sensor, set your camera to record raw files (Figure 7-1). These files will be fully processed later in the Adobe Camera Raw workflow described later in this chapter.

The raw setting within your camera typically also captures a JPEG file for preview purposes, as computers without Photoshop or Lightroom installed may not be able to preview raw photographs. It is extremely rare to have problems with your camera recording digital files of any kind, raw or JPEG. However, make it a habit to use the largest JPEG capture when using the camera raw setting. Your memory card will fill much faster, but your large JPEG file can act as a backup if something goes wrong with the raw file (and vice versa).

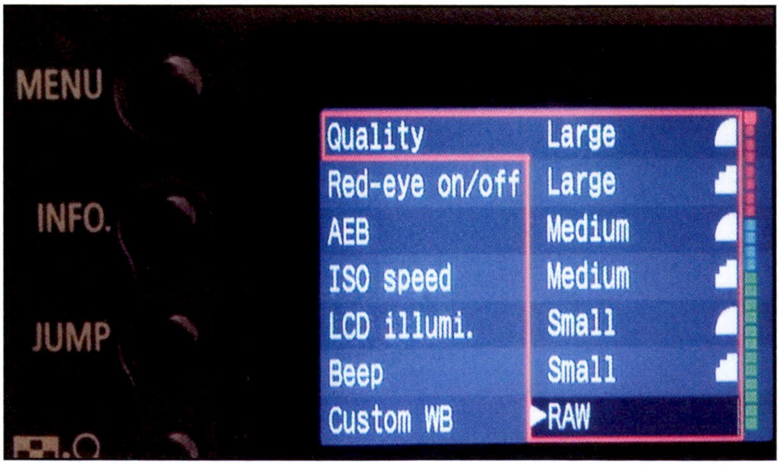

Figure 7-1

The raw function is an excellent way to capture a digital image, as it allows you to take advantage of the full dynamic range of your camera. It is the equivalent of unprocessed film and allows for extensive nondestructive editing.

Photo © KS.

Digital Displays

You'll recall that each photosite on a CMOS sensor is capable of collecting two types of information: tones (values) and a single color (red, green, or blue). Your computer displays the file as a photograph on your monitor. The monitor's image is made up of pixels too, but here, the term *pixel* takes on a different meaning. Pixels in the digital darkroom are tiny squares of gray or color. Each pixel can be black, white, or one shade of gray in a grayscale image, or it can be a color mixed from red, green, and blue components in a color image. Each pixel can display only one color at a time.

Most JPEG color images from digital cameras have 8 bits (0s or 1s) for each of the Red, Green, and Blue color channels (Figure 7-2). Therefore, a color image consists of 24 (8 bits × 3 channels = 24), 0s or 1s in each pixel. This is known as a 24-bit image. If you take the number of options (either 0 or 1 equals two options) and multiply that to the 8th power for an 8-bit image, you'll see that 2^8 is 256. Each color channel is capable of 256 different **intensity values** for each primary color. Intensity value translates to a measurement of brightness (ranging from darkest to lightest).

> ### NOTE
>
> 8 bits = 1 byte
>
> 1024 bytes = 1 kilobyte (KB or K)
>
> 1024 KB = 1 megabyte (MB)
>
> 1024 MB = 1 gigabyte (GB)

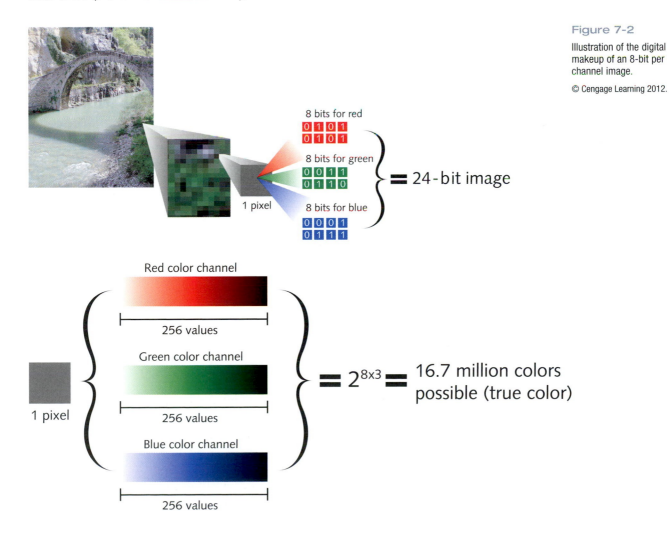

Figure 7-2

Illustration of the digital makeup of an 8-bit per channel image.

© Cengage Learning 2012.

Figure 7-3

A file in Grayscale mode
has only one color channel.
There are several ways
of creating images with
grayscale *appearance* in
Photoshop. Only if you go
to Image > Mode and change
your file to Grayscale mode
do you actually have a
grayscale file.

Photo © KS.

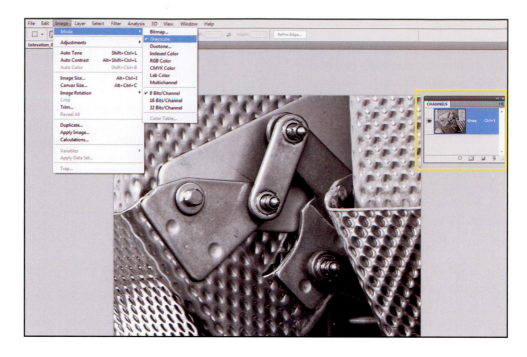

Because a pixel in a color image contains components of all three color channels, an image is capable of holding up to $2^{8 \times 3}$ or 16,777,216 (approximately 16.7 million) different colors. This number is considered **true color** and renders images in what we typically consider photographic-quality color.

Images without color are called **grayscale** and have only one visual component—that being intensity, also called *tonality* or *brightness* (Figure 7-3). Grayscale photographs contain only one color channel (Gray). Although many people call grayscale images "black and white," there is a distinct difference between these two on the computer. A digital **black-and-white image** is made up of either black or white pixels—there are no shades of gray.

Resolution

Resolution refers to the number and size of the pixels in your digital file. Resolution can be described either as the number of pixels contained in the entire file (a method frequently used by Web designers) or by the file's width/height dimension plus a pixel-per-inch calculation. Although both are accurate, photographers generally use the latter method to describe resolution and is the method used for the vast majority of this text.

Resolution is measured in the number of pixels across a linear inch of the photograph. Desktop and film scanners are capable of scanning in photographs at a variety of resolutions. Typical resolutions are 72 pixels per inch (ppi) (considered *low resolution*) and may go as high as 4,000 ppi or higher (extremely *high resolution*) in film scanners. As resolution settings increase, more digital information is captured.

Opening the Digital File

The purpose of this chapter is to help you understand the new digital workflow using Bridge, Adobe Camera Raw, and Photoshop. The digital workflow begins by transferring your file from your camera to the computer. Digital cameras frequently come with their own software and wire connectors that give you quick access to the digital files on your camera. Many photographers remove the storage disk from their cameras and use a memory card reader to transfer their files. Either way, Adobe Bridge will be the best portal to download and save your digital photos.

Start the Adobe Bridge software program in one of two ways: Either start the Adobe Bridge program from your Start-up menu, or start Adobe Photoshop, go to the File menu, and select BROWSE IN BRIDGE. Bridge will start up for you.

Adobe Bridge has a combination of image organizing and file management capabilities you will find very helpful. Adobe Bridge will download, rename, and make copies of your files, all in one move. This is advantageous, as you should always back up your digital files as soon as possible. Memory cards can go bad, and they need frequent reformatting. Either one of these circumstances would result in the loss of your photographs.

In Bridge, go to FILE GET > PHOTOS FROM CAMERA. This opens the Photo Downloader window within Bridge (Figure 7-4). Beside SOURCE, select your camera or your memory card (if you're using a memory card reader) from the drop-down menu. Under IMPORT SETTINGS, locate a folder to store your images. You can also create and name a new subfolder if you wish.

Under RENAME FILES, select a name for all of the files in your camera or memory card. Your custom name may be any of the presets in the drop-down menu, or you

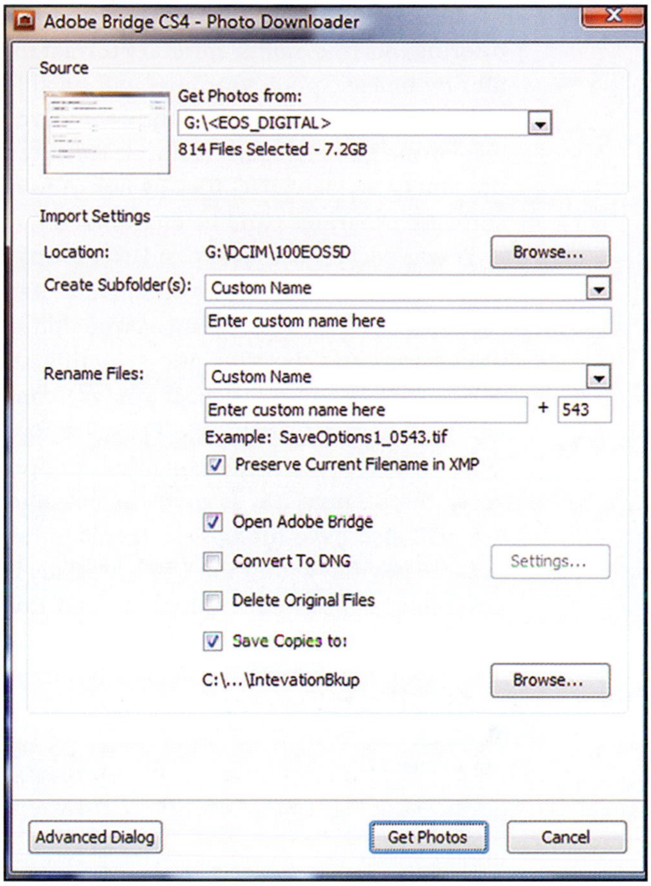

Figure 7-4

GO TO FILE > GET PHOTOS FROM CAMERA… in Bridge to open the Photo Downloader window.

Photo © KS.

can type in your own custom name. This renaming process will give you much more informative, searchable file names than your camera automatically creates.

It is advisable to PRESERVE your CURRENT FILENAME IN XMP, so if for some reason you need the original file names, they will be available to you. XMP (extensible metadata platform) is a separate data file that resides with your image file. It includes the file name, identifying information, and data about your camera settings for each file. You will learn more about XMP metadata in Chapter 15.

Some photographers are converting all of their digital images to DNG file formats. The DNG format was created by Adobe in response to many camera manufacturers creating their own digital raw formats (such as .nef by Nikon, .raf by Fuji, .mrw by Minolta, and .crw by Canon). Unless you have the accompanying proprietary software, you may not be able to open one of these raw formats. It is hoped that by offering this free, nonproprietary format for all raw images, photographers will be able to open all raw files in the future, regardless of the camera manufacturer. However, the ability to open DNG files by non-Adobe software programs can't be guaranteed.

If you decide to CONVERT to DNG format, CLICK on the box beside the option and then CLICK on SETTINGS. You will have the option of compressing the files and selecting an image conversion method. If you are converting raw files to DNG, the PRESERVE RAW IMAGE is the recommended method to preserve the original file as much as possible. You will also have the option to embed the original raw file within the DNG file. This is advisable, as your entire unprocessed raw file will be available to you later. However, it also means that your DNG files will be larger.

Many photographers don't use the Convert to DNG option, so their photographs are downloaded in the format the camera saves on the memory card. These would typically be JPEG and/or raw files.

Under the RENAME FILES function is an option to SAVE COPIES TO: and a Browse button. It is highly recommended that you use this feature, as it is far safer to have two copies of your digital files than one copy alone. Get in the habit of immediately backing up all of your photographs.

Once you have made all of your decisions, CLICK on the GET PHOTOS button at the bottom of the Photo Downloader window. Bridge will copy and rename your photographs as you specified.

File Organization in Bridge

Before you know it, you will have hundreds of digital images and will need a way to organize them. Adobe Bridge gives you several tools to do so. Open Bridge if you haven't already done so.

Folders and Favorites in Bridge

CLICK on the FOLDERS panel in the upper left corner of the Bridge window (Figure 7-5). The Folders panel acts as any other listing of folders on your computer. You can copy, paste, delete, and move files across folders in Bridge. At the top center of the Bridge window, look for the ESSENTIALS button and make sure it is active. Along the bottom right side of the Bridge window, you will see a slider that allows you to zoom in or out of the file thumbnails.

The Favorites panel allows you to create shortcuts to specific folders you frequently use. To create a shortcut to a folder, use the Folders panel first. CTRL-CLICK (RIGHT-CLICK) on the folder and select ADD TO FAVORITES (Figure 7-6). A shortcut to that folder will appear on the Favorites panel.

When viewing files in a folder (either through the Folders or Favorites panel), you are working with the photographs within their original folders. Most of the time this works well, but there are times when the Collections function of Bridge is very helpful.

Collections in Bridge

There will be times when you want to access a photograph for more than one use. Perhaps you are using one photograph in a class assignment, a poster for yourself, and a calendar within a page layout program. It would be a disadvantage to have three separate files of that one photograph. If you made any changes to the photograph in one file, they wouldn't be changed in the other two files.

Bridge's Collections function is similar to a folder containing shortcuts to your image files. You store shortcuts in Collections without copying, moving, or renaming the actual file. You could have one collection for your class assignment, one for your poster, and one for your calendar and could drag and drop your photograph into each of those collections. Start a new collection by CLICKING on the NEW COLLECTION button at the bottom of the Collections panel (Figure 7-7).

You can open any file from any collection and make changes to it. When you save the file, it saves back to its original folder (wherever that is). The file's icon within the collection reflects the changes you have made. If a particular file was included in

several collections, all of the file's icons within the various collections will reflect those changes even though you only made the changes on the original file.

Figure 7-8 shows you how Bridge was used in the organization of this textbook.

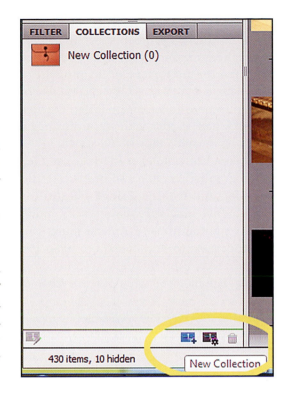

Figure 7-7

The Collections folder within Bridge. To start a new Collection, CLICK on the NEW COLLECTION (blue) button in the lower right corner of the Collections panel.

Photo © KS.

Figure 7-8

The collections used for the organization of this textbook.

Photo © KS.

There are some 500 photographs, illustrations, and screen captures from photographers around the world in this text. Imagine the nightmare of keeping all of those images organized! By careful use of the Collections functions in Bridge, the files could be kept in collections according to the chapters in which they would appear.

Bridge Collections aren't just used for photographs. Any file can be placed into a collection, making Bridge helpful for documents and spreadsheets as much as for photographs. To place images in a Collections folder, CLICK AND DRAG the IMAGE'S ICON directly into the Collections folder. The file itself will not move from its original folder. You have simply created a shortcut to that file.

CLICK on a Collections folder to see icons of the images placed in that folder. DOUBLE-CLICK the image icon to open the original file. CTRL-CLICK (RIGHT-CLICK) the image icon and SELECT OPEN IN CAMERA RAW to open the file in the Adobe Camera Raw window.

Labeling and Rating Photographs in Bridge

You will no doubt take far more photographs than you need for any given project. Slight variances in lighting conditions, camera angles, or placement of elements within your photographs will make some images stronger than others. Bridge allows you to rate individual photographs and to sort them by using the Filter function.

Select the images you want to rate by clicking once on each photo, going to the Label menu, and selecting the rating you wish (Figure 7-9). It is totally up to you to decide which label to use for your organizational needs. You can rate any grouping of images by selecting multiple images and applying the rating all at once.

CLICK on the FILTER PANEL beside the Collections panel on the left side of the Bridge window. CLICK ONCE on the STAR RATING you gave your images. CLICK OFF the NO RATING CHECK in the same window so images without ratings won't be visible. Now only the images you gave that particular rating to should be visible in your window (Figure 7-10). The rating function

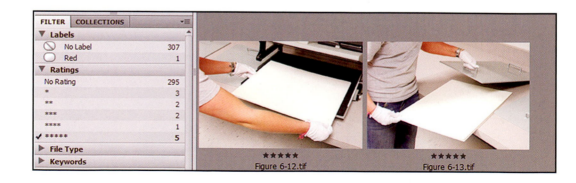

saves an enormous amount of time by preventing the need for constant sorting of images.

When you are ready to see all of your images again, CLICK the NO RATING button again. ALL of the images should now be visible.

Opening a File in Adobe Camera Raw

You will begin by opening your file in Adobe Camera Raw (ACR). Whether your file was captured in raw, JPEG, or TIFF format, the procedure is the same. CTRL-CLICK (RIGHT-CLICK) on your file and select OPEN IN CAMERA RAW (Figure 7-11). Your file will open within the ACR window.

ACR gives you tools to make color and tonal adjustments, set the resolution, and make other **global corrections** (corrections or adjustments to the entire image) before opening the file in Photoshop. The advantage of making global corrections in ACR is that the original file remains unchanged. The adjustments you make are saved in a separate file (known as an **XMP sidecar file**) attached to the original file. The original pixels can remain unchanged until you open the file in Photoshop. This is the first step in pixel preservation.

It is considered good practice to make all of the adjustments you can to the file in ACR. Later, in Photoshop, you can

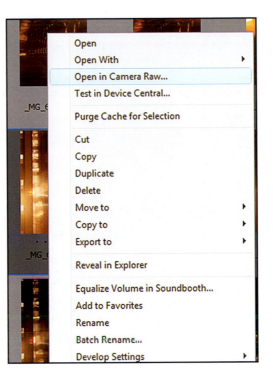

Figure 7-11

CTRL-CLICK (RIGHT-CLICK) on an image and SELECT OPEN IN CAMERA RAW.

Photo © KS.

fine-tune those adjustments and do further compositing or retouching in localized areas (called **localized corrections** or localized adjustments).

Initial Adjustments in ACR

On the right side of the ACR window, look for icons similar to those shown in Figure 7-12. Make sure the Basic icon (far left in the series) is clicked. This reveals the basic global adjustments available to you.

Why use camera raw settings in your camera if you can open JPEG and TIFF files in Adobe Camera Raw?

Because of ACR's nondestructive editing capabilities, all files can benefit from being initially edited in ACR, whether they are raw (available only on some cameras) or JPEG files (which all digital cameras can capture). Raw files include a greater dynamic range than most JPEG files, and therefore the ACR exposure adjustments give you the opportunity to retrieve shadow and highlight information beyond the limits of a JPEG capture. That alone is worth using the raw setting if it is available on your camera.

Figure 7-12

Select the Basic icon (circled in yellow).

Photo © KS.

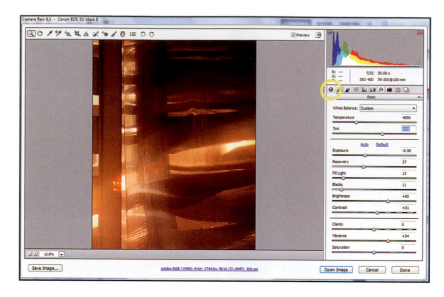

Set the White Balance

If you are working on a camera raw file, the colors in the image have not yet been made into pixels. A camera raw file is grayscale information only, and therefore you can assign any color balance you wish to your file. The default color balance is As Shot (Figure 7-13). Several other options are listed in the drop-down window.

If you are opening a TIFF or JPEG file, your options are limited to As Shot, Auto, or Custom. The microprocessor within your camera has already set the colors during the processing of the file, so you will have fewer

color balancing options than you would have if you were working with raw files.

When your camera captures raw files, the camera's microprocessor is bypassed and the color information is not permanently set. Raw files are basically grayscale files to which any color balance option can be applied. When working with raw files in ACR, your White Balance options will look like those in Figure 7-14.

Available to any type of file you are opening, the Custom option allows you to use the Temperature (blue/yellow slider) and Tint (magenta/green) sliders to tweak

Figure 7-13 (left)

The As Shot option is the default color balance.

Figure 7-14 (right)

Because the color information in raw files hasn't yet been applied to the file, you will see several more options for White Balance in ACR.

Photos 7-13 and 7-14 © KS.

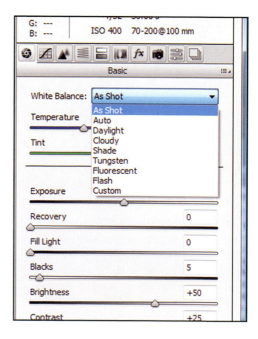

your image's color balance. By moving both sliders, you can alter the red/cyan color balance in your image. Only when your monitor is properly calibrated (see Chapter 10) can you trust the color balance you see when moving these sliders. Select a color balance that matches your intentions for your photograph.

Exposure

Below the White Balance section of ACR is the Exposure section, which includes sliders for exposure, recovery, fill light, blacks, brightness, and contrast (Figure 7-15). In the top right corner of ACR is a histogram showing the values of pixels for each of the individual color channels of Red, Green, and Blue. Yellow represents areas where Red and Green channels overlap; cyan, areas where Blue and Green channels overlap; and magenta, areas where Red and Blue channels overlap. White represents areas where all three color channels overlap.

Begin your work by moving the Exposure slider until your image has the exposure you want. Take care to watch the histogram as you move the slider. The left side of the histogram represents the shadow values, with the farthest left point being the Black Point; the right side, the highlight values, with the farthest right point being the White Point. You can push the pixels so far to the right or left that highlight and shadow detail is lost, or **clipped**. If you see a vertical line on the far right or far left of the histogram (such as for the highlights in the Red channel and the shadows in the Blue channel in Figure 7-15), you have clipped those values. If all three color channels are clipped, those pixels will be either pure white (if highlights) or pure black (if shadows) and will contain absolutely no visible detail.

In this particular image, the light source is creating a bright specular highlight that isn't supposed to contain detail. It is permissible to have that region go to pure white, so the clipped pixels in the highlight area aren't of great concern. Because the photographer isn't concerned about having shadow detail in the darkest areas of the

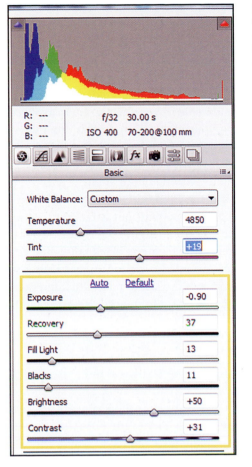

Figure 7-15

The Histogram, at the top right corner of ACR, and the Exposure sliders (in yellow).

Photo © KS.

image, the tiny clipped portion of the Blue channel isn't of concern. The photographer made this aesthetic decision; not everyone will agree with her decisions.

As you learned in an earlier chapter, it is better to slightly overexpose a digital image rather than underexpose it. Shadow details tend to contain more digital noise that becomes more evident if you lighten shadow areas. In ACR, you can push your exposure to a slight overexposure, slightly clipping the highlight values. You can recover the detail within those pixels in your next step.

The Recovery slider lowers the values of the brightest pixels in the image. Move the Recovery slider to the right until you see the clipped highlight pixels within the histogram move away from the right edge. Unless you have a specular highlight within your photograph, your goal is to not have any vertical line on the right side of the histogram.

The next step in processing your image is to move the Black slider until you are satisfied with the shadow areas of your photograph. Moving the Black slider to the right darkens your shadow values; moving it to the left lightens your shadow values. Watch the left side of your histogram to avoid clipping your shadow areas. You don't want to see a vertical line on the left side of the histogram unless your image has pure black regions with no detail at all.

Use the Fill Light slider to brighten your shadow areas without affecting the highlights. The Fill Light slider pulls low-value pixels away from the black point, just as the Recovery slider pulled high-value pixels away from the white point. Pushing the Fill Light slider far to the right may reveal digital noise in your shadow areas.

The Brightness function in ACR affects the overall brightness of your image by flattening the shadows and expanding the highlights of the photo. This step should be taken only after the Exposure, Recovery, Blacks, and Fill Light adjustments have been made. Remember to watch the white and black points in the histogram to prevent clipping.

The Contrast slider increases or decreases the contrast in your image by simultaneously moving the highlight and shadow values of the pixels. Make adjustments with the Brightness and Contrast sliders simultaneously until the appearance of the photograph matches your intentions.

Color Quality Adjustments

The Clarity, Vibrance, and Saturation sliders at the bottom of the window affect the quality of color within your photographs. The Clarity slider adjusts the contrast in response to an average brightness of neighboring pixels. If your overall image seems rather flat (low-contrast) or hazy, try making a Clarity adjustment to increase the contrast of the midtones within the image.

The Vibrance control increases or decreases the color intensity while keeping the colors within their own color family. This means you can increase the intensity of the colors without having them appear unnatural or garish.

Unlike the Vibrance control, the Saturation control increases the saturation of colors to the point that they don't look natural. Compare the colors in Figures 7-16, 7-17, and 7-18. Figure 7-16 is the color balance of the portrait when it was first taken. In Figure 7-17, the Vibrance slider was used to give the colors a little more saturation. In Figure 7-18, the Vibrance slider was left

Figure 7-16

The original color balance of the file.

Photo © KS.

Figure 7-17

Vibrance only was added in ACR.

Photo © KS.

Figure 7-18

Saturation only was added in ACR.

Photo © KS.

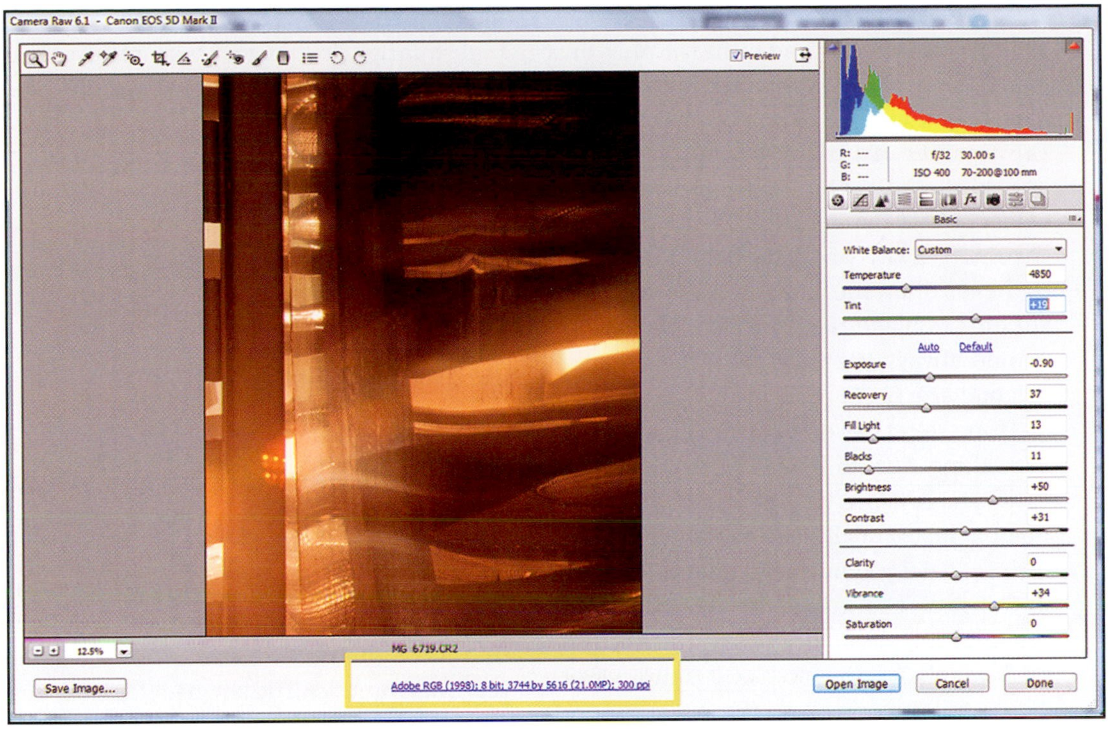

Figure 7-19

Look at the center bottom of the ACR window for the Workflow Options link.

Photo © KS.

at 0, and the Saturation slider was used to the same percentage that the Vibrance slider had been used in Figure 7-17. The colors in Figure 7-17 look more natural yet give the image's colors additional life.

Setting the Color Space, Resolution, and Bit Depth

Once you have your file adjusted as you see fit, it's time to set the color space, resolution, and bit depth of your file. The resolution is determined in part by the megapixel size of your camera, but the image can be resized as needed before you ever leave the Adobe Camera Raw window.

Look at the bottom center of the ACR window, within the yellow box shown in Figure 7-19 to find the blue Workflow Options link. Click on the link to open the Workflow Options dialog box (Figure 7-20). Select the color space you want to use, typically Adobe RGB (1998). You will learn more about color spaces in Chapter 10.

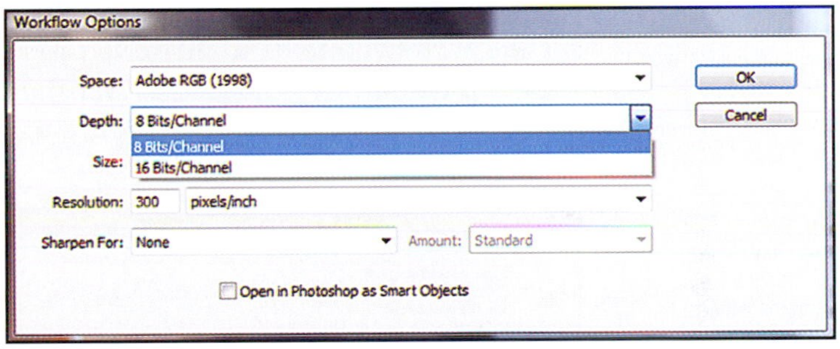

Under the Depth option, select 16-bits/ Channel if you need to do any retouching or local adjustments on the image. This will give you thousands more levels of value between pure black and pure white, allowing for smoother changes if you lighten or darken local areas within the file. If you are sure you won't be making any changes, use 8-bits/Channel instead. You will notice that the file size of a 16-bit/ Channel file is considerably larger than that of an 8-bit/Channel file.

Figure 7-20

The Workflow Options dialog box.

Photo © KS.

The Size option includes several presets. All but one preset has either a plus or a minus sign within its name (Figure 7-21). The preset *without* a plus or minus sign is the number of pixels your camera's sensor captured. Select this preset. If you select one of the smaller file sizes, you are throwing away pixel information before you ever open the file. Although there are reasons to make files smaller later on, you should always open and save the file at its original size first.

If you select one of the larger file sizes, you are asking ACR to invent more pixels than your camera captured. There is no guarantee that the image quality will remain as good as the original if you invent additional pixels.

Set the resolution you want for your file (Figure 7-22). This does not add or subtract pixels from your file; it simply sizes the individual pixels so the ppi measurement meets your needs. Most inkjet printers print well at 240 ppi. Photographs destined for the Web need to be at 72 or 96 ppi so they can be quickly uploaded to websites. If your photograph will be published, it will

likely need to be set to 300 ppi to obtain a high quality print. CLICK AND DRAG across the number in the Resolution window and type in the resolution you want.

The Sharpen option is available here, but it is recommended that you not use these Sharpen presets. You will learn about sharpening in greater detail in Chapter 8. CLICK OK to close the Workflow Options dialog box.

Straightening and Cropping in Adobe Camera Raw

At this stage, remember that you are still doing nondestructive editing to your file. Your original file hasn't changed in any way. The next steps might seem like techniques that will alter the original file, but that isn't the case. Your actions will be recorded and will take effect when you open your file in Photoshop, but the original file will remain unchanged.

Straightening Your Image

Despite your best efforts, you may make photographs in which objects should be (but aren't) vertical. You will also make images that would be compositionally stronger if portions of them could be cropped. Look across the top menu in the ACR dialog box (Figure 7-23). The Crop tool (on the left within the yellow box) and Straighten tool (on the right within the yellow box) will crop and straighten your photographs yet leave your complete original file intact. If you later choose to crop the file in a different manner, or if the straightening you do causes other problems, you will be able to return to the original file and rework the image for better results.

To straighten your image, SELECT the STRAIGHTEN TOOL. CLICK AND DRAG a line that goes along an object within the scene that should be either vertical or horizontal (Figure 7-24). When you release the mouse, you will see a bounding box showing the boundaries of the newly straightened image. If you are satisfied with the image

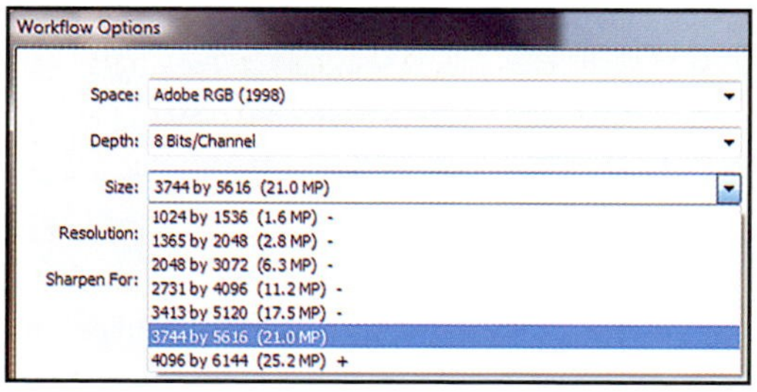

Figure 7-21 (left)

The size options in the Workflow Options dialog box. Select the listing *without* a plus or minus side beside it.

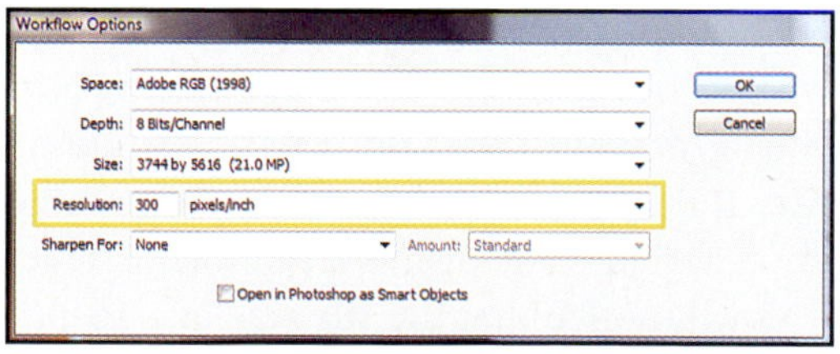

Figure 7-22 (middle)

Select the resolution you want for your file.

Figure 7-23 (bottom)

The Crop and Straighten tools at the top of the ACR window.

Photos 7-21 through 7-23 © KS.

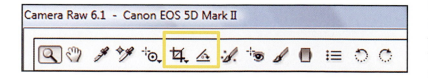

you now see, PRESS the RETURN (ENTER) key to finalize the straightening process. If you want to try the procedure again, press the ESCAPE key and start again.

When you are ready to open the file in Photoshop, it will open as a straightened image. However, because you are still doing nondestructive editing, the original digital file will remain as it was without the straightening completed.

Cropping Your Image

CLICK and HOLD your mouse on the CROP TOOL to see the available presets (Figure 7-25). Select one of the preset width-to-height ratios, or select NORMAL to simply click and drag over your image to select the cropping you wish. If you select one of the width-to-height proportional presets, you'll note that you will be restricted to only that width/height ratio when you click and drag over your image.

Where to crop your image is an important aesthetic decision. This is the time to slow down, carefully look at your entire photograph, and decide where the points of visual interest are. If something within your photograph detracts from your visual story, crop it out. Bring your viewers' eyes to the essence of your image and crop everything else.

The photograph in Figure 7-26 was made in a food manufacturing plant. Light was reflecting from the large oven's metallic surface, creating an interesting abstract design. The oven was powered off at the time, but the color temperature of the light very conveniently created a fiery-appearing environment.

This is the JPEG-captured file as the camera originally captured the image. Some parts of this image are more visually interesting than others. Several cropping

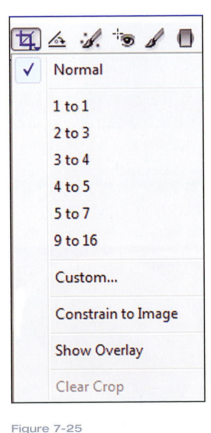

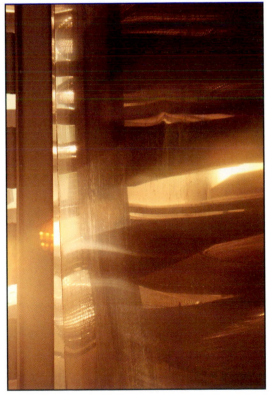

Figure 7-24

CLICK AND DRAG the Straighten tool along a vertical or horizontal line within the image.

Photo © KS.

Figure 7-25

Width-to-height ratio options for the Cropping tool.

Photo © KS.

Figure 7-26

The photograph as it was made, with no cropping applied.

Photo © KS.

options could be successful with an image like this (Figure 7-27). Using ACR to crop your image, you keep the crop nondestructive and can later reopen the file and crop the original image in a different manner.

To actually crop your image, CLICK AND DRAG the CROP TOOL on your image, then ADJUST THE EDGES of the bounding box until you are satisfied with what you see. Either PRESS the RETURN (ENTER) key or DOUBLE-CLICK INSIDE THE BOUNDING BOX to set the crop.

Removing Chromatic Aberration

Depending on the quality of a camera's lens, a colored border may appear between the bright and dark areas within your photograph. This can happen if your lens doesn't focus the red, green, and blue components to the exact same conversion point, creating fringes of color. It typically occurs along light/dark boundaries or along the edges of your image. The close-up section of Figure 7-28 shows this type of **chromatic aberration**.

 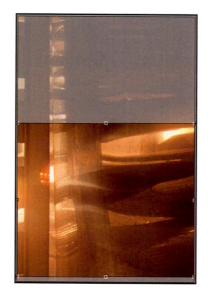 

Figure 7-27

These screen captures show three possible croppings for this photograph. It is possible that none of these cropped images would be an exact ratio that matches one of the cropping tool's presets. It's more important to crop the photograph to the exact dimensions that best tell the visual story rather than to match any preset.

Photo © KS.

Figure 7-28

Notice the colored fringe along the edge of the window frame (expanded area).

Photo © Eddie Tapp (www. eddietapp.com).

Figure 7-29

Click on the Lens Corrections button on the right side of the ACR window.

Photo © Eddie Tapp (www. eddietapp.com).

Figure 7-30

These settings were used to correct the chromatic aberration.

Photo © Eddie Tapp (www. eddietapp.com).

To correct for chromatic aberration, CLICK on the LENS CORRECTIONS button on the right side of the ACR window (Figure 7-29). MOVE the Red/Cyan Fringe and Blue/Yellow Fringe sliders until the chromatic aberration disappears. In the Defringe drop-down menu, you can SELECT None, Highlight Edges, or All Edges for your correction. In this situation, Highlight Edges worked well with the settings shown in Figure 7-30.

Saving and Opening Options

It's time to save the work you have accomplished thus far. There are several options at this stage. The first is to click on Done in the lower right corner of the ACR window (Figure 7-31).

When you click on Done, you are telling ACR that you have completed all adjustments and are ready to view the final results of your work. The file will briefly disappear and then reopen in ACR as the cropped/straightened/adjusted image.

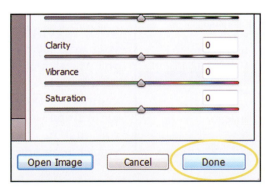

Figure 7-31

The Done button in the bottom right corner of the ACR window.

Photo © KS.

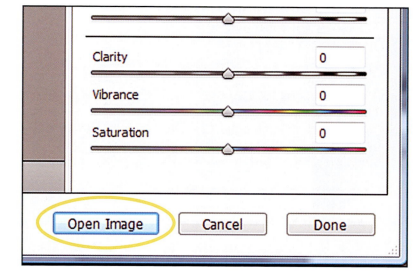

Window	Help
Arrange	▶
Workspace	▶
Extensions	▶
3D	
Actions	
Adjustments	
Animation	
Brush	
Brush Presets	
Channels	
Character	
Clone Source	
Color	
Histogram	
History	
Info	
Layer Comps	
✓ Layers	
Masks	
Measurement Log	
Navigator	
Notes	
Paragraph	

To actually save the file, CLICK on SAVE IMAGE in the left lower corner of the ACR window (Figure 7-32). The Save Image function gives you file format options and allows you to choose a destination folder for your file. If you have cropped your original file, you are also able to preserve the cropped pixels within your new file, just in case you change your mind on the cropping you have completed. In Photoshop, you can later go to IMAGE > REVEAL ALL to see the original uncropped state of your photograph.

Because the author plans to continue working on this file in Photoshop, she selected Photoshop (.psd) as the file format (Figure 7-33). If she later adds layers, the Photoshop format will be ideal as it automatically preserves layers on future saves. The Photoshop format is the only format that will also preserve all of the pixels cropped in ACR.

Other Save format options include creation of file naming conventions that can be applied to several files at a time. The same file naming options are available through Adobe Bridge as well. A separate option to Save Image is the Open Image option in the right lower corner of the ACR window (Figure 7-34). CLICK on OPEN IMAGE to open the file with all its adjustments in Photoshop. If you would rather open the original file without any adjustments, you can hold down the OPTION (ALT) key and CLICK on OPEN IMAGE.

If you hold down the SHIFT KEY and CLICK on OPEN, you will open your file as a Smart Object. This is the most pixel-preserving of all the Open options; Photoshop opens a file comprised of, and still linked to, the original file within the ACR window.

If you can't see your Layers panel in Photoshop, go to WINDOW > LAYERS (Figure 7-35). Although most Open options will result in your Photoshop document in a Background layer, the Open as Smart

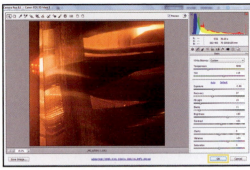

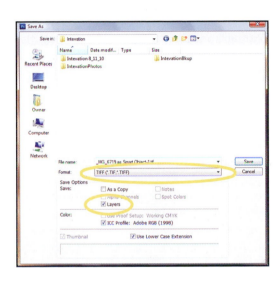

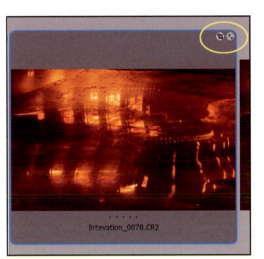

Object (SHIFT-CLICK on OPEN in ACR) option results in a single Smart Object layer (Figure 7-36). If you double-click on the Smart Object layer icon in the Layers palette, you can make new adjustments in the ACR window. After you have completed your adjustments, you will find an OK button in the lower right corner of ACR (in the yellow box in Figure 7-37). Click OK and you will be returned to the newly updated file in Photoshop.

Even though the Smart Object layer is the only current layer in this file, Photoshop treats it differently than a typical Background layer. To prevent any risk of accidentally flattening the file, save it as a Photoshop document as you continue to work in Photoshop. If you choose to save it as a TIFF document, be sure that you preserve the layers in the TIFF options box (Figure 7-38).

The XMP Sidecar

As you'll recall, you have been instructed to open your images through the ACR program because it provides nondestructive editing to preserve the quality of your pixels. As you complete the image-editing process in ACR and save your file, all of the ACR settings and cropping information are saved in an attached XMP (Extensible Metadata Platform) file called an *XMP sidecar*. The XMP information remains available when you reopen your files in Adobe Bridge. The thumbnail images with XMP sidecars have a small icon (Figure 7-39) showing that the images have been edited in ACR.

More in Adobe Camera Raw

We have barely scratched the surface of what the ACR software holds. You have learned enough to get started with files in Photoshop, and the information you learn in Chapter 8 could be completed in either ACR or in Photoshop. For now, you'll learn the basics of Photoshop.

Working in Adobe Photoshop

Before working with a photograph in Photoshop, we'll examine the basics of the software program. This text assumes that you are working in Photoshop CS5, but older versions of Photoshop have many of the same functions as the CS5 version.

It is recommended that you open all photographs in ACR to begin the editing process. However, it is also possible to simply open a file in Photoshop. Changing resolution or cropping are destructive edits in Photoshop and should be judiciously applied. There is no XMP sidecar to get you back to the original file if you change your mind later. A safer method is to open files as a Smart Object.

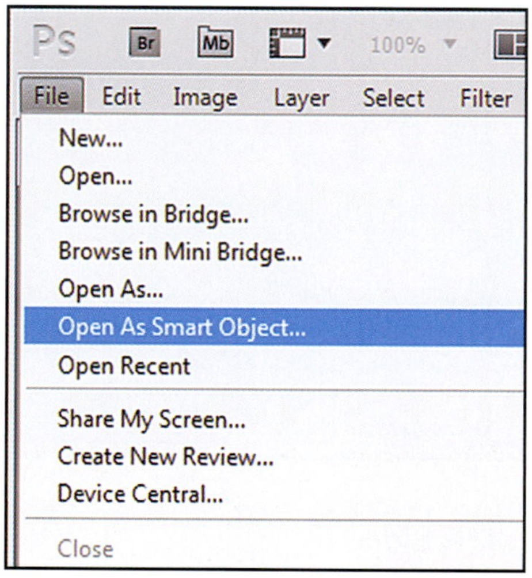

Opening a Photograph

Start up Photoshop. Go to the FILE menu and CLICK on OPEN AS SMART OBJECT... (Figure 7-40). Select a photograph to open.

Now CLICK on the ZOOM TOOL toward the bottom of the right column in the Tools palette (Figure 7-41). Release your finger on the mouse and move your cursor onto the photograph. Now CLICK until you're at the magnification you want, or CLICK AND DRAG over a section of the photograph. You'll zoom directly into that area.

Continue clicking until you've zoomed in as close as you can go. You'll see small squares of color. These squares are the pixels that comprise your photograph (Figure 7-42).

Hold down the OPTION (ALT) key, and you'll see the Zoom tool's plus sign turn into a minus sign. Keep holding the OPTION (ALT) key down as you click your mouse on your canvas. You'll zoom back out of your canvas.

Figure 7-40

Go to File > OPEN AS SMART OBJECT...

Photo © KS.

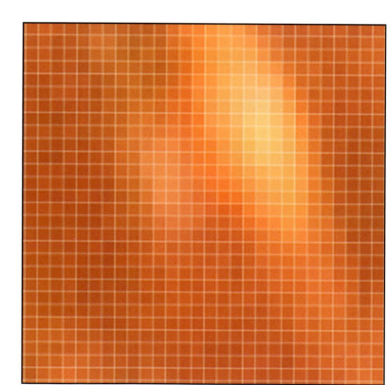

Figure 7-41 (left)

The Zoom tool (circled) in Adobe Photoshop.

Figure 7-42 (right)

A close-up view of the pixels that comprise a photograph. The white grid is new in later versions of Photoshop and exists for close-up viewing purposes only. It is not actually a portion of the file.

Photos 7-41 and 7-42 © KS.

Setting the Resolution

Every image you work on in Photoshop is made up of pixels. The more ppi you have, the greater the resolution of that file. For an image to print well, it needs to be higher resolution. An image going to a high-quality commercial press will require up to 300 ppi. An image being printed on a desktop printer will usually print well at 180–240 ppi, although you may need to do some testing to determine what resolution works best for your printer.

If you didn't set your resolution in ACR, it should be your first step in Photoshop. Go to the IMAGE menu and CLICK on IMAGE SIZE (Figure 7-43). The Pixel Dimensions section at the top of that dialog box tells you how many megabytes of disk (or hard drive) space the file takes up (Figure 7-44). It also gives you the exact number of pixels across the width and height of the file. Web designers most often use this information. The Document Size section is much more helpful to photographers and gives the width, height, and resolution of the file.

You can change the pixel-per-inch resolution at any time. First, UNCHECK (or deselect) the RESAMPLE IMAGE option (Figure 7-45). Now CLICK AND DRAG over the number in the RESOLUTION box. Key in another number. Watch what happens to the width and height numbers as you do this (Figure 7-46).

If you put in a resolution number higher than the original, the width and height will decrease. If you put in a resolution number lower than the original, the width and height will increase. That's because

Figure 7-43

IMAGE > IMAGE SIZE.

Photo © KS.

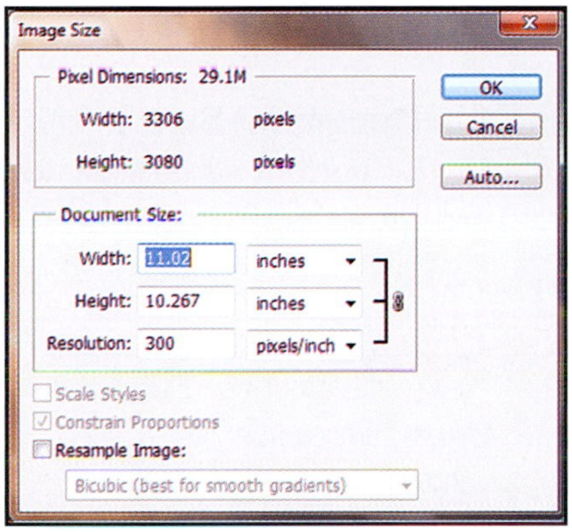

Figure 7-44

Image Size dialog box.

Photo © KS.

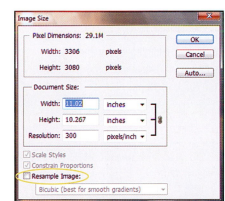

Figure 7-45

Make sure the Resample Image box is unchecked.

Photo © KS.

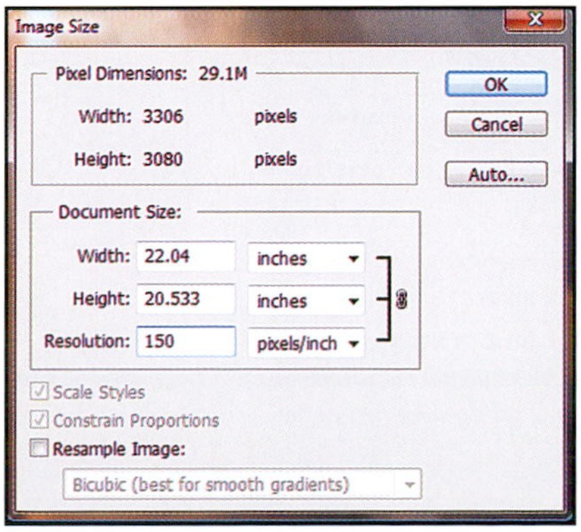

Figure 7-46

CLICK AND DRAG over the Resolution and change it to a different number. Watch what happens to the Document Width and Height.

Photo © KS.

the *number of pixels* isn't changing—all of the pixels are simply changing size. The Document Size tells you how big the image would be if you printed it at the given resolution. As you change the pixel-per-inch resolution, the Document Size tells you the new dimensions of the image.

Think of having a specific number of marbles in a jar. If all of those marbles suddenly shrank, they'd take up much less space in that jar. If the marbles suddenly expanded, they would take up more space in the jar. In Photoshop, the size of your document changes depending on the size of the pixels in your image.

Changing the Document Size

Now CLICK in the bottom square beside RESAMPLE IMAGE to select it, and you will

see a check mark (Figure 7-47). You just changed the rules. The Resample Image function either invents or throws away pixels, which changes the document size. Photoshop best handles this task when set on Bicubic, so make sure the Resample Image option is set to Bicubic. Different Bicubic options such as Bicubic Smoother and Bicubic Sharper are available, depending on whether you are increasing or decreasing your file size.

Photoshop can invent new pixels and still retain good image quality, but only up to a point. Increasing the number of pixels by more than 50% *in addition to* the original pixels can decrease image quality.

To ask Photoshop to invent or throw away pixels, SELECT both CONSTRAIN PROPORTIONS and RESAMPLE IMAGE option boxes. Now CLICK AND DRAG across either the WIDTH OR HEIGHT box and INCREASE OR DECREASE its number (Figure 7-48). The other dimension (height or width) will change automatically—the Constrain Proportions option prevents a squished photograph.

Notice the Pixel Dimensions at the top of the Image Size dialog box (Figure 7-49). The new file size shows up reflecting the change you made. The Pixel Dimensions also shows you how large the file was before you made the changes. This is proof that you're changing the number of pixels in the image. You have

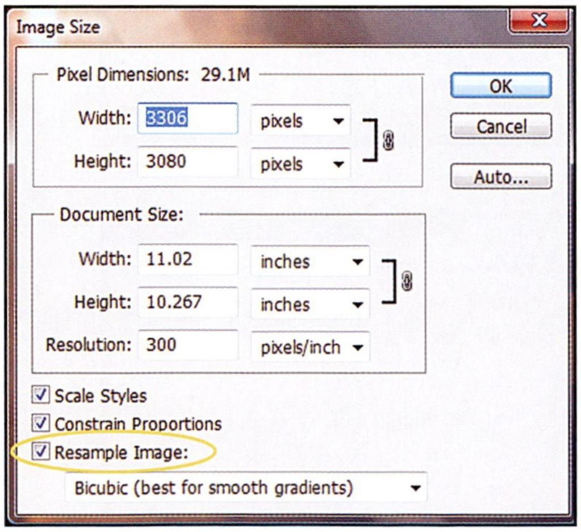

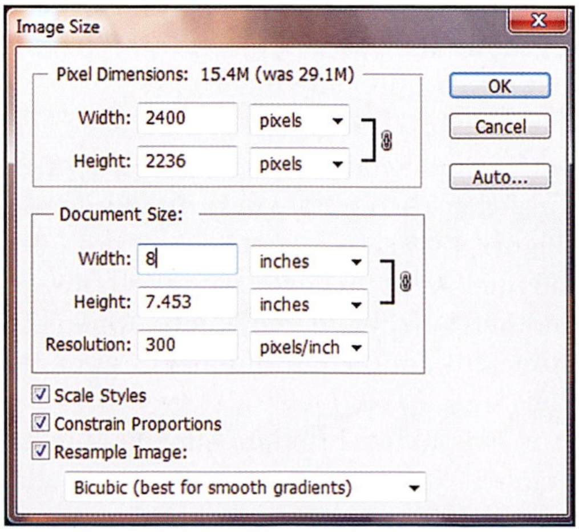

Figure 7-47 (left)

The RESAMPLE IMAGE and the CONSTRAIN PROPORTIONS boxes are now clicked ON.

Figure 7-48 (right)

Changing the Document Width also changes the Document Height and vice versa. The resolution remains the same.

Photos 7-47 and 7-48 © KS.

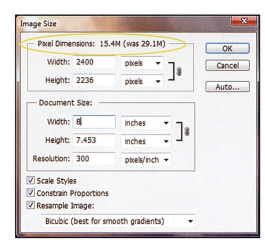

Figure 7-49

The Pixel Dimensions have now changed, as image data have been discarded from the file.

Photo © KS.

either added or discarded image data, depending on whether you increased or decreased one of the Document Width or Height dimensions.

Be careful not to go over the "150 % rule." In the Pixel Dimensions section, the Width and Height numbers are measured in pixels. Change the measurement selection from pixels to percent by HOLDING DOWN the PIXEL box in either the Width or Height box and DRAG UP TO SELECT PERCENT (Figure 7-50). Now, change the number in the box to 150 (Figure 7-51). That means you're going to keep all the original pixels (100%) and add an additional 50% of pixels to equal 150%. Now look at the Document Size. The new width and height values show the largest size this file can be and still stay within the 150% rule. You aren't required to change a file size by 150%—that's just the limit of what you can safely do. Any percentage less than 150% is fine; any percentage greater than that is violating the 150% rule.

There is no limit to the number of pixels you can throw away. However, once the file has been made smaller, you MUST follow the 150% rule if you want to make that small file larger in the future. Therefore, it's always best to permanently save a file at its largest size. Then, if you change the file to a smaller size, rename that file when you save it so you'll still have the large original file in storage.

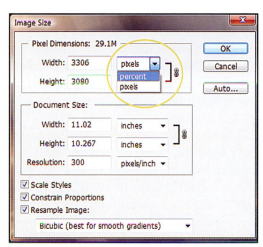

Figure 7-50

Change the Pixel Dimensions measurement to Percent.

Photo © KS.

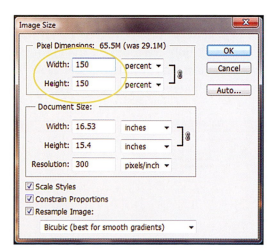

Figure 7-51

Change the width or height value to 150. This is the most you can safely increase the size of your image.

Photo © KS.

Saving Files

If you previously saved your downloaded files in Adobe Bridge, you can go to FILE > SAVE in Photoshop, and the old file will be replaced by the current file. If you wish to rename the file to preserve the original file you were working on, go to the FILE menu and choose the SAVE AS...option. Here, you can name the file and select the destination folder. Select the destination folder, and name your file by DRAGGING YOUR CURSOR over the old file name and typing in a new name. Below the SAVE AS...text field, you'll see FORMAT. If your file has layers (anything other than the Background layer), it is safest to save it in the PHOTOSHOP (.psd) format. If you only have only a Background layer, you can save it in either the TIFF or the Photoshop format (Figure 7-52).

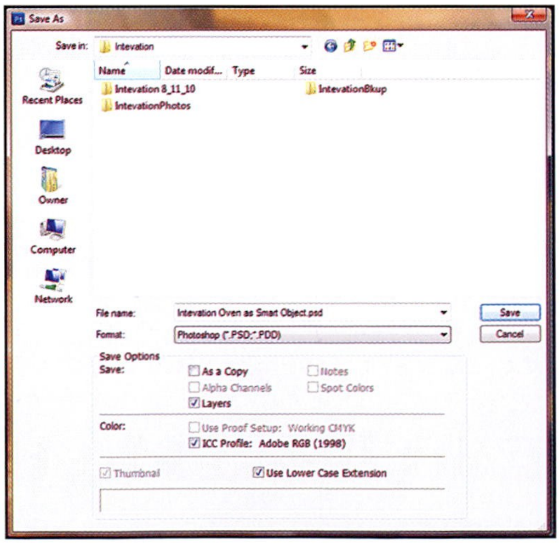

In the SAVE OPTIONS section, you will see several choices. Make sure ALPHA CHANNELS and LAYERS are CHECKED if you have alpha channels and layers in your file. (If you have no alpha channels, the option will be grayed out.) Don't check Annotations or Spot Colors.

In the COLOR section, CLICK on ICC COLOR PROFILE. You will learn more about ICC profiles in Chapter 10. Double-check everything now: Your file name is at the top of the dialog box, you've given the file the name, and you've saved the file as a Photoshop or TIFF format. You've told the computer to save the Alpha Channels and the Layers if your file contains them, and the ICC Color Profile is selected. Now, CLICK on SAVE, and you have saved the file.

Two Choices of Saving Files

From here on, you have two choices of saving files. As you continue to work on your file, you can go back to the FILE menu and choose SAVE. Doing so updates the existing file to show the new changes you have made. If you go to the File menu and the Save option is grayed out, you haven't made any changes to your file since the last time you saved it.

An alternative to this is to go to FILE > SAVE AS...where you have the option of giving this file a NEW NAME. If you give the file a new name, you will end up with two files: the first file you saved *plus* a new file showing the most recent changes you have made.

Whatever saving method you choose, *save your files often.* Computers crash for no apparent reason, and saving your files often decreases the risk of total catastrophe. Professional photographic organizations highly recommended that you routinely back up your saved files to an external hard drive or other memory device. It is far safer to have your file on two computers than just on one. The safest method of all is to keep one copy of your important files in a separate building from the one where you typically work. If there is a house fire and you lose your home computer, duplicate files stored at your office will be extremely valuable to you.

Figure 7-52

The Photoshop SAVE As...window.

Photo © KS.

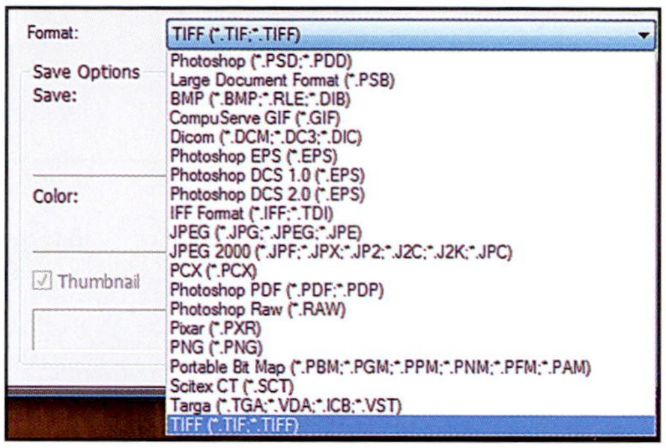

Figure 7-53

File format options in Photoshop.

Photo © KS.

File Formats

Photoshop is capable of saving many different kinds of files (Figure 7-53). Each file format serves a different purpose. For the purposes of this text, there are three formats important for you to understand.

TIFF stands for "tagged information file format." TIFF (.tif) files are relatively universal in that many software programs can open them. Although TIFF files can save layers, it's preferable to save files with layers in the Photoshop (.psd) format.

The **Photoshop** (.psd) format is used whenever you are working with layers in Photoshop. This file format can only be guaranteed to open in Photoshop (all versions) and the Adobe InDesign (CS4 and up) page layout program, but it safely maintains all of the layering you create during your digital darkroom work.

Almost all digital cameras save files in **JPEG** (.jpg) format. These images are compressed into smaller file sizes than Photoshop or TIFF file formats. This compression works fine in digital cameras, but you don't want to repeatedly save your files in JPEG format. Once the JPEG files are on your computer, save them as TIFF or Photoshop images.

The JPEG format is a **lossy compression** format. As you repeatedly change and then save a JPEG file, you'll slowly lose some of the color information in the file. Opening and closing a JPEG file alone won't damage it—it's the repeated opening, changing, and saving of the file that ultimately damages it. Remember to save your JPEG files as TIFF or Photoshop files as soon as possible when you download them. This can be automatically accomplished when downloading and renaming your digital images in Adobe Bridge.

Summary

Using Adobe Bridge's downloading and renaming features is the most efficient way of transferring your digital images from your camera. Bridge also gives you backup capabilities as the files are being downloaded, and its organizational features will help you keep track of your files.

The new digital workflow includes opening all photographs in Adobe Camera Raw because of its nondestructive image-editing capabilities. Pixels and resolution are the raw ingredients of your images. The more pixels you have, the bigger an image you can create. Pixel preservation is of utmost importance in the digital workflow.

Take the time to read through your digital camera's manual. Look for any reference to image size, image quality, or file size. Set your camera to the highest image quality you can obtain. Resolution features in Adobe Photoshop allow for resizing of photographs.

Save your files often, and save them in more than one place.

The following Table 7-1 is a synopsis of the tasks and techniques covered in this chapter. Refer to the page listed in this table to refresh your memory on exact procedures.

Table 7-1

Synopsis of Tasks and Techniques in Chapter 7

© Cengage Learning 2012

Digital Darkroom Tasks	First Solution	Alternate Solutions	Page Reference
Open File in ACR.	In Adobe Bridge: Ctrl-click (Right-click) image and Open in Camera Raw	In Photoshop: File > Open as Smart Object.	187
Select Color Balance.	Raw file: Select the color balance in ACR (several options). Use Temperature and Tint sliders as needed.	JPEG or TIFF file: Select the color balance in ACR (fewer options). Use Temperature and Tint sliders as needed.	188
Change the exposure.	Either raw or JPEG files: Use Exposure, Recovery, Fill Lights, Blacks, Brightness, and Contrast sliders. Carefully watch your histogram to prevent clipping.	JPEG files have the same options, but you won't have the same flexibility with exposure.	189
Remove chromatic aberration.	In ACR: Use Lens Correction and Chromatic Aberration sliders.		194
Straighten or Crop an image.	In ACR: Use the Crop and Straighten tools.		192
Set the file resolution.	Select the resolution in the ACR Workflow Options dialog box.	Go to Image > Image size in Photoshop to set the resolution.	191
Set the bit depth.	Select the bit depth in the ACR Workflow Options dialog box.		191
Open the file in Photoshop.	Shift-click the Open button in ACR to open the file as a Smart Object in Photoshop.	Click the Open button in ACR to open the file in Photoshop.	198
Save your file in Photoshop.	File > Save or File Save as (Photoshop)		202

EXERCISES

1. Consult your camera's manual to learn how to set the image quality settings. Set your camera to the highest quality settings possible.

2. Use Adobe Camera Raw to develop five distinctly different images from one of your digital photographs. Use the White Balance and Exposure functions to make changes that result in a variety of images.

3. Color balance can be an aesthetic consideration. Some of the oldest color photographs have a peculiar color balance that says "vintage" to many viewers. Go to the Prints & Photographs Online Catalog for the Farm Security Administration/Office of War Information Color Photographs: http://www.loc.gov/pictures/search/?st=grid&c=100&co=fsac and look at the color balance of the vintage photographs. Study the economic and social status of the era during which the FSA was involved with photographing the American condition. Make at least three new photographs in the genre of these photos, including subject matter, composition, and color balance. Work within Adobe Camera Raw to obtain the color balance you see in these images.

4. Study Norman Rockwell's illustrations at: http://www.americanillustration.org/artists/rockwell/rockwell.html and compare his illustrations and color balance to those in the Prints & Photographs Online Catalog. Become aware of how the color balance of many of Rockwell's paintings was similar to those of early color photography.

5. In the By the Decade section (Appendix A), read the 1931–1940 through 1941–1950 sections to better understand the time in which the Farm Security Administration photographs were made.

FURTHER READING

- DAYLEY, Lisa DaNae and Brad Dayley. *Photoshop CS5 Bible.* Hoboken, NJ. Wiley, 2010.

- EVENING, Martin. *Adobe Photoshop CS5 for Photographers: A Professional Image Editor's Guide to the Creative Use of Photoshop for the Macintosh and PC.* Oxford, U.K: Elsevier, Ltd., 2010.

- SCHEWE, Jeff, and Bruce Frasier. *Real World Camera Raw with Adobe Photoshop CS5.* Berkeley, CA: Peachpit Press, 2010.

Magic.

Photo © Elizabeth Brooke.

CHAPTER

8

Image Development in Photoshop

- Develop an aesthetic awareness of values in an image.

- Use Photoshop's Merge to HDR function to maximize dynamic range.

- Use a variety of Photoshop tools to make selections.

- Use adjustment layers to fine-tune the values and colors within an image.

- Use pixel layers derived from Background or other layers for additional changes.

Every photography student needs to challenge the assumption that the photograph your camera delivers is the final photograph. Nothing could be further from the truth! This chapter introduces concepts and methods that will further develop an image toward your intention and also gives you the Photoshop skills you will need to accomplish this goal. This chapter will be written in the first person, as it will be helpful to observe the thought processes of a photographer (the author) when describing, evaluating, and working on a single image.

The Merge to HDR function within Photoshop (used in this chapter) is definitely not necessary all the time, but the particular scene I selected was in need of special treatment. Be assured that the vast majority of images you make don't need to be started in any way other than FILE > OPEN IN ADOBE CAMERA RAW.

Evaluating a Scene

The digital darkroom phase of photography actually begins before you make a photograph. As you view a scene you're going to photograph, pay attention to what's most important in that scene. Which areas can be in or out of focus? How bright do you want the highlights to be? Do you want visual detail within the highlights and/or shadows? Within the range of values in your scene, would you like the portions of the scene currently of midtone value to be represented darker or lighter in your final image? All of these questions give you an idea of how to select an exposure for that scene. It also alerts you to changes you might want to make to the resulting image in the digital darkroom.

It might be helpful to think of different values according to the Zone System. You will recall that Zone III is the darkest zone that includes visible detail, whereas Zone VIII is the lightest zone that includes visible detail, and Zone V is considered middle gray. Do your best to examine your scene and decide how bright or dark you want each area

within that scene to be. Capture the best visual information you can in your exposure, being particularly careful to use an exposure that captures detail where you want it.

The goal of any exposure is to give you the raw ingredients (detail and pixels) to create the image you want. However, there are times when the dynamic range of your scene far exceeds that of your camera. This happens frequently in sunlit scenes where highlights are very bright and shadows are very dark. You may need a darker-than-desired exposure to capture highlight detail, forcing your shadow areas into too low a zone. You might need a lighter-than-desired exposure to capture shadow detail, forcing your highlight areas into too high a zone.

Taking multiple photographs at different exposures is a viable option in the digital darkroom. Photoshop can take a series of photographs and combine them, using the best of each exposure, to come up with a single exposure containing detail throughout the entire image. This process is called Merge to HDR (High Dynamic Range).

Aesthetic and Compositional Assessment of Your Photograph

When you view your photograph in Photoshop, take the viewer's perspective and think about what he/she will notice in the image. What stands out to you? What were you hoping would stand out? If you lightened or darkened specific areas within the photograph, would you enrich the viewer's experience? Would those changes help the image match what you remembered about that scene?

Compare the values of your image to the values you observed in the actual scene. Are there areas you wished could be lighter or darker? Look at the regions that fall into the midtone range. Are they as light or as dark as you wish? Is there adequate visual distinction between different regions? Would some change enhance the distinction between those regions?

By way of example, the photographs you see in Figure 8-1 will evolve according to my thought process. You may or may not agree with my aesthetic decisions, and that's fine. Hopefully, the information presented here will spark ideas for your own photographs. Throughout the chapter, I will be using and explaining a variety of valuable Photoshop tools. You will learn how to use several features in this chapter and more in Chapter 9.

When I was invited to photograph the interior of a new potato manufacturing plant, I came across the scene shown in Figures 8-1. I was struck by the metal's luminosity. It felt very three-dimensional, with power and strength throughout. Everything was so crisp and clean that the geometry of the individual elements really stood out. The entire scene was monochromatic in color, reflecting the hues of the overhead lights.

I took note that the top surface of the wheel (in the center of the photo) was at least 1 stop brighter than that of the table on which it sat. I knew I wanted to have

detail within the wheel's surface, so I didn't want it to be any brighter than Zone VIII.

The chain apparatus was a high contrast area as well. The top of the chain was about ½ stop darker than the top surface of the wheel, and I still wanted it to have a sense of luminosity. To differentiate between the wheel and the top of the chain, I thought about placing that portion of the image at Zone VI–VII. Because I wanted a distinct difference between the chain top and sides, I made a note to create the chain sides approximately 3 stops darker in value. That meant that the chain sides would be considerably darker than they were in reality. As an artist, I allowed myself to make that decision.

The side wall and base of the stand were around 8 stops darker than the top surface of the wheel. If I placed the top of the wheel at Zone VIII, the side wall would be Zone 0 and would be completely black with no detail. It was at this point that I knew I needed to make multiple exposures to combine for a final image.

The Initial Exposures and Merge to HDR

The dynamic range of my camera's sensor is good, but it was no match for the range between highlights and shadows in this scene. I proceeded to make a series of four photographs using a tripod and a **cable release**, a cord extending from the camera that trips the shutter without your needing to touch the camera. I made a series of four different exposures, 1 full stop brighter than the next, starting with a short enough shutter speed to maintain detail within the brightest portion of the scene. The second photo used a shutter speed 1 stop longer than the first. The third photo used a shutter speed 1 stop longer than the second photo, etc.

Because I wanted great depth of field, I set the aperture to f/32 for all four exposures and set the camera to Aperture Priority because I didn't want the depth of field to change between all four photographs.

The ISO remained at 400 for all four photos. I chose an ISO of 400 because I wanted fine-grain images, but I didn't want such long shutter speeds that the exposure time itself introduced digital noise.

I downloaded my photos using Adobe Bridge and then went into Photoshop. In Photoshop, I went to FILE > AUTOMATE > MERGE TO HDR PRO ... and selected the four JPEG photographs you saw in Figure 8-1

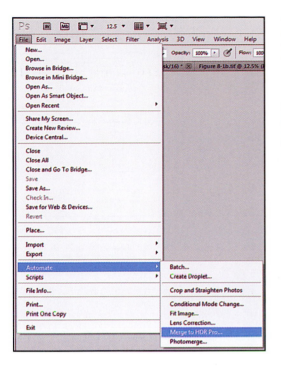

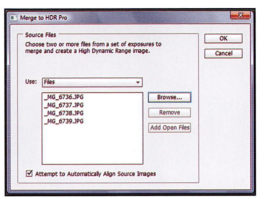

Figure 8-2 (left)

Photoshop's Merge to HDR function makes use of the dynamic ranges of multiple identical scenes photographed with different exposures. It was important not to vary the aperture during the exposures as it could have affected the depth of field.

Figure 8-3 (right)

The four JPEGS were selected for the merge. Because even a tripod may not be perfect with this job, the Attempt to Automatically Align Source Images was checked.

Photos 8-2 and 8-3 © KS.

(Figures 8-2 and 8-3). Photoshop's Merge to HDR Pro function combines the four images, according to the Camera EXIF exposure metadata of each photograph, and then gives options for how highlights, midtones, and shadows should be applied to the final merged photograph. The goal of using Merge to HDR Pro is to compress all of the tonal information from the original multiple photographs into a single, lower dynamic range version of the scene.

After calculating for a minute or two, Photoshop presented me with the photograph and options shown in Figure 8-4. It seemed quite flat without much highlight or shadow differentiation, so I started working with the options on the right.

Merge to HDR Pro Options

These options are available in Photoshop CS5. If you have a previous version of Photoshop, you may have different available options.

I kept the Mode set at 16-bit to take advantage of the much greater number of tonal values in 16-bit versus 8-bit files. I also kept the Local Adaptation set of options, which allowed me to make changes according to my own perception of the image.

The Edge Glow options work together as an overall contrast control. A low radius setting makes the image seem rather flat. A higher radius level increases the overall contrast. The Strength slider adjusts the strength of the effect. I used the Zoom function in the left lower corner to zoom in to 100% magnification before making any adjustments (circled in yellow in Figure 8-5). As I adjusted the Edge Glow radius and strength sliders, I was careful not to allow halos to form around the edges of high-contrast areas. By HOLDING DOWN the SPACEBAR, my cursor turned into the Hand tool, allowing me to CLICK AND DRAG around the image to look for problem areas. My major concern was to not allow a halo to develop around the bright rectangular tooth in the middle of the image (circled in cyan in Figure 8-5).

The Tone and Detail controls include Gamma, Exposure, Detail, Shadow, and Highlight. The default Gamma setting is approximately halfway between showing no contrast between highlights and shadows and showing full contrast between highlights and shadows. Pushing the Gamma to the left includes more contrast, whereas pushing it to the right includes less contrast derived from the original multiple images.

After making the adjustment to the Gamma slider, I adjusted the overall brightness of the image by moving the Exposure slider. This slider is highly sensitive, so it was important to watch the highlights and shadows in the image as I made the adjustment. My goal was to place the highlights and shadows at the exact

The combined photographs had much less contrast than desired and seemed rather flat.

Photo © KS.

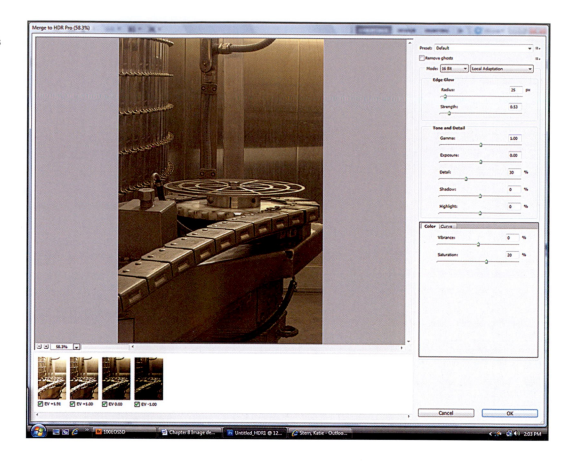

The small, bright rectangular tooth in the middle region of the photograph was a concern. If I moved the Edge Glow radius and strength sliders too high, a halo developed around that tooth. I had to be satisfied with a slightly lower setting to preserve the sense of luminosity of that tooth without creating a halo.

Photo © KS.

tonal values I wanted them, given that this slider affects both at the same time. Later I would work with the shadows independently of the highlights.

The Detail slider allowed me to adjust the contrast within the midtones of the image, much like the Clarity slider works in Adobe Camera Raw. Even moving the Detail slider a little bit dramatically increased the sense of dimension within this particular photograph. I loved the effect but noticed that the bright tooth in the center of the photo started producing a halo around it again. I backed off on the Detail slider enough to eliminate the halo, knowing I could make local adjustments to the contrast within the image later.

The Shadow and Highlight sliders fine-tune the shadows independently of the highlights, and vice versa. When using these sliders, I kept my eye on the darkest shadow areas and the brightest highlight areas to make sure image detail was maintained at the values I wanted them.

Under the Color section, I chose to severely decrease the saturation. I didn't want to go totally gray, as I planned on increasing some of the contrast within the image by keeping some sections a bit yellow (warm) and introducing a small amount of blue (cool) to other sections. This would hopefully be a near-subliminal difference that would generate a sense of depth within the image. I brought the Saturation down to −65% and left the Vibrance at 0%.

The Toning Curve (the Curve tab beside the Color tab) allows you to make final adjustments to the overall contrast within the image. A toning curve is incredibly powerful, and I chose to leave this one alone in favor of using the same Curves function in a different way within Photoshop. You'll learn more about Curves soon.

Figure 8-6 shows the final settings before I clicked OK. Then, I rather impatiently waited for Photoshop to make all of the adjustments I had requested and to open the file.

Figure 8-6

The final HDR image settings before I clicked OK.

Photo © KS.

Selections and Adjustment Layers

When the file arrived in Photoshop, my first task was to save it. HDR files automatically come into Photoshop as 16-bit images, which is excellent given the fact that I planned on making more adjustments. You will notice upon saving such a file that your file format options are somewhat limited. Photoshop (.psd) format was ideal because it allowed me to add and save layers as I went along.

My global decisions were complete. My next task was to change localized regions of the photograph in hopes of bringing out the machinery's nuances. Recalling what I visualized when making the photographs, I wanted to create a little more contrast between the wheel/chain region and the background region. One way to do this would have been to simply darken the back wall, but it held highlight and shadow values that gave a sense of metal to its texture. I chose instead to add a bit of blue (the color opposite of yellow) to the background so it would contrast slightly with the slight warm tone of the rest of the image. Because this photograph is in the RGB color mode, it was easy to add another color.

Making the Selection

Photoshop allows you to select any region of a photograph and do something to it. Several tools specialize in making selections, including the Marquis, Lasso, Quick Selection, and Magic Wand tools. The Quick Selection and Magic Wand tools are nested together within the Tools panel, so you see only one or the other at a time. If you hold your mouse down on the tool, you can then select whichever tool you need from the fly-out menu (Figure 8-7).

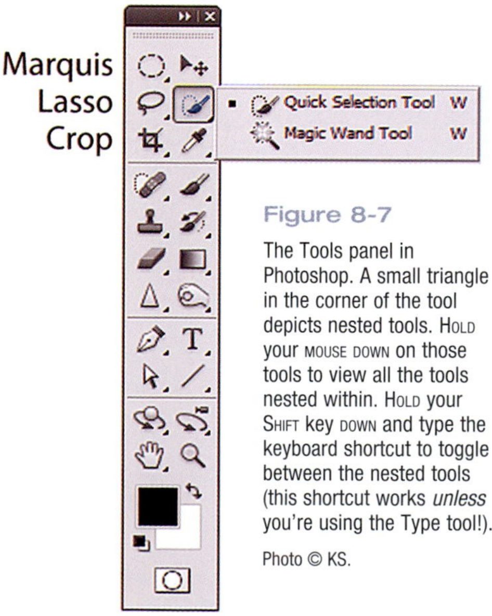

Marquis
Lasso
Crop

Quick Selection Tool W
Magic Wand Tool W

Figure 8-7

The Tools panel in Photoshop. A small triangle in the corner of the tool depicts nested tools. HOLD your MOUSE DOWN on those tools to view all the tools nested within. HOLD your SHIFT key DOWN and type the keyboard shortcut to toggle between the nested tools (this shortcut works *unless* you're using the Type tool!).

Photo © KS.

When you rest your cursor over any tool, its name and keyboard shortcut will appear. Knowing the keyboard shortcuts is a major time-saver when using Photoshop. Instead of moving your mouse to the Tools panel to select a new tool, simply type the shortcut key on your keyboard and the tool will be selected. If nested tools have the same keyboard shortcut, HOLD your SHIFT key DOWN and type the keyboard shortcut repeatedly to toggle through the nested tools.

The Marquee and Lasso Tools

The Marquee tool selects specific areas in either rectangular or elliptical shapes. With either the Rectangular or Elliptical Marquee tool selected, first SELECT the tool in the Tool panel by CLICKING on the TOOL and then LETTING GO with your MOUSE. Bring your cursor into the photograph and CLICK AND DRAG over an area within the photograph. When you release the mouse, you will see a selected area outlined in moving dotted lines (called "marching ants" by many Photoshop users). Whatever task you apply next to this photograph will only alter the region of the photograph within that selected area. The rest of the photograph won't change.

Every selection tool within Photoshop creates selected areas but does it in different fashions. The Lasso tool is a free-form click-and-drag tool that allows you to select whatever shape you need. Nested with the Lasso tool is the Polygonal Lasso tool that creates straight lines between anchor points. If you need to select an area bordered by straight lines, use the Polygonal Lasso tool. CLICK ONCE on EACH CORNER of the area, being sure to CLICK BACK on the BEGINNING POINT to complete your selection.

Although very helpful at times, the Polygonal Lasso tool can be frustrating. I've had more students make emergency phone calls as a result of problems with the Polygonal Lasso tool than with any other aspect of Photoshop. If for any reason your Polygonal Lasso tool gets out of control and flies off the page, simply DOUBLE-CLICK wherever you are, and the tool will automatically close the selection loop and give you a working selection.

If you aren't satisfied with a selection, you can deselect that area by going to the SELECT menu at the top of the Photoshop window and come down to DESELECT. CMND (CTRL)-D is the keyboard shortcut, and it's one you should quickly memorize.

If my initial selection isn't quite right, I can *add* to my selection by HOLDING DOWN the SHIFT key and CLICKING AND DRAGGING outside my originally selected area. I can *subtract* from my selection by HOLDING DOWN the OPTION (ALT) key and CLICKING AND DRAGGING across my originally selected area. If I'm using the Lasso tool to do this, I need to create a rather complete drag that starts and ends near the same point. Drawing a single line with starting and ending points distant from each other doesn't work with the Lasso tool.

Because I want to select the back wall of this room, the Rectangular Marquee and Lasso tools could both be helpful to me. I started with the Rectangular Marquee tool (Figure 8-8). As soon as I zoomed in to make an accurate selection, I noticed some smudging along the back wall. If this were photojournalism, I may have needed to keep the smudges. Because this was to be a fine art project, I could decide whether or not to keep them. I chose to keep them for the time being because they added to the metal's texture.

Once I had my initial selection, I held my SHIFT key DOWN to add to my selection and continued to CLICK AND DRAG. When the Rectangular Marquee tool ceased to be helpful, I switched to the LASSO tool to continue adding to my selection. Switching between different selection tools is perfectly acceptable. Figure 8-9 shows the Lasso tool adding to the selection I made with the Rectangular Marquee tool (note the plus sign on the Lasso tool's icon in the photo, designating that my Shift key was held down). By the time I had completed using these tools, I had the selection shown in Figure 8-10.

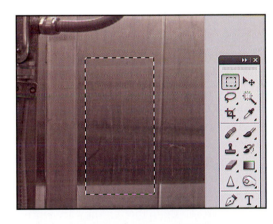

Figure 8-8

Results of my first click and drag with the Rectangular Marquee tool.

Photo © KS.

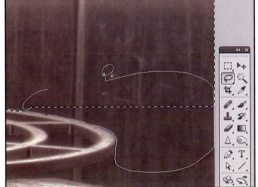

Figure 8-9

Adding to my selection with the LASSO tool, holding the SHIFT key to add to my selection and holding the OPTION (ALT) key to subtract from my selection as needed.

Photo © KS.

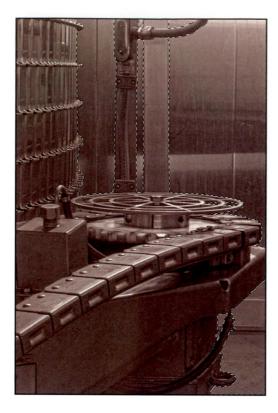

Alpha Channels

Partway through the selection process, I was getting tired and feared losing all of my selection work. I decided to create an **alpha channel** to save this selection. An alpha channel resides in the Channels palette, underneath the individual color channels. It is essentially a map of the pixels selected when using selection tools. The shape and position of that selection is recorded in the alpha channel. Even though they are stored with the color channels, alpha channels' characteristics are entirely different.

It can take a long time to create an accurate selection, so it's helpful to save that selected shape and position along the way in case you get interrupted. Once you have made a selection, CLICK on the SAVE SELECTION AS CHANNEL button at the bottom of the Channels palette (circled in yellow in Figure 8-11). By default, the name of the channel is Alpha 1. To change its name, DOUBLE-CLICK on the CHANNEL'S NAME and type in a new name. Click anywhere else to finalize the name change.

Using Alpha Channels

Alpha channels are extremely helpful in a variety of ways. Most importantly, they give you access to a previous selection. HOLD the CMND (CTRL) key DOWN and CLICK on the NAME of the alpha channel (not the icon). The selection will reappear in your photograph.

Another way of making an alpha channel from a selection is to go to SELECT > SAVE SELECTION (Figure 8-12). This is exactly the same as clicking the Save selection within the Channels panel. The next dialog box (Figure 8-13) allows you to name and save the channel as a new channel.

If you accumulate several alpha channels, the SELECT > SAVE SELECTION menu will allow you to add to or subtract from existing channels. This can save enormous amounts of time when creating multiple selections within an image.

Sharing and Reusing Alpha Channels

Alpha channels can also be moved from one image to another. CLICK AND DRAG the NAME OF THE ALPHA CHANNEL from the Channels panel into a different photograph. When you release your mouse, the alpha channel will appear in that file's Channels panel.

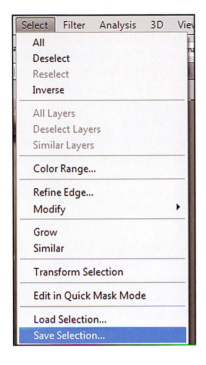

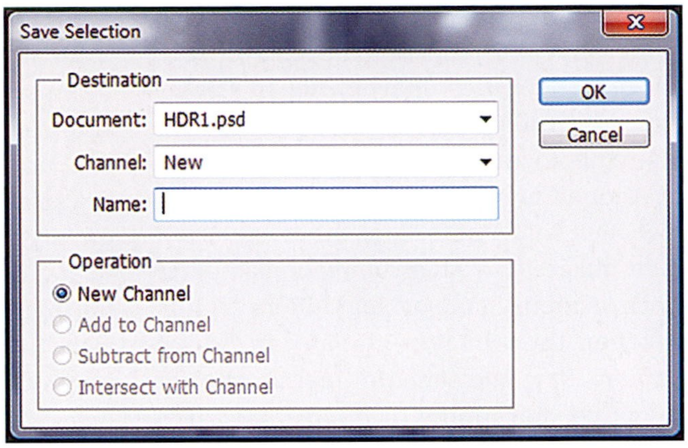

Figure 8-12 (left)

SELECT > SAVE SELECTION.

Figure 8-13 (right)

NAME your new alpha
channel and SAVE it as
a new channel.

Photos 8-12 and 8-13 © KS.

This practice allows for all kinds of creativity. You can select the shape of an object in one photograph, create an alpha channel, and move the alpha channel to another file. In the new file's Channels panel, create a selection from the alpha channel and use it to make changes within the new image.

You can even make an alpha channel from an entire photograph. Select an entire photograph with the Rectangular Marquee tool. Then create a new alpha channel from that selection. This is a grayscale alpha channel that can be used in multitudes of creative ways.

Fine-Tuning Edges

Back to my machinery image. Once the overall selection was made, I zoomed in to 100% magnification and went around every edge, adding or subtracting from my selection all the while. Making a good, worthwhile selection is time-consuming, but this work separates a good Photoshop user from lesser knowledgeable users. My work is only as good as my selections.

To quickly zoom in to 100% magnification, DOUBLE-CLICK on the Zoom tool (looks like a magnifying glass) in the Tools panel.

Alternately, you can type 100% in the Magnification box in the left lower corner of the Photoshop window. Critical Photoshop work is always done at 100% magnification.

Each time I made significant progress, I created a new alpha channel and threw away the old one by CLICKING AND DRAGGING it down to the tiny TRASH CAN in the lower right corner of the Channels panel. Then I saved my file (FILE > SAVE). Saving my file as a Photoshop (.psd) document automatically saved the alpha channel.

Evaluating Edges

When I looked closely at the edges within my image, I noticed they were very slightly blurry despite my use of an f/32 aperture. I have several options here, including using one of Photoshop's Sharpen or Unsharp Mask filters to sharpen the image before finalizing any selection. For the purposes of this demonstration, I will move forward and show you how to use the Refine Edge tool to accommodate for soft edges.

> **NOTE**
>
> To quickly get back out of a zoomed-in magnification, DOUBLE-CLICK the HAND tool in the Tools panel to fit the entire image within the window. Alternately, CMND (CTRL)-0 (zero) also zooms the image out until it fits in the window.

The truth is, all digital photographs need some sharpening. The camera's micro-processor applies sharpening to JPEG-captured files during the JPEG capture. Many photographers sharpen their images in Adobe Camera Raw before ever bringing them into Photoshop. Others sharpen their images only after completing all other work on them. Some photographers slightly sharpen their images globally in Adobe Camera Raw and then do final touches of selective sharpening in Photoshop when they have completed all other adjustments. You will learn more about how to sharpen images in Chapter 9. In the meantime, the soft edges within this photograph are perfect for the training you are receiving here.

Because the Marquis and Lasso tools create hard-edged selections, any color or tonal adjustment I make to this selected area of the photo couldn't exactly match the image itself, creating an unnatural appearance to the adjustment. I needed to adjust the edges of the selection so they matched the visual softness of my photograph's edges.

Refining Edges

With my selection in place and active, I went to SELECT > REFINE EDGE ... in Photoshop (Figure 8-14). Photoshop's Refine Edge function allows me to adjust the edge of my selection so it better matches the edge quality in my photograph. I chose to zoom in at 100% magnification to the small hooks on the left side of the image. Any critical work like this should only be done at 100% magnification. Under EDGE DETECTION, I CLICKED OFF SMART RADIUS and INCREASED THE RADIUS of the selection edge so the selection would be more gradual along its borders. It takes a while for Photoshop to process a selection edge, so patience was in order until I could see the preview of the change I had made.

As you can see in Figure 8-15, a RADIUS of 15 pixels was too much. I backed off until I saw the same gradual shift that I had seen in the actual image. In this case, the resulting RADIUS setting was 3 pixels (Figure 8-16). Given that the resolution of this file was 300 ppi, 3 pixels measured only 1/100th of an inch. That wasn't much, but it was enough to make a difference in the quality of this selection.

Under the ADJUST EDGE section of the REFINE EDGE panel, I chose to FEATHER the selection. The FEATHER slider softens the edges of the selection, slightly blurring the edges. A 2-pixel feather seemed about right.

Figure 8-14 (left)
SELECT > REFINE EDGE.

Figure 8-15 (right)
REFINE EDGE with a RADIUS setting of 15 pixels was too much.

Photos 8-14 and 8-15 © KS.

Select	Filter	Analysis	3D	V

All
Deselect
Reselect
Inverse

All Layers
Deselect Layers
Similar Layers

Color Range...

Refine Edge...
Modify ▶

Grow
Similar

Transform Selection

Edit in Quick Mask Mode

Load Selection...
Save Selection...

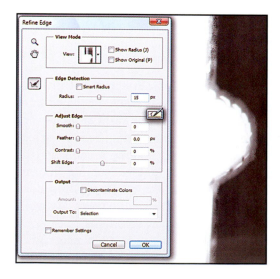

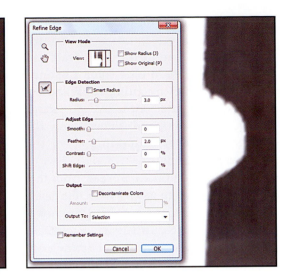

> **NOTE**
>
> SMART RADIUS is an option that frequently improves a masked edge, especially when trying to select a person's hair from a background. Use a rather high RADIUS adjustment and CLICK the SMART RADIUS option to help make those challenging separations.

Any adjustment I would make to this portion of the image would now gradually come into play.

In this photograph, I am creating a selection to which I will make a simple change in color or value. However, this is also how I would create a selection of pixels from one image to move into another photograph. When doing photomontage work (combining different portions of photographs together), the color of selection edges can bleed over into the new photograph. If you are planning to move a selection of pixels into a new photograph, CLICK on the DECONTAMINATE COLORS option in the REFINE EDGE OUTPUT section. Then use the AMOUNT slider just enough to remove any color along the edges. This avoids giving away the fact that these pixels came from a different photograph.

In the OUTPUT to section of the REFINE EDGE dialog box, I chose SELECTION (the default option) and CLICKED OK (Figure 8-17). The changes I made in REFINE EDGE became a part of my selection. That meant my alpha channel was no longer accurate. I threw the alpha channel in the trash can at the bottom of the Channels panel and created a new alpha channel. Then I saved the file.

> **NOTE**
>
> I could have used the SMOOTH slider, but that slider doesn't round off corners. Because there weren't any perfectly sharp corners in my image at 100% magnification, the SMOOTH slider wouldn't have been quite as effective. The CONTRAST slider makes soft edges of a selection more crisp, exactly the opposite of what I needed.

Adjustment Layers

It took over an hour to create that selection to my satisfaction. After saving the alpha channel and saving the file, I could finally make my first local adjustment. Local adjustments are changes you make to certain parts of an image, not the entire image. Best practices in Photoshop dictate that I not make any permanent changes to the pixels in this file until I have finished all editing. Pixel preservation still rules.

Photoshop's answer to pixel preservation is adjustment layers. In this case, I wanted to change the hue of the back wall and floor to a very slight blue color. I opened my Layers panel by going to WINDOW > LAYERS (F7 is the keyboard shortcut). The initial Layers panel showed only the Background layer containing all of the photograph's pixels.

Because I had taken a break from this project, I needed to get my selection back. I opened my Channels panel (WINDOW > CHANNELS) and CMND (CTRL)-CLICKED in the name box for my alpha channel. My selection showed up again.

Photoshop has a variety of **adjustment layers** that allow you to make nondestructive editing decisions for all or parts of your image. Adjustment layers essentially create suggestions of what your image might look like if you were to flatten the layers. However, the pixels on the Background layer do not change color or tonal value until you actually flatten the layers. You can DOUBLE-CLICK on the ICON of an ADJUSTMENT LAYER at any time and change the adjustment levels to your satisfaction. Besides being good for pixel preservation, this ability to change the amount or type of adjustment at any time is very reassuring, as you can make initial changes and tweak them later.

Types of Adjustment Layers

Several types of adjustment layers are available in Photoshop. I started with the Color Balance adjustment layer for this project and later used the Levels and Curves adjustment layers. It is worth noting that many of these adjustments are also available in Adobe Camera Raw and can be applied globally or locally to a photograph before ever opening the photo in Photoshop.

To see the types of adjustment layers available, CLICK on the HALF-BLACK, HALF-WHITE CIRCULAR icon at the bottom of the Layers panel (Figure 8-18).

The top three adjustment varieties (Solid color, Gradient, and Pattern) are often used in graphic illustrations and won't be discussed here. The next four (Brightness, Levels, Curves, and Exposure) change the values of brightness of your photograph, but they can also be applied to individual color channels to alter the color balance of sections of your image.

The next six options (Vibrance, Hue/Saturation, Color Balance, Black & White, Photo Filter, and Channel Mixer) are highly creative and offer powerful adjustments to the colors in your images. The Black & White adjustment layer is highly recommended when you want to change a color image to grayscale. Being slightly older in the Photoshop world, the Channel Mixer used to be the method of choice for changing a color image to grayscale. You could try both to see which works best with your color photographs.

The final five options are highly individual. Invert will change your image from a positive to a negative. Posterize, Threshold, and Gradient Map dramatically alter the pixels for graphical purposes. Selective Color will alter the amount of ink used to print a color photograph using cyan, magenta, yellow, and black inks.

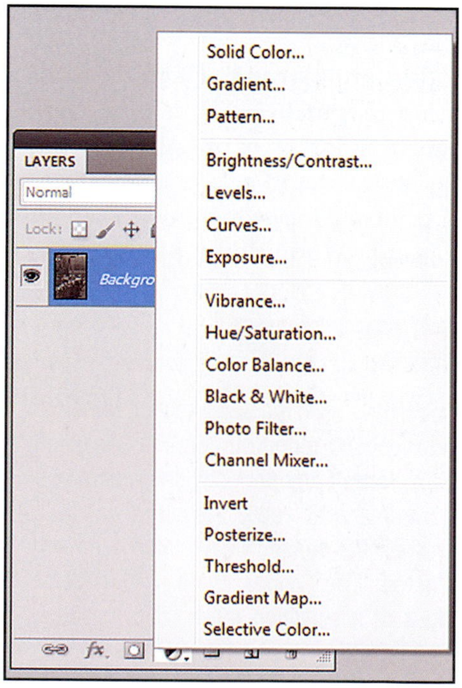

Figure 8-18

Types of adjustment layers available in Photoshop.

Photo © KS.

Working in an Adjustment Layer

For my project, I decided to create a new adjustment layer for Color Balance. I CLICKED on the NEW FILL or ADJUSTMENT LAYER icon in the Layers panel (circled in yellow in Figure 8-19) and chose COLOR BALANCE. Several things happened at once. An Adjustment panel appeared, giving me sliders for each of Cyan/Red, Magenta/ Green, and Yellow/Blue. I also saw a new layer above my Background layer in the Layers panel. My selection had disappeared from the photograph, but its shape appeared in a mask (circled in magenta in Figure 8-19) on the Color Balance adjustment layer. Finally, my Channels panel showed a Color Balance alpha-like channel under the individual color channels. This isn't really an alpha channel. In fact, it will completely disappear unless I am active on that particular adjustment layer in the Layers panel.

Because I wanted a slight blue hue in the selected areas of my photograph, I started with MIDTONES selected in the top option in the Adjustments panel and moved the Blue slider to a +3 value. I then selected the SHADOWS option and added slightly more blue (+4) to the shadow values. Shadows typically have a slight blue tinge to them, so this added to the subtlety of the change. The result of my color balance adjustment is shown in Figure 8-20.

If I'm not totally satisfied with this visual effect, I have two options. I can DOUBLE-CLICK on the LAYER thumbnail of the Color Balance adjustment layer and make additional color balance changes. I could also decrease the overall effect of the Color Balance adjustment layer by lowering the opacity of the layer itself. Figure 8-21 shows the location of both the Layer thumbnail and the Opacity slider within my Layers panel. Both of these changes are nondestructive and don't affect the pixels residing in the Background layer.

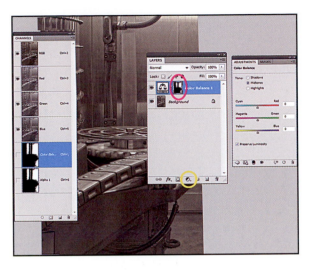

Figure 8-19

The new color balance adjustment layer and the accompanying layer mask (circled in magenta). Photoshop also created a temporary Color Balance channel in the Channels panel that will disappear any time I leave the Color Balance adjustment layer in the Layers panel.

Photo © KS.

Figure 8-20

After making the color balance adjustment to my selection, I could better distinguish the foreground and background elements within the photograph.

Photo © KS.

Figure 8-21

Additional changes can be made by DOUBLE-CLICKING on the ADJUSTMENT LAYER'S THUMBNAIL and changing the adjustment values. The Opacity slider will change the opacity of the layer effect from 0–100%.

Tonal Value Adjustments

I decided to work with the values in the foreground elements, as I had hoped the top of the metal belt and wheel could be brighter. I also wanted more contrast on the large metal container on the left. Finally, I wanted the prongs on the big metal container to be lighter and stand out a little more. All of these are tonal value changes. Levels and

Curves adjustment layers are valuable for these kinds of changes.

The first task was to make a selection of everything but the background. It took me a long time to make that first selection, but this selection would be easy. I held my CMND (CTRL) key DOWN and CLICKED on the MASK icon in the Color Balance layer to bring my selection back (Figure 8-22).

When I saw my selection in the photograph again, I went to the SELECT menu at the top of Photoshop and came down to INVERSE. Now everything that was previously selected wasn't selected any more, and all pixels not previously selected were selected (Figure 8-23). The feathering I had created in my earlier selection was simply reversed in degree; so, the new selected area feathered away at its edges.

I chose to make a new alpha channel out of this new selection. Now the Channels panel showed two different alpha channels. This wasn't a totally necessary step, but it is good insurance. Layer masks can be painted on and altered in multitudes of ways; so, it was best to create that new alpha channel right away (Figure 8-24). Then I saved my file.

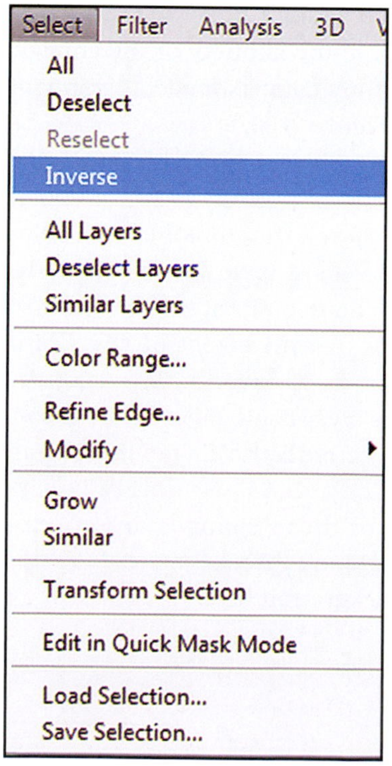

Figure 8-22 (left)

CMND (CTRL)-CLICK on any layer MASK icon (circled in yellow) to create a selection from that mask.

Figure 8-23 (right)

Go to the SELECT menu at the top of the Photoshop window and come down to INVERSE to select the pixels not previously selected and to deselect all previously selected pixels.

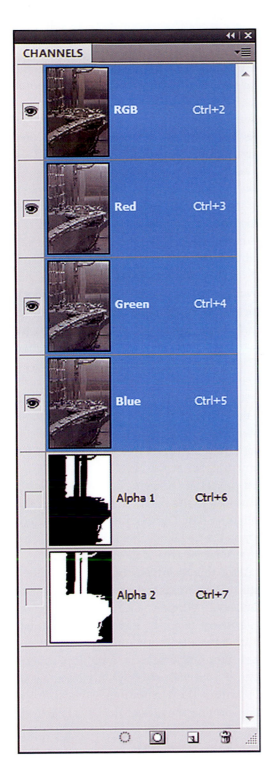

Levels and Curves Adjustments

As you will recall from Chapter 3, the histogram of an image shows where the pixel tonal values fall from total darkness to total brightness. A Levels adjustment layer will allow you to lighten or darken the midtones.

It will also allow you to move the white and black points to increase the contrast within an image.

If you want to lighten or darken the midtones of your image, start an adjustment layer for Levels by CLICKING on the HALF-CIRCLE icon at the bottom of the Layers panel and selecting Levels. The Adjustments panel will show the histogram depicting the levels at which the pixels are falling. There are two sections to the Levels dialog box, the Input Levels and Output Levels. I use only the Input Levels for the vast majority of my image editing.

The MIDDLE INPUT SLIDER is the gray triangle in the middle of the base of the Input Levels histogram (circled in yellow in Figure 8-25). Moving the middle input slider to the left lightens the midtones of the image without affecting the brightest highlights or the darkest shadows. Moving it to the right darkens the midtones without affecting the brightest highlights or the darkest shadows. Overall, though, a Levels adjustment layer will not give you the same kind of control that a Curves adjustment layer will give you.

I decided against the Levels adjustment layer, as simply modifying the midtones of the image didn't give the effect I wanted.

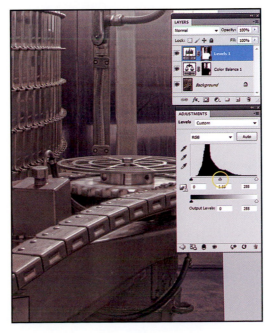

Figure 8-26

The Curves adjustment layer. When I selected the TARGET ADJUSTMENT tool (circled in yellow), my cursor moved to the photograph and when I CLICKED AND DRAGGED directly on an element in the photo I wanted to change, Photoshop set an anchor point on the Curve and changed the value of the pixels falling in that area of the histogram. The eyedroppers shown in the magenta triangle can be used to set the Black Point, White Point, and Middle Gray Point within the image.

Photo © KS.

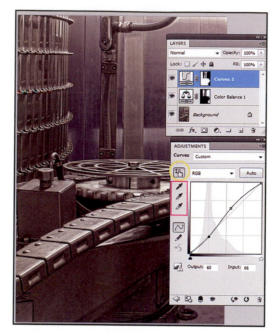

To discard the layer, I CLICKED AND DRAGGED it to the TRASH CAN at the bottom of the Layers panel. When I released the mouse, the layer disappeared. I then reactivated my selection by CMND (CTRL)-CLICKING on the new alpha channel (called Alpha 2 in the Channels panel). Then I CLICKED on the NEW FILL or ADJUSTMENT LAYER icon and selected CURVES.

Having the histogram built into the Curves box is extremely helpful. It allows you to visualize the White Point (in the upper right corner of the Curves box) and the Black Point (in the lower left corner of the Curves box), and where the pixels are falling within the Levels histogram. Just as working in the Levels adjustment layer, the Curves graph allows you to make tonal adjustments in a nondestructive adjustment layer. Changes you make here will be reflected within your image, but they won't change the values of your Background layer until you flatten all of the layers.

In Curves, you can click a new anchor point on the diagonal line and drag your cursor to reshape the curve. You can place several points along this curve and drag to affect the tonal values at the corresponding point in the histogram. Steeper lines within the curve depict greater contrast. Shallower lines within the curve depict less contrast.

A horizontal line will create a plan gray blotch void of detail within your photograph. The Curves function is powerful, and it doesn't take much to destroy your image. Start with just two or three anchor points and look at the results in your image. It is always safest to make changes at 100% magnification of your file.

A new feature in Photoshop CS5 is the TARGET ADJUSTMENT tool circled in yellow in Figure 8-26. I clicked on that tool and then brought my cursor into the image. I placed the cursor on the top surface of the metal belt and dragged upward. Then I placed the cursor on the side of the metal belt and dragged downward. When I did, I began to see much more contrast between the top and side of the belt. The Curves box shows Photoshop's placement of anchor points on the diagonal Curves line when I first clicked the pixels in the image. When I moved my cursor upward, the motion forced the anchor point upward on the graph and those pixels became lighter. Later, when I clicked a side area of the belt and moved my cursor downward, the anchor point was set at the level of brightness of those pixels. My dragging downward lowered the values of the pixels in that region of the histogram. The Curves effect happened not only on the metal belt, but it happened in the entire selected area of the photograph.

All of this took place only in the regions within the unmasked area of the adjustment layer. Whenever a selection is active in an image (e.g., you have marching ants), Photoshop automatically creates a layer mask when you start a new adjustment layer. If you click directly on a layer mask icon within the Layers panel (watch for a frame around the mask to know it is active),

NOTE

Be absolutely certain your layer mask is selected within the Layers panel before you begin painting on your image! Look for a white frame around the mask before you start painting on the photograph.

you can actually paint onto the photograph (not the layer mask) using a Brush tool and can change the areas that are affected by that adjustment layer (Figure 8-27). The layer mask will reflect the changes made by painting directly onto the image.

Painting with white as the Foreground Color with the Curves adjustment layer mask active would add regions affected by the changes made by that adjustment layer. Painting with black as the Foreground Color with the adjustment layer mask active would subtract regions affected by the adjustment layer changes. Any changes made by painting into a layer mask will not be reflected in any previously saved alpha channel.

Setting Black, Gray, and White Points within Curves

Along the side of the Curves box, you can see three eyedroppers (within the magenta rectangle in Figure 8-27). You can use these eyedroppers to set the Black Point, Gray Point, and White Point within the image. It's highly advisable that you HOLD DOWN the OPTION (ALT) KEY IMMEDIATELY AFTER using these tools to see what areas were clipped (forced to pure black or pure white). Figure 8-28 shows a severe shadow clipping because I purposely used the Black Point eyedropper on a dark gray area for demonstration purposes. The white regions you see in Figure 8-28 fall within the black-and-white points of the histogram; so, they're fine. The problem areas are identified by color (for clipped color channels) or black (for areas clipped in all of the channels). These regions of the photograph will now be totally black and show no detail at all. I immediately did an EDIT-UNDO (CMND-Z or CTRL-Z) to undo that Curves Black Point setting.

The White Point eyedropper works in much the fashion, in that it creates a value of pure white within the image. I clicked on a region I thought was the brightest portion of the file and then checked my change by HOLDING DOWN the OPTION (ALT) key (Figure 8-29). Now regions of black fall within the Black and White Points of the histogram. Any white or colored areas fall beyond the

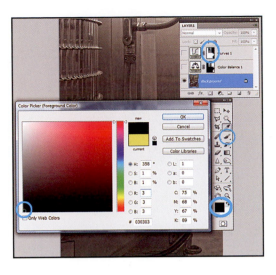

Figure 8-27

The Brush tool and Foreground Color box are circled in cyan within the Tools panel. An adjustment layer mask is circled in the Layers panel. Clicking in the large colored window within the Color Picker as shown will give you a new Foreground Color.

Photo © KS.

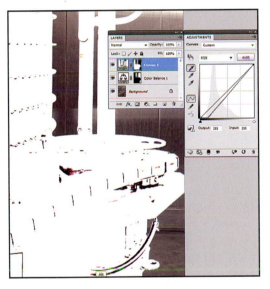

Figure 8-28

When using one of the Black Point, Gray Point, or White Point eyedroppers, hold down the OPTION (ALT) key to check for clipping. In this scenario, the Black Point eyedropper was used on a dark gray area. The tonal values of all pixels darker than this point were forced to black. This includes all colored and black areas in this image.

Photo © KS.

NOTE

The Foreground Color is the more forward of the two large squares at the bottom of the Tools panel. DOUBLE-CLICK on it to select a new color from Photoshop's Color Picker. First, SELECT the hue from the thin rainbow strip. Then CLICK anywhere within the larger color rectangle to select a new color. Then CLICK OK. Your new color will appear as the Foreground Color in the Tools panel. If you are active on a layer mask, any colored selection for Foreground Color will change to a grayscale color. It will only retain its true hue if you have clicked on (meaning you're active on) a layer containing pixels, such as the Background layer in this file.

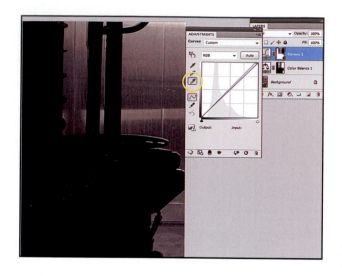

Manual Evaluation of Values

Because I prefer to manually check the values of my image, I went to WINDOW > INFO. I then selected the EYEDROPPER tool in the Tools panel (both the Eyedropper tool and Info palette are circled in yellow in Figure 8-30). I also selected the 5 × 5 SAMPLE OPTION for the Eyedropper tool in the upper left corner of the Photoshop window (Figure 8-31). This would ensure that when I rested my mouse over an area of the photograph, a region of 5 pixels by 5 pixels would be sampled instead of a single pixel. This creates a slight blending of the underlying pixels, instead of selecting the value of just one pixel alone.

The Eyedropper tool gives me a numerical assessment of the values in my image. I can rest my cursor over any region of my photograph and check the Info panel to see its RGB values. Each color channel in the Info panel represents 256 values, whether the photograph is in 8-bit or in 16-bit mode. The range of each color channel in the Color or Info panel goes from 0–255. In the RGB color system, black is represented by a value of 0 in each channel; white, by a value of 255.

The Info panel also includes a CMYK reading. I can read either numbering system within that panel, depending on my needs. With experience, I can equate given RGB or CMYK values to specific colors. If a person has problems with color vision, these numerical values become extremely valuable.

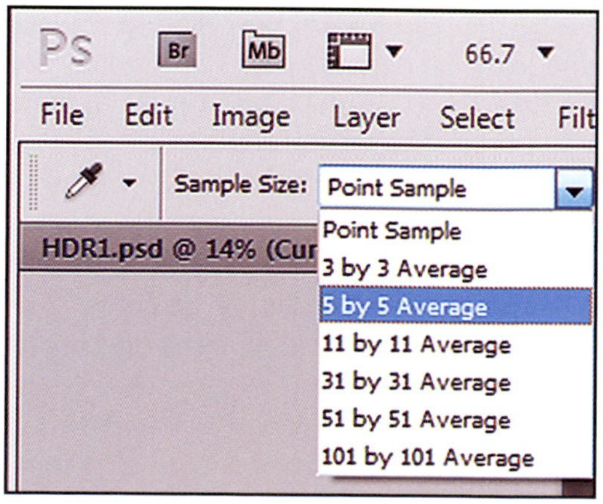

Figure 8-29

After clicking on my photograph using the White Point eyedropper in the Curves window, I held down my OPTION (ALT) key to check for White Point clipping. The areas covered in black are fine. The colored or pure white areas have been clipped. The pure white areas would show absolutely no detail within the image.

Photo © KS.

White Point and are clipped. Because I don't want any areas of pure white in my image, I immediately did an EDIT > UNDO (CMND-Z OR CTRL-Z) to eliminate this change.

It is up to you to decide if these eyedroppers within Curves are valuable to you. It all depends on whether or not you want pure black or pure white regions within your photographs. It is possible to double-click on each eyedropper and set a new White Point, Gray Point, or Black Point value for each eyedropper. This is something I do when evaluating photographs before sending them to press, as a professional press run frequently demands very slightly lighter shadows than pure black and very slightly darker highlights than pure white.

Figure 8-30 (left)

Go to Window > Info to view the Info panel. Click the EYEDROPPER tool in the Tools panel to sample the values of pixels in the image.

Figure 8-31 (right)

Almost every tool in Photoshop has separate options that show up in the upper left corner of Photoshop. These options change, depending on the tool you are currently using. Here, I chose a 5 × 5 sample for the Eyedropper tool.

Photos 8-30 and 8-31 © KS.

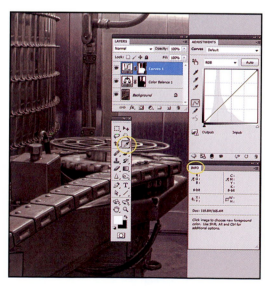

Quick Mask Mode

That's enough information about evaluating the tonal values in a photograph for now. It's time to get back to work. Even though the selection where I changed the Curves looks good when zoomed out, it isn't good enough yet. I want to better differentiate the tiny hooks along the large container on the left portion of the photograph. Another helpful selection tool is Photoshop's Quick Mask. Quick Mask is an excellent method for making selections of tiny regions and regions with soft edges. Soft shadows and items out of focus also fit into this category.

Look at the bottom of your Tools panel for the Quick Mask button (circled in yellow in Figure 8-32). CLICK on that button, and you have moved into Photoshop's Quick Mask mode. Photoshop's Quick Mask allows you to use the Brush tool to paint a selection. When you paint with a black foreground color, you paint a mask onto your photograph. The mask isn't permanent even though it is typically colored. The colored portions of this mask show you exactly where your selection will be when you exit Quick Mask mode.

I started by DOUBLE-CLICKING on the QUICK MASK button at the bottom of the Tools panel. This brings up the Quick Mask Options dialog box (Figure 8-33). By default, you will paint in masked (non-selected) areas when you paint in Quick Mask mode. You can decide if this default works for you or not. Depending on the size of the selection, I sometimes prefer to work in opposite fashion, having the color overlay indicate the selected areas instead. To make this change within the Quick Mask Options, CLICK on SELECTED AREAS instead of Masked Areas. Then CLICK OK. Now as you work, your selected areas will be designated with a color overlay in Quick Mask mode.

Because the regions I needed were so small, I thought it would be easier to use the cover overlay indicating the selected areas. I made that change in Quick Mask Options before moving forward.

Just for future reference, be aware that you can change the color of your mask in the Quick Mask Options box. This is very helpful if you are trying to paint a selection/mask with the same overlay color as your photograph. CLICK on the COLOR SQUARE in the Quick Mask Options box to select a new color for your mask (Figure 8-34).

Figure 8-32

CLICKING on the QUICK MASK button at the bottom of the Tools panel puts you into Quick Mask mode.

Photo © KS.

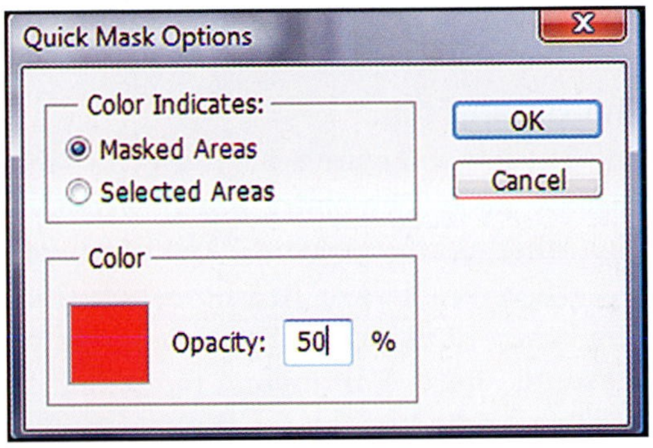

Figure 8-33

DOUBLE-CLICK on the QUICK MASK button in the Tools panel to open the Quick Mask Options dialog box.

Photo © KS.

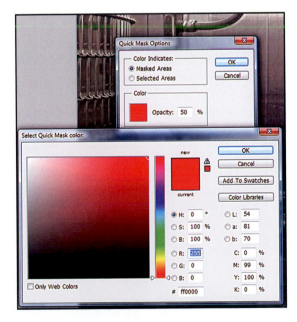

Figure 8-34

You can select a color of mask that Quick Mask will use. CLICK on the COLOR SQUARE in the Quick Mask Options box to open Photoshop's Color Picker. Select a new color and click OK.

Photo © KS.

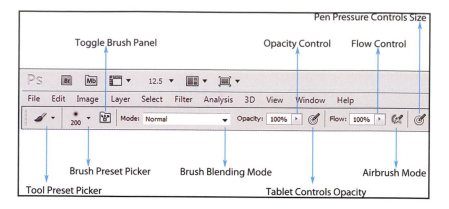

Figure 8-35

Brush tool on the Tools panel.

Photo © KS.

Brush Tool   B
Pencil Tool   B
Color Replacement Tool   B
Mixer Brush Tool   B

Toggle Brush Panel   Opacity Control   Flow Control   Pen Pressure Controls Size

Brush Preset Picker   Brush Blending Mode   Airbrush Mode

Tool Preset Picker   Tablet Controls Opacity

Figure 8-36

The Brush Tool Options bar appears when you SELECT the Brush tool in the Tools panel.

Photo © KS.

The Brush Tool

The Brush tool (Figure 8-35) is used to paint a Quick Mask. The entire Brush system in Photoshop is very powerful and continues to garner new power in Photoshop CS5. The basics of using the Brush tool will be presented here. For anyone interested in creating painted renditions of photographs, I recommend that you spend a lot of time learning and experimenting with the Brush panel (WINDOW > BRUSHES).

As soon as you CLICK on the BRUSH tool, the Options menu changes to the Brush Options at the top of the Photoshop window. Refer to Figure 8-36 as you read on.

Select a brush size by CLICKING on the BRUSH PRESET PICKER. Then select the size brush and the softness you want to use. Brush sizes are measured in pixels. The small icons give you a sense of how soft or

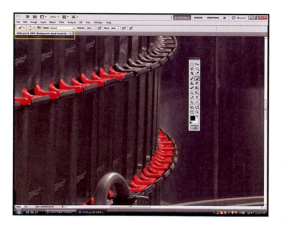

Figure 8-37

Painting with red mask in Quick Mask. Note the top bar gives the name of the file and the percentage of magnification (100%). I am on the Background layer and currently active in Quick Mask. My file is currently 16 bits/pixel bit depth.

Photo © KS.

> **NOTE**
>
> The size brush you need will depend in part on the resolution of your file. If your file is 300 ppi resolution, a 10-pixel brush will be very small. That same 10-pixel brush would look much larger on a 72 ppi resolution file.

hard the brush edge is. CLICK on a BRUSH icon to make it your active brush.

I selected a brush size of 24 pixels and a soft edge to begin my painting. It's important that I match the softness of the brush edge to the softness of my image's edges. Black is my foreground color. I clicked and dragged to paint the mask onto the prongs.

The Opacity Control within the Brushes Options bar allows you to select a percentage of opacity for the brush. The opacity of the mask itself is set by default to 50% in Quick Mask (Figure 8-37). The Brush tool works independently of this mask opacity. If I use 80% opacity for the Brush tool, only 80% strength will be used to paint the mask. Later, when making changes to the areas selected by the mask, any changes I make will only be applied at 80% strength in those areas. In similar fashion, the edge quality of my soft-edged brush will create a diminishing opacity along the brush edges.

I can change my brush size and brush softness at any time without returning to the Brush Preset Picker. To change the size of a brush, CLICK on the LEFT or RIGHT BRACKET keys just to the right of the letter "P" on your keyboard. The left bracket key decreases the brush size; the right bracket key, increases the brush size. As you use the bracket keys, Photoshop jumps from one preset brush to the next. You can watch this happen by opening the Brush Preset Picker and select one brush. Then use the right and left bracket keys on your keyboard to select different presets.

To change the softness of any brush you're using, HOLD the SHIFT key DOWN and then use the right and left bracket keys. Use the SHIFT-RIGHT BRACKET key to make the brush edge harder; the SHIFT-LEFT BRACKET key, to make it softer. Note that the softness bracket key shortcuts only work when you are using one of the round brush presets.

As I paint with the Brush tool and black as my foreground color, I am painting the mask onto the photograph. If I use the double arrow beside the Foreground and Background colors in the Tools panel, I can reverse the Foreground and Background colors (Figure 8-38). If my Foreground and Background colors aren't black and white when I start up Quick Mask, I can make them black and white by clicking on the small black and white squares in the lower left corner of the Tools panel. Because I have to reverse Foreground and Background colors so often, I tap the letter X on my keyboard to toggle them back and forth. X is the keyboard shortcut for reversing the Foreground and Background colors.

When I completed the painting of the areas I wanted to select, I exited Quick Mask by CLICKING again on the QUICK MASK button at the bottom of the Tools panel. The same button that brings you into Quick Mask also gets you out of it.

Pixel-Based Layers

Now I have a selected area in my photograph (Figure 8-39). Because I used a brush with feathered edges, I can't assume that the marching ant selection I see is an accurate rendition of my true selection. Trust Quick Mask, not the shape the marching ants create!

With any selection comes a host of options. I could start an adjustment layer, and Photoshop would automatically use the selection to mask any changes I would make. Another option is to make a new pixel layer

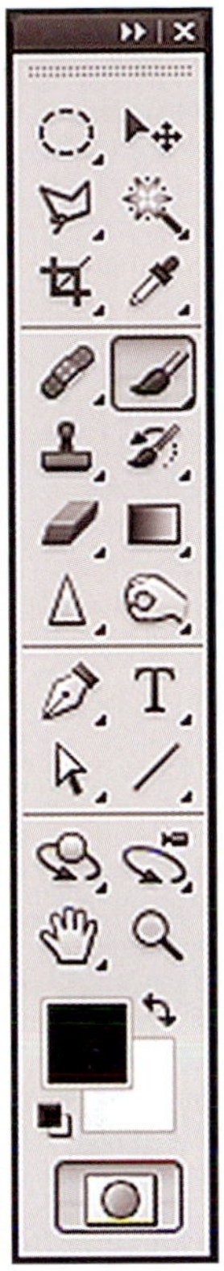

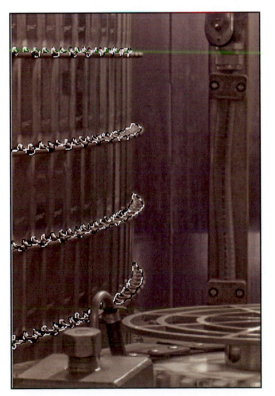

Figure 8-38

Use the default icon in the left lower corner to quickly make black your Foreground color and white your Background color. Use the double arrow to reverse the two colors, or remember the keyboard shortcut of tapping the letter X to reverse the two colors.

Photo © KS.

Figure 8-39 (bottom right)

When you are finished working in Quick Mask, CLICK the QUICK MASK button again in your Tools panel. The mask will revert to a selection.

Photo © KS.

Figure 8-40 (top left)

Layer 1 is currently visible, showing the prongs I had selected using Quick Mask. The Background layer's EYEBALL is turned OFF so you can't see its pixels.

Figure 8-41 (top right)

By DRAGGING and DROPPING Layer 1 above the adjustment layers, those adjustment layers no longer have any effect on the Layer 1 pixels.

Figure 8-42 (bottom left)

Hold down the OPTION (ALT) key before CLICKING on the NEW FILL or ADJUSTMENT LAYER icon, and then select USE PREVIOUS LAYER TO CREATE CLIPPING MASK. This prevents the new adjustment layer from affecting the Background layer as well.

Photos 8-40 through 8-42 © KS.

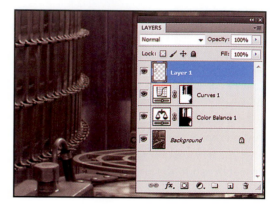

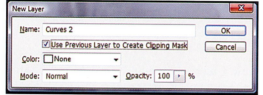

of the selected areas. This would give me a different set of options. To make a new layer from pixels on an existing layer, I CLICKED on the BACKGROUND LAYER to make it the active layer. Then I went to LAYER > NEW > LAYER VIA COPY. The keyboard shortcut is CMND (CTRL)-J. Instead of working on adjustment layers, LAYER > NEW > LAYER VIA COPY created a layer (called *Layer 1*) with pixels on it. The pixels within the selected area were copied from the Background layer onto a new layer.

Working with pixel layers is like working with layers of cellophane. You can see through the various layers unless some pixels cover other pixels. In this case, you shouldn't see any difference between the new and Background layers because you haven't moved the pixels. You can turn off the eyeball just to the left of the Background layer to make that layer invisible (Figure 8-40). The only pixels you will see are the pixels on Layer 1. The checkerboard pattern you see is the base layer of Photoshop. TURN ON the Background layer's EYEBALL back on to view those pixels again.

The use of LAYER > NEW > LAYER VIA COPY copies the pixels to a new layer directly above the current layer. In this example, the adjustment layers I worked on earlier are above Layer 1, so any effect they have on the Background layer also affects the

pixels in Layer 1. That's exactly what I want here. If for any reason I didn't want the adjustment layers to affect the new pixels, I could CLICK AND DRAG Layer 1 and drop it above the adjustment layers. Since adjustment layers affect *only* the pixels on layers below them, the Layer 1 pixels wouldn't be affected (Figure 8-41).

I want to increase the contrast of the pixels on Layer 1. The best way of doing this is to create a Curves adjustment layer. However, I don't want the effects of the new adjustment layer to affect the Background layer at the same time. I assigned an adjustment layer to only one pixel layer by holding down my OPTION (ALT) key before CLICKING on the NEW FILL or ADJUSTMENT LAYER icon. When I saw the dialog box shown in Figure 8-42, I selected USE PREVIOUS LAYER TO CREATE CLIPPING MASK. Photoshop finds the edges to my pixels in Layer 1 and applies the new adjustment layer to only those regions where pixels exist on that layer.

I zoomed in to 100% magnification so I could carefully watch the changes being made. To create more contrast within Layer 1, I placed two anchor points on the Curves box. The first was at the ¼-tone (shadow) range, the other was on the ¾-tone (highlight) range. By dragging the ¼-tone point to the right and dragging the ¾-tone point to the left, I created an S-shaped curve that *increased* the contrast within the image (Figure 8-43). I was especially careful not to allow the curve line to bump against either side of the box, as that would effectively move the Black or White Point and could cause clipping of shadow and highlight pixels.

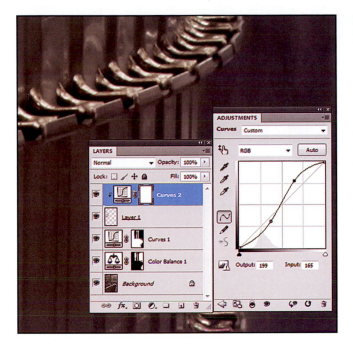

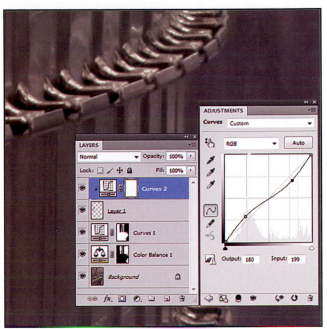

Figure 8-43

An S-shaped curve increases the contrast of your image.

Photo © KS.

Figure 8-44

An inverted S-shaped curve decreases the contrast of your image

Photo © KS.

If I had wanted to decrease the amount of contrast, instead of increasing it, I would have moved the ¼-tone point to the right and moved the ¾-tone point to the left. This creates an inverted-S shape that decreases contrast within the image (Figure 8-44).

Continuing the Artistic Process

The entire process of lightening and darkening various areas of this photograph spanned a series of days. Sometimes I knew I had made a good decision; other times I had to live with my changes until other areas fell into place. The beauty of working with adjustment layers is that you can adjust as you go without damaging underlying pixels. I continued to make various selections and adjusting those selected areas throughout the process.

The final rendition of this image appears in Figure 8-45. You will quickly notice that this image barely resembles the examples you have been seeing throughout this chapter. I kept some changes and discarded others. In the end, I went with a grayscale rendition of the scene. You may have decided to make different changes if this had been your

Figure 8-45

This is the final rendition of this project. It was converted to grayscale by going to IMAGE > MODE > GRAYSCALE and was also converted from 16-bit to 8-bit.

Photo © KS.

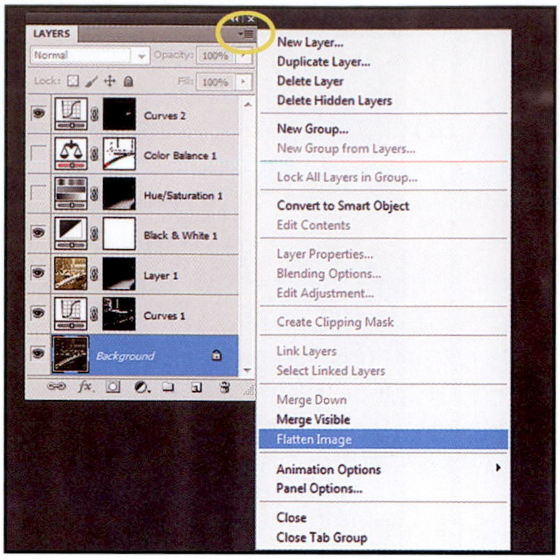

Figure 8-46 (left)

CLICK on the Layer panel's FLY-OUT menu (circled in yellow) and select FLATTEN IMAGE. Then save your file with a different name. The file with all of your layers will be available if you decide to make changes in the future.

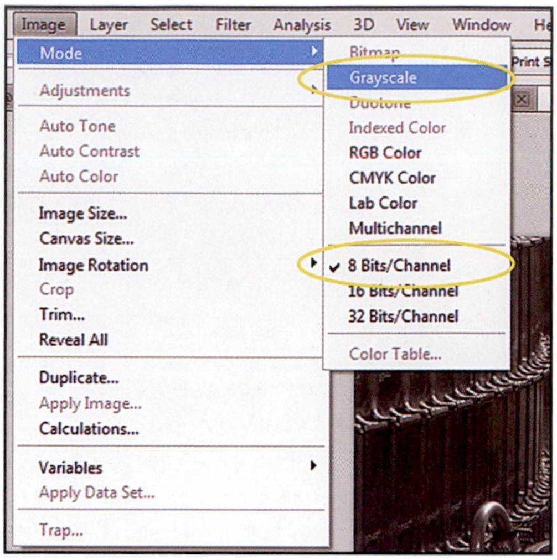

Figure 8-47 (right)

The final file was converted to grayscale by going to IMAGE > MODE > GRAYSCALE and was also converted from 16-bit to 8-bit.

Photos 8-46 and 8-47 © KS.

photograph, and that's fine. It is up to you to decide how your photographs will look.

I flattened the layers by going to the FLY-OUT menu on the Layers panel and selecting FLATTEN IMAGE (Figure 8-46). It was important for me to flatten the image before changing the file to Grayscale mode because some of the adjustment layers would have been discarded if I had changed the mode before flattening the layers.

My final task was to create a grayscale, 8-bit file. I went to IMAGE > MODE > GRAYSCALE to discard the color information. In the same window, I converted the file from 16-bit to 8-bit (Figure 8-47). Then I saved the file with a *different name* to preserve the file with all of the adjustment layers.

In Chapter 9, you will learn about selection tools related to color. You will also learn about sharpening your photo and making any changes to color balance you might need.

Summary

Merge to HDR is a viable option if your scene holds a greater dynamic range than your camera can record. Taking multiple photographs of the same scene and varying your exposures will give you opportunities to get detail into your highlights and shadows.

It is helpful to make note of the light being reflected from your scene when you make the photograph. Later, you can use the digital darkroom to make adjustments in tonality to localized regions of the photograph. Your goal should be to have your final image meet your intentions, whether you ultimately choose to render your image close to its original values or change the values of selected areas according to your desires.

Table 8-1 lists the Photoshop-related tools and commands from this chapter. Use this table as a shortcut to find the tools and procedures you need:

Table 8-1
Photoshop-Related Tools and Commands in Chapter 8

© Cengage Learning 2012

Digital Darkroom Tasks	First Solution	Alternate Solutions	Page Reference
Merge to HDR	In Adobe Bridge: TOOLS > PHOTOSHOP > MERGE TO HDR.	In Photoshop: FILE > AUTOMATE > MERGE TO HDR.	211
Making a selection in Photoshop	Rectangular or Elliptical Marquee tool. Lasso tool. Quick Mask mode.	HOLD the SHIFT key DOWN and use a selection tool to add to a selection. HOLD the Option (ALT) key DOWN and use a selection tool to subtract from a selection.	214

Alpha channels	WINDOW > CHANNELS to view the Channels panel. CLICK on the NEW CHANNEL icon to create a new alpha channel. CMND-(CTRL)-CLICK on the ALPHA CHANNEL to make an alpha channel an active selection.	Once you have a selection, go to the SELECT menu and choose SAVE SELECTION. Go to the SELECT menu and choose LOAD SELECTION. Select the alpha channel you want to load into a selection.	216
Modify the border of a selection	Go to the SELECT menu and choose REFINE EDGE.		218
Adjustment layers	To make a new global adjustment layer, CLICK on the CREATE NEW FILL or ADJUSTMENT LAYER icon at the bottom of the Layers panel. To make a new localized adjustment layer, HAVE AN ACTIVE SELECTION before clicking on the NEW FILL or ADJUSTMENT LAYER icon. To make an adjustment layer affect only the pixel layer immediately below it, HOLD DOWN the OPTION (ALT) key before CLICKING on the NEW FILL or ADJUSTMENT LAYER icon. Then CLICK the option: USE PREVIOUS LAYER TO CREATE CLIPPING MASK.	Go to the LAYERS menu and select NEW ADJUSTMENT LAYER. To change the opacity of an adjustment layer, use the OPACITY SLIDER at the top of the Layers panel to decrease the layer's opacity.	219
Work with layer masks	Layer masks automatically appear if you have a selection before starting a new adjustment layer. You can assign a layer mask to a layer containing pixels by CLICKING on the ADD LAYER MASK icon at the bottom of the Layers panel.	Go to IMAGE > IMAGE SIZE in Photoshop to set the resolution. You can create a selection from a layer mask by HOLDING DOWN your CMND(CTRL) key and CLICKING on a layer mask (either adjustment or pixel layer masks work).	224
Adjusting contrast in your photograph	CREATE A CURVES ADJUSTMENT LAYER and place two anchor points on the curve: one at the ¼-tone and one at the ¾-tone. An S-shaped curve increases contrast; an inverted S-shaped curve decreases contrast.	USE THE TARGET ADJUSTMENT tool within the Curves dialog box. CLICK AND DRAG directly on your photograph to lighten or darken values within the image.	230
Check for clipping	After you have used the White or Black Eyedropper tools in the Curves dialog box, HOLD DOWN your OPTION (ALT) key to see if any values have been clipped to pure white or pure black.		225
Using the Quick Mask mode	CLICK the QUICK MASK button at the bottom of the Tools panel to get into and get out of Quick Mask. SELECT the BRUSH tool and paint with black to paint in a mask. Paint with white to paint out a mask. TAP the letter X on your keyboard to toggle the Foreground and Background colors in the Tools panel.	DOUBLE-CLICK on the QUICK MASK button at the bottom of the Tools panel to change the options from Masked areas to SELECTED areas. You can select a color of mask that Quick Mask will use. CLICK on the COLOR SQUARE in the QUICK MASK OPTIONS box to open Photoshop's Color Picker. SELECT a new color and CLICK OK.	227
Flatten your image	CTRL-(RIGHT)-CLICK on any layer and SELECT FLATTEN IMAGE.	CLICK on the FLY-OUT menu in the Layers panel and SELECT FLATTEN IMAGE.	232
Convert to Grayscale mode	IMAGE > MODE > GRAYSCALE.		232

1. Start from home and carry your camera and tripod 15 minutes in any direction. You can be walking, riding a bicycle, or driving. Wherever you end up, look around you and find visually interesting things to photograph. Make a few photographs that simply document your surroundings. Then look for the following and make photographs that:

    A. Help a viewer get a sense of what the place looks and feels like.

    B. Get closer to individual objects and celebrate their form, color, or graphical quality.

    C. Give the viewer a sense of what kind of activity takes place there.

    D. Move in closer and create abstract images from close-up views of the surroundings.

2. Select a scene with high contrast and, with a tripod, create a series of bracketed exposures at that scene. Use the Merge to HDR functions in Bridge or Photoshop to combine the individual exposures into one photograph. From there, work within Photoshop to change the contrast and values of local regions within the photograph, similar to the project discussed in this chapter.

3. Select a nonprofit organization that would be interested in having a student photographer make photographs.

    A. Read the chapter on best business practices in this text. Look on the ASMP website (http://asmp.org/tutorials/property-and-model-releases.html) to learn about the importance of obtaining model releases when photographing people. Download the sample model release from the ASMP website and make copies of it.

B. Go to the organization's location and photographically document the place and its people. Listen to people talk about the organization and learn what is important to them. Use composition and lighting to bring that message through in your photographs. Have any people you have photographed sign your model releases.

C. Meet with the organization and share your photographs with them. Get feedback on the images you made. Which images best helped tell the organization's story? Which images aren't quite as strong?

FURTHER READING

- DAVIS, Harold and Phyllis Davis. *The Photoshop Darkroom: Creative Digital Post-Processing.* Oxford, U.K: Elsevier, Ltd., 2010.

- JOHNSON, Chris. *The Practical Zone System for Film and Digital Photography.* 4th Ed. Oxford, U.K: Elsevier, Ltd., 2007.

- EVENING, Martin. *Adobe Photoshop CS5 for Photographers: A Professional Image Editor's Guide to the Creative Use of Photoshop for the Macintosh and PC.* Oxford, U.K: Elsevier, Ltd., 2010.

- NIGHTINGALE, David. *Practical HDR: A Complete Guide to Creating High Dynamic Range Images with Your Digital SLR.* Oxford, U.K: Elsevier, Ltd., 2009.

Felice Frankel
Science Photographer

Science photographer Felice Frankel holds concurrent positions at Harvard Medical School's Systems Biology and the Massachusetts Institute of Technology. Working in collaboration with scientists and engineers, Frankel's images have been published in over 300 journal articles and/or covers. She is author of *Envisioning Science, The Design and Craft of the Science Image* (MIT Press); *No Small Matter, Science on the Nanoscale,* with George M. Whitesides (Harvard University Press); *On the Surface of Things, Images of the Extraordinary in Science* (Harvard University Press), co-authored with George Whitesides; and *Modern Landscape Architecture, Redefining the Garden,* with Jory Johnson (Abbeville Press).

Describe your photographic work.

My work is about the visual communication of science and scientific ideas. I help researchers communicate their research. The images I make support their work, trying to help them communicate their scientific ideas with images that explain and support those ideas. My scientific photography isn't about me. It's very much a collaborative effort between the scientists and me.

I have a bachelor's degree in biology. I became an amateur photographer and later became a professional architecture and landscape photographer. On a fellowship at Harvard, I had the opportunity to get back to science.

I met a particular Harvard chemist whose work was about to be published in a journal. I thought I could make a better photograph of their research and did so. Incredibly, it made the cover of the journal. I carved a niche for myself by helping researchers use cameras, microscopes, and other scientific tools to obtain better visualizations of their research. I bring in a photographer's point of view, but with a scientific bent.

What training did you receive in photography?

I am totally self-taught in photography. I've had no formal training. No school teaches what I do.

When I was photographing architecture, I was working with film in the predigital era. I had to make a lot of previews with Polaroid instant film so I could see the approximate results I would get on film. Even then, I was never quite sure, for example, if the color balance worked. I never knew until the film came back. But now, because I can see the digital photo so quickly, I find myself taking more chances.

My technical knowledge is very important because when you know how to make a photo better and anticipate problems, it frees you up to do a better job. I see many photographers who are so involved with camera techniques that they lose their creativity. For me, it's important to consider the aesthetics of the photograph and how it conveys information to the viewer.

Technical rigor is important in my work, but I must also be very honest in my photographs. Whenever I color images that could only be captured as a black-and-white image because of the equipment used, I always indicate that I have done so in the caption. Honesty and integrity are paramount. Anything I do to a photograph is documented when it is printed in a scientific journal. I can't take artistic license and create something without that documentation.

How did you learn how to use complex scientific equipment to take photographs?

I taught myself how to take microscopic photos. I come to the microscope as a photographer, not a microscopist. When I work with more sophisticated equipment, I will work with the technician. I know what I want to get on screen, so I select the samples and compose

Photo © Felice Frankel.

the photograph. The technician captures the actual image. I know what the machine can do, but it's faster to have the technician working the machine. I'm acting as an art director that point.

What advice do you have for someone interested in being a science photographer?

If you really want to do this, you have to show your ability to make pictures better than the researcher can make. It worked for me because I gave the researchers something they couldn't do. Perhaps the scientist didn't have time, or maybe she just didn't know how to make a better photograph.

Find a lab whose results are clearly visual. And just as important, find the researchers who are interested in enhancing their presentations and submissions. If they aren't, forget it. This isn't something you can push onto people. Volunteer your services and make something for them. All you need is one prominently placed scientist who recognizes your skills and value to get a foot in the door.

A lot of luck was also involved with my success. I had a book out called *Modern Landscape Architecture*, and that book opened the door for me to work at Harvard.

Anyone who wants to do this must have at least a science background or have a strong interest in the sciences. Understand the scientific vocabulary and a lot of what is happening in the lab. You don't have to know everything. And if you are photographing a new area about which you know very little, you must acknowledge what you don't know. The worst thing is to pretend that you know something to researchers. You don't need to be an expert, but you need to know the basics. If it's biology, you need to do your homework in that particular area. Read the articles the scientists have published. If you can't grasp the articles' content, don't offer to work for that researcher.

What sort of photographs should an aspiring science photographer show to researchers?

Showing researchers wonderful landscapes or portraits won't translate to the researcher into an understanding of what you can do as a science photographer. You may know that the way you handled light in one portfolio piece could enhance a photo of a microscopic organism, but the scientists won't catch on. If they're working on something that is reminiscent of something you see around you, take the photos of things around you. They'll be able to translate that image more easily.

Man of the Ranch.

Photo © KS.

CHAPTER

9

Final Touches and Creative Options

Chapter Learning Objectives

- Use both Adobe Camera Raw and Photoshop's arsenal of retouching tools to complete minor clean up of an image.

- Apply the noise reduction capabilities of Adobe Camera Raw and Photoshop.

- Use a variety of selection tools to work with and combine images in Photoshop.

- Use pixel-based layers and layer masks for retouching and photomontage work.

- Apply a variety of sharpen commands in Adobe Camera Raw and Photoshop to sharpen an image.

- Use either Adobe Camera Raw or Photoshop to straighten and crop an image.

- Use Photoshop's History panel to undo work and create snapshots for additional retouching.

Photoshop is a set of incredibly powerful tools, but it is a mechanical means to an end. Your artistic vision must guide the use of Photoshop's tools. It is all too easy to allow Photoshop to determine the outcome of a photograph.

Some of Photoshop's features have presets (called *default settings*) that make temporary decisions when you first open them. A considerable amount of research went into devising default settings, and therefore they enhance many, but not all, photographs. Learn about the tools and then move beyond their presets. Good design work entails challenging every default ever created. Otherwise, you are limited by a generic assumption of what might look good instead of what works best for your image.

Cleaning and Fine-Tuning Tools

Despite your best efforts, there will be things you want to change within a photograph. A small spot, piece of garbage, or a facial blemish might need to be removed so it will not detract attention from the rest of your photograph. Photoshop's retouching tools are very powerful allies for cleaning up your photographs.

Each retouching tool does some things better than others. It's helpful to know how to use each tool so you can try a variety of solutions to a problem area. This portion of the chapter will introduce each tool and its options. The example photos used will include a variety of images from color to grayscale, formal to informal, in hope that you will get an idea of when each tool is most valuable.

Spot Removal Tool in Adobe Camera Raw

The first time you have access to a retouching tool is actually in Adobe Camera Raw (ACR). The Spot Removal tool (circled in yellow in Figure 9-1) can be used to make corrections in small areas of your image.

First, ZOOM IN TO 100% MAGNIFICATION by selecting 100% from the menu in the left lower corner of the ACR window (Figure 9-2). HOLD DOWN YOUR SPACEBAR key to obtain the HAND tool, allowing you to click and drag around the image as needed. When you release the Spacebar key, your cursor will return to your most recently used tool.

The SPOT REMOVAL tool has presets that appear on the right side of the ACR window, directly below the histogram. There are two options for the tool: Heal and Clone. The Heal option is most helpful for removing small skin blemishes (Figure 9-3) while keeping the luminosity and texture realistic. In copying existing pixels and using those pixels to replace areas that need retouching, the Clone option tends to have soft, diffuse edges that can mask the texture of the underlying surface.

MOVE the RADIUS slider up until your cursor's circle extends beyond the edge of the blemish you want to retouch. The Radius cursor has the same keyboard shortcuts as the Brush tool in Photoshop. Use the RIGHT BRACKET key to increase the size of the brush, and use the LEFT BRACKET key to decrease the brush size. Keep the Opacity slider at 100% for full effect of the tool.

Camera Raw 6.1 - JPEG

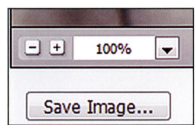

100%

Save Image...

CLICK ONCE on the blemish and let go of your mouse. You will immediately see two circles. The red circle is the original circle you placed with your cursor. The green circle is the sample point from which new pixels will be derived (Figure 9-4). Be very aware of the color, tonal value, and texture of the sampled area; and make sure it matches the color, tonal value, and texture of the area being repaired.

CLICK AND DRAG the GREEN CIRCLE as needed until you have a good match in the two circles. As you drag the green circle to new areas, the pixels within the RED CIRCLE will give you a preview of how that area will look (Figure 9-5).

When you are satisfied with the results, move your cursor to the next blemish and CLICK again. Alternately, you can CLICK AND DRAG out your source point, and the Radius slider will automatically keep track of the size change. Be sure to create a source point with a radius larger than the blemish you are retouching. The Spot Removal tool samples from the surrounding area to ensure a good blend.

As long as you are active on the Spot Removal tool, you will continue to see your dotted circles. When you switch to any other tool across the top toolbar in ACR, the dotted

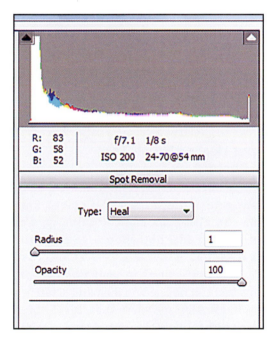

R: 83	f/7.1 1/8 s
G: 58	
B: 52	ISO 200 24-70@54 mm

Spot Removal

Type: Heal

Radius   1

Opacity   100

circles will disappear. They will reappear if you return to the Spot Removal tool.

Because you are working in ACR, these are nondestructive editing changes. They can be reversed by CLICK-ING on the CLEAR ALL button at the bottom of the Spot Removal options panel (Figure 9-6). When you open the file in Photoshop, remember to SELECT 16-BITS/CHANNEL in the Workflow Options dialog box

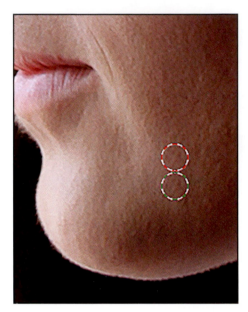

Figure 9-4

CLICK on the blemish you want to retouch, and let go with your mouse. The red circle covers the area you are retouching. The green circle is the sampling point from which the repairs will come.

Photo © KS.

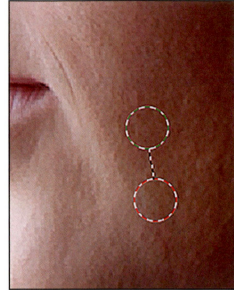

Figure 9-5

The GREEN CIRCLE can be CLICKED AND DRAGGED until the color, value, and texture of your sample point matches your source point (the RED CIRCLE).

Photo © KS.

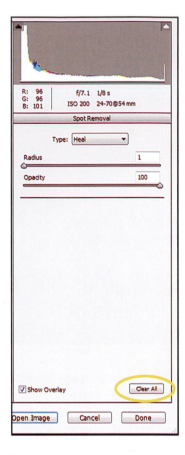

Figure 9-6

Use the CLEAR ALL button to remove all Spot Removal changes in Adobe Camera Raw.

Photo © KS.

(bottom center of the ACR window) if you are planning to make more retouching or tonal value/color modifications.

Spot Healing Brush Tool in Photoshop

It may not be practical for you to do all of your retouching in Adobe Camera Raw. You can also complete the same type of retouching in Photoshop. Use the SPOT HEALING BRUSH tool (Figure 9-7) to correct small imperfections in your photograph. This tool can be used on dust and scratches or on wrinkles and blemishes. It has three types of healing: Proximity Match, Create Texture, and Content-Aware (Figure 9-8).

The PROXIMITY MATCH option uses pixels around the edge of the selected area to find a region to use as a patch. The CREATE TEXTURE option uses pixels within the selected area to create a texture. You may need to click and drag through an area a second time to pick up more texture.

The CONTENT-AWARE option compares nearby image content to the area being retouched. It attempts to realistically

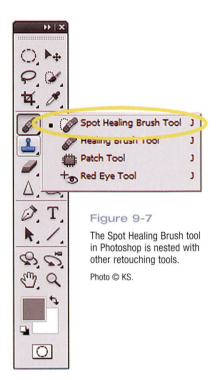

Figure 9-7

The Spot Healing Brush tool in Photoshop is nested with other retouching tools.

Photo © KS.

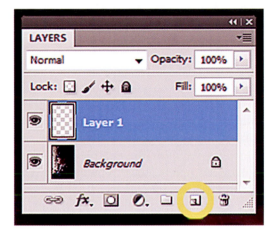

Ps [Br] [Mb] [⬚▾] 100% ▾ [⬚▾] [⬚▾]

File   Edit   Image   Layer   Select   Filter   Analysis   3D   View   Window   Help

[✎]▾ ●▾ Mode: Normal ▾ Type: ⦿ Proximity Match ○ Create Texture ○ Content-Aware ☐ Sample All Layers
       19

maintain key details such as shadows and edges of objects. This is the option to use if you are trying to remove a person or object from a scene. Be sure to click and drag over enough area to include a good sampling of the surrounding region. Use the SAMPLE ALL LAYERS option if you have several pixel-based layers.

Many photographers like to work on layers in case something goes wrong with their retouching methods. To do this, start a new layer by CLICKING on the CREATE A NEW LAYER icon at the bottom of the Layers panel (Figure 9-9). Be sure you are active on Layer 1 (it should be blue). If you aren't active on Layer 1, CLICK ONCE on the LAYER 1 rectangle in the Layers panel to make it active.

Now when you do your retouching, the Spot Removal tool will create the retouched pixels on the new layer. If you decide later that you don't want to keep those changes, you can throw the entire layer away by DRAGGING it to the TRASH CAN just to the right of the New Layer icon in the Layers panel. All of the pixels residing on that layer will be discarded.

Select the SPOT HEALING BRUSH tool and choose a brush size that extends

slightly beyond the blemish you are retouching. Select a brush hardness/softness that works for your project. Some experimentation might be needed to select good brush size and softness settings. Bring your cursor over the blemish area and CLICK to select that area. You will see a dark spot appear, showing you the selected area. When you release your mouse, the blemish is replaced by new pixels sampled from the surrounding area (Figure 9-10).

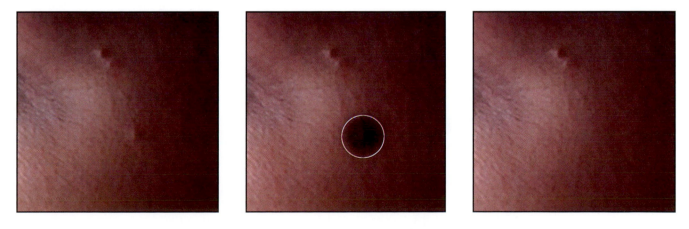

Figure 9-10

Example of using the Spot Healing Brush tool. (left) Before. (center) CLICK on the blemish. (right) Release the mouse and the blemish is gone.
Photo © KS.

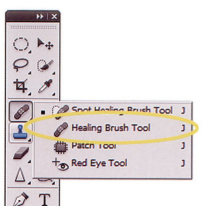

Figure 9-11

The Healing Brush tool in Photoshop.

Photo © KS.

The Healing Brush tool (Figure 9-11) paints with pixels sampled from a different area of the photograph. It compares the color and value of the sampled pixels to replace the pixels in the retouch area. The Healing Brush tool is better than the Spot Healing Brush tool if you need to replace larger areas or to copy pixels from regions distant from the retouching area.

Select the HEALING BRUSH tool. Then look across the top of the Photoshop window to view the options for this tool (Figure 9-12). Note in particular the source and Sample areas. CLICK on SAMPLED, and then SELECT ALL LAYERS from the Sample box. Keep the Aligned box unchecked for now.

To select an area to sample, first select a brush size appropriate for your project. Then HOLD DOWN your OPTION (ALT) key and CLICK on the region you wish to sample (Figure 9-13a). Then release your mouse. Photoshop samples those pixels regardless of the layer on which they reside.

After you have released your mouse, move your cursor over the area to be retouched (Figure 9-13b). You will notice that your cursor will show a preview of the

sampled pixels. If the sample matches the surroundings of the area to be retouched, CLICK ONCE to complete the retouching. If the cursor preview doesn't match the surroundings, sample from a different region instead. Figure 9-13c shows a good result of using the Healing Brush tool.

Because you did not click the Aligned box in the Healing Brush options (refer again to Figure 9-12), your sample point will remain the same even if you move your cursor to a new region to be retouched. Sometimes this works well, but many times it isn't satisfactory. Go back now and CLICK on the ALIGNED button within the Healing Brush Options (Figure 9-14). Sample an area the same way as before, move your cursor away from your sampling point, and CLICK over the blemish to produce the desired retouching.

When you move your cursor to the next blemish, the sampling point moves the same distance and angle as your cursor. This may or may not produce a desirable sampling point, so it is safest to resample often while you are doing retouching work. Always click a few times in a region instead of clicking and dragging your cursor. Resample after 6–8 clicks of the mouse. By frequently sampling several areas, you are likely to obtain a better retouching result.

Patch Tool

Photoshop's PATCH tool is a click-and-drag function that only works on a single layer (Figure 9-15). Despite this unfortunate issue, it is a very quick way to do minor retouching. First, CLICK AND DRAG around an area

Figure 9-12

Use the SAMPLED source and select ALL LAYERS. Keep the Aligned box unchecked.

Photo © KS.

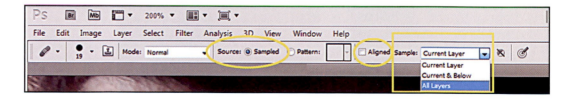

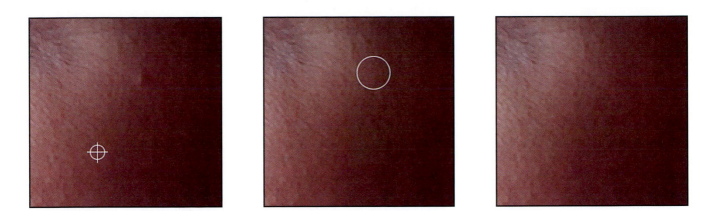

Figure 9-13

(left) Hold down your Option (Alt) key and click once on the area you want to sample. (center) Then release your mouse. Move your cursor to the region to be retouched. (right) Click to complete the retouching.

Photo © KS.

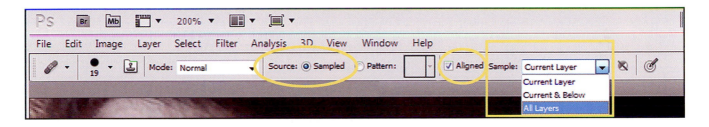

to be retouched. Once you see a selection, reach with your cursor inside that selection and drag it to a region you wish to sample. When you release your mouse, Photoshop will sample that region and replace the originally selected area with pixels from the sampled region (Figure 9-16).

To begin a new retouch, simply click and drag around another problem area. You can use the Cmnd (Ctrl)-D keyboard shortcut to deselect at any time. As your eye becomes trained to see similar colors and tonal values, your retouching can become relatively fast. Just remember that you can't copy pixels onto a separate layer with the Patch tool. Any retouching actually changes the color and tonal values of the retouched pixels (also known as **destructive editing**). Although not ideal, it is the only way the Patch tool currently functions.

A nice feature of the Patch tool is that your originally selected area gives you a preview of the sampling regions as you drag the selection around. This makes it quite easy to find a sampled region that will work for you.

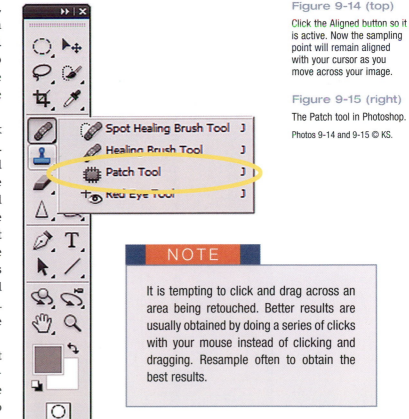

Figure 9-14 (top)

Click the Aligned button so it is active. Now the sampling point will remain aligned with your cursor as you move across your image.

Figure 9-15 (right)

The Patch tool in Photoshop.

Photos 9-14 and 9-15 © KS.

NOTE

It is tempting to click and drag across an area being retouched. Better results are usually obtained by doing a series of clicks with your mouse instead of clicking and dragging. Resample often to obtain the best results.

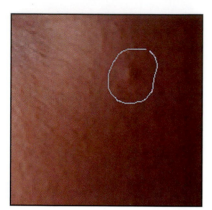 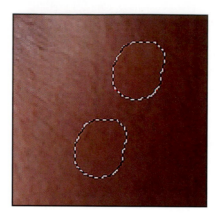 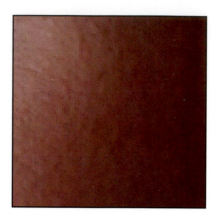

Figure 9-16

(left) CLICK AND DRAG a free-form selection with the Patch tool. (center) DRAG the selected area to a sampling region that matches the color and tonal value you need. (right) When you release your mouse, the effect is complete.

Photo © KS.

The History Panel

As you do your retouching, things will undoubtedly go wrong. Photoshop gives you one undo by the CMND (CTRL)-Z keyboard shortcut. There are times when that isn't enough. Go to WINDOW > HISTORY to open the History panel (Figure 9-17). The History panel shows the last 20 actions you have taken on your file. By CLICKING the ACTION NAMES (called *History states*) going from the bottom upward, you can undo several steps. Once you are back to the state you want your file to be in, simply continue working on your file. All of the history states below your selected state will disappear. Unfortunately, the History states don't remain with your file when you close it. The History panel will start collecting states when you reopen your file.

Creating Snapshots

The History panel has several powerful functions, including creating snapshots of your file by using the CAMERA at the bottom of the History panel (Figure 9-18). A **snapshot** is a temporarily saved state of your file and appears at the top of your History panel (Figure 9-19).

Snapshots are valuable if you need to return to a state of the image more than 20 steps before. By CLICKING on the SNAPSHOT box, that state of your file becomes the image you see in the Photoshop window. The History list is grayed out, and you can essentially start from that point again.

Snapshots are not retained after you close the file. If you want to create different permanent states of your file, don't use the History panel. Save the file with different names as you work, creating several files independent of Photoshop. You can open any of those images and work from them in the future. It is helpful to include the date within the name of your saved files so you can easily identify the most recent versions of the file.

Figure 9-17

Go to WINDOW > HISTORY to open Photoshop's History panel.

Photo © KS.

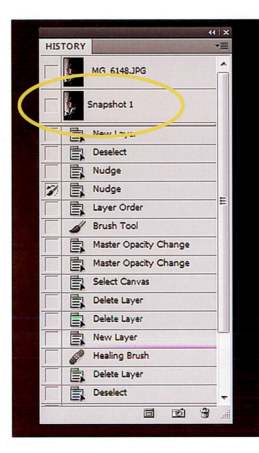

Using Photoshop Help

There are many creative and useful ways to use the History panel, including painting from a previous snapshot by using the History Brush tool in the Tools panel. In Photoshop, go to HELP > PHOTOSHOP HELP (Figure 9-20) and type "History Panel" in the Search box. Photoshop's Help menu takes you to an amazingly intricate, informative, and helpful resource called Adobe Community Help. As you become more comfortable with the techniques taught in this text, consult Adobe Community Help to learn more about Photoshop's tools and functions.

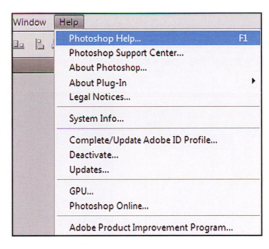

Handling Dust and Noise

Photoshop's filter capabilities comprise special effects for the creative Photoshop user. They also provide phenomenal tools for fine-tuning your photograph. Specific filters frequently used to enhance photographs are the Dust & Scratches and Reduce Noise filters. Both reside under the Noise category in the Filters panel (Figure 9-21). The noise reduction capabilities of Adobe Camera Raw are very powerful; so ACR is the best choice for dealing with digital noise.

The Dust & Scratches Filter

Figure 9-22 is a cropped portion of a much larger photo. It has been enlarged to show the areas needing retouching. This particular image was scanned from a 35 mm transparency and had dust on it when it was scanned. You can see the dust most easily in the blue sky. You will also note that this image has a crooked building in the background. You will learn how to remedy that later.

Go to FILTER > NOISE > DUST & SCRATCHES. When the dialog box opens, the default settings for the Dust & Scratches filter go to work. Set the THRESHOLD level to 0 so you get the full effect of the filter. The Threshold value determines how different the pixels should be before considering them dust or cratches.

DRAG the RADIUS slider left or right to increase or decrease the size of the area searched for those dissimilar pixels assumed to be dust or scratches (Figure 9-23). As you increase the Radius, your photograph will blur. Use the absolute least amount of Radius required to get rid of the dust and scratches.

Once you have set your Radius slider to the desired level, increase the Threshold until the defects are eliminated. Again, be aware of the blurriness the filter induces and stop before your photograph is noticeably blurry.

If you have a sky filled with dust as in Figure 9-22, you can minimize the damage of the Dust & Scratches filter by using the LASSO tool to encircle the dusty spots. Create a selection around one dust spot, HOLD DOWN your SHIFT key to add to your selection, and continue circling dust spots

Figure 9-21 (bottom left)

Dust & Scratches and Reduce Noise are two Photoshop filters used for retouching.

Figure 9-22 (bottom right)

This photo is a close-up of the dust marks on an old scanned slide.

Photos 9-21 and 9-22 © KS.

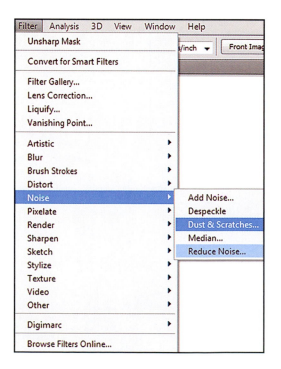

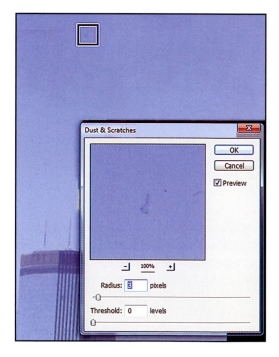

Figure 9-23

Begin with the Threshold at 0 and SLIDE the Radius to a level that diminishes or eliminates the dust or scratch. When you bring your cursor into the photo, it converts to a square. CLICK over a dust particle or scratch to see it in the filter's preview box. Be sure the preview is at 100% magnification.

Photo © KS.

with the Lasso tool (Figure 9-24). When you apply the Dust & Scratches filter, only the selected areas will be affected.

As you continue to work, you can reapply the Dust & Scratches filter by using the keyboard shortcut of CMND (CTRL)-F. This shortcut repeats your last filter at its same settings. You can find this option at the top of the Filters drop-down menu.

Don't try to eliminate all dust and scratches if doing so would introduce too much blur to your image. Instead,

use the Dust & Scratches filter to take care of the small problems. Then use the retouching tools discussed earlier in this chapter to clean up the remaining blemishes.

Noise Reduction in Adobe Camera Raw

You have read about digital noise and its causes in earlier chapters of this text. Digital noise falls into two categories: chroma (color) and luminance (which resembles traditional film grain).

The photo you see in Figure 9-25 was taken at night with an ISO of 3200 and

Figure 9-24

Go to FILTERS > LAST FILTER to reapply the filter at the same settings you most recently used. The keyboard shortcut is CMND (CTRL)-F.

Photo © KS.

Figure 9-25

The digital noise in the shadows of this photo was caused by the high ISO setting. Go to the DETAIL section (circled in yellow) to find the NOISE REDUCTION settings for luminance and color.

Photo © KS.

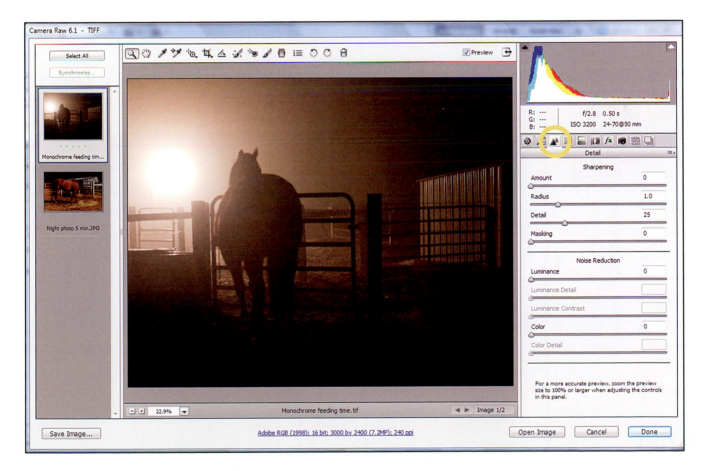

Figure 9-26

SELECT ALL to select all of the photographs you opened in ACR. Then CLICK on SYNCHRONIZE to open the Synchronize options window.

Photo © KS.

shutter speed of 0.5 second. This photo was purposely made at a high ISO setting in a high-contrast environment to show the digital noise caused by using high ISO camera settings. Note that there is considerably more noise in the shadows than there is in the highlights. It has been opened in Adobe Camera Raw because of the noise reduction capabilities there. The Noise filter in Photoshop works in similar fashion; so, the information presented here is valid for both applications.

One strong reason for effecting noise reduction in Adobe Camera Raw is that the settings you create for one photograph can be applied to several photographs at once. This is true regardless of whether you are working on noise reduction or any other function in ACR. Working with multiple photos at once prevents you from having to apply each ACR setting to every individual photograph. In Figure 9-25, two photos have been opened at once by selecting both in Bridge, then CTRL (RIGHT)-CLICKING and selecting OPEN IN CAMERA RAW. Both images will appear in the left-hand column of the ACR window. You can select several images at once and open them in ACR.

You can work on one file in ACR and, if the settings will also work on your other photographs, CLICK ON SELECT ALL in the top left corner of the ACR window (Figure 9-26). When all of the images are selected, CLICK ON SYNCHRONIZE . . . to bring up the Synchronize options window. Select the aspects of the photograph you want to apply to all photos and then CLICK OK. The drop-down menu in the Settings window gives you a quick menu for selecting individual categories (Figure 9-27). When you CLICK OK, all of the selected settings will be applied to your photographs.

The Noise Reduction sliders in ACR control luminance separately from color. Before using these functions, ZOOM IN TO 100% MAGNIFICATION by CLICKING on 100% in the lower left corner of the photo window (Figure 9-28).

The LUMINANCE slider controls the strength of the noise reduction. Because any noise reduction blurs your image, use as little strength as needed to improve your photograph. The LUMINANCE DETAIL slider acts as a threshold and attempts to maintain the sharp edges in the photograph. Higher levels of Luminance Detail will

Figure 9-27 (left)

The Synchronize options window in ACR.

Figure 9-28 (right)

ZOOM IN TO 100% MAGNIFICATION before applying any amount to the Noise Reduction sliders.

Photos 9-27 and 9-28 © KS.

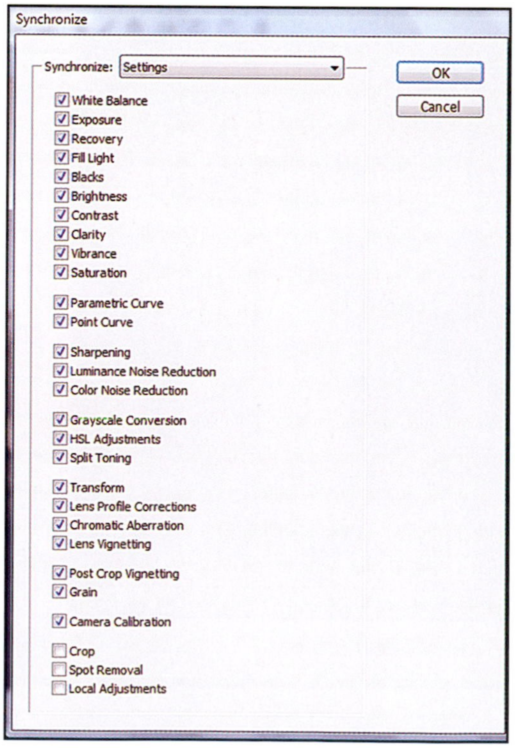

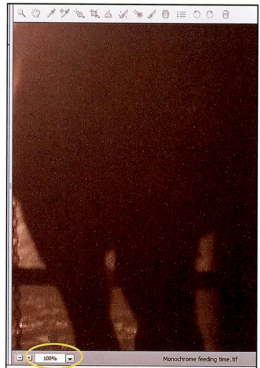

maintain your sharp edges in the photo, but it will also reduce the smoothing in the rest of the photograph.

The Luminance Contrast slider affects the contrast of texture in the photograph. Smoothest results are obtained by dragging the slider to 0. As you drag the slider to the right, more texture contrast is maintained. However, you do need to watch for mottling of some areas; so, be sure to scroll through the image as you work to check for problem areas. The Luminance Contrast slider has a greater effect when the Luminance Detail slider is set to a low value. If you are using a relatively high Luminance Detail setting, the Luminance Contrast setting won't have nearly as much impact. Figure 9-29 shows the settings used and the resulting image.

Color noise tends to appear as magenta/green speckles in high-ISO photos or in photos made with long shutter speeds. The photograph in Figure 9-30 was made on a full moon night with available light only. The 5-minute shutter speed (camera in Bulb mode) created an eerie sense of motion and daylight. It also provided an excellent example of chroma noise (Figure 9-31).

The Color slider in ACR separates color information from luminance and smooths the stray pixels that you see as speckles. Increasing the Color slider can cause blending (sometimes called *bleeding*) of the colors along sharp colored borders. This can cause color details to become mottled or desaturated. The Color Detail slider will help prevent this blending. Again, check your entire photograph by clicking and dragging with the Hand tool to examine every area of the image before deciding on your final noise reduction settings. Figure 9-32 shows the settings used and results obtained. In this case, the blurriness of the horse in motion allowed for rather substantial noise reduction settings.

Figure 9-29

Results of using Luminance noise reduction controls in ACR.

Photo © KS.

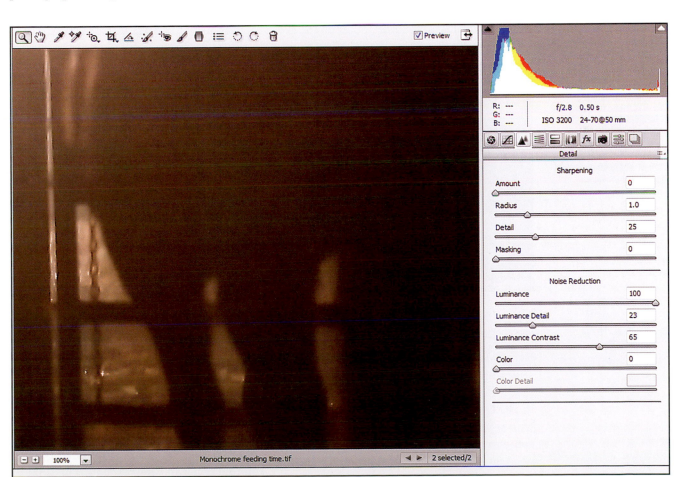

Figure 9-30 (top)

A 5-minute exposure on a full moon night captured this available light photograph. Aperture setting was f/5.6 and ISO was 400. As a result of the low light conditions, focusing the camera had to be performed manually in the dark.

Figure 9-31 (bottom left)

Zoomed in to 100% magnification, the magenta speckles (chroma noise) become more evident.

Figure 9-32 (bottom right)

The results of chroma noise reduction.

Photos 9-30 through 9-32 © KS.

Sharpening Images

Every digital photograph requires some sharpening, regardless of its source (camera or scanner). If you photograph in JPEG or TIFF only, the microprocessor within your camera sharpens the image to some extent. Those images probably won't need much, if any, further sharpening. If you

photograph in camera raw, no sharpening is applied until you open the file in Adobe Camera Raw. Either way, it is up to you to determine how much sharpening your images need.

Under no circumstances will ACR's or Photoshop's sharpening tools be able to solve all blur issues. A truly out-of-focus photograph can't be rescued. The goal of sharpening is to create more tonal contrast along the sharp edges of objects without destroying the smooth texture in areas without sharp edges. A person's face, for instance, has areas of sharp edges around the eyelashes, lips, teeth, and nose. Areas of smooth texture include the forehead, cheeks, and chin. If all areas of a person's photograph were treated with equal sharpness, the detailed areas would look good, but the smooth areas would appear gritty. The ACR Sharpening options optimize the sharp edges of an image and provide controls to prevent destruction of the smooth areas of that image.

The Adobe Camera Raw Sharpening functions are a part of the Details panel. To demonstrate the first two Sharpening functions, Figure 9-33 will be used. It was made with available window light only, an ISO of 200, f/7.1, and a shutter speed of ⅛ second. Figure 9-34 shows how the image looked at 100% magnification in ACR before any sharpening was applied.

The Sharpening function of ACR consists of four sliders, including Amount, Radius, Detail, and Masking. The AMOUNT and RADIUS sliders are concerned with how much sharpening takes place and across how many pixels. Before using either one, set the image view magnification to 100%. Otherwise, you can't accurately judge the sharpening effect.

The Amount slider is exactly that. Push the slider to the right to increase the amount of sharpening. The default setting is 25% if you're sharpening a raw file. If you are working with a JPEG or TIFF file in ACR, the software assumes that your camera's microprocessor has already completed some sharpening. The default Amount setting for JPEG and TIFF files is 0.

The Radius slider determines the width of the sharpening effect. You will notice an effect across small details in your photo with a small Radius setting. This is good for fine details, but a greater radius will be needed to sharpen slightly blurry areas, such as a marginally sharp edge of a building as a result of shallow depth of field when the image was made.

Together, the Amount and Radius sliders make an image appear sharper by creating halos of light along the visual edges within the photograph. These halos become brighter with an increased Amount and wider with an increased Radius. Your goal in sharpening an image is to obtain good detail sharpness without allowing viewers to perceive halos in your photograph.

The remaining two sliders under Sharpening are the DETAIL and MASKING sliders. Both of these sliders maintain sharpened areas but decrease the distracting halos. The Detail slider allows you to push the Amount slider higher than you otherwise could while suppressing the visibility of the corresponding halo. The Detail slider is best kept to a low value, as too high a value can exaggerate noise in the image.

The Masking slider selects portions of an image that doesn't contain sharp edges and masks out the Sharpening effect in those areas. It evaluates the photograph and makes decisions along areas with color or value contrast. Areas of high contrast (such as eyelashes) remain sharpened, whereas smooth areas (such as a person's cheeks) are masked out. This prevents areas such as the model's skin from becoming gritty in appearance. The masking calculations can take a little while to process; so, you might notice a slight delay as you change the Masking slider value.

Figure 9-35 shows the values and results of sharpening in ACR. The eyelashes and eyebrows are in sharper focus, but the skin tones have not been allowed to become grainy.

Photoshop Sharpening Tools

Many photographers begin the sharpening process in ACR to get some level of sharpness going forward into Photoshop.

They leave the final sharpening for Photoshop. This method of dual sharpening is beneficial when combining two or more photographs in Photoshop. Each pixel layer can be individually sharpened, increasing the likelihood that you can match the sharpness of all of the combined images. Matching sharpness of images is one way of ensuring that your composite image will look natural.

Photoshop has several sharpening tools. The two most helpful to photographers are the SMART SHARPEN and the UNSHARP MASK filters. Both are nested within the Sharpen filter (Figure 9-36). The Unsharp Mask filter is older and more widely used; so, it will be discussed first.

Unsharp Mask

The name Unsharp Mask comes from a very old printing technique using a negative and a slightly out-of-focus positive of the same negative. When sandwiched together and printed, the resulting print appeared sharper than the original negative printed alone.

Unlike the Sharpening tool in ACR, the Unsharp Mask filter can't find edges within a photograph. It works by internally

Figure 9-35 (left)

For this image an Amount of 94, Radius of 1.7, Detail of 4, and Masking of 51 produced optimum results.

Figure 9-36 (right)

Smart Sharpen and Unsharp Mask are two powerful sharpening filters in Photoshop.

Photos 9-35 and 9-36 © KS.

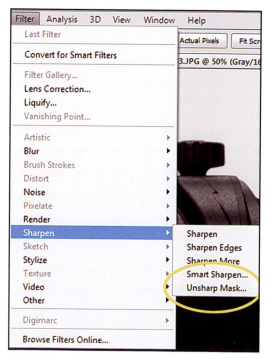

creating a slightly blurred duplicate of the image (which you won't see) and comparing the edge values of the surrounding pixels on both the original and the blurred versions. Depending on the Unsharp Mask settings used (Figure 9-37), varying amounts of overlying pixels are cancelled out. The net effect is a visual increase in image sharpness.

Overall contrast of the photograph is increased as a result of using the Unsharp Mask filter. This can be demonstrated by watching the histogram of your photograph before and after sharpening (Figure 9-38).

The Unsharp Mask filter increases the contrast of neighboring edge pixels. Selecting the exact pixels to be affected is the job of the Radius and Threshold sliders.

The Radius slider determines the breadth of the geographical region that pixels are compared. A Radius value around 1.5–2.2 pixels is recommended for high-resolution (300 ppi) images. A lower Radius value (around 0.5 pixel) works better for screen captures or other low-resolution photographs. When using the Unsharp Mask filter, set the Radius value before moving the Amount slider.

The Amount slider works just as it does in the Sharpening section of ACR. Greater values in the Amount slider will produce more contrast along the edges of the selected areas. It is important to be zoomed in to 100% magnification to view the effects of the Amount slider. Halos around areas of contrast appear with higher Amount levels. When a halo begins to appear,

decrease the Amount value until the halo disappears.

Threshold controls how similar in value (not color) pixels must be to their adjacent pixels before the Sharpen filter affects them. A value of 0 means all pixels in the photo are analyzed. Raising the Threshold excludes pixels very similar in value, such as skin tones and regions of sky in a photo. Excessive use of the Threshold amount can create patchy regions on a photograph; so, be very conservative when setting the Threshold. The author has never needed a Threshold value greater than 4, and a Threshold value greater than 5 is not recommended.

Smart Sharpen

Photoshop's Smart Sharpen filter allows you to sharpen highlight areas separately from shadow areas. Go to FILTER > SHARPEN SMART SHARPEN and CLICK on the ADVANCED tab to see the options in Figure 9-39. Begin your work using the Sharpen tab.

The Amount and Radius work in Smart Sharpen the same way they do with the Unsharp Mask filter. The REMOVE drop-down menu offers three different types of blur to ask Smart Sharpen to remove. GAUSSIAN BLUR (the default setting) is a generalized sense of blur. THE LENS BLUR sharpens details with better precision than Gaussian Blur, and it also tends to avoid the halos that result from the Unsharp Mask filter. The MOTION BLUR attempts to remove the blurred effect of making photographs while moving the camera or from too long a shutter speed. The angle of the motion in the photo can be entered in the window provided, or you can CLICK AND DRAG the CIRCULAR icon just to the right of the angle window (Figure 9-40).

You have the option of CLICKING the MORE ACCURATE box. Doing so gives more accurate results to the Smart Sharpen filter. This also might have the effect of sharpening the digital noise within your photograph; so, be sure to closely examine the results of the Smart Sharpen filter after it is applied. As before, the filter should be used with your photograph set to 100% magnification.

To use the Smart Sharpen filter, first make your SHARPEN decisions in the Sharpen tab. Once you have selected your Amount, Radius, and Remove decisions, CLICK on the SHADOW or HIGHLIGHT tab. Each of these tabs has settings that affect only the shadows or the highlights of the image.

The FADE AMOUNT setting conceals more of the sharpening effect as you increase its value. Smaller values gradually fade the sharpening. This setting fades back the sharpen effects if the highlights or shadows of your image appear a little too sharp after you have set basic Sharpen values.

The TONAL WIDTH slider controls the range of values being modified by the Fade Amount setting. Higher values in the Tonal Width slider result in a greater range of values being affected by the Fade Amount setting.

The RADIUS slider works the same way here as it did in the Unsharp Mask filter. A higher Radius value sets a greater

Figure 9-39

Photoshop's Smart Sharpen Advanced options.

Photo © KS.

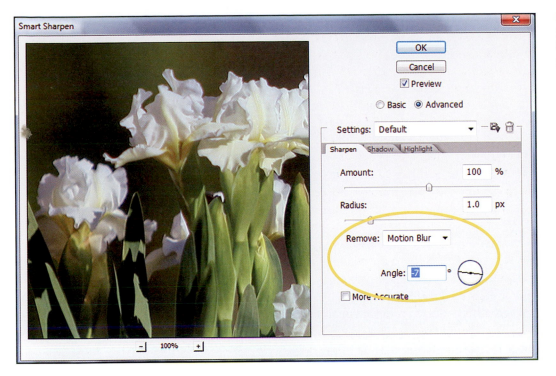

sampling size of the region that determines whether a given pixel falls into highlights or shadows.

Determining Which Sharpening Tool to Use

Photographs vary widely according to values, color, focus, and sharpness. No single sharpening tool can be considered better or worse than any other. Try each tool on a variety of photographs until you get the feel for what works best on a specific type of image.

Straightening Images in Photoshop

You learned earlier how to straighten a photograph in Adobe Camera Raw. Photoshop's Ruler tool is also excellent for this purpose.

The Ruler Tool

The Ruler tool is nested with the Eyedropper tool in Photoshop (Figure 9-41). It is a click-and-drag tool that measures the angle of the resulting dotted line. It works well if you need to correct a crooked photograph. It also works well to measure the angle of

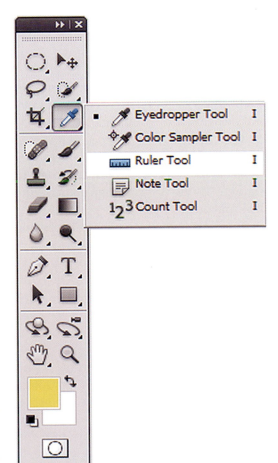

Figure 9-41

The Ruler tool in Photoshop.

Photo © KS.

motion within a photograph. That angle can then be placed in the Angle box of the Remove Motion Blur portion of the Smart Sharpen filter.

Figure 9-42 was made with a tripod, but it still isn't exactly vertical. The RULER tool will measure the exact angle of the vertical wall. ZOOM IN until an edge that should be vertical (or horizontal) is visible. CLICK AND DRAG the RULER tool along that edge. In Figure 9-43, the start and stop points of the click and drag are circled.

Go up to the menu at the top of Photoshop and select IMAGE > IMAGE ROTATION > ARBITRARY (Figure 9-44). Photoshop measures the angle and direction required to make the Ruler measurement exactly vertical or horizontal (Figure 9-45). All you need to do is CLICK OK, and the entire canvas is rotated for you.

Figure 9-46 shows the results of the image rotation. There is clearly a problem with color in the background. As Photoshop rotates an existing canvas, it ensures the entire existing photograph fits into the canvas and enlarges the canvas as needed. New pixels are created using whatever color was present in your Background

Color box on the Tools panel. In this case, that color was yellow. Your next step will be to crop the unwanted pixels.

The Crop Tool

Photoshop's CROP tool (Figure 9-47) has several important options at the top of the Photoshop window (Figure 9-48). If you need to constrain your width and height proportions as you crop an image, enter that information into the corresponding boxes. If for example you are measuring for an 8-inch by 10-inch print, ENTER "8 in" and "10 in" into the width and height boxes.

Although Photoshop offers a RESOLUTION box as well, use this box with discretion. If you want to throw away pixels from a large file, it is acceptable to insert your required resolution here. However, Photoshop will invent pixels if you enter a width, height, and resolution that ultimately require the invention of additional pixels. It is far safer to LEAVE THE RESOLUTION BOX EMPTY in the Crop options and deal with resolution through IMAGE > IMAGE SIZE after you have cropped the image.

After entering a width and height, CLICK AND DRAG the CROP tool within the photograph to create the cropped area. The box margins (called the *bounding box*) will be constrained to your designated proportions. CLICK AND DRAG a CORNER to cover more or less area of your photograph.

When you are satisfied with the crop, PRESS your RETURN (ENTER) key to complete the crop. You can also DOUBLE-CLICK

somewhere inside the bounding box, provided you don't double-click in the exact center, to complete the crop.

If you prefer to CLICK AND DRAG the CROP tool without a width and height proportion, CLICK on the CLEAR button in the top options bar (Figure 9-49) and the width and height information will disappear. Now you have a free-form click-and-drag tool that will allow you to crop without restrictions.

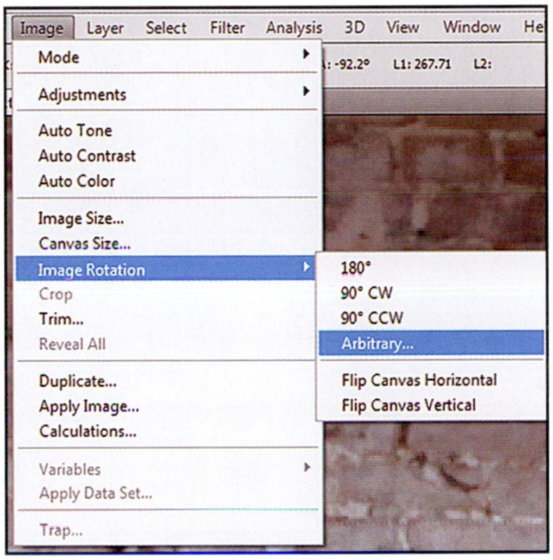

Figure 9-43 (left)

CLICK AND DRAG the RULER tool along the line that should be vertical.

Figure 9-44 (top right)

Go to IMAGE > IMAGE ROTATION > ARBITRARY.

Figure 9-45 (bottom right)

The Amount and direction (clockwise or counterclockwise) will already be filled in for you.

Photos 9-43 through 9-45 © KS.

Figure 9-46 (left)

After the image was rotated, Photoshop filled in the missing pixels with the color of the Background Color square in the Tools panel.

Figure 9-47 (right)

Photoshop's Crop tool.

Photos 9-46 and 9-47 © KS.

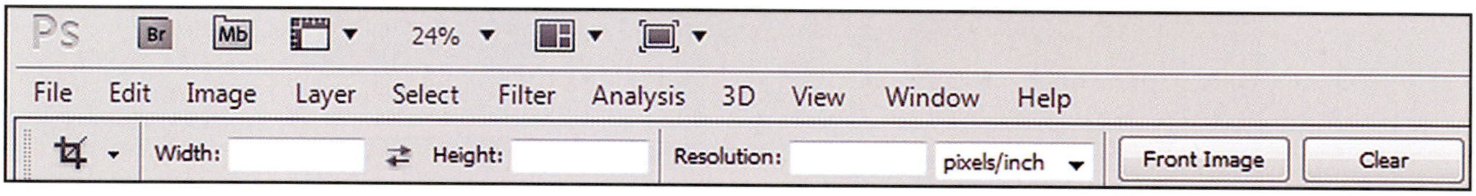

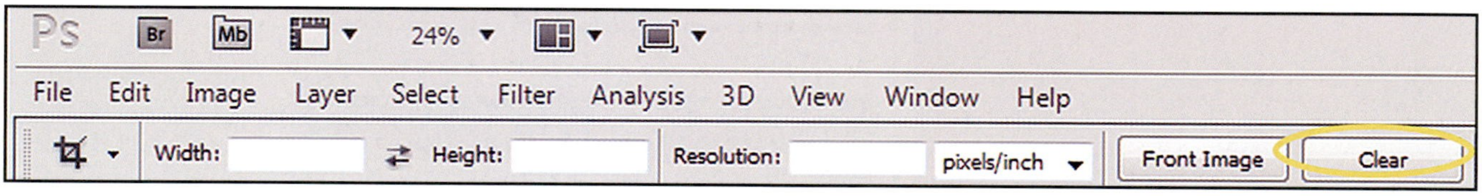

Figure 9-48 (top)

Options for the Crop tool.

Figure 9-49 (bottom)

The Clear button in the Crop Options clears the Width, Height, and Resolution windows.

Photos 9-48 and 9-49 © KS.

Combining Photographs

Photoshop was not the first manipulator of photography. In the late 1800s, negatives were made from thin glass plates coated with light-sensitive chemical emulsions. When exposed to mercury vapors in a darkroom, the emulsion produced the photographic negatives. It wasn't long before artists realized they could paint or draw onto the negatives, producing white clouds in an otherwise plain sky. Areas of density were added to glass plate negatives, producing lighter regions on the resulting print.

Advertisers and graphic designers became intrigued with photography shortly after its infancy. Early twentieth-century Russian posters showed a propensity for cutting up photographs and creating collages from the various print pieces plus other printed materials. With the advent of Photoshop, photographers and designers alike quickly pushed the creative envelope and explored new avenues of self expression.

Of all the possible uses of Photoshop, combining photographs is one of the most ubiquitous and creative. Still, it's worth remembering that the best work comes from creativity with a purpose. If you know what you are trying to say with your images and hold true to that purpose, your work will be more thought-provoking and memorable.

Preparation for Photomontage Work

Before beginning your work with multiple photographs, it is worth reviewing some important subjects taught in earlier chapters. Resolution, in particular, can be an issue when working with more than one photograph.

If your various files are not of the same resolution, something unexpected will happen when you combine them. A donating file (the file from which pixels are selected and moved) set to 300 ppi resolution has 300 linear pixels to every inch. If a receiving file (the file that receives the donating file's pixels) has only 72 ppi resolution, the pixels from the 300 ppi image will sharply increase in size when the two photos are combined. The number of pixels doesn't change, but the pixel size is translated to the new ppi resolution.

For example, a series of pixels 200 pixels wide and 100 pixels high within a 300 ppi file takes up ⅔-inch width and ⅓-inch height. If you move those pixels to a file set to 72 ppi, the same pixels will measure an approximate 2.8-inch width and 1.4-inch height.

Compare the lighting, tonal values, color temperature, and contrast from one photograph to another before combining them. Portrait photographers, in particular, must be careful when adding people to existing photographs. If one person is lit from a different direction or has more or less contrast than the other people in the photo, that person will stand out. Viewers may not be able to identify exactly why they don't think the photograph is right, but they won't feel comfortable with it.

There are several methods for moving pixels from one photograph to another. The easiest is to have two files open at once in Photoshop. In the donating file, go to SELECT > ALL in the top menu. Copy the files by going to EDIT > COPY or CMND (CTRL)-C. Click on the receiving file and go to EDIT > PASTE or CMND (CTRL)-V. The copied pixels will appear on their own layer in the receiving file.

Any time you have a selected area on a photograph, the selected pixels will be the only pixels copied and pasted using this method. Areas of partial selection (such as a feathered edge) will be copied at the same transparency as they had in the donating file.

A second method of moving pixels uses Photoshop's MOVE tool (Figure 9-50) to CLICK AND DRAG pixels from one file to another. As you drag the pixels away from a Background layer, the empty space fills will pixels of the current Background Color in the Tools panel. This isn't permanent. As soon as you have dragged the pixels to the receiving file and released your mouse, the donating file will return to its original appearance.

This demonstration involves selecting the red leaf in Figure 9-51 and moving the leaf to a less-cluttered background. Possible selection tools include the QUICK SELECTION tool (Figure 9-52) and COLOR RANGE, a powerful selection mechanism under the Select menu.

The Quick Selection tool selects pixels according to their color. It finds borders as you click and drag through an area. The brush tip used by the Quick Selection tool can be resized by using the RIGHT and LEFT BRACKET keys to the right of the letter P on your keyboard. This tool is particularly good at selecting areas with sharp color borders.

A quick click and drag through the leaf selected the leaf. Like other selection tools in Photoshop, holding down the SHIFT key and clicking in the photograph adds to a selection. Holding down the OPTION (ALT) key subtracts from a selection. In this case, HOLDING DOWN the SHIFT key and DRAGGING through a portion of the stem of the leaf added the stem to the selection (Figure 9-53). From this point, either the

Figure 9-50

Photoshop's Move tool.

Photo © KS.

Figure 9-51

The goal of this exercise is to select the red leaf and its stem. (see right and below right)

Photo © KS.

Figure 9-52

Photoshop's Quick Selection tool.

Photo © KS.

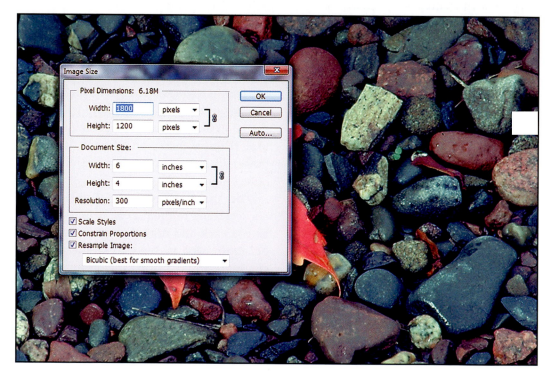

Lasso tool or Quick Mask would be appropriate for fine-tuning the selection.

A second method of selection by color is Photoshop's Color Range command. Color Range selects a specified range of color within either an existing selection or within an entire image.

The Color Range command is preferred over the Quick Selection tool because of its ability to make partial selections based on similar colors. Although the Quick Selection tool always makes initial selections with hard edges, the Color Range command feathers (makes partially transparent) its selection, depending on the similarity of other colors being selected.

Go to SELECT > COLOR RANGE in the top left corner of the Photoshop window. Figure 9-54 shows the resulting Color Range command window. When you invoke the Color Range command, your cursor automatically becomes an Eyedropper tool. CLICKING ONCE within the bright red portion of the leaf created the preview seen in Figure 9-54. The white areas in the preview window show the selected area. Gray areas are partially selected, and black areas are not selected.

The FUZZINESS slider controls the range of colors collected for the selection. In this demonstration, a higher Fuzziness amount would select a greater variety of the reds in the leaf. A lower Fuzziness amount would select fewer reds and make the current selection smaller.

Selecting LOCALIZED COLOR CLUSTERS builds a more accurate selection. It also allows you to use the Range slider, which restricts the geographic range being selected. Because some of the pebbles also contain red, moving the Range slider to the right restricts the geographic selection to the area of the red leaf alone.

To add to the selected area, you can either hold the SHIFT key and CLICK in the leaf again, or you can HOLD the SHIFT key and CLICK directly in the preview of the Color Range window. Figure 9-55 shows the results of Shift-clicking in the preview and modifying the Fuzziness and Range values. CLICKING OK in the Color Range window closes the window and creates the selection in the photograph (Figure 9-56).

The marching ants of this selection show a sharp border, but the feathering the Color Range command created is evident when the selection is viewed in the Quick Mask mode (Figure 9-57). The marching ant selection is clearly not telling the entire story and should not be used to judge the actual selection.

Once the selection is finalized using any combination of selection tools, use the MOVE tool to CLICK AND DRAG the leaf to a different file. The selection can be copied

and pasted into a different file, or you can use the MOVE tool to CLICK AND DRAG the selection up to the tab of a different open file (Figure 9-58).

Hold your cursor on the tab for the receiving file until that file opens on your screen. Still holding down the mouse key, DRAG the selection to the canvas of that file. Then release the mouse. Your selected pixels will appear on their own layer within the receiving file.

In this example, the receiving file was in Grayscale mode (Figure 9-59). If dragged onto the existing receiving file, the leaf would have become grayscale because

Figure 9-53

SHIFT-CLICKING the leaf's stem added it to the existing selection.

Photo © KS.

Figure 9-54

The Color Range command window after CLICKING ONCE in the red leaf.

Photo © KS.

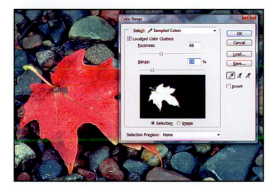

Figure 9-55

The selection after adjusting the Fuzziness and Range sliders.

Photo © KS.

**Figure 9-56
(top left)**

The marching ants do not tell the full story of what is or is not selected after using the Color Range command.

**Figure 9-57
(top right)**

The green mask in Quick Mask shows feathering along some edges of the selection. This feathering is not represented by the marching ant selection in Figure 9-56. Quick Mask provides a much better picture of what is or is not selected after using the Color Range command.

**Figure 9-58
(middle)**

Using the Move tool, CLICK AND DRAG the selection to the tab of another open file. Continue to HOLD DOWN the MOUSE key until you can drag the selected pixels onto the receiving photograph.

**Figure 9-59
(bottom)**

IMAGE > MODE shows you the Color mode of that file. In this case, the file was grayscale. Any colored pixels added to this file would have been converted to grayscale by the Color mode.

Photos 9-56 through 9-59 © KS.

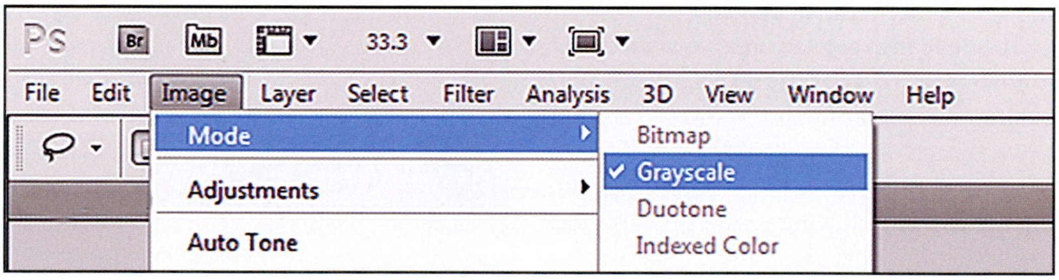

the file itself couldn't represent color. Before bringing the leaf into the receiving file, it was changed to RGB Color (Figure 9-60) so the leaf could retain its color. Figure 9-61 shows the leaf in its new environment and on its own layer.

Working with Pixel Layers and Layer Masks

Once you have a new layer containing pixels in your file, you can do anything to those pixels independently of the Background layer. Any filter will apply only to the existing pixels on the active layer. Changing the opacity of an individual layer will change only the opacity of the pixels residing on that layer.

Pixel layers can also have layer masks applied to them. Figure 9-62 shows where to CLICK on the LAYERS panel to introduce a layer mask to a pixel layer. Once the mask is in place, use the BRUSH tool to paint either black (which hides pixels) or white (which reveals pixels) or shades of gray (which makes pixels transparent). (See Figure 9-63.) Be sure you are clicked on the layer mask itself before painting with the Brush tool.

Transforming Pixels

In this exercise, the leaf appeared somewhat larger than desired. Going to EDIT > TRANSFORM gives you several options on reshaping your existing pixels (Figure 9-64). Each option gives you a bounding box with corners that can be clicked and dragged. When you have completed your transformation, press the RETURN (ENTER) key or DOUBLE-CLICK inside the BOUNDING BOX.

Using the keyboard shortcut of CMND (CTRL)-T gives you a free-form transformation tool. The bounding box appears around the pixels within the layer. HOLD DOWN the SHIFT key and DRAG one corner to make the pixels smaller. Resting your cursor just outside one of the corners gives you a double-arrow icon representing the Rotate function. Be aware that it is always safer to make a pixel selection smaller, not larger. Photoshop must invent new pixels if you choose to enlarge an area with the Transform or Free Transform functions. If you decide against your transformation, PRESS the ESCAPE key to remove the bounding box and cancel the transformation.

Layer Blending Modes

Even more creativity exists within layer blending modes (Figure 9-65). Each layer, other than the Background Layer, can be

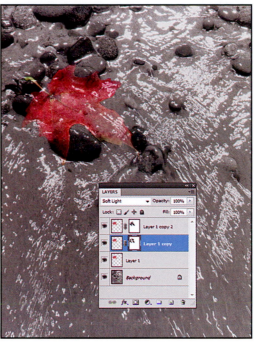

Figure 9-66 (left)

Changing this layer's blending mode to SOFT LIGHT helped blend the leaf into the water.

Figure 9-67 (right)

Duplicate layers, blending modes, and layer masks all contributed to the final product.

Photos 9-66 and 9-67 © KS.

set to a different mode. Each blending mode compares pixels on the active layer to the pixels below that layer and applies a different algorithm to that layer, changing its appearance.

The leaf appears out of place in this scene. Changing the blending mode to SOFT LIGHT dramatically improves its appearance. However, some of the rocks are showing through the leaf (Figure 9-66).

This situation was remedied by DUPLICATING LAYER 1 two times, creating a total of three leaf layers. By concealing some of each leaf by painting into its respective layer mask, a much more realistic image evolved. Figure 9-67 is a screen capture of the final image showing the layers and their respective layer masks.

Learning More While Being Careful

The information presented thus far in Chapters 7, 8, and 9 cover the essentials of working with digital photographs. Once you learn and apply these skills to your photographs, you will have an enormous amount of control over the appearance of your final images.

The digital darkroom offers expansive ways to alter photographs that would be far more challenging in a traditional darkroom. No introductory photography textbook can begin to teach you everything there is to know about Photoshop's capabilities.

The goal of this text is to explain the best uses of Photoshop and why certain functions are important to preserve the quality of your image. In the process, you have also learned some terminology used by any Photoshop book, magazine, or tutorial. Having learned the basics, you will be able to easily pick up new Photoshop skills.

When you do, remember that pixel preservation is of paramount importance. Because this manner of thinking is not universal, you will come across tutorials that include potentially damaging steps. If possible, learn what you can and then adapt the information in ways that yield the same results without causing pixel damage. Work in layers and adjustment layers whenever you can. Always watch your histogram to prevent unwanted clipping of highlights and shadows. Zoom in to 100% magnification and carefully examine every inch of your photograph to observe the effect of actions throughout your photograph.

Summary

Many of the creative processes available in Photoshop depend on a clear notion of what you want to do with an image. The procedures and tools discussed in this chapter are summarized in Table 9-1. Refer to the page listed in this table to refresh your memory on exact procedures.

Table 9-1
Procedures and Tools in Chapter 9
© Cengage Learning 2012

Digital Darkroom Tasks	First Solution	Alternate Solutions	Page Reference
Retouching small blemishes.	Spot Removal Tool in ACR (Heal option)	Spot Healing Brush tool in Photoshop (Proximity Match option). Create a new layer for retouching	243
		Healing Brush tool in Photoshop	
		Patch tool in Photoshop (only works on existing layer)	244
Remove a large section of an image (such as a person).	Spot Healing Brush Tool in Photoshop (Content-aware option)		243
Retouching Dust or Scratches.	Filter > Noise > Dust & Scratches (Photoshop)	Spot Healing Brush tool in Photoshop (Proximity Match option)	243
		Patch tool in Photoshop (only works on existing layer)	
Reduce digital noise.	Noise Reduction sliders in ACR	Filter > Noise > Reduce Noise (Photoshop)	248
Sharpen an image.	Sharpening function in ACR	Filter > Sharpen > Unsharp mask (Photoshop)	252
		Filter >Sharpen > Smart Sharpen (Photoshop)	
Straighten an image.	Straighten tool in ACR	Ruler tool in Photoshop	257
Crop an image.	Crop tool in ACR	Crop tool in Photoshop	258
Selection tools.	Quick Selection Tool (Photoshop)		261
	Select > Color > Range (Photoshop)		
Transforming pixels on pixel layers.	Select > All and Edit > Transform (Photoshop)		266
Layer Blending Modes.	(Photoshop)		266

EXERCISES

1. Create a series of 10 photographs that tell a visual narrative. Two typical stages of visual narrative include a complicating event and a resolution. Within this visual narrative, the complicating event will arise over time within the photographic series. It also implies things that have happened before the first photo and things will continue to happen after the last photo.

   Within visual narratives, not all of the details need to be clearly spelled out. Your audience will fill in details and add to your narrative by using their own imaginations.

2. Create one single image that tells enough of the visual narrative to give your viewers context to the complicating event without giving away the resolution. It can suggest possible resolutions without revealing one ultimate solution. The individual photograph should imply a before, during, and after sense of time despite the lack of resolution. It should immediately engage the viewer's imagination.

3. The artistic movement called surrealism became active across Europe and the United States in the 1930s and 1940s. Read the information on these decades in the By the Decade section (Appendix A) to better understand how and why surrealism came about. Consider how Photoshop's photomontage capabilities relate to this era.

FURTHER READING

- THE SMITHSONIAN INSTITUTE has developed a website called "Click! Photography Changes Everything" (www.click.si.edu). Here you will find a collection of essays and stories by invited contributors and visitors discussing how photography has shaped our culture and lives.

- WITTMANN, M., "Time, Extended: Hiroshi Sugimoto with Gilles Deleuze." *Image [&] Narrative* [e-journal], Vol.X, issue 1 (2009). Available: http://www.imageandnarrative.be/Images_de_l_invisible/Wittmann.htm

- BROWN, Ainsley, "René Magritte and Paul Éluard: An International and Interartistic Dialogue." *Image & Narrative* [e-journal], Vol. VI, issue 3(13) (2005). Available: http://www.imageandnarrative.be/inarchive/surrealism/brown.htm

- MCCLOUD, Scott. *Understanding Comics.* New York: Harper Collins Publishers, 1993. Although this book is outside of the immediate photographic realm, it is an excellent resource for visual storytelling.

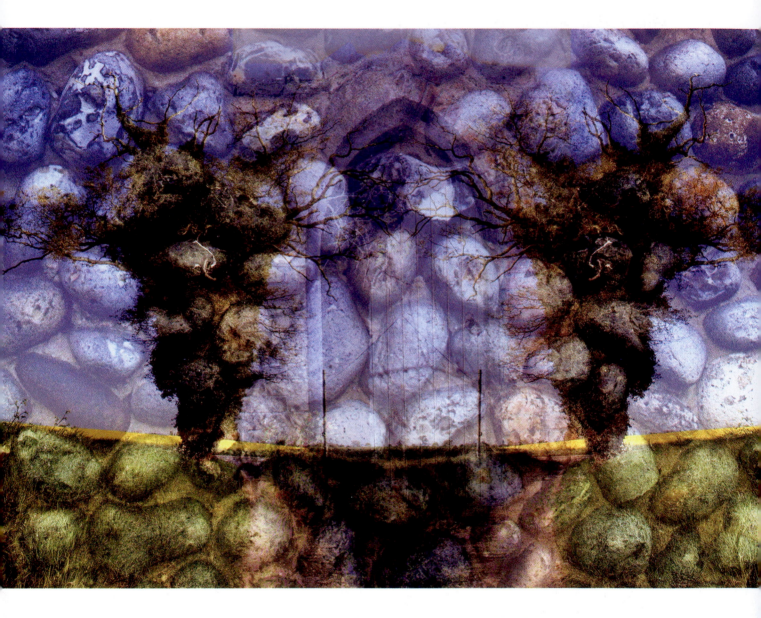

Hidden History. Limited edition archival pigment print, 23" × 34.5".

Photo © Trish Simonite, 2007.

CHAPTER

10

Digital Color Management and Printing

- Know the evolution of color management policies.

- Define the various methods of measuring color presented in this chapter.

- Explain how color measurement is different from color perception.

- Select the proper color setting in your digital camera.

- Select industry-standard color settings in Photoshop.

- Identify and/or obtain ICC profiles for your printer.

- Research longevity data for your type of printer, printer inks, and paper.

- Work with your printer's utility to assure high quality prints.

Obtaining a good print of your digital photograph can be challenging. Your prints may turn out darker, lighter, or have a different color cast than what you see on your screen. If you work on a digital file at home and later bring it to your classroom, the image may not look the same on your classroom's computer as it did on your home computer. When printing successful digital photographs or working with one file across multiple computers, color management is of utmost importance. Digital color management ensures the continuity of appearance of your files as they move from your camera to your computer and, ultimately, from your computer to a printed photograph.

The information in this chapter is technical in nature. The goal is to bring all of your digital equipment to an industry standard of color rendition so that you, the creative photographer, can predict how your final images will look when printed. Without these controls, your camera, monitor, and/or printer can take over and wreak havoc on the appearance of your printed photographs. None of these techniques is difficult; each is simply very important.

History of Digital Color Management

When digital photography started, people were taught to match the appearance of *their* photos on *their* monitor with *their* printer's output. It didn't make any difference if one person's printer didn't print the same color balance as someone else's printer as long as everything worked at home.

Problems arose when digital photography grew in popularity and professional labs started printing people's digital files. The color balance of prints from outside labs was unpredictable and sometimes downright disastrous. Images on people's monitors might match their own printer's output, but it was a gamble to send a file to a commercial printer for printing. There was no way to predict a print's color balance because there was no color communication between the home and lab computers. Something needed to change.

Professionals studying color management moved toward a different philosophy. Instead of telling people to match the images on their monitors to their prints,

the digital photography industry began to encourage people to calibrate (specify color settings for) their cameras, monitors, and printers to match an industry-standard color and density. If all photographers began using that single industry standard as a target for calibration, the chances of having all monitors and printers print very similar colors would greatly increase.

This change in thinking was of critical importance in the history of digital photography. It took a lot of work on the part of many people, but the success has been overwhelming. This industry standard has become much easier to attain with recent advances in technology. To better understand the issues involved with matching an industry standard, we'll take a closer look at color management.

The Role of Digital Color Management

Digital color management was designed to create communication between digital information governing light-generated colors and digital information governing printers' ink-generated colors. By developing a language that cameras, scanners, computers, and printers (collectively called **devices** in color management terms) can all understand, translation of color information across different devices became possible.

Luckily for us, color management has become relatively easy in recent years. Camera manufacturers, creators of software like Adobe Photoshop, and printer and scanner manufacturers have all jumped on the color management bandwagon. The following information will be helpful to everyone interested in gaining control over the color and density of their printed digital images. It will take you far longer to learn about digital color management than to do it. Nevertheless, the concepts are important to understand.

Mechanical Means of Measuring Color

Historically, the first step in creating a language that defined color was to invent machines to measure the wavelengths of light reflected from a print or displayed on a monitor. Two such machines are described in the following sections.

Spectrophotometers

Spectrophotometers are mechanical devices that measure the wavelengths of color within the visible spectrum. They are used to measure light waves reflecting from printed photographs. The data collected by spectrophotometers help us understand how a given color is going to appear under a variety of lighting conditions. Information gathered from spectrophotometers is called **spectral data**.

Colorimeters

Colorimeters are mechanical devices that measure amounts of color being emitted from computer monitors or other displays. They contain a set of filters similar to the red, green, and blue cones found in the human eye; therefore, they emulate our perception of color. Information gathered from colorimeters is called **colorimetric data**.

Color Spaces, Gamuts, and Profiling Devices

To define the colors available to a camera sensor, photographers take a picture of an industry-standard print of colored squares with a digital camera. Then they use a spectrophotometer and specialized software that measure and record the color of the individual squares. The resulting spectral data is mapped onto a three-dimensional graph. The three-dimensional space that contains all of the colors represented in the graph is called a **color space**. The **gamut** of colors is the subset of all possible colors that appear within a given color space. This process is called **profiling** a camera.

Color Models

Cameras of the same make and model can differ slightly in their color gamuts as a result of manufacturing tolerances (Figure 10-1).

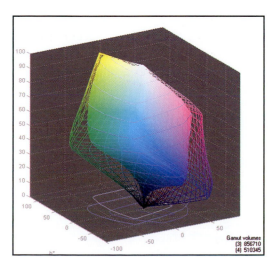

Figure 10-1

Imatest Corporation created Gamutvision, a software program that plots color information in three-dimensional form and allows you to compare one color space to another color space. In this example, the graphic shows that a camera's color space (represented by the wireframe) contains more colors than the color space of an inkjet printer (represented by the solid color). Learn more at www.imatest.com.

Photo © Imatest LLC, 2010.

The age of a camera can also slightly alter its color gamut. Because of this, it became helpful for scientists to define these color spaces separate from the cameras that produce them and call them **color models**.

ProPhoto RGB

ProPhoto RGB is the widest of all color models, yet the majority of digital cameras can't make use of it. That may change in the future. At the time of this writing, most monitors can't display all of the colors available in the ProPhoto RGB color model.

RGB

Having three channels of color data, RGB is the most common color model. "R" stands for the Red channel and contains all of the data associated with the red components of your image. "G" stands for the Green channel and contains all data associated with the green components. "B" stands for the Blue channel and contains all data associated

with the blue components of your image. Data from all three channels combine in the RGB Composite channel to give you the image you see on your screen.

You can see these channels if you open the Channels panel in Photoshop. If you can't see your Channels panel, go to WINDOW > CHANNELS (Figure 10-2). If you have an RGB file open, you will see RGB channels (Figure 10-3). By default, the individual channels appear as grayscale images. Although this can be changed in Photoshop's Preferences panel, most photographers leave them as grayscale.

The RGB color model is considered **device dependent** because each camera or scanner uses internal systems to assign the numeric RGB values. Each camera may be slightly different in its sensor or software composition; hence, the RGB color values of a given scene may shift slightly when you use different cameras to photograph that scene.

CieL*a*b

The **CieL*a*b** (or just *L*a*b* or even *Lab*) mode, a second color model, is also comprised of three separate channels of information. "L" stands for the lightness

Figure 10-2

In Photoshop, go to WINDOW > CHANNELS to view the Channels panel.

Photo © KS.

Window   Help

Arrange   ▶
Workspace   ▶

Extensions   ▶

3D
✓ Actions
Adjustments
Animation
Brush
Brush Presets
Channels
Character
Clone Source
Color
Histogram
History
Info
Layer Comps
Layers

Figure 10-3

The RGB color channels.

Photo © KS.

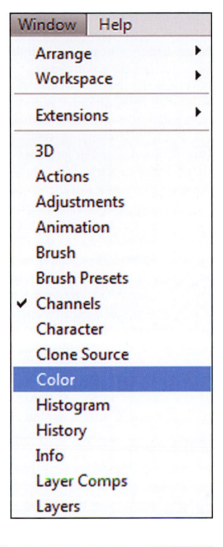

Figure 10-4 (left)

The CieL*a*b color channels.

Figure 10-5 (right)

Go to WINDOW > COLOR to open Photoshop's Color panel.

Photos 10-4 and 10-5 © KS.

channel and represents density (range from light to dark) information ranging from black through shades of gray to white. The "a" channel represents redness-to-greenness, and the "b" channel represents blueness-to-yellowness (Figure 10-4). Together, these three channels of information define the various colors of your photograph in a language computers can understand.

There is one very important difference between the L*a*b mode and all of the other color modes discussed here. L*a*b is a **device independent** color system; that is, L*a*b, unlike other color systems, does not depend on devices such as your camera or scanner to assign the color values to individual pixels. These color values come from highly specialized spectrophotometers. Because they do not rely on any device to generate the colors, L*a*b's color values are the only truly consistent values available in digital color systems.

The Color panel in Photoshop gives you the opportunity to use color sliders to represent any of these color models. If you can't see your Color panel, go to WINDOW > COLOR (Figure 10-5). HOLD DOWN the FLY-OUT TRIANGLE in the upper right corner of the panel. You will see a variety of color models available (Figure 10-6). CLICK on the model you want to use, and it will become active in your color panel.

Figure 10-6

The fly-out menu on the Color panel allows you to select HSB sliders.

Photo © KS.

This does not change the actual color model of your image; it simply changes how the colors within your photograph are represented within the Color panel.

Within the list of color model sliders is one called *HSB*. Although not a true color model like RGB or CieL*a*b, these sliders are worth understanding. HSB stands for Hue, Saturation, and Brightness.

"H" stands for the hue channel and identifies the characteristic we call *color*. A blue hue looks different to us than does a red or orange hue. A green hue appears different than does a yellow or brown hue. In the HSB model, hue is identified independently of saturation or brightness. The "S" in HSB stands for the saturation channel and represents the purity of a color. Red light is perceived as strong red unless that particular light also had elements of blue and green that combine to dull the red color. The more a color contains elements of other colors, the less saturated it appears to us. We perceive a fully desaturated color as gray. Last, the "B" stands for the brightness channel in the HSB sliders. It is similar to the Lightness channel in the L*a*b color model.

The HSB sliders are very helpful if you want to carefully alter a color you are using for painting or retouching an image. By moving the saturation or brightness

sliders independently of the hue slider, you can keep a new color within its original color family. This is a very useful capability when doing photographic retouching.

Note that choosing a different set of color sliders within the Color panel *does not* mean you have changed the color engine that is currently running Photoshop. That only takes place when you choose a different color mode for your entire file, first by choosing the IMAGE menu and then changing the mode. You'll learn how to do this next.

Photoshop's Color Modes

Photoshop does not capture color. That's the job of your camera or scanner. Photoshop's job is to take the color information from your files and work with it by interpreting the numeric color information in your file and mapping it to a predefined color model. Each of the color modes described here—and more—is available in Photoshop.

Go to IMAGE > MODE and see all of the different color modes you could use in Photoshop (Figure 10-7). The list beginning with Bitmap and continuing through Multichannel are all different color modes. They all display color and/or density information differently.

Although all modes have their roles to play, the RGB, HSB, and Lab listings are the ones you'll use the most. You may also use the Grayscale mode if you have created grayscale images from digital files. You will soon learn how to set the color mode in Photoshop's color settings and in your digital camera. For now, though, step away from Photoshop to learn about other factors that affect digital color management.

The Human Factor in Digital Color Management

We see different colors because all the objects we see absorb certain wavelengths of light and reflect other wavelengths of light. Our eyes and brains translate these light wavelengths as color.

The rod and cone cells within your eyes are responsible for vision. Each cone is

Figure 10-7

To show Photoshop's available color modes, go to IMAGE > MODE.

Photo © KS.

sensitive to only one of three colors: red, green, or blue. Your eyes also contain millions of rods, which are light-sensitive but not color-sensitive cells. Rod and cone data combine in your brain to produce your sense of vision.

Issues of Perception

How you *perceive* color (in other words, how you think color looks) is based on two separate factors: the physical reflected wavelengths (the stimulus) and your brain's interpretation of those wavelengths (color sensation). Issues in human perception alone prevent the mechanical RGB, L*a*b, or HSL color modes from being perfect as sole color management devices. This muddies the water of any purely mechanical means of working with color and causes color management to be an elusive beast. Here are some of the issues:

■ **Simultaneous contrast** occurs when two squares of the exact same color are surrounded by different colors, as shown in Figures 4–49 and 4–50. Our perception of those two original squares tells us they are two different colors. Human perception of one color is altered by other colors closely surrounding it, and mechanical means of measuring color can't account for this fact. Spectrophotometers and colorimeters were created to measure solid patches of color, which isn't the same as looking at photographs. You view photographs as a series of colors beside other colors, and therefore your perception of any specific color will change depending on the colors surrounding it.

■ **Cone fatigue** occurs if you stare at one color long enough. Those cones become incapable of accurately reading color wavelengths entering your eye (Figure 10-8). This becomes critically important when designing a workspace for your digital darkroom. If the walls in your room are even slightly pink, yellow, or green, your eyes' cones become fatigued by that color; and you are prone to creating images that aren't properly color balanced. Your brain will

compensate with the opposite color without your realizing it. Prints may look color-corrected to you while you're working, but you may perceive a color cast in those prints after you have left your workroom and later return to the prints.

■ **Metamerism** is a function of human perception. Metamerism allows us to print a photo of a real object, such as an apple or orange, that looks exactly like the real object even though no red or orange ink is used to make the print. Almost all color printers use a combination of cyan (similar to aquamarine), magenta, yellow, and black inks to reproduce the colors we see on the printed page. A saturated red hue would be reproduced by combining magenta and yellow (Figure 10-9). A slightly different red hue (Figure 10-10) would be represented by percentages of all four printing colors.

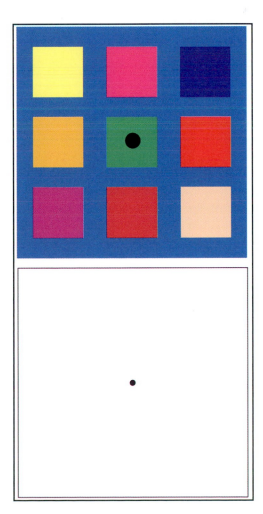

Figure 10-8

A demonstration of cone fatigue. Stare at the black dot in the top rectangle for about a minute. Then look at the black dot in the white rectangle below it. Faint images of the opposite (complementary) color will begin to appear on the page.

Photo © KS.

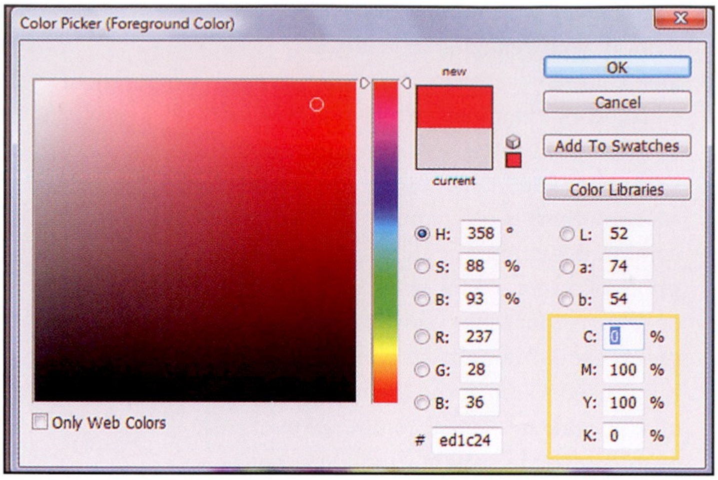

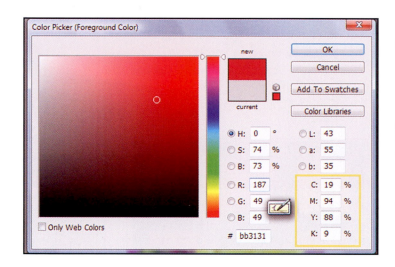

Take the following steps to ensure a color-neutral environment:

- Paint your walls white or a color-neutral gray. The Munsell Corporation sells a standard gray neutral paint for this purpose.
- Cover your windows to prevent sunlight from entering your workspace. As it travels across the sky, the sun changes color temperature. Reflections of that light can hit your monitor and alter your color vision.
- Always let your monitor remain on (and not asleep) for at least 30 minutes before doing any monitor calibration or critical color work on files. Take this time to do file management instead, such as downloading and naming files, backing up files, etc.
- If you use a light source within your workroom, consider using a light that has an approximate 5,000° K (daylight balanced) color temperature.

Steps in Digital Color Management

By now you're beginning to understand the complexities of color management. Even though mechanical processes can move you a long way toward color management, your human eye must still be the final judge of a properly color balanced image. Nevertheless, it's in your best interest to get all the color management control you can from mechanical methods *before* relying on your eyes for final color matching.

Trish Simonite, the photographer who made the opening image for Chapter 10, creates photographic prints from her images. Color management for her is of utmost importance, as she must deal with color issues across different media. Read her message in the Artist Statement.

Step One: Calibrate Your Monitor

Color experts around the world convened an International Color Consortium (ICC) and developed a highly specific standard for the display of color on computer monitors. The goal of this group was to define this standard for everyone so that monitors across the world would show color and density the same way.

Figure 10-9 (top)

Photoshop's Color Picker demonstrates the printing ink colors required to represent this saturated red color. Double-Click on the Foreground Color at the bottom of the Tools panel to invoke the Color Picker.

Figure 10-10 (bottom)

The printing ink colors required to represent this particular red color.

Photos 10-9 and 10-10 © KS.

- Although metamerism in general is good, one side effect of metamerism is that a print viewed under one light source may look different when viewed under a different light source. If your workroom is lit with fluorescent lights, your prints will appear to have a given color balance under those lights. If you move the print to a different room lit with, say, incandescent lights, the print's color balance may appear different to you. The best solution to this problem is to view a print under the same lighting conditions as the room where you intend to display it.

Control Your Surroundings

Because your vision influences color perception, controlling digital color also means controlling your work environment.

Trish Simonite

Even though there are specific procedures that allow you to print the image very close to what you see on the screen, printing is still an art and you may need to make minor adjustments to the image in order to achieve your goal. The goal is that the image should communicate the content that expresses your intent.

The most important thing when dealing with color management is to calibrate your monitor. The second is to download the ICC profiles for your specific paper.

Your first step in color management is to calibrate your monitor to that industry standard. Although it's possible to calibrate your monitor without any third-party hardware and software, it isn't recommended. Instead, spend some very worthwhile money on a package that includes a colorimeter and software that measures the color output of your monitor and brings your monitor's settings to that industry standard.

The products listed below are specifically used to calibrate monitors and are very easy to use. Without advocating one product over another, here are some products available at the writing of this text:

- Eye-one Display 2 by X-Rite,
- X-rite i1Display LT,
- ColorVision ColorPlus and
- Pantone® Huey™.

All of these products come with a colorimeter that plugs into your computer and measures the color your monitor displays. Once you've installed the colorimeter and accompanying software, running the program is an easy task. The software measures the color display of your monitor and creates a file of information called a **monitor profile**. This profile sends your monitor instructions on how to display specific colors and densities to match the industry standard defined by the International Color Consortium.

A word about laptops: Because the brightness of a laptop display dramatically changes, depending on its angle of view, serious digital work on laptops should be avoided. Laptops are good for carrying and transferring files, and they can certainly be used to check an image's composition, depth of field, or focus. In addition, a laptop can run Photoshop, which can evaluate your photographs' exposures with its histogram functions. However, laptops are *not* adequate for critical color or density work.

Before calibrating your monitor, be sure to have your monitor's display on full time for at least 30 minutes. A monitor's color balance changes as it warms up; so, you don't want to run the software before then. Make sure you have your monitor's sleep function turned off because the monitor needs to stay on during the entire calibration procedure.

It's a good idea to calibrate your monitor at least once per month. Monitors fall out of calibration over time, and older monitors may need calibrating more often. If you are doing critical color work, calibrate your monitor weekly or even more often.

Step Two: Set Your Camera's Color Mode

Digital cameras rely on their built-in color collecting and color interpreting methods to display and record color. Your camera's sensor contains photoreceptors that collect light information. Each photoreceptor is covered with either a red, green, or blue filter and therefore collects either red, green, or blue digital information. There are typically more green photoreceptors than there are red or blue photoreceptors because the human eye is particularly sensitive to variations in green hues.

The **gamut of a sensor** refers to the range of colors it can collect. A sensor's gamut is a function of its photoreceptors and the camera's built-in microprocessor that interprets the data captured by those photoreceptors. Cameras with wider color gamuts can record a wider range of colors from a scene. The most common color gamuts captured by 35 mm digital cameras are:

- **Adobe RGB (1998)**, or simply **Adobe RGB**, is the gamut frequently used by professional photographers. It has the widest color space of all the color gamuts listed here.
- **sRGB** has a significantly smaller gamut than Adobe RGB (1998) and is the gamut recommended by many printing labs. The thought is that if the printing labs can reproduce only the colors within the sRGB gamut, there's no reason to capture more color information in your digital files. It's worth noting that sRGB is often the only color gamut available in many consumer-level cameras.
- **CMYK** captures only the color information that can be reproduced in a CMYK color printout. This is a considerably smaller gamut than either of the above-listed color gamuts. Even if you intend to send your color photographs to a commercial press that uses only CMYK colors, it's not recommended that you use this color gamut in your camera. Capturing a wider gamut of color gives you greater options in the long run. You can convert your files to CMYK in Photoshop if you need to.
- **Gray, Grayscale, or Black-and-White** captures only density information and no color information at all. Even if you intend to change your images to grayscale, this is not a recommended gamut for the initial image capture. There are many creative ways to change a color image to grayscale in Photoshop. Capture color information by using an Adobe RGB or sRGB color gamut first, and change your images to grayscale in the digital darkroom instead.

Check your camera's manual to see what color gamuts (frequently called *color modes* in camera manuals) your camera can use. If possible, set your camera mode to Adobe RGB. That way you will be collecting the most color information you can represent on your monitor. If Adobe RGB isn't available on your camera, choose sRGB instead.

Differences in sensors, and differences in the software that interpret the sensor's information, can cause one digital camera to display a specific scene slightly differently than another digital camera would display that scene. The color balance and/or density of the resulting photographs can be different even though the scene and lighting conditions were the same.

Step Three: Select Industry-Standard Color Settings in Photoshop

Now it's time to match up your camera's color settings to those in Photoshop. Open Photoshop and go to EDIT > COLOR SETTINGS (Figure 10-11). For the RGB Working Space, choose the same color mode you set in your camera (Figure 10-12). There's no need to change any of the other working spaces for now as they pertain to output for commercial printing purposes. If your camera is set to Adobe RGB (1998) or Adobe RGB mode, choose the Adobe RGB (1998) working space in Photoshop. If your camera is set to sRGB mode, select the sRGB working space in Photoshop.

In the Color Management Policies section of the Color Settings window, SELECT PRESERVE EMBEDDED PROFILE. This tells Photoshop to honor the camera's color mode when the image was made.

Profile mismatches occur when your camera's color mode setting is different than the working color space within Photoshop. For instance, let's say your camera is set to the sRGB color mode, and your working space in Photoshop is Adobe RGB (1998). When you open the sRGB file in Photoshop, you have a profile mismatch.

In the same Color Settings window under Profile Mismatches, make sure ASK

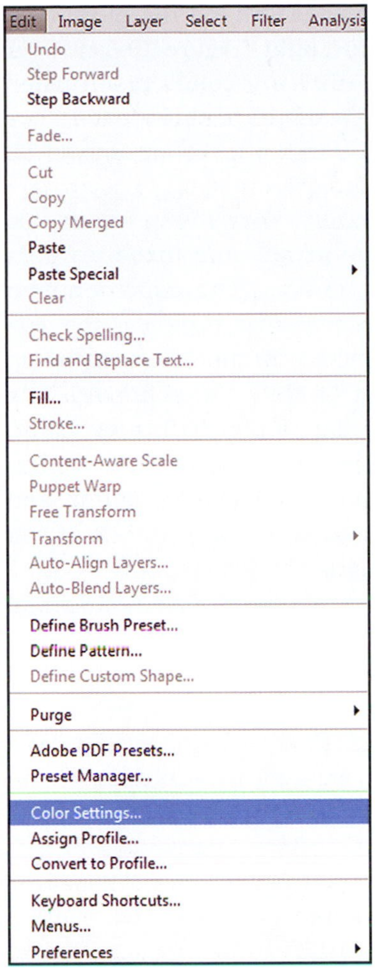

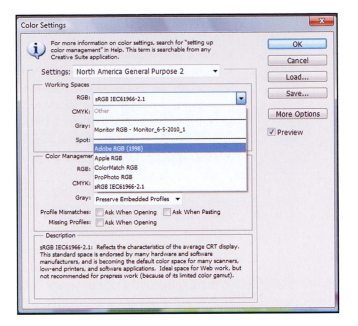

Figure 10-11

EDIT > COLOR SETTINGS.

Photo © KS.

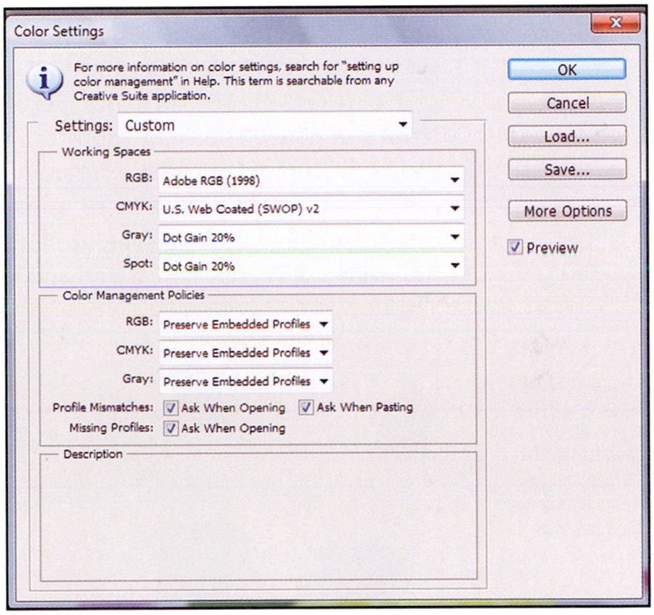

Figure 10-12 (right top)

SELECT ADOBE RGB 1998 from the RGB drop-down menu.

Figure 10-13 (right bottom)

Under Color Management Policies, SELECT PRESERVE EMBEDDED PROFILES. Under Profile Mismatches, SELECT ASK WHEN OPENING and ASK WHEN PASTING. Also under Profile Mismatches, SELECT ASK WHEN OPENING.

Photos 10-12 and 10-13 © KS.

WHEN OPENING and ASK WHEN PASTING are selected. Under Missing Profiles, ASK WHEN OPENING should be selected (Figure 10-13). Each time you open a file in Photoshop, the color mode used to capture that image will be retained. But if you're pasting a portion of a photograph with a different mode, you'll have the option of changing that digital photograph's color mode to your working color space.

Under Color Management Policies: RGB, SELECT PRESERVE EMBEDDED PROFILES. If you happen to come across a file that doesn't have an embedded profile, Photoshop will ask you how you want to handle the file. The best solution will be to assign the file your RGB WORKING SPACE. Every photograph should have a color profile assigned to it before you work on it in Photoshop.

CLICK OK in the upper right corner of the Color Settings window to save your color settings. Now your photograph's color information will work with the color settings in Photoshop.

Use External Color Management Tools

In Chapter 11, you will be given instruction on using a gray card to set a custom white balance within your digital camera. This technique is helpful in color management, as it helps neutralize any color casts in your photographs before pixels are ever created.

Color management begins with the camera and continues throughout the photographic and digital darkroom processes. If you learn color management and thoroughly apply the techniques discussed here to your photographic workflow, those techniques become excellent habits. Color management isn't an option for serious photographers; it is an absolute necessity.

Making Digital Color Prints

Color management continues into the printing process. Translating the color information from Photoshop to the color settings in your printer is the final step of color management. First, you'll learn the differences between color produced by light and color produced by inks.

Light Color Versus Printing Color

One issue confronting photographers and printers deals with the physics of light and color. The light monitors use is based on combining different amounts of red, green, and blue light. Red, green, and blue represent a color system called the **additive color system**. When red, green, and blue light are added together, they result in white light (Figure 10-14). Over 16.7 million different colors result when varying levels of these three colors are combined in varying levels of density on computer monitors.

Unfortunately, very few printers use light to make prints, and those printers are very expensive. The most common type of consumer-level printer is the inkjet printer, which requires a completely different set of colors to achieve a mix of colors similar to the RGB color space. Inkjet printers use cyan (a color similar to light turquoise), magenta, yellow, and black in combination to print all of the printable colors.

Three of these colors (cyan, magenta, and yellow) combine to create near-black ink. Therefore, cyan, magenta, and yellow combine to make the **subtractive color system** (Figure 10-15). However, a little black ink is commonly added to make the black richer and darker. A digital color photograph can be printed with only four colors of ink. This is called the **CMYK color system** (*K* represents black). The collection of colors that can be created by mixing cyan, magenta, yellow, and black inks comprise the CMYK color space.

The sad fact is that we can never print all of the colors within the RGB color space with CMYK inks. The CMYK color space is

Figure 10-14 (left)

Red, green, and blue lights combined together make white light (the additive color system). Blue and green light combine to create cyan light. Red plus green light combine to create yellow light.

Figure 10-15 (right)

Cyan, magenta, and yellow inks combined together create black ink (the subtractive color system).

Photos 10-14 and 10-15
© Cengage Learning 2012.

Hint: Never show a client a richly colored photo on your computer monitor if it will later be printed on a CMYK press. Your client will ask you why you lost all of those deeply saturated colors! Instead, go to VIEW > PROOF COLORS to show a preview of what the file will look like after it is printed with CMYK inks. Go back to VIEW > PROOF COLORS again to turn off the preview.

considerably smaller than the RGB color space; so, a mixture of cyan, magenta, yellow, and black inks simply can't reproduce the full 16.7 million colors visible on monitors. Many modern inkjet printers are compensating for this fact by using more than four colors of ink, but any CMYK-based printer will still reproduce fewer colors than the same file contains in the Adobe RGB color space on your monitor.

To make the best of this situation, it's critical that the color information of your file be converted to a highly specific printer profile. By converting the digital profile to your printer's profile, you're ensuring as close a match as possible between the digital file and the final print.

Printer Profiles

A printer's ICC profile takes into consideration factors such as your inkjet printer's manufacturer and model, the brand of inks installed in the printer, and the exact type of paper being used. Each printer model comes with a set of ICC profiles made specifically for that model. These profiles download to your computer when you install the software for your printer.

Digital printing papers can be separated by manufacturer, surface (matt, glossy, etc.) and weight (plain, heavy, etc.). Each paper has both chemical and surface qualities that affect the way color inks appear on it. Even if you're printing with pure magenta ink, for example, the appearance of that ink may vary when printed on different paper types.

Your digital photograph's color mode is known as a **source profile**. A printer's profile is called a **destination profile**. When you're ready to print your photograph, you need to convert your source profile to the destination profile. You do this by going up to EDIT and choosing CONVERT TO PROFILE (Figure 10-16). Find your printer's profile in the drop-down menu and select it.

The task of Convert to Profile is to change a digital photograph's color profile while maintaining the color appearance of the source file to the greatest extent possible. If you happen to have your Info Panel open when you convert a file to a different profile, you may notice that the actual RGB numbers of specific pixels change when

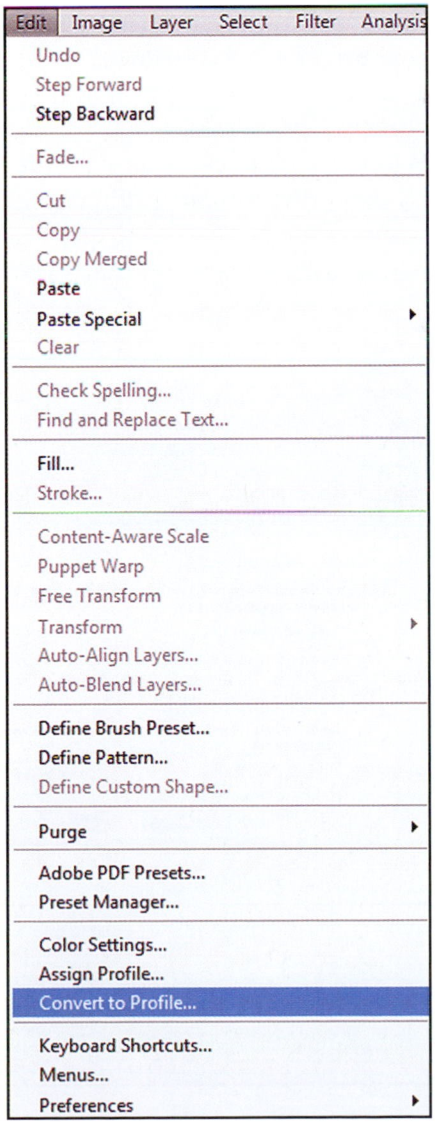

Figure 10-16

EDIT > CONVERT TO PROFILE.

Photo © KS.

the new profile is applied. That is to be expected. The important thing is that your print looks as close as possible to the image on your monitor.

Preparing Your Printer

Every inkjet printer requires maintenance to ensure high-quality prints. The ink comes from tiny nozzles in the ink cartridge, and those nozzles can easily clog. The result is an unacceptable print with faint lines running through a portion of it. To address this issue, read your printer's manual to learn about the maintenance options (sometimes called the *printer utility*) for your printer (Figure 10-17). In particular, look for "Nozzle Check" and "Print Head Alignment" capabilities. Run these maintenance procedures any time your print quality goes down.

Nozzle Check

When the ink cartridges' nozzles get clogged, they cannot properly spray ink

onto the print. Running a nozzle check before you print your file will let you know if this will be an issue. Load plain (not photo quality) paper into your printer, and run the nozzle check from the printer's utility. Your printer will print out a pattern showing ink coming from each print head in succession (Figure 10-18).

Carefully examine the pattern. If you see small gaps in any of the lines, your print heads need to be cleaned. Return to the printer utility software and CLICK on the HEAD CLEANING UTILITY. The printer will automatically clean the print heads. Once the cleaning is complete, print the nozzle check again. The nozzle check pattern should be 100% correct before you proceed. You may need to repeat the head cleaning procedure several times until the nozzle check prints correctly (Figure 10-19).

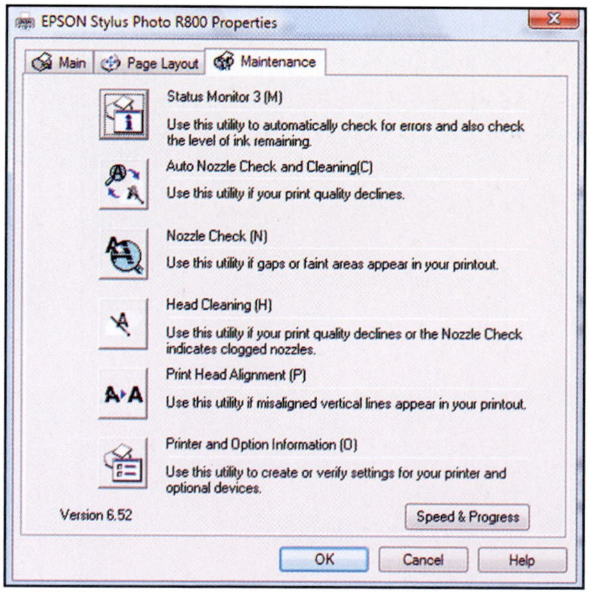

Figure 10-17

This printer's utility functions are listed under the Maintenance tab. Consult your printer's manual on how to locate your printer's utility functions.

Photo © KS.

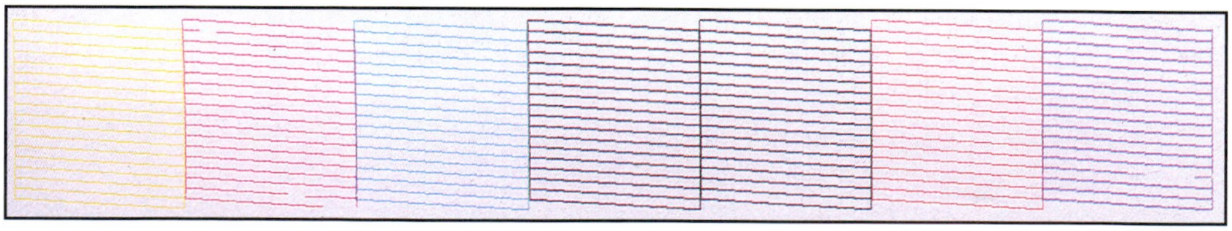

Figure 10-18

Look closely at the printout's thin lines and check for any gaps. In this printout, the patterns second to the left and at the far right have significant gaps.

Photo © KS.

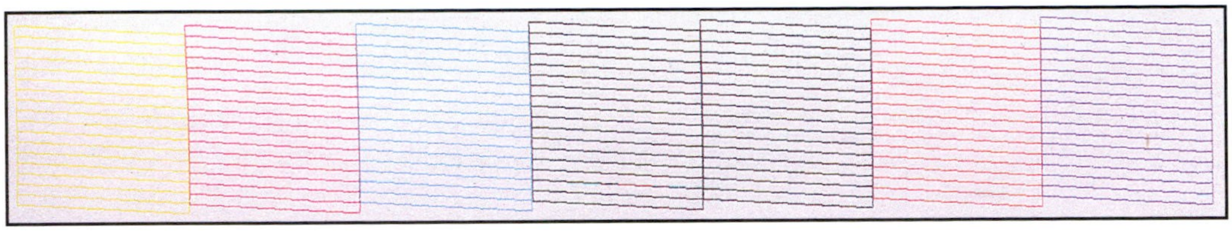

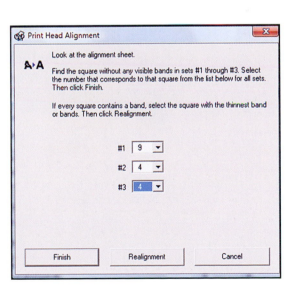

Figure 10-19

After print head cleaning is complete, run the nozzle check again. You should see a complete pattern like this one.

Photo © KS.

Print Head Alignment

If the print heads are out of alignment, your print quality can also be poor with linear gaps. To check for this possibility, use the PRINT HEAD ALIGNMENT UTILITY for your printer. Some printers have an automatic print head alignment function. For purposes of this demonstration, the manual function was used.

Print out the pattern as shown in Figure 10-20. Your pattern may differ somewhat, depending on your manufacturer's software. In this example, small vertical lines are visible in most of the squares. Your task is to select the individual square for rows 1, 2, and 3 that seem the most solid. Each solid square's number is transferred to the utility's dialog box. In this example, numbers 9, 4, and 4 were selected (Figure 10-21). Then the print head utility was run again.

This procedure was repeated two more times before achieving solid squares in the #5 spot in rows 1, 2, and 3 (Figures 10-22 and 10-23).

Again, this example is from the printer manufacturer for this machine. Your printer's print head alignment utility may be different in appearance. The important thing is to make sure your print heads are aligned and your inkjet nozzles are unclogged before you try to print your photograph.

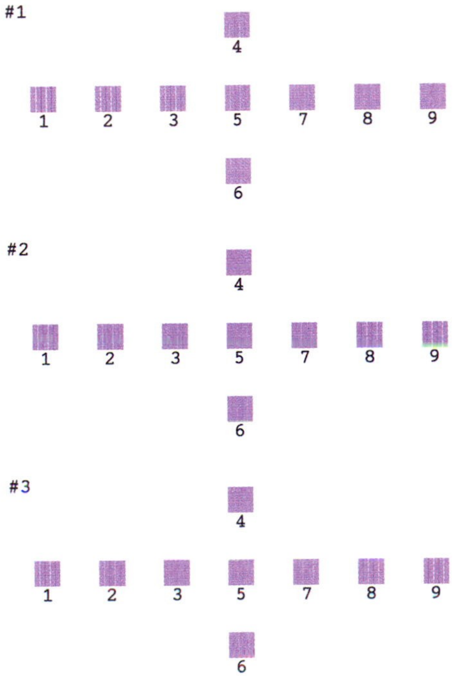

Printer Preferences

This information will vary somewhat depending on your printer manufacturer. When you go to FILE > PRINT, look for a COLOR MANAGEMENT section set up in the printer window. Common options for this section are Document or Proof. SELECT DOCUMENT (Figure 10-24) unless you are sending your file to a commercial printer.

Figure 10-20

Select the squares in rows 1, 2, and 3 that appear the most solid.

Photo © KS.

Figure 10-21

Enter these numbers into the printer utility's menu. Then run the print head alignment again.

Photo © KS.

**Figure 10-22
(left)**

The second printout
(not shown) was
closer, but minor
adjustments were
still needed.

**Figure 10-23
(right)**

The most solid square
should be in position #5
across all three rows,
as in this example.

Photos 10-22 and 10-23
© KS.

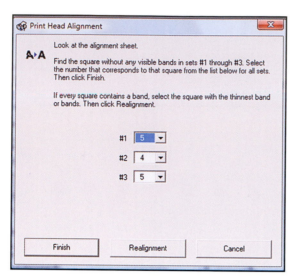

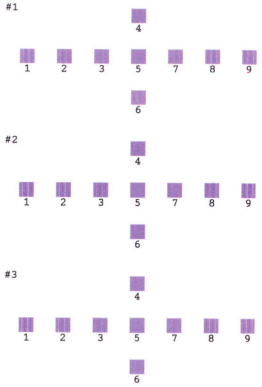

Figure 10-24

Go to FILE > PRINT and look
for the COLOR MANAGEMENT
section. Consult your
printer's manual if you
can't locate it.

Photo © KS.

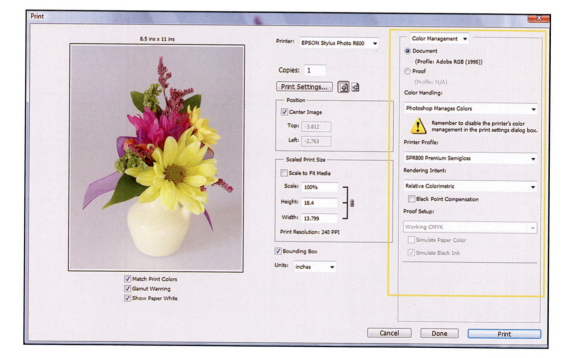

Within that same window, look for a section called COLOR HANDLING. This is an important component of your printer's software. In the drop-down menu, SELECT PHOTOSHOP MANAGES COLORS. You are doing all of your color management in Photoshop; so, you don't want your printer to step in at this stage and take over.

Click on PRINTER PROFILE and select the printer you are currently using. Under RENDERING INTENT, SELECT RELATIVE COLORIMETRIC. This will be the best choice most of the time. If you are in particular need of saturated colors, you might try PERCEPTUAL RENDERING INTENT to increase color saturation.

If your printer has a BLACK POINT COMPENSATION button, CLICK it ON. This will help Photoshop and your printer properly translate the blacks of the Photoshop file to the blacks within the printer's color gamut.

Your final step will be to disable color management in the printer's dialog box. CLICK ON PRINT in your printer software. You may need to go to the Advanced

settings in that dialog box. Look for a section called COLOR MANAGEMENT or ICC/ICM PROFILE. TURN this function OFF so that your printer will not be able to make any unwanted color adjustments (Figure 10-25).

Select the type of paper you will be using, and also select the paper size and orientation. If possible, select the highest dpi (dots per inch) function available for your printer.

You are finally ready to CLICK on the PRINT button. If you have followed all of the steps of color management, your print should closely resemble the image you see on your screen. However, do not assume the two images will look exactly the same. Your monitor is showing colors created by light, not by ink. Your monitor and your print are also in two separate color spaces (RGB and CMYK), so it is not likely that they will perfectly match. However, they should be very close.

Digital Print Permanence

You have probably seen old color prints from the 1950s or later that have yellowed and faded. This is an issue of print permanence, and it is a direct function of the dyes used to make those prints.

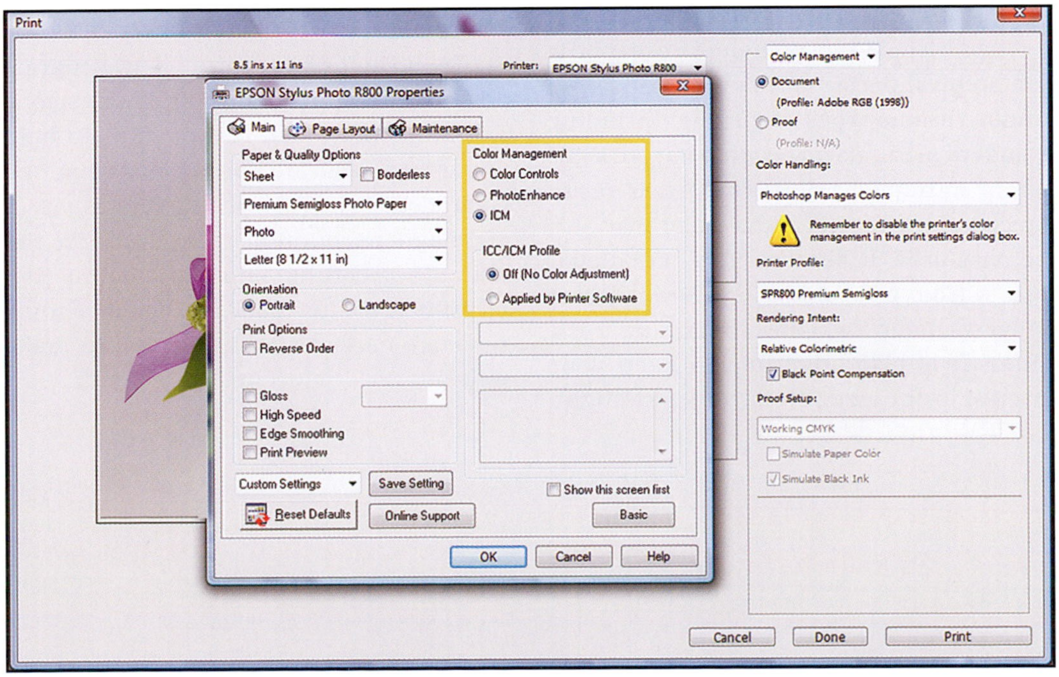

Figure 10-25

TURN OFF the printer's COLOR MANAGEMENT function as shown here.

Photo © KS.

Technological breakthroughs since that time have greatly extended the life of color prints made with dyes.

Digital printing has a similar history. When digital printing first became popular, manufacturers used unrealistic data in their advertising. Some manufacturers stated their digital prints could last 20–30 years or longer. When photographers used those printers, they were sorely disappointed. Some prints started to fade or change color within a matter of weeks or months, not years.

Henry Welhelm, a scientist involved in the study of darkroom photographic print permanence, became prominent on the Internet as a tester of digital print permanence. He set up a series of large light banks to simulate accelerated decay of color in digital prints. Keeping track of the printer, printing inks, and papers being used, Wilhelm began publishing his findings online. His website (www.wilhelm-research.com) became a trusted source of information regarding print permanence. Wilhelm's research provides abundant information about the importance of using specific papers, inks, and printers to obtain long-term print permanence. If you are looking for a new printer, inks, or paper for printing your digital photographs, it's a good idea to check his website before making a purchase.

Also included in Wilhelm's research is the archival permanence of images stored under various types of glazing; including standard glass, glazing containing a UV filter, or unframed prints. The print's resistance to high humidity and water may also be measured. It became clear that digital prints from most inkjet printers will last longest under a glazing containing a UV filter. It is also advisable to keep your framed print away from direct sunlight.

These precautions will slow, but will not eliminate, fading from UV light.

A second excellent resource for archival information of digital prints is the Image Permanence Institute (www.imagepermanenceinstitute.org). This non-profit organization is a university-based laboratory devoted to preservation research and education. It is sponsored by the Rochester Institute of Technology and the Society for Imaging Science and Technology. The Image Permanence Institute goes beyond the question of print permanence and investigates sustainable practices in environmental management and preservation. It also helps develop ISO Standards for imaging media and preservation and offers informational websites and e-newsletters for interested readers.

Summary

Color management is a technical, but very necessary, part of working with digital equipment. Without these controls set into place, you will not have predictable results when printing your digital images.

Digital color management begins with understanding the available color spaces and the color modes that utilize them. These color modes apply to digital cameras and scanners and are an integral part of Photoshop's color engine.

The advent of ICC profiles was a great advancement in digital color management. Digital printers use ICC profiles to help ensure an accurate conversion from one color mode to another within Photoshop.

Image permanence depends on the use of a carefully selected combination of printer, printer inks, and paper. Online resources are available for you to make well-informed selections.

EXERCISES

1. Look in Appendix A, By the Decade: 1941–1950 and 1951–1960 to learn about the era that color photography was first becoming popular.

2. Investigate the film noir style of movies and relate that style to photography by Edward Weston, Alfred Stieglitz, Paul Caponigro, and Paul Strand.

3. Investigate the abstract expressionism movement that started in 1945 and relate it to photography. How can photography be used as a medium for abstract expressionism?

4. Identify on your computer every aspect of color management available to you in Photoshop and in your printing software. Then make a series of small prints using a variety of ICC profiles to visualize the difference these profiles make.

5. Read your camera's manual to learn how to set your camera's color space.

6. Go online and find ICC profiles available for your printer.

FURTHER READING

- Fraser, Bruce, Chris Murphy, and Fred Bunting. *Real World Color Management.* 2nd ed. Berkeley, CA: Peachpit Press, 2004.

- Rodney, Andrew. *Color Management for Photographers: Hands-on Techniques for Photoshop Users.* Burlington, MA: Focal Press/ Elsevier, 2005.

- DeWolfe, George. *Digital Masters: B&W Printing: Creating the Digital Master Print.* New York: Lark Books, 2009.

- DeWolfe, George. *George DeWolfe's Digital Photography Fine Print Workshop.* New York: McGraw-Hill Osborne Media, 2006.

Books III – From the series: *The secret of Books.*

CHAPTER

11

Working with Light

- Define the components of your sense of vision and how these components relate to photography.

- Summarize the importance of light in photography.

- Explore the effects of different lighting conditions on photography.

- Describe color temperature and its effect on photography.

- Recognize the potential problems when photographing with multiple light sources.

- Use a digital camera's custom white balance function.

- Become aware of the different qualities and directions of light and how they affect photography.

- Describe how commercial and portrait photographers handle lighting requirements.

- Demonstrate basic skills in classic portrait photography.

Light is of the utmost importance in photography. The word "photography" is derived from Greek words meaning "writing with light." You have actually been studying light throughout this text, but in conjunction with camera and darkroom functions. In this chapter, you'll learn more about light itself and how to control light to improve your photographs.

An understanding of light includes a basic understanding of how you see. Vision is critical in photography, and there are similarities between how your eyes and your camera process light. We will begin the study of light by looking at your sense of vision.

Human Vision

Your eyes are responsible for gathering, focusing, and transmitting visual information to your brain. Over 70% of all the sensory receptors in your body are in your eyes. You'll begin the study of vision by examining the basic anatomy of the eye.

The Eye

The **cornea**, the clear, colorless outer covering, is responsible for protecting your eye from foreign particles and environmental irritants (Figure 11-1). Behind the cornea is the **iris**, the colored portion of your eye. It is a muscle that automatically contracts and expands, depending on the amount of light in your environment. The **pupil** is the center hole that allows light to enter your eye. By contracting and expanding in response to the light in your environment, your iris controls the amount of light coming through the pupil and falling on the back of your eye.

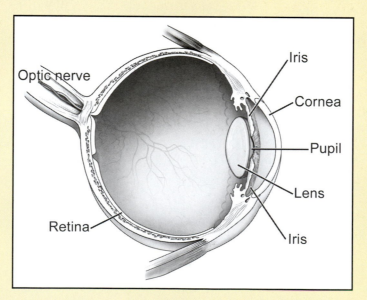

Figure 11-1

Diagram of the human eye.

Photo courtesy of National Eye Institute, National Institutes of Health (NEI/NIH).

The **lens** of your eye is a gelatinous disc, convex on both sides, residing immediately behind your iris. The lens bends the light coming into your eye so that the image converges, flips upside down, and falls on the rods and cones in the back of your eye. Muscles on either side of the lens contract and expand, reshaping the lens and resulting in near-instantaneous focus, regardless of the distance between you and the object on which you're focusing.

The lining in the back of your eye, the **retina** contains 125 million specialized photoreceptor cells, with 7 million cells responsible for color vision and 118 million cells responsible for grayscale (black-and-white) vision. Your eye's photoreceptors transform light information into electrical impulses.

Several layers of nerve cells, so small as to not hamper vision, lie just above the retina. These nerve cells gather the electrical impulses from your photoreceptors and carry them into your brain. Your brain is responsible for interpreting these electrical impulses, with the net result being your perception of the visual information.

Photoreceptors

Each eye has millions of photoreceptors on the retina, most of them opposite the pupil. There are two major categories of photoreceptors, rods and cones. **Rods** are responsible for collecting and interpreting light in terms of black, white, and shades of gray. They are incapable of interpreting color information. Rods are responsible for your ability to see at night.

Cones are responsible for color vision. Sensitive to only one of three colors—red, green, or blue—each cone can be identified as being red-sensitive, green-sensitive, or blue-sensitive. Although they work very well during the day and in artificial light, cones aren't very good at gathering color information in low-light conditions. As a result, our color vision in relatively dark surroundings is very poor and we see more in shades of gray.

Sensory Nerves and Optic Nerve

A very fine, nearly invisible network of **sensory nerves** (or *neural network*) covers the rods and cones in your eyes. The neural network converges at the **optic nerve**, the major nerve that transports the electrical impulses to the brain.

Visual Perception

So far, you've learned about how your eye and brain allow you to see. That's only half the story. Once the light information enters your brain, a variety of factors influence what part of your surroundings actually capture your attention. This is called perception, which is different from strict visual information. Perception determines what you notice in a scene, how you recognize shapes and colors, how you feel about the scene, and how you recall the visual information.

It takes prior knowledge to identify items in a photograph. It takes life experiences to process the visual information and identify the most important aspects of a scene. Hence, perception invokes your emotions and makes you feel something about the photograph. Without your brain's capacity to remember and learn from prior experiences, most photographs wouldn't have much meaning for you.

In addition, your own goals and expectations, memories, and minute-to-minute thoughts alter your attention to the visual information entering your brain. This fact is important not only when you are creating photographs, but also when you listen to people critiquing your photographs. Every viewer of your photographs has expectations, memories, learned responses, and general opinions developed over years of living. Those thoughts and experiences alter what a viewer will notice and how he/she will react to your images.

Human Vision and the Camera

As digital photography was developed, experts referred to the rod and cone functions to develop the sensors responsible for digital image capture. Table 11-1 offers a rough translation between the human eye and cameras/digital captures.

Light and Electromagnetic Radiation

Light is a form of energy that physicists call **electromagnetic radiation** that travels in tiny packages called **photons**. Photons travel through your camera's lens and strike the film or digital sensors, starting the production of an image.

Studying these wavelike motions reveals how color is associated with light. You are probably familiar with the historical work that Sir Isaac Newton conducted in 1665. Newton passed a white light through a prism and observed the rainbow of colors on the other side. He determined that white light is comprised of all of the colors combined: red, orange, yellow, green, blue, indigo, and violet. Together these colors comprise the spectrum of colors visible to the human eye (Figure 11-2).

Light and Color

The electromagnetic field of visible light fluctuates at a variety of speeds, creating differences in the wavelengths of that energy. The amount of space between the peaks of each wave is measured in *hertz*, or more commonly, *megahertz* (1,000,000 hertz). A hertz is the number of wavelengths that pass a marker within a single second. We identify the different frequencies as color.

Table 11-1
Eye-Camera Correlation
© Cengage Learning 2012

Human eye	Function	Camera equivalent
Eyelid	allows light in or blocks light	Shutter
Lens	focuses the scene to a specific point at the back of the dark chamber	Lens
Pupil	a hole that lets light enter an enclosed dark chamber	Aperture
Iris	A muscle or mechanical piece that increases or decreases size of opening	Diaphragm
Photoreceptors	Process light, convert light to a form that can be sent to brain or recorded.	Film or ccd/cmos
Brain	Processes the information to form an image	Darkroom\computer.
Camera body	Dark chamber of the eye.	Space between the lens and film (camera) or the lens and fovea (eye).
Normal field of vision	160 degrees horizontally and 135 degrees vertically	"normal" focal length lens
Curvature of cornea and lens	Bends light toward a focal point in the interior of the eye	Bends light toward a focal point in the interior of the camera

Equally as important to photographers is what happens when light reflects off of objects. Every object has a physical property that determines which wavelengths of light will be absorbed and which will be reflected. An object we identify as red absorbs all visible wavelengths other than red. The absorbed energy is typically changed into heat energy and ceases to be light energy.

How We See Color and Tones

The red, green, and blue photoreceptors in your eyes are similar to the red, green, and blue color systems used in computer monitors, video cameras, and digital sensors. Your brain takes the color information and reads the various mixtures of these three colors, resulting in your ability to see the visible spectrum of light.

The rods in your eyes are similar to the **tonal values** (range in brightness) used in monitors and cameras. The tonal range from darkest dark to brightest light is a grayscale range containing no color information. *Values* are specific points along the tonal range. An image with mostly high values is relatively light, whereas an image with mostly low values is relatively dark (Figure 11-3).

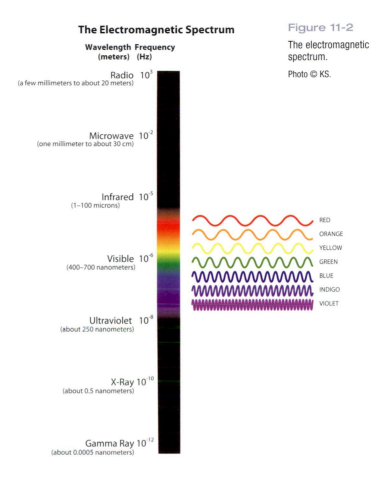

The Electromagnetic Spectrum

Wavelength (meters)	Frequency (Hz)
Radio (a few millimeters to about 20 meters)	10^3
Microwave (one millimeter to about 30 cm)	10^{-2}
Infrared (1–100 microns)	10^{-5}
Visible (400–700 nanometers)	10^{-6}
Ultraviolet (about 250 nanometers)	10^{-8}
X-Ray (about 0.5 nanometers)	10^{-10}
Gamma Ray (about 0.0005 nanometers)	10^{-12}

RED
ORANGE
YELLOW
GREEN
BLUE
INDIGO
VIOLET

Figure 11-2

The electromagnetic spectrum.

Photo © KS.

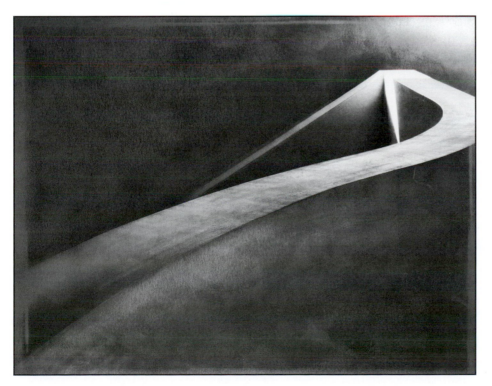

Figure 11-3

Capp Street 3. Tonal values are always grayscale. This image consists of a wide range of tonal values from very light to very dark.

Photo © Barry Brukoff, 2005. Capp Street 3. www.brukoffphoto.com.

Your digital camera captures red, green, and blue color information, and the corresponding tonal information, on its photoreceptors and translates that information to a digital form that Photoshop and other image-editing software programs can read. Photoshop stores the red, green, and blue color information in separate color channels and makes visible one composite color channel on screen, allowing you to see millions of colors on your monitor. The tonal range from dark to bright is also represented within each color channel (Figure 11-4).

Pay Attention to Light

When you take a photograph, you aren't recording an object, person, or scene—you are recording the light reflecting off that object, person, or scene. The light bouncing from the scene goes through the lens and comes into contact with your camera's film or digital sensor. This may seem like splitting hairs, but it's actually very important. Photographers do pay attention to the person or object they are photographing, but they pay at least as much or more attention to *the light reflecting off* that subject. How they work with that light—and how they choose to record it onto film—is an integral part of creating a successful photograph.

Set up a collection of solid objects in a row on a table. Using only one small light source such as a lamp or flashlight, look at the shadows the objects cast. Note the direction and quality of the shadows. Do this with several light sources from varying distances. Note that despite changes of light sources, all of the objects within the group will cast the same quality of shadows. In other words, it isn't just the object itself that's dictating what the shadows look like; it's also the size, quality, and distance of the light source that determine how the shadows appear.

Shadows help you visually interpret your world. Highlights and shadows give you a three-dimensional read of whatever you see. This is particularly important when you're trying to get the feel of a three-dimensional image on a two-dimensional print.

Fast and Slow Falloff

The sun is the most convenient light source for photographers. It is very large, but it's also very far away. This effectively makes the sun a small light source from a very great distance. Because light rays from distant sources tend to run parallel to each other, the light is highly directional. When the light rays strike a three-dimensional form, only the side of the form closest to the light source

Figure 11-4

Illustration of photosites within a sensor and the resulting channels in Photoshop.

Photos © KS.

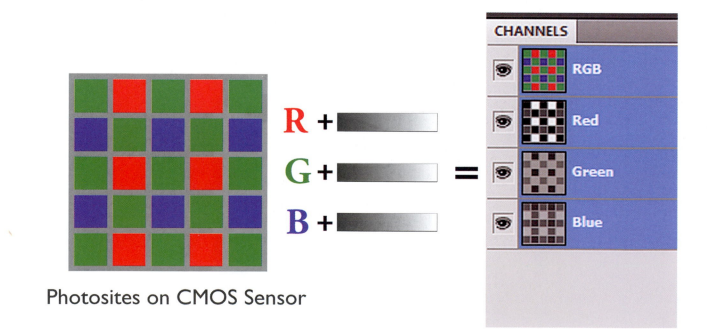

Photosites on CMOS Sensor

will be lit. As the form's surface curves, fewer of the light rays strike it, causing decreasing brightness. The side of the form opposite the light source receives no direct light rays.

Falloff is the word used to describe the space where the brightest area on a three-dimensional form transforms to darkness. **Fast falloff** is the term used when the length of falloff is very short, appearing as a relatively sharp line of demarcation (Figure 11-5a). **Slow falloff** is the term used when the length of falloff is longer, resulting in a broader space between the brightest and darkest surfaces (Figure 11-5b).

Cloudy days change the sun from a small to a very large light source. The clouds' moisture diffuses (redirects) the light rays into countless multiple directions. These light rays strike your subject from multiple directions, creating a decreased range of tonal values between the highlight and shadow sides of your three-dimensional form. Highlights are not as bright, and shadows are not as dark as they are when lit by small, distant light sources. Photographers tend to prefer cloudy days because it's far easier to create more contrast in an image via darkroom or digital techniques than it is to reduce the contrast in an image.

Contrast of Tonal Values

The amount of tonal contrast within an image is described in relation to the full tonal range, the range from the darkest dark (pure black) to the brightest bright (pure white). The full tonal range always remains the same. The tonal values of the scene you're photographing will fall somewhere on that full tonal range.

High-contrast images have values that fall on a broad subset of the full tonal range. Very high-contrast images have the majority of pixels falling in the highlight

Figure 11-5a

An example of fast falloff. The light source is small and distant from the model, resulting in sharp-edged shadows.

Photo © KS.

Figure 11-5b

An example of slow falloff. The light source is larger and closer to the model, resulting in shadows with a softer, more gradual edge. Note the gradual shadow around the model's nose.

Photo © KS.

and the shadow areas with few pixels falling in the midtones (Figures 11-6a and 11-6b).

Low-contrast images have values that fall on a much narrower subset of the full tonal range (Figures 11-7a and 11-7b).

It doesn't matter where on the tonal range the pixels fall. Overall light images, just as overall dark images, can have high contrast (Figures 11-8 and 11-9). The important factor is the breadth of tonal range found within your image, not the overall brightness or darkness of your image.

Figures 11-6a and 11-6b

Lost Shoes. Note the large spike in the highlight and shadow areas of the histogram. This is a high-contrast photograph.

Photo © Heinz Baumann Photography.

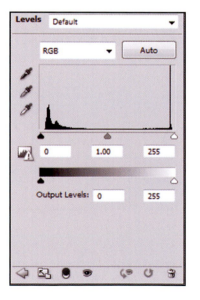

Figures 11-7a and 11-7b

Hollywood. The histogram shows that all of the pixels fall in the midtone to highlight range. This is a low-contrast photograph because all of the pixels fall into only a small portion of the histogram.

Photo © Heinz Baumann Photography.

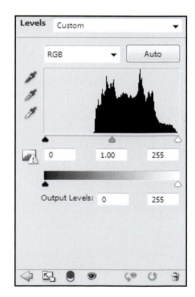

Figure 11-8

Orchid. This photo is high contrast because of the dark pixels in the insect, but it is still overall a light photograph.

Photo © Heniz Baumann Photography.

Color Temperature

Light's electromagnetic energy can be described by its color temperatures, measured in degrees Kelvin (° K). Although cameras and film record different color temperatures as variations in color, your brain accommodates for these changes and reads different light sources as "white" light.

Manufacturers calibrate most films and digital sensors to daylight balance, or approximately 5500° K. Incandescent light, such as light created by the common light bulb, is around 2400° K. Because most film and digital sensors aren't calibrated to this color temperature, photographs made with incandescent light sources appear yellow.

Fluorescent light (found in the long tubular lights in many offices and homes) range from 3000 to 4500° K. Photographs made with fluorescent light sources appear green or greenish yellow. Figure 11-10 is a list of some of the more common light sources and their approximate color temperatures.

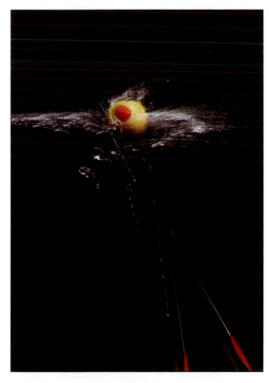

Figure 11-9

Olive. This is a high-contrast photograph because of the brightness of the reflections on the liquid, but it is still overall a dark photograph.

Photo © Heniz Baumann Photography.

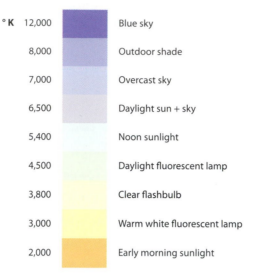

Color Temperatures in Degrees Kelvin (° K)

° K		
12,000		Blue sky
8,000		Outdoor shade
7,000		Overcast sky
6,500		Daylight sun + sky
5,400		Noon sunlight
4,500		Daylight fluorescent lamp
3,800		Clear flashbulb
3,000		Warm white fluorescent lamp
2,000		Early morning sunlight

There is a plethora of lights on the market, each with a different color temperature. The same type of light (such as halogen or tungsten) may have a different color temperature, depending on the manufacturer.

Color Correction Filters

If you are a film-based photographer, you can purchase lens filters to correct a color balance issue. First, determine the color temperature of your light source. The best way to find out is to look at the actual light bulb and read the brand name. Then check with the manufacturer to learn its color temperature.

Color correcting (cc) filters come in a variety of strengths and colors (Figure 11-11). Each filter changes the color temperature of light entering your lens to a daylight color temperature. These filters can be very strong in color, or they can be very mild. A 5 cc red filter adds 5 units (a relatively small amount) of red to your scene. A 20 cc green filter (a stronger color) adds 20 units of green to your scene. These filters can be stacked together and placed in front of your lens as needed.

Many filters, other than color correcting filters, are available to photographers. Some go well beyond the goal of color correction and purposely colorize an entire scene (Figure 11-12).

Multiple Light Sources

Difficulties arise when a photographer is faced with multiple light sources. The best case scenario is to have all light sources be the same style and brand and have the same age of light bulb. This system fails if there is also light coming into the scene through a window, as the daylight will probably be a different color temperature from the interior lights.

Commercial photographers handle this issue by either covering windows with black plastic (available through garden centers) or by waiting until nightfall to make photographs. It's also possible to exchange existing light bulbs with bulbs of different color temperatures so the various light sources will match.

If an overhead light source tends to turn a scene green but photographers need to use a daylight-balanced flash, they can cover the flash with a green color correction filter. In essence, the photographers are colorizing the light coming from the flash to the same color temperature as the overhead light source.

Photographers then use a color correction filter (probably magenta in this case) on the lens front to color correct both the ambient and flash light.

Custom White Balance

Some digital cameras are capable of analyzing a light source and creating a special color temperature correction setting, called a **custom white balance**, to record the scene with natural colors and without a color cast. Photographers who use this feature have the greatest chance of getting properly color-balanced images, no matter what the light source (Figure 11-13).

You'll need to follow the instructions in your manual to learn how to create a custom white balance. Generally, though, the procedure is as follows:

- Take a photograph of a white or gray board or piece of paper in the same lighting conditions as the subject you're photographing. Gray cards, available from many camera shops, are great for this purpose. Bring the card close enough to the camera so that the gray fills the viewfinder, and then photograph the card (Figure 11-14).
- Find the custom white balance function on your camera (you'll need to consult your manual to find this). When you set the function to CUSTOM WHITE BALANCE, you will be asked you to select a photograph to act as the source. Select your photograph of the gray card.

- Your camera will read the color temperature of the gray card and make calibration adjustments for its white balance. As long as you use that custom white balance setting under those lighting conditions, your photographs will be color-balanced. Compare Figure 11-14 (poorly color-balanced) with Figure 11-15 (custom white balanced).

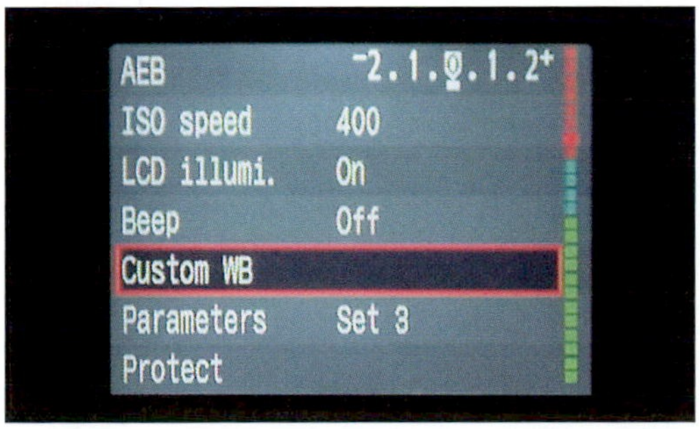

Figure 11-13 (bottom left)

Many digital cameras allow you to create a custom white balance. Check your digital camera owner's manual to see how to use this feature.

Figure 11-14 (left)

The top photo was made in the shade of late afternoon with the digital camera set to daylight balance. The gray card (bottom photo) was photographed with the same ambient light. Outdoors, shady areas reflect more blue than do sunny areas.

Figure 11-15 (below)

This photo was made after the camera was set to CUSTOM WHITE BALANCE using the gray card photo in Figure 11-14. The color balance of the scene looks much warmer.

Photos 11-13 through 11-15 © KS.

External Methods to Achieve Color Balance

Other methods to achieve good color balance include working with a specialized color chart, such as a commercially-made color chart (Figure 11-16). This chart contains squares of color at known color values. When photographed, these squares can be color-balanced using Photoshop's Curves functions.

Another method to achieve color balance is by photographing a commercially-made color target and using the white, gray, and black point eyedroppers in Adobe Camera Raw to define a color neutral balance for the image. ACR reads the small colored squares and creates a color- and tonal-correcting curve (Figures 11-17 and 11-18). When the curve is applied to the photograph(s), excellent tonal and color balance are achieved (Figure 11-19).

Directional Light

Describing light calls for a specialized vocabulary. Throughout this text, we have been discussing highlights, midtones, and shadows. Now you'll learn how to describe the light falling on your subjects.

Light can fall on subjects from a variety of directions. Look at the diagrams and corresponding examples in this chapter. Notice where the highlights and shadows fall on the subjects. Look at the edges of the subjects to examine the lighting effects for each direction and light source.

Front light is light falling on the side of your subject that's directly facing your camera. The light source is directly

Figure 11-16 (left)

A commercially-made target color chart.

Figure 11-17 (center)

This is the color balance captured by the camera set to Automatic White Balance. It didn't seem far off from color neutral at the time the photograph was made.

Figure 11-18 (bottom left)

The color chart was photographed under the same lighting conditions. The resulting photograph was used to set the white, gray, and black point in ACR and to determine a proper tonal and color correction curve.

Figure 11-19 (bottom right)

The resulting color correction curve was applied to this image. Compare this image to the one in Figure 11-17.

Photos 11-16 through 11-19 © KS.

behind the camera. Although frequently used, front light acts to somewhat flatten the subject (Figure 11-20).

Sidelight is light falling on either the left or right side of your subject. The light source is to either side of the camera. Sidelight brings out the texture in your subject and tends to make it appear more three-dimensional (Figure 11-21).

Backlight takes place when the photographer meters for the background light instead of the light that is hitting the subject (Figure 11-22). When the background light is strong, the subject itself may be rendered nearly or totally black in the photograph. This is called a *silhouette*.

When the subject is backlit by a light source positioned a little higher than the subject, rim lighting is visible along the edge of your subject. Rim light is a slight overflow of light that helps to separate your subject from the background. Your subject is very dark, other than being surrounded by the rim lighting (Figure 11-23).

Surface Quality

Light can be transmitted, reflected, or absorbed by surfaces. These terms are not absolute, as most surfaces reflect some light wavelengths and absorb other light wavelengths. The surface quality of the object you're photographing has a large impact on how light reflects off of it.

Figure 11-20 (left)
Front light.

Figure 11-21 (right)
Side light.

Photos 11-20 and 11-21
© Phil Ziesemer.

Figure 11-22 (left)
Backlight.

Figure 11-23 (right)
Rim lighting.

Photos 11-22 and 11-23
© Phil Ziesemer.

Figure 11-24a

The angle of incidence equals the angle of reflection for very smooth surfaces like mirrors or polished objects. These are called *direct reflections*.

Photo © KS.

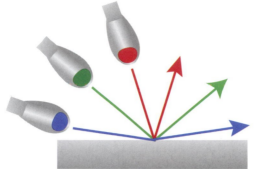

Light rays are reflected at an equal angle away from the object as the angle with which it struck the object. A law of physics states that the angle of incidence equals the angle of reflection (Figures 11-24a and 11-24b). In other words, if a light source strikes a smooth object at a 45-degree angle, it will be reflected at a 45-degree angle away from the object.

Direct and Diffuse Reflections

Rougher surfaces tend to reflect light in many more directions, scattering the light rays. Look at the surfaces in Figure 11-25. All of the surfaces are red, and all have approximately the same tonal value. Depending on the surface quality of the object, the light rays are being reflected in one general direction (called *direct reflection*) or in scattered directions (called *diffuse reflection*). Smooth, polished surfaces, especially mirrors, create a direct reflection of the light source, whereas rough-textured objects (which comprise the majority of surfaces) produce diffuse reflections.

Transmission of Light

Light is *transmitted* (passed) through glass, air, thin plastic, and clear water (Figure 11-26). Most objects transmit some light rays and reflect other light rays. An object made of glass or clear plastic can

Figure 11-24b

This massive public sculpture called *Cloud Gate* resides in Millennium Park in Chicago, Illinois. Its mirror-like surface reflects passersby, creating a visually interesting and very interactive piece of art. The British artist Anish Kapoor designed *Cloud Gate*.

Photo © KS.

Figure 11-25

All of these surfaces are approximately the same tonal value. The direction of light reflecting off these surfaces varies dramatically, depending on the surface quality of the objects, producing varying ratios of direct reflection to diffuse reflection.

Photo © KS.

bend, or *refract*, the light rays as they are transmitted through the material.

Predicting Qualities of Reflected Light

Experimentation is by far the best teacher for learning about qualities of light. Following are some concepts to keep in mind as you learn to observe direct and diffuse reflections of light.

- All white objects produce a substantial amount of diffuse reflected light, regardless of the object's surface.
- Colored and dark objects produce lesser amounts of diffuse reflections, depending on their surface quality and tonality, because so much of the light is absorbed into the object and isn't reflected at all.
- The light source and its proximity to the object being photographed determine whether reflected light will be direct or diffuse. The closer the light source is to the subject, the broader it is in relation to the size of the subject, offering greater opportunity for diffuse reflection.
- Dark-colored objects absorb light in large amounts. It takes more light to properly expose a very dark object than it does a white object because of the dark objects' rate of absorption. Photographing dark objects with large light sources close to the object will frequently improve your results.

Any object reflects some light, making it visible, and selectively absorbs other light. The light rays an object reflects gives that object its color. The object absorbs all other wavelengths, making those colors invisible (Figure 11-27).

Polarizing Filter

Because diffused light scatters in multiple directions, it can produce reflections and glare you may not want in your photograph. A polarizing filter (Figure 11-28) prevents diffused reflected light from reaching your film/sensor by allowing only direct reflected light into your lens. This

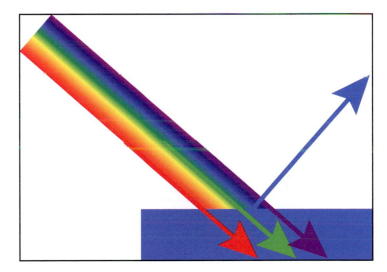

Figure 11-26 (top)

Triple Glass Refraction. Light is refracted by glass.

Photo © Alex Saberi.

Figure 11-27 (middle)

Illustration of light being absorbed if not reflected as color.

Photo © KS.

Figure 11-28 (bottom)

A polarizing filter.

Photo © Georgois Alexandris/ iStockphoto.

reduces the glare and slight desaturation of colors that can result from strong diffused reflections. Using a polarizing filter under the right conditions will remove reflections from water or windows, darken a blue sky, and increase the contrast within clouds, making them stand out dramatically against the blue sky.

A polarizing filter consists of two pieces of glass in a setting that allows one glass piece to rotate independently of the other. When attached to the camera lens, the outer glass can be rotated to give varying amounts of polarization (Figures 11-29 and 11-30).

There are two types of polarizing filters: linear and circular. The type you will need

Figure 11-29

Fort Pickens, Pensacola Beach, Florida. This photograph was made in the early afternoon on a sunny day. The sunlight reflected as glare off of the canon and its housing. Exposure: 1/500 second at f/8, ISO 200.

Photo © KS.

Figure 11-30

Fort Pickens, Pensacola Beach, Florida. This photograph was taken moments later with a polarizing filter turned to full polarization. Exposure: 1/125 second at f/8, ISO 200. The camera's light meter automatically made the shutter speed 2 stops longer to compensate for the loss of light caused by the polarizing filter. The black cannon now appears much darker than it does in Figure 11-29. The orange structure also darkened a little, but not as much as the black cannon.

Photo © KS.

depends on the camera you use. Purchase a circular polarizing filter if you work with an autofocus lens and/or a through-the-lens metering system. Your camera manufacturer will also have instructions on which one to use. Be sure to use the recommended type of polarizing filter.

Predicting Qualities of Polarized Light

As you use a polarizing filter, keep these concepts in mind:

- Dark objects produce weaker diffuse reflection than do light objects; their response to a polarizing filter is potentially far greater than that of light objects, depending on the direction of the polarizing filter in relation to the reflected light rays (Figures 11-29 and 11-30).

- A white object photographed with and without a polarizing filter looks very similar in both photographs (Figures 11-31a and 11-31b). White objects produce so much diffuse reflection that polarizing filters have

Figure 11-31a

This image was made without a polarizing filter. The blue sky is washed out, and the reflections in the pool mask the water's color.

Photo © KS.

Figure 11-31b

This image was made a few minutes later with a polarizing filter. The sky and grass are much darker, but the white clouds remain equally as bright as in the unpolarized image. The water's color can now be seen because the reflections are gone.

Photo © KS.

very little effect on them, regardless of the angle of the light source.

■ Shiny objects reflect mostly direct light; so, their response to a polarizing filter will depend predominantly on the direction of the light source striking the object.

■ A polarizing filter eliminates reflections of light rays running perpendicular to it, but the filter has no effect on light rays running parallel to it. As a result, you won't see changes in your images if you're photographing directly into or directly away from the sun early in the morning or late in the evening.

■ When photographing outdoors, a polarizing filter will have the most effect if the sun is on either side of you or directly overhead. The polarizing filter will have little or no effect on cloudy days.

Polarizing filters always add 2 stops of density to your exposure. You lose 2 stops of light any time you use a polarizing filter. If you are using a camera that can do Through the Lens (TTL) metering, your light meter will give you a reading that takes the filter's presence into consideration. You won't need to make any changes.

If you are using a camera that doesn't have an internal light meter (such as a pinhole or large-format camera), you will need to add 2 stops of light to your exposure. You can do this by increasing the aperture size by 2 stops or lengthening the shutter speed by 2 stops.

Using a Polarizing Filter as a Neutral Density Filter

Because you can select the amount of polarized effect you want by turning the outer glass in the polarizing filter, you can effectively turn off the polarizing effect and use the filter as a neutral density filter. In essence, you are decreasing the amount of all light coming into the lens. This can be helpful if you need a slower shutter speed than you can obtain any other way (Figure 11-32).

Attach your polarizing filter to your lens, and select the amount of polarization by

turning the outer piece and watching the results through your viewfinder. Results can range from no polarization effect (in which your filter is simply acting as a neutral density filter) to full polarization. Either way, you lose 2 stops of light.

Ultraviolet (UV) Filter

Ultraviolet (UV) light falls outside of the visible spectrum of electromagnetic energy, but it can still affect your photographs. UV light creates a slight hazy appearance and decreases the overall contrast in your images.

A UV filter blocks ultraviolet light and decreases the haze in your image. It also acts as an excellent lens protector, taking any day-to-day bumps and scratches and keeping your lens glass undamaged. A new UV filter is far less expensive than a new lens (Figure 11-33).

A Sense of Play

Depending on what you're trying to convey or express with your photographs, your choice of lighting will directly impact the quality and strength of your message. Different lighting conditions alter the prominence of objects, change the reflections evident in the photo, and evoke specific moods in your photographs.

When you plan and make photographs, experiment with your light sources. Try different sizes of light sources and alter their direction and distance from your subject. Play with unusual and unexpected light

Figure 11-32

This image was made using a polarizing filter. Because it was a cloudy day, the filter had little or no effect on the diffuse reflections. However, it did have the effect of darkening the scene by 2 stops, allowing for a longer shutter speed. The slower shutter speed gave a milky appearance to the running water. Photo taken with a 4 × 5 field camera. Exposure: 16 seconds at f/64, ISO 100.

Photo© KS.

sources to see how they might impact your photographs. Use unusual angles, directions, and quantities of light. The more you experiment with light, the better creativity and control you will develop.

Portrait and Commercial Photography

Formal portrait photography requires special attention to lighting conditions. The position, direction, height, and quality of light sources in the studio and/or outdoors directly impact

Figure 11-33

Close-up photo of a UV filter. The *77* you see on the lens is the size of filter that fits that particular lens.

Photo © Janaka Dharmasena/ ShutterStock.

Figure 11-34

A daylight-balanced strobe light.

Figure 11-35 (left bottom)

Many cameras can accept a remote power unit for use with slave units (left) or a removable flash unit (right).

Figure 11-36 (right top)

The modeling light and flash tube on a strobe head.

Figure 11-37 (right bottom)

The hand in this photo is pointing to the modeling light. The ring-shaped light behind the model's finger is the flash tube.

Photos 11-34 through 11-37
© Phil Ziesemer.

the quality of the photographs made. You are about to be introduced to the equipment used in a typical photographic studio. The examples of how these various studio lights affect the resulting photographs will help you control whatever sources of light you use to make photographs.

Portrait and commercial photographers use daylight-balanced studio lights called **strobe lights** (Figure 11-34). The light source (sometimes called *strobe head*) comes in three general models:

1. Models requiring an external battery pack and cords connecting the strobe head to the battery pack;
2. Standalone plug-in models using a power cord plugged into the strobe head and a standard wall outlet; and
3. Small battery-powered models typically attached directly to cameras.

Some models have a built-in **slave**, an electronic device that detects a flash from other strobes and fires its own strobe. No wiring to connect these strobes to each other is required. Many small battery-powered models accept external slaves that several vendors manufacture, eliminating the need for the strobe to be attached to the camera (Figure 11-35).

At least one strobe or remote device needs to connect to the camera. You may need a hot shoe adapter that connects directly to your camera and accepts a synch (short for synchronization) cord. Synch chords come in various lengths. One end attaches to your hot shoe adapter; the other end, to the strobe head.

Strobe Heads

Strobe heads typically have two lights: a modeling light and a flash tube (Figure 11-36). The modeling light can be as simple as a common tungsten light bulb, or it can be proprietary to the manufacturer of that head (Figure 11-37). A constant light,

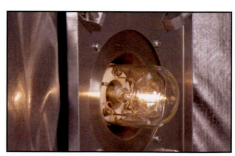

the modeling light is used to illuminate your scene and give you a sense of the quality, amount, and direction of light hitting your subject. However, it is nowhere near as bright as the flash tube and may or may not be daylight-balanced.

Some modeling lights automatically turn off when the flash tube fires, whereas others automatically change to a dimmer light level. There is usually a short recycling time before the modeling light comes back on, usually when the unit is fully charged again. The flash tube is daylight-balanced. It emits a very fast (around 1/000 second) bright light.

The strobe head has built-in power levels that allow you to increase or decrease the output of light emitted from the unit (Figure 11-38). This is, in part, how the exposure is controlled. A lower output results in a darker photograph; a higher output, a lighter photograph.

Most strobe heads are shipped with a **parabola**, a parabolic-shaped cover that channels and directs the light (Figure 11-39), protects the tubes, and provides a holder for umbrellas, softboxes, and other light modifiers. Parabolas are removable to accommodate some of those modifiers.

Studio lights are mounted onto light stands (Figure 11-40). Light stands come in a variety of sizes, strengths, diameters, and heights. Some are portable and can be packed for off-site photography, and others

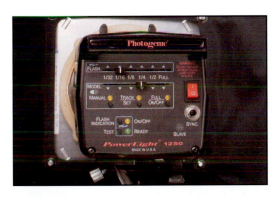

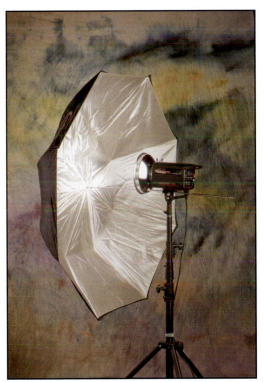

Figure 11-38 (top left)

The power levels on the back of the strobe head.

Figure 11-39 (bottom left)

The parabola, the silver reflector behind the flash tube and modeling light, frequently comes packaged with strobe lights. Parabolas come in a variety of sizes and styles. The black metal pieces connected to this parabola are called *barn doors*.

Figure 11-40 (right)

A studio light with an umbrella on a light stand.

Photos 11-38 through 11-40
© Phil Ziesemer.

NOTE

Use of small strobes for commercial work and portraiture is becoming immensely popular. To learn more, go to www.strobist.com.

Safety Tips for Handling Flash Tubes

Flash tubes are extremely fragile and get very hot. DO NOT touch the tube with your bare hands. The oil in your skin can cause it to overheat and explode. Wear clean cotton gloves to install new flash tubes.

are fixed with roller bases for studio use. Light stands need to be large and strong enough to steadily hold whatever lights, plus light modifiers, are attached to them. A wide base is particularly important for use with large modifiers.

A **boom** is another form of light stand allowing you to mount a strobe head directly over your subject. Booms can be attached to the ceiling or used with counterweights on traditional light stands. Several possible connectors are available to attach booms to light stands.

Light Modifiers

Umbrellas, softboxes (Figure 11-41), barn doors, gobos, louvers, grids, scrims, snoots, and reflectors are all tools of the studio photographer. Each has a different effect on the strobe light, but the overall goal is the same: Control the quality, quantity, and direction of light striking the subject.

- Softboxes and umbrellas change a small light source into a larger light source.
- Barn doors narrow the light source in one or more directions.

- Gobos (short for go-betweens) are boards mounted somewhere between the strobe and the camera. They block light spilling from the strobe onto the subject. They are also used to prevent lens flares.
- Louvres, grids, and scrims can be made of metal, plastic, or fabric. They create a directional quality to the light and can be used at an angle to skim the light across the surface of a subject.
- Snoots attach to the parabola of strobes and strongly funnel the light source into a narrow stream of light.

Reflectors range from white sheets of paper to large pieces of plastic or fabric stretched across a frame (Figure 11-42). They are used on the side opposite the light source and bounce light onto the unlit side of the subject. Clamps of various sizes are used to attach the reflectors to support structures.

White and silver reflectors reflect the same color of light as the source light (Figure 11-43). Gold reflectors change the color temperature of the daylight-balanced strobe hitting the subject to warm up the scene. The light source can be pointed directly at the reflector, which in turn is pointed toward the subject. Aluminum or silver reflectors create a harsher light with more contrast than does a white reflector.

Commercial and portrait photographers use all kinds of light modifiers that alter the quality and/or direction of light striking the subject. The utmost control of light makes a critical difference in the success or failure of the photographer's work. Not only is the lighting equipment expensive, but it also takes years of training and practice to become proficient in using it.

**Figure 11-41
(top left)**

A softbox attached to a studio strobe.

**Figure 11-42
(bottom left)**

Reflectors come in a large variety of shapes, sizes, and colors.

**Figure 11-43
(bottom right)**

A white reflector on the left; a gold reflector on the right.

Photos 11-41 through 11-43
© Phil Ziesemer.

Many of the photographs in this text were selected because of the quality of light in them. Heinz Baumann, who created the chapter-opening photograph, offers more information about how the photograph was made. Read the information in the Artist Statement, below, about his equipment and thought process. Now that you have learned about studio lighting, this information should be familiar to you.

The Classic Portrait

Good portrait photography relies on good lighting, posing, composition, choice of surroundings, and personal rapport with the subject. But without good lighting, excellent management of the rest of that list won't matter. You can't make a good portrait if you don't have good light.

Portraiture is as creative an area as you will find in photography. However, there are industry-standard starting points for classic portraiture when you're first learning portraiture. You'll begin by thinking of a person's head, shoulders, and face as a three-dimensional object and apply your knowledge of lighting to that area.

Although portraits can be made wherever there is enough light, this section assumes that you're working in a studio with light sources on movable stands. The person you're photographing will be referred to as your model.

Observing Basic Light

You can use any light source you have available for this exercise. You'll start with one light and will later add more.

Begin with one small light source (Figure 11-44). Later you can modify your light to a large light source by adding an umbrella or softbox. Remember that the quality of light falloff is determined by the source size and distance from the subject. Starting with a small light source will make the effect of your light easier to see.

Your studio should have a simple backdrop and allow the model to sit at least 6 feet in front of the backdrop (Figure 11-45). Otherwise, you will see your model's shadow on the backdrop in the photograph.

Artist Statement

Heinz Baumann

- **Title: Books** III—From the series: The Secret of Books
- Use: Still life; Book cover study

About the Equipment:

- Camera: Cambo Ultima 23 D view camera
- Lens: Schneider Apo Digitar 90mm f/4.5 Copal 0
- Digital Back: Leaf Aptus 75
- Lighting: Electronic flash Elinchrom; Softbox and projections spot
- Computer: PowerMac, MacBookPro
- Software: Leaf Capture 11, Adobe CS4
- Props and set: Old books, herbs, candle etc; Background old wood.

About the Lighting:

The intention was to create a Dutch ambience, a warm atmosphere "product" shot on the busy desk of a former scientist.

The main light is a 145 × 145 cm softbox above the center of the set, supplemented by a bounce in front of the subject. A projections spot with a gobo are placed behind. The flash with projection optics and gobo was used to create textured lighting effects and shadows.

Simple lighting can create a warm tone picture. The props were chosen to match the mood of the picture.

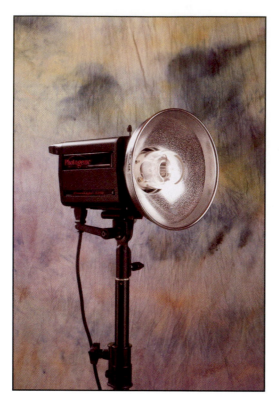

Posing Your Model

The most basic approach to posing a model involves the following considerations:

- Have your model sit at about a 30- to 45-degree angle to the camera.
- Have your model cross the leg nearest the camera over the leg farthest from the camera.
- Bring the arm closest to the camera back toward the camera.
- Cross the arm farthest from the camera over the legs so it is closer to the camera.
- Have the model's head pointing toward the light source, but bring the eyes back toward the camera.
- Ask the model to cock his/her head very slightly to the side.
- For long-haired models, bring the hair closest to the camera in back of the shoulder, and bring the hair farthest from the camera in front of the shoulder.

Basic Classic Lighting

Similar to styles in clothing, architecture, and automobiles, portraiture lighting styles have evolved over the decades.

Hollywood styles of portraiture in the 1930s and 1940s are quite distinct, with the woman receiving very soft, broad light and the man receiving light with much faster falloff.

For the past two decades, that difference has considerably decreased. Men and women now receive essentially the same amount of light for formal portraiture. The latest trend seems to be more dramatic lighting for portraiture. More contrast between the right and left sides of the face has replaced the flat lighting of the earlier Hollywood styles.

In this section, you will learn the role of each light in a basic classic portrait setting. You will also learn how to measure the amount of light coming from each light source.

Key Light

The main light used for a portrait, the **key light** is generally set off to the side of, and slightly above, your model (Figure 11-46). The role of the key light is to create a sense of three-dimensional form.

The shadow created by your model's nose determines the height of the key light. That shadow should fall slightly below the nose (Figure 11-47).

Watching where the shadow of the model's nose falls on the side of the face farthest from the light source determines the subject-to-key light distance. The nose casts a shadow onto the cheek, and the lack of light source on the model's far side creates shadow on that side of the head. The only lit portion of the far side of the model's face should be a triangle on the cheek and eye.

Broad Lighting

Because your model is not directly facing the camera, you have two choices for positioning the key light. Look at your model's ears. **Broad lighting** means you place the key light on the same side as the ear facing the camera (Figure 11-48). It doesn't matter if the ear is covered with hair or not.

Advantages of Broad Lighting

- Broad lighting is flattering for people with thin, long faces.
- Broad lighting can help avoid glare in eyeglasses.

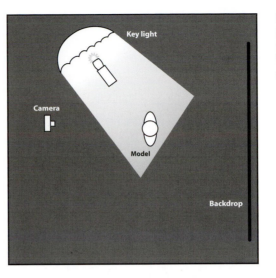

Figure 11-46

Diagram of the position of the key light in relation to the camera and model.

Photo © KS.

Disadvantages of Broad Lighting

- Broad lighting tends to broaden the appearance of the face and isn't as flattering on people with medium or heavier faces.

Short Lighting

Short lighting means you place the key light on the opposite side of the ear facing the camera (Figure 11-49). The light illuminates the far side of the face at its

Figure 11-47 (left)

Proper positioning of a key light. Note the nose shadow and triangle of light on the cheek farthest from the light source.

Figure 11-48 (right)

Example of broad lighting. The key light is coming in from the right.

Photos 11-47 and 11-48 © Phil Ziesemer.

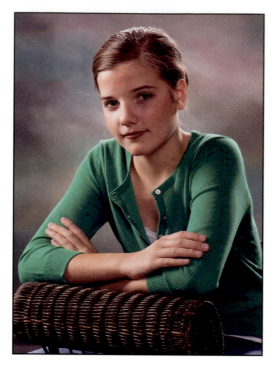

greatest strength, and the side of the face facing the camera is more in shadow.

Advantages of Short Lighting

- Short lighting tends to narrow the appearance of the face and is flattering on people with medium or heavier faces.

Disadvantages of Short Lighting

- Short lighting is less flattering for people with thin, long faces because it makes the face look even narrower.
- Short lighting can cause glare in eyeglasses.

Look Right? Look Left?

Your model has been positioned at an angle to the camera, but which direction is best? Look at your model's eyes. Humans are not exactly symmetrical, and it's common for people to have one eye larger than the other. Position your model so the smaller eye is closer to the camera than the larger eye. If your model's eyes are equal in size, it doesn't matter which direction you choose. Some people have a distinct preference for one side of their face over the other. It's a

good idea to honor that preference, at least for the vast majority of your photographs.

Attach an umbrella to your strobe light (Figure 11-50). You will need to point the strobe away from your model so it points toward the umbrella. Position the light so the umbrella faces your model. This light appears yellow because only the modeling light (an incandescent light with a warm color temperature) is currently on.

Now that you have posed your model and discovered the proper position for the key light, put an umbrella or softbox on your light source to make it a much larger source. Note the tremendous difference this makes in how the light illuminates your model (Figure 11-51). The nose shadow has much slower falloff. The triangle of light on the side of the model's face opposite the light source is much broader with slower falloff into shadow areas.

When deciding how close the light source with umbrella or softbox should be to your model, look for the triangle of light on the model's face. That triangle of light should include the model's eye, just to its far corner. The triangle's lowest point should extend down approximately to the lip line.

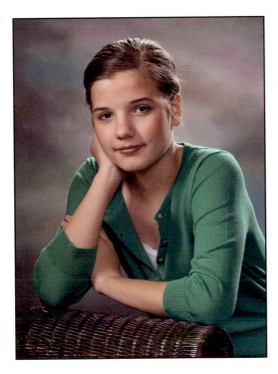

Figure 11-51 (left)

An umbrella has been added to the key light. Note the much slower falloff in the shadows. In this photograph, an additional light was set up above and behind the model to act as a hair light. This explains the additional illumination on her shoulders and head, and the far left side of her face.

Figure 11-52 (right)

Flat lighting.

Photos 11-51 and 11-52 © Phil Ziesemer.

Examples of Incorrect Key Lighting

- Too much of the model's face is lit (Figure 11-52). You lose the sense of three-dimensional form. This is sometimes called *flat lighting*. **Reason and solution:** The light source is too close to your model. Back the light source away from your model.

- Only half of the model's face is lit (Figure 11-53). There is no triangle of light on the unlit side of the model's face. **Reason and solution:** The light source is too far in back of the subject. Move the light source closer to the camera while watching for the triangle of light on your model's cheek.

- The model's eyes are in shadow (Figure 11-54). The triangle of light is too low. This is sometimes called *raccoon eyes*. **Reason and solution:** The light source is too high. Lower your light source until light illuminates your model's eyes.

- The model's eyes and forehead are lit, but not the cheek (Figure 11-55). The triangle of light is no longer triangular in

Figure 11-53

No triangle of light on the model's cheek.

Photo © Phil Ziesemer.

shape. **Reason and solution**: The light source is too low. The nose is casting a shadow across the cheek where the triangle of light should be. Raise your light source until light illuminates your model's eyes and cheeks.

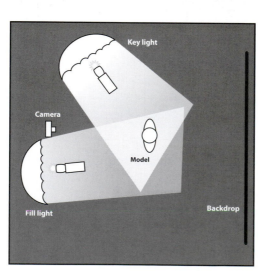

The Fill Light

A second light source, known as the **fill light**, fills in the shadows of your model. The strength of a fill light is highly variable and depends on what mood you want to convey in the portrait. A strong fill light tends to express a happy or positive mood. A weak fill light, which leaves considerable shadow, can express a powerful or negative attitude.

The fill light is typically a large light source (a light with umbrella or softbox) set just to the side of, and immediately behind, the camera (Figures 11-56a and 11-56b). It illuminates the entire face (hence, the term "fill light").

The power of the light source is personal preference, but it is typically set to a fraction (¼–¾) of the power of the key light. It is a good practice to evaluate the fill light strength by examining the resulting photographs while the model is still in the studio. Look at your lights' power levels and their distance from your model. Close observation and practice will teach you where to set your fill light.

Example of Incorrect Fill Lighting

The fill light is creating cross shadows on the key lit side of the model's face

(Figure 11-57). Although faint, the shadow created by the model's nose is distracting. **Reason and solution:** The fill light isn't directly beside the camera. Bring the fill light source closer to the camera, and watch your model until the shadow disappears. You may also need to use a larger umbrella or soft light to soften the fill light.

The Background Light

A background light is sometimes used to help separate your model's hair and shoulders from the dark background. It is typically a relatively small light source placed very low and directly behind the model, and pointed upward toward the backdrop. The resulting light falloff creates a pleasing gradient of light behind the model.

Photographers typically use lights at lower levels of power than the key or fill lights to create a good background light. The goal of the background light is to separate subject from background, not overpower the entire portrait.

The position of the fill light is decided by looking through your camera and watching for separation of your subject from the background (Figure 11-58). The light should be brightest at the model's shoulders and fall off slowly until it loses all power above the model's head. All hair should be separated from the background with the background light, but the light's power at the top of the model's head is less than where it falls behind the model's shoulders.

The background light should be broad enough to span the width of the model's shoulders, but not be so broad as to illuminate the entire background behind the model. There should be some light falloff at the upper corners of your portrait.

Examples of Incorrect Background Lighting

- The background is brighter than the highlights on the model's face (Figure 11-59). The background has become the brightest part of the portrait and is distracting. **Reason and solution:** The background light's

Figure 11-57

Cross shadows on the key lit side of the face. Look very closely at the shadows around and underneath the model's nose.

Photo © Phil Ziesemer.

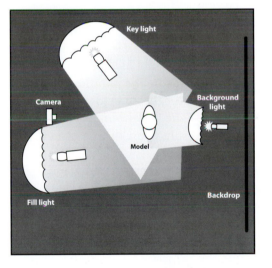

Figure 11-58

Placement of a background light.

Photo © KS.

power is set too high. Lower the power level until the issue is resolved.

- The background is so dark that the model's shoulders aren't separated from the background (Figure 11-60). It appears that the model blends directly into the background. **Reason and solution:** The background light's power is set too low. Raise the power level until the issue is resolved. You may also need to check the direction of the light to make sure it is pointing upward but still facing the background.

- The model's arms are separated from the background, but the shoulders or head is not (Figure 11-61). The hair and shoulders still blend into the background. **Reason and solution:** The background light is too low. Point it higher on the background while observing the results through your camera.

- The entire background is brightly lit with no falloff in the upper corners (Figure 11-62). There is excellent separation of the model from the background, but the background is bright and overpowering. **Reason and solution:** The background light is too

broad and/or too bright. First, try lowering the power of the background light and check the results. If the light is still too broad, move the light source closer to your model, away from the background. This will result in the light falling onto a smaller space on the background. If that solution isn't enough, consider using a light modifier such as a snoot to narrow your light source.

■ The background light separates the center portion of the model, but not the shoulders along the edge of the image (Figure 11-63). There is excellent separation of the model directly behind the neck, but it doesn't continue throughout the shoulders. **Reason and solution:** The background light is too narrow. Move the light source closer to your model. This will result in the light falling onto a wider space on the background.

The Hair Light

A **hair light** is the final touch to your classic portrait. It adds dimension and a spark of interest to your portrait by illuminating the top of your model's head and highlighting the tops of the shoulders. Good hair light is subtle and never prominent in the image. It should never be so strong as to be immediately noticeable.

Suspended by a boom overhead, the hair light is typically a small- to medium-sized light source such as a strobe with a softbox (Figure 11-64). It is positioned above and slightly behind the model. The hair light should never come so far forward as to illuminate the model's nose.

Place the hair light on the same side of the subject as the key light. The model's hair color determines the power of the hair light. A model with blond hair will need less hair light than a model with dark hair. Never use a hair light on a bald person.

Watch out for lens flare. If your hair light is set to an angle that allows the light to fall directly on the camera lens, flare can result. Either move the light, or use a directional device such as a barn door or gobo to block the flare from the camera lens.

If possible, place both the key light and the hair light on the same side as the part in your model's hair. This will eliminate the possibility of creating an unwanted shadow.

Figure 11-63 (left)

The background light is too narrow.

Figure 11-64 (right)

A strobe head with a softbox set high on a boom acts as a hair light.

Photos 11-63 and 11-64
© Phil Ziesemer.

- The tip of your model's nose is receiving light from the hair light (Figure 11-65). This makes the nose much brighter than it should be. You may also see light striking your model's forehead. **Reason and solution:** Your hair light is positioned too far forward. Bring the hair light close to the background, away from the camera.
- The model's hair looks good, but the hair light is causing flare on the lens. Lens flares are caused by light sources reflecting across the various pieces of glass within your lens. Lens flare from a small light source results in bright spots and streaks. In Figure 11-66, the broad light source has washed out the entire photograph. **Reason and solution:** Try repositioning the hair light so you don't get lens flare, but you still have the lighting effect you want on the model's hair. If that isn't possible, use a gobo to block the unwanted light.

Lighting Ratios

The key, fill, background, and hair lights are used at various ratios of power and/or distance to flatter the model and evoke an emotional connection with the viewer. The ratio between the key and fill lights are the predominant method of achieving these goals. The **lighting ratio** is the mathematical ratio of power levels between the two lights.

It is your decision how dark the shadows will be in relation to the highlights in your portraiture. Selecting a lighting ratio that helps tell your model's story is a powerful creative tool. It is helpful to study the Inverse Square Law in order to understand lighting ratios.

The Inverse Square Law

Diffuse reflections (which comprise the majority of light reflected off of your model) get brighter if you move the light source closer to your model. This change in brightness can be calculated with the **inverse square law**, which states that light intensity is inversely proportional to the square of the distance (Figure 11-67).

If you double the distance from the light source to your model, you will get only one-fourth of the original illumination. This law applies mainly to a small light source, not light that has been diffused by umbrellas or other light modifiers. There may be a

Figure 11-65 (left)

The hair light is positioned too far forward.

Figure 11-66 (right)

The hair light is causing an overall flare.

Photos 11-65 and 11-66
© Phil Ziesemer.

little less falloff with diffused light sources. However, the concept is still important.

Use a handheld incident flash meter when measuring lighting ratios. The light meter gives you f-stop values that determine the differences in strength of the individual light sources. Measure only one light source at a time and turn off all other light sources while taking the readings. Meter from the position of your model's face, always pointing the light meter toward the camera.

Two-to-One (2:1) Lighting Ratio

If your key and fill lights are set to equal power and are the same distance from your subject, your light meter reading for each light (measured independently with the other light turned off) will be the same. Your lighting ratio is 2:1 (Figure 11-68). The result is very even lighting across your model's face with only a very slight difference in lighting between the two sides of the face.

This doesn't make sense until you remember that the fill light actually falls on both sides of your model's face. The fill light is added to the key light when calculating lighting ratios ($2^0 = 1$ key light unit +1 fill light unit).

It might be helpful to think about the light in units of power. In a 2:1 lighting ratio, 1 unit of light comes from the key light and 1 comes from the fill light to equal a total of 2 units

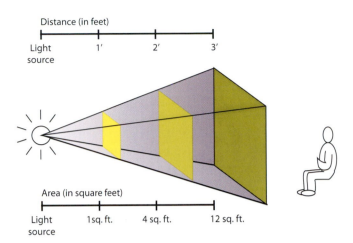

of light. If both your key light and fill light measure equal readings on your light meter, 2 units of light (key plus fill) are striking one side of the face, and 1 unit of light (fill light only) is striking the other side of the face. Therefore, you have a 2:1 lighting ratio.

Three-to-One (3:1) Lighting Ratio

If your key light is 1 stop brighter than your fill light, you have a 3:1 ratio. If your key light metered at f/11, your fill light would meter at f/8, a 1-stop difference (Figure 11-69).

In a 3:1 lighting ratio, 2 units of light come from the key light and 1 comes from the fill light to equal a total of 3 units of light ($2^1 = 2$ key light units + 1 fill light unit). Three

Figure 11-67
The inverse square law.
Photo © KS.

Figure 11-68 (left)
A lighting ratio of 2:1

Figure 11-69 (right)
A lighting ratio of 3:1.
Photos 11-68 and 11-69 © KS.

units of light (key plus fill) are striking one side of the face, and 1 unit of light (fill light only) is striking the other side of the face. Therefore, you have a 3:1 lighting ratio. Your model's face will be slightly lighter on the side facing the key light.

A 3:1 ratio is very popular in portrait photography. It gives enough visual difference to the two sides of the model's face to give a sense of three-dimensional form, but it doesn't create so much contrast as to cause problems with dark shadows when the image is printed.

Five-to-One (5:1) Lighting Ratio

If your key light is 2 stops brighter than your fill light, you have a 5:1 ratio ($2^2 = 4$ key light units + 1 fill light unit). If your key light meters at f/11, your fill light would meter at f/5.6 (Figure 11-70). You would see a greater difference between the key and fill sides of your model, but the fill side would still be easily visible.

In a 5:1 lighting ratio, 4 units of light come from the key light and 1 comes from the fill light to equal a total of 5 units of light. Five units of light (key plus fill) are striking one side of the face, and 1 unit of light (fill light only) is striking the other side of the face. Therefore, you have a 5:1 lighting ratio.

A 5:1 lighting ratio is considered dramatic lighting for portraiture.

Nine-to-One (9:1) Lighting Ratio

If your key light is 3e stops brighter than your fill light, you have a 9:1 ratio, a difference of 3 full stops ($2^3 = 8$ key light units + 1 fill light unit). If your key light meters at f/11, your fill light would need to measure at f/4 (Figure 11-71). You would see considerably more difference between the key and fill sides of your model's face. A 9:1 ratio is considered very dramatic lighting for portraiture.

In a 9:1 lighting ratio, 8 units of light come from the key light and 1 comes from the fill light to equal a total of 9 units of light. Nine units of light (key plus fill) are striking one side of the face, and 1 unit of light (fill light only) is striking the other side of the face. Therefore, you have a 9:1 lighting ratio.

Benefits of Using Lighting Ratios

Using lighting ratios gives you a lot of consistency and control as you make your images. Think of the benefit of using equal lighting ratios on photographs you will later composite together in Photoshop. Even if you make five different portraits with the same lighting ratio, all five people could be composited into one photograph without seeing an obvious change in lighting conditions.

Figure 11-70 (left)
A lighting ratio of 5:1.

Figure 11-71 (right)
A lighting ratio of 9:1.
Photos 11-70 and 11-71 © KS.

It's quite common for portrait photographers to add a person into an existing photograph. If the lighting ratios for the two images were different, the added person would stand out dramatically from the other people in the photograph.

Balancing Flash and Ambient Lighting

Lighting ratios are also very helpful when balancing flash and ambient lighting conditions. Outdoor portraiture can be greatly enhanced by adding a small amount of fill light via your on-camera flash unit or studio strobe to the model's face. The sunlight is the ambient light, and your fill light is provided by your flash.

Begin by taking a light meter reading of the ambient light. Select your aperture and shutter speed to create a good exposure of the ambient light. Then take a flash meter reading of your flash or strobe unit. Your meter should register between ½–1½ stops *under* your ambient light meter reading. Be sure your camera's ISO is set to the same value as the flash meter. By experimenting with varying amounts of fill flash, you will be able to make very natural-looking photographs with your model's face well illuminated (Figure 11-72).

Summary

It is difficult to overstate the importance of light and its applications to photography. Observing and evaluating the light falling on your subjects will help you to become a better photographer.

The tremendous variations in light qualities, color temperatures, and reflections offer many opportunities for experimentation. Become playful in your thought processes. Photograph objects simply because the lighting is great. Try using unlikely light sources such as black lights, car headlamps, candles, mirrors, Christmas tree lights, penlights, and anything else you can think of. Let go of your expectations of what constitutes a "good" photograph and look for ways to be inventive in your experiments. Later, during the process of evaluation, you can determine if the results could be valuable in future photographic endeavors.

Studio lights are used in specific distances, directions, and intensities to produce portraits. Understanding lighting ratios and the various qualities of light available with studio strobes will make you a better photographer.

Figure 11-72

Ola. The fill flash used for this photograph illuminated the dancer enough to give highlights to his face, but wasn't so strong as to plunge the background into darkness. The result is a photograph that celebrates the joy of the moment.

Photo © Muema.

FURTHER READING

- HUNTER, Fil; Steven Biver, and Paul Fuqua. *Light Science & Magic: An Introduction to Photographic Lighting.* 3rd Ed. Oxford, UK: Elsevier Inc., 2007.

- HURTER, Bill. *Group Portrait Photography Handbook.* Buffalo, NY: Amherst Media, Inc., 2003.

- POOLE, Richard. *The Lighting Workshop.* Christchurch, New Zealand: Photoretreat.

- SEXTON, John. *Quiet Light.* Boston: Little, Brown, and Co., 1990.

- WACKER, J. D. *Master Posing Guide for Portrait Photographers.* Buffalo, NY: Amherst Media, Inc., 2001.

1. Cast off all expectations and be creative while completing this exercise. Assume there's no right or wrong, and you cannot fail. Select one object that is large enough to photograph easily, but small enough to carry around with you. Photograph the object under a variety of lighting conditions, both indoors and outdoors. Think of unusual light sources such as Christmas tree lights, black lights, penlights, mirrors reflecting lights, car headlights, etc. The more unusual, the better. Don't worry about your images being *good*, just experiment and enjoy the creative process.

2. Do online searches for photos and videos involving painting with light (sometimes called light graffiti). These are images created by photographers wearing dark clothes and shining flashlights or other light sources in various patterns while the camera shutter remains open. Create your own light graffiti images.

3. Practice the portraiture information provided in this chapter. Work with models that have patience and are willing to let you work through the ups and downs of being a student photographer. Make photographs of different lighting ratios and compare them to see the effect of the different ratios.

4. Evaluate images you have previously made by examining the lighting conditions and thinking about the mood they create. Which light sources create an air of mystery? Humor? Interest? Boredom? How could you have improved these images by controlling the lighting conditions?

NOTES

NOTES

W. Morgan Rockhill
Commercial Photographer

Please tell me about your photography.

I've been a commercial photographer for many years. My job is to help my clients sell their products by showcasing them to their best advantage. I'm passionate about tone, texture, and light. I specialize in creating images in which I treat each of the material surfaces of a product to each one's best advantage. Soft light makes shiny things look good, but textured items die. So I need to use mixed lighting and multiple, composited image layers to enhance each feature of each object. I change the lighting and the angles of light so each surface is shown to its best advantage.

How did you get started in commercial photography?

I studied fine art photography in school and worked as an assistant in a photo studio for a summer. I learned the basics there. I was taught to never quit, to always try to make it better. If something isn't working, start over. It should be easy. If it's not easy, you're probably doing something wrong.

I started my own business after that very short assistant work. I learned mostly by not knowing what was impossible, and I always pushed the envelope. Fortunately, someone gave me a break, took a chance, and hired me for my first job. I worked hard and didn't make much money in the beginning. Eventually, I had a studio with several talented employees in Rhode Island.

Years later, I moved out of the city and I went back to being a one-man shop in order to have total control over my work. However, because I no longer have employees, I don't make money unless I'm taking pictures. If I stop doing photography, the income stops. It's not a business so much as a profession, and not something I can retire on.

What is your photographic process?

My job is to highlight, define, and bring out the essence of each element of the object being photographed. I photograph a lot of watches. Watches have textured faces, glossy areas, and polished bezels that need full surround lighting. I may take 15 to 20 photographic captures in which nothing changes but the lighting. Then I combine the images in Photoshop layers to reveal the best of each capture.

Isn't that time-consuming?

Yes! But I have clients who are willing to pay for that time. I have been able to retain a group of clients who highly value the quality of the work I do. Excellent photography translates to increased sales. This was proven when clients went to other photographers who didn't take the same care in making images that I do. The photography was cheaper but their sales went down. When they returned to my photography, their sales went back up.

How do you analyze an object you're photographing?

I look for the inspiration inherent within the object. I sit with the object and ask myself how I can tell the "story" of that object. How would I draw it? For example, glass is transparent and shiny, and the object has a specific shape. These things must be part of the visual story on film.

I also ask my client what story he is trying to tell. I need to know my client's intent. Is it an ad shot or a catalog shot? An advertisement includes context like mood or story; an impression of sexuality or speed or softness. A product photograph for a catalog is an entirely different story and a different price point. What does the object look like? What are people really buying? That's what I'm thinking about for a catalog photograph. Most people find that a good, simple catalog shot that

Photo © W. Morgan Rockhill (www.morganrockhill.com)

defines forms, textures, materials, surfaces, and colors is worth the money they spend on it.

Tell us about your studio and how you obtain new clients.

My clients rarely come to my studio. My office is 54 miles from the nearest traffic light! That makes it very difficult for me to secure new clients. I don't exactly run into art directors while delivering jobs to agencies. In fact, I've only met one of my current clients face-to-face. So I'll find potential clients who I think may be a good fit and ask them to send a product and a standard photo of the product to me. I'll do a photograph for free to show them the difference in the quality of the photographs I create. I offer to let the client put my photograph on the client's Web site on alternate days and see if sales go up on the days my photograph is shown. My work proves its own worth.

What keeps you interested in the field of commercial photography?

In 1972, Xerox was doing a TV series on the human body. On one show, they had the first open heart surgery ever filmed for television. The show made me realize that heart surgeons might do thousands of coronary bypass surgeries in their careers. I understood that if you're going to do something for many years of your life, it isn't *what* you do, it's *how* you do it and *with whom* you do it that determines your life and its rewards.

I just finished photographing 95 wristwatches that had a lot in common. They were variations on a theme. When writing a novel the best story is still some variation on the theme of "boy meets girl." What I bring to each repetition of the "story" is that variation. It's the craft and the passion. I work independently so I can afford to do that.

How do you charge for your services?

Traditionally, photographers used to charge by the day or half day, but now, in the digital world, it seems that I charge by the minute. Actually most jobs are individually contracted on a specifically estimated price for the project based on my estimate of the time required. For me, the whole passion is the craft. That's what an artist, especially a photographer, does. I'll take a photo of something you see every day but in a way someone else has never noticed. As artists we see differently than other people; so, we see what others miss.

Traditionally, photographers used to charge by the day or half day, but now, in the digital world, it seems that I charge by the minute. Actually most jobs are individually contracted on a specifically estimated price for the project based on my estimate of the time required. For me, the whole passion is the craft. That's what an artist, especially a photographer, does. I'll take a photo of something you see every day but in a way someone else has never noticed. As artists we see differently than other people; so, we see what others miss.

What advice would you have for aspiring commercial photographers?

Drawing is critically important. If you want to be a product photographer, you must learn how to draw in order to understand lighting. That's the only way to learn the visual language. Drawing gives you the visual clues that help you define size, shape, and perspective. You learn that if you draw a circle and shade it, you have a ping pong ball. How do you make it a shiny ball? It's the reflective edge that defines the surface finish. You don't get rid of the reflections; you just get them in the place you want them to be.

Study impressionism. Photographing something realistically may not be the best solution.

By studying impressionism, you learn that instead of rendering, what we're after is really just an impression of an object. What are the fundamental visual clues? Sometimes that's more important than the technical details. What are the minimum words in the visual vocabulary needed to make an effective statement? What is the minimum number of notes you need to play to say "shiny"? It all comes from working with light.

What was the best advice given to you about commercial photography?

It came from my first boss, Dick Richards. He said, "Never forget for one minute that the reason we are here in this studio today is to sell our client's product." Many commercial photographers and art directors make pretty pictures and get awards. That's what weekends are for. Clients pay you to sell their products.

How has digital photography changed the field of commercial photography?

It has been a bittersweet revolution. Over the past ten years, with the advances in digital cameras, anybody can take a picture and put it on the Internet. It's so easy that with virtually no skills anyone can take a moderately reasonable picture and get it into a computer system. This has cut the entire bottom off the pyramid of the business model. All of the "bread-and-butter" work essentially went away. This has brought all but the top photographers' work way down the pay scale.

I consider myself very fortunate. I am able to live and work in the wilderness. I have diversified into graphics as well. I also now work with inventing, producing, and marketing products. Photography is no longer my sole source of income. So I only want to work for people if I feel that I'm the best photographer for the job.

Still Life with Summer Bouquet, Cherries and Figs.

Photo © Mitch Eckert, 2009. Mitch is an Assistant Professor at the University of Louisville, Kentucky, USA.

12

Composition

- Describe the role of strong composition in photographs.

- Identify compositional variables that photographers can control.

- Develop an awareness of techniques that will aid in creating well-composed photographs.

- Read about the stock photography profession.

- Identify design elements in existing photographs.

- Examine your own photographs for compositional elements.

Photography is filled with anticipation, excitement, satisfaction, and disappointment. Imagine this scenario: You've made what you consider a fantastic photograph. You show it to your friends who stare quizzically at it. The seconds tick by. Can't they see what you see in the image? Don't they think it's a great image? Why are you getting blank stares from these people?

If this hasn't happened to you yet, it probably will. It is part of being a photographer. Not every photograph you make is going to be successful in communicating what you saw and felt to other people. Something blatantly obvious to you will be nearly invisible to someone else. This chapter is intended to help you minimize these frustrating moments.

Composition and Visual Communication

Part of becoming a good photographer involves stepping back from a scene long enough to look at it with a different frame of mind. New photographers tend to look through the camera and notice only the elements that initially caught their attention within the scene. Only the most pertinent and meaningful elements penetrate the photographers' consciousness. Everything else within the scene tends to be ignored.

You will become a better photographer when you change your thought process to seeing every scene as a flat, two-dimensional form inside your camera. Every inch of a photograph contributes to its overall feel and message. What you perceive as an important element within the scene lies (in two-dimensional form) directly alongside or on top of other elements within the photograph, regardless of whether or not those elements are close together in real life (Figure 12-1). Which elements will your viewers see first? How do the various elements relate to each other? How will your viewer discern the most relevant aspects of your photograph?

Photographer Mitch Eckert made the image that opened this chapter. For him, even the two-dimensional form can be a creative canvas onto which he can build texture and purpose. Read the Artist Statement to learn more about his work.

Composition is the arrangement of elements within your photograph and how those elements are captured within your scene, and it has a great deal to do with how your viewers will respond to your photographs. You can't always control composition (Figure 12-2), but you always need to consider it when making photographs. The more you practice making and capturing good compositions, the better your photographs will become.

There are no hard-and-fast directions for crafting good compositions. There are no "rules of composition" written in stone. A creative photographer starts by acknowledging that compositional issues exist and then finds ways of breaking all traditional conventions, if necessary, to convey the intention for the photograph. Your intention in making a photograph will guide your decisions about composition.

Mitch Eckert

Still Life with Summer Bouquet, Cherries, and Figs is part of a larger body of work in which I was investigating the genre of still life. With the Dutch masters as inspiration, I arranged objects on a table mimicking compositional strategies, lighting, and color relationships to form an aesthetically pleasing arrangement.

I photographed the still life with a digital camera and printed the image using an inexpensive inkjet printer. While I found the image to be quite beautiful, it lacked vitality. Out of frustration I crumpled the photograph along with many others and threw them away. When the time came to dispose of the wadded up pieces of paper, I took one from the recycle bin and at that moment had an epiphany. The unintended result of my act of frustration was an aged and richly textured surface evocative of the crackleur surfaces of old still life paintings that I so admire.

Using a flatbed scanner, I made a record of the image and printed the final work on a wide-format inkjet printer on fine-quality printmaking paper imported from Germany.

Gestalt and Image Composition

It is helpful to understand what draws viewers to a visual piece (photograph, painting, or drawing) and what might be considered visually interesting to them. Photographers make use of psychological research that has revealed important facts about how people interact with visual information.

During the 1920s, German psychologists developed a theory of mind and brain called **gestalt** (a German word generally meaning the "essence or shape of an entity's complete form, or the unified whole of an entity"). Gestalt psychology describes the human brain as holistic with self-organizing tendencies. Gestalt theory gives us a platform to predict how viewers will perceive visual elements. You may have heard the phrase, "the whole is greater than the sum of its parts." This phrase stems from gestalt theory.

Five principles of gestalt theory apply to visual studies. They are similarity, continuation, closure, proximity, and figure/ground. Each will be briefly discussed here. Later in the chapter, you will see a variety of compositions in photographs, including some that directly relate to these principles.

Similarity
When you have several similar elements within a photograph, your brain perceives them as a group or pattern. The viewer will quickly notice one dissimilar element, or one element outside the overall pattern, within that photograph.

Continuation
If there is a line or curve within the photograph, your eyes will naturally follow it. Even if the physical line stops, your eyes will continue in the direction of that line

unless another element forces your eyes to change direction. Lines can be directly visible (as in a road or sidewalk), or they can be implied (such as following a person's gaze within the photograph).

Closure

Elements may be incomplete within your image because they exist along the edge of the photograph, or they may be overlapped by other elements within the photograph. Your mind still perceives these elements as complete.

Proximity

Proximity means how close elements are to each other. If elements are dispersed across a relatively large space, your brain perceives them as separate. However, if those elements are close to each other within the print, your mind tends to group them together and cease seeing them as individual elements. As a result, multiple elements used in close proximity can create an altogether different shape.

Figure/Ground

Your brain can bring to attention individual elements separate from the background of their environment. When you look at a plate of food on a table, you notice the food, plate, and perhaps the silverware. The table itself, a tablecloth, and a centerpiece on the table receive far less attention. The element you are likely going to pay attention to is called the figure. The surrounding area is called the ground. Interesting compositions can result from careful balance of figure and ground when making photographs.

Additional Issues of Perception

Gestalt theory helps you think of how elements might be perceived, depending on their organization within the photograph. There are other facts about human perception that stem from psychological theory and testing. The following are additional thoughts to consider as you make your photographs:

Lights versus Darks

The eye is drawn first to the area of greatest contrast (light vs. dark) in an image. (See the photograph by Alison Hahn, Figure 12-3.) Areas that are lighter (highlights) are viewed before areas that are darker (shadows).

As a photographer, you must decide how light the lightest portion of the photograph should be. If it's a very dark image, the lightest area might be no lighter than dark gray. On the other hand, if the image is very light overall, the lightest area may be only slightly darker than the paper itself.

Specular highlights are very bright areas, such as light bouncing off chrome or headlights or other light sources within the photograph. These highlights may be rendered as light as the paper itself. When the specular highlight appears in a model's eye, it's called a **catchlight**. Catchlights are important when photographing people and animals, as they help the subjects seem alive (Figure 12-4).

An image whose visual information is mostly lighter than middle gray is considered a **high-key image** (Figure 12-5);

Figure 12-3

Longevity.

Copyright 2010 Alison Hahn.

Alison Hahn

My current body of work explores the aesthetic importance of Dutch still life paintings during the seventeenth century, referred to as "Vanitas." The term *vanitas* is the Latin word for "emptiness," and the Dutch still life painters during the Golden Age depicted the transient nature of life through symbols such as overripe fruit, withering flowers, skulls, and smoke. Exquisite details, objects bathed in glowing light, and the symbolic use of foodstuffs and objects from nature in various phases of the life cycle conveyed hidden messages about mortality and the brevity of life. The photographs in "Vanitas" evoke similar emotions of drama, mystery, and awe through the painterly details of high-resolution scans.

For my current interest in photography, I use a flatbed scanner to construct fabricated landscapes. I use photographic imagery as the background and layer the scanning surface with transparencies, soil, plant material, and water to compose the foreground, middle ground, and background in a single image. As an artist, I draw on my affinity for the natural world to create visual metaphors that represent personal narratives and universal experiences of loss, absence, and transformation. By using organic specimens from the land in various stages of the life cycle, I am referring to the topography of the psychic terrain as well. Each image reveals a passionate story of the inner life.

The appeal of the flatbed scanner as an expressive photography tool is inspired by many of its inherent characteristics. The scanner creates a shallow depth of space in an image by illuminating the image from beneath the glass. The falling off of light and focus depicts the details and shapes in an image in a compelling and mysterious way, and the illusion of space is deceptive. In some images, subtle shadows are created on the background photograph, and oftentimes an object will cast dual shadows as result of being illuminated and photographed by a moving source. Most importantly, the magnification of minute details by scanning is visually fascinating and symbolically parallels an interest in the "examined life."

Figure 12-4

The white reflections in this girl's eyes are catchlights. They make her seem more alive, and they also show us that a softbox was probably used to light her face.

Photo © JGW Images.

Figure 12-5

A high-key image.

Photo © Phil Ziesemer, Merrill, Wisconsin.

an image mostly darker than middle gray, a **low-key image** (Figure 12-6). Christian Fletcher's photograph is also a good example of the gestalt principle of similarity. The one human form stands out from the background of shadows and the building.

Shapes

Our eyes tend to complete geometric shapes, even though the shapes themselves may not be complete. In the Japanese garden image (Figure 12-7), the photographer used a slow camera shutter speed to capture leaves being moved by the water's current. The resulting sense of motion suggests a series of circles from the trail of leaves. This is a good example of how our minds complete incomplete shapes, following the gestalt principle of closure.

Our eyes tend to find the simplest solution to visual information. We try to make sense out of visual chaos in the quickest, most efficient way possible and quickly discern patterns—whether colors, objects, or lines create them. In Figure 12-8, the thorns on the plant stalk are seen as a unified whole and a pattern of the plant, in part because they are in close proximity to each other.

Figure 12-6

A low-key image.

Photo © Christian Fletcher, Photo Images Dunsborough, Western Australia.

Figure 12-7

Swirling Leaves in a Pond with Waterfall.

Photo © Design Pics/Dan Sherwood/Getty Images.

This photograph is also an excellent example of how photographers can manipulate the gestalt principle of figure/ground. It may take a viewer several seconds to decipher foreground versus background in the image as a result of the photographer's compositional decision.

Foreground versus Background

Foreground elements generally appear larger in a photograph than do background elements. This feature of visual perception is taken for granted. We use visual clues of size to help us determine distances of objects from us. In a two-dimensional form such as a photograph, the differences in size from one visual element to another helps give a sense of depth. In Figure 12-9, the lamp appears to be wider than the tree trunk in the distance.

Format of the Photograph

A **horizontal format** (a photo wider than it is tall) tends to lend a sense of peace or stability to the photograph (Figure 12-10). Margaret Bourke-White was one of the first photographers for *Life Magazine*. Her compositions were strong and purposeful, selectively using horizontal or vertical formats, depending on the subject matter of the photographs.

Figure 12-9

A Good Day for Reading. Foreground elements look larger than background elements.

Photo © Christopher Mattison. See more of Chris's photos at www.earthimagephotography.com.

Figure 12-10

Indian leader Mohandas Gandhi reading as he sits cross-legged on floor next to a spinning wheel that looms in the foreground as a symbol of India's struggle for independence, at home.

Photo © Margaret Bourke-White/ Time Life Pictures/Getty Images.

A **vertical format** (a photo taller than it is wide) tends to give a sense of strength or power to the photograph. Figure 12-11 is a good example. Lewis Hine photographed during a similar time period to Margaret Bourke-White. Hine, a sociologist and photographer, used his photography as a tool to encourage social reform.

A **square format** can be a beautiful shape; it is created by 2¼ square medium-format cameras, or it can be cropped from a larger horizontal or vertical image (Figure 12-12).

The Horizon Line

The **horizon line** is traditionally the line where the sky meets the ground. Whether real or imaginary, the horizon line within the photo tends to divide the scene into sections. In Figure 12-13, the horizon line is quite low in the photograph. The photographer made this decision so he could include more of the waterfall in the image.

Horizon lines can be placed anywhere in the photograph. In Figure 12-14, the photographer chose to place the horizon line in the center of the image and to include the reflection in the foreground.

Photographs with centered horizon lines tend to lend a sense of peacefulness to the photograph. In this photo, there is interesting visual information in both the top and bottom halves of the photograph.

The horizon line can also be put in unusual positions, even diagonally, which results from the photographer holding the camera at a 45-degree angle to the horizon (Figure 12-15). Diagonal lines of any kind tend to add energy to a scene. It divides a scene into triangles, which are strong visual elements in a composition.

Figure 12-14

Maroon Bells, Colorado.

Photo © KS.

Figure 12-15

Fishermen, south Thailand/Post tsunami.

Photo © Cedric Arnold, Bangkok, Thailand.

Figure 12-16

Glacier Park, Montana. 4 × 5 transparency with field camera, aperture of f/64. Shutter speed not recorded.

Photo © KS.

Colors in the Photograph

Objects closest to us have the greatest contrast of values and the most saturated colors. As objects recede from the foreground, contrast decreases and colors lose their saturation, meaning they become more gray (Figure 12-16). This phenomenon is known as **atmospheric perspective.** Leonardo da Vinci first used atmospheric perspective. His famous painting, *The Mona Lisa*, is a good example of atmospheric perspective.

Images containing mostly yellows, oranges, reds, or browns are considered warm-toned images. Several photographic printing methods yield warm-toned prints, including this albumen print by Julia Margaret Cameron in 1866 (Figure 12-17). Derived from eggs, albumen became a part of the emulsion used for prints. Albumen printing was very popular during Cameron's time. This photograph is also a good example of the gestalt principle of continuation. The model's eyes are looking downward and to the side, creating an implied line your eyes will follow.

Images containing mostly blues and greens are considered cool-toned images (Figure 12-18). The cool tones can be

Figure 12-17

Beatrice by Julia Margaret Cameron.

© SSPL/NMeM/Royal Photographic Society/Getty Images.

Figure 12-18

Blues and greens comprise a cool color palette.

Photo © Mark Mawson, Australia.

atmospheric (as in a foggy day), or they can be the result of the colors of elements within the photograph. This photograph is a good example of the gestalt principle of proximity. Although there are dozens of lines from the waves, your mind groups them together and treats them as the water's surface. The waves are not perceived as individual objects. The image is also a good example of implied continuation, as you assume the swimmer is going to continue swimming in the direction in which she is pointed.

A warm-toned element within an otherwise cool-toned image (or a cool-toned element within an otherwise warm-toned image) will stand out from its surroundings. In Figure 12-19, the presence of green light contrasts dramatically with the woman's red lipstick, adding to the sense of discomfort and alienation within the image.

Colors themselves carry culturally related emotional connotations; hence, colors must be carefully considered if images will be used in worldwide advertising publications. Use of the wrong colors can send damaging messages to viewers, potentially offending an entire culture and wasting the thousands of dollars spent to create and publish the advertisement.

For example, brides in the United States traditionally wear white. Brides in India traditionally wear red, as it is believed that wearing white could bring bad luck (Figure 12-20). An advertisement including a bride in white would not be appropriate for a traditional Indian audience.

The Path Through the Photograph

The gestalt principle of continuation plays a very important role in how your viewers' eyes will travel through your photograph. Lines, either real or implied, are followed through a composition. As the line of one element leads to another across elements, your viewer is led through the photograph.

Think about what you want your viewer to notice first in your photograph. How will you make that happen? Arrange the

Figure 12-19 (below)

Crimson Shroud. The green color cast from fluorescent lighting contrasts sharply with the red lipstick and makeup containers on the floor, emphasizing a young woman hiding her insecurities behind her makeup.

Photo © Renee M. Haas, Photographer.

Figure 12-20 (right)

Brides in India wear red dresses for the wedding ceremony.

Photo © Anyka/Shutterstock.

elements within your photograph to create perceived lines. Look at the scene as if it were already a two-dimensional photograph, and look for overlapping features and real or perceived lines.

Continuation is not the only principle that determines how a viewer's eyes will travel through your photograph. Where is the area of greatest contrast? That's where the viewer's eyes typically go first. Where is the area of greatest focus? People tend to gravitate first to elements in focus rather than those out of focus (Figure 12-21).

Which elements do you notice first, second, third, etc.? Is that the order of importance that you want to have your viewers register? Do the elements create enough visual interest to keep your viewers involved with the photograph for more than a few seconds? Does the visual story evoke an emotional connection with the viewers?

Figure 12-21

Woman with Kimono and Fan in Hagi, Japan. The photographer's choices of depth of field and selective focus were critical to the visual story being told.

Photo © Magdalene Solé, Photographer.

Figure 12-22 (top)

Life on the Farm. As you look at this photo, observe how your eyes travel through it.

Photo © Erika Schultz, Seattle Times.

Figure 12-23 (bottom)

The strong shapes this image form suggested leading lines that guide the viewer's eye through the photograph. The dark edges keep the viewer's eyes from leaving the image.

Photo © Michele Clement Photography.

The image in Figure 12-22 at first appears complex in composition, but it contains leading lines and areas of visual interest that keep you looking at the image and finding significant visual information. The subject matter, excellent composition, and dramatic lighting help viewers respond on an emotional level to the photograph.

Edges of the Photograph

What, if anything, will the photographic edges hold to keep your viewers' eyes traveling within the photograph and not falling off the edge? The shapes in Figure 12-23 create a suggested leading line for viewers to follow. The dark areas surrounding the stone tend to direct viewers from the edges of the image back into the photograph.

Some photographers slightly darken the edges or corners of a photograph, creating a visual barrier to keep the viewer's eyes within the photo. This process is called *vignetting* and can be subtle or strong. It can be accomplished with compositional elements or prephotographic lighting control, or it can be completed in the darkroom or in Photoshop. It is a frequent natural occurrence when using wide-angle lenses or pinhole cameras.

Movement within the Photograph

Viewers tend to assume that motion will be continuing if they perceive something as "moving" within the photograph. A person's line of vision can also be perceived as movement within a photo. Therefore, it is important to decide where to place a person within the photograph. It is usually considered good composition to allow some extra space into which the person can look (Figure 12-24).

Perspective and Depth

Perspective gives a sense of three-dimensional depth to a two-dimensional image (Figure 12-25). We are accustomed to seeing depth in our everyday world. A row of trees is tallest where it is closest to us; shortest, at its farthest distance from us. A train track appears widest where we're standing beside it; narrowest, at the farthest visual distance from us.

Because a photograph is a two-dimensional image, depth lies within the viewer's perception, not in physical reality. You can choose whether to have shallow or great depth of field, choosing your aperture and lens' focal length accordingly (as discussed in Chapter 3). Photographer Shannon Faulk shares her thought process as she prepares for a photo session in the Artist Statement (see also Figure 12-26).

Figure 12-24

Belarusian Zdislav Endzheichik sows winter wheat. In this image, space is wisely left for both people to look into. If the left side of the image were cropped closer to the woman, her space would seem crowded.

Photo © AP Images/Sergei Grits.

Figure 12-25

Subterranean.

Photo © John Smith Images.

Mergers

Mergers are unexpected intersections within a composition that result from a three-dimensional space being captured on a two-dimensional surface like a photograph (Figure 12-27). It may or may not be possible to avoid mergers, depending on the area surrounding your scene and the timing of the action you are photographing. As you become more proficient in photography, you will begin to see mergers before you record them on your camera. However, that doesn't mean you will always be able to avoid them. A question arises as to what to do about mergers in your images. If you are a fine art photographer, it is permissible to alter the photograph with retouching processes after the camera captures the image.

Photojournalists, on the other hand, must follow extremely stringent rules about altering photographs. Photographer John Filo won a Pulitzer Prize for the photograph in Figure 12-27. He was at the right place at the right moment to capture the emotional horror of a young woman kneeling over the body of a Kent State student. The fence post directly behind her head constitutes a merger, but rules applied to photojournalists may not allow its removal. The photograph remains visually and emotionally powerful regardless of the merger's presence.

Figure 12-27

John Filo took this famous photograph during the Kent State shootings in 1970.

Photo © John Filo.

Shannon Faulk

Equipment

- Canon EOS 1Ds Mark 2
- Canon 14 mm L Series Lens
- 2 Profoto 7B Battery Powered Strobes
- 2 Profoto Grid Reflectors
- 2, 30-Degree Grids
- Pocket Wizards, 1 Transceiver, 2 Receivers
- 4 Bogen Aluminum 13' Light Stands
- 2 knuckles for Flag Stands
- 2 Road Rags/Black Flags

Camera Settings

- I set the camera to Manual exposure, ISO/100, f/8 @ 1/200th, white balance 5800K.
- ISO/100. I could have gone higher, but my ambient light allowed me to keep it low.
- Aperture f/8. I wanted my background to be slightly out of focus to separate the subject from the background.
- Shutter Speed 1/200th. Pocket wizards that fire my strobes require sync speeds at or below 1/250th.
- 5800K, Manual White Balance, Think of the WB setting as film, daylight film is 5600K. I like my images a bit warmer (especially in shade) so I set it to 5800K and leave it. Forget AWB (auto white balance); it is too unpredictable.

Day of Shoot

This particular location had been in the back of my mind for years. I never had the perfect model to make the shot really stand out until I found this particular model using the website Model Mayhem. It's a website for young professionals looking for free images for their modeling portfolios.

On the day of the shoot, I arrive at least 30 minutes early to make sure cars were not blocking the background. I also like setting up everything before the model shows up. Doing so allows you the time needed to connect with the model when he or she arrives. It also gives you time to slow things down a bit, decide what clothes are to be worn, and also to explain what it is you want during the shoot.

At the location, I pull out my camera and frame my shot or shots. Once I have found my first shot, I put my camera on a tripod to mark the location. Now it's time to find my exposure, keeping in mind of course, f-stop, shutter speed, ISO.

I wanted the ambient exposure to be about 1 stop underexposed, which led me to f/8. Check the shutter speed to see if it falls within the sync speed that my camera and pocket wizards require, which I set to 1/200th of a second. Lastly, I check my ISO to make sure I haven't inadvertently left it too high, which can happen, ruining an entire shoot if it's left above 640, at least on my Canon 1Ds Mark 2.

Now that I have the camera set and in position, I can start setting up my Profoto lights and Flags. I start with setting up the stands first about head high for this particular shot. Then the Profoto heads are put on stands, along with the grid reflectors and 30-degree grids. Next is the Flags that are attached to stands using knuckles typically used on C-stands, but work just as well on aluminum stands.

Placing all the lights equidistant to the camera is ideal for consistent exposures from your lights. In this case, the lights were set to either side of the model about 10 feet from the subject. Using the grids will help keep the light off the ground and focused on the model. Next, place the Flags between the lights and the lens at about half the distance.

Using my Canon's timer control, I can set it to 10 sec countdown and use myself as the model to start testing the light. Having the lights set to the same settings and at equal distances from the model allows me not to use a flash meter, but to adjust using my histogram on my camera's LCD. So, I push the trigger, walk to the model's mark.

Preparation is the key.

Now that I've tested the shot, I can wait on the model and feel confident that everything will look great.

Composing a Photograph

Carefully select which areas of a scene to include in—or exclude from—your image. An image with a centered subject can sometimes become more visually interesting if it is composed in a different fashion. For example, you can leave out a very light, empty, boring sky so that a more interesting foreground can hold your viewer's attention.

Framing and Cropping Decisions

Images made with 35 mm film-based cameras are rectangles. They are rarely a width and height ratio that fit neatly onto a printed page (Figure 12-28). When they make an 8 × 10-inch print from a 35 mm photograph, printers can't fit the entire image onto the page. This is very frustrating

for photographers who want to have their entire images printed (Figure 12-29).

If you are in this situation, request that a *full-frame print* be made of your image. A full-frame print includes all of the visual information on the original image. The full-frame print will be 7 × 10 inches, which will leave a wider border along the long sides of your photo. This can be covered with a mat when the photograph is matted and framed.

Figure 12-28

An original, uncropped 35 mm photograph.

Photo © KS.

Figure 12-29

The photograph is shown here as if it were cropped to an 8 × 10-inch print. The darker side borders will be trimmed off when the print is made.

Photo © KS.

Framing a Photograph In-Camera

Cropping can take place both before and after you make the photograph. It is far more efficient to carefully compose your image before making the photograph to avoid additional cropping . This is called **framing the photograph in-camera**. If you are forced to crop off a lot of your photograph because the interesting part is only a small portion of the image, the quality of the resulting image will decrease. You are essentially forcing a small amount of film or digital information to expand to a large space, and that isn't always feasible.

When you look through your camera, look carefully in each corner and in the middle of the scene to determine if there is important visual information there (Figure 12-30). If not, bring your camera closer to the subject while watching for any stray objects that are entering your photograph along its edges. After you are satisfied that the corners and edges of the photograph look the way you want them to, look in the middle area of the photograph. Again, include only the elements you want to see there.

The Rule of Thirds

There are no hard-and-fast rules of cropping, but there is a **rule of thirds** based on a fifteenth-century art history concept of the Golden Mean or Golden Section. Very briefly described, the Golden Mean states that important elements are more visually interesting when they appear in specific areas of a rectangle; elements that fall within other areas of the photograph will have less visual interest.

The rule of thirds is used to determine those areas of interest, which are at the four intersections of four imaginary lines drawn to divide the composition into thirds horizontally and again vertically (Figures 12-31 through 12-33). Because most 35 mm, some medium-format, and large-format cameras create rectangular photographs, the rule of thirds can be an important aid in composing better, more engaging photographs. Again, this is not a hard-and-fast rule, but it does give photographers a starting point when composing photographs.

Figure 12-30 (above)

Look in each corner and then in the middle of the scene (indicated here with stars) before pushing the shutter button.

Photo © KS.

Figure 12-31 (below)

Lines showing the rule of thirds division. Placing important compositional elements at any of these intersections can make the photograph more visually interesting.

Photo © KS.

Figure 12-32

Two men walk past the headquarters of the German postal and logistics group Deutsche Post AG in Bonn 09/03/2010. Photographer Ina Fassbender followed the rule of thirds when determining where to place the people within this scene. This photo also follows the gestalt principle of similarity, as the paneled walls form a pattern broken by the two human figures.

Photo © REUTERS/Ina Fassbender.

Figure 12-33

Famine in Niger 2005. Two members of the Africa Muslim Agency attempt to brace the front gate as thousands of mothers carrying their malnourished children try to push into the therapeutic feeding center in Maradi, Niger. A stampede began after the Nigerien police drove their truck through the crowd killing a mother and child, according to witnesses. At the beginning of the week, the center gave away 22 tons of free millet and caused a massive crowd around three sides during the following distribution day. The therapeutic feeding center distributes food and accommodates about 200 people with medical, food, and housing for about a week. A combination of severe drought and a locust plague has caused a food shortage, which has affected at least 2 million people in Niger and about 5 million in the region. Niger is one of the poorest countries in the world.

Photo © Omar Vega/ZUMApress.com.

Remove Clutter

As the photographer, you are responsible for the content of every square inch of your photograph. Include only visual material that supports your intention. Too many elements can prevent your viewers from seeing or understanding why you made a particular photograph. For instance, the elegance and power of Fan Ho's image is based on simplicity (Figure 12-34).

When deciding how close or far away from your subject to set your camera and tripod, look frequently through the camera's viewfinder. Keep the most significant portions of your photograph and eliminate the areas that don't lend additional important visual information. The resulting photograph will have much more impact for your viewer.

Figure 12-34

Approaching Shadow, 1954 by Fan Ho.

Photo courtesy of Modernbook Gallery.

Removing the clutter from a scene doesn't mean all of your images must be as minimal as Fan Ho's image. It means that everything within the frame supports the story you are trying to tell. Alfred Eisenstaed was a prolific photographer during the mid-1900s. The image in Figure 12-35 contains numerous elements that, together, give a sense of time and place in history. Every element supports the visual story.

White Space

If you are making images for publication or advertisement, you may need to purposely leave some space in your photograph for text. When photographers work with advertising agencies, the art director may ask the photographer to leave one section of a photograph with minimal visual information so that text can be later dropped into place. That empty space is called **white space**, regardless of what color it actually is in the photograph (Figure 12-36).

Figure 12-35

VJ Day Times Square 1945. A jubilant American sailor clutching a white-uniformed nurse in a back-bending, passionate kiss as he vents his joy while thousands jam Times Square to celebrate the long-awaited victory over Japan.

Photo © Alfred Eisenstaedt/Getty Images.

Figure 12-36

White space gives graphic designers space for advertising text or additional photos.

Photo © Angelique Ambrosio.

If the advertising agency plans to use white text, the white space should be very dark or black; if they will be using black text, the white space may be white, gray, or a pastel color. It might also be a part of the photograph that is severely out of focus so as not to distract from the text.

Stock Photography

Working with an advertising agency requires extreme attention to detail and good communication between the art director and the photographer. The art director may go so far as to provide drawings, showing the photographer how the scene should be set up. Lighting, composition, color balance, and visual interest all become critical in such a project.

Stock photographers must consider potential white space in some of the photographs they make in order to meet written contracts with **stock photo agencies**. These agencies market photographs to potential publishers around the world on behalf of their contracted photographers. Once a publisher chooses a photograph for a specific publication, a contract is drawn up between the stock photo agency and the publisher. The agency receives a fee, and the photographer receives a specific percentage of that fee, depending on the contract with that agency.

Stock photographers try to guess in advance how publishers might use their photographs (see Chuck Pefley's Professional Profile at the end of Chapter 15). Because these photographs frequently end up in advertisements, the photographers often leave white space for potential text within the composition.

Leading Lines

Leading lines are visual elements within a photograph that draw the viewer's eyes through the image. The lines can be strongly visible, such as a fence line, or they can be suggested, such as a person pointing to something far away (Figure 12-37). By using leading lines to bring attention to specific places within a photograph, the photographer can emphasize the important elements of the composition.

Figure 12-37

Boatride. The leading lines created by the waves point directly to the child's finger and give context to the scene.

Photo © Allan Davey.

When using leading lines of any kind, make sure you place something interesting and important at the end of those lines. It's a visual disappointment to have leading lines that lead viewers on a journey, but have no interesting final destination.

Patterns

Our world is filled with visual repetitions. These repetitions form patterns within images and can be visually interesting. An image filled with a pattern can be made more visually interesting by dynamically altering that pattern in one portion of the image. The pattern sets up a visual rhythm, and a break in that rhythm creates a point of visual interest (Figure 12-38).

A Touch of Color

Many patterns, such as leaves, repetitive lines, or ripples in a pond, will often be rather monochromatic. A monochromatic image might be any color, but it's generally a very narrow range of that color. A close-up photograph of a green leaf would be a good example.

When using a monochromatic background, photographers can add a small element of a starkly different color to the image, and that element will stand out against the monochromatic background. This is an excellent way of adding contrast to an image and bringing the viewer's eye directly to that element. The greater the contrast in color between the object and its background, the easier it is for the viewer to see the intended element (Figure 12-39).

Figure 12-38

Patterns appear in many nature- and scientific-based photographs. This is a polarized light micrograph of a liquid crystal.

Photo © Karen Neill/LCI, Wellcome Images. Visit the Wellcome Image Collection at http://images.wellcome.ac.uk/.

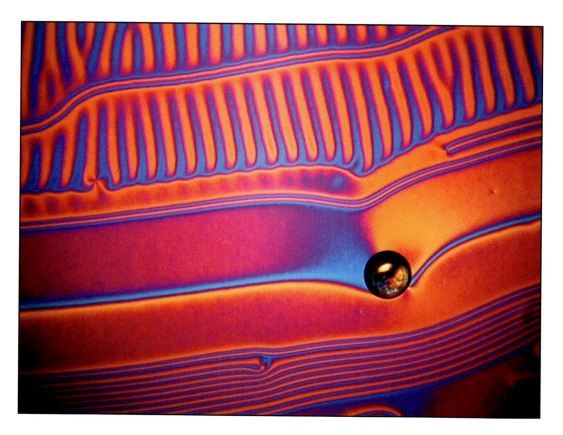

Figure 12-39

Waterlily.

Photo © Anne Geddes, 2010. See more of Anne's collection of
photographs at www.annegeddes.com.

When using touches of color, it is helpful to know a little about the **color wheel**, which is an artistic tool that painters use to choose and mix various colors. There are three primary colors on the color wheel: red, blue, and yellow (Figure 12-40). These primary colors can't be achieved by mixing any other colors together.

For each of these primary colors, there is an opposite or "complementary" color. When a color and its complement are mixed together, they cancel each other; and the artist is left with gray. Red and green are complementary pigment colors, as are yellow and violet, and blue and orange (Figure 12-41).

If you want to use a color that will stand out vividly against a monochromatic background, you would do well to choose an object in the color opposite of your background color as Anne Geddes did in Figure 12-39.

Remember that these colors are color complements when using paints and other pigmented materials. When dealing with light—as you do in a color darkroom or on the computer—the color complements change slightly. Red and cyan (a color close to aquamarine) are opposites, as are green and magenta, and blue and yellow (Figure 12-42). You can successfully use these color complementary pairs for touch of color compositions as well.

Motion as Contrast

A photograph that shows motion in some areas and stationary elements in other areas is using motion as contrast. In Figure 12-43, a relatively long shutter speed of ½-second stops the potter's action, but allows the potter's wheel to show active motion. The camera was set to shutter priority (Tv) mode, and a tripod was used to steady the camera. In Figure 12-44, the train seems to be standing still. However, the ground around the train gives you the visual clue showing the motion of the train.

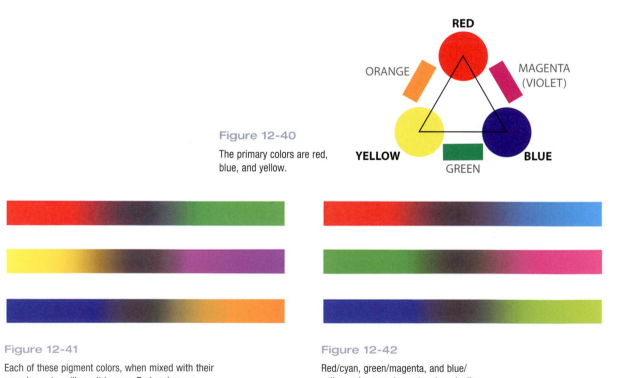

Figure 12-40

The primary colors are red, blue, and yellow.

Figure 12-41

Each of these pigment colors, when mixed with their complements, will result in gray. Red and green pigments are complementary, as are yellow and violet, and blue and orange.

Figure 12-42

Red/cyan, green/magenta, and blue/ yellow color complements when dealing with light.

Figure 12-43

An example of contrast
via motion.

Photo © KS.

Figure 12-44

Something's afoot: A woman
sits between carriages
on a train as it travels to
Mymensing from Dhaka,
capital of Bangladesh,
on Sept. 20. Millions of
Bangladeshis were traveling
home from the capital to
celebrate the Muslim Eid
al-Fitr holiday, which marks
the end of the fasting month
of Ramadan.

Photo by Andrew Biraj/Reuters.

Experiment with Your Compositions

Remember that there are no hard-and-fast rules of composition. It could be that changing the orientation of an existing photograph will create a totally different image. In Figure 12-45, the photographer chose to rotate his photograph by 90 degrees to arrive at a completely different image.

Further exploration can come from taking time with your subject matter. When you approach a subject, plan on spending a lot of time with it—not just a few minutes, but hours, days, or even weeks. Create an entire series of photographs, and plan on editing the results later (Figures 12-46 and 12-47).

Don't be afraid to experiment to find a variety of visual solutions. Come closer to your subject. Move farther away. Change the positioning of the horizon line in the photograph. Look to the left or right of the existing scene, or even behind you, to see what else might be of interest. Rotate the camera to unusual angles. Lie on your back. Stand on a ladder. Get on your hands and knees. The possibilities are endless, provided you are open to them.

Summary

The information in this chapter is meant to offer you a starting point with which to explore composition. These are by no means hard-and-fast rules. In fact, the rules are frequently broken with excellent results. If you think you see a strong composition, make a photograph of it. Then work more with the individual elements within the scene to see if you can strengthen its composition.

Composition is a tool to help you convey your intention to your viewers. When learning about composition, it can be very helpful to show your photographs to viewers who aren't aware of your intention for the images. If the viewers give you feedback demonstrating that they understand and agree that your message is clear, you have begun to achieve your goal. If they don't, look again at the composition of your images to determine what changes will help you improve the image's visual communication.

Figure 12-45

White Rose.

Photo © Chris Walker, 2009.

Figure 12-46

Girasole, Umbria, 1999.

Photo © Jeff Curto.

Figure 12-47

Girasole, Chianti, 1998.

Photo © Jeff Curto.

1. Look at photographs in a variety of advertisements and evaluate the composition of the images. How does the composition lead your eye through the photograph? Which elements stand out? How does the composition help to make the advertising message clear?

2. Look at the background and edges of your photographs. Are there elements that distract the viewer? If so, would cropping the photograph help eliminate those distractions?

3. Place an overlay, such as acetate or tracing paper, on top of some of your favorite photographs. Draw a line depicting how your eye travels through the photograph. What elements within the photograph keep your eye from leaving the image? What leading lines exist within the photograph?

4. Research photographs by Diane Arbus, Mary Ellen Mark, Lewis Hine, and Margaret Bourke-White. Compare and contrast the use of composition by the first two photographers with the use of composition by the other photographers. How do the compositions strengthen the intentions of the photographers?

5. Select one object or a series of objects in your everyday environment. Over a period of several days and at different times each day, write down what you notice about the shape, position, background, and lighting conditions of that scene. After keeping a journal of this information over several days, decide what it is that you find most visually interesting about that scene. Then make photographs of the scene that best portray what you found to be most interesting. Use your knowledge of lighting and composition to strengthen your intentions.

6. Look at the compositions in paintings from the Renaissance, including paintings by Rafael, Leonardo da Vinci, Michelangelo, Bellini, and Giorgione. Use these compositions as inspiration for your own photographic compositions.

FURTHER READING

- DYCHEMIN, David. *Within the Frame: The Journey of Photographic Vision.* Berkeley, CA: New Riders Press, 2009.

- GRILL, Tom, and Mark Scanlon. *Photographic Composition: Guidelines for Total Image Control Through Effective Design.* New York: Watson-Guptill Publications, 1990.

- LANDA, Robin. *Graphic Design Solutions.* 3rd ed. Clifton Park, NY: Thomson Delmar Learning, 2006.

- LAUER, David A., and Stephen Pentak. *Design Basics.* 5th ed. Fort Worth, TX: Harcourt Brace College Publishers, 2000.

- ZELANSKI, Paul, and Mary Pat Fisher. *The Art of Seeing.* 8th ed. Upper Saddle River, NJ: Prentice Hall, 2010.

Concrete Euphoria: Singapore River.

Courtesy of Mintio, Republic of Singapore.

CHAPTER

13

Critiquing Photographs

- Understand the concept of critiquing a photograph.

- Become aware of different purposes for photographs.

- Develop an understanding of intentions for photography.

- Learn what questions to ask as you critique photographs.

- Understand how different kinds of photographic organizations might critique photographs.

Critiquing is a careful, evaluative process that involves answering a series of questions; in this case, those questions refer to a photograph. Many students are terrified of having their photographs critiqued. The word itself conjures the fear of hearing people say they don't like your photograph or that you did something very wrong when making the photograph. A good critique, though, is far removed from that scenario; it answers questions about why the photograph was made, whether it meets the photographer's intentions, and what might be changed to better match the photograph to those intentions (Figure 13-1). In this chapter, you'll learn how to look at, evaluate, and critique photographs.

Reasons for Making Photographs

Chapter 1 of this text discussed various reasons for making photographs. You'll recall that those reasons included decoration, personal symbolism, persuasion, and recording of events.

Many photographers express in writing the reason for making their photographs. This documentation, called an **Artist Statement**, give viewers insights regarding the photographer's thoughts regarding their works. Read the Artist Statement from Mintio, the photographer who made the image found at the beginning of this chapter.

Another reason to make photographs involves using those images later as a visual reference to an item, person, or scene. Police officers photograph crime scenes, and realtors photograph homes going

Figure 13-1

Most people would consider this a dull picture of a partially burned box, but there was a story behind it. A student had unknowingly driven his car over the box and was dragging it directly under the car's engine, causing sparks and flames that could have been disastrous. Someone cared enough for the student's safety to shout, stop the driver, and dislodge the smoking box from the underside of the car. It was a very close call. The photograph serves as a reminder to the photographer to keep her eyes open and help others when she can. Without knowing the story behind it, the photo could be misunderstood and/or harshly critiqued by others.

© Cengage Learning 2012.

Mintio

"Concrete Euphoria" is a photoseries that explores of the ever-changing mega cities of Asia. The artist sees Asian mega-cities as sites of relentless progress as Asia constantly tries to remake itself in urban development. Created entirely within the camera, the abstraction of the landscapes is created by multiple exposures within a single frame. The artist works from 4–16 exposures per frame, and these exposures can vary from a fraction of a second to several hours.

In the genre of contemporary landscape images, the artist views the camera as a tool to translate the experience of being in a physical space into a two-dimensional map. Through the kaleidoscope-like multiple exposures, the camera takes a step to render familiar places as fantastical and sublime: elements within the cityscape such as streetlights, road signs, buildings intersect to create stark symbols amidst the confusion. In some images, almost inno-

cently, religious and political symbols emerge: we can see crosses, swastikas, and grids. Wonder is created in the way the fragmented details rework and reassemble themselves into something new.

Much of the beauty of the details comes from the fact that this series was shot with a large-format camera, on 4 × 5 film transparencies. The scale of the images and their resolution allow the viewers to appreciate the pattern-like quality of the image at a distance and engage with the minute and intricate details up close. Occasionally, with the capacity of the medium, subtle differences in between the exposures are revealed—for example, amidst the towering buildings viewers can spot a passing airplane in the sky or a worker in a construction site. Working with long exposures at varied timings also allows the artist to create variations and changes within the seemingly repetitive pattern.

up for sale. To show damage or changes to the environment, scientists and people interested in environmental changes make photographs (Figures 13-2 and 13-3).

Making personal photographs for purposes of self-expression involves extensive thought, preparation, and post-production work. For these artists, composing the scene means taking responsibility for every square inch of the area to be included in the photograph. If it's an outdoor scene, unwanted items (such as trash or vehicles) in the scene are moved or removed. Stray branches or dead pieces of grass are removed from the area surrounding a beautiful flower. Highlights and shadows caused by bright sunlight and surrounding bushes are evaluated and controlled or eliminated. People are moved in or out of the scene, or they will be carefully posed

within the scene. These photographers wait until the light and atmospheric conditions are exactly what they want before making the photograph.

If it's an indoor scene or studio setup, the photographer will take equal care to ensure that only what is truly desired for the photograph will be there. Backgrounds and props, such as tables and chairs, will be carefully composed. Light is carefully controlled. Positioning of elements, including people, within the photograph is carefully staged (Figure 13-4).

After taking considerable effort to get the best possible photograph on film or digital media, these artists then go to the traditional darkroom or computer to continue fine-tuning the image. They may change the highlights, shadows, color balance, and cropping of their photographs until the images strongly relate to their own artistic vision.

Figure 13-2

Mount St. Helens before its
major eruption in 1980.

Photograph courtesy U.S. Forest
Service, 1973.

Figure 13-3

Mount St. Helens two years
after its 1980 eruption.

Photograph courtesy Lyn
Topinka, USGS.

Figure 13-4

Photo © Kemal Kamil.

Steps in Critiquing Individual Photographs

Your first task in critiquing a photograph is to determine which style of photograph you are viewing. If it's a snapshot quickly taken while enjoying a party with friends or the recording of an important crime scene, an in-depth critique may not be appropriate. But for photographs that are created to convey a message, tell a visual story, or evoke the viewer's emotional response, an in-depth critique can help you understand and appreciate the photograph. This is the type of photography that will be discussed for the remainder of this chapter.

Your reaction to a photograph will vary, depending on your life experiences, knowledge of photography, and knowledge of the subject matter within the photograph. Because each person's approach to a photograph is different, critiques of any given photograph will differ from one person to the next.

It is very common for photographers to have differing opinions on the handling of an image. The following Artist Statement holds an example of an e-mail conversation between two photographers discussing two different croppings of a single image (refer to Figures 13-5 and 13-6).

Questions to Ask about an Individual Photograph

Following are some general questions to ask when viewing a photograph. Your answers will formulate your final critique.

- Describe the photograph. What does it look like? Color, grayscale, or areas of each?
- What is the subject matter in the photograph?
- Can you tell from which social era it came? What clues give you that information?
- Does the photograph give you a sense of time (day or night, long exposure or short exposure)? What clues give you that information?

Figure 13-5

"Spirit of Hope."

Photo © Andrew Van der Merwe, Cape Town, South Africa. Andrew sculpts letters into sand and then photographs them. See more of his work at http://www.behance.net/Gallery/African-beach-calligraphy-doodles/284641.

Two Photographers Discussing Croppings of an Image

From: S. Mattingly
Sent: October 11 10:45 AM
To: D. A. Salinger
Subject: Croppings of "Spirit of Hope"
Attachments: Spirit of Hope(1).jpg; Spirit of Hope(2).jpg

There are distinct compositional and, therefore, conceptual differences between these two images. The uncropped version has the sun centered horizontally and the horizon line centered vertically. I get an overwhelming sense of peace, stability, and power. The small figure in the sand is the one bright spot that lends a sense of mystery and aberrant energy to the image. His mission seems in contrast to the rest of the image.

From: D.A. Salinger
Sent: October 11 11:03 AM
To: S. Mattingly
Subject: RE: Croppings of "Spirit of Hope"
Attachments:

The cropped version has a much higher horizon line and only implies the presence of the sun via the reflection in the water. As a result, it invokes a different thought process from the viewer. It's more mysterious and less stable than the square image. I almost feel like the bright figure is leading the dulled crowd in a crusade, but unfortunately all of the energy is within the single figure.

From: S. Mattingly
Sent: October 11 11:52 AM
To: D. A. Salinger
Subject: RE: Croppings of "Spirit of Hope"
Attachments:

I'm with you on how the horizontally cropped version implies the sun, and to imply something is usually better than stating it bluntly, but I decided this image was a special case. Sure, the cropped version implies the sun; but the full version, with the physical connection clear, is able to go beyond that and somehow hint at a more abstract, spiritual connection. Instead of focusing only on the running figure, one is compelled to consider the relationship between the two. Here, a jumbled mass of meaningless letters and symbols is energized by a single individual, charging in, armed with nothing but enlightenment. This piece is dedicated to the vision and determination of enlightened individuals such as William Wilberforce, Mahatma Gandhi, Martin Luther King, and Nelson Mandela who have brought cultural, political, and judicial change to oppressive regimes and given meaning and hope to the lives of countless others.

Figure 13-6
A cropped version of "Spirit of Hope."

Photo © Andrew Van der Merwe.

- What can you discern about the camera's aperture, shutter speed, and ISO settings when the photograph was made? What visual clues lead you to your conclusions?
- What was the approximate focal length of the lens? Wide angle? Telephoto? What leads you to your conclusion?
- What were the lighting conditions when the photograph was made? Do you think flash was used at all? Can you discern the distance, direction, and color temperature of light source(s)?
- What was the vantage point of the camera when the photograph was made? Was the camera low to the ground, at eye level, overhead, or somewhere in between?
- Did the photograph have an emotional impact on you when you first saw it? What emotions did the photograph trigger in you?
- What emotional response do you think the photographer was trying to evoke in a viewer? Did the photographer's intention match your emotional reaction?

- What concept or idea do you think the photographer was trying to portray with the photograph?
- Do you think the photographer was successful in translating these thoughts into a visual form? What aspects of the photograph lead you to this conclusion?
- Considering your thoughts on the lighting, choice of lens, vantage point, aperture, shutter speed, and ISO the photographer used, what could the photographer have done differently to strengthen the message?
- Do the following elements help or hurt what you perceive as the concept of the photograph?
  - Cropping of the photo
  - Density (lightness or darkness) in the overall photograph
  - Contrast (the range between the lightest and darkest areas of the photo)
  - Details (or lack thereof) in shadows and highlights
  - Depth of field
  - Composition

Figure 13-7

"Shattered, 2010."

Photo © Zelda Zinn 2010, Santa Monica, California, USA. See more of Zelda's work at www.zeldazinn.com.

Artist Statement

Zelda Zinn

I saw the image of the little girl, a carte de visite, and was immediately taken with her wide-eyed gaze. She reminded me of Alice in Wonderland, innocent and worldly at the same time. This photo could be seen in several ways: as an image on a glass plate that was disintegrating, or in a more metaphorical sense, as a comment on one's life: that the past was fixed and could not be undone. This girl stares out at us from history, but we cannot view her except through the broken, imperfect prism of our time.

- Color (if it's a color image) such as color balance, brightness or dullness of the colors, and how the colors relate to each other within the photograph
■ What changes would you make if you could have made the photograph yourself?

Formulating Your Opinion

Notice that you haven't yet been asked if you like the image. Until you have thoroughly answered the previous questions, you won't have credible arguments to support your like/dislike response. Once you have answered these questions in as much detail as you can, then it's time to formulate your opinion of the photograph. Base your opinion on the answers you gave to these questions.

The critique of a photograph requires a thorough investigation of its content. It forces you to put yourself in the shoes of the photographer, the observer, and the people, scene, and/or event within the photograph. Further discussion can include reference to similar images you've seen before. They may be other photographs, or they could

be paintings or drawings of similar subject matter. Those other images may add more context to your thoughts on the photograph you are critiquing. How are those images similar? How are they different from the photograph you're critiquing? Is photography the best medium for the subject matter included in this photograph? Would a drawing or painting have been more effective? Why or why not?

The following photograph by David Julian is called *The Log Soldiers* (Figure 13-8). Answer the questions listed previously as you look at this photograph. Although there are clearly two photographs here, the photographer chose to combine them and display them as a single image. Take this information into consideration as you do this exercise.

Critiquing a Collection of Photographs

Just as an individual photograph can be critiqued, so can an entire collection of works be critiqued. A collection typically is based on a single theme or concept, and the images are frequently made with one style

Figure 13-8
The Log Soldiers.
Photo © 2007, David Julian.

of visual expression. This style is typically consistent over the entire collection. Style, in this application, could mean that all of the photos are black-and-white, or all the photos are color. The photographs might conjure memories of an earlier time, or they could give a sense of the future. Whatever the style is, it remains consistent across all the photographs in the collection.

Questions to Ask about a Collection of Photographs

Following are some general questions to ask when viewing a collection of photographs. Your answers will formulate your final critique.

- Describe the collection of photographs as a whole. What does it look like? Color? Grayscale?
- What are the similarities and differences in subject matter across the collection?
- What story does the collection tell?
- Within that story, how does each photograph within that collection help tell that story?
- Do some of the photographs have better storytelling ability than others?
- Are all of the images important to the collection? Are there any that could be removed and still tell an equally strong story?

- When you look at all of the photographs in the collection, are there any that don't seem to belong to the rest of the collection? What makes this (or these) photograph(s) different?
- Ask the questions listed earlier for critiquing of individual photographs to each of the photographs in the collection. Given those answers, do you think the photographer might have used the photographic tools to better advantage in making any of the photographs?
- What do you think the photographer was trying to say with this collection? Does the collection match the photographer's intention?
- What other photographs could the photographer have made to further tell the intended story?

Fine art photographers often photograph a series of images that, as a whole, tell a visual story. Photojournalists and documentary photographers notice and bring to our attention things other people might entirely miss. Every photograph within the series is like a piece of a puzzle, in that it adds to your understanding of the photographer's intentions. See the photographs (Figures 13-9a through 13-9e) and the Artist Statement by Colleen Mullins; you can view more images in her portfolio at www.colleenmullins.com.

Artist Statement

Colleen Mullins

This work is an examination of the urban forest of New Orleans, forever altered by a 70% canopy loss at the hands of Katrina in 2005, that has since suffered unbelievable indignities at the hands of man.

We have a strange relationship with nature as urban dwellers. And we seemingly hold a cultural belief that if it is an Eden we planted, we have eminent domain over the territory it occupies. While sometimes their deformities can be perceived as comical, the impact of this loss will be faced by New Orleans residents returning home for years to come. Absent street signs, and often the houses themselves, these trees are frequently the only signifiers to tell me that I've returned to a site to photograph. Imagine if the tree was not a marker for a photograph, but a marker for your home.

Figure 13-9a

Photo © 2010 Colleen Mullins,
Minneapolis, Minnesota.

Figure 13-9b

Photo © 2010 Colleen Mullins.

Photographic Installations

Photography is no longer only a print on a sheet of paper. There are new possibilities for photographers at every turn. Printing processes include printing onto fabric, metal, plastic, rocks, wood, and many other substrates. Each process can be used to help tell a story. By looking into new possibilities, you can find unusual or brand new ways to enhance the message you are trying to convey with your photographs.

Photographic installations don't stop at the two-dimensional form. They use the three-dimensional room in which they are hung to further shape the viewer's experience. Rooms may be dark or brightly lit, and the walls may be covered or plain. The arrangement of space between and around photographs guide the viewer through the imagery.

Thoughts on Being Critiqued or Judged

Because of the diversity of images possible with photography, it's quite likely that different individuals, photography groups, and organizations will offer conflicting ideas when critiquing images. Although some people offer critiques of images, others are asked to judge images in competitions. These judges may or may not use the same criteria as those listed earlier in this chapter.

Every judge of a fine art competition will bring his or her own knowledge, experience, and opinions to the judging process. Judges of portrait photography, such as in competitions for the Professional Photographers of America (PPA), have a different set of criteria from those that fine art judges may use. Judges of local or regional camera clubs may have yet another set of criteria for judging. No individual set of criteria is better or worse than any other set.

Learn what you can by entering a variety of competitions and having your photographs judged. Try not to take the judge's negative comments personally. Take whatever constructive information you can from the experience and use it for making future photographs.

Artist Statement

Ginger Owen-Murakami in collaboration with Vicki Van Ameyden

Artists, Vicki Van Ameyden and I have been cooperating as a team on projects for the last three years. While recognizing the need to work large scale and in multiples in order to build sculptural or experiential environments, our projects have centered on content derived from discussions of our parallel life journeys.

History Cairn and *Kite Piece* are projects that were inspired by the subsequent and serendipitous acquirement of family photo albums as heirlooms due to the deaths of family members. Framing our ideas around the nostalgia generated from remembering our past through picture albums, we contemplated basic life stages: infancy (birth), youth, adulthood, old age, and ultimately death. We built two installations speaking directly to two of life's stages: youth and death. *History Cairn* references a burial mound, whereas, in *Kite Piece* a young girl's dress is tethered to images of "her" past. This work represents a communal conversation on the influence of family history.

Summary

Critiquing photographs is not a quick and simple process of deciding whether or not you like an image. It is a thought-provoking process requiring the use of observational skills learned through making and studying photographs. Learning more about photography will enhance your critiquing skills.

Take the time to read artist's statements available from artists of all mediums. Visit art museums and art galleries to view current displays. You will gain a greater respect for that artist's works and develop a better understanding of how artists reveal the intentions for their works of art.

When critiquing both your own work and the work of others, ask the questions presented in this chapter to gain a much better understanding of why the work was created. Then complete the critique by formulating your opinion on whether the artwork was successful.

EXERCISES

1. Select one of the photographs in this chapter and critique it by answering the questions presented in this unit.

2. Select a documentary photograph from a news magazine or *National Geographic* and critique it by answering the questions presented in this unit.

3. Do a search on the Internet for fine art photographers. Read their artist's statements and view their work. Formulate an opinion about whether or not their statements support their works.

4. Critique one of your own photographs by answering the questions presented in this unit. Given your answers, what might you do to strengthen your photograph?

5. Select one portrait painting of the great masters of Europe: Rembrandt, Leonardo da Vinci, Titian, Michelangelo, Jan van Eyck, or Raphael. Do research on the life and times of the painter, including the social climate in which the painter lived. Study the composition, various elements, and backgrounds of the painted portrait. Then create a photographic portrait that uses similar composition and lighting of the painting within your photograph. Vary the elements such as clothing, props, and background to emphasize the differences between the social climates of the two eras (15th or 16th century and today's modern society). Prepare a written paper that discusses why you created the portrait the way you did.

FURTHER READING

■ ADAMS, Robert. *Beauty in Photography: Essays in Defense of Traditional Values*. 2nd ed. New York: Aperture Foundation, 1989.

■ BARRETT, Terry. *Criticizing Photographs*. 3rd ed. New York: McGraw-Hill, 1999.

■ COLEMAN, A. D. *The Digital Evolution: Visual Communication in the Electronic Age*. Portland, OR: Nazraeli Press, 1998.

■ KISSICK, John. *Art: Context and Criticism*. 2nd ed. New York: McGraw-Hill, 1995.

■ MITCHELL, William J. *The Reconfigured Eye: Visual Truth in the Post-Photographic Era*. Cambridge, MA: MIT Press, 1992.

■ SONTAG, Susan. *On Photography*. New York: Picador USA, 1977.

Lluvia de Angeles, taken at the Parque General San Martin-Provincia de Mendoza, Argentina.

Photo © Carlos Alberto Bau/iStockphoto.

14

Copyright Law

Chapter Learning Objectives

- Identify the main components of U.S. copyright law.

- Define copyright law terms such as *copyright owner*, *derivative*, *fair use*, *public domain*, and *royalty free*.

- Determine whether or not a work falls under copyright law.

- Identify your photographs with your copyright information.

- Understand how rights can be transferred and under what conditions a transfer can take place.

- Identify the various licensing conditions that Creative Commons offers.

- Explain how you can register your copyrighted works.

It was a stunning scene with flowers going from floor to ceiling as far as the eye could see. The Philadelphia International Flower Show 2010 was a grandeur event that begged to be photographed (Figure 14-1). People were taking pictures at every turn. But what reproduction rights did this give the photographers? Who owned the copyright to the floral arrangements? Could people sell their images? Publish them? Make greeting cards out of them? What rights do artists and photographers have? How can you as a photographer protect your images? These questions are answered within the details of U.S. copyright law.

Few federal laws so immediately affect photographers as copyright law. Your photographs are protected by it, and every person is bound to it. This chapter covers the United States copyright law as it applies to photographers and digital artists.

What Works Can Be Copyrighted?

Photographs are only one category of copyrighted materials. Copyright law covers other creative works, including writings, paintings, drawings, sculptures, jewelry, songs and sound recordings, dances, theater productions, plays, videotapes, and website designs.

As soon as you push your camera's shutter button, you immediately own copyright to the resulting image. You don't need to register it, write anything down, or identify it with your name or copyright symbol. United States federal law says you are the **copyright owner**.

Copyright ownership gives you specific rights pertaining to your photographic images. You have the right to:

- Make copies or alter your photograph in any way you choose;
- Display your photographic images;
- Distribute your photographic images by print, film, or digital file;
- Sell your photographic images;
- License other people to use your photographic images and charge those people for that license; and
- Create derivatives (alterations) of your photographic images, including small alterations such as cropping, retouching, layering, or other larger modifications and adaptations (Figure 14-2).

It is the image itself, not the print or digital file, that is copyrighted. You own copyright to your image regardless of whether it's printed and hung on a wall, shown in a website, used in an advertisement, or stored on a disk. It could be printed on fabric, wood, metal, or brick. The copyright remains yours.

The first formal moment of copyright coverage occurs when your photograph or other creative work is fixed in a **tangible form**. For photographers, the tangible form is typically either film or the digital file. Your photographic negative is a

Figure 14-1

This floral sculpture of a giraffe designed by Adriene Presti, AIFD, was displayed as a part of "Exhibition South Africa: The Mighty Togo" in the Philadelphia International Flower Show 2010. As the designer, she holds copyright to this sculpture. Before taking any photos at the flower show, the author asked permission from the show organizers to make photographs. Permission was granted. However, that permission was only to make photographs. It would not have allowed the author to publish this image without further permission from the copyright owner.

Photo © KS.

Figure 14-2

The image above and the four on the following page are all derivatives of Adriene Presti's floral sculpture.

Photos © KS.

Figure 14-2

(continued)

Photos © KS.

tangible form, as is a file stored on your camera's memory card. You receive copyright protection at the moment of fixation on either film or memory card. If you have combined two or more of your own photographs (*not* anyone else's) on your computer, you own copyright to the new image as soon as you save that file.

Exceptions to Copyright Law

Copyright law has few exceptions, one being if the federal government produced the creative work. All photographs that federal employees create in the scope of their professional work are in the **public domain** and anyone can use them. For example, photographs that the Hubble Telescope takes are public domain and not covered by copyright law (Figure 14-3).

Current copyright law states that copyright owners maintain copyright protection for life plus 70 years. For an anonymous work, a pseudonymous work, or a work made for hire (work you do while employed by a company), the copyright endures for a term of 95 years from the year of its first publication or a term of 120 years from the year of its creation, whichever expires first. This has been a part of copyright law since 1978. These terms of copyright protection have changed over the years, depending on federal legislation. Because the legislation has changed several times, it is wise to consult the comprehensive charts available through the Copyright Office website (www.copyright.gov) if you're curious about works created before 1978.

> ### NOTE
>
> ### Photographs from the Hubble Telescope
>
> Photographs that the Hubble Telescope takes are actually grayscale images to which color is applied for scientific and/or aesthetic purposes. Read more at http://hubblesite.org/gallery/behind_the_pictures/meaning_of_color.

Notice of Copyright Ownership

Many people are familiar with ©, the official copyright symbol, which is part of the proper notice of copyright ownership. The full proper notice is as follows: © year, name. To type the copyright symbol on a Mac computer, hold down the OPTION key and type the letter "g." To type the copyright symbol on a PC computer, hold down the ALT key. While holding down the ALT key, type "0169" on the NUMERIC KEYPAD of your keyboard (this works in Photoshop). Then release the ALT key. You'll see the © on your screen. In Microsoft Word, you can also hold the CONTROL and ALT keys and type the letter "c." However, this technique doesn't work in Photoshop.

It is not necessary to place the copyright notice on your photographs. As a result of an amendment to the copyright law in 1986, your images are protected regardless of whether you use the formal notice. However, it's advisable that you do so to alert other people that you are the copyright owner. It is particularly advisable to put the copyright notice on any prints you sell.

Exclusive and Nonexclusive Rights

Rights protected by copyright law can be transferred to other people in two different ways: exclusive and nonexclusive rights. **Exclusive rights** include all rights to copy, display, change, sell, or license the photograph. If you transfer exclusive rights of your image to someone else, you will no longer have any right to keep, sell, display, or otherwise use the photograph again. It's like selling an original work of art that can't be reproduced. Transfer of exclusive rights can only be completed with a written agreement. It can't be done verbally.

Nonexclusive rights allow someone else to use your photograph while you still maintain the copyright. A nonexclusive transfer might be any of the following:

Figure 14-3

Light Echoes from Red Supergiant Star
V838 Monocerotis – October 2004.

Photo by NASA, ESA and H.E. Bond (*STScI*).

- You agree to let a friend use a photo of yours on his website.
- You agree to let the local newspaper print your photograph, with or without payment, depending on the agreement.
- You agree to let a magazine use your photograph on its front cover for a designated fee or for free.
- You agree to allow an artist to paint the image of your photograph and sell that painting. Whether or not you charge a fee for this right is up to you.
- You allow a major corporation to use one of your photos for a greeting card. The corporation wants you to refrain from licensing that photo for any other greeting card use for a period of three years.

Nonexclusive rights can be transferred without a written agreement, but it is *definitely* not recommended. It is always best to write down any agreement on transfer of rights. In fact, all of these transfers of rights are best handled with a written contract.

Work for Hire

When a company employs you to produce work for that company and its customers, you are in a **work for hire** situation. Under most circumstances, the company you are working for will own copyright to any creative work you produce.

It is very important to agree on copyright ownership before you start working for an individual or a company. If you are a freelancer hired to take photos for a

NOTE

Learn More about Working with Contracts

See chapter 15, Best Practices, to learn more about working with contracts.

specific event or need, sign a contract that stipulates who will own copyright to your photographs *before* you do the work. Claiming copyright afterwards, without a signed agreement, is often very difficult. This is one of the greatest sources of frustration and financial loss for student photographers. Make all agreements in writing and have both parties sign the contract, before any work begins.

Registering Your Photographs

Copyright protection of your photographs begins at the moment you make the photograph. If you find out that someone has copied your photograph without your permission, you can file a **legal claim** (legal complaint) against that person. A claim could include the following:

- You can tell the person to stop using your photograph and/or return the print to you.
- You can require a reasonable payment for the use of the photograph. However, you would have additional protections if you register your photographs with the U.S. Copyright Office *before* you file a copyright claim. These additional protections include:
  - You can seek statutory damages ($750–$30,000, or up to $150,000, if you can prove the infringement was willful).
  - You can seek payment of your attorneys' fees.

If you haven't registered your photographs with the Copyright Office before you file a claim, you are not allowed to seek statutory damages or payment of your attorneys' fees. Copyright registration is relatively easy, thanks to online registration at www.copyright.gov/forms. You can register your photographs in large groups, instead of individually, saving lots of time and money. Published and unpublished works need to be filed in separate groups.

Fair Use Doctrine

Certain circumstances allow people to use copyrighted works of any kind, regardless of who owns copyright to them. The **Fair Use Doctrine** was added to federal copyright law to free use of copyrighted works for purposes of education, research, and criticism, among others. Because these three purposes might influence how you make or use photographs, they will be discussed here.

Education and Research

It is permissible for you and your professors or teachers to copy short excerpts of copyrighted material (including photographs) and include them in reports or class handouts, provided the use of the excerpts is strictly for educational purposes. It is also permissible to do "copy exercises" to help you learn new skills. An example would be a class exercise that requires you to create to the best of your ability a copy of a famous, copyrighted photograph, drawing, or painting. Such exercises are covered by the Fair Use Doctrine. However, you do not have the right to further copy, sell, or disseminate that work.

Criticism

If an author is writing about a copyrighted work, such as a newspaper article about the strong and weak points of a local art show, it is permissible to use copyrighted images from that art show to illustrate the points the author makes. Note that it is *not* permissible to use a photograph to simply illustrate that same story. The photograph must be absolutely required to make sense of the author's commentary.

Use of Copyrighted Photographs for Collage Work

This may be the most misunderstood aspect of copyright law. There are several common assumptions about copyright law. See how your understanding compares to these facts:

1. *Assumption:* If you change a copyrighted work by a given percentage, you don't need to ask the copyright owner's permission to use that work.
   Fact: This is not true. If a copyright owner can recognize his/her work within your own work, you can be sued for copyright infringement. There is no safe percentage of change. Any questionable use could be brought to a judge and jury to decide if copyright law had been broken.
2. *Assumption:* You can take a part of a copyrighted image to incorporate into your photomontage without asking the copyright owner's permission.
   Fact: Again, this is not true if the copyright owner could identify the portion of copyrighted image you took. Any recognizable use of a copyrighted image subjects you to charges of copyright infringement and could be brought to a judge and jury to decide if copyright law had been broken.
3. *Assumption*: You can take any image off the Internet and use it in your own photomontage work without asking the copyright owner's permission.
   Fact: Just because an image is on the Internet doesn't mean it is copyright free. Someone owns copyright to it, and you need to find the copyright owner and ask permission.

Royalty-Free Photographs

Photographs may be sold either individually or in bundles, either over the Internet or via CD/DVD. If an image is listed as royalty free, you have the right to reuse it for almost any purpose after you have purchased it. The purchase price covers the usage. You don't need to ask for further permission.

Many clip art services work this way. If you do an online search for free photographs or free clip art, you will find dozens of websites offering that service. However, *be very careful* about using these websites! Carefully read the full Terms of Use for any royalty-free images you find on the Internet. Sometimes you can use images without asking permission, if you use them for nonprofit purposes. However, those terms may require permission if you are going to sell your photomontage or put it on a T-shirt and sell the T-shirts.

The bottom line is this: Read the Terms of Use on every website offering royalty-free artwork of any kind, including photography.

Derivatives

A **derivative** is a copy of an original work. "Copy" could mean any of the following:

- You make prints with different burning and dodging from an original negative or digital file so the resulting prints look slightly different.
- You knowingly produce a painting or drawing that resembles a copyrighted image, whether the original image is a photograph, painting, drawing, or sculpture.
- You download a copyrighted photograph from the Internet and alter it in Photoshop until it is different from, but still recognizable as being from, the original.
- You download or scan a copyrighted image and use a recognizable portion of that image in a photomontage.
- You're working for an advertising agency that wants to use a copyrighted image with a specific look and feel. The agency isn't willing to pay the fee to use that photo; so, they hire you to go out and create an image that closely resembles the copyrighted image. Even though you're the person behind the camera, you are knowingly creating a derivative of a copyrighted image.

If you are the copyright owner of all the original images in these examples, you have the right to do all of this work. If you aren't the copyright owner, you need written permission from the copyright owner to perform any of these tasks. If you do not have that permission to do these tasks, you are breaking copyright law.

How Images Are Compared

Let's look a little closer at the advertising agency example. A judge and jury will look at the photograph's aspects under the photographer's control when trying to decide whether a photographer has created a derivative of a copyrighted image. These aspects can include any or all of the following:

- Similar posing of the models, props, or other components of the image;
- Similar lighting, whether natural light or strobe light, was used;
- Angle of view and perspective of the two images, covering both the photographer's vantage point and the choice of focal length of the lens;
- Similar background used in the photograph, including anything from a scenic photo taken by a lake, to a cityscape in a specific city, to a similar background created in a studio;
- Shading, including similar uses of highlight and shadow effects in both images; and
- Color, including a particular overall hue to the image or use of the same color in specific elements in both photos.

Scenes a Faire

There's no doubt that an image made of a particular building will always look like that building. It's impossible to make a photograph of the building in a totally unique way. This concept is covered in the **scenes a faire** portion of copyright law. It stipulates that the components of a scene that must be contained in any photo of that scene (such as the shape of the building or its surrounding buildings) are not copyrightable. A photo of the Golden Gate Bridge in San Francisco, for example, would probably not be copyrightable unless there was another extremely unusual element within the photograph.

This chapter's opening image is a good example of a scenes a faire situation. This fountain in Argentina could be photographed thousands of times.

Many of those photographs will no doubt look similar. There is no danger of one photographer being allowed to hold copyright to the entire fountain and all photographs of that fountain. However, if a photographer were to capture an unusual image of the fountain (perhaps if the background held a particular person or if there was something else unusual within the image), then that photographer could have a stronger case to own copyright for that particular image.

The Best Copyright Solution

The best solution to any of these issues is to obtain the copyright owner's written permission before using any copyrighted image. The written agreement should include the following:

- Identification of the copyright owner and the person interested in using the photograph;
- Identification and/or description of the photograph itself;
- Terms of use, such as:
  - How many times the interested person can use the image (one time right, continuous right for a specified period of time, etc.);
  - Date of the agreement and how long the agreement is in effect;
  - How the photograph will be used (print media, online, website) and, if applicable, the size of use (front cover full page, ¼ page, etc.), and the distribution (worldwide, single country, local, etc.); and
  - What the interested person should do if an extension of permission is needed;
- Contact information for both the copyright owner and the person interested in the photograph;
- A place for signatures of the copyright owner and the person using the photograph; and
- The date of the agreement written somewhere on the page.

It's worth noting at this stage that you don't need to be afraid of unknowingly photographing something that another person in the world has also photographed. If someone else were to charge you of copyright violation, that person would have to prove that you had direct access to that person's image. In the same manner, you would have to prove that someone else had access to your photograph before you could claim a copyright violation.

Copyright License Conditions

Artists want not only recognition for their works, but they also seek protection for their works. To secure that protection, artists can enter into a variety of copyright license conditions. Some artists prefer to selectively share their works with others, allowing specific uses of their works that don't require written permission. Creative Commons was developed to meet the needs of artists who wanted a combination of sharing and protection of their works.

Creative Commons: The Basic Licenses

Recognizing the need to share photographs and other copyrighted works with the world, Creative Commons (www.creativecommons.org) has created a variety of licenses that work alongside copyright law and allow specific usage of copyrighted works without the need to ask permission to use them. Creative Commons offers artists of all kinds four different categories of license conditions. The next four headings give a brief description of each category.

Attribution

Under the **attribution** condition, the copyright owner allows others to copy, distribute, display, and perform the copyrighted work and any derivative works based on that work. Other people are required to give the copyright owner credit exactly as requested within the license.

Share-Alike

Under the **share-alike** condition, the copyright owner allows others to distribute derivative works only under a license identical to the one that the copyright owner originally placed on the work.

Noncommercial

Under the **noncommercial** condition, the copyright owner allows others to copy, distribute, display, and perform the work and any derivative works based on that work, provided the use is for noncommercial purposes only. The copyright owner would separately negotiate any commercial use of the work.

No Derivative Works

Under the **no derivative works** license condition, the copyright owner allows others to copy, distribute, display, and perform only verbatim (unchanged) copies of the work; no derivative works are permissible.

Mix of License Conditions

Copyright owners can mix the four license conditions discussed above to arrive at a variety of licenses. This lends even more flexibility to the Creative Commons' licenses.

Attribution Share-Alike

Under the **attribution share-alike** condition, the copyright owner allows others to use the image for any purpose, including creating derivatives from it, provided they credit the copyright owner *and* license their new creations under the identical terms of the Creative Commons license.

Attribution No-Derivatives

Under the **attribution no-derivatives** condition, the copyright owner allows redistribution, commercial and noncommercial, of the work, provided that work is passed along unchanged and in whole and with credit to the copyright owner.

Attribution Noncommercial

Under the **attribution noncommercial condition**, the copyright owner allows others to use, change, and build upon the work, but only for noncommercial purposes and provided that derivative works acknowledge the copyright owner, although users are not required to license the derivative works on the same terms as the copyright owner's original license.

Attribution Noncommercial Share-Alike

Under the **attribution noncommercial share-alike condition**, the copyright owner allows others to use the work, including derivative works, and change it in any way they wish, provided the use is for noncommercial purposes and that users credit the copyright owner and license their new creations under the same terms as the copyright owner's original license.

Attribution Noncommercial No-Derivatives

The **attribution noncommercial no-derivatives condition** is the most restrictive of the five mixes of licenses. Under this condition, the copyright owner allows others to download works and share them with others, provided the users mention the copyright owner, provide a link to the copyright owner, make no changes to the works, and do not use the works for commercial purposes.

GNU Free Documentation License (GNUFDL)

A form of licensure similar to the Creative Commons license group, the GNU Free Documentation License makes a manual, textbook, or other functional and useful document "free" in the sense that the works can be freely copied and redistributed, modified or unmodified, and used either commercially or noncommercially. The license preserves for the author and publisher a way to get credit for the work, although the original authors will not be responsible for the modifications that others make. Any modified works must also be licensed as free.

Although the GNU Free Documentation License is primarily used in creation of text for manuals and textbooks, JPG and PNG files can also be assigned this license. The entire GNU Free Documentation License can be found at www.gnu.org.

Wikimedia Commons

Wikimedia Commons (http://commons.wikimedia.org) is a database of more than 5.5 million media files. Here you can find photographs, videos, and sound files that have been donated under Creative Commons licenses for everyone's benefit. If you so choose, you can also contribute your works to this nonprofit organization.

Images and other media files are free, in that users are allowed to copy, use, and modify any file according to the license listed for each file, as long as they credit the source and the authors. The Wikimedia Commons database itself and its texts are licensed under the Creative Commons' attribution share-alike license.

To make the best use of Wikimedia Commons, register and log in whenever you want to upload or download files. You can participate in Wikimedia Commons by contributing your work, your file management skills, or your time by organizing files or moving files into relevant subcategories.

Protecting Your Copyrighted Images

In Chapter 15, Professional Practices, you will be given information on how to apply electronic information to your digital files to protect them from copyright violation. This is becoming increasingly important in our digital society. Taking steps to protect your images from copyright infringement is of critical importance. You've worked hard for your images. Now, you will learn how to make sure they remain yours.

Summary

The U.S. government assumes that all citizens have knowledge of federal copyright law. Claiming ignorance of the law is not an effective defense if copyright law is broken. Copyright law protects you as a photographer from having your creative works stolen. It also charges you with being responsible and careful when thinking about using other people's creative works.

It is always best to err on the side of caution if you are considering using the creative works of someone else. Ask permission. You will be amazed at how often you get a positive response.

Contact the Photographer

If you plan to use an image found in Wikimedia Commons, it is still a good idea to contact the photographer of that image. One of the author's students contacted a photographer and told him how she wanted to use the image. The photographer was completely unaware that his image had been placed in Wikimedia Commons. This may be an extremely unusual case; however, your best practice will always be to contact the photographer.

1. Write a short paper on the copyright law, what you see as its strengths and weaknesses.

2. Select at least one photo you have made and assign a Creative Commons license to it. Be sure you are comfortable with sharing this image with others according to the Creative Commons license you assign to it.

3. Go to http://commons.wikimedia.org and discover all the types of media available with the Creative Commons' licenses. Upload the image you used for Exercise #2 to this website.

4. Investigate two active national organizations that act as advocates for photographers regarding copyright law issues:

   A. Professional Photographers of America (PPA), www.ppa.com

   B. American Society of Media Photographers (ASMP), www.asmp.org

5. Do an online search for "Shepard Fairey, President Obama, and Mannie Garcia" to read about the copyright lawsuit over Fairey's use of a photo of President Obama made by Mannie Garcia. Write a short paper giving your opinion on whether or not Shepard Fairey violated copyright law. Support your opinion with facts from the websites you reviewed in previous exercises for this chapter.

6. Explore *Photo District News* at www.pdn.com. PDN is a comprehensive news magazine covering many issues regarding photographers. It also sponsors an annual student photography contest. Read and report on at least three articles regarding contemporary issues such as licensing and copyright law.

FURTHER READING

- VISIT www.copyright.gov and explore the information on this website.

- VISIT http://creativecommons.org/about/licenses/ to learn more about the different Creative Commons' licenses.

- VISIT the American Society of Media Photographer's (ASMP) website at http://asmp.org/content/registration-counts to get additional training in copyright law.

Jeff Richter
Wildlife/Nature Photographer

Photo © Jeff Richter, www.jeffrichterphoto.com.

Jeff Richter's images have been used in publications of The Nature Conservancy, Sierra Club, Audubon, NorthWord Press, Willow Creek Press, BrownTrout, Wisconsin Trails, and Loonwatch, among others. He sold his photographs through his northern Wisconsin gallery for over ten years. Jeff chose to self-publish books of his photography, and the results have been beyond his expectations. His first book, *Seasons of the North*, was published in 2003. Since that time he has published two more books, *White Deer: Ghosts of the Forest* and *Pure Superior: Photographs of Lake Superior*. Read more about Jeff at his website, www.naturepressbooks.com.

Jeff, you supported yourself through gallery sales and publications of your images for many years. Why did you decide to publish a book of your photographs?

I had developed a solid portfolio of nature images over the previous several years. I approached a publishing company, and they were interested in my book idea. However, during negotiations it became obvious that I was going to make very little income through another publisher. Instead, I took the plunge into self-publishing.

It changed my life. The book was a success, and the notoriety was completely overwhelming. I was on Public Radio and on television five different times. There were interviews, newspaper articles, and calls from people who loved the book.

How did you plan for the publication?

I had very little in the way of a business plan in the beginning. When I get a notion to do something, I dive into it and figure it out as I go. But there were some factors that made a huge difference. I had run a nature photography gallery for many years, so I knew I had a strong following of people who liked my work. That alone told me I would do at least well enough to recoup the cost of publishing the book.

What did you learn from the self-publishing experience?

I was able to create the exact book and text I wanted, which was great. The concept of selling the book was new to me. I was on the hook to sell and market the book myself. It required my getting in the car and driving to every book store, gift store, and gallery that I thought might be interested in carrying the book. I go on loops of hundreds of miles in each direction every couple of months to revisit stores. I prefer face-to-face contact with store owners. Because of the personal contact, the store owners are generous with how they display the book and recommend it to their customers.

What has this success done to your photography?

I feel even more pressure to expand my work and to make better, stronger images than those included in the last book. The book idea is also a fun way to approach shooting. I have a goal in mind and think about how I can tell a story. The individual image becomes a part of a whole instead of telling the whole story within the single image.

The success I've had has also cut into my time for photography. I'm a one-man show. I maintain the business in a way that gives me a lot of flexibility. I have to be fiercely protective of the space between the business and photographic opportunities. I have to be able to pick up and leave when I need to get photography done. I still enjoy nothing more than the creative process of being in the field with a camera.

As a result of the time pressures, I've become more efficient with my photography. I get a little smarter about the time I spend out in the field. If you're a good photographer, you should be making a better image than you did last week or last year. If you aren't pushing yourself, you're going backwards.

What advice would you give a photographer who is thinking about self-publishing a photography book?

- Ideally, make sure your photographs are better than anyone else's photos of the same subject matter. That's a very important way to get your work noticed.

- Don't be afraid to do the self-publishing if you can afford it. Look toward doing short print runs to get started, because you won't need tens of thousands of dollars to do 5,000 books like I did.

- Don't be afraid to get out and show the book. That's the only way it's going to get sold.

- Hire a good graphic designer, someone who has been in the publishing world. It's really helpful if you can find a designer experienced with the design and marketing of a book. I had no idea of the technical and business issues involved with the designing and printing process. My graphic designer was immensely helpful with all of that work.

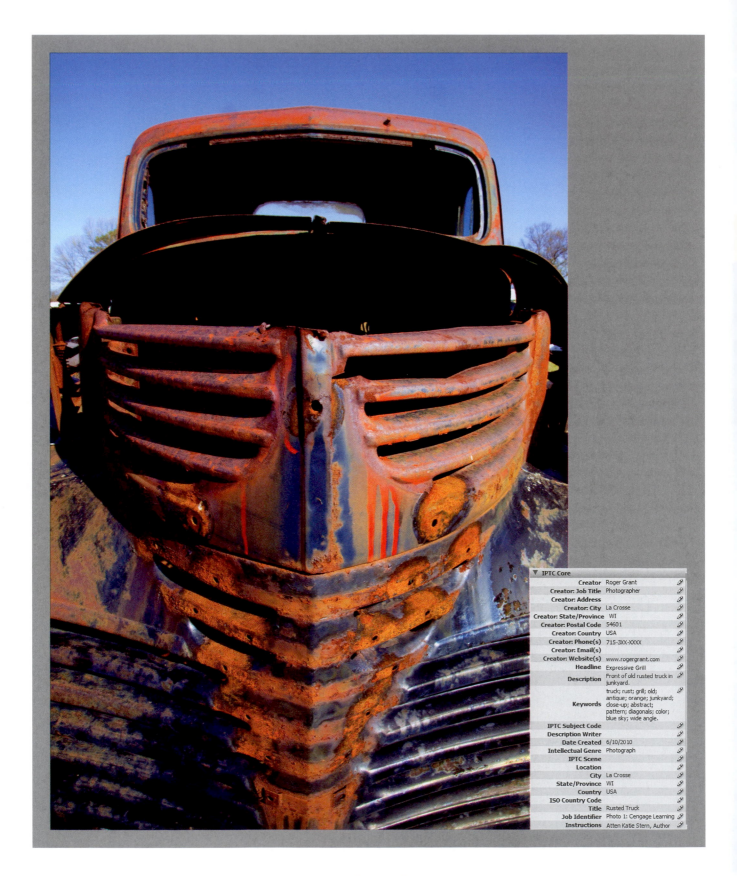

The IPTC Core panel in the image displays:

▼ IPTC Core

Creator	Roger Grant
Creator: Job Title	Photographer
Creator: Address	
Creator: City	La Crosse
Creator: State/Province	WI
Creator: Postal Code	54601
Creator: Country	USA
Creator: Phone(s)	715-3XX-XXXX
Creator: Email(s)	
Creator: Website(s)	www.rogergrant.com
Headline	Expressive Grill
Description	Front of old rusted truck in junkyard.
Keywords	truck; rust; grill; old; antique; orange; junkyard; close-up; abstract; pattern; diagonals; color; blue sky; wide angle.
IPTC Subject Code	
Description Writer	
Date Created	6/10/2010
Intellectual Genre	Photograph
IPTC Scene	
Location	
City	La Crosse
State/Province	WI
Country	USA
ISO Country Code	
Title	Rusted Truck
Job Identifier	Photo 1: Cengage Learning
Instructions	Atten Katie Stern, Author

Expressive Grill.

Photo © Roger Grant.

15

Best Practices

Chapter Learning Objectives

- Become aware of the Orphan Works Act history in U.S. Congress.

- Organize your images by assigning them metadata in Bridge.

- Protect your images by adding IPTC Core information in Bridge.

- Become aware of different usage rights for publication of photography.

- Know when you need a model or property release.

In recent years, there has been a strong political push toward making some copyrighted works usable by museums, libraries, publishers, writers, and individuals. Large collections of photographs, paintings, drawings, sculptures, and musical or theatrical scores can't be used by people because there is no copyright listed and/or the artist simply can't be found. Groups interested in gaining access to these works have put pressure on politicians to do something about it.

Orphan Works Act: Protecting Your Copyrighted Images

In 2006, the first Orphan Works Act was introduced in Congress. An **orphan work** is one protected under copyright law but whose copyright owner cannot be identified or located. In general, the Orphan Works Act would have allowed individuals or organizations to use orphan works for any purpose free of charge, provided the individuals or organizations could show in good faith that they tried to find the copyright owner.

The 2006 bill died in committee and never came to the House Floor for discussion or vote. However, another version of the Orphan Works Act arose in 2008 with a strong push for reform. The Senate passed this version in September 2008, but the House of Representatives did not act on it before adjourning and allowed the bill to die. At the date of this writing, a new bill has not been introduced. However, the general consensus is that some version of earlier Orphan Works Acts will eventually become law.

This probability should be an alert to all photographers. Even though copyright law states you own copyright to every image you make, your images are not necessarily safe from others using them. You need to take steps to clearly identify yourself as the copyright owner and to give your contact information in a way that will follow your photographs wherever you send them. In addition, you should make your contact information available to people who might need to find you for copyright permission purposes.

Photographer Registry

Because finding a copyright owner is oftentimes difficult, there has been a worldwide movement toward making photographers' contact information available to anyone who needs it. The Photographer Registry (www.photographerregistry.com) is a website formed specifically to help retailers, consumers, media buyers, and others to locate the copyright owner of a particular photograph they want to reproduce. In so doing, the Photographer Registry hopes to help reduce the risk of copyright infringement for everyone.

Through the Photographer Registry, photographers can create a free account, enter their contact information, and even change that contact information at any time. Several professional photographic organizations support the registry, which is an excellent first step in protecting the copyright of your images.

Electronic Identification of Photographs

In this section, you will learn how to electronically identify your images and help protect them from copyright infringement. Tools within Adobe Bridge and Photoshop will attach your copyright and contact information to your images. Bridge, which ships with the Adobe Suite, is available to all Photoshop users.

In Photoshop, go to FILE > BROWSE IN BRIDGE (Figure 15-1), or simply start up Adobe Bridge separately from Photoshop. CLICK on the FOLDERS tab and locate the folder containing your images. Open the folder. Across the top right menu, CLICK on ESSENTIALS (Figure 15-2). Your images will be visible in the window below. In the lower right corner, you will find the Thumbnail size slider. Move the slider to the right or left to increase or decrease the size of your thumbnails (Figure 15-3). CLICK ONCE on one of your photographs to make it active.

In a side window, you will find a panel called METADATA (Figure 15-4). The Metadata panel could be on the right or the left side of the Bridge window when you open Bridge. The exposure information (outlined in red) that your camera generated includes some of the properties of your image capture. Here, you will find the f-stop, aperture, ISO setting, and the camera's metering setting when you made

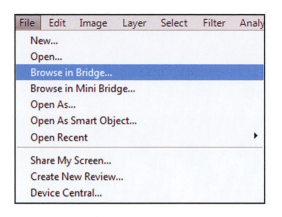

Figure 15-1

BROWSE IN BRIDGE will open the Adobe Bridge software program.

Figure 15-2

Look across the top of the Bridge window to find the ESSENTIALS tab.

Figure 15-3

Look for this Thumbnail size slider in the lower right corner of the Bridge window.

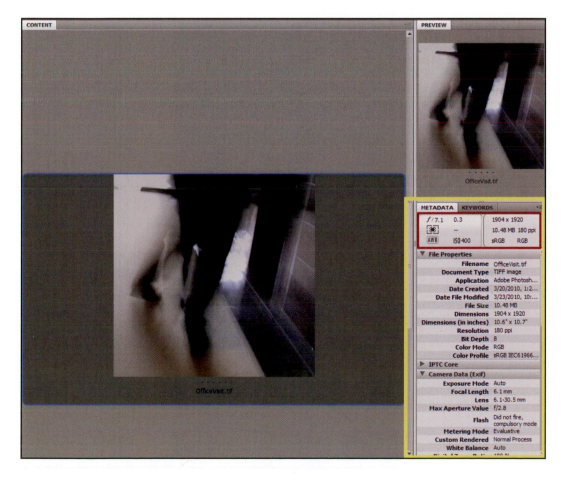

Figure 15-4

The Metadata panel in Bridge. The information outlined in red shows the exposure information for that image.

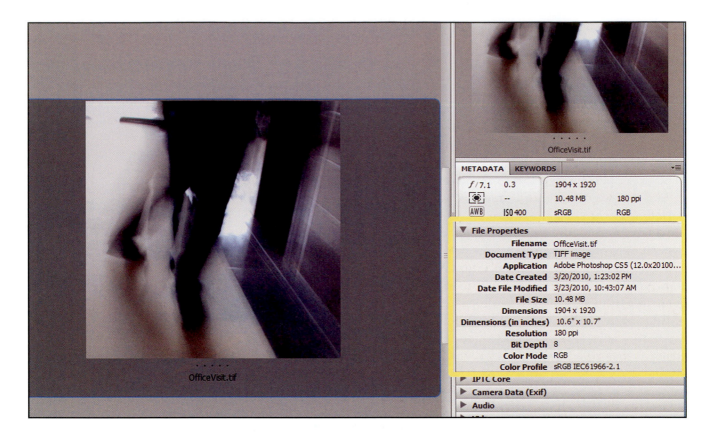

Figure 15-5 (top)

The File Properties section of the Metadata panel.

Figure 15-6 (bottom left)

The IPTC Core section of the Metadata panel.

the photograph. On the right, you can also see the file dimensions in pixels, the file size in megabytes, the file's current ppi resolution, and the file's color mode. Bridge is clearly an invaluable analysis tool as you learn how to use aperture and shutter speed to your creative advantage.

File Properties

File Properties (Figure 15-5) data include the file name, document type, date and time created, the date the file was last modified, the file size and current dimensions, and the file's current resolution. This information is very helpful as you are glancing through dozens or hundreds of images within your folders. You can filter for images according to these file properties, allowing you to easily find images made on a certain date, having a certain focal length, or with a certain white balance, etc.

IPTC Core

Beneath the File Properties in the Metadata panel is the IPTC Core section (Figure 15-6). **IPTC** stands for the

International Press Telecommunications Council, the group that approved the IPTC Core specification in 2004. IPTC Core displays editable metadata, including lines for your name, address, telephone number, website, e-mail address, headline, description, and a variety of other options. IPTC Core metadata are of primary importance to identifying your images and protecting your copyright, especially with the recent legislative push toward a future version of the Orphan Works Act.

Unfortunately, most websites do not maintain copyright information on photographs. All metadata, including IPTC Core information, are stripped if you use Photoshop's Save for Web and Devices function. If you are going to use your images on a website and want them to be safe from copyright violations, make them sufficiently small in size to be unusable. You can also ask the Web master to include your copyright on the photograph or within a caption on the website.

Although your camera generates Exif data, you will create your own IPTC Core data. You can apply the IPTC Core data to your photographs one at a time or to many images at once. It's a good idea to group your photographs together by IPTC Core elements such as location, date taken, etc., before assigning the metadata template. This makes application of IPTC Core data much more efficient. You will learn how to apply IPTC Core metadata within this chapter.

Camera (Exif) Data

Look in the CAMERA DATA (EXIF) section of the Metadata panel (Figure 15-7). Exif (Exchangeable Image File Format) data include characteristics of the camera used to capture the image. It is not the same data as that shown at the top of the Metadata panel, in that the camera and lens *capabilities* are shown, *not* the actual aperture, shutter speed, and ISO used to make that particular image. It also gives you additional information (including the focal length of a zoom lens when the image was made), the white balance setting, and the

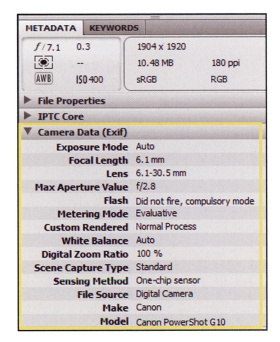

Figure 15-7

The Camera data (Exif) section of the Metadata panel. This is different from the information shown in Figure 15-4.

exposure mode and includes the make and model of your camera.

Organizations such as UPDIG (Universal Photographic Digital Imaging Guidelines) and ASMP (American Society of Media Photographers) highly recommend that you allow all camera-generated metadata to remain intact as a part of your file. However, if for some reason you need to remove Exif data from your digital file, you can do so by opening the image in Photoshop, then copying the image and pasting it into a new Photoshop document. The Exif data will not follow the pixel information.

Keywords

Because you can make photographs by the thousands, it's difficult to keep track of them. What if someone asks you for a copy of the great family photo you took at a birthday party three years ago? How long would it take you to find that image?

Keywords are essential to help you organize and locate your photographs. After you have assigned keywords to your photographs, you can search for images containing those keywords in Adobe Bridge (Figure 15-8). All photographs containing those keywords will then appear on your screen.

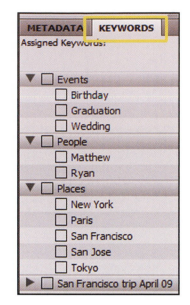

Keywords can include subject matter, location, date, event, person's name, or any other aspect of a photograph for which you might want to search. Use as many keywords as you can think of for each photograph. Think in both general and specific terms. A birthday party image might benefit from keywords that indicate the event, the event's date, the birthday person's name, location, names of relatives, etc.

Stock photo agencies depend on keywords to search databases that can include more than a million images. **Photo buyers** (people who are looking for images to use in publications) contact a stock photo agency and ask to see photos that contain specific subject matter, place and/or time, mood, colors, etc., according to their needs. The stock photo agency pulls a series of photographs that contain those keywords in their metadata. Photo buyers look through the collection and select which image to use. The stock photo agency draws up a contract for the photo's usage and delivers the photo after payment is made. The person who photographed the image is paid a commission based on a contractual agreement with the stock photo agency.

Stock photographers are responsible for giving each of their photographs descriptions and keywords before sending them to the stock photo agency. The keywords can

be both broad and specific, but they must be accurate. Assigning proper keywords assures photographers that photo buyers interested in that subject matter will see their images. Figure 15-9b shows the metadata Chuck Pefley wrote to accompany his photo in Figure 15-9a. Learn more about Chuck Pefley's photographic business in the Professional Profile at the end of this chapter.

Many stock photo agencies, including (but not limited to) Corbis, Tony Stone, Getty Images, Masterfile, Magnum Photos, iStockPhoto, and Shutterstock have online services that allow photo buyers to do keyword-based searches online. Several smaller (also called *microstock*) stock photo agencies also have online search capabilities.

Creating Metadata Templates

Start up Adobe Bridge and look in the top menu for Tools. CLICK ON TOOLS > CREATE METADATA TEMPLATE (Figure 15-10). Enter a name in the Template Name box. Then fill in all of the information you would like to attach to your images (Figure 15-11). Depending on the breadth of your project, you can create a different template for each of the different groupings of images you have. Be sure to fill in keywords as well. Then CLICK on SAVE.

Figure 15-9b

A screen capture of the metadata Chuck Pefley created for the photo in Figure 15-9a.

Photo © Chuck Pefley.

Figure 15-9a

This photograph could be used for a variety of purposes, including transportation, city scenery, engineering, or travel publications.

Photo © Chuck Pefley (www.chuckpefley.com).

Tools	Window	Help
Batch Rename...		
Device Central...		
Create Metadata Template...		
Edit Metadata Template		▶
Append Metadata		▶
Replace Metadata		▶

Figure 15-10

Create your own metadata template in Bridge by going to Tools > Create Metadata Template.

In Bridge, select all of the images appropriate for your new metadata template. Once you have selected the files, you have two choices. If you go to Tools > Replace Metadata, and then choose the template name, all existing metadata will be replaced. If you left a field blank in your template, the resulting metadata will not include information in that field even if it had information there before.

A safer method is to click on Tools > Append Metadata, and then choose the template name (Figure 15-12). The information that replaces a blank field will be appended to your metadata. However, information that already existed in the metadata will not be replaced. You will see the new metadata in the IPTC Core metadata palette (Figure 15-13).

Figure 15-11 (near right)

Name the template and fill in as much of the form as you wish.

Figure 15-12 (far right)

To apply a metadata template to your files, click on Tools > Append Metadata and select the metadata form you wish to use.

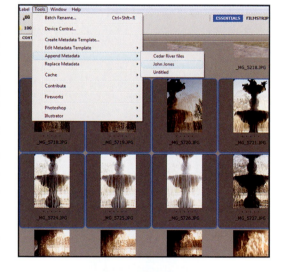

Figure 15-13

The new metadata is appended and is now a part of your files.

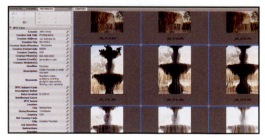

If you later decide to make changes to the metadata of an individual image, select that image. Then look in the IPTC Core palette. To the right of each field you will see a pencil icon. CLICK on the ICON of one field, and you will be able to directly enter data into any of the fields (Figure 15-14). Use your Tab key to move from one field to the next. When you're finished, CLICK on the APPLY button at the bottom of the Metadata panel. You can also press your RETURN (ENTER) key to set the changes. If you want to cancel the changes, CLICK on the CANCEL button at the bottom of the Metadata panel.

There is a second method of adding or editing metadata in either Bridge or in Photoshop. Go to FILE > FILE INFO (Figure 15-15). Here, you can add or change information, copyright data, etc., to one or more files (Figure 15-16).

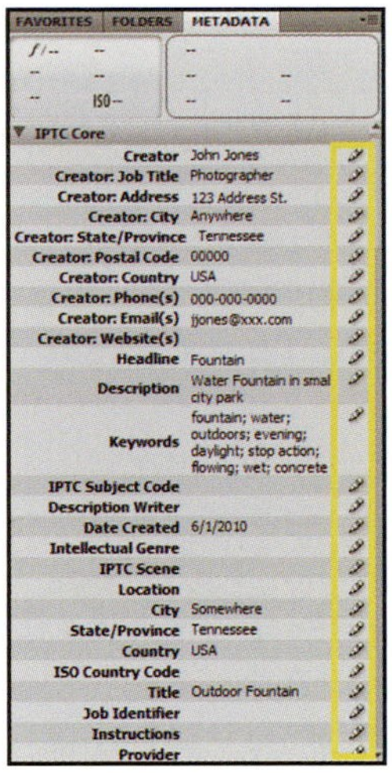

Figure 15-14

CLICK on any of the PENCIL icons along the right side of your metadata to make changes to it.

Figure 15-15

Both Photoshop and Bridge allow you to enter or edit some metadata by going to FILE > FILE INFO.

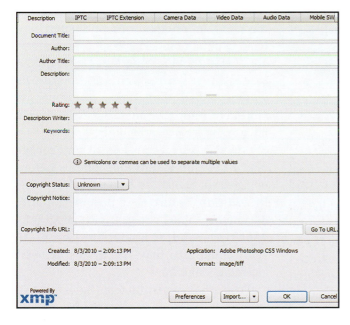

Figure 15-16

The File Info window in Photoshop CS5.

Business-Related Forms

The creative side of photography is most enticing to people. Sometimes it's difficult to pull away long enough to learn the business side; yet there are legal issues and business forms that pertain to both amateur and professional photographers.

If you are even remotely interested in selling your photographs or having them published, you need to be aware of the more common business forms that photographers use. Some photographers find it difficult to bring up issues of forms and contracts with potential models or photo buyers, but it is imperative that you become comfortable with these practices. If you don't, you could have your photographs used with no compensation even if compensation was verbally promised to you. Worse yet, you could end up owing someone money.

Publication Rights

Getting an offer to have a photograph published is an exciting event. The first time you receive such an offer, you may be reluctant to talk about fees or permissions for fear of having the offer dissolve. However, gather your courage and be prepared to bring up these subjects. You can decide whether to charge for the publication of your image. You can also ask if that photo buyer typically pays a customary fee. If not, then it will be up to you to decide what (if anything) to charge.

It is also important to set the rights for the publication. A one-time right will give the photo buyer the right to publish your photograph in one publication only. That is, the photograph can't be republished in a different document and/or on a website without your written permission. Depending on the publisher's needs, you may grant other rights. Perhaps a publisher would want rights to publish your photo in a series of greeting cards, requiring an added permission beyond one-time rights. In requesting the rights, this publisher might stipulate that you cannot allow other publishers to publish your photo in any other greeting cards for a specified period of time.

A different publisher might request all rights to your photograph, which could mean that your photo could be used in that publisher's books, websites, calendars, and brochures for as long as it wishes. If you grant all rights of one of your photographs to a publisher, you lose the right to use that photograph again or have that photograph published by anyone else. This is clearly something you need to know before handing over a digital file.

Whatever agreement you make with the prospective publisher, be sure to write a paper-based (not e-mail message) contract that specifies the exact usage of the image. Include both the rights granted and the payment information. Make sure the document is dated, and have the prospective publisher sign the document before

NOTE

Go to www.asmp.org to learn more about licensing of photographs. SELECT LICENSING from the QUICK LINKS field on the home page. Whatever you do, get a signed agreement before delivering your digital file. Students, in particular, are prone to skipping this step and getting financially burned in the process. Don't let it happen to you!

delivering the digital file. Keep the signed document on file forever. Some publishers have their own contracts for photographers to sign. If you receive such a contract, make sure you understand every part of it and ask questions as needed.

Model Releases

If you are even the least bit interested in having your photographs published, you need to obtain model releases for recognizable people in your photographs. A **model release** is a written contract that allows you to publish photographs of the people you have photographed. Because people have rights to privacy, photographers must obtain written permission of any recognizable person within their photos before using those photos for trade or advertising. In addition, before they become binding documents, model releases for photographs depicting children under the age of 18 years must also have a parent's or legal guardian's signature.

To protect yourself from lawsuit, ask your models (or other recognizable people in your photos) to sign a model release at the time you make the photographs. Carry several copies of a model release form (and also a pen) in your camera bag. Be sure all model releases have been signed and dated before you submit images for publication or place them for sale in art fairs or galleries. Ask yourself these questions:

- Do your images include people who could recognize themselves?

- Could you possibly earn money from the images either in print or online form or as a publication?
- Could a company use the photographs for advertising or marketing purposes?

If your answer to any of these questions is *yes*, you need to obtain a model release before selling the photo or submitting it for publication.

However, if you want to use a photograph for news reporting or for social, political, or economic commentary, the First Amendment allows you to do so without obtaining model releases. Ask yourself these questions:

- Do your photographs depict a current event that would be appropriate for newspaper coverage?
- Do your photographs illustrate a point you're making in an editorial or other social, political, or economic commentary?

If your answer to any of these questions is *yes*, you do not need to obtain a model release, *provided* that you earn income specifically for these uses. If, however, your current or future plans include using the images for advertising or promotion, you will need to secure model releases.

Professional organizations like the American Society of Media Photographers (ASMP) and Professional Photographers of America (PPA) have developed model releases for their members. These forms include the following essential components:

- A written understanding of what the photographer may do with the photograph,
- A payment of some form to the model, and
- The model's signature and the date the model signed the release.

As a legal, written contract, a model release is not binding unless something of value has exchanged hands. Therefore, you need to make some form of payment to the model for the release to be binding. That payment could be money (amount negotiable), it could be a print of the best image, or it could be something else that the model considers valuable. Whatever the agreement is, make good on your promise; otherwise, the model release is invalid.

If you promise to send a photograph to a person, *be sure to follow through on your promise*. Nothing could damage your reputation—or the reputation of photographers in general—more than making a promise and not following through on it. If you're the type of person who may forget to follow through on promises, make a small monetary payment to your models, rather than promising something for the future. Even a single dollar would satisfy this requirement, if the model considers that sufficient exchange value for a signature.

Asking for the Signature

One of the toughest things to do as a photographer is to incorporate business practices into an artistic moment. If you do your homework as a photographer, you will almost always have your camera with you for those unexpected moments when the subject matter, light, composition, and atmospheric conditions all add up to an unusually beautiful image.

If that image includes a person you don't know, it is worth your while to introduce yourself after you have made the photograph. If you have a digital camera, show the person the photo in the back of your camera and explain who you are. Explain that you might someday wish to have your photographs published and ask if the person might be willing to sign a model release giving you permission to use the photo. It has been this author's experience that very few people, even if total strangers, refuse this request.

If you are photographing people for a specific purpose (perhaps for a class project or for a client), ask the model(s) to sign the model release *before* the photo session begins. If, for some reason, the model leaves without signing the form or if you forget to ask for the signature, you can't use the photos in publication or earn any income from them. Ask for the signature early and in a matter-of-fact fashion, and get it over with. Then enjoy the photo session.

If you have photographed someone you don't know in either a studio or casual setting, it is helpful to give that person some form of identification. A business card works well for this purpose because it increases your credibility and helps build confidence for yourself and others. If you offer a print to people you have photographed, the business card also gives them a way to reach you if they have questions. However, it is still your responsibility to send a promised print to these people even if you don't hear from them again.

Property Release

A few occasions will merit a signed property release before using photographs of someone's house, pet, car, or other material object. Most government buildings do not require property releases. However, photographing a famous house or privately owned company building might require a property release before you could earn income from that photograph. It is always safer to get a property release if there is any question at all about ownership. Many releases are written to cover both model and property permissions and can be used under both circumstances.

Special Circumstances

Your model release should cover issues of digital manipulation or alteration of the photograph, including using that person's photograph within other photographs. Otherwise, you may not have permission to composite photographs of that person with other photographs or to make other changes within Photoshop.

Although a well-written model release will cover the vast majority of possible uses of an image, it will not cover everything. If you are asked to have the photo published in a poster or advertisement that challenges the model's perceived sex, religion, politics, health, or living habits, you need to secure a specific release from the model for that use. For example, a health organization may want a photograph to use in an AIDS poster campaign. If there is any chance that people viewing the poster might perceive the model as having AIDS, the model must first sign a special release specifically for that use. The original signed model release, in this case, would not be enough to keep you legally safe.

Keeping Good Records

After you have obtained the signed model release, write a few notes on the back of the form to remind you of where the photo was made and what the people/scene looked like; that way, you can match the form to the photographs you have made. It's quite common to hear from a person you have photographed months or years after the fact. Many people also appreciate hearing if their photograph is published in a magazine or calendar, and your notes on that model release can help you make that connection.

Model releases should always be kept in a safe, yet accessible place. Never throw them away, even if you think they won't be of value to you in the future. Some publishers ask for copies of a model release before publishing a photograph. If you can't produce the release, your photo won't be published. Further, the signed release is your protection against any future legal action on the part of the model. Although rare, this could happen. Keeping the original model release on file will serve you well in a legal situation.

Summary

If you are interested in becoming a professional photographer, you must learn the ins and outs of professional business practices. By using Bridge to identify your photographs and entering keywords to search for them, you will save yourself an immense amount of time and headaches in the future. Start identifying your photographs with keywords now, and keep up this practice for as long as you make photographs.

If you are interested in earning an income from your photographs, you need to use model releases and to secure signatures of people in your photographs. Contact ASMP or PPA to learn more about the legal aspects of photography.

EXERCISES

1. Go to Photographer Registry (www.photographerregistry.com) and register yourself as a photographer.

2. Go into Adobe Bridge and use the TOOLS > CREATE METADATA TEMPLATE to create your own template.

3. Append that metadata template to your images.

4. Apply keywords to your images using the techniques discussed in this chapter.

5. Label your images according to a labeling system that makes sense to you.

FURTHER READING

- VISIT the ASMP website (www.asmp.org) and CLICK on BUSINESS RESOURCES to learn more about the business aspects of photography.

- VISIT the UPDIG website (www.updig.org) to learn about the latest recommendations for digital image management.

- VISIT www.dpbestflow.org to learn about training opportunities in your area. Educational downloads available on this website have Creative Commons licenses.

- AMERICAN SOCIETY OF MEDIA PHOTOGRAPHERS. *Professional Business Practices in Photography, 7th Ed.* New York: Allworth Press, 2008.

- Krogh, Peter. *The DAM Book: Digital Asset Management for Photographers, 2nd Ed.* Sebastopol, CA: O'Reilly Media, 2009.

Chuck Pefley

Stock Photographer (www.chuckpefley.com)

First a disclaimer: There are probably almost as many different approaches to the photography business, stock and otherwise, as there are photographers on this planet. Having said that, I will define a "stock photograph" as any "existing" photographic image that is available from any source for licensing by any end user to satisfy a visual communications need.

What do you do? Describe your stock photography business.

I enjoy making pictures. I am a very visual person. Shooting stock allows me to photograph situations and things that attract me and fulfill my personal vision. In other words, I make pictures that satisfy ME. I am the initial client and my photographic efforts must first and foremost please me. If there is some future financial gain to be had from the photo, that's a bonus. If not, I'm still a happy camper because I've satisfied my inner creative urge.

What prompted you to go into stock photography?

I began my photography business in 1976, back in the dark ages of film, manual focus lenses, and manual exposure cameras. Photography was appealing to me for several reasons: autonomy, business ownership, glamorous lifestyle, and it looked like a lot of fun. Despite the struggles and uncertainties along the way, I'm happy with my choice.

What previous experience and training did you have before entering the field of stock photography?

None. Along the way, I've done a lot of reading of books and magazines, talked to a lot of photographers, gone to many seminars. Knowledge is a cumulative process. Trial and error has played a major role, as has keen observation. Perhaps the most important aspect of a good photographic education is self-criticism—that ability to honestly look at one's own work and judge it beside that of others and in the process learn how to change and grow.

How did you research stock photo agencies, and how did you make contact with them? Do those procedures still work today?

Magazine and textbooks usually give credit lines beside photographs. Agencies can be identified in this way. Source books usually list agencies. Word of mouth among photographers. But remember, I started almost 30 years ago. Living in Seattle, I was lucky to have a couple of strong agencies I could visit in person. That's how I started. I joined AllStock. A few years later, AllStock was bought by Tony Stone Worldwide Images. A few years later, Tony Stone was bought by Getty Images. Today, Getty is the largest agency in the world marketplace. So, through a series of circumstances outside my direct control, I moved from a small local agency into the largest picture supplier in the world. Luck, persistence, and being in the right place at the right time all played a part.

Over the years since joining Allstock, I've been approached by other agencies and have approached others as well. I'm a firm believer in two things: (1) Don't put all your work in one place, and (2) pursue "nonexclusive" relationships. There are basically two kinds of agency contract relationships. One is exclusive. The other is not. Of exclusivity, there are various flavors . . . image exclusive where a photographer is not able to place a similar or sister image given to the image exclusive agency with any other agency. The photographer is, however, free to place nonsimilar images with other agencies. There is also an arrangement that is known as "agency-exclusive." Under this agreement, a photographer agrees to put all his/her work with that agency only. Of course, the hard part of any agency/photographer relationship is the fact that the agency reserves the right to decide which images, if any, are accepted for representation. In the case of an agency-exclusive contract, should the agency refuse any images offered by the photographer, those images are basically dead since the photographer may not offer them to any other agency. Not a good deal in my opinion.

A nonexclusive agency relationship/contract is one where the photographer is free to offer the same and/or similar images to other agencies simultaneously. This can be beneficial in that each agency will have its own set of strengths and weaknesses. Therefore, an agency that is good in the textbook market might be weak in the corporate lifestyle market. Another agency might excel in animal images, and another might specialize in transportation. It's necessary to look at the strengths and weaknesses of the respective agencies and realize that each one will have its own forte.

What national or international organizations act as advocates for stock photographers?

SAA, or Stock Artists Alliance (http://www.stockartists.com), is the only national organization I'm aware of that was created specifically for the advocacy of stock photographers. This organization grew out of contract negotiations between stock photographers and Getty Images a few years ago. It became painfully apparent that unless independent stock photographers banded together and acted as a group, those large and powerful agencies would call all the shots. SAA was born from this conflict and has matured and broadened its mandate to include all stock photographers and is not agency specific or focused any longer.

Most of the national photography groups like ASMP—American Society of Media Photographers (http://www.asmp.org), PPA—Professional Photographers of America (http://www.ppa.com), NPPA—National Press Photographers Association (http://www.nppa.org), EP—Editorial Photographers (http://www.editorialphoto.com), etc., all have some links to the stock business but are more focused on other aspects of the photography trade.

Glass staircase,
Apple Computer Store,
Fifth Avenue,
Manhattan,
New York, NY.
Photo © Chuck Pefley.

What personal qualities do you think successful stock photographers have?

- Insatiable curiosity;
- Visual skills;
- A need to make pictures;
- Business skills, including accounting and negotiation;
- Marketing skills;
- Self-motivation—ability to create your own projects and see them to completion;
- Organizational skill, both in the studio/office and in the field on location;
- People skills when dealing with strangers, models, authorities, and clients;
- Attention to detail; and
- Attention to detail—yes, I've repeated myself.

What are some of the pros and cons of a stock photography business?

Extremely crowded marketplace, especially when compared to what was available 20 years ago.

What advice would you give to aspiring stock photographers?

First, follow your dreams. Don't let anybody tell you it's not possible or you can't do it. Second, don't give up. Keep making photos and keep knocking on doors. Third, and this is perhaps hardest of all, don't sell yourself short. Keep your pricing competitive. Photography is one of the few businesses where the clients/customers seem to think they can dictate how much YOUR work is worth. No matter how hungry you are, ask for a fair fee. Last time I bought a camera, the store told ME how much it was—not the other way around.

What business skills do stock photographers need?

The business skills needed by anybody in small business are considerable. Stock photography is no different. Accounting skills and the ability to understand legal contracts are paramount. However, both of these can be hired—for a fee, of course. Communication skills, both written and oral, are also very important. The ability to convey your message succinctly and in a way that's understandable to a person not in the photo business is necessary. Too often we assume the other person understands our terminology: transparency, chrome, contact sheet, proof, long glass, fisheye, etc. The more time we spend talking to other photographers and immersing ourselves in our craft, the more likely we are to assume everybody knows what we're talking about. In this digital age, communication skills are perhaps even more important as technical terms like TIFF, JPEG, raw, pixel, etc., that are so prevalent in our everyday language.

How has the stock photo business/industry been changed over the last 20 years?

Undoubtedly the biggest change in stock photography, indeed, in the whole photographic industry, has been brought about through technology. Twenty years ago, we all used film. For stock, that meant transparency or slide film in most instances. Good photographers learned to fill the frame with everything they needed to complete their message because that piece of transparent film was the final image or finished product presented to the stock agency or client. Post-processing to correct minor flaws, tweak color or contrast, and cropping the image via Photoshop weren't options. Today the use of Photoshop and similar computer software is the norm.

How has the stock photo business/industry been changed by the advances in digital photography and the Internet?

The real question is: "**How hasn't** the stock photo business been changed by digital photography and the Internet?" An answer to this question lies in the basic concept of copyright and the licensing of those rights. According to the U.S. copyright law, the ownership of an image is vested in the creator of that image at the moment it is created. As the owner of an image, you automatically have the rights to control how that image is used and to receive fair compensation for that use. The idea of copyright is to make it financially possible for creators to continue to be creative . . . and this has not changed . . . yet. What has changed is the continued and constant downward pressure on license fees and the willingness of many to allow usage for the princely sum of a dollar or two . . . or simply for the thrill of seeing their image published online.

The Internet and the proliferation of affordable digital cameras (and cell phones) now make it possible for nearly everybody to make somewhat acceptable images. And herein lies the problem faced by the stock photographer today. Much of the population thinks all that is necessary is a digital camera, being in the right place at the right time, and clicking the shutter. The computer takes care of everything else. Unique skill, training, and years of experience have been supplanted by the popular belief that "digital = easy and automatic" and "I can do that myself—so why should I pay for a picture?"

In order to succeed in today's stock photography marketplace, it is necessary, more than ever before, to find your own unique vision, as well as a narrow niche. Gone are the days when it was possible to make a good living via stock sales of nothing more than city skylines, for instance. Today, it is necessary to specialize in things such as couples, babies, endangered species, traffic, helicopters, motorcycles, working cowboys, bank presidents, etc. Pretty sunsets and mountain vistas, while fun to make and popular with our friends, mostly do not pay the bills any longer. In short, everyone now is a "photographer."

How has social networking (Facebook, Twitter, etc.) changed how you share your photography?

I really don't use social networking to sell my work. However, I do use these networks to keep in touch with ideas and trends, as well as a way of sharing photos I make that probably have little commercial or editorial value but do have significant "friend" value.

How do you keep yourself interested in photography as a profession?

Photographic image making is a lifestyle for me. I find I "need" to make images and learned many years ago that I'm frustrated when I can't scratch a visual itch. Therefore, it is imperative that I carry a camera with me—always, no matter if I'm simply going to the grocery store, taking a walk, or driving across town. It is probably redundant, but if you don't have a camera (of some kind), you cannot make photographs. Simple, isn't it?

For many years, I found myself being very productive for relative short periods of time, like a 2- or 3-week road trip. This intense production was always followed by 3 to 6 weeks of relative inactivity. When I realized this was my pattern a few years ago, I decided to commit myself to producing one (at least) useable image everyday. Knowing myself all too well, I knew the only way for me to make this happen, week in and out, was to make a public commitment; thus, my One-A-Day Mostly Seattle photo blog was born. As I write this, I'm close to 900 continuous days of blog publication. The surprising thing is that I've made a significant number of salable images as a direct result of my blogging promise to myself. Daily exercise, whether preparing to run a marathon or a stock photography career, is necessary for success.

NOTES

Appendix A: By the Decade

Photography

1834: William Henry Fox Talbot created permanent (negative) images using paper soaked in silver chloride and fixed with a salt solution. He then created positive images by contact printing the negative onto another sheet of paper.

1837: Daguerre's first daguerreotype—the first permanent image that needed under 30 minutes of light exposure. It was a direct positive method that created the final print only and was the first photographic process that made commercial photography practical.

1839: (January) Englishman William Henry Fox Talbot presented to the Royal Society of London a paper on photogenic drawing and permanent camera obscura images made with photosensitive silver salts on paper (salt prints). Unlike the daguerreotype, Talbot's system could create many prints from one negative.

(March) American Samuel F. B. Morse was in Paris to promote his telegraph. He met Daguerre and returned to New York to teach the process. Among his pupils was Mathew Brady.

John Herschel made the first glass plate negative.

1840: The first American patent in photography was issued to Alexander Wolcott for his camera.

World History

1829: Australia was claimed as a British territory.

1838: The first Anglo-Afghan war began when the British Governor of India launched an attack on Afghanistan.

American History

1829: William Burt received the first U.S. patent for a typewriter.

1831: The first U.S.-built locomotive pulled a passenger train for the first time.

The first U.S. steam engine train run.

1833: Chicago incorporated as a village with approximately 200 inhabitants.

1834: *The Man*, the first U.S. Labor newspaper, was published.

The U.S. Congress created the Indian Territory (now Oklahoma).

1836: Texas declared its independence from Mexico.

The U.S. Congress formed the Territory of Wisconsin.

1837: Oberlin College admitted both men and women to its freshman class. Oberlin was one of the earliest colleges to allow women and people of color to attend.

The Panic of 1837 started the Great Depression.

continues on next page

1838: The Underground Railroad began, helping enslaved people escape from the South and flee northward.

Samuel Morse's telegraph system was publicly demonstrated.

U.S. Presidents

Andrew Jackson (1829–1837)

Martin Van Buren (1837–1841)

Art

In full swing, the Romantic era started in approximately 1820 and continued until the early 1900s. Artists included Ferdinand Victor Eugène Delacroix and Joseph Mallord William Turner.

The Barbizon School of French landscape painting was opened. Theodore Rousseau, one of the school's founders, rejected the classical painting style in favor of direct observation from nature. Other leaders were Georges Michel, Jean-Francois Millet, and Jean-Baptiste-Camille Corot. The school was influential in the eventual development of impressionism.

The Hudson River school (American) was comprised of landscape painters who had been influenced by the Romantic movement. Its founder was Thomas Cole. Other artists included Frederic Edwin Church, John Frederick Kensett, and Sanford Robinson Gifford. These three painters later founded the Metropolitan Museum of Art in New York City. Thomas Moran, another Hudson River School artist, played a major role in the creation of Yellowstone National Park. Park proponents presented Moran's sketches and paintings to members of Congress. Congress later established the National Park system.

Music

1830: Hector Berlioz wrote his *Symphony Fantastique* and premiered it in Paris.

1835: Frédéric Chopin's *Grand Polonaise Brillante* premiered in Paris, France.

Literary

1830: Oliver Wendell Holmes published *Old Ironsides*, a poem about a ship called the *U.S.S. Constitution*.

BY THE DECADE:
1841–1850

Photography

1841: William Henry Fox Talbot patented the Calotype process, the first negative-positive process making possible the first multiple copies.

1842: Cyanotype printing, a printing-out process resulting in a white image on blue background, was developed.

1843: The first advertisement with a photograph, made in Philadelphia, PA, appeared.

Anna Atkins produced *British Algae,* an album illustrated with cyanotype photographs.

In the United States, the photographic enlarger was invented, allowing enlargements to be made from negatives.

1844: William Henry Fox Talbot published *Pencil of Nature,* the first book with photographic illustrations (glued-in calotypes).

1845: Mathew Brady opened a portrait studio in New York.

1846: In Germany, Zeiss began to manufacture photographic lenses.

1847: Niepce De St. Victor discovered the albumen printing process.

World History

1840s: The Hungry Forties: a large part of the Irish peasantry starved to death, and the condition of the English workers was also miserable. Potato blight destroyed three-quarters of the crop. It was a period of rapid industrial development and social unrest.

1843: The Free Church of Scotland seceded from the Church of Scotland.

1846: Henry Rawlinson deciphered cuneiform writing, the key to studying Babylonian history.

1847: The first *Merriam-Webster Dictionary* was published.

The telegraph was first used as a business tool.

1848: *The Communist Manifesto* by Marx and Engels was published in German.

A revolution in Paris brought the expulsion of King Louis-Philippe and established a Second Republic in France under Louis Napoleon (1808–1873).

1850: Western Australia became a penal colony.

American History

1841: The first American women graduated from a university.

1844: Samuel Morse's telegraph connected Washington with Baltimore.

1850: The number of U.S. public libraries tripled over the previous 25 years.

The paper bag was invented.

U.S. Presidents

William Henry Harrison (1841)

John Tyler (1841–1845)

James K. Polk (1845–1849)

Zachary Taylor (1849–1850)

Art

1841: George Cruikshank opened The New School of Portrait-Painting.

1842: The first commercial Christmas card was printed.

1849: Gustave Courbet painted *The Stone Breakers*.

1850: Jean-FranLois Millet painted *The Sower*.

continues on next page

Music

1841: Adolphe Sax Belgian invented the saxophone (patented in 1846).

Schumann composed Symphony no. 1 in B-flat Major, op. 38 *(The Spring)*.

1842: The New York Philharmonic Society was founded.

1843: Mendelssohn composed the music to Shakespeare's *A Midsummer Night's Dream*.

1844: Verdi composed *Ernani* in Venice.

1846: Electric lighting was installed at the Opera in Paris.

1850: Robert Schumann composed his third symphony, the *Rhenish*.

Literary/Books

1841: The *New York Tribune* began publication.

James Fenimore Cooper wrote *The Deerslayer*.

Ralph Waldo Emerson wrote *Self-Reliance*.

The first type-composing machine was used in London.

1845: Edgar Allen Poe wrote *The Raven*.

1847: Charlotte Brontë wrote *Wuthering Heights*.

1849: Henry David Thoreau wrote his essay *The Duty of Civil Disobedience*.

1850: Nathaniel Hawthorne wrote *The Scarlet Letter*.

Theater/Broadway

1843: The Theatre Regulation Act of 1843 banned drinking in legitimate theaters.

1844: The first music house opened in London.

1851–1860

Photography

1851: Frederick Scott Archer announced the invention of the wet collodion process, requiring only 2 or 3 seconds of light exposure.

1854: Adolphe Disderi developed *carte-de-visite* photography in Paris. The public used these pocket-sized prints as calling cards.

1856: Photojournalism began with pictures of the Crimean War.

1859: The Sutton was the first patented panoramic camera.

The wide-angle lens was invented for cameras.

1860: Mathew Brady took a photographic portrait of Abraham Lincoln.

World History

1851: Victoria separated from New South Wales.

1854: The Treaty of Kanagawa was signed. It brought Japan's closed feudal monarchy into the world community.

George Boole developed a logic system on which future computers would depend.

American History

1852: Massachusetts was the first state to enact a compulsory education law.

1853: Henry Steinway (Heinrich E. Steinweg) began the New York firm of piano manufacturers.

U.S. Navy Commodore Matthew Perry (1794–1858) sailed into Edo Bay and demanded that Japan open its harbors to American trade.

1854: The telegraph brought news of the Crimean War.

U.S. Presidents

Millard Fillmore (1850–1853)

Franklin Pierce (1853–1857)

James Buchanan (1857–1861)

Art

1857: Currier & Ives prints entered the market.

Music

1853: Richard Wagner published the librettos to *Der Ring des Nibelungen (The Ring Cycle)*, considered one of the most ambitious musical projects ever undertaken by a single person.

1857: Johannes Brahms composed his Piano Concerto no. 1.

1858: Offenbach wrote *Orphee aux enfers*, an operetta.

1859: The French Opera House, the first great opera house in America, was built in New Orleans.

1860: The slave trade introduced West African rhythms, work songs, chants, and spirituals to America; these genres strongly influenced blues and jazz.

Literary/Books

1851: Herman Melville wrote *Moby Dick*.

Hawthorne wrote *The House of the Seven Gables*.

1852: Harriet Beecher Stowe wrote *Uncle Tom's Cabin*.

1854: Thoreau published *Walden*.

continues on next page

BY THE DECADE:
1851–1860 *continued*

1855: Walt Whitman published *Leaves of Grass.*

Longfellow wrote *Song of Hiawatha.*

The first edition of Herbert Spencer's *Principles of Psychology* was published.

1859: Charles Darwin published *Origin of Species.*

Dickens wrote *A Tale of Two Cities.*

1860: Dickens wrote *Great Expectations.*

260 magazines were published in the United States.

Theater/Broadway

1851: Stephen Foster wrote *Old Folks at Home.*

Verdi composed *Rigoletto* in Venice.

BY THE DECADE:
1861–1870

Photography

1861: James Clerk Maxwell demonstrated a projected color photographic image using three different color filters: red, green, and blue (London).

1861–65: Mathew Brady and staff (mostly staff) photographed the American Civil War, exposing 7,000 negatives.

1866: Photos of Yosemite Valley helped to pass laws to protect U.S. scenic places.

1869: In France, color photography was invented using cyan, magenta, and yellow (subtractive method).

1870 (circa): The U.S. Congress sent photographers out to the West. The most famous photographers were William Jackson and Timothy O'Sullivan.

1870: William Jackson's Yellowstone photographs aided efforts to preserve U.S. heritage.

World History

1862: Giovanna Caselli invented the pantelegraph, allowing a person to transmit a photograph over wires.

1864: French and English Labour leaders in London established the first International Workingmen's Association.

1864: Marx drew up his *Inaugural Address*—a much more moderate document than *The Communist Manifesto.*

1867: The transportation of convicts to Western Australia ceased.

1869: Marx's German followers founded the Eisenach Party (SAP) [South German Party].

American History

1861: The Confederacy attacked Fort Sumter, a U.S. Army post, starting the American Civil War.

The telegraph brought the Pony Express to an abrupt end.

1862: Paper money was first distributed in the United States.

1863: President Lincoln issued the Emancipation Proclamation.

The Southern Confederacy banned alien voting rights in its Constitution.

Abraham Lincoln's Gettysburg Address was short, but unforgettable.

William Bullock invented the rotary web-fed letterpress.

1865: Louis Pasteur published his theory that germs spread disease.

The Thirteenth Amendment was signed, abolishing slavery throughout the United States.

1866: Atlantic cable unites Europe and the United States with instant communication.

1869: Susan B. Anthony and Elizabeth Cady Stanton formed the National Woman Suffrage Association. Its primary goal was to achieve voting rights for women by means of a congressional amendment to the Constitution.

U.S. Presidents

Abraham Lincoln (1861–1865)

Andrew Johnson (1865–1869)

Ulysses S. Grant (1869–1877)

continues on next page

1861–1870 *continued*

Art

1835–1870: Photography was hurting the business of painters. The new invention was dubbed "the foe-to-graphic art." In particular, artists who specialized in miniature portraits suffered.

1862: Jean-Auguste Ingres painted *The Turkish Bath.*

1863: Painter Edouard Manet shocked the art world with *Luncheon on the Grass.*

Music

1867: Johann Strauss wrote his waltz *The Blue Danube.*

Charles Gound wrote the opera *Romeo and Juliet.*

1868: Edward Grieg wrote *Piano Concerto in A Minor.*

Brahms wrote *A German Requiem.*

Literary/Books

1863: Edward Everett Hale wrote *The Man Without a Country.*

1865: "Lewis Carroll" published *Alice's Adventures in Wonderland.*

Mark Twain wrote *The Celebrated Jumping Frog of Calaveras County.*

1866: Fyodor Dostoevsky published *Crime and Punishment.*

1867: Marx completed Volume I of *Das Kapital.*

Louisa May Alcott published *Little Women.*

1868–1869: Charles Darwin's *The Descent of Man* was published.

1869: *The People's Literary Companion* was the first mail-order periodical.

Leo Tolstoy's *War and Peace* was published.

Postcards became popular in Austria.

1870: More than 5,000 newspapers were published in the United States.

Dance

1860s: Waltz *La Veilers* was popular.

1861: A Burlesque dancer's costume fully bares her legs on stage, abandoning tights.

1866: Gitana waltz was popular.

1870: Léo Delibes' ballet *Coppélia* debuted.

Theater/Broadway

1862: Victor Hugo's *Les Misérables* debuted.

1865: Tony Pastor opened the first variety theater in New York.

1868: Burlesque officially arrived with Lydia Thompson at New York's Woods Theater.

Film

1861: Coleman Sellers invented the Kinematoscope, a crude movie projector.

BY THE DECADE:
1871–1880

Photography

1871: Richard Leach Maddox invented the gelatin dry plate silver bromide process.

1872–1878: British photographer Eadweard Muybridge took the first successful photographs of motion.

1874: Photography and impressionism began to intermingle. Artists Cézanne and Gauguin exhibited prints. George Davidson contended that a sharp photograph was not always desired. His photograph *The Onion Field* (1890) used rough-surfaced paper and a soft-focus technique.

1877: Van der Weyde opened the first studio lit by electric light, permitting exposures of 2–3 seconds for a carte-de-visite.

Photography began to be used as a means of promoting social reform. Pioneers included Richard Beard, John Thomson, Thomas Annan, and Paul Martin (all British or Scot) and Jacob Riis and Lewis Hine (USA).

1880: George Eastman set up Eastman Dry Plate Company.

The first halftone photograph appeared in a daily newspaper, *The New York Graphic*.

World History

1870–1871: Franco-Prussian War. Otto von Bismarck became the Chancellor of the German Empire after defeating the French in the Franco-Prussian War.

1875: German social democrats (ADAV and SAP) merged on the basis of The Gotha Programme.

1877: Ten years following publication of the first magazine, Japan published 200 magazines in Japan.

1879: In Leipzig, Wilhelm Wundt started the world's first laboratory of experimental psychology.

American History

1871: End of Treaty Making, an act by Congress, ended the era of treaty making with Indian Nations, under the assumption that Indians were conquered.

1872: Susan B. Anthony cast a ballot and was arrested for it.

The first Montgomery Ward mail-order catalog was published.

1873: The U.S. postcard debuted; its cost was one penny.

Scientists May and Smith experimented with selenium and light, opening the door for transforming images into electronic signals.

1875: Civil Rights Act of 1875 was passed.

1876: Bell invented the telephone.

National Baseball League was founded.

Herbert Spencer applied evolution to society and coined the phrase, "the survival of the fittest."

1877: Thomas Edison invented the phonograph.

The Boarding School era required all Native American children to attend an off-reservation boarding school and learn the ways of the dominant culture.

1879: The first Congress of Trade Unions was held.

1880: The United States had about 50,000 telephones.

U.S. Presidents

Ulysses S. Grant (1869–1877)

Rutherford B. Hayes (1877–1881)

continues on next page

Art

1860s–1880: Impressionism revolutionized art. To the impressionists, art could be rendered completely through light and color.

1872: Impressionism still reigned.

James McNeill Whistler painted a portrait of his mother.

1876: Edgar Degas painted *The Glass of Absinthe.*

1877: Impressionist Camille Pissarro painted *Red Roofs.*

1880: Modern art was born.

Advertising copywriting became an occupation.

A halftone photograph, *Shantytown*, appeared in a newspaper.

Music

1871: Verdi's opera *Aida* debuted.

1874: Modest Mussorgsky composed *Pictures from an Exhibition.*

1876: In Norway, Edvard Grieg composed the *Peer Gynt Suite.*

1879: Brahms composed Violin Concerto in D.

1880: Tchaikovsky composed the *1812 Overture.*

Antonin Dvorak composed Symphony no. 1.

Richard Strauss composed Symphony in D Minor.

Literary/Books

1876: Mark Twain's *Adventures of Tom Sawyer* was the first typed novel.

1877: Anna Sewell wrote *Black Beauty: The Autobiography of a Horse.*

Charles Peirce founded American pragmatism by writing *The Fixation of Belief.*

1880: Carlo Collodi wrote *Pinocchio: The Story of a Puppet.*

Dance

1874: Glide waltz (a.k.a.: Boston) was popular.

1877: Tchaikovsky's ballet *Swan Lake* debuted.

1880: The Virginia reel became popular.

Theater/Broadway

1871: Gilbert and Sullivan's *Thespis* was performed at London's Gaiety Theatre.

Verdi's *Aïda* premiered in Cairo.

1879: When Nora left her husband in Henrik Ibsen's *A Doll's House*, audiences at Copenhagen's Royal Theatre were shocked.

BY THE DECADE:
1881–1890

Photography

1881: The twin-lens reflex camera was invented.

1884: The Stebbing Automatic camera was the first production model to use roll film.

1885: Eastman American Film was introduced—the first transparent photographic film.

A disguised spy camera was invented in Germany.

1888: Kodak box cameras made picture taking simple. The "snapshot" was born.

George Eastman introduced the Kodak camera, which used paper photographic film wound onto rollers. He registered the name Kodak at the same time. The slogan was "You press the button—we do the rest."

National Geographic was first published.

World History

1887: Gramophone played flat discs.

1889: The railway network between Australian cities of Adelaide, Brisbane, Melbourne, and Sydney was completed.

1890: In Germany, Ferdinand Braun invented the cathode ray tube.

American History

1881: Clara Barton assisted in founding the American Red Cross.

Women entered the business world via their skills with the typewriter.

1882: The Chinese Exclusion Act of 1882 excluded Chinese (and all Asian) workers from specific industries.

1883: Thomas Edison invented the light bulb.

The Civil Rights Act of 1875 was ruled unconstitutional by the Supreme Court.

1884: Long-distance phone calls were now possible.

1887: The Dawes Act (General Allotment Act) dropped the land base of Native Americans from approximately 150 million acres to 49 million acres.

The Interstate Commerce Commission was established.

1888: Congress established the Department of Labor.

1890: The Sherman Anti-Trust Act, the first major regulatory law passed by Congress, attempted to curb the growth of monopolies.

Wyoming entered the Union as the first state to have women's suffrage.

Mississippi adopted a state constitution imposing a poll tax, literacy test, and other devices aimed at preventing African Americans from voting.

U.S. Presidents

James A. Garfield (1881)

Chester A. Arthur (1881–1885)

Grover Cleveland (1885–1889)

Benjamin Harrison (1889–1893)

Art

1885–1920: Post-impressionism was practiced by a group of artists (Cézanne, van Gogh, Seurat, and Gauguin, primarily) who moved past Impressionism.

1885: Vincent van Gogh painted *The Potato Eaters*.

1886: Pointillist painter Georges-Pierre Seurat painted *Bathing at Asnieres*.

1888: Vincent van Gogh painted *Sidewalk Café*.

continues on next page

BY THE DECADE:
1881–1890 *continued*

Music

1880s: Ragtime was born.

1885: Brahms composed his Fourth Symphony.

Franz Liszt completed the *Hungarian Rhapsodies*.

Gilbert and Sullivan's operetta *The Mikado* infuriated the Japanese.

1888: Tchaikovsky composed his Fifth Symphony.

Nikolai Rimsky-Korsakov composed *Scheherazade*.

1890: Tchaikovsky composed a ballet called *Sleeping Beauty*.

Literary/Books

1882: The city of Boston banned Walt Whitman's *Leaves of Grass*.

1884: Mark Twain wrote *Adventures of Huckleberry Finn*.

1885: Robert Louis Stevenson wrote *A Child's Garden of Verses* and *Prince Otto*.

1886: Friedrich Wilhelm Nietzsche wrote *Beyond Good and Evil*.

1890: William James's *Principles of Psychology* moved the field toward science.

How the Other Half Lives by Jacob Riis depicted life in city slums.

Emily Dickinson's first book of poems was published.

Dance

1880: Ashland polka gained popularity.

1888: Knickerbocker waltz became popular.

Newport dance became popular.

1889: Cakewalk became fashionable with Sam T. Jack's *Creole Show*.

1890: Modern dance emerged when choreographers and dancers begin to rebel against traditional ballet.

1890: Tango became popular.

Tchaikovsky wrote his ballet *Sleeping Beauty*.

Theater/Broadway

1881: The first modern cabaret, *Le Chat Noir (The Black Cat),* opened in Paris.

London's Savoy Theatre opened, the first theater to be lit by electricity.

Vaudeville debuted at Tony Pastor's New 14th Street Theater in New York.

1883: The Metropolitan Opera House opened in New York with Gounod's *Faust*.

Film

1889: William Dickson synchronized motion pictures with phonograph.

BY THE DECADE:
1891–1900

Photography

1890s: The first halftone photographic reproductions appeared in daily papers.

1891: The telephoto lens was made for the camera.

1892: Frederick Ives invented the natural color photographic system.

1895: The Pocket Kodak camera was announced.

1896: Kodak introduced the first capture medium, a photographic paper, designed specifically for x-ray image capture.

1900: The first of the famous Kodak Brownie cameras was introduced. It sold for $1 and used film that sold for 15¢ a roll.

World History

1891: The National Australian Convention met and agreed on adopting the name Commonwealth of Australia.

The first international phone call via submarine cable took place between London and Paris.

1897: In England, the Marconi Company started a wireless telegraphy business.

1898: Newspapers, led by Hearst and Pulitzer, helped push the United States into war with Spain.

1899: The Australian Labor Party took power in Queensland, becoming the first trade union party to do so anywhere in the world.

Marconi radio equipment was installed in British warships.

Economist Thorsten Veblen coined the term "conspicuous consumption."

1900: In China, the Boxer Rebellion began.

1900: Max Planck introduced the quantum theory hypothesis.

American History

1891: The Populist Party was formed at the national level in Cincinnati, Ohio.

1893: Colorado was the first state to adopt an amendment granting women the right to vote. Utah and Idaho followed suit in 1896.

1896: The National Association of Colored Women was formed.

Plessy v. Ferguson—this Supreme Court decision upheld a "separate, but equal" doctrine.

1898: New York State passed a law against misleading advertising.

Columbia University School of Social Work was opened.

1900: Noncitizen voting rights were rapidly disappearing. By 1900, only 11 states still retained them.

In the United States, 562 cities had more than one daily newspaper; New York City had 29.

U.S. Presidents

Grover Cleveland (1893–1897)

William McKinley (1897–1901)

Art

1891: Claude Monet painted *Haystacks*.

1892: Mary Cassatt painted *The Bath*.

Paul Cézanne painted *The Card Players*.

Robinson founded the Linked Ring, a group of photographers based in London, that pledged to enhance photography as a fine art, rather than as a science.

1893: The first major exhibition of the Linked Ring took place and was known as the Photographic Salon.

Norwegian artist Edvard Munch painted *The Scream*.

continues on next page

1896: The first comic strip, *The Yellow Kid,* appeared in *The New York American.*

1897: Paul Gauguin painted *Nevermore.*

1898: Rodin sculpted *The Kiss.*

1900: Rodin sculpted *The Thinker.*

Henri Matisse began the Fauvist movement in painting.

Music

1891: Gustav Mahler composed Symphony no. 1.

1892: Bruckner composed Symphony no. 8.

1894: Sibelius composed *Finlandia.*

Claude Debussy composed *Prelude to Afternoon of a Fawn.*

1896: Giacomo Puccini wrote *La Bohème,* an opera.

John Philip Sousa composed "Stars and Stripes Forever."

1897: Scott Joplin, James Scott, and Joseph Lamb popularized ragtime.

1900: The modern music era began.

Literary/Books

1892: Arthur Conan Doyle's *The Adventures of Sherlock Holmes* was published.

1894: George Bernard Shaw wrote *Arms and the Man.*

1898: H. G. Wells's *The War of the Worlds* brought the "Martians" and panic to the public.

1900: An estimated 1,800 magazines were being published in the United States.

Joseph Conrad wrote *Lord Jim.*

Sigmund Freud wrote *The Interpretation of Dreams.*

Dance

1892: Tchaikovsky wrote his ballet *The Nutcracker.*

1893: The striptease was born in Paris.

1900: Oscar Schlemmer became a leader in abstract dance with his *Triadic Ballet.*

Theater/Broadway

1890: *Uncle Tom's Cabin* premiered.

1891: Carnegie Hall opened in New York.

1894: Wilde succeeded again with *The Importance of Being Earnest.*

Film

1894: *Fred Ott's Sneeze,* a film made using Edison's Kinetograph in 1893, became the first officially copyrighted film.

1895: Auguste and Louis Lumiere of France invented the Cinematographe. This is considered to be the birth of film.

1898: The U.S. Army forbade camera operators to enter Cuba during the Spanish-American War.

1900: Much of Europe and Japan began to make movies.

BY THE DECADE:
1901–1910

Photography

1902: The Kodak Developing Machine made it possible for amateurs to process their own film without a darkroom.

Alfred Stieglitz organized the "Photo Secessionist" show in New York.

1905: Alfred Stieglitz and Edward Steichen opened a photo art gallery in New York City. It was later known simply as "291."

Picture postcards were the new fad.

1907: The Lumiere brothers in France manufactured the first commercial color film, the Autochrome plates.

A photograph was transmitted by wire across France.

1909: The U.S. National Child Labor Committee hired Lewis Hine to photograph children working in factories.

World History

1901: Australia became an independent nation.

1903: A plague hit India.

The Russo-Japanese War began.

1905: The Russian Revolution of 1905 began.

1908: Turks revolted in the Ottoman Empire.

1909: Plastic was invented.

1910: The Mexican Revolution started.

American History

1901: President McKinley was assassinated. Vice President Theodore Roosevelt took over as President.

1902: Congress passed the Chinese Exclusion Act.

1903: Wilbur and Orville Wright made the first heavier-than-air flight at Kitty Hawk, North Carolina.

1906: Kellogg's started selling Corn Flakes.

1908: Henry Ford introduced the Model T.

1909: National Association for the Advancement of Colored People was founded.

Major revision of the U.S. Copyright Act protected authors and composers.

1910: Only 13.5% of Americans completed high school; 2.7% had college degrees.

Hallmark Cards started.

U.S. Presidents

Theodore Roosevelt (1901–1909)

William Howard Taft (1909–1913)

Art

1904: French sculptor Frédéric-Auguste Bartholdi created the Statute of Liberty.

1907: Picasso and Braque introduced cubism.

1908: Artist Gustav Klimt painted *The Kiss.*

1909: The art nouveau style, also called the *new style*, emerged.

1910: Frank Lloyd Wright completed the Robie House near Chicago.

Henri Matisse painted *The Red Studio.*

Music

1901: Mahler's Fourth Symphony, his most popular, debuted in Munich.

1902: Claude Debussy introduced musical impressionism with *Pelléas and Mélisande.*

continues on next page

BY THE DECADE:
1901–1910 *continued*

1904: Giacomo Puccini's opera *Madame Butterfly* debuted.

1906: In Chicago, the jukebox was invented.

1908: Bela Bartok composed String Quartet no. 1.

1909: Richard Strauss wrote *Elektra,* an opera.

1910: Classical music closed its Romantic period.

Igor Stravinsky composed his *Firebird Suite.*

Literary/Books

1901: Andrew Carnegie began to build public libraries across the United States.

Booker T. Washington wrote *Up From Slavery*.

1902: Muckraking began with a Lincoln Steffens' article in *McClure's Magazine.*

Beatrix Potter self-published *The Tale of Peter Rabbit.*

Arthur Conan Doyle wrote *The Hound of the Baskervilles.*

1906: Upton Sinclair wrote *The Jungle.*

Dance

1905: In Berlin, Isadora Duncan opened the first school of modern dance.

1910: The soft-shoe became popular.

The South American tango gained popularity in Europe and the United States.

Broadway/Theater

1907: The first *Ziegfeld Follies* was staged in New York.

Movie/Television

1904: Narrative film emerged as the dominant form.

1905: The first movie theater, or nickelodeon, was opened in Pittsburgh.

1908: *Dr. Jekyll and Mr. Hyde,* the first horror film, lasted 16 minutes.

1909: Film companies began buying screen rights to books and plays.

1910: There were about 9,000 movie theaters in the United States. Average films were 10–12 minutes in length.

Science/Technology

1902: Images can be transferred by photoelectric scanning.

1905: Einstein proposed his theory of relativity.

1905: Freud published his theory of sexuality.

1907: The first electric washing machine was produced.

1909: A radio distress signal saved 1,700 lives after ships collided.

BY THE DECADE:
1911–1920

Photography

1911: Rotogravure was first used in production of photographs for magazines.

1912: The Speed Graphic camera was introduced and became the standard for newspaper photographers.

1913: The first 35 mm still camera was developed.

1914: The Leica camera was developed in Germany.

1917: Kodak developed aerial cameras and trained aerial photographers during World War I.

1920: Photojournalism was born when printing technology supported mass production.

World History

1911: The Chinese Revolution began.

1912: The *Titanic* struck an iceberg and sank.

1914: World War I began when Germany declared war on Russia and France.

Great Britain and Japan declared war on Germany.

1917: The Russian Revolution started.

1919: Shortwave radio was invented.

The Treaty of Versailles ended World War I.

1920: The bubonic plague hit India.

The League of Nations was established.

KDKA radio began a regular schedule, starting the era of radio broadcasting.

American History

1911: The National Progressive Republican League was founded.

Arizona became a state.

1913: Henry Ford created the assembly line.

1914: Unions were gaining power.

1917: The United States entered World War I.

1919: The "Great Migration" began (southern African Americans to northern cities).

1920: The Harlem Renaissance began.

With the passage of the Nineteenth Amendment, women were given the right to vote.

Prohibition went into effect, dividing the country into wet and dry states.

The American Civil Liberties Union (ACLU) was founded.

Art

1911: Pablo Picasso began creating cubist collages.

Marc Chagall painted *I and the Village.*

1913: Matisse coined the term "cubism."

The Armory Show in New York City introduced modern European art to the United States.

1916: The Dada movement began in Zurich.

Norman Rockwell drew his first *Saturday Evening Post* cover.

1917: Austrian Egon Schiele's painted *The Embrace.*

Music

1912: Luigi Russolo founded the Italian futurist movement with *Futurista.*

1914: ASCAP was founded to protect music copyrights.

1915: Classic New Orleans jazz was gaining in popularity.

1917: Prokofiev composed his Classical Symphony, op. 25.

Ottorino Respighi composed *Fontaane de Roma.*

1918: Bela Bartok composed *Bluebeard's Castle,* an opera.

Igor Stravinsky composed *Histoire du Soldat.*

continues on next page

1919: Jazz arrived in Europe.

Othmar Schoek composed the opera *Don Ranudo.*

Chicago became the home of jazz.

Literary/Books

1911: *Photoplay,* the first movie fan magazine, began publication.

Ambrose Bierce wrote *The Devil's Dictionary.*

The Concise Oxford Dictionary was published.

Emma Goldman wrote *Anarchism and Other Essays.*

1912: Carl Jung's *Psychology of the Unconscious* initiated analytical psychology.

George Moore wrote *Ethics.*

1916: Russian anarchist Mikhail Bakunin wrote *God and the State.*

1920: Edith Wharton's *The Age of Innocence* depicted a callous New York society.

1920: Sinclair Lewis wrote *Main Street.*

Dance

1912: Maurice Ravel's ballet, *Daphnis and Chloe.*

1913: Darktown Follies opened in Harlem.

Igor Stravinsky composed the ballet *Le Sacre du Printemps* in Paris.

1914: Richard Strauss's ballet *Josephs Legende* opened in Paris.

1917: Many variations of the fox trot, waltz, tango, and kangaroo hop were favorite dances.

Theater/Broadway

1917: Busomi's *Turandot* and *Harlequin* (two one-act operas) debuted.

1920: Eugene O'Neill's play *Beyond the Horizon* marked the beginning of modern American drama.

Film

1912: The first U.S. feature film, *Oliver Twist,* was released.

1913: *Gertie the Dinosaur,* the first animated cartoon, required 10,000 drawings.

1915: Charlie Chaplin debuted his Little Tramp character in *Kid Auto Races At Venice.*

1916: Filmmaker D. W. Griffith's three-hour Civil War epic, *The Birth of a Nation,* defined the language of film.

1920: The movement of German film expressionism was established with Robert Wiene's *The Cabinet of Dr. Caligari.*

BY THE DECADE:
1921–1930

Photography

1921: Photographs could be transmitted by wire across the Atlantic.

Man Ray began making photograms ("rayographs").

1923: Kodak introduced home movie equipment.

1925: André Kertész began an eleven-year project photographing street life in Paris.

1927: General Electric invented the modern flash bulb.

1928: Kodak introduced 16 mm Kodacolor film for motion pictures.

1930: Published photos showed Americans the effects of the Depression.

World History

1921: Irish Free State was proclaimed.

1922: Kemal Atatürk founded modern Turkey.

Mussolini marched on Rome.

1923: Hitler was jailed after a failed coup.

The Teapot Dome Scandal occurred.

1929: The Vienna Circle and its theory of logical positivism was founded.

American History

1921: George Washington Carver presented new ideas on agriculture to the House of Representatives.

1923: U.S. Steel began instituting an 8-hour work day.

Harlem's Cotton Club opened with all-black performances for white-only audiences.

1924: The Julliard School opened in New York.

Radio hook-ups broadcast Democratic and Republican conventions.

1925: The Scopes trial publicized the debate over evolution versus the Bible.

1927: Charles Lindbergh flew the *Spirit of St. Louis* from New York to Paris.

1928: Penicillin was discovered.

Schenectady, New York, hosted the first scheduled television broadcasts.

1929: The stock market crashed, marking the beginning of the Great Depression.

Walt Disney Productions was formed.

1930: "Golden Age" of radio began.

U.S. Presidents

Warren G. Harding (1921–1923)

Calvin Coolidge (1923–1929)

Herbert Hoover (1929–1933)

Art

1922–1939: Surrealism was emerging.

1922: Paul Klee painted *Twittering Machine*.

Archaeologist Howard Carter discovered the Egyptian tomb of King Tutankhamen.

1925: The term "art deco" was coined from The Exposition des Arts Decoratifs held in Paris.

Raymond Hood designed the Radio City Music Hall auditorium and foyer.

1930: Grant Wood painted *American Gothic*.

continues on next page

1921–1930 *continued*

Music

1924: Ottorino Respighi composed *The Pines of Rome.*

George Gershwin wrote his symphonic jazz, *Rhapsody in Blue.*

1925: Dmitri Shostakovich composed his First Symphony.

Grand Ole Opry began in Nashville as "WSM Barn Dance."

1928: Maurice Ravel composed *Bolero.*

1929: Les Paul invented the electric guitar.

Literary/Books

1922: Emily Post published *Etiquette.*

1923: *Time,* the weekly news magazine, started publication.

1924: E. M. Forster wrote *A Passage to India.*

1925: F. Scott Fitzgerald wrote *The Great Gatsby.*

Hitler published *Mein Kampf.*

Ernest Hemingway wrote *In Our Time.*

1927: Martin Heidegger's *Being and Time* helped found modern existentialism.

Dance

1926: Martha Graham led the American modern dance movement.

1928: The newest dance craze was the Charleston.

Theater/Broadway

1921: Eugene O'Neill's play *Anna Christie* opened and later won the Pulitzer for drama.

1924: George Gershwin's *Rhapsody in Blue* opened in New York.

1929: Hollywood made its first original musical, *The Broadway Melody.*

Film

1922: Robert Flaherty's *Nanook of the North* was the first feature film documentary.

1927: Warner Brothers produced and debuted *The Jazz Singer,* the first feature-length talkie.

1929: Walt Disney introduced animated cartoons with synchronized sound: *Galloping Gaucho* and *Steamboat Willie.*

BY THE DECADE:
1931–1940

Photography

1931: Harold "Doc" Edgerton developed strobe photography at MIT.

Exposure meters went on sale.

1932: Group f/64 was formed.

The first 8 mm amateur motion-picture film, cameras, and projectors were introduced.

1934: Fuji Photo Film was founded.

1935: Kodak's Kodachrome became the first amateur color film.

The Farm Security Administration hired photographers to record rural hardships.

1936: *Life* began publication in 1936 and introduced photo essays.

World History

1932: Scientists split the atom.

1933: Adolf Hitler became Chancellor of Germany and established the first Nazi concentration camp.

1935: The Spanish Civil War began.

1937: The Hindenberg disaster occurred.

Japan invaded China.

1938: Hitler annexed Austria.

1939: World War II began.

1940: The Lascaux caves were discovered in France.

American History

1931: Al Capone was imprisoned for income tax evasion.

1932: The New Deal Era began with formation of the CWA, CCC, PWA, and TVA.

Amelia Earhardt was the first woman to fly solo across the Atlantic.

1933: Prohibition ended in the United States.

The first real comic book, *Funnies on Parade,* went on the newsstands.

1934: The Dust Bowl began.

1935: The first telephone call was made around the world.

1939: The first commercial flight was made over the Atlantic.

1940: Only 24% of American adults completed high school.

Of all adult males in the United States, only 5.5% of them had college diplomas; of all adult females, only 3.8%.

U.S. Presidents

Franklin D. Roosevelt (1933–1945)

Art

1931: Salvador Dali painted *Persistence of Memory.*

Georgia O'Keeffe painted *Red, White, and Blue.*

1934: René Magritte painted *The Human Condition.*

1936: Diego Rivera completed his mural *The History of Mexico.*

1937: Pablo Picasso painted *Guernica.*

Georges Braque painted *Woman with a Mandolin.*

Music

1931: New radio singers Bing Crosby and the Mills Brothers entertained audiences.

1932: Jazz composer Duke Ellington wrote *It Don't Mean a Thing, If It Ain't Got That Swing,* foretelling the swing era of the 1930s and 1940s.

1935: Benny Goodman was named "King of Swing."

continues on next page

1936: Sergei Prokofiev composed *Peter and the Wolf.*

1937: Béla Bartók's masterpiece *Music for Strings, Percussion and Celesta* premieres in Basel

1940: Big bands dominate popular music.

Literary/Books

1932: Aldous Huxley wrote his classic *Brave New World.*

1934: P. L. Travers wrote *Mary Poppins.*

Agatha Christie wrote *Murder on the Orient Express.*

1936: Margaret Mitchell wrote *Gone with the Wind.*

1937: John Steinbeck wrote *Of Mice and Men.*

J. R. R. Tolkien wrote *The Hobbit.*

1939: John Steinbeck's *The Grapes of Wrath* described the Dust Bowl migration.

1940: Hemingway wrote *For Whom the Bell Tolls,* a novel of the Spanish Civil War.

Richard Wright wrote *Native Son.*

Dance

1931–32: Savoy style Lindy (a.k.a., smooth Lindy, West Coast swing, slow Lindy) became popular.

1934: Benny Goodman on NBC's *Let's Dance* started the big band swing era on radio.

The jitterbug accompanied the Big Band era.

Theater/Broadway

1934: Cole Porter's musical *Anything Goes* went on Broadway.

1935: George Gershwin's *Porgy and Bess* debuted on Broadway.

1938: Thornton Wilder wrote his Pulitzer Prize play *Our Town.*

Orson Welles's radio drama *War of the Worlds* caused national panic.

1940: Chaplin's *The Great Dictator* parodied Hitler and Mussolini.

Film

1932: Rouben Mamoulian's musical *Love Me Tonight* smoothly integrated the songs into the film's plotline.

1939: Some of the greatest films ever made were released, including *Gone with the Wind, The Hunchback of Notre Dame, Mr. Smith Goes to Washington, Ninotchka, Stagecoach, The Wizard of Oz,* and *Wuthering Heights.*

1940: Disney released its animated feature film masterpiece *Pinocchio.*

Bob Hope and Bing Crosby starred in *Road to Singapore.*

BY THE DECADE:
1941–1950

Photography

1941: Kodak marketed the Ektra camera with a shutter speed range from 1/1000 to 1 second.

1942: Kodak's Kodacolor print film debuted.

Margaret Bourke-White, Robert Capa, Carl Mydans, and W. Eugene Smith covered the war for *Life* magazine.

1946: Kodak marketed Kodak Ektachrome transparency sheet film.

1947: Henri Cartier-Bresson, Robert Capa, and David Seymour started the Magnum Picture Agency.

1948: Edwin Land marketed the Polaroid camera, an instant picture process.

Hasselblad in Sweden debuted its first medium-format SLR.

1949: East German Zeiss developed the Contax S, the first SLR with a pentaprism viewfinder.

World History

Early- to mid-1940s: The Nazi German Holocaust killed an estimated six million Jews and many non-Jews.

1941: Mohandas Gandhi explained passive resistance in *Constructive Programme*.

1942: Japan bombed Darwin, Broome, and Queensland in Australia.

1945: Germany surrendered. Japan surrendered. World War II officially ended.

The United Nations was established.

1946: The Second Red Scare (Cold War) started and continued through the mid-1950s.

1948: Gandhi was assassinated.

The policy of Apartheid began.

1949: Communists were victors in the Chinese Revolution.

1950: The Korean War, a civil war between North and South Korea, started.

American History

1941: Pearl Harbor was attacked; United States entered World War II.

Manhattan Project began.

1942–45: United States interred into camps more than 110,000 Japanese people based on their ethnicity.

1944: "White Primary" laws excluding African Americans from voting were declared unconstitutional.

1947: Chuck Yeager broke the sound barrier.

1948: *The Ed Sullivan Show* debuted on television.

1949: The Whirlwind at MIT was the first real-time computer.

1950: The Korean War began.

Senator Joseph McCarthy began a witch hunt for Communists.

1950: McCarthyism began an era of massive distrust.

The Billy Graham Evangelistic Association was started.

U.S. Presidents

Harry S Truman (1945–1953)

Art

1942: Artist Edward Hopper painted *Nighthawks*.

1943: Norman Rockwell drew "The Four Freedoms" cover of *The Saturday Evening Post*.

1943: Artist "Grandma" Moses painted *Sugaring Off*.

1945: Abstract expressionism began. This movement discarded everything, including recognizable forms, except self-expression and raw emotion.

continues on next page

Music

1942: *Chattanooga Choo Choo* became the first gold record.

1943: Béla Bartók composed *Concerto for Orchestra.*

1944: Aaron Copland composed *Appalachian Spring.*

Leonard Bernstein composed the musical *On the Town.*

1948: Columbia Records introduced the long-playing vinyl record.

1948: Leo Fender invented the Fender electric guitar.

Literary/Books

1943: *Being and Nothingness* expounded Sartre's philosophy of existentialism.

1945: George Orwell's *Animal Farm* portrayed totalitarianism and communism.

1946: Dr. Spock published *The Common Book of Baby and Child Care.*

Robert Penn Warren wrote *All the King's Men.*

1948: B. F. Skinner's *Walden Two* discussed behaviorism.

1949: George Orwell wrote *1984.*

Dance

1943: The continuing dance craze was the jitterbug.

1946: The New York City Ballet was started.

Theater/Broadway

1943: *Oklahoma* was the first theatrical musical that dealt with serious subjects.

1945: Tennessee Williams's play *The Glass Menagerie* debuted.

1946: On Broadway, Irving Berlin's *Annie Get Your Gun* was highly successful.

1947: Tennessee Williams's *A Streetcar Named Desire* opened on Broadway.

1949: Arthur Miller's Pulitzer Prize play *Death of a Salesman* premiered.

Film

1941: The first film noir was John Huston's *The Maltese Falcon.*

1942: *Casablanca* premiered in New York.

BY THE DECADE:
1951–1960

Photography

1951: The low-priced Brownie 8 mm movie camera was introduced.

1954: Eastman Kodak introduced high-speed Tri-X film.

1957: Russell Kirsch made the first digital image on a computer. The image measured 176 pixels on a side.

1958: Kodak's Cavalcade was the company's first fully automatic color slide projector.

1960: Garry Winogrand began photographing people on New York City streets.

World History

1953: Julius and Ethel Rosenberg were executed for espionage.

1954: The first atomic submarine was launched.

1955: The Warsaw Pact was signed.

1956: The Hungarian Revolution began.

Khrushchev denounced Stalin.

First transatlantic telephone calls were made by submarine cable.

1957: The launch of the Soviet satellite *Sputnik* alarmed the United States, and the Space Age began.

1959: Castro became dictator of Cuba.

1960: *Tiros I* was launched as the first weather satellite.

American History

1951: The Mattachine Society, the first national gay rights organization, was formed.

Color television was introduced.

1952: Richard Nixon's Checkers speech saved his political career.

Polio vaccine was created.

1953: The Termination Act dissolved Native nations and absolved the U.S. government of prior treaty obligations.

1954: *Brown vs. Board of Education's* Supreme Court ruling made segregation in public schools unconstitutional.

1955: Rosa Parks refused to give up her bus seat for a white man.

1958: NASA was founded.

1959: The microchip was developed, enabling the computer revolution.

Xerox manufactured a plain paper copier.

1960: Television sets were in 7 of 8 U.S. homes.

The Kennedy–Nixon presidential debate was televised.

1960: Lasers were invented.

U.S. Presidents

Dwight D. Eisenhower (1953–1961)

Art

1953: Jackson Pollock painted the abstract expressionist *Blue Poles*.

1955: Edward Steichen curated the *Family of Man* exhibit at New York's Museum of Modern Art.

1958: John Whitney, Sr., used an analog computer to make art animation in the United States.

Inspired by mundane aspects of American culture, pop art began.

continues on next page

Music

1951: Cleveland disc jockey Alan Freed's phrase "rock 'n' roll" promoted rhythm and blues to white audiences.

1954: *Rock Around the Clock* by Bill Haley and the Comets became a huge hit.

1955: Elvis Presley became the first rock star.

1958: The Country Music Association was established in Nashville.

1960: John Coltrane formed a quartet and initiated jazz's New Wave movement.

Literary/Books

1951: Marine biologist Rachel Carson wrote *The Sea Around Us.*

1952: *The Revised Standard Version of the Bible* was published.

Hemingway completed *The Old Man and the Sea.*

E. B. White wrote *Charlotte's Web,* a children's story.

1954: William Golding wrote *Lord of the Flies.*

Tolkien published the first book of his trilogy, *The Fellowship of the Ring.*

1956: John F. Kennedy wrote short biographies, *Profiles in Courage.*

Dance

1956: Joffrey Ballet of Chicago was started.

1958: Rock and roll (swing) brought new dances including the twist.

Alvin Ailey established the American Dance Theater.

Theater/Broadway

1951: *Paint Your Wagon* opened on Broadway.

1955: Tennessee Williams's *Cat on a Hot Tin Roof* opened on Broadway.

1957: Leonard Bernstein's *West Side Story* debuted on Broadway.

Film

1951: Rodgers and Hammerstein's *The King and I* premiered.

A Streetcar Named Desire was the first film ever to win three acting Oscars.

The government's HUAC investigated communism in the film industry.

1952: Robert E. Wise's allegorical *The Day the Earth Stood Still* was released.

1958: *Island in the Sun* featured the first kiss between a white actress (Joan Fontaine) and a black actor (Harry Belafonte) in a movie.

1960: Alfred Hitchcock's *Psycho* was released.

BY THE DECADE:
1961–1970

Photography

1963: The line of Kodak Instamatic cameras was introduced. More than 50 million Instamatic cameras were produced by 1970.

Polaroid Corporation's research team invented the first instant color picture material.

The first purpose-built underwater camera, the Nikonos, was introduced.

The Society for Photographic Education held its first national conference.

1965: Fuji Photo Film U.S.A., Inc. began as a six-person office in the Empire State Building.

1966: Earth-rise photo was captured by Kodak's lunar module camera.

1968: Photograph of the Earth was taken from the moon.

1969: Astronauts sent live photographs from the moon to a worldwide audience.

World History

1961: The Bay of Pigs invasion was a peak of the Cold War.

The Berlin Wall was built.

Soviets launched the first man into space.

1964: Nelson Mandela was sentenced to life in prison in South Africa.

1966: China's Cultural Revolution began.

American History

1960s: The civil rights movement gained momentum with protests and freedom rides.

1962: The Cuban Missile Crisis began.

1963: President John F. Kennedy was assassinated.

1964: The Civil Rights Act passed.

The Wilderness Act passed.

Mariner IV sent television images from Mars.

1965: The United States sent troops to Vietnam, the first war to be televised.

1966: The psychedelic scene started in San Francisco.

1968: Martin Luther King, Jr., was assassinated in Memphis, Tennessee.

1969: Neil Armstrong became the first human to set foot on the moon.

1970: National Guard troops fired into an anti-war demonstration at Kent State University in Ohio, killing four students.

IBM introduced computer floppy disks.

Of all U.S. adults, 55% had completed high school.

Movie tickets sold in the United States dropped from 3 billion plus in 1950 to under 1 billion.

National Public Radio was founded.

U.S. Presidents

John F. Kennedy (1961–1963)

Lyndon B. Johnson (1963–1969)

Richard Nixon (1969–1974)

Art

1962: Andy Warhol exhibited his *Campbell's Soup Can,* a work of pop art.

1963: Charles Csuri made his first computer-generated artwork (United States).

1964: Op art was introduced, defined as illusion because of its mathematically based composition.

1969: Pop art movement's Claes Oldenburg made large sculptures like *Lipstick.*

continues on next page

1961–1970 *continued*

Music

1961: Robert Moog and Herbert Deutsch created the voltage-controlled synthesizer.

Berry Bordy founded Motown and promoted the slogan "Black and White Together."

1963: Folk singer Bob Dylan popularized protest songs.

1964: England's Beatles became wildly popular in the United States.

1965: The Byrds's version of Bob Dylan's *Mr. Tambourine Man* introduced "folk rock."

1968: Walter Carlos released *Switched-On Bach.*

The Reggae scene started in Jamaica.

The Grateful Dead, Jefferson Airplane, and Jimi Hendrix popularized psychedelic rock.

1969: The Woodstock Music and Art Fair took place in Bethel, New York.

Literary/Books

1961: Harper Lee won the Pulitzer Prize for *To Kill a Mockingbird.*

1962: Rachel Carson's *Silent Spring* lead to a ban on DDT and other pesticides.

1963: Betty Friedan's influential book *The Feminine Mystique* formulated the modern women's rights movement.

Jacques Cousteau wrote *The Living Sea.*

1969: Mario Puzo's novel *The Godfather* was published.

Dance

1962: A dance concert held in New York marked the beginning of the Judson movement and postmodern dance.

1966: The frug, the locomotion, the hitchhiker, the Freddie, and the Watusi were popular dances with rock-n'roll.

1970: Texas two-step was popular with country Western music.

Theater/Broadway

1960s: "Performance Art" started in the United States.

1962: Edward Albee's play *Who's Afraid of Virginia Woolf?* opened.

1968: The rock musical *Hair* opened on Broadway.

1970: On Broadway, *Jesus Christ Superstar* created a sensation.

Film

1968: *2001: A Space Odyssey, Funny Girl,* and *Rosemary's Baby* were highly popular movies.

BY THE DECADE:
1971–1980

Photography

1972: Polaroid invented a camera capable of focusing by itself.

Kodak introduced 110-format cameras with 13 × 17 mm frames.

1973: Polaroid introduced one-step instant photography with the SX-70 camera.

1977: Cindy Sherman began work on *Untitled Film Stills.*

1978: Japan's Konica invented the point-and-shoot, auto-focus camera.

1980: DX coding enabled certain cameras to automatically set the film speed.

World History

1973: The Vietnam cease fire agreement with the United States was signed during the Paris Peace talks. U.S. troops pulled out of Vietnam.

1979: Margaret Thatcher became the first woman Prime Minister of Great Britain.

Kakadu National Park and the Great Barrier Reef Marine Park in Australia were both made official.

American History

1972: *The Washington Post* began Watergate reporting that eventually resulted in President Nixon's resignation.

1973: The Endangered Species Act was passed.

Roe v. Wade established a woman's legal right to abortion.

The American Psychiatric Association removed homosexuality from its official list of mental disorders.

1974: President Nixon resigned.

1978: The American Indian Religious Freedom Act was passed, attempting to restore Native nations' right to practice religion and ceremony.

1979: A nuclear accident occurred at Three Mile Island.

U.S. Presidents

Richard Nixon (1969–1974)

Gerald R. Ford (1974–1977)

Jimmy Carter (1977–1981)

Art

1970s: Postmodernism was the movement during this decade.

Body art gained in popularity.

Performance art was popular. Artists took their art directly to a public forum.

1971: The world's first museum-based solo exhibition of computer-generated art: Manfred Mohr, *Musee d'Art Modern,* Paris.

Late-1970s: Neoconceptualism, neoexpressionism, and feminist art began.

Music

Early-1970s: The Moody Blues, Electric Light Orchestra, and Pink Floyd combined classical styles with rock. Synthesizers became popular instruments.

1973: Reggae music arrived from Jamaica.

1977: Elvis Presley died at Graceland at the age of 42.

1978: Sony introduced the Walkman.

Hip hop—a blend of rock, jazz, and soul with African drumming—was born in the South Bronx.

1979: Rap music grew beyond the streets of New York.

continues on next page

BY THE DECADE:
1971–1980 *continued*

Literary/Books

1971: John Rawls wrote *A Theory of Justice.*

B. F. Skinner wrote *Beyond Freedom and Dignity.*

1972: The first regular issue of *Ms.* magazine was published in July.

1973: Erica Jong wrote *Fear of Flying.*

1975: Frances Lappé's *Diet for a Small Planet* opposed meat.

1978: Will Eisner's *A Contract with God* was the first graphic novel.

Dance

1974: Premier Russian dancer Mikhail Baryshnikov defected and joined the American Ballet Theatre.

1980: Disco was the rage.

Broadway/Theater

1979: The Sondheim musical *Sweeney Todd* appeared on Broadway.

Movie/Television

1972: *Deep Throat* started a porn industry explosion.

1976: Small satellite dishes started to appear in residential backyards.

Barbara Walters became the first woman to anchor a U.S. network newscast.

1977: George Lucas released his space opera *Star Wars.*

Steven Spielberg wrote and directed *Close Encounters of the Third Kind.*

Saturday Night Fever sparked the "disco inferno."

1979: *The China Syndrome* foreshadowed the Three Mile Island meltdown.

1980: CNN, the 24-hour news channel, started reporting.

Science/Technology

1971: The Wang 1200 was the first word processor.

1972: Pong was the first home video game.

1974: The word "Internet" entered the American vocabulary.

1975: Bill Gates and Paul Allen started Microsoft.

1977: The Apple II microcomputer was a bestseller. Other bestsellers were the Commodore Pet and the TRS-80.

Nintendo began to sell computer games.

1978: Atari's arcade game *Football* introduced video sports.

Louise Brown was the first test-tube baby born outside the womb.

1979: News groups arrived on the Internet.

BY THE DECADE:
1981–1990

Photography

1982: Sony demonstrated its Mavica still video camera.

1984: Canon demonstrated its first electronic still camera.

1985: Pixar introduced a digital imaging processor.

Minolta introduced the world's first autofocus SLR system.

1986: Fuji introduced the Quicksnap, a disposable camera.

1987: Kodak announced the Fling, its first one-time-use camera.

1988: Kodak Ektapress Gold film was the first color negative film created especially for photojournalists.

1990: Eastman Kodak announced Photo CD as a digital image storage medium.

Adobe Photoshop 1.0 was introduced for Apple Macintosh computers.

World History

1981: A new illness was named AIDS.

1982: The Reagan and Bush (George H. W.) administrations began supporting death squads in El Salvador and the Contras in Nicaragua.

1983: The U.S. Embassy in Beirut was bombed.

1984: Two bodyguards killed Indira Gandhi, India's Prime Minister.

1985: Scientists discovered a hole in the earth's ozone layer.

Mikhail Gorbachev called for glasnost and perestroika.

1986: The Chernobyl nuclear accident took place.

The U.S.S.R. launched the Mir Space Station.

1989: The Berlin Wall was destroyed, unifying Germany.

Students were massacred in China's Tiananmen Square.

1990: Nelson Mandela was freed from a South African jail.

American History

1981: The first woman was appointed to the U.S. Supreme Court.

Reagan fired almost 13,000 striking air traffic controllers.

1983: Cabbage Patch Kids swept the nation as its newest fad.

1983: Sally Ride became the first American woman in space.

1986: The space shuttle *Challenger* exploded.

1988: Indian Gaming Regulatory Act allowed gambling operations on Indian lands.

1989: Exxon's tanker Valdez spilled millions of gallons of oil on Alaska's coastline.

1990: The Hubble telescope was launched into space.

Of all American adults, 85% had completed high school.

U.S. Presidents

Ronald Reagan (1981–1989)

George H. W. Bush (1989–1993)

Art

1980s: Contemporary art gained a foothold in the art world.

Multiculturalism was prominent.

The graffiti movement saw a rise in popularity.

1986: Andy Warhol used an Amiga for a self-portrait and portrait of singer Deborah Harry.

continues on next page

BY THE DECADE:
1981–1990 *continued*

Music

1981: MTV, a music video channel, debuted on cable TV.

1983: Audio music cassettes outsold LP records.

1986: The garage scene started in New York at the "Paradise Garage" club.

1988: The rave scene started in London with the *Summer of Love*.

Literary/Books

1984: William Gibson coined the term "cyberspace" in his novel *Neuromancer*.

Several large U.S. newspapers began offering online text versions.

Tom Clancy wrote *The Hunt For Red October* and *Red Storm Rising*.

1988: Stephen Hawking wrote *A Brief History of Time*.

1989: B. F. Skinner wrote *The Origins of Cognitive Thought*.

1990: Michael Crichton completed his blockbuster novel, *Jurassic Park*.

Broadway/Theater

1981: *Cats* opened and became Broadway's longest-running play.

1984: Broadway's Pulitzer Prize-winning musical by Stephen Sondheim *Sunday in the Park with George* debuted.

1986: The musical *Phantom of the Opera* was on Broadway.

Movie/Television

1982: Movies included *E.T., Tootsie, The Verdict, Missing,* and *Das Boot*.

1985: The first Blockbuster Video store opened in Dallas.

1987: From Japan came the *Anime* cartoon film.

1988: *Who Framed Roger Rabbit?* introduced the blending of animated imagery and real people.

1989: *TV Guide* put Oprah Winfrey's head on Ann-Margret's body for its cover image.

Science/Technology

1981: IBM introduced the personal computer (PC).

1982: Within a year or so, 5.5 million PCs had been sold.

1983: *Time* named the computer as "Man" of the Year for 1982.

1984: The first Macintosh computer was sold.

1986: International standards were set for audio, video, and digital recording.

1988: The first data crime was reported.

1989: Researchers tried to index the exploding Internet, but couldn't keep up.

1990: The World Wide Web originated at CERN in Europe.

BY THE DECADE:
1991–2000

Photography

1991: Kodak's Professional Digital Camera System (DCS) enabled photojournalists to take electronic pictures.

1993: Adobe Photoshop became available for Windows computers.

Photojournalists and studio photographers switched to digital cameras.

1996: Kodak introduced the Advanced Photo System (APS).

1997: Kodak produced the first point-and-shoot digital camera.

1998: Megapixel cameras became available at the consumer level.

2000: Snapfish was launched.

World History

1991: The United States launched Operation Desert Storm.

South Africa repealed apartheid laws.

The Soviet Union was divided into 15 newly independent republics, and the Soviet Communist Party officially ceased to exist.

1993: The North American Free Trade Agreement (NAFTA) went into effect.

1994: Nelson Mandela was elected President of South Africa.

The Rwandan genocide began.

1995: A gas attack took place in a Tokyo subway.

Israeli Prime Minister Yitzhak Rabin was assassinated.

1996: Mad cow disease was found in Britain.

1997: Hong Kong was returned to China.

Princess Diana died in a car crash.

Scientists cloned sheep for the first time.

1999: The Panama Canal was returned to Panama.

American History

1992: Riots raged in Los Angeles after the Rodney King verdict.

1993: The World Trade Center was bombed.

1995: Oklahoma City bombing shook the American heartland.

1996: The Unabomber was arrested.

1997: *Pathfinder* sent back images of Mars.

1998: President Clinton was impeached but wasn't forced out of office.

2000: Congress passes the Children's Internet Protection Act.

One in four American adults held college degrees.

U.S. Presidents

Bill Clinton (1993–2001)

Art

1994: Lowbrow was born of underground or "street" culture and poked fun at convention.

Lowbrow artist extraordinaire Robert Williams founded *Juxtapoz* magazine.

2000: Body art, including tattoos and piercings, gained popularity in the United States.

Web sites became more complex by using video, sound, and motion, allowing the public to visit art museums online.

continues on next page

Music

1991: Seattle band Nirvana started grunge music with *Smells Like Teen Spirit*.

1992: Compact disc music sales surpass sales of cassette tapes.

1993: "The Macarena," a song by Los Del Rio, was released.

1994: The most popular radio format in the United States was country music.

1998: Music industry was up in arms as people downloaded MP3 sound files for free.

2000: Court action prompted Napster to stop distributing copyrighted music for free.

Literary/Books

1995: Amazon.com started selling books online.

1997: Novelist Charles Frazier wrote *Cold Mountain*.

1998: J. K. Rowling wrote *Harry Potter and the Sorcerer's Stone*.

In the United States alone, 50,000 publishers released 70,000 book titles in one year.

2000: People started reading e-books on book-size electronic units.

Dance

1994: Country line dancing gained popularity.

1995: *Riverdance—The Show,* the first Irish dance show, opened in Dublin.

1996: "The Macarena" was popular.

Movie/Television

1991: Denver viewers could order movies at home from a list of more than 1,000 titles.

Disney's *Beauty and the Beast* was nominated for Best Picture.

1993: Steven Spielberg's *Jurassic Park* was released.

1994: Best Picture winner was *Forrest Gump*.

Digital satellite TV service, DirecTV, became available in the United States.

1995: *Toy Story* was released, the first computer-generated feature-length film.

1998: *The Last Broadcast* was the first desktop feature film.

1999: TiVO debuted.

Science/Technology

1991: The Internet was made available for commercial use.

1992: Tim Berners-Lee developed the software and protocol for the World Wide Web (www).

1994: Netscape launched Navigator.

1996: Microsoft released Internet Explorer.

The World Wide Web held more than 100,000 pages and was growing fast.

The World Exposition was the first world's fair held on the Internet.

1998: Traffic on the Internet was doubling every 100 days.

An estimated number of World Wide Web pages: 300 million.

An estimated number of Web pages added each day: 1.5 million.

1999: 150 million Internet users could access more than 800 million Web pages.

2000: The dot.com industry crashed.

BY THE DECADE:
2001–2010

Photography

2003: Nikon and Canon attributed 80% of their sales to digital camera bodies. Film sales dropped dramatically in the industrialized countries.

2003: Canon shocked the digital camera market with the 6 megapixel, under $1,000 Canon Digital Rebel (300D).

Photobucket was launched.

2004: Photos by two rover vehicles were beamed back from Mars.

Photokina 2004 showed over 100 new digital photographic products in Cologne, Germany.

Kodak ceased to manufacture film-based cameras.

Some new digital cameras were sporting MPEG 4 video technology.

2005: Canon EOS 5D, the first consumer-priced full-frame digital SLR, with a 24 × 36 mm CMOS sensor, sold for $3000.

Cell phone cameras reportedly outsold other cameras at a rate of 4:1.

2007: London observers use cell phone cameras to document the aftermath of the London public transportation attacks.

2008: Polaroid ceased production of all instant-film products.

2009: Kodak Corporation ceased manufacturing of Kodachrome film.

White House official photographer Pete Souza began uploading White House photographs to Flickr.

World History

2002: The Euro became legal tender in twelve European Union countries.

The first SARS virus outbreak was identified in the Far East.

2003: A World Summit of the Information Society met in Switzerland.

2004: A major earthquake and tsunami caused the deaths of nearly 290,000 in Sri Lanka, India, Indonesia, Thailand, Malaysia, and other countries around the rim of the Indian Ocean.

2005: Terrorist bomb attacks took place on London's public transport system.

A major earthquake in Kashmir killed nearly 80,000 people.

Global warming remained controversial but continued to be a major concern of scientists and environmentalists.

2006: A Danish newspaper printed several cartoons negatively depicting Muhammed. Angry Muslim demonstrators violently demonstrated against Denmark and other nations where newspapers reprinted the cartoons.

2007: Gordon Brown replaced Tony Blair as Prime Minister of Great Britain.

A National Intelligence Estimate says "with high confidence" that Iran froze its nuclear weapons program in 2003. This contradicts a similar report written in 2005 that stated Iran was determined to continue developing such weapons.

2008: Prime Minister Hashim Thaci of Kosovo declared independence from Serbia.

Cuban president Fidel Castro stepped down after 49 years in power.

More than 170 people are killed and about 300 are wounded in a series of attacks on several landmarks and commercial hubs in Mumbai, India.

continues on next page

2001–2010 *continued*

2009: H1N1 virus has killed as many as 103 people in Mexico, assumed to be the epicenter of the world-wide outbreak.

A North Korean court convicted American journalists Euna Lee and Laura Ling of "illegal entry" and sentenced them to 12 years in a labor prison. The journalists were working on a story about North Korean refugees.

In compliance with the Status of Forces Agreement between Iraq and the United States, U.S. troops withdrew from Iraqi cities and transferred the responsibility of Iraqi cities' security to Iraqi troops.

Japan's opposition party (the Democrats) was elected over the Liberal Democrats, who have dominated Japanese politics for nearly 50 years.

U.S. Presidents

George W. Bush (2001–2009)

Barack Obama (2009–)

American History

2001: Three hijacked aircraft attacks by Al-Quaeda demolished New York's World Trade Center and damaged the Pentagon.

President George W. Bush launched the War on Terrorism. Economic globalization continued at an unprecedented pace.

The Patriot Act was enacted.

2002: No Child Left Behind Act reformed public education.

Enron and other major corporations experienced scandals from accounting fraud, costing employees and stockholders millions of dollars.

2003: Congress authorized force against Iraq, allowing President Bush to lead the nation into a controversial war.

Space shuttle *Columbia* broke apart over Texas, killing all seven astronauts on board.

2005: Hurricane Katrina hit Louisiana, devastating New Orleans and the Mississippi coast.

3D Cellular launched wireless communication tools that caused the cellular industry to blossom.

China became the largest consumer of integrated circuits in the world.

2006: President Bush renewed the Patriot Act, defiantly stating that he is not bound by its requirement to tell Congress how the law is being used or applied.

2008: The U.S. government intervened in the U.S. financial system to avoid a crisis. The Federal Reserve outlined a $200 billion loan program that allowed the country's biggest banks borrow Treasury securities at discounted rates.

Senator Barack Obama won the Presidential election over Senator John McCain.

2009: Barack Obama, the first African-American president, took office.

Art

2002: Nam June Paik created Transmission, a 33-foot-tall tower with neon lights and lasers.

Manifesta 4, the European Biennale of Contemporary Art, was held in Frankfurt, Germany.

2008: Three men wearing ski masks stole four pieces of artwork from the Zurich Museum in one of the largest art robberies in history. Taken were a Cezanne, a Degas, a van Gogh, and a Monet, with a combined value of $163 million.

Music

2001: Apple's iPod music player skyrocketed in popularity.

Napster was barred from offering its online music file sharing service.

2003: iTunes music store offered tunes for 99 cents.

2001–2010 *continued*

2004: The evolving iPod held 10,000 tunes, but fit into a shirt pocket.

2005: Willie Nelson's *Countryman* album was released.

2007: NPR Music was launched as a free online music discovery destination devoted to music genres that commercial media neglected.

Movie/Television

2001: J. K. Rowling's *Harry Potter and the Sorcerer's Stone* was released. The first of J. R. R. Tolkien's fantasy books was also released in movie form: *The Lord of the Rings: The Fellowship of the Ring*.

2002: MTV reportedly reached 250 million homes worldwide.

George Lucas's *Star Wars: Episode II* was released.

2004: Michael Moore's controversial *Fahrenheit 9/11* won the top prize at the Palme D'Or at the Cannes Film Festival.

Directed by Mel Gibson, *The Passion of the Christ* was both praised and criticized.

98% of all U.S. homes had a color television.

2005: Reality television became a well-established sector of television programming.

Technology

2001: Americans spent more on electronic games than they did on movie tickets.

More than half of all Americans have used the Internet.

Instant messaging grew in popularity.

2002: Cheap, handheld computers were a big sales item.

Many dot.com businesses failed.

2003: Cell phones added computer and Internet capabilities.

2004: There were 1.5 billion cell phones worldwide.

Google received 138,000 requests a minute in 90 languages.

One in every five people under the age of 30 say the Internet is the main information source.

Flickr was launched.

Wi-fi cell phone/cameras are replacing some computers.

University of San Diego offers degree in wireless communication.

2005: Hewlett Packard purchased Snapfish, launched in 2000.

2007: The Dodge and Burn Blog, a blog about diversity in photography, was initiated (http://dodgeburn.blogspot.com).

2008: David Hobby, author of the Strobist.com blog and generally considered founder of the Strobist photographic movement, quit his job at *The Baltimore Sun*. Hi blog (www.strobist.com) had reached an online monthly readership of over 300,000 photographers from 175 countries.

2009: Flicker contains 3 billion photographs.

2010: Three groups of historic NASA images were released on The Commons on Flickr. A collaboration between Flickr, the space agency and the Internet Archive made the release possible.

NOTES

List of Photographers

This list is presented as a launching point for further investigation into photography. These names come from all eras of photography and represent a cross section of many styles of photography.

Abbott, Berenice
Adams, Ansel
Arbus, Diane
Archer, Frederick Scott
Arnold, Eve
Atget, Eugène
Atkins, Anna
Avedon, Richard
Bacon, Francis
Baldessari, John
Barmbaum, Bruce
Bayer, Herbert
Bellocq, E. J.
Bernhard, Ruth
Blossfeldt, Karl
Blumenfeld, Erwin
Bourke-White, Margaret
Brady, Mathew
Brandt, Bill
Brassaï
Burtynsky, Edward
Bravo, Manuel Alvarez
Callahan, Harry
Cameron, Julia Margaret
Capa, Robert
Caponigro, John Paul
Caponigro, Paul
Carroll, Lewis
Cartier-Bresson, Henri
Christina Z. Anderson
Close, Chuck
Coburn, Alvin Langdon
Cohen, Mark

Cohn, Alfred
Collier, John, Jr.
Cunningham, Imogen
Curtis, Edward S.
Daguerre, Louis-Jacques-Mandé
DeCarava, Roy
Degas, Edgar
Dennis, Lisl
Doisneau, Robert
Eakins, Thomas
Edgerton, Harold
Edwards, John Paul
Eggleston, William
Eisenstaedt, Alfred
Emerson, Peter Henry
Ernst, Max
Estes, Richard
Evans, Frederick
Evans, Walker
Frank, Robert
Freund, Gisèle
Friedlander, Lee
Geddes, Anne
Giacomelli, Mario
Gilpin, Laura
Goldblatt, David
Goldsworthy, Andy
Grosz, George
Gutmann, John
Haas, Ernst
Hagemayer, Johan
Hall, Job
Henri, Florence
Hine, Lewis
Hockney, David
Horst, Horst P.
Hugnet, Georges
Hume, David
Ingalls, Bill
Izis (Isreal Bidermanas)

Jackson, William Henry
Jacobi, Lotte
Josephson, Kenneth
Kanaga, Consuelo
Kansuke, Yamamoto
Karsh, Yousuf
Käsebier, Gertrude
Kenna, Michael
Kern, Pascal
Kertész, André
Killip, Chris
Kimura, Ihei
Klee, Paul
Klein, William
Kosuth, Joseph
Kruger, Barbara
Lachapelle, David
Lafont, Suzanne
Lange, Dorothea
Lanting, Frans
Lartigue, Jacques-Henri
Laughlin, Clarence John
Leibovitz, Annie
Le Secq, Henri
Levine, Sherrie
Levinstein, Leon
Levinthal, David
Levitt, Helen
Link, O. Winston
Lissitzky, El
Long, Richard
Maddox, Richard Leach
Maisel, Jay
Man Ray (Emmanuel Radnitzky)
Mann, Sally
McCurry, Steve
McSavaney, Ray
Meatyard, Ralph Eugene
Meyerowitz, Joel
Michaels, Duane

Model, Lisette
Modotti, Tina
Moon, Sarah
Muench, David
Muybridge, Eadweard
Newhall, Beaumont
Newman, Arnold
Newton, Helmut
Nixon, Nicholas
Orkin, Ruth
O'Sullivan, Timothy
Outerbridge, Paul, Jr.
Parks, Gordon
Penn, Irving
Porter, Eliot
Ray, Man
Riis, Jacob

Rodchenko, Alexander
Rosenthal, Joe
Salgado, Sebastião
Sander, August
Sato, Tokihiro
Sexton, John
Sherman, Cindy
Shore, Stephen
Smith, W. Eugene
Soloway, Eddie
Sommer, Frederick
Steichen, Edward
Stieglitz, Alfred
Stock, Dennis
Strand, Paul
Stromberg, Tony
Sugimoto, Hiroshi

Talbot, William Henry Fox
Tenneson, Joyce
Tress, Arthur
Uelsmann, Jerry
Versace, Vincent
Vestal, David
Warhol, Andy
Watkins, Carleton
Weese, Carl
Weston, Brett
Weston, Cole
Weston, Edward
White, Minor
Winogrand, Garry
Wolfe, Art

Glossary

A

Absorption (of chemicals): penetration of darkroom chemicals through the skin, a hazard of using and working with darkroom chemicals.

Accelerator: a chemical that creates the alkaline environment required by the developing agents. The accelerator has an effect on the contrast of the resulting negative.

Additive color system: a color system consisting of combinations of red, green, and blue. When combined, these three colors create white light on a monitor and are used in computer, television, and video equipment.

Adobe RGB: the collection (gamut) of colors frequently used by professional photographers. Adobe RGB has the widest color space of all the color gamuts available on most cameras.

Acrylic glazing: a mounting material that is an excellent choice when shipping framed photographs because there is less chance for breakage than if glass were used. This material scratches very easily, however.

Adjustment layer: a layer without pixels, an adjustment layer creates visual changes in your image without physically changing the pixels in underlying layers.

Alpha channel: a map of a selected area within the photograph. An alpha channel allows you to reselect the same pixels previously selected. Alpha channels are stored underneath the color channels in the Channels palette within Photoshop.

Angle of coverage: in regard to large-format lenses, the angle of coverage is the maximum image area of usable quality captured by a given lens. Depending on their design, two lenses with the same focal length may have different angles of coverage.

Angle of view: the portion of the scene that the lens sees. The angle of view is sometimes called the *image circle*.

Antihalation coating: in black-and-white and color negative films, a coating that prevents light from reflecting back through the emulsion and further exposing the silver halide crystals; also known as *antihalation backing*.

Aperture: the actual opening in a lens created by the diaphragm. Its size dictates the amount of light allowed through the lens as you make a photograph.

Aperture Priority (Av) mode: a camera mode that allows you to select an aperture setting according to the depth of field you want for your photo.

Archival: the ability of a photographic print to last several years without fading or suffering a shift in color.

Archival processing: the additional care and processing that photographers take to preserve their images.

Artist Statement: documentation that gives viewers insights regarding the photographer's thoughts regarding his or her works.

Atmospheric perspective: a phenomenon that makes objects closest to us have the greatest contrast of values and the most saturated colors. As objects recede from the foreground, their contrast decreases and colors lose their saturation, meaning they become more gray.

Attribution condition: a copyright license condition whereby the copyright owner allows others to copy, distribute, display, and perform the copyrighted work and any derivative works based on that work, provided they give the copyright owner credit exactly as requested.

Attribution no-derivatives condition: a copyright license condition whereby the copyright owner allows redistribution, commercial and noncommercial, of the work, provided that work is passed along unchanged and in whole and with credit to the copyright owner.

Attribution noncommercial condition: a copyright license condition whereby the copyright owner allows others to use, change, and build upon the work, but only for noncommercial purposes and provided that derivative works acknowledge the copyright owner, although users are not required to license the derivative works on the same terms as the copyright owner's original license.

Attribution noncommercial no-derivatives condition: a copyright license condition whereby the copyright owner allows others to download works and share them with others, provided the users mention the copyright owner, provide a link to the copyright owner, make no changes to the works, and do not use the works for commercial purposes.

Attribution noncommercial share-alike condition: a copyright license condition whereby the copyright owner allows others to use the work, including derivative works, and change it in any way they wish, provided the use is for noncommercial purposes and that users credit the copyright owner and license their new creations under the same terms as the copyright owner's original license.

Attribution share-alike condition: a copyright license condition whereby the copyright owner allows others to use the image for any purpose, including creating derivatives from it, provided they credit the copyright owner *and* license their new creations under the identical terms of the Creative Commons license.

B

Backlight: a condition where the light source is behind the subject and is aimed toward the camera. Backlighting can produce interesting lighting conditions, such as rim light and silhouettes.

Back paper: an archival liner paper attached to the back of wooden frames to keep dust and insects out.

Bit depth: a reference to the number of colors that can be displayed within an image. The greater the bit depth, the more colors available to be used in an image.

Bits: digital bits of information in binary code (0s and 1s).

Black point: the point at which pixels have a value of 0 in each of the Red, Green, and Blue channels in the RGB color system, or they have the value of 100% in each of the Cyan, Magenta, Yellow, and Black channels of the CMYK color system; also called *pure darkness.*

Black-and-white image: an image made up of either black or white pixels; a black-and-white image has no shades of gray.

Blocked-up shadows: an exposure that falls on the shoulder or toe of a characteristic curve. That part of the exposure will not be able to render clear separation between the tones, resulting in dark areas with little or no detail.

Blooming: the point where light information hitting photosites starts to spill over to other photosites, producing a featureless white spot. A purple fringe is visible when those white areas within the photograph are adjacent to very dark areas.

Blown-out highlights: the result of overexposure that causes a loss of detail in the lightest portion of a photograph.

Boom: a form of light stand that allows mounting of a strobe head directly over the subject; can be attached to the ceiling or used with counterweights on traditional light stands.

Brightness: a term loosely equivalent to light. In Photoshop, brightness is used in relation to the range of visible light ranging from pure black to pure white within a photograph.

Brightness range (levels): the range of values used within a photograph. A low-contrast photograph uses a narrower brightness range than a high-contrast photograph. All digital photographs can have the capacity of using the entire available brightness range from pure black to pure white in Photoshop.

Broad lighting: placement of the key light on the same side as the ear facing the camera.

Bulb mode: a camera mode that allows the camera's shutter to remain open as long as the shutter button is pushed.

Burning: in the darkroom, exposing selective areas of a photographic image to more light beyond the straight exposure time. Burning darkens the print in those selected areas.

C

C-41: a rather general term given to the process for developing many kinds of color print film.

Cable release: a cord extending from the camera that trips the shutter without your needing to touch the camera.

Camera raw file: an image file consisting of sensor information that has been collected but not yet processed by the camera's microprocessor.

Catchlight: a specular highlight that appears in a model's eye. A catchlight is most often a reflection of the light source.

Center-weighted averaging: the metering system of a camera takes the entire scene into account, but gives more attention to the center of the frame (where photographers often compose a scene). The metering system gives more "weight" to the center of the frame when choosing a proper exposure.

Characteristic curve: a graph representing the film's response to light during an exposure. The characteristic curve reveals the differences in how contrast is recorded by different kinds of film.

Charge-coupled device (CCD): a solid-state imager (sensor) that converts light coming through the lens into electronic signals. Because of high costs, most digital cameras have switched to a different solid-state sensor called CMOS.

Chromatic aberration: a fringing of color along areas of great contrast, caused by the camera lens failing to focus different wavelengths of light onto the same focal plane.

Chromogenic film: black-and-white film containing dye couplers along with silver halide. During the development process, dye couplers in chromogenic film produce black dye instead of colored dyes. Chromogenic film uses the same processing procedures as color print film.

CieL*a*b*: a device-independent color model comprised of three separate channels of information: "L" for lightness, "a" for redness-to-greenness, and "b" for blueness-to-yellowness.

Clipped: an area of a photograph that registers as pure white or pure black on the histogram. This term is frequently used when a highlight or shadow has been shifted to pure white or pure black in Levels or Curves, therefore losing the detail previously available in those portions of the photograph. It can also be used to define over- or underexposure during a digital photographic capture or scan.

Closing (stopping) down the aperture: decreasing the diameter of the aperture or changing the f-stop to a smaller opening, such as from f/4 to f/5.6.

CMOS (complementary metal-oxide semiconductor): a sensor that collects light coming through the lens and converts it to electronic signals. Although a CMOS sensor may not be able to match the quality of the imaged created by CCDs, its smaller size and much lower cost make CMOS sensors the ideal choice for most consumer digital cameras.

CMYK: a color gamut (collection of colors) that includes only the colors that can be reproduced in a color printout using cyan, magenta, yellow, and black inks; a considerably smaller gamut than either Adobe RGB or sRGB.

CMYK color system: a color system based on mixing cyan, magenta, yellow, and black inks.

Color cast: a shift in color within a photograph. A color cast creates an image that doesn't look the proper color.

Colorimeter: a mechanical device that measures amounts of color being emitted from computer monitors or other displays.

Colorimetric data: information gathered from colorimeters.

Color models: color spaces that are defined separately from the cameras that produce them.

Color spaces: the combination of color system (mode) information plus a scale to quantify the amount of color components. Plotted out, color spaces show all of the possible color combination within a three-dimensional space.

Color systems (modes): computer language that allows computers to identify and represent colors. The most commonly used color systems are RGB (Red, Green, and Blue, CMYK (Cyan, Magenta, Yellow, and Black), grayscale (including black, white, and all shades of gray in between), and CieL*a*b (including separate channels for Lightness [L], red-green [a], and blue-yellow [b]).

Color wheel: an artistic tool that painters use to choose and mix various colors.

Composition: the aesthetic arrangement of the various elements within a photograph. The photographer is responsible for making decisions about what visual elements the photograph will contain and why they are present or mindfully eliminated.

Cone fatigue: when the eyes' cones become incapable of accurately reading color wavelengths entering the eyes because of staring at a color for long periods of time.

Cones: photoreceptors in the eye that are responsible for color vision; sensitive to only one of three colors—red, green, or blue—each cone can be identified as being red-sensitive, green-sensitive, or blue-sensitive.

Conservation mount board: a mount board made of chemically treated wood pulp and available in buffered and unbuffered versions, with the unbuffered versions suitable for mounting photographs.

Contact print: a single print made of a series of negatives placed directly onto light-sensitive photographic paper.

Contact print frame: a combination of glass plus a sturdy backing between which negatives and photographic paper are placed.

Contrast: a measurement of the range from darkness to brightness that a sensor or film can record; also known as *dynamic range*. When discussing contrast in an image, contrast is the amount of difference between the highlights and the shadows within the image.

Copyright owner: a person who has made a creative work. When applied to photography, the copyright owner is the person who pushed the shutter button and made the photograph that is fixed onto film or memory card.

Cornea: the clear, colorless outer covering your eye. It is responsible for protecting your eye from foreign particles and environmental irritants.

Correct exposure: meaning that the film negative (or digital information) produces a photograph in which the light areas and light-colored objects are as light as expected and the shadows and dark objects are as dark as expected from the scene being photographed.

Cotton museum mount board: a mount board made of 100% cotton fiber, a material known to be stable over decades of use; unbuffered versions suitable for mounting photographs.

Covering power (coverage): a measurement of the size of the image a lens makes inside the camera. Different lenses of the same focal length are manufactured to produce a variety of angles of coverage.

Critiquing: the assessment of a photograph, which includes the description of the photograph, a discussion of subject matter, composition, relationship of the appearance of the photo to the intention of the photographer, and whether the photograph supports that intention.

Custom white balance: a feature of some digital cameras that are capable of analyzing a light source and creating a special color temperature correction setting to record the scene with natural colors and without a color cast.

D

Densitometer: a device used to measure the density of film and to plot the shape of a film's characteristic curve. Densitometers can also be used to measure the density of prints.

Density: the build-up of silver in the exposed frames on the negative. The darker areas within a negative are considered denser than the lighter areas.

Depth of field: how much of a scene is in focus from close to the camera to distant from the camera. Depth of field is a function of aperture; a wide-open aperture such as f/4 results in a shallow depth of field, and a narrow aperture such as f/22 will record a scene with a greater depth of field.

Derivative: a copy of a copyrighted work such as a photograph, including small alterations such as cropping, retouching, and layering; or other larger modifications and adaptations, including creating a photomontage from a series of copyrighted photographs.

Destination profile: a series of instructions as to how digital color information will be represented when output; for example, your printer's profile.

Destructive editing: any photo editing that actually changes the color and tonal values of the pixels.

Developer: a chemical used to develop exposed photographic materials.

Developing agent: an organic compound that reduces the exposed silver halide crystals in film to metallic silver. The most common developing agents in developers are metol, phenidone hydroquinone, amidol, or glycin. Sometimes a specific developer will have a blend of these agents.

Device-dependent (-specific): software that pertains to a specific printer, camera, or scanner. New digital cameras and scanners come with software to load onto the computer, allowing the computer to recognize the new device.

Device-independent: when a system, program, or color model does not need to depend on devices, such as cameras or scanners, to interpret or assign the system's codes or values. An example is the CieL*a*b color mode.

Devices: collectively, what cameras, scanners, computers, and printers are called.

Diaphragm: an arrangement of flat, thin pieces of metal that overlap and work together inside the lens to create a variable-sized opening for the light to pass through.

Dodging: in the darkroom, using a light-blocking device to block the enlarger light from striking predetermined areas of a photographic print. Dodging subtracts exposure time from the straight print exposure and results in lightening those selected areas.

Dry down: the phenomenon of prints darkening slightly as they dry in the darkroom. Dry down is a significant factor when determining the optimum exposure time for prints.

DX code: a magnetic code that tells the camera what the film's speed (ISO) is and automatically sets that ISO value in the camera's metering system. If your camera can't read the DX code, you must use a dial on your camera to manually select the proper film speed.

Dynamic range: the breadth of the range of contrast between pure black and pure white that film or digital cameras can record.

E

18% (middle) gray: the average between pure black and pure white. 18% gray is what the light meter renders all exposures unless the photographer overrides the light meter when making the exposure.

Electromagnetic radiation: a form of energy, or *light*.

Enlarger: the machine used to print negatives.

Exclusive rights: all rights to copy, display, change, sell, or license your creative work (documents, images, etc.).

Exif (Exchangeable Image File Format) data: include characteristics of the camera used to capture the image—camera and lens capabilities, focal length of a zoom lens, white balance setting, exposure mode, and the make and model of the camera.

Exposure: the recording of light from the scene in front of the camera. The word "exposure" in photographic terms means that light has been allowed to reach the film (traditional) or light sensor (digital).

Exposure equivalents: the combinations of aperture and shutter speed that will yield the exact same exposure for a given scene. Exposure equivalents are accurate, provided there are no changes in lighting conditions or film speed/ISO settings.

Exposure latitude: a measure of the forgiveness of a film to be overexposed or underexposed and still produce a relatively good print.

Expressive photography: an image created with the intention of reflecting inner thoughts.

F

Fair Use Doctrine: added to federal copyright law to free use of copyrighted works for purposes of education, research, and criticism, among other purposes.

Falloff: the area where a bright area on a three-dimensional form transforms to darkness.

Fast falloff: when the length of falloff is very short, appearing as a relatively sharp line of demarcation between highlight and shadow.

Fast lens: a lens with unusually wide aperture capabilities. Aperture settings of 1.4 or 2.8 allow photographers to use faster shutter speeds because so much light can enter the lens.

Fill light: typically a large light source (a light with umbrella or softbox) set just to the side of, and behind, the camera; illuminates the entire face (hence, the term "fill light").

Filler board: a mat board placed behind the mounted print to take up any empty space between the mounted print and the back edge of the frame.

Film grain: the empty space between the particles of silver on film. When negatives from higher ISO films are enlarged to prints, the empty space between the particles of silver on the film can make the prints appear grainy.

Film plane: the place inside the camera where the film rests, ready to be exposed to light. Film must be exactly parallel to the lens to ensure that every portion is exposed and focused identically.

Film plane shutter: found in film-based SLR and viewfinder cameras, this shutter is mounted toward the back of the camera body, just in front of the film plane; synonymous with *focal plane shutter*.

Film speed (ISO or ASA): a numeric representation (100, 200, 400, etc.) of a film's sensitivity to light. It is related to the size of the silver halide particles within the film. The finer the particles, the more light is needed to transform the silver halide particles into the latent image state. As film speed increases, film grain becomes larger and less light is required to make correct exposures.

Film washer: a specialized film reel holder with a connecting tube hooked up to a water faucet.

Finishes: paper textures such as glossy, matte, and low-luster.

Fixed focal length (prime) lens: a lens designed with a single, or unchangeable, focal length.

Flat image: a photograph with too little contrast.

Focal length: a measurement of the distance from the principal plane (outer edge) of the lens to the rear nodal point, the point at which light rays converge inside the lens to a single point; usually measured in millimeters.

Focal-plane shutter: a multiple-component shutter mounted toward the back of the camera body, just forward of the film plane, where the film travels. During an exposure, the shutter opens for a preset length of time, allowing for an exposure of varying speeds, depending on the shutter speed set for that photograph; synonymous with *film-plane shutter*.

Frame: an individual image recorded on the film or digital recording media. A "frame" is one photograph.

Framing the photo in-camera: carefully composing your image before making the photograph to avoid additional cropping in post-production.

Front light: a condition where the light source is directly behind the camera and aimed directly at the subject. Front light acts to somewhat flatten the subject.

f-stop (relative aperture): a measurement found by dividing the focal length of a lens by the effective diameter of its aperture.

Full stop: a specific incremental difference in light between one exposure setting and another. Changing the aperture or the shutter speed to exactly double or cut in half the amount of light for the exposure is changing that setting by 1 full stop. A 1-second shutter speed allows exactly 1 full stop more exposure of light than a half-second. Changing the aperture from f/5.6 to f/8, or f/16 to f/11, is a full-stop change.

Full-frame print: a print that includes all of the visual information on the original 35 mm negative.

G

Gamma (midtone): the middle gray value range of an image falling between the highlight and shadow areas of an image.

Gamut: the subset of all possible colors that appear within a given color space.

Gamut of a sensor: the range of colors a camera's sensor can collect.

Gating: the time during which a camera's sensor is collecting light information coming through the lens.

Gestalt: a German word generally meaning the "essence or shape of an entity's complete form, or the unified whole of an entity."

Glass: as a mounting material, comes in two forms, standard and nonglare etched glass, with the latter perhaps containing acid and therefore not a good choice for mounting photographs.

Glazing: the material covering the photograph and mat board, typically consisting of glass or acrylic sheets.

Global corrections: corrections to the entire image.

Graded photographic papers: these darkroom papers range from grade 1 (to dramatically decrease contrast) to grade 4 (to dramatically increase contrast). A grade 2 paper is considered to be the best paper for normal-contrast negatives.

Gray card: a camera accessory manufactured to give 18% gray reflectance.

Grayscale: an image whose pixels contain only black, white, or shades of gray.

H

Hair light: the light in a classic portrait that adds dimension and spark of interest by illuminating the top of the model's head and highlighting the tops of the model's shoulders.

Hardening agent: a chemical compound that hardens the emulsion of the film to help protect it from scratching.

High-key image: an image with visual information mostly lighter than middle gray.

Highlights: bright areas in a scene or photograph that contain details that add to your understanding of the image.

Horizon line: traditionally, the line where the sky meets the ground. Whether real or imaginary, the horizon line within the photo tends to divide the scene into sections.

Horizontal format: a photo that is wider than it is tall. Horizontal formats tend to lend a sense of peace or stability to the photograph.

I

Image circle: a circular image projected onto the film or sensor as light passes through the lens. It always extends beyond the rectangle perimeter of the film or sensor, allowing the film or sensor to capture a rectangular (or square) image.

Image stabilization (IS): a function that some cameras have, allowing them to steady themselves enough to compensate for natural *camera shake*, or movement from handholding a camera.

Incident light: the available light that happens to be falling onto your object, regardless of the light source.

Ingestion: to take in as if for digestion; can take place if food or beverages are brought into a room containing darkroom chemicals.

Inhalation (of chemical vapors): breathing in; a hazard when using and working with darkroom chemicals.

Intensity value: a measurement of brightness (ranging from darkest to lightest).

Intentions: the photographer's thoughts about a photograph, including answers to the following questions: What do you want to photograph? Why do you want to photograph it? What message are you trying to send to your viewers? What action or reaction do you hope to elicit from your viewers?

Inverse square law: a law of physics that states light intensity is inversely proportional to the square of the distance.

IPTC: the International Press Telecommunications Council, the group that approved the IPTC Core specification in 2004.

Iris: behind the cornea, the colored portion of your eye.

ISO (or ASA): an agreed-upon standard of measurement of the sensitivity of film or digital sensor to light.

J

JPEG (.jpg): a format that compresses images into smaller file sizes than do the Photoshop or TIFF file formats.

K

Key light: the main light used for a portrait. A key light is generally set off to the side of, and slightly above, your model, creating a sense of three-dimensional form.

Keystoning: the deformity observed when a photograph is made with the camera on a different plane than the flat structure being photographed. The classic keystoning example is seen when a camera is tilted back to photograph a tall building. The top of the building appears much narrower than the bottom of the building.

L

Latent image: the combination of light striking, and influencing, a yet undeveloped roll of film or sheet of photographic paper. The potential is there, but without chemical intervention, the film remains opaque or the paper remains white.

Layer mask: a Photoshop function that allows you to hide pixels on a layer without actually erasing those pixels. A layer mask can be created for any layer other than the Background layer.

Leading lines: elements within the composition of a photograph that lead the viewer's eyes through the photograph.

Leaf shutter: a series of individual, spring-mounted metal leaves that move in an extremely fast, synchronous pattern to allow light into the camera, allowing almost all of the light from the scene to enter the camera at the same time.

Leakage current: when heat generated in the CCD or CMOS sensor creates an electrical signal indistinguishable from the signal originating from light coming through the lens. Leakage current is sometimes called *dark current*.

Legal claim: a legal complaint.

Lens: a gelatinous disc, convex on both sides, residing immediately behind the iris. Bending the light coming into your eye, the lens changes shape as you focus your eyes to different distances.

Lens flare: rays from a bright light source hitting the lens at an obtuse angle, scattering light into the final image. Lens flares can create unexpected bright spots and/or wash out an image, leaving it lighter than intended.

Lighting ratio: the mathematical ratio of power levels between the key and fill lights.

Light-tight: meaning that light coming through the lens during an exposure is the only light that can reach the camera's film or sensor.

Lignin: a naturally occurring substance in wood that can damage prints.

Localized corrections: compositing or retouching corrections made in localized areas.

Lossy compression: a method of saving a digital file that compresses the digital information by throwing away small amounts of color information.

Low-key image: an image with visual information mostly darker than middle gray.

M

Macro setting: this lens feature allows a shorter minimum focusing distance than the same lens built without a macro setting. Some zoom lenses also come with macro settings.

Manual (M) mode: a camera mode that allows you to set both the aperture and shutter speed.

Mat board: a mount board with a colored and/or textured surface on one side, which is not acid-free and should not be used to mount photographs; best used as an overmat.

Megapixels: the number of pixels digital cameras are capable of gathering during an exposure. A 6-megapixel camera can gather approximately 18 MB of information.

Merger: an unexpected, funny, or frustrating intersection that is typically seen only after the photograph has been taken and shown to someone else. An example would be a telephone pole that seems to stick out of someone's head.

Metamerism: a function of human perception that allows us to print a photo of a real object, such as an apple or orange, that looks to us exactly like the real object even though no red or orange ink is used to make the print.

Middle gray: the halfway point between the brightest possible value (white) and the darkest possible value (black).

Middle Input slider (Midpoint Gamma slider): the gray triangle midpoint between the Black point and the White point on the Levels input histogram. Moving the Midpoint Gamma slider to the right will darken the middle values of an image; moving it to the left will lighten the middle values of an image.

Midtone: a reflected light value that falls between the highlights and the shadows; an area of medium brightness in a scene or photograph.

Minimum focusing distance: the least distance the camera can be set from the subject and have that subject come into focus. All lenses have a minimum focusing distance.

Model release: a written contract that allows you to publish photographs of the people you have photographed.

Monitor profile: a file of information, including how color will be displayed, about a specific monitor.

N

Negative: as a photographic exposure is created, reflected light strikes the film surface. Once processed, the light-sensitive film reacts by turning darker where the scene's light was brighter, and becomes increasingly transparent where the scene's light was darker. A photographic print is produced from a negative.

No derivative works condition: a copyright license condition whereby the copyright owner allows others to copy, distribute, display, and perform only verbatim (unchanged) copies of the work; no derivative works are permissible.

Noise: a phenomenon that occurs when CMOS sensors misread the electronic information, creating visual flecks that don't match the rest of an image.

Noncommercial condition: a copyright license condition whereby the copyright owner allows others to copy, distribute, display, and perform the work and any derivative works based on that work, provided the use is for noncommercial purposes only; the copyright owner would separately negotiate any commercial use of the work.

Nondestructive editing: image editing that changes the *appearance* of the pixels without changing the actual color or values of the original pixels.

Nonexclusive rights: when one allows another to use a copyrighted creative work (photographs, etc.) for a specified purpose or period of time, but not permanently.

Normal focal length: the view from left to right within a scene approximately equal to the field of vision with only one eye open. It can also be thought of as the approximate length of the diagonal of the camera's format. The diagonal length of a single frame of a 35 mm film (a single negative on a roll of 35 mm film) is approximately 50 mm. A normal lens is one that neither enlarges (draws objects in a scene closer) nor widens the view (pushes objects in a scene back). On 35 mm cameras, a 50 mm lens is considered normal.

O

Opening up the aperture: increasing the diameter of the aperture; changing the f-stop to a larger opening, such as from f/11 to f/8.

Optical coating: a lens coating that increases the actual transmission of light to the camera. Optical coatings also reduce the amount of scattered light within the lens itself, therefore reducing the possibility of lens flare.

Optic nerve: where the neural network, or the network of sensory nerves, converges; the major nerve that transports the electrical impulses to the brain.

Orphan work: a work protected under copyright law but whose copyright owner cannot be identified or located.

Overexposure: allowing an exposure of more light than needed to reach the photographically sensitive material. Shadow (dark) areas will be lighter than expected, and lighter areas may be so light as to not record detail. Overexposure can be an intentional tool used by knowledgeable photographers who wish to impart aesthetic qualities.

Overmat: a mat with a window in it to cover the borders of the photograph and to ensure that the print lies flat.

P

Parabola: a parabolic-shaped cover that channels and directs the light of a strobe head.

Parallax: a phenomenon causing a visual discrepancy between what is seen through the viewfinder and what the camera ultimately records, risking pictures that are slightly low and off center, even though the scene was perfectly composed when seen through the viewfinder.

Penetration (of chemicals): absorption of chemicals through broken skin; a hazard of using and working with darkroom chemicals.

Pentaprism: located above the mirror of an SLR camera, a pentaprism reverts the image to right-side up so you can see the scene as it appears when viewed in the real world.

Perception: different from strict visual information, perception determines what you notice in a scene and how you recognize shapes and colors.

Perspective: the art of giving realistic, expected depth to a two-dimensional image. We are accustomed to seeing depth in our everyday world. A row of trees is tallest where it is closet to us, yet shortest at its farthest distance from us.

pH: a measurement of the acidity or alkalinity of a substance.

Photo buyer: a person looking for images to use in publications.

Photons: tiny particles of light.

Photoshop (.psd): format used whenever you are working with layers in Photoshop; format can only be guaranteed to open in Photoshop (all versions) and the Adobe InDesign (CS4 and up) page layout program; safely maintains all of the layering you create during your digital darkroom work.

Photosite: one section of the grid of a light-sensitive section of a CMOS or CCD sensor. Also loosely referred to as a *pixel*, an acronym for picture elements. Each individual photosite creates 1 pixel of information in the final image.

Pinhole camera: a simple, light-tight box with a tiny hole on one side and a method of holding film on the opposite side. The earliest form of camera, the pinhole camera has no lens.

Pixel: an acronym for "picture element." A pixel is one tiny square within the photograph. It can represent any 1 of 16.7 million different colors, but it can only be one color at any given time.

Pixel preservation (nondestructive editing): the practice of using Adjustment layers to suggest changes to pixels without actually affecting the changes on those pixels. The final change takes place only once when the layers are flattened in the final image.

Pixel wasteland: regions close to the Black or White points on a histogram that contain no pixels.

Point-and-shoot: a term used for cameras with few controls. Either the camera determines exposure and focus settings automatically or there are limited adjustments designed into the device. Point-and-shoot cameras frequently have a rangefinder optical system.

Positive: another term for "positive" would be "as the scene looked." Areas that were dark in the scene appear dark in the print; areas that were light in the scene appear light in the print.

Posterization: the shifting of colors within a photograph due to changes within Levels or Curves, resulting in many values that have no pixels on a histogram.

Preservative: a chemical compound added to developer to keep it fresh over time. Developers tend to oxidize rapidly in water, rendering them useless for film processing. The preservative retards this oxidation process.

Prime lens: a lens that has only one fixed focal length; to change how much to photograph within a scene, you need to move toward or away from that scene to make the change.

Principal plane: the plane including the point of the lens farthest distant from the camera body.

Profiling: the act of measuring and identifying the gamut of colors that a particular camera or other device renders.

Profile mismatch: occurs when your camera's color mode setting is different than the working color space within Photoshop.

Program mode: a camera mode that typically reads the film's or camera's ISO setting and then invokes your camera's light meter to select the proper aperture and shutter speed for the exposure.

Public domain: a category of creative works that is not protected by copyright law. Works in the public domain may be used without need for copyright permission.

Pupil: the hole in the iris that allows light to pass through the front of your eye.

R

Rangefinder optical system: the device that separates the viewfinder from the lens making the image. The viewfinder itself is placed above and often to the side of the lens; therefore, the viewfinder doesn't point to the exact spot as the lens.

Rear nodal point: the point at which the incoming light rays converge to a single point. The image traveling through the lens flips upside down at the rear nodal point.

Raw conversion: when a camera's ADC converts the analog information to digital information, conducts a variety of image-altering procedures, and creates a JPEG image.

Reflection loss: the amount of light reflected back from the lens. Reflection loss, whenever light moves from air to glass, is typically about 7%. Modern antireflection optical coatings are capable of reducing the reflection loss to less than 0.5%.

Reflective light meter: an in-camera meter that measures the amount of light reflected from the scene and sets the exposure accordingly.

Replenisher: an agent that is added to the developer tank to help restore the developer to full activity.

Resolution: the number of pixels that fall across a linear inch. The resolution of an image is given as pixels per inch (ppi).

Restrainer: included in developers, restrainers prevent the developing agents from affecting any silver halide crystals that have been exposed to small amounts of light. Without a restrainer, some of this slightly exposed silver halide would change to metallic silver.

Retina: the lining in the back of your eye, containing 125 million specialized photoreceptor cells that transform light information into electrical impulses.

Rim light: light illuminating the edge of a subject when the subject is backlit. Rim light is a slight overflow of light that helps to separate the subject from the background; the subject is also fully visible while being surrounded by the rim lighting.

Rods: photoreceptors in the eye that are responsible for collecting and interpreting light in terms of black, white, and shades of gray.

Rule of thirds: used to determine those areas of interest, which are at the four intersections of four imaginary lines drawn to divide the composition into thirds horizontally and again vertically.

S

Safelight: an amber-colored (yellow) light used in darkrooms during black-and-white printing. Photographic paper is sensitive to blue light. Because blue and orange are opposites on the color wheel, photographic paper doesn't respond to low intensities of amber-colored light.

Safelight fog: a phenomenon that occurs when photographic paper is exposed to a safelight for a long period of time, or if a darkroom safelight is too bright. Safelight fog can darken the highlights of a print.

Scenes a faire: a portion of copyright law that stipulates that components of a scene that must be contained in any photo of that scene (such as the shape of the building or its surrounding buildings) are not copyright protected.

Scheimpflug principle: a law of physics that describes the increased depth of field you get by tilting the front lens of a large-format camera forward while keeping the film plane in its original position.

Sensory nerves of the eye: a very fine, nearly invisible network of nerves that covers the rods and cones in the eyes, gathering visual information collected by photoreceptors and transporting it to the optic nerve and ultimately to the brain.

Shadows: dark areas in a scene, slide (transparency), or print that may contain detail or may be too dark to hold any detail.

Share alike condition: a copyright license condition whereby the copyright owner allows others to distribute derivative works only under a license identical to the one that the copyright owner originally placed on the work.

Short lighting: when the key light is placed on the opposite side of the model's ear facing the camera.

Shutter: a mechanical barrier inside a camera that prevents light from contacting the film or sensor, except when the photographer opens and closes it when creating a photograph.

Shutter Priority (Tv) mode: a camera mode that allows you to select a shutter speed setting according to your need to stop action in your scene.

Shutter speed: the length of time the shutter remains open during a photographic exposure. Many advanced cameras are capable of shutter speeds ranging from 1/4,000 second to "bulb," which allows a photographer to lock a shutter open indefinitely, sometimes for hours.

Sidelight: a condition where the light source is to either side of the camera. Sidelight brings out the texture in the subject and tends to make it appear more three-dimensional.

Silhouette: an image in which the subject is so dark as to be nearly or totally void of detail, and the surrounding scene is lighter and almost always contains much more visual information. A silhouette is most often backlit.

Silver gelatin print: a black-and-white print made in a traditional darkroom; this term differentiates a traditional darkroom black-and-white print from an inkjet print that might look similar to it.

Simultaneous contrast: occurs when two squares of the exact same color are surrounded by different colors, causing the viewer to think the two squares are different in color.

Slave: an electronic device that detects a flash from other strobes and fires its own strobe.

Slope of a characteristic curve: The portion of a characteristic curve that correlates with the midtones in an image. The portion of an image that falls on the slope of a characteristic curve will have good separation between tones, allowing a considerable amount of detail to be rendered in the photograph.

Slow falloff: a lighting condition in which the length of light falloff is longer, resulting in a broader space between the brightest and darkest portions of an object's surface.

Slow lens: a lens with unusually narrow maximum aperture capabilities. Maximum aperture settings of 5.6 or 8.0 force photographers to use unusually long shutter speeds to compensate for the decreased amount of light entering the lens.

SLR camera: a single-lens reflex camera uses an optical system involving a mirror and pentaprism inside the camera. The image seen in the viewfinder is the same as the image being taken in by the lens. There is no issue of parallax with SLR cameras.

Snapshot: a quick, minimally planned photographic capture of a scene.

Source profile: for example, the colors your scanner or digital camera can capture.

Spectral data: color information gathered from spectrophotometers.

Spectrophotometer: a mechanical device that measures the wavelengths of color within the visible spectrum; typically used to measure color on printed materials.

Specular highlights: very bright areas created by light bouncing off chrome, headlights, or other highly reflective surfaces within the photograph.

Square format: a photo with equal height and width. Many older and medium-format cameras use square-format film.

sRGB: the gamut of colors recommended by many printing labs; has a significantly smaller gamut than Adobe RGB.

Standard mount board: a mount board made of unpurified wood pulp that slowly breaks down over time, subjecting a print to acidity and potential damage.

Stock photo agency: a business that promotes (on behalf of photographers) a wide range of photographic images to advertisers and publishers for the purpose of publication.

Stock photographer: a photographer who creates photographs with the intention of selling various publication rights to publishers.

Stock solution: a powder or liquid concentrate form that needs to be mixed with water and stored in dark (brown or black) plastic containers; considerably stronger than the solution actually used to develop film or photographic paper.

Straight exposure: when all areas of a darkroom print are exposed equally without burning or dodging. Straight exposures reveal areas that require burning (additional exposure) or dodging (less exposure).

Straight print: a print made of an entire negative at a single exposure.

Strobe lights: daylight-balanced studio flash units.

Subtractive color system: a color system consisting of combinations of cyan, magenta, yellow, and black. Together these four colors create black. They are the four colors of ink used in most color printing processes.

Sunny f/16 Rule, the: when photographing outdoors on a sunny day, use the following formula: 1/ISO = shutter speed at an aperture of f/16.

T

Tangible form: for photographers, typically either film or the digital file.

Telephoto lens: a lens with a focal length longer than 50 mm in 35 mm cameras. Telephoto lenses act like binoculars in that they narrow the field of view and also magnify the scene.

Telephoto view: a field of view that is narrower than usual where objects in the frame appear closer to the photographer than they would with a normal lens.

TIFF: "tagged information file format," (.tif); relatively universal image file format in that many software programs can open them.

Tonal values: range in brightness, or *values* along the tonal range between pure black and pure white; always given in grayscale terms and completely separate from color.

True color: the capacity for a computer to display 16.7 million different colors.

U

Underexposure: an exposure of less light than needed to properly record a scene onto film or sensor. Shadow areas are darker than expected and may not contain intended detail. Lighter areas are darker than expected. Accomplished photographers can intentionally use underexposure to impart aesthetic qualities.

V

Value: the range of black through progressively lighter grays to white within an image; typically described as *light*, *medium*, or *dark*.

Variable contrast photographic paper: paper that requires a filter, the choice of which dictates the resulting contrast of the negative, to be inserted under the lens on the enlarger head; the filters are numbered by grades, grade 1 (to dramatically lower contrast) by half-grades to grade 4 (to dramatically increase contrast).

Vertical format: an image wider than it is tall.

Viewfinder: in a camera, a small window through which one looks to compose and focus the scene one is photographing.

Viewfinder camera: a camera design that uses a rangefinder optical system. Many point-and-shoot cameras use this system.

Vignetting: darkening of an image's corners by cutting off or shading the corners of a photograph. Vignetting can also be added in post-production in Photoshop.

W

White point: the point at which pixels have a value of 255 in each Red, Green, and Blue channel in the RGB color system, or they have the value of 0% in each of the Cyan, Magenta, Yellow, and Black channel of the CMYK color system.

White space: any section of a photograph with minimal visual information so that text can be dropped into place later on. That empty space is called *white space*, regardless of what color it actually is in the photograph.

Wide-angle lens: a lens with a focal length shorter than 50 mm in 35 mm cameras. Wide-angle lenses allow photography of large areas, such as mountains or football stadiums.

Wide-angle view: a broader, wider field of view than a normal view. Typically, objects in the wide field of view appear to be farther away from the photographer than they would with a normal lens.

Work for hire: when a company employs a person to produce creative work and then maintains and owns the copyright for that work.

Working solution: a stock solution further diluted with water.

X

XMP sidecar file: a separate file, attached to the original file, containing adjustments made to an original file.

Z

Zone System: a system of evaluating reflected light and exposure values that Ansel Adams introduced to the photographic world in his book, *The Negative*, in 1981.

Zoom lens: a lens with variable focal length capability. Typically, a zoom lens ranges from medium wide-angle to medium telephoto ability and can be infinitely varied between the two.

Index

A

absorption (of chemicals), 102
accelerator, 105
acrylic glazing, 164
additive color, 282
adjustment layer, 219
Adobe Bridge, 183–184, 196–197, 202–203, 402–403
    collections, 185–186
    file organizations, 184
    labeling, 186–187
    opening, 183–184
    rating, 186–187
Adobe Camera Raw
    bit depth, 191–192
    chromatic aberration, removal, 194–195
    color balancing, 188–189
    exposure, 189–190
    image capturing, 180
    image cropping, 193–194
    image sharpening, 252–254
    initial adjustment, 187
    noise reduction, 249–252
    opening, 187, 195–197
    quality adjustments, color, 190–191
    resolution, 191–192
    saving option, 195–197
    space setting, 191
    spot removal tool, 240–242
    straightening, 192–193
    XMP Sidecar, editing, 197
Adobe Photoshop
    color modes in, 276
    combining in, 260
    document size, changing of, 200–201
    dust and scratches filter, 248–249
    formatting, 203
    help menu, 247
    history panel, 246
    layer masks, 265–267
    opening, 198
    patch tool, 244–245
    pixel layers, 265–267
    resolution, 199–200
    saving options, 202
    sharpening tools, 253
    Smart Sharpen filter in, 256–257
    spot healing brush tool, 242–244
    tips, effective use, 267 *See also* image development, Adobe Photoshop
Adobe RGB, 280
African American Museum, 5
alpha channel, 216
angle of coverage, 42
angle of view, 42
antihalation coating, 99
aperture, 30–31
    in Aperture Priority mode, 73, 74
    explanation of, 30–34
    matching your intention, 84–85
    opening up and closing down (or stopping down), 73
    in Program mode, 72–73
Aperture Priority mode (Av), 73–74
    closing down, 73
    opening up, 73 *See also* depth of field
archival, 162
archival processing
    definition, 150
    steps, involved in, 150–151
Artist statement
    Detroit Disassembled (Moore), 12
    image combination (Lirakis), 17
    emphasizing the elements, 144
    color management (Simonite), 279
    lighting techniques (Baumann), 313
    compositional strategies (Eckert), 336
    high-resolution scans (Hahn), 339
    shooting preparation (Faulk), 351
    reassembling (Mintio), 369
    image cropping (Mattingly and Salinger), 372
    metaphorical expression (Zinn), 374
    urban forest Katrina damages (Mullins), 376
    family history (Murakam and Ameyden), 380
ASA (American Standards Association), 86
    film speed, 86
atmospheric perspective, 345
attribution condition, 394
attribution no-derivatives condition, 395
attribution noncommercial condition, 395
attribution noncommercial no-derivatives condition, 395
attribution noncommercial share-alike condition, 395
attribution share-alike condition, 395

B

background light, 319
    hair lighting in, 321–322
    incorrect, examples, 319–321
backlight, 303
back paper, 164
battery care, 50
bit depth, 80–82
bits, 37
black-and-white, chemistry of
    developer, 104–105
    fixer, 105
    hypo clearing agents, 106
    replenisher, 105
    stop bath, 105
    threading, 106
    washer, 106
black-and-white film developing, 103
black-and-white film, processing, 108–111
    canister measurement, 106
    contrast control, 116
    equipments, assembling, 107–108
    exposure, 117
    location, selection, 107
    push processing, 116–117
    storage, 111–112

temperature, chemicals, 107
threading, 106 *See also* 4 × 5 sheet
film, loading and developing
black-and-white image, 182
black point, 80
blocked-up shadows, 75 *See also*
underexposure
blooming, 71
blown-out highlights, 75 *See also*
overexposure
boom, 312
bracketing, 68
brightness, 78
brightness range (levels), 78
broad lighting, 315
burning and dodging
documentation of, 148–150
in the traditional darkroom, 144–148
Bulb mode, 74
burning, 144
business-related forms, 409

C

C-41, 121
cable release, 209
camera body, 26–32
camera lenses, 26–30
focusing distances in, 28
optional functions, 28–30
types, 26–28
camera, protection
dirt and dust, 48
fresh water, 47
from salt conditions, 47
heat, 46
humidity, 46
tips, 47
travel concerns, 47
camera raw files, 180
cameras
body of, 26
early history, 23–24
point-and-shoot, 25 *See also specific*
cameras
camera settings
Aperture Priority mode (Av), 73, 74
camera raw, 180
custom white balance, 301
Manual mode (M), 74
Program mode (P), 72–73
Shutter Priority mode (Tv), 74
camera types
cell phone cameras, 44
digital camera sensors, 34–36

large-format (monorail) cameras,
41–44
medium-format cameras, 39–40
pinhole cameras, 23, 40–41
plastic cameras, 40
point-and-shoot cameras, 25
SLR (single-lens reflex) cameras, 25
viewfinder cameras, 24
catchlight, 337
CCD (charge-coupled device), 36
Cedar Rapids, 5
cell phone cameras, 44
center-weighted averaging, 62
characteristic curves of film, 99–101
chromatic aberration, 194
chromogenic film, 99
CieL*a*b color mode, 274–276
clipped, 189
closing (stopping) down the aperture, 73
CMOS (complementary metal-oxide
semiconductor), 36
image, saving, 38
sensor sizes, 36–38
CMYK (cyan, magenta, yellow, black) color
mode, 280, 282–283
collage work, copyrighted photographs, 392
collection of photographs
critiquing, 375–376
questioning, 376–379
color
in composition of photos, 345,
358–360
in different cultures, 119
perception, 119–120
primary and secondary
colors, 360
temperature in light, 299–302
color films
C-41 processing, 121–122
color creation in, 120–121
E-6 processing, 122–123
impact, on photography, 119
perception, 119–120
processing of, 118 *See also* color
print, processing of
colorimeters, 273
colorimetric data, 273
color models, 273
color perception
composition issues, 279
cone fatigue, 277
metamerism, 277–278
simultaneous contrast, 277
surroundings, controlling of, 278

color print, processing of, 152–153
filtration system, 152
color spaces, 273–276
color systems (modes)
additive color, 121
CieL*a*b, 274–276
CMYK (cyan, magenta, yellow, black),
280, 282–283
RGB (red, green, blue), 274
subtractive color, 282
color temperature, 299–300
color wheel, 360
commercial and studio photography, 312–313
composition
closure, 337
clutter removal, 355–356
edges, 348
experiment possibilities, 362
figure/ground, 337
foreground *vs.* background, 341
format, 342
framing and cropping decisions in,
352–353
gestalt, 336, 346–347
horizon line, 343–344
leading lines, 357
mergers, 350
motion, contrast and, 360
moving within, 349
patterns, 357
perspective and depth, 349
proximity, 336
role of color in, 345–346
shapes, 340–342
similarity, 336
stock photography, 357
touching, color, 358–360
visual communication and, 334–335
white spacing in, 356–357 *See also*
rule of thirds
composition of photographs
colors, 345, 358–360
contrast, 297–299
definition of, 334
foreground *vs.* background, 229
format, 342–343
full-frame *vs.* cropped, 352
horizontal line, 343–344
leading lines, 348, 357
lights *vs.* darks, 337–338
mergers, 350
movement in and through, 349
patterns, 358
perspective and depth, 349–350

rule of thirds, 353–354
shapes, 340–342
white space, 356–357
condenser enlargers, 132–134
cone fatigue, 277
cones, 293
conservation mount board, 163
contact print, 137–140
exposure in, 137–138, 140
contact print frame, 137
contrast, 116
copyright laws, 385
education and research, 392
exceptions, 389
exclusive and nonexclusive rights,
389–391
ownership rights, 389
registration, photographs, 391
scenes a faire, 393–394
solutions, 394
work for hire, 391
copyright license conditions, 394–396 See
also specific licenses
copyright owner, 386
cornea, 292
correct exposures, 26, 61
cotton museum mount board, 163
coverage or covering power of lenses, 43
critiquing photographs, 367–380
explanation of, 369, 371
judging, images, 380
opinions vs., 375
questions to ask, 371–375
ways to be critiqued, 375–380
crop tool, 258–259
custom white balance, 301

D

darkroom printing
practicing of, 130
safelight, 130–131 See also enlarger
darkroom, safety requirements
children, 103
inhalation, 103
penetration and absorption, chemicals, 102–103
pets, 103
pregnant women, 103
darkroom (traditional) setup, 102–103
densitometer, 99
density, 86
depth of field
aperture controls and, 82–83
apparent (not real), 27

button preview, 85–86
creativity in, 84–85
examples of shallow and great,
82–83
preview, 85
using a small aperture opening, 83
using different lenses, 26–28
derivatives
definition, 393
destination profile, 283
destructive editing, 245
developer, 104
developing agent, 105
device-dependent (-specific), 274
device independent, 275
devices, 273
diaphragm, 29–30, 59
diffusion enlargers, 134
digital camera sensors, 34–36
digital color management
CieL*a*b, 274–276
color models, 273–274
external tools, 281–282
history, 272
human factor, 276–277. See also
color perception
ProPhoto RGB, 274
RGB, 274
role in photography, 272–273
steps in, 277–281
types, mechanical means, 273
digital color print
head alignment, 285
ICC profiles, 283–284
light color vs., 282–283
nozzle check, 284
permanence, 287–288
preferences, 285–287
preparing, 284
digital images
16-bit vs. 8-bit, 211, 226
color spaces, 273–276
color systems (modes)
CieL*a*b, 274–276
CMYK (cyan, magenta, yellow,
black), 280, 282–283
RGB (red, green, blue), 274
evaluating images on the computer,
77–78
flattening images, 190, 197, 232
grayscale vs. black-and-white
images, 280, 293
image quality, 179–180
ISO settings, 88

monitor
calibration, 278–279
displays, 181–182
resolution, 182
types of noise, 88–89 See also
photoshop computer software
digital ISO setting
exposure equivalents, 59
film speed, 86–88
mode settings, 72–74, 82
random noise, 88
digital medium-format cameras, 39
digital noise
leakage current, 89–90
random noise, 88–89
row and column noise, 90
types, 88–90
digital photograph
displays, 181–182
image quality in, 179
quality settings, 179–180
resolution, 182 See also specific
designing software
dodging, 144
dry down, 143
dust
in digital sensor, 49
in internal mirror, 49
DX code, 87
dynamic range, 70–72, 209

E

18% or middle gray, 61, 65–66
electromagnetic radiation, 294
electronic identification, 402–405
camera (Exif) data, 405
file properties, 404
IPTC core, 404–405
keywords, 405–406
metadata templates, creation,
406–409
enlarger, 131–132
easel alignment in, 134
lens and aperture, 133–134
types of, 131–133
exclusive rights, 389
Exif (Exchangeable Image File Format)
data, 405
exposure
aesthetic decisions, 59–60, 76–77,
82–84
critical elements, 59
equivalents in, 59
evaluation, 77–78

learning techniques, 90 *See also* good exposure
exposure latitude, 101
exposure lock metering, 63–65
exposures
  aesthetic aspects, 82–86
  bracketing, 68
  correct exposures, 26, 61
  definition of, 23, 90
  equivalents, 59
  evaluation of, 77–78
  exposure compensation (overriding), 65
  latitude, 101
  overexposure and underexposure, 75, 90
  technical aspects
    dynamic range, 70–72, 209
    film speed (ISO or ASA), 86–90
expressive photography
  definition, 7

F

Fair Use Doctrine, 392
falloff, 297
fast falloff, 297
fast lens, 32
fiber-based papers, 136
field of vision, 26–27
file formats
  camera raw, 180
  JPEG (Joint Photographic Experts Group), 180
  Photoshop, 180
  TIFF (tagged information file format), 203
fill light, 318
filler board, 164
film
  black-and-white negative, 99
  characteristic curves, 99
  chromogenic, 99
  color
    components of, 118
    kinds of, 121–122
    traditional printing, 136–137
  exposure latitude, 101
  processing steps and materials
    black-and-white negative, 99
    color, C-41 processing, 121–122
    color, E-6 processing, 122–123
  sizes, 39
  speed (ISO or ASA), 59, 61, 86–90, 116
film grain, 86, 118

film plane, 33
  shutter, 33
film speed (ISO or ASA), 86
film washer, 106
filters
  color correction, 300
  UV filters, 308
finishes, 136
fixed focal length (or prime) lenses, 25, 28
flat image, 142
flattening images, 190, 197, 232
focal lengths, 25–27, 31
focal-plane shutters, 33
4 × 5 sheet film, loading and developing
  exposure evaluation, 115
  sheet film holders, 112–115
frames, 39, 164
  hanging accessories, 164
framing the photograph in-camera, 353
front light, 302
f-stop (relative aperture)
  lists of, 30–32
full stop, 32
full-frame print, 352

G

gamma (midtone), 211
gamut, 273
gamut of a sensor, 280
gating, 34
gestalt, 336
glass, 164
glazing, 164
global corrections, 187
GNU Free Documentation License, 395–396
good exposure
  definition, 90
graded papers, 134
graded photographic papers, 134
gray card, 64
grayscale, 280, 293

H

hair light, 321
half-stop, 32
handheld meters, 69–70
  incident lighting, 69–70
  lighting sources, option, 70
hardening agent, 106
Henry Wilhelm Imaging, 288
high-contrast image, 99, 211, 297
high-key image, 337, 339
highlights, 61

histogram
  brightness levels, 78–79
  interpretation, 80
horizontal format, 342
horizontal line, 343–345
Huth & Booth Photographic Artists, 174–175

I

ICC profiles, 283–284
image circle, 43
image development, Adobe Photoshop
  adjustment layers, 219–222
  alpha channels, 216–217
  Brush tool operations, 228–229
  color balancing, 221
  curves box, adjustments, 225–226
  edges, 217–219
  HDR merging, 209
    Pro options, 211–213
  levels adjustments, 223–225
  lightening and darkening process, 231–232
  pixel-based layers, 229–231
  Quick Mask mode, 227
  selection, 214
    Lasso tool, 214–215
    Marquee tool, 214–215
  straightening images. *See* ruler tool
  tonal value adjustments, 222–223
  values, manual evaluation of, 226
image stabilization (IS), 28
incident light, 69
individual photographs
  critiquing, 370
  questioning, 371–375
infrared film
  developing, 124
  digital cameras and, 124–125
  effective usage, 123
  film speed, 124
  image focusing, 124
  printing, 124
  purchasing, 124
  storing, 124
  traveling, 124
ingestion, 102
inhalation (of chemical vapors), 103
intensity value, 181
intentions, 16
  definition, 16
intentions for photographs
  with color temperature, 299
  and composition, 362
  by controlling the aperture, 84–85

by controlling the exposure, 76–78
with lighting, 303
questions to ask, 371
reasons for making photographs, 368–370
using burning and dodging, 144
using the histogram in photoshop, 78–80
using the Shutter Priority mode, 74
inverse square law, 322
IPTC, 404
iris, 292
ISO (or ASA), 86
ISO (International Standards Organization)
film speed, 86–88 See also digital ISO setting
ISO 200, 87, 118, 124, 253
ISO 400, 87, 124
ISO 18902, 163
ISO 18916, 163

J

JPEG (Joint Photographic Experts Group), 180, 203

K

key light, 314
keystoning, 42
Kodak gray card, 86, 121

L

large-format cameras, 41–44
perspective control in, 42–43
Scheimpflug principle, 42
view and coverage angle, 43–44
latent image, 86, 100, 105
layer mask, 265
leading lines, 348, 357
leaf shutter, 34
leakage current, 89–90
learning, 11, 18
legal claim, 391
lens, 25, 26
lens covers and shades, 28–29
lens diameter, 31
lens flares, 29–30
lenses
coverage or covering power, 43
explanation of, 26–27
fixed focal length (or prime) lenses, 25, 28
image circle, 43
lens covers and shades, 28–29

lens diameter, 31
macro settings, 28
normal lenses, 26, 43
optical coatings, 30
reflection loss, 30
slow lens, 32
telephoto lenses, 26–27, 43, 84
wide-angle lenses, 27, 43
zoom lenses, 25, 27–28
light
and color temperature, 299–300
commercial photography lighting, 309
custom white balance, 301
directions of, 302–303
lights vs. darks, 337–338
multiple light sources, 300–301
seeing shadows, 60
studio lighting, 310–311
lighting ratios, 322–325
balancing flash, 325
benefits of, 324–325
five-to-one (5:1), 324
inverse square law, 322
nine-to-one (9:1), 324
three-to-one (3:1), 323–324
two-to-one (3:1), 323
light meters, 26
exposure compensation (overriding), 65
exposure lock metering, 63–65
hand held, 69–70
matrix meters, 63
purpose of, 26, 61
reflective meters, 61
spot meters, 61
light, reflecting off, 60, 67–68
objects and, 61
reality vs. imagination in, 60–61
reflective meters, 61
light source
basics, 313–314
broad lighting, 315
vs. color, 294–295
custom white balancing, 301
directional light, 302–303
electromagnetic radiation, 294
external methods, 302
falloffs, fast and slow, 296–297
fill light, 318
incorrect, examples, 318–319
importance of, 296
key light, 314–315
incorrect, examples, 317
modifiers, 312–313

multiple, 300–301
portraiture, 309–310, 313
posing, model, 314
short lighting, 315
strobe heads, 310–312
tonal values, 295–296
contrast in, 297–298 See also surface quality
light-tight box, 26
lignin, 163
localized corrections, 187
lossy compression, 203
low-contrast image, 79, 116, 190, 298
low-key image, 340

M

macro settings, 28
Manual mode (M), 74
mat board, 163
Materials Safety Data Sheets (MSDS), 103
matrix meters, 63
medium-format cameras, 39–40
megapixels, 179, 191
mergers, 350
metal frames, 164
metamerism, 277
metering modes, camera
center-weighted averaging, 62
exposure compensation, 65–67
exposure lock metering, 63–65
matrix meters, 63
spot meters, 61–63
meters. See light meters
middle gray, 60
middle input slider (midpoint gamma slider), 223
midtone, 60
minimum focusing distance, 28
mixing and storing chemicals, 104
model releases, 410–411
property release, 412
record keeping, 412
signature, 411–412
special circumstances, 412
mode settings, 72
Aperture Priority mode, 73–74
Bulb mode, 74–75
Manual mode, 74
Program mode, 72
Shutter Priority (Tv) mode, 74
monitor
calibration, 278–279
displays, 181–182
profile, 279

monorail cameras, 41
mount board
    conservation, 163
    cotton museum, 163
    standard, 163
mounting methods
    alternatives, 172
    cold, 170–172
    dry, 165–168
    hinge, 170
    mat board, cutting and measuring of,
        168–169
    presentation portfolios, 172

N

negatives, 23, 86, 99
no derivative works condition, 395
noise, 38
noise (digital), 88–90
noncommercial condition, 395
nondestructive editing, 178
nonexclusive rights, 389
normal focal length, 40
normal lenses, 26, 43
Notes, technical points
    Operation Photo Rescue, 6
    photographic opportunities, 11
    parallax issues, 24
    image stabilization (IS) function, 29
    f-stop measurement, 31
    f-stop calculations, 31
    aperture values, 31
    leaf shutter, 34
    meter reading instructions, 64
    print film, shadows exposure, 101
    transparency Film, highlights
        exposure, 101
    ingestion, 102
    lights, usage of, 107
    canister lid operation, 108
    stop bath, 110
    silver filtration systems, 110
    lids removal, 114
    old axiom
        for print film, 117
        for slide film, 117
    burn/dodge requirements, 150
    mount board
        signing, 170
        sticky notes removal, 171
    computer commands, 179
    raw file capturing, 180
    intensity values, 181
    Adobe updation, 183

renaming process, 183
zoom out operation, short cut to, 199
Edit > Undo process, 200
image size, resetting of, 201
save operations, 202, 203
tools panel, 214
addition and deletion, 215
zoom in operation, 217
SMART RADIUS options, 219
edge selection, 219
layers panel, 224, 249
color selection, 225, 229
Brush tool, 228, 229
retouching methods, 245
combining techniques, 261
previewing, 283
ink and paper, quality of, 284
ICC profile, 287
polarized filter removal, 308
strobes usage, 311
cropping decisions, 352, 355
Hubble Telescope, 389
contract, working on, 391
licensing, 410

O

opening up the aperture, 73
Operation Photo Rescue, 5
    website, 6
optical coatings, 30
optic nerve, 293
orphan work, 402
overexposure, 64, 75, 90
overmat, 163

P

parabola, 311
parallax, 24–25
patterns, 358
Pefley, Chuck, 414–417
penetration (of chemicals), 102
pentaprism, 25
perception, 119
perspective, 349
pH, 162
photo buyer, 406
photographer registry, 402
photographic installations, 380
photographic papers
    filters and, 134–135
    types of, 136
photographic print (the positive),
    23–24
photography

credibility creation, 16
importance of, 6
making, 16
purposes of, 6–8
society and, 8–10
photomontage work, 260–264
photons, 37
photoshop computer software
    alpha channels, 216–217, 222
    brightness/contrast function
        concerns, 189–190
    burn and dodge tools, 144–150
    camera raw files, 180
    changing the document size,
        200–201
    cleaning and fine-tuning tools
        crop tool, 258–260
        dust & scratches filter, 248
        unsharp mask filter, 254–255
    color settings, 280–281
    file formats, 203
    foreground and background colors,
        229
    Info palette, 226
    introduction to, 198–201
    opening a photograph, 198
    printing
        ICC profiles, 283–284
    Quick Mask mode, 227–229, 263
    saving files, 202–203
    setting the resolution, 199–200
    tools palette (the Toolbox), 198
    transform functions, 266
    using layers and the Layers palette
        curves, 223–226
        layer masks, 265
        levels, 223–226
        make new layers, 230
        saving files with layers, 202
    using selections, 214–216
    using selection tools
        Brush tool, 228–229
        Color Range tool, 262–263
        Lasso tool, 214–216
        Magic Wand tool, 214
        Marquee tool, 214–216
    using the histogram, 78–80
photoshop (.psd), 203
photosites, 37–38, 88
pinhole cameras, 23, 40–41
pixels
    in digital images, 181–182,
        198–201
    in photosites, 37

pixel preservation or nondestructive editing, 178
plastic cameras, 40
point-and-shoot cameras, 25
polarizing filter, 305–307
    as neutral density filter, 308
    concept, 307–308
positive images, 23
posterization, 81
preservative, 105
preview depth of field button, 85–86
primary and secondary colors, 360
prime lens. *See* fixed focal length (or prime) lenses
principal plane, 26
printing
    image cropping, 134
    preparation of, 136–137
    size of, 134
    step by step process, 138–140, 141–143
    testing in, 140–141 *See also* contact print; photographic papers
Professional Photographers of America (PPA), 380
Professional Profiles
    Betty Huth and Ed Booth, 174–175
    Chuck Pefley, 414–417
    Dick and Barbara Waltenberry, 53–55
    Felice Frankel, 236–237
    Jeff Richter, 398–399
    Michael Kamber, 157–159
    R. J. Hinkle, 94–95
    W. Morgan Rockhill, 329–331
profiling, 273
profile mismatch, 280
Program mode (P), 72
publication rights, 410 *See also* copyright laws
public domain, 389
pupil, 292

R

rangefinder optical system, 24
raw conversion, 180
rear nodal point, 26
reflection loss, 30
reflective light meter, 66
reflective meters, 61
replenisher, 105
resin-coated (RC) papers, 136

resolution
    of cell phone cameras, 44
    in digital images, 182
    setting in Photoshop, 199–200
restrainer, 105
retina, 293
retouching, 151–152
RGB (red, green, blue) color mode, 274
rim lighting, 303
rods, 293
royalty-free photographs, 392–393
rule of thirds, 353–354
ruler tool, 255–258

S

safelight, 130
safelight fog, 130
scanners, 273–274
scenes a faire, 393
Scheimpflug principle, 42
sensory nerves of the eye, 293
shadows, 61
share alike condition, 395
short lighting, 315
shutter, 25–26
Shutter Priority mode (Tv), 74
shutter speeds, 32, 33–34, 59
sidelight, 303
silhouette, 72, 303
silver gelatin print, 136
simultaneous contrast, 277
slave, 310
slope of a characteristic curve, 100
slow falloff, 296
slow lens, 32
SLR (single-lens reflex) cameras, 25
    mirror in, 25
snapshot photos, 11, 246
source profile, 283
spectral data, 273
spectrophotometers, 273
specular highlights, 337
spot meters, 61
square format, 343
sRGB, 280
standard mount board, 163
stock photo agency, 406
stock photographer, 357
stock photography, 357
stock solution, 104

stopping down the aperture, 73
straight exposure, 145–148
straight print, 143
strobe lights, 310
subtractive color, 282
Sunny f/16 Rule, 70
sunscreen and insect repellent, 50
surface quality, 303–305
    direct and diffuse reflections, 304
        concepts, 305
    transmission, lighting, 304–305

T

tangible form, 386
telephoto lenses, 26–27, 43, 84
telephoto view, 25
test prints, 140–143
TIFF (tagged information file format), 203
tonal values, 295
true color, 182

U

ultraviolet (UV) filters, 308–309
underexposure, 75
unsharp mask, 254–255

V

value, 60
variable contrast photographic paper, 134
vertical format, 343
viewfinder, 24
viewfinder cameras, 24–25
viewfinder focusing aids, 24
vignetting, 29

W

white point, 80
white space, 356–357
wide-angle lenses, 27, 43
wide-angle view, 25
Wikimedia Commons, 396
work for hire, 391
working solution, 104

X

XMP sidecar file, 187

Z

zone system, 67–68, 143–144
zoom lenses, 25, 27–28